Literate Lives

Teaching Reading & Writing in Elementary Classrooms

THE WILEY BICENTENNIAL—KNOWLEDGE FOR GENERATIONS

Each generation has its unique needs and aspirations. When Charles Wiley first opened his small printing shop in lower Manhattan in 1807, it was a generation of boundless potential searching for an identity. And we were there, helping to define a new American literary tradition. Over half a century later, in the midst of the Second Industrial Revolution, it was a generation focused on building the future. Once again, we were there, supplying the critical scientific, technical, and engineering knowledge that helped frame the world. Throughout the 20th Century, and into the new millennium, nations began to reach out beyond their own borders and a new international community was born. Wiley was there, expanding its operations around the world to enable a global exchange of ideas, opinions, and know-how.

For 200 years, Wiley has been an integral part of each generation's journey, enabling the flow of information and understanding necessary to meet their needs and fulfill their aspirations. Today, bold new technologies are changing the way we live and learn. Wiley will be there, providing you the must-have knowledge you need to imagine new worlds, new possibilities, and new opportunities.

Generations come and go, but you can always count on Wiley to provide you the knowledge you need, when and where you need it!

WILLIAM J. PESCE
PRESIDENT AND CHIEF EXECUTIVE OFFICER

PETER BOOTH WILEY
CHAIRMAN OF THE BOARD

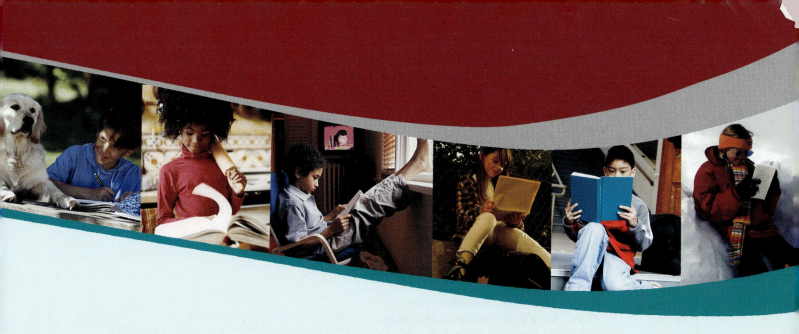

Literate Lives

Teaching Reading & Writing in Elementary Classrooms

Amy Seely Flint

Georgia State University

BICENTENNIAL
1807
WILEY
2007
BICENTENNIAL

John Wiley & Sons, Inc.

VICE PRESIDENT & PUBLISHER   **Jay O'Callaghan**
ACQUISITIONS EDITOR   **Robert Johnston**
SENIOR DEVELOPMENT EDITOR   **Ellen Ford**
PRODUCTION EDITOR   **Nicole Repasky**
MARKETING MANAGER   **Jeff Rucker**
SENIOR DESIGNER   **Madelyn Lesure**
PRODUCTION MANAGEMENT SERVICES   **Ingrao Associates**
SENIOR ILLUSTRATION EDITOR   **Sandra Rigby**
SENIOR PHOTO EDITOR   **Lisa Gee**
EDITORIAL ASSISTANT   **Carrie Tupa**
MEDIA EDITOR   **Lynn Pearlman**
COVER DESIGNER   **Madelyn Lesure**
COVER IMAGES
    girl in snow   **Photodisc/Punchstock**
    boy with dog   **Photodisc/Punchstock**
    girl in kitchen   **Flynn Larsen/Photonica/Getty Images**
    boy on steps   **Blend/Punchstock**
    girl with skates   **Spencer Rowell/Taxi/Getty Images**
    boy in room   **Digital Vision/Punchstock**
Bicentennial Logo Design   **Richard J. Pacifico**

This book was set in 11/13 Minion by Prepare Inc. and printed and bound by Courier/Kendallville. The cover was printed by Courier/Kendallville.

This book is printed on acid free paper. ∞

To order books or for customer service, please call 1-800-CALL WILEY (225-5945).

Library of Congress Cataloging-in-Publication Data
Flint, Amy Seely.
    Literate lives: teaching reading & writing in elementary classrooms/Amy Seely Flint.
        p. cm.
    Includes index.
    ISBN 978-0-471-65298-4 (pbk.)
    1. Language arts (Elementary)—United States. 2. Reading (Elementary)—United States.
    3. English language—Composition and exercises—Study and teaching (Elementary)—
    United States. I. Title.
    LB1576.F4844 2008
    372..6—dc22
                                                    2007025173

About the Author

Amy Seely Flint is an Associate Professor at Georgia State University. She regularly teaches courses in language and literacy for initial certification students, master degree students, and doctoral students. Dr. Flint works closely with teachers at a local elementary school, providing weekly professional development sessions in literacy development. Dr. Flint has received a number of grants to support teachers as they engage in professional development opportunities focused on literacy development. She was an elementary teacher for a number of years in Atlanta, Georgia, and Los Angeles, California.

After receiving her Ph.D from the University of California, Berkeley, Dr. Flint accepted a position at Indiana University in Bloomington, Indiana. While at Indiana University, Dr. Flint was selected to be a principle investigator and member of the National Commission on Excellence in Elementary Teacher Preparation for Reading Instruction, sponsored by the International Reading Association. She was also involved in the Critical Literacy Study Group, a collaborative of colleagues, teachers, and preservice teachers that researched the role of critical literacy in elementary classrooms. She served as President of the Whole Language Umbrella and was a member of the executive board for the National Council of Teachers of English.

Dr. Flint is a co-author, *Buried Treasures in the Classroom: Using Hidden Influences to Enhance Literacy Teaching and Learning* (with Dr. Mary Riordan-Karlsson, published by International Reading Association, 2002) and numerous articles in *Journal of Literacy Research, Language Arts, The Reading Teacher, Elementary School Journal,* and *Young Child.* She has authored chapters in *Learning to Teach Reading: Setting the Research Agenda* (edited by Cathy Roller, published by International Reading Association, 2001) and *Improving Reading and Literacy in Grades 1-5* (edited by E P. St. John, S. Loester, and J. Barzdell, published by Corwin Press, 2003).

Dr. Flint is an avid reader, traveler, and tennis player. She lives with her husband, Michael; dog, Stella; and two cats, Belle and Sweet Pea.

Preface

An emerging view of the reading process

Teaching children to read and write is daunting. There are federal and state pressures and mandates that insist that all children will learn to read and write by the time they finish third grade. Media reporters and politicians focus on failing test scores and schools. Literacy programs and curricular structures promise to teach children to read and write. Parents and caregivers hold on to the notion that reading and writing activities look like those of their childhoods. Children enter through classroom doors with expectations of learning to read and write. And there are teachers. Teachers know that reading and writing are incredibly complex and sophisticated processes that demand much from the young child. Teachers also know that children are quite competent and capable of becoming readers and writers.

This book is designed to meet the challenges and needs of teacher candidates in elementary education programs. *Literate Lives: Teaching Reading and Writing in Elementary Classrooms* invites readers to consider the complexities of the reading process in diverse settings. Students in a recent course of mine created a poem that I believe captures the meaning and essence of this book.

> *The important thing about knowing your readers is that they are all different.*
> *It is true to say that they all have different interests, backgrounds, and confidence levels.*
> *Some may have language barriers and some just struggle.*
> *They might be missing literacy skills or they might be missing teeth.*
> *But, the important thing to know about your readers is that they are all different indeed.*
>
> **Lindsay Childs, Valerie Curry, and Hyo Eun Lee**

The reading methods course and audience for the text

Undergraduate students aiming to be elementary teachers are generally accepted into Teacher Education programs in their junior year of college. They begin a series of methods courses whereby they learn how to teach various content areas (reading, language arts, math, science, social studies, etc.). Most teacher education programs offer at least six hours of literacy-focused course work because reading and writing are central in elementary classrooms. While there are many different configurations of the literacy courses in teacher education programs, all elementary teacher education students are expected to take at least one course focused on the reading process and how to teach children to read. A reading methods course typically focuses on:

- preparing teacher candidates to teach reading at the elementary level
- introducing various issues related to language, language learning, and the teaching of reading
- addressing various approaches to reading, content area reading, literature discussions, phonics, phonemic awareness, vocabulary, fluency, and what role each of these plays in curriculum planning

This book is designed to meet the needs of undergraduate teacher candidates, as well as graduate students in alternative certification programs, preparing to teach reading at the elementary level.

Framework and focus

The text introduces teacher candidates to the notion that reading is a complex, multilayered process that begins early in a child's life. Reading, by all accounts, is more than decoding symbols on a page. While this is one component of the reading process, it is important for teacher candidates to see a broader, more complete picture of reading. Given the role that reading plays in the elementary school curriculum, it is imperative that teachers have a well-developed understanding of the reading process and what it means to be a teacher of readers.

In the book, I cover major theories and application strategies of the reading process as well as current debates in the field. However, *Literate Lives: Teaching Reading and Writing in Elementary Classrooms* incorporates a framework that I believe makes it a unique text on the market. This framework builds upon the following themes:

- believing that literacy is based in social, cultural, and historical contexts;
- assuming an inquiry stance (being 'problem posers' and wondering 'why');
- using "kidwatching" (Goodman, 1985) as an assessment tool to make informed instructional decisions;
- recognizing and using the multiple literacies that children bring to the classroom; and
- lingering and reflecting on one's decisions in light of what one knows and believes.

There is a recursive nature to this framework whereby what one comes to know and believe is based on understandings about children, literacy development, and reflections on what occurred.

The reading process from a socio-critical perspective

Perhaps the most central idea in understanding the reading process from a socio-critical perspective is that reading (and more broadly, literacy) is a socially, culturally, and historically situated construct. Teachers' beliefs about literacy development (how reading is learned and what literacy is for) determine the types of reading events and activities that will take place in the classroom. These beliefs are based on values, attitudes, knowledge, histories as readers, and networks of interactions with others. These practices then become the ways in which reading is defined for a particular community (namely students, teachers, parents, and administrators).

Recognizing that reading is more than breaking the code, each chapter offers vignettes and strategy work that demonstrates literacy from a critical perspective. The vignettes highlight children and teachers from diverse settings and backgrounds. A socio-critical perspective involves readers taking on multiple perspectives, engaging in social action, disrupting the commonplace, and focusing on socio-political issues (Lewison, Flint, & Van Sluys, 2002).

Inquiry stance

Operating with an inquiry stance is critical to being an effective teacher, and in particular, an effective reading teacher. An inquiry stance is one that positions the teacher as a "problem poser" (Freire, 1973), asking questions about the ways in which children come to make sense of squiggles on a page. With an inquiry stance, a teacher considers that there may be more than one way to approach the teaching of reading. This opens up the possibility for viewing literacy in a more complex and dynamic fashion, rather than in a "one size fits all" formula. Teachers working from an inquiry stance begin with what they know and juxtapose this knowledge with new perspectives. In doing so, they come to new insights while continuing to ask more questions.

Throughout each of the chapters, readers are asked to assume an inquiry stance. The vignettes of teachers and children in reading events enable readers to consider a range of possible responses and reactions. The various possible interpretations are further examined as theories and strategies are shared.

Kidwatching

Kidwatching, a term first coined by Yetta Goodman (1985), is related to notions of inquiry. As teachers "kidwatch" or closely observe the responses and behaviors of children engaged in reading events, they can then construct a range of hypotheses that leads to further inquiry and wonderment. The hypotheses enable teachers to open up and consider a variety of possible strategies that promote and support readers in the process.

Establishing this idea of kidwatching early in the book and maintaining a focus on children's demonstrations of their understandings of the reading process supports the larger conceptual picture that reading is a socially and critically mediated endeavor. Readers are encouraged to try out some of their kidwatching skills on the vignettes presented, as well as in the *Invitations for the Classroom*.

Multiple literacies and texts

Children quickly learn to identify important icons such as McDonald's®, Coca-cola™, Nike®, favorite cereal brands, and cartoon characters' names such as Sponge Bob™, Mickey Mouse™, and Blue™. The early attempts often occur without explicit attention or instruction. Rather, children are immersed in the environmental print around them. Later they begin reading Pokemon™ and Yugio™ trading cards, Harry Potter series books, stories from reading anthologies, Eye Witness books, and surfing Internet websites for information on a hobby or interest. The notion of text will be expanded to include a variety of materials, including "everyday" materials such as advertisements, trading cards, and posters. Readers will broaden their own conceptions of what counts in literacy events to include home and community practices (Moll, Amanti, Neff & Gonzalez, 1992).

Lingering and reflecting

A final thread woven throughout the framework is the notion of lingering and reflecting. Returning to and lingering over key concepts presented in the chapters support readers as they begin to envision a reading curriculum that is meaningful for the children they are teaching. Revealing uncertainties about the reading process and how to become effective teachers of readers contributes to one's growth and development. *Creating Connections* are reflective points of discussion that are included in each chapter to encourage readers to pause and linger over what has been presented. The new information should be juxtaposed with current understandings and experiences, all of which lead to posing new questions and beginning new inquiries into the reading process.

The guiding principles presented in the framework are highlighted throughout the chapters. Readers will become quite familiar with these ideas and how they play out when teaching reading, whether it is in the first few years of school or in the middle and later elementary school years.

Pedagogical elements

The text is written to provide both the historical and theoretical foundations of teaching reading, writing, and literacy as well as to provide sufficient practical information and real-world applications so that the beginning teacher has the tools and confidence needed to begin a successful career as a teacher of literacy.

• Each chapter opens with a vignette highlighting teaching decisions made by current teachers and reading specialists in the field. Following the vignette, *I Wonder* questions are asked to generate reflective thinking. The vignette and follow-up questions set the stage for the key concepts that are introduced in the chapter.

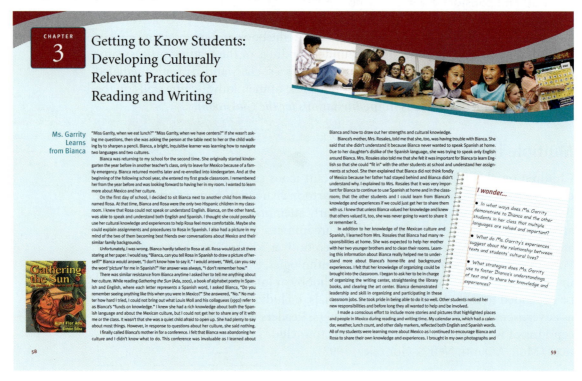

Chapter Overview

Young children bring a multitude of personal experiences from home and community settings (e.g., preschools, day-cares, libraries, etc.) as they begin to understand the world of print. They learn what print is, how it works, and why it is used. Kadin's interactions with *Hop on Pop* and *Bubblegum, Bubblegum* illustrate that these early "hands on" experiences with text contribute to literacy development. His budding literacy-like behavior (pretend reading of *Bubblegum*) suggests that he is engaging in the early intellectual work of reading and writing.

Becoming literate is a developmental process that begins early in a child's life through interactions with family members and caregivers in a variety of settings. The National Association of Early Childhood Education and the International Reading Association note that when teachers, daycare providers, and caregivers support early literacy practices in school and home settings, they are helping young children foster and sustain their interest and enjoyment of reading and writing (NAECY, 1998). Teachers and caregivers can facilitate these early literacy practices in many ways as children enter the literacy landscape. This chapter focuses on the literacy practice for children prior to entering formal school experiences, most notably kindergarten, and addresses the following questions:

- What is the difference between a reading readiness perspective and an emergent literacy perspective toward literacy learning?
- What are the dimensions of emergent literacy knowledge?
- How do environmental print and technology support early literacy development?
- What are some strategies and invitations to facilitate emergent literacy knowledge?

Historical beginnings of emergent literacy

Over the years, researchers have developed theories for when and how a child learns to read and write. When do children realize that symbols on a page actually hold meaning? How do children access and mediate written text for their own purposes? Some theorists focused on children's maturation levels and concluded that children

• A *Chapter Overview* further introduces the chapter theme and asks several *Guiding Questions* for students to think about as they progress through each chapter.

• Numerous photos, tables, illustrations, and examples of real student work illustrate the text. These examples provide an important visual component so that new teachers can see how the classroom might look, or how a student might respond to a reading or writing assignment.

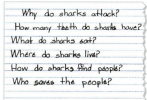

• **Creating Connections** boxes are integrated throughout the chapters. These are reflective questions or tasks that readers think about or do in order to juxtapose text material with their own experiences. These Creating Connections elements are numbered for ease of referencing or assigning.

> **Creating Connections 2.3**
> Review the English/Language Arts standards for speaking in your state. What aspects of oral language development do the standards focus on? How are issues of power reflected in the standards?

> **Creating Connections 3.8**
> Conduct a read-aloud event with a small group of children. Consider the goals and materials for the event. Notice the interaction patterns that you and the students engage in. What assessments will you use to determine effectiveness of the read-aloud event?
> Share your experiences with a classmate.

> **Creating Connections 2.1**
> Make a list of common words that you use that are relatively "new" to our lexicon. Examples may include: BLOG, fast-track, globalization, ipod, etc.
> Where did these words come from?
> How often do you use these words?

Through language we create versions or storylines of the social and natural worlds that position people in relation to power (Wilson–Keenan, Solsken, & Willett, 2001). It is readily apparent in many state departments of education (e.g., Virginia, Indiana, New Jersey) that some forms of English have more power than others. "Standard English" is the language of power in the United States. Students in grades K–12 are expected to achieve particular oral language standards, such as "speak in complete, coherent sentences," "stay on topic when speaking," and "tell an experience or creative story in a logical sequence" (Indiana: http://www.doe.state.in.us/standards/Docs-TeacherEdition/Teacher-EnglishLA-081303.pdf), or "use conventions of English, including grammar and appropriate forms of address" and "use clear, concise, organized language" (New Jersey: http://www.state.nj.us/njded/frameworks/lal/chapt2.pdf). It is also noted in Virginia that a Standards ... a full command of the English language ... and their rich speaking and writing ... va.us/main/sol/solview.cfm?curriculum... a particular way of speaking (Standard ... and dialects, such as African-American ... palachian. In many instances, when ch ... tic forms, they are seen as not having t ... social success. Teachers will routinely ... questions in Standard English, or they ... of saying something. In either case, the ... of language that is necessary for success ...

The three assumptions regarding l ... evolving and dynamic; (2) language pr ... (3) language practices reflect power and ... sider as they interact and work with chil ... gest that how children talk and what ... community. Recall that in the opening vignette, we can see how Ms. Jacobs comes to value Angie's language use as she negotiates classroom literacy events. The next section offers a discussion on language variation, attitudes, and policies that play an important role in how students respond to and participate in classroom discourse.

Language practices are dialogic and evolving

Language users are always in the process of refining their language use. Children

In the sec ... nizes that lea ... courages stud ... variety of wa ... loguing with ... questions dra ... In doing so, s ... reflect upon p ...

Ms. Jacobs works to understand all the ways in whi ... aims to develop a *cultural match* among the studen ... Developing curriculum that is culturally relevan ...

Variations in oral language

> **Creating Connections 2.4**
> How would you complete the following statements?
> It _____ (feeling, emotion, stance) when people say _____.
> When I hear them say this, it makes me think they _____.
> In small groups, consider how your peers responded to the statements. What attitudes, assumptions, and beliefs are apparent in the statements?

Language (oral and written) is the means by which teachers and students impart information, construct new understandings, represent relationships, ask questions, and reflect on what they know and understand. How language is used in the classroom and the values and attitudes speakers/listeners carry in relation to what they say/hear play an important role in how teachers and students begin to position themselves and others in the learning community. Language, not only the specific language a family speaks (Spanish, English, Cantonese), but the dialect and forms of language help define identity and mark membership in particular groups who have shared knowledge and shared meanings. A

---

morpheme
Smallest linguistic unit that carries meaning.

Words can also carry different meanings beca ... A *morpheme* is the smallest linguistic unit that ca ... be considered *free*, such as ... may be *bound*, meaning that ... and prefixes such as -ed, -ing ... change the meaning of the w ... (dog + s [plural]), "teacher ... word "pretend" has only on ... it does not alter the meaning ... iar word, they may search fo ... note that many of these wor ... words are not connected in meaning to the o ... inside of fragrant; play inside of display). Te ... morphemes is particularly helpful in understa ... English in speaking, reading, and writing.

Additionally, vocabulary knowledge supp ... ied contexts and for multiple purposes (Ric ... (2005) comment that learners move from no ... acquainted with it, to attaining a deeper and r ... the word in different ways. Nagy and Scott (20 ... in vocabulary development should go beyon ... sary definitions. Chapters 7 and 8 present a numbe ... cabulary work.

> **TECHNOLOGY LINK**
> http://www.childrenslibrary.org/
> Access digital copies of children's books from all over the world written in their original languages.

propriate to the time, place, audience, and purpose ... validation of the child's language and culture, wh ... maintained, stress to be reduced, and education to ... to the core curriculum is provided" (Necochea & (

Literacy events, such as literature discussions a ... students to take risks in language development. Th ... ideas using their primary language without interfe ... usage. Students are more at ease interacting with o ... in the texts, thereby expanding their knowledge ar ... questions (why, how come, when). By the time chil ... mastered nearly all of the complexities of language ... ability, children express their needs, thoughts, and ... ade, Trey's mother asked Trey if he wanted to take ... ool lunch? Trey responded rather quizzically, "How ... unch?" His mother explained that there is a menu ... it to see what will be served that day. Trey was quite ... I'll buy lunch on days they have artichokes." ... n when formalized instruction or learning does not ... g child and those in the immediate surroundings?

> **TECHNOLOGY LINK**
> http://www.childdevelopmentinfo.com/development/current_research_language_development.shtml
> This site provides a list of current research on language development.

• Marginal **Key Terms** definitions call out important new terminology that students need to understand and remember. In addition, there are several marginal **Technology Links** in every chapter that give students additional web resources for research and important information relevant to the chapter topics.

---

syntax
The study of the rules or "patterned relations" that govern the way words combine.

Syntactics: the structure of language

Syntax is the study of the systematic ways in ... organized and related to one another. The syntax ... another within a sentence or paragraph. This cue ... liday's notion of learning about language. Reader ... the language's grammar to know the likelihood of ... next word in a sentence. When a reader comes t ...

• **Did You Know. . .** is a feature that offers interesting and relevant information about various aspects of teaching literacy. These are often useful topics for further class discussion.

• **Invitation for the Classroom** assignments are highly practical, real-world opportunities for readers to bring something they have learned into the class and apply it to the children they will be teaching.

> ### Did you know...
> In the Indianapolis Public School district, there are two schools, known as the Cent ... for Inquiry (CFI), that embrace the inquiry model for schooling (http://www.302.ip ... k12.in.us/). There is also a Center for Inquiry in Columbia, South Caroli ... (http://www2.richland2.org/cfi/).
> Recent testing data on the ISTEP (Indiana Statewide Testing for Educational Progres ... shows that students attending CFI in Indianapolis have a higher average percent ... in English/Language Arts and Math than do students across the stat ...
>
> | Year | State Average (public and nonpublic) | Cente |
> |---|---|---|
> | 2002–03 | 68.7% | |
> | 2003–04 | 71.0% | |
> | 2004–05 | 71.7% | |
> | 2005–06 | 72.9% | |

> ### Invitation for the classroom
> Interview a small group of students about their perceptions and understandings of what reading and writing are for. Possible questions to ask include:
> 1. Why do people read? Write?
> 2. How did you learn to read? Write?
> 3. Who helps you with your reading? Writing?
> 4. What do you do when you have trouble reading text? Writing?
> 5. What types of things do you like to read? Write?
> 6. Who do you know who is a good reader? Writer?
> 7. How would you help someone who is having trouble reading? Writing?

> ### Did you know...
> There are many different terms used for children who enter into classrooms speaking languages other than English.
> **English Language Learner (ELL)** is a term used for students who first learn a language other than English in their home and community (U.S. born or immigrant) and ... English as a new language.
> **... glish Proficient (LEP)** is another term that classifies children based on ... age proficiency. The child may have some knowledge but is not fully pro-
> ... s include:
> ... English speaker, language minority student, ESL (English as a Second Lan- ... dent, ENL (English as a New Language), or bilingual student.

> ### Invitation for the classroom
> #### Languages around the World
> Read *If the World Were a Village* (Smith, 2002). Engage students in a discussion about languages used in the world. Compare the information on Table 2.1.
> Additionally, collect samples of text in other languages.
> 1. What are the purpose and function of the text?
> 2. How is print placed on the page?
> 3. What strategies do you use to make sense of the text?

Chapter Overview

Young children bring a multitude of personal experiences from home and community settings (e.g., preschools, day-cares, libraries, etc.) as they begin to understand the world of print. They learn what print is, how it works, and why it is used. Kadin's interactions with *Hop on Pop* and *Bubblegum, Bubblegum* illustrate that these early "hands on" experiences with text contribute to literacy development. His budding literacy-like behavior (pretend reading of *Bubblegum*) suggests that he is engaging in the early intellectual work of reading and writing.

Becoming literate is a developmental process that begins early in a child's life through interactions with family members and caregivers in a variety of settings. The National Association of Early Childhood Education and the International Reading Association note that when teachers, daycare providers, and caregivers support early literacy practices in school and home settings, they are helping young children foster and sustain their interest and enjoyment for reading and writing (NAECY, 1998). Teachers and caregivers can facilitate these early literacy practices in many ways as children enter the literacy landscape. This chapter focuses on the literacy practice for children prior to entering formal school experiences, most notably kindergarten, and addresses the following questions:

- What is the difference between a reading readiness perspective and an emergent literacy perspective toward literacy learning?
- What are the dimensions of emergent literacy knowledge?
- How do environmental print and technology support early literacy development?
- What are some strategies and invitations to facilitate emergent literacy knowledge?

📖 Historical beginnings of emergent literacy

Over the years, researchers have developed theories for when and how a child learns to read and write. When do children realize that symbols on a page actually hold meaning? How do children access and mediate written text for their own purposes? Some theorists focused on children's maturation levels and concluded that children

• A *Chapter Overview* further introduces the chapter theme and asks several *Guiding Questions* for students to think about as they progress through each chapter.

• Numerous photos, tables, illustrations, and examples of real student work illustrate the text. These examples provide an important visual component so that new teachers can see how the classroom might look, or how a student might respond to a reading or writing assignment.

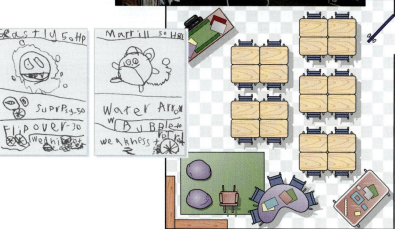

• *Creating Connections* boxes are integrated throughout the chapters. These are reflective questions or tasks that readers think about or do in order to juxtapose text material with their own experiences. These Creating Connections elements are numbered for ease of referencing or assigning.

Creating Connections 2.3

Review the English/Language Arts standards for speaking in your state. What aspects of oral language development do the standards focus on? How are issues of power reflected in the standards?

Creating Connections 3.8

Conduct a read-aloud event with a small group of children. Consider the goals and materials for the event. Notice the interaction patterns that you and the students engage in. What assessments will you use to determine effectiveness of the read-aloud event?

Share your experiences with a classmate.

Creating Connections 2.1

Make a list of common words that you use that are relatively "new" to our lexicon. Examples may include: BLOG, fast-track, globalization, ipod, etc.

Where did these words come from?
How often do you use these words?

Language practices are dialogic and evolving

Language users are always in the process of refining their language use. Children

---

Ms. Jacobs works to understand all the ways in whi... aims to develop a *cultural match* among the studen... Developing curriculum that is culturally relevan...

Variations in oral language

Language (oral and written) is the means by which teachers and students impart information, construct new understandings, represent relationships, ask questions, and reflect on what they know and understand. How language is used in the classroom and the values and attitudes speakers/listeners carry in relation to what they say/hear play an important role in how teachers and students begin to position themselves and others in the learning community. Language, not only the specific language a family speaks (Spanish, English, Cantonese), but the dialect and forms of language help define identity and mark membership in particular groups who have shared knowledge and shared meanings. A

Creating Connections 2.4

How would you complete the following statements?
It _____ (feeling, emotion, stance) when people say _____.
When I hear them say this, it makes me think they _____.
In small groups, consider how your peers responded to the statements. What attitudes, assumptions, and beliefs are apparent in the statements?

---

morpheme
Smallest linguistic unit that carries meaning.

Words can also carry different meanings beca... A *morpheme* is the smallest linguistic unit that ca... be considered *free*, such as t... may be *bound*, meaning that... and prefixes such as -ed, -ing... change the meaning of the w... (dog + s [plural]), "teacher... word "pretend" has only on... it does not alter the meaning... iar word, they may search f... note that many of these wor... words are not connected in meaning to the or... inside of fragrant; play inside of display). Te... morphemes is particularly helpful in understa... English in speaking, reading, and writing.

Additionally, vocabulary knowledge supp... ied contexts and for multiple purposes (Ric... (2005) comment that learners move from no... acquainted with it, to attaining a deeper and r... the word in different ways. Nagy and Scott (2... in vocabulary development should go beyond... sary definitions. Chapters 7 and 8 present a numbe... cabulary work.

Syntactics: the structure of language

syntax
The study of the rules or "patterned relations" that govern the way words combine.

Syntax is the study of the systematic ways in... organized and related to one another. The syntax... another within a sentence or paragraph. This cue... liday's notion of learning about language. Reade... the language's grammar to know the likelihood of... next word in a sentence. When a reader comes t...

TECHNOLOGY LINK
http://www.childrenslibrary.org/
Access digital copies of children's books from all over the world written in their original languages.

---

propriate to the time, place, audience, and purpose... validation of the child's language and culture, wh... maintained, stress to be reduced, and education to... to the core curriculum is provided" (Necochea &...

Literacy events, such as literature discussions a... students to take risks in language development. Th... ideas using their primary language without interfe... usage. Students are more at ease interacting with... in the texts, thereby expanding their knowledge ar... questions (why, how come, when). By the time chil... mastered nearly all of the complexities of language... ability, children express their needs, thoughts, and... ade, Trey's mother asked Trey if he wanted to take... ool lunch. Trey responded rather quizzically, "How... unch?" His mother explained that there is a menu... t to see what will be served that day. Trey was quite... I'll buy lunch on days they have artichokes."... n when formalized instruction or learning does not... child and those in the immediate surroundings?

TECHNOLOGY LINK
http://www.childdevelopmentinfo.com/development/current_research_language_development.shtml
This site provides a list of current research on language development.

• Marginal *Key Terms* definitions call out important new terminology that students need to understand and remember. In addition, there are several marginal *Technology Links* in every chapter that give students additional web resources for research and important information relevant to the chapter topics.

Did you know...

In the Indianapolis Public School district, there are two schools, known as the Cent... for Inquiry (CFI), that embrace the inquiry model for schooling (http://www.302.ip... k12.in.us/). There is also a Center for Inquiry in Columbia, South Caroli... (http://www2.richland2.org/cfi/).

Recent testing data on the ISTEP (Indiana Statewide Testing for Educational Progres... shows that students attending CFI in Indianapolis have a higher average percent... in English/Language Arts and Math than do students across the sta...

Year	State Average (public and nonpublic)	Center...
2002–03	68.7%	
2003–04	71.0%	
2004–05	71.7%	
2005–06	72.9%	

Invitation for the classroom

Interview a small group of students about their perceptions and understandings of what reading and writing are for. Possible questions to ask include:

1. Why do people read? Write?
2. How did you learn to read? Write?
3. Who helps you with your reading? Writing?
4. What do you do when you have trouble reading text? Writing?
5. What types of things do you like to read? Write?
6. Who do you know who is a good reader? Writer?
7. How would you help someone who is having trouble reading? Writing?

Did you know...

There are many different terms used for children who enter into classrooms speaking languages other than English.

English Language Learner (ELL) is a term used for students who first learn a language other than English in their home and community (U.S. born or immigrant) and English as a new language.

...glish Proficient (LEP) is another term that classifies children based on... age proficiency. The child may have some knowledge but is not fully pro...

...s include:

...English speaker, language minority student, ESL (English as a Second Lan... ...dent, ENL (English as a New Language), or bilingual student.

• *Did You Know. . .* is a feature that offers interesting and relevant information about various aspects of teaching literacy. These are often useful topics for further class discussion.

• *Invitation for the Classroom* assignments are highly practical, real-world opportunities for readers to bring something they have learned into the class and apply it to the children they will be teaching.

Invitation for the classroom

Languages around the World

Read *If the World Were a Village* (Smith, 2002). Engage students in a discussion about languages used in the world. Compare the information on Table 2.1.

Additionally, collect samples of text in other languages.

1. What are the purpose and function of the text?
2. How is print placed on the page?
3. What strategies do you use to make sense of the text?

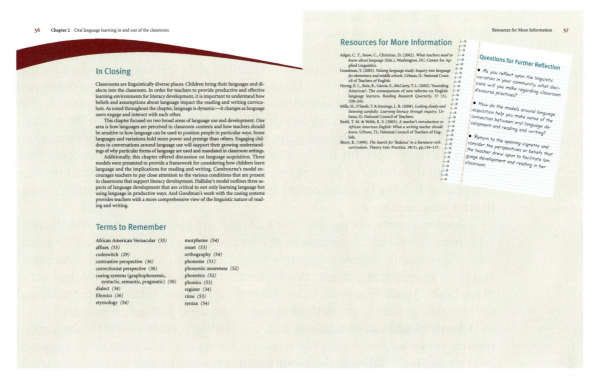

- Each chapter ends with ***In Closing***, a brief summary of the main points of the chapter, as well as a review list of ***Terms to Remember*** and ***Resources for More Information***. Final ***Questions for Further Reflection*** encourage readers to tie together what has been learned in each chapter.

Concepts to be addressed in the chapters— organization of the book

The framework for viewing reading as a socially and critically situated endeavor provides a coherent structure to build understandings of the reading process. *Part I: Gaining a Knowledge Base about Reading and Learners* discusses the underlying beliefs and ideologies about reading operating in classrooms, how teachers come to know their students' reading behaviors and purposes, and various reading models and culturally relevant curricular approaches to support effective instructional decision making. Building from a theoretical discussion of why people read, readers of this text are introduced to initial assessment strategies that highlight students' reading behaviors and interests as a means for establishing an effective reading program. In light of this information, readers are introduced to various reading models and curricular approaches/programs that support different theoretical positions.

Beginning with a conversation of why it is important to operate from a belief system, **Chapter 1** discusses various definitions of reading (how one defines reading will determine which theoretical model and instructional practices a teacher uses) and what it means to be literate in the twenty-first century. A broader understanding of literacy is presented in this chapter, expanding current thinking of what constitutes text and literacy practices. As part of this discussion, the reader also comes to see how important it is to value literacy practices that are not always seen as viable practices in classroom contexts. Because No Child Left Behind legislation is driving literacy reform efforts, readers are introduced to the central issues related to this legislation. Recent legislative mandates and the current emphasis on phonemic awareness and decoding strategies in beginning reading instruction will be addressed.

Chapter 2 addresses the role of oral language in learning to read and write. Guiding assumptions about oral language are developed, followed by a discussion of issues, policies, and practices related to language diversity in the classroom. The chapter then addresses oral language development by introducing how Brian Cambourne's conditions are relevant to literacy learning. Michael Halliday's model establishes a framework for thinking about curricular practices in the classroom. Three central domains of language development are discussed. The chapter then moves to addressing language cueing systems (graphophonemic, semantic, syntactic, and pragmatic).

Chapter 3 continues the discussion of diversity by focusing on culturally relevant literacy practices. A discussion of core principles for working with linguistically and culturally diverse students is provided, as well as the role of community and home in supporting literacy development. Initial assessments enable the teacher to establish a baseline to work from. Through interviews, interest inventories, and surveys, teachers can begin to think about the students in their classrooms.

Chapter 4 addresses reading models. The reading models involve thinking about reading from a bottom-up approach (phonics and skills) and a top down approach (whole language). Adding to these long standing reading models are two more: transactional and critical literacy. The later two models invite the reader to consider the larger purposes for reading and how readers are positioned in particular ways.

Chapter 5 introduces various reading programs and approaches that are theoretically linked to the reading models presented in Chapter 4. Discussions about how teachers' implicit and explicit beliefs about literacy development will connect to the instructional approaches they implement. The reader/writer workshop structure is presented as a way to organize literacy instruction in the classroom. This approach integrates reading and writing, thereby showing how teachers use reader/writer notebooks, authentic literature, mini lessons, and conferences in their teaching.

Part II Understanding the Reading Process in Classrooms introduces the reader to significant components of the reading process (word analysis, fluency, comprehension, vocabulary development, critical practices). Because these components do not stand alone (in the reading process or in instruction), the reader will learn about these components inside of classroom reading instruction. The chapters highlight primary, intermediate, and advanced practices in reading and writing. By gaining an insider's view of what happens in classroom practices, readers see reading instruction in authentic contexts.

Chapter 6 begins a discussion on emergent literacy in preschool settings. Through the work of Marie Clay and Elizabeth Sulzby, readers understand the differences between reading readiness and emergent literacy. As readers come to know various emergent literacy classrooms, they are introduced to strategies and children's literature that support these initial steps into literacy. Young children's demonstrations of authentic uses of literacy are highlighted as they construct signs and other texts for play centers. Included in this chapter is a list of predictable and rhyming texts that encourage emergent readers to attend to phonemic awareness.

Chapter 7 focuses on literacy development in primary classrooms. Inside this chapter, readers will come to know early primary teachers who implement a range of instructional practices and approaches to best meet the needs of their students. The vignettes highlight how teachers can differentiate instruction in early literacy classrooms. The four-resource model is highlighted as a way to think about the reading process in the early grades. A focused discussion on code breaking practices, such as onset and rime patterns, initial and ending consonant patterns, word chunking, word walls, word sorting, and have-a-go strategy, are a part of this chapter. The other practices are also addressed, and readers come to appreciate the importance of reading aloud to young children and conducting initial literature discussions. Shared reading and guided reading are highlighted as instructional structures to facilitate the reading process. Throughout the chapter, titles of children's books are offered. Additionally, connections to state standards and benchmarks are provided.

Chapter 8 addresses intermediate and accomplished readers and writers. This chapter follows a similar pattern as Chapter 7 in addressing the reading process from the four-resource model perspective. Vignettes and examples are threaded throughout the chapter. Work samples from readers and writers (grades 3–6) are included. Highlighted in Chapter 8 are ways to engage students in meaningful and effective literature discussions as well as ways to increase fluency in reading. How to implement these varied literature discussion formats and how to effectively assess the reading progress of students are included in this chapter. Strategies such as DRTA, QAR's, QuICS, and story mapping are just a few to be mentioned. Connections to benchmarks and standards conclude the chapter.

Chapter 9 returns to the notion of assessment. Formal and informal reading and writing assessments are addressed. Various assessment strategies are shared including miscue analysis, running records, anecdotal note taking, reading conferences, and checklists. Vignettes provided in this chapter enable readers to gain an understanding of how assessment can be used to inform instruction.

The third section of the book, *Part III: Refining Effective Instruction*, focuses on refining effective literacy instruction. Readers learn about stance and interpretive authority that contribute to meaning making. Content area literacy and inquiry are introduced to the reader as a means for reading to learn.

Chapter 10 addresses the hidden influences in the reading process, namely stance, interpretive authority, and social positioning. Reader response theories (Langer, 1995; Rosenblatt, 1938/1978) frame this chapter. Examples of how misalignments and alignments in teacher and student stances result in different responses and ways of interacting with text and each other.

Chapter 11 offers a discussion on providing opportunities for children to engage in inquiry projects and how technology can support children's literacy development. Having children conduct inquiry projects supports viewing literacy as a tool for understanding the world. Content area reading strategies for working with textbook reading are shared. How to evaluate reading and writing software programs and websites are also discussed in this chapter.

Chapter 12, the concluding chapter, offers a discussion on struggling readers. This chapter focuses on approaches and strategies that highlight motivation, interest, and ways of making the reading process more accessible for those that have not found reading to be an easy endeavor. Because struggling readers often receive additional support and remediation, school-wide programs such as Success for All, 4-blocks, Reading Recovery, and Literacy Collaborative are discussed. The chapter concludes with a return discussion of the guiding principles established in Chapter 1.

Instructor and student supplements

For instructors

- **Instructor's Manual:** Designed to help instructors maximize student learning, the Instructor's Manual presents the author's teaching philosophy, contains sample syllabi and chapter outlines as well as ideas for in-class discussion, and ideas for in-class and out-of-class activities. Prepared by Pam Summers at SUNY Cortland.

- **Test Bank:** The Test Bank is a comprehensive testing package that allows instructors to tailor examinations to chapter objectives, learning skills and content. It includes traditional types of questions (i.e., true-false, multiple-choice, matching, and short answer), as well as open-ended essay questions. Prepared by Karla Broadus at the University of Texas-San Antonio.

- **PowerPoint slides:** The PowerPoint slides aid professors in visually presenting the key concepts found in each chapter of the text. Intended as a lecture guide, the PowerPoint slides present material in a concise format that enables easy note-taking. Prepared by Geri Mohler at the California State University, Bakersfield.

- **Video:** A collection of literacy video is available free to adopting professors. These video clips cover the most important topics in literacy instruction.

- **The Wiley Faculty Network:** The Wiley Faculty Network (WFN) is a faculty-to-faculty network promoting the professional development and training. The WFN facilitates the exchange of best practices, connects teachers with technology, and helps to enhance instructional efficiency and effectiveness. The WFN provides training and professional development with online seminars, peer-to-peer exchanges of experiences and ideas, personalized consulting and sharing of resources. For more information on the Wiley Faculty Network, please contact your local Wiley representative. Go to www.WhereFacultyConnect.com, or call 1-866-4FACULTY.

- **Wiley Library of Children's Books:** A library of ten children's books (many referenced in the text) is available to adopters for use in their reading methods class.

For students

- **Study Guide:** The Study Guide includes pre- and post-chapter assessment questions including true-false, multiple-choice, short-answer, and essay.

- **Web Resources and Technology Links:** This resource provides links to major websites cited in the chapter text as well as other web resources for students. Prepared by Amy Flint of Georgia State University.

- **Links to National and State Standards**

- **The Book Companion Site:** (www.wiley.com/college/flint) contains additional support materials that will help students develop an understanding of course concepts and teaching methodologies and strategies.

- **CliffsTestPrep® Guides:** Often, future teachers have a lot riding on one standardized exam. In a few nerve-wracking hours, students are tested on years of learning in their chosen field. Designed specifically to help students prepare for their exams, CliffsTestPrep® guides provide focused review and practice to boost students' confidence and scores.

All CliffsTestPrep® guides are written by experienced educators who are not only experts on the subject matter, but who are also test-prep specialists and familiar with the exams. These guides can help students score higher on many standardized exams including the PRAXIS, CSET, FTCE, RICA and more. Each book includes proven test-taking strategies, sample questions, and practice exams—complete with answer and explanations.

A substantial discount is offered when CliffsTestPrep® guides are packaged with *Literate Lives*. For more information, to request an examination copy or to place an order, contact your local Wiley Sales Representative.

Acknowledgments

It is important for me to thank a number of people who have supported me throughout the development of this text. First and foremost, my husband Michael's unwavering enthusiasm and support has been instrumental in keeping me focused on the project. My early mentors at Berkeley, Robert Ruddell and Anne Haas Dyson, provided me with a foundation for literacy practices that was more than just one size fits all. My colleagues, mentors, and friends at Indiana University and Georgia State University include Mitzi Lewison, Dorothy Menosky, Jerry Harste, Carolyn Burke, Christine Leland, Peggy Albers, and Mary Ariail. Their insights and perspectives on the various drafts supported my own growth and development in critical and holistic practices. Geeta Verma, also at Georgia State University, offered much encouragement over many cups of coffee as I worked to meet deadline after deadline. Katie Van Sluys at DePaul University with me and Tasha Tropp Laman at University of South Carolina participated in many "author's circles" (Short, Harste w/Burke, 1996) as I worked on revision after revision.

I would also like to thank the countless teachers and graduate students I have worked with over the years. Their work with children in classrooms is what makes not only this text possible but provides the inspiration that high-quality, effective, critical literacy practices can occur and must occur for future generations. In particular, the teachers who shared their classroom stories for the vignettes include Jane Hammel, Natasha Adams, Megan Garrity, Maysee Young Herr, Elizabeth Binns, Katherine Simon, Leslie Bell, Donna Taylor, Kevin Gallagher, Rise Reiner, and Jennifer Laughlin. The graduate students who reviewed chapters as well as collected research material include Teresa Fisher, Tommy Fredrick, Meadow Graham, Katherine Simon, Jennifer Ureno, and Li Xu.

This text would not have occurred without the patience and support of the Wiley staff: Robert Johnston, Aquisitions Editor; Ellen Ford, Senior Developmental Editor; Maddy Lesure, Senior Designer; Nicole Repasky, Production Editor; Suzanne Ingrao, Outside Production Manager; Sandra Rigby, Senior Illustration Editor; Lisa Gee, Senior Photo Editor; and Jeff Rucker, Marketing Manager.

Creating a literacy methods textbook is a huge endeavor that involves many drafts and revisions. I would like to thank all of the reviewers and colleagues who so graciously shared their time, expertise, and energy with me as the chapters came to life. Reviewers of the book include:

Marcia Baghban, *Queens College*

Beverly Bell, *Ohio University Zanesville*

Katherine Blanchard, *University of North Texas*

Terri Brandvold, *Idaho State University*

Sharon Brickman, *Oklahoma City University*

Karla Broadus, *University of Texas San Antonio*

Mary Jo Campbell, *Edinboro University of Pennsylvania*

Jean Casey, *California State University Long Beach*

Grant Cioffi, *University of New Hampshire*

Martha Dillner, *University of Houston Clear Lake*
Joel Dworkin, *University of Texas Austin*
Mary Ann Dzama, *George Mason University*
Susie Emond, *Saginaw Valley State University*
Virginia Goatley, *SUNY at Albany*
Margaret Golden, *Dominican University of California*
Barbara Griffin, *Cameron University*
Gail Halmstead, *University of Wisconsin Eau Claire*
Roberta Herter, *California Polytechnic State University*
Wendy Hope, *St. Joseph's College*
Rosalind Horowitz, *University of Texas San Antonio*
Laveria Hutchison, *University of Houston*
Nancy Kennedy, *Lewis University*
Tasha Tropp Laman, *University of South Carolina*
David Lund, *Southern Utah University*
Doug Macisaac, *Stetson University*
Barbara Malspina, *Gavilan College*
Dixie Massey, *Pacific Lutheran University*
James McCan, *Nova Southeastern University*
Nikki Merchant, *Slippery Rock University*
Tracey Meyerhoffer, *College of Southern Ohio*

Virginia Modia, *LaSalle University*
Candice Moench, *Wayne State University*
Geri Mohler, *California State University Bakersfield*
Sherrie Pardieck, *Bradley University*
Elizabeth Pearsall, *Wayne State University*
Bertha Perez, *University of Texas San Antonio*
Margaret Policastro, *Roosevelt University*
Audrey Quinlan, *Seton Hill University*
Larry Rice, *Humboldt State University*
Dan Roccio, *Maryville University*
Suzanne Rose, *Slippery Rock University*
Karen Samson, *Chicago State University*
Michelle Schroeder, *Idaho State University*
Patsy Self, *Florida International University*
Deborah Setliff, *Tennessee Tech University*
Maureen Spelman, *Saint Xavier University*
Barbara Sposet, *Baldwin-Wallace College*
Sarah Spruce, *Olivet Nazarene University*
Pamela Summers, *SUNY College at Cortland*
Frank Tavano, *De Paul University*
Ann Teberg, *Whitworth College*
Kim Truesdell, *Buffalo State College*
Katie Van Sluys, *DePaul University*
Nancy Witherell, *Bridgewater State college*
Deborah Wooten, *University of Tennessee*
Lilliana Zecker, *DePaul University*

I am also grateful to those colleagues who participated in focus groups to discuss their courses, students, and their issues. The interactive feedback provided by these sessions is invaluable to an author in refining and focusing writing of any text. To these I also send many thanks for their interest and comments:

Gwynne Ellen Ash, *Texas State University*
Kathy Brashears, *Tennessee Tech University*
Lendi Bland, *Emporia State University*
Amy Broemmel, *University of Tennessee*
Sharon Brickman, *Oklahoma City University*
Cynthia Carson, *University of Toledo*
Faye Deters, *Eastern Kentucky University*
Marie Donovan, *DePaul University*
Claudia Eliason, *Weber State University*
Scott C. Greenwood, *West Chester University*
Deborah Gurvitz, *National Louis University*
Ana Harris, *Austin Peay State University*
Helen Hoffner, *Holy Family University*
Daniel Holm, *Indiana University South Bend*

Judy Lambert, *University of Wisconsin Oshkosh*
Mary H. Mosley, *University of Central Arkansas*
Katheeen Sanders, *Fort Hays State University*
Sally W. Simpson, *Tri-State University*
Rosemary Siring, *Montana State University Billings*
Sandra Stokes, *University of Wisconsin Green Bay*
Frank Tavano, *DePaul University*
Ann Teberg, *Whitworth College*
Shelley Hong Xu, *California State University, Long Beach*
Lilliana Zecker, *DePaul University*

Brief Contents

Contents

Part III: *Refining Effective Instruction*

Literate Lives

Teaching Reading & Writing
in Elementary Classrooms

Examining Literacy in the Twenty-First Century

Discovering What Makes a Good Reader and a Good Teacher of Readers

Quantez entered my third grade classroom as a transfer student from another school across town. Unlike most of my students whose parents dropped them off, walked, or rode their bikes, Quantez rode the city bus to school. He returned home the same way and played with siblings and cousins until his mom returned home from work. Quantez did not participate in piano lessons, Little League, or Boy Scouts—common after-school activities for the community in which the school was located. In the classroom, he struggled with literacy events. He did not easily read the third grade reading basal or effectively answer questions related to the readings. The stories in the reading anthology were not connected to what Quantez knew about the world and his experiences. His writings were meager. Quantez did not respond well to the prompts provided during writing time. By all accounts, Quantez was on his way to being a school failure in literacy practices.

It was my first year of teaching. Like many first year teachers, I relied on a teacher's manual to make decisions about how to teach reading. Students were grouped into three ability groups, and each group met with me daily to read aloud and answer comprehension questions from a reading textbook. I followed the sequence of stories provided in the teacher's manual. Students worked on reading skills, such as vocabulary, predicting, sequencing, and comprehension, by completing worksheets connected to each story. These skills were determined by the prepackaged reading curriculum used in the classroom. My understandings of the reading process did not include using authentic pieces of literature, working with others, challenging the status quo, or considering multiple perspectives. Literacy was seen as "one size fits all;" and for the most part, I had a "one size fits all" classroom.

Ten years later I was a researcher in a fourth grade classroom. Robert and Elaine, two struggling and reluctant readers in a fourth grade classroom reminded me of Quantez and the difficulties he faced in my classroom literacy program. Like Quantez, Robert and Elaine brought to the classroom different kinds of experiences and knowledge than what was perceived as being valued or important. Robert experienced great difficulty with school-defined reading events (e.g., orally reading *Island of the Blue Dolphin* and responding to a series of comprehension questions; defining words from the story; composing a summary paragraph of the chapter, etc.). The reading selections held little, if any, personal connection for him. Elaine's struggles were defined by her desire to see literacy events as social opportunities to work and share with others (e.g., small group literature discussions were more helpful to Elaine than working on a list of questions by herself). Robert's and Elaine's ways of constructing understandings of text were not aligned with the teacher's. Consequently, these two readers did not succeed in this classroom.

Much has changed since my first year of teaching. We now have solid research on the benefits of children working in groups, oral and written language development, brain

research, and authentic literature. After years of working with children, teachers, colleagues, and teacher candidates, I have come to see Quantez, Robert, and Elaine not as "struggling and reluctant" but as insightful and engaged when the reading materials and events were more similar to their interests and community practices. I remember Quantez heading excitedly with a self-selected book toward our "reading rocket" (a refrigerator box and a flashlight transformed into a rocket shooting through space). I vividly recall conversations with Robert and Elaine in self-selected literature discussions and how they easily connected characters' experiences to their own. What these literacy stories suggest is that literacy is not static and "one size fits all" but rather dynamic and multifaceted.

Over the years, I have come to understand the connection between my beliefs about literacy development (how reading is learned and what literacy is for) and the types of reading events and activities that can take place in the classroom. My beliefs are based on values, attitudes, knowledge, history as a reader, and networks of interactions with others. These practices then become the ways in which reading is defined for a particular community (namely students, teachers, parents, and administrators). From my work as a teacher, researcher, and teacher educator, I now have a view of literacy that is socially and critically situated.

I wonder...

- What experiences have you had in classroom settings that remind you of Quantez, Robert, or Elaine?

- What would you say are some guiding assumptions about literacy that were prevalent in these two classrooms?

- These two classrooms used traditional reading textbooks (also known as basal reading materials) to conduct reading instruction. What other options are you familiar with that the teachers might have considered?

3

Chapter Overview

Teaching children to read and write is intensely interactive, intellectually complex, engaging, and challenging. Teachers must decide on how to best meet the needs and challenges of all their learners in the classroom. At the same time, teachers must be mindful of standards, benchmarks, and other outside pressures that make their daily mark on instruction. The teachers in the opening vignette operated with some implicit assumptions about literacy development. In Quantez's classroom, literacy was a static and universal experience. All children received essentially the same curriculum, working through the same skills at the same time. In Robert and Elaine's classroom, the teacher also viewed literacy in a one size fits all perspective. She did not consider her students' life experiences as contributions to literacy development. In order to understand how these assumptions are formed and what it means for literacy instruction, this chapter focuses on the following questions:

- What does it mean to read and write in the twenty-first century?
- How do various models of schooling impact literacy teaching and learning?
- What are the guiding principles for effective and meaningful literacy development in elementary classrooms?
- What role does *No Child Left Behind* have in literacy instruction in today's classrooms?
- How does one's personal vision impact literacy development and teaching?

The gap: Literacy practices in school and outside of school

Creating Connections 1.1

Create a timeline of five to ten significant literacy moments in your life. These events can be both positive and negative. When do you remember learning to read? What books did you love as a child? Who has had an influence on your literacy life? What about writing events?

TECHNOLOGY LINK

www.blogger.com

Create your own blog to respond to the *I Wonder* questions, *Creating Connections*, and *Further Questions* presented throughout the book.

When asked what literacy is and how to teach literacy to young children, many people offer singular definitions that literacy involves reading and writing print-based materials. They have images of children reading school textbooks and writing book reports and essays. People generally hold on to such explanations because these descriptions often reflect their own elementary school backgrounds. There is a prevailing belief that how they learned to read and write will work for the new generation. What is not considered, however, is how incredibly different children's experiences around texts are in the twenty-first century.

Students in today's elementary classrooms were born into a kaleidoscope of images, print, and sounds. They are constantly bombarded with visual, audio, and print technologies that provide endless possibilities for interpretation and meaning making. Favorite characters from books are now seen on small and large screens (TV, movies, videogames), emblazoned on t-shirts and other personal belongings, and are a source for interactive websites and other multimedia venues. Children are able to navigate effortlessly among the many formats of technology, as well as interact with these formats at the same time. Children growing up in the twenty-first century understand the fluidity of images, words, logos, and icons; they attend to not only the print on a page but also to the topographical design of a page in print or on the screen (Moss, 2001). They pay attention to layout, captions, and the visual presentation of information. Moreover, as children interact with a range of textual materials and resources, they come to participate in broader descriptions of reading and writing.

Email, blogs, websites, text messages, novels, list-servs, picture books, essays, textbooks, newspapers, magazines, instant messaging, reports, chatrooms, music lists, and graphic novels are just a few of the textual resources that children access as they construct meaning in classrooms and in their daily lives. And while students engage with this vast array of textual materials in a variety of settings, classroom contexts continue to reflect a more static and traditional view of what "counts" in literacy practices. Given the speed with which technologies advance, there seems to be an ever widening gap between the literacy experiences offered in school, and those available for students outside school walls. In classrooms, literacy

is often approached from a print-based, linear perspective; while literacy uses outside of school have a pervasiveness of flexibility and multimodality. In order to make sense of our current literacy practices for elementary-aged students, it is important to consider the views people have about literacy development, how schools are organized to achieve particular goals, and how federal policies and mandates drive these actions.

Perspectives on what it means to be literate

[T]he views that people have of what literacy involves, of what counts as being literate, what they see as "real" or appropriate uses of reading and writing skills, the ways people actually read and write in their daily lives, these all reflect and promote values, beliefs, assumptions and practices, which shape the way life is lived within a given society and, in turn, influence which interests are promoted or undermined as a consequence of how life is lived there. (Lankshear & Lawler, 1993, p. 43)

We must look at our beliefs about reading and writing. What does it mean to be literate? Is it enough for the reader to be able to read at a fifth grade level; or must the reader be able to critically think about what he or she has read? Our beliefs about what it means to be literate inform how we teach reading and writing. **Ideologies** are systems of beliefs people carry with them as they navigate their daily living. These beliefs are cultural, gendered, religious, historical, political, and social. As systems, they function to create a view of reality that is seemingly commonplace. In the United States, for example, it is expected or commonplace that children will become proficient readers and writers, and that these practices will be learned in school. Four and five year olds anxiously await kindergarten because they believe it is a place where they will learn to read. It is also expected that nine and ten year olds will easily navigate expository material in textbooks. And current literacy practices in classrooms indicate that another common belief is that standardized tests are an adequate method for documenting students' skills and abilities in reading and writing.

TECHNOLOGY LINK
http://amlainfo.org/
The Alliance for Media Literate America is the largest organization promoting media literacy.

ideologies
Systems of beliefs that people carry with them as they navigate their daily living.

Creating Connections 1.2
- What is reading? Write your response on a note card. Share your response with three other classmates and collectively rewrite a definition of reading.
- Review a sample of texts (picture books, young adult novels, adult novels, magazines, websites, textbooks, advertisements). What does one need to know to successfully read and understand the different texts?
- As a group, summarize, compare, and evaluate the most important aspects of reading.

Ideologies about reading and writing development are based on values and always involve social contexts and histories. The past three decades have demonstrated that there are competing perspectives on the purpose for literacy development. For some, literacy development should create productive citizens and members of the workforce. For others, literacy should transform the world, and in the process value diverse viewpoints, experiences, and histories of those involved (Cardiero–Kaplan, 2002). At the center of all the debates on literacy teaching and learning is how people define literacy, and ultimately, how they define schooling. The next section details three possible ways of thinking about schooling practices and the impact on literacy development. The impact of these policies and mandates can be felt in the classroom through the types of materials and activities available to teachers and students.

Models of schooling that impact literacy development

The implicit theories and ideologies that people hold about literacy, learning, and teaching contribute greatly to the ways in which schools are structured and organized. These theories are the very fabric of how society views the purpose of schooling. The context in which children learn to read and write can vary tremendously, from traditional models of instruction to more progressive and critical models. In the following discussion, three models of schooling are presented along with how the model of schooling impacts the nature of literacy instruction in particular classrooms.

Learning is about skill building: Industrial model

industrial model

A model of education which focuses on standardization.

The **industrial model** of schooling has persisted throughout the twentieth century and now into the twenty-first. Schooling practices designed according to this model are developed to be efficient, uniform, and competitive. The ideological perspective in the industrial model is meant to create a workforce that is compliant, punctual, and accountable. In some respects, not much has changed over the years. The technologies may be more sophisticated but the pedagogy and the environment over very

The Industrial Model for schooling emphasizes an "assembly line" model with standardized materials and events.

much the same. Seymor Papert (1993) commented that someone from the nineteenth century could enter a contemporary classroom and know at a glance where they are.

In an industrial model there is a push to create uniformity across schools, irrespective of the context in which they exist. This means that all students should be provided with essentially the same content and curriculum that focus on mastery of identified standards. Reading and writing skills often move from simple to complex. In doing so, all learners are expected to attain the same understandings (Leland & Kasten, 2002).

While there are alternative models of schooling throughout the United States (see the next section on inquiry and critical), a driving force that is keeping many schools in an industrial model is **No Child Left Behind (NCLB)**, which is federal legislation enacted to improve the state of education in the United States. NCLB and the Reading First Initiative (which provides federal money to states) hold schools accountable for achieving adequate yearly progress (AYP) in the areas of literacy and mathematics. Given that accountability is a significant aspect of the industrial model, schools use standardized assessments to judge whether or not students accomplish the desired outcome of meeting state standards. All children in grades three through eight are tested annually in math and reading/language arts. Test scores are then measured against other schools and districts. Schools not achieving desired progress will be placed on a "needs improvement" list and targeted for additional support or curriculum changes. If schools do not improve in a period of three years, there are sanctions for closing the school down (see The Role of *No Child Left Behind* on Literacy Instruction for more information).

The industrial model for education focuses on standardization and having students in an "assembly line." Therefore, literacy materials are standardized with an emphasis on skills. Students complete reading worksheets and other activities focused on attaining accuracy. Performance is critical. The teacher often evaluates the quality of the performance by measuring student work against predetermined standards and other benchmarks. For example, a teacher in a fifth grade classroom considers how students respond on an activity sheet attached to *Olive's Ocean* by Kevin Henkes (2003) that focuses on characterization, plot, and setting. This work is then displayed on a bulletin board with teacher comments that address the standard. Little room exists for students to construct their own version or interpretation. Students are held accountable for demonstrating a level of proficiency in a literacy task before moving on to the next skill or to a higher level.

To further highlight an industrial model for schooling, consider Ms. Day's first grade classroom. Ms. Day teaches at a school where pressure from NCLB policies and directives to improve standardized test scores dominates the teachers' conversations during weekly grade level meetings. Ms. Day implements a prescriptive literacy program that focuses on discrete skills in the reading process. In one particular lesson early in the school year, Ms. Day asks her struggling readers to manipulate magnetic letters to form a list of words that is in the same word family (*mat, fat, cat, rat, sat,* etc.). Students then complete a worksheet that has them matching the words with pictures. Students write the words at the bottom of the page. In later lessons, Ms. Day has students read from a decodable text that emphasizes the rime pattern of -at. Students read such sentences as "Up went the cat. The cat saw a rat. The rat sat on the mat." Reading and writing instruction from this viewpoint concentrate on sounds, letters, and direct comprehension of text in a sequential order. The lesson is offered because it is part of a publisher's prescribed curriculum.

No Child Left Behind (NCLB)
Federal legislation to improve the state of education.

TECHNOLOGY LINK
http://www.ed.gov/nclb/landing.jhtml
U.S. Department of Education's official website for *No Child Left Behind (NCLB)*.

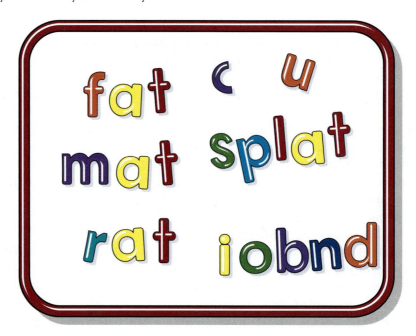

Given the lack of flexibility in the prescribed program, Ms. Day is not able to take into consideration her students' experiences with words and texts. She does not acknowledge how some of her students have had many experiences with the stories *The Cat in the Hat* (Dr. Seuss, 1967) and Eric Carle's *Have You Seen My Cat?* (1997). Conversations with other grade level teachers remind Ms. Day of the constant pressure to move students through the curriculum, while attending to such standards and benchmarks as "Students know and use word analysis skills and strategies to comprehend new words encountered in text."

Investigating a question: Inquiry model

inquiry model

Suggests that learning is best achieved when students make decisions about their own learning process.

In contrast to the industrial model of education, where the focus is on compliance and accountability, an ***inquiry model*** of schooling promotes the notion that schools should represent one's real life. There is not a "one size fits all" perspective, but learning and teaching can take many forms depending on the students and teachers in the classrooms. The goal of education should be to "cultivate productive differences" (Eisner, 1990).

In the early part of the twentieth century, John Dewey advocated developing curriculum with students' interests in mind. An inquiry model suggests that learning is best achieved when students are invited to participate in making decisions about their learning process: for example, locating topics and interests to study; choosing materials to use; finding ways to represent their learning (e.g., powerpoint slides, reports, dioramas). The tasks and activities are authentic and meaningful to the learners as they discover the world in which they live. Reading and writing instruction expands to include texts commonly used in settings outside of classrooms (e.g., newspapers, news magazines, websites). Within an inquiry model, teachers facilitate students' learning rather than direct it. There is an emphasis on "lifelong learning" that is critical in nature and not dependent on standards or minimums (Leland & Kasten, 2002).

TECHNOLOGY LINK

http://www.inquiry.uiuc.
edu/index.php

The Inquiry Page is more than a website. It's a dynamic virtual community where inquiry-based education can be discussed, resources and experiences shared, and innovative approaches explored in a collaborative environment.

The inquiry model of education recognizes diversity and multiple ways of knowing. Inquiry is learning from knowledge domains and using the habits of mind of writers, scientists, artists, and historians. The inquiry model values and affirms the cultural knowledge and language practices students bring to the classroom. Literacy is not a competitive enterprise where some kids succeed and others fail; but rather literacy development is collaborative with students working together on various questions and projects.

Imagine Ms. Day's ideological perspectives shifting from an industrial model to an inquiry model. Her literacy curriculum embraces a greater degree of flexibility and authenticity. She acknowledges and values that children come to school with different experiences, interests, and strengths. The focus for her curriculum is not just on skills, but on meaning making. Her role shifts from transmitter of information to demonstrator of different ways of learning, such as offering art as a way to respond to texts, investigation centers for students to pursue questions, and writing centers to explore different genres. Discussions about various topics are more conversational in nature. Meanings are drawn from the text as well as personal experiences.

Ms. Day's reading curriculum is not defined by a particular prescriptive program (learning the -at word family), but by students' current interests. Ms. Day's students live in an ocean side community and they expressed an interest in the recent shark attacks off the coast of Florida. To build on this interest, Ms. Day creates a text set on different kinds of sharks, including picture books, websites, and newspaper articles on the attacks and ocean safety. Additionally, Ms. Day made available books on tape and the computer for those students that may need more support in reading the text. The readability of the texts in the set is not controlled as it is in the prescribed reading program. The literacy events and practices include sustained and authentic uses of texts for seeking information and answering inquiry questions. Children immerse themselves into the inquiry by reading and writing about sharks and shark attacks. They work collaboratively in groups that are organized according to the different questions being pursued. Reading and writing in an inquiry model are for purposes that will make a difference in the lives of students as they learn about the habitats and life cycles of sharks and ocean safety.

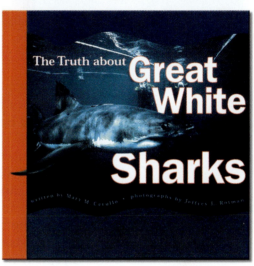

Texts and materials used for an inquiry into shark attacks.

Problematizing the status quo: Critical model

The industrial model requires students to know the basics but not to question or challenge the perspectives presented in the text. The inquiry model focuses on students' personal interests. A third model of schooling, the ***critical model***, raises questions about power, gender, social structures, and identity, offering a more global context for learning. In a critical model of education, the conversation focuses on the ways which various literacy and cultural practices privilege and/or marginalize people. Moreover, teaching and learning are seen as political acts.

The critical model challenges long-held commonplace beliefs and understandings. A critical literacy ideology encourages students to interrogate the text and the curriculum, wondering whose voice is missing and how the story might be told from a different perspective. So when third graders read biographies of notable Americans, such as presidents, civil rights advocates, and inventors, they begin to

critical model

Raises questions about power, gender, social structures, and identity, offering a more global context for learning.

Why do sharks attack?

How many teeth do sharks have?

What do sharks eat?

Where do sharks live?

How do sharks find people?

Who saves the people?

Questions posed by first graders studying sharks and the environment.

question why others are not included on the list (e.g., Native Americans, Hispanics, artists). Texts are placed within historical and cultural contexts that provide a sense of place. A critical literacy ideology empowers students and teachers to actively participate in a democracy and move literacy beyond text and into social action. Many educators and parents believe that this critical perspective is not appropriate for younger children—the texts are too difficult; the issues too complex. While there may be a need for more scaffolding and demonstration, young children are capable of considering socially significant and important issues (Chaffel, Flint, Pomeroy, & Hammel 2007; Heffernan & Lewison, 2005; Lewison, Flint, & Van Sluys, 2002).

If Ms. Day operated from a critical ideology perspective, her literacy curriculum would invite students to examine questions related to social issues such as the environment, global weather patterns, and pollution that may lead to sharks swimming in shallow water. Students may begin to investigate and interrogate current environmental policies and practices. Similar to the inquiry model, the texts are not controlled or prescribed, enabling children to glean information from a variety of sources.

The models of schooling as discussed here are found in classrooms throughout the country. In many classrooms, current federal legislation and policy (NCLB and Reading First Initiatives) have teachers and students focused on a more functional view of literacy—learning discrete skills from a prescribed curriculum. Some schools, however, are working from an inquiry model where the curriculum is student centered and students collaborate across ages and grades to understand the different functions that literacy may serve. Even fewer schools have in place a critical model. And yet, a critical literacy ideology recognizes that reading and writing do not take place in a vacuum but occur in larger social, cultural, political, and historical contexts.

What lies beneath these three models of schooling are assumptions about teaching and learning. The industrial model presupposes that the "content of what

Did you know...

In the Indianapolis Public School district, there are two schools, known as the Center for Inquiry (CFI), that embrace the inquiry model for schooling (http://www.302.ips.k12.in.us/). There is also a Center for Inquiry in Columbia, South Carolina (http://www2.richland2.org/cfi/).

Recent testing data on the ISTEP (Indiana Statewide Testing for Educational Progress) shows that students attending CFI in Indianapolis have a higher average percentile in English/Language Arts and Math than do students across the state.

Year	State Average (public and nonpublic)	Center for Inquiry
2002–03	68.7%	63.9%
2003–04	71.0%	74.2%
2004–05	71.7%	75.6%
2005–06	72.9%	78.7%

an educated person should learn was assumed to be universal; [therefore] all learners received the same curriculum" (Leland & Kasten, 2002, p. 8). The inquiry and critical models of schooling are rooted in significantly different assumptions, including the premise that learning occurs when students have opportunities to construct understandings with others, to explore their own interests, and to consider socially significant and real-life issues.

One of the goals of this text is to help teachers bridge the chasm between the literacy experiences students have outside of school and their literacy learning in the classroom. Recent educational research and theory [e.g., New Literacy Studies (Barton & Hamilton, 2000; Street, 1995), Critical Theory (Freire, 1973; Shannon, 1990), Social Constructivism (Vygotsky, 1978), and Reader Response (Rosenblatt, 1978)] suggest useful guidelines for teaching literacy today. In the next section several guiding principles for effective literacy instruction are examined.

Six guiding principles for teaching reading and writing in the twenty-first century

The industrial model of schooling has outlived its usefulness in preparing students for their futures. With the rapid growth and expansion of technology, participation in a variety of literacy events and practices is more accessible than ever before. Children have access to classmates in other parts of the world; are reading texts that are available on the Web; and are creating new formats and designs for information. Although the industrial model is readily available because of the ideological perspectives in federal mandates such as *No Child Left Behind* legislation, it is critical to consider classroom literacy practices and decisions beyond the narrow scope of NCLB.

The following guiding principles for teaching reading and writing present a broad perspective of literacy development and set the foundation for each chapter in this book.

The first of these six principles declares that reading and writing are not isolated, but rather involve social and cultural understandings. The second principle notes that literacy should be purposeful and take social goals into consideration. The third principle states that some approaches to literacy are more influential than others. Fourth, literacy is learned through inquiry. Fifth, students use their knowledge and experience to learn to read. The sixth principle suggests that everyday types of materials and multimodal texts can be used to teach reading and writing.

Principle #1: Literacy practices are socially and culturally constructed.

What does it mean that literacy is "socially and culturally constructed and situated?" The focus is not on the specific skills a reader or writer can do, but rather the relationships that are established (Hamilton & Barton, 2001). Any time people are engaged in reading and writing events, they are constructing social relationships with others. When you think of someone reading, or writing, do you envision someone alone at home, in the library, or maybe on public transportation? That's a common way to think about reading and writing, but often, we read and write with others. Particularly in classroom settings, reading and writing events involve groups of readers and writers. Classrooms are collections of racial, ethnic, and cultural groups. This diversity is a resource. The different ways students respond to and create meaning are valued. Children often interact

Literacy is collaborative and connected to life experiences of the students.

with each other and the teacher as they work in reading groups, participate in book discussions, and share their writing with peers. These activities recognize the cultural and linguistic diversity that students have as they enter the classroom. Furthermore, these activities point to the fact that literacy development is socially situated.

How does this work in the classroom? Children learn how to *do* literacy as a result of being a member of a group, whether the membership is in a family, a neighborhood, a place of worship, or as a member in a classroom. Because they are members of these groups, children observe others engaged in a variety of literacy practices. For example, Rory, age 3, observes his mother creating and using a grocery list when going to the store. He watches her write out the list of needed items, and while at the store, he also watches as she crosses off the items as they are placed in the shopping cart. These brief encounters with text are authentic venues for how reading and writing are used to accomplish particular tasks in the world. Other home literacy practices occur because they have meaning and are useful in people's lives—for example, writing phone messages, reading the mail, surfing the on-screen TV guide for a particular television show, reading the newspaper, selecting an option on the DVD, having a story routine during nap and bedtime, and reading Internet sites. Children learn that literacy involves and extends to many people and has many goals.

Looking at what people do with literacy, with whom, when, and how is central to the concept of literacy as a social practice. Children also learn that different literacy events have different expectations. Completing a skills worksheet requires a particular way of being (quiet and individual), as does engaging in a literature discussion about a favorite story (knowing group etiquette and sharing ideas). Children become aware of what is expected of them, what is important with regards to the literacy event, and how to meet teachers' and group members' goals. When completing a worksheet, children figure out that there is often just one answer, while in a literature discussion they discover that the teacher may value multiple interpretations. Literacy practices, then, are not just about learning a particular set of skills; literacy also includes learning how to be socialized into particular social practices in particular settings (Bloome & Katz, 1997). For example, students need to know how to discuss their ideas in a group setting, and how to write down and present their ideas to others. This is all part of literacy. Literacy practices do not exist in isolation. They are a part of social relationships and networks. In this way, literacy is a socially and culturally situated practice.

Principle #2: Literacy practices are purposeful.

We use different literacy practices to achieve different goals. Barton and Hamilton (1998) identify a number of reasons why people engage with literacy practices:

- to organize their lives (agendas, daily journal);
- communicate with others (letters, email, and instant messages);
- entertain (novels, and greeting cards);
- document experiences (memoir, and poems);
- make sense of their worlds (books and Internet sites); and

- participate in social life beyond their immediate context (reading about others).

Reading and writing practices in classroom settings can be organized in ways that are authentic and purposeful, as the above list suggests. Most of these events are social; meanings are constructed as a result of working together. There are abundant opportunities in classrooms to engage children in real-life, social experiences involving literacy. Reading and writing logs, journals, daily agendas, and plans for inquiry projects help children to organize their time during the instructional day. To communicate with others, children write letters, email, and text messages. Reading and writing events inside other disciplines (social studies, math, science, etc.) can be designed to support learning concepts and making meaning. Such practices might include reading informational texts, recording facts in learning journals, documenting questions, engaging in discussions, presenting newly learned information, creating powerpoint slides, and other activities. The personal narratives, poems, essays, and other texts students compose during writer's workshop are opportunities to document their lived experiences. Students may read literature selections for entertainment. Reading literature also encourages learning beyond the immediate context in which they live. All of these support the idea that people read and write for a reason.

> ### Creating Connections 1.3
>
> Observe a classroom's literacy block of time. What are the types of literacy events that occur during this time? Pay close attention to how the teacher and students interact with each other. What are the types of roles they take on in the literacy events? What are the purposes for these literacy events? Discuss your impressions with classmates.

Principle #3: Literacy practices contain ideologies and values.

Literacy practices are not neutral. They carry with them values, ideologies, and beliefs about how the world should be organized and operate. Recall the discussion on ideological perspectives and models of schooling. Some literacy practices are more valued in an industrial model (decontextualized vocabulary skills) and others in an inquiry or critical model (reading authentic texts to support vocabulary development). Brian Street (1984, 1995) introduced two perspectives around literacy: autonomous and ideological.

AUTONOMOUS MODEL. An *autonomous model* suggests that literacy practices are cultural and context free; that literacy in and of itself will affect social and cognitive functions. Adult and basic literacy programs often operate with this perspective—that if the person learns to read and write, he or she will be a better citizen with a brighter economic future (Quigly, 1997; Terry, 2006). Yet this perspective does not consider the social and economic conditions of their lives. Literacy is seen as neutral and universal. The National Institute of Literacy, a federal agency designed to promote literacy development from early childhood to adulthood, operates from an autonomous perspective of literacy. It is an agency that is charged with overseeing No Child Left Behind's singular view of the reading process. This particular view of literacy is held up as the standard, that is, what everyone should strive for.

To illustrate an autonomous view at the classroom level, schools-based literacy practices are often seen outside the context of everyday life. The practices and events one engages in during school are usually separate from everyday practices found in the larger social context. Students are asked to complete skill sheets and respond to

autonomous model

Sets of literacy skills and competencies are separate from the situations in which they are used.

literature in ways that are very much defined by the school. Take, for instance, how literature is usually read in the classroom. Children are regularly expected to answer low-level, literal questions that do not enhance the quality of the reading experience, such as "What are the characters' names in *Harry Potter*?" Ocassionally, inferential questions are asked (What would you do if you were Harry?). On their own, however, students may spontaneously share their excitement while reading *Harry Potter* (Rowling, 1998) by discussing favorite characters and reenacting various scenes. In doing so, children address more complex and sophisticated themes of the story.

School literacy practices often position literacy as an individual exercise, whereby reading and writing are privileged over oral language or other meaning making systems (e.g., drama, art, music). The work students and teachers do around reading and writing is accepted as natural and inevitable (Hall, 1998). There are no questions about whether or not children should strive to a particular standard or achieve a particular basic skill. The autonomous model assumes that children should reach a specific standard of skill; there is no questioning of this approach to literacy. Skills and standards are established as "givens." To challenge such an idea would seem as though one does not care about standards.

IDEOLOGICAL MODEL. Counter to the autonomous model is what Street (1984) refers to as the ***ideological model***. This model of literacy takes into consideration the ideologies and values that are associated with the people engaged in the literacy practices. In other words, literacy practices are embedded in a particular world view and these practices are a part of the cultural milieu. An ideological model suggests that literacy practices are related to people's everyday lives.

> **ideological model**
>
> Literacy is not a generalized culture-free process, but a set of specific practices in particular social contexts.

When teachers and students assume an ideological model of literacy, they engage in literacy practices that are meaningful and purposeful to those involved. These practices offer opportunities to legitimize uses of literacy outside of school contexts; to value alternative ways of meaning making (oral, drawing, music, movement); and to recognize that literacy is collaborative. From an ideological perspective, then, classroom literacy practices are connected to the life experiences of the students. In Ms. Barwick's third grade classroom, the students express interest in the recent immigration protest rallies. Many of the students are from Mexico and Central America. They have life experiences in border crossing. Collaboratively, students read and write about these events as they shape their own understandings about immigration policies and practices in the United States. They write letters to city officials, hold debates, and problematize the issues that are confronting their families.

Principle #4: Literacy practices are learned through inquiry.

Operating with an inquiry stance is critical to being an effective teacher, and in particular, an effective reading teacher. In Chapter 11, an inquiry curriculum is discussed in more detail. An inquiry stance is one that positions the teacher as a "problem poser" (Freire, 1985), asking questions about the ways in which children come to make sense of squiggles on a page. With an inquiry stance, a teacher considers that there may be more than one way to approach the teaching of reading and writing. Inquiry is not so much seeking the right answer because there often is not a singular answer, but rather seeking

> ### *Creating Connections* 1.4
>
> 1. What has been your experience with an autonomous model of literacy? With an ideological model?
> 2. What benefits or difficulties might occur if more 'givens' about literacy development were challenged?
> 3. What would a classroom that uses authentic texts for literacy development look like?
>
> Share your responses with classmates in class or through your blog.

resolutions to questions and issues. This opens the possibility for viewing literacy in a more complex and dynamic fashion, rather than in a one size fits all formula. Teachers working from an inquiry stance begin with what they know and juxtapose this knowledge with new perspectives. In doing so, they come to new insights while continuing to ask more questions.

Inquiry implies a "need or want to know" premise. For teachers the emphasis is on nurturing inquiry attitudes or habits of mind. Students who actively make observations, collect, analyze, synthesize information, and draw conclusions are developing useful problem-solving and learning skills. To illustrate, students in Ms. Cunningham's fourth grade classroom are studying their local community and they engage in a series of questions around the contributions people have made to their community, historical markers in the community, and the history of the monuments in the community. The students use a number of resources including text sets, interviews, photographs, and a field trip. The knowledge and skills students acquire in this inquiry can be applied to future "need to know" situations that students will encounter both at school and at work. Another benefit that inquiry-based learning offers is the development of habits of mind that can last a lifetime and guide learning and creative thinking (http://www.thirteen.org/edonline/concept2class/inquiry/).

Children learn to participate in literacy events in a variety of places

Principle #5: Literacy practices invite readers and writers to use their background knowledge and cultural understandings to make sense of texts.

Children come into school bringing their varied linguistic backgrounds and personal experiences. A child's cultural context and experience (e.g., What types of texts are available at home? Is English the child's second, third, or fourth language?) plays a significant role in which literacy events and practices are valued in the home and community in relation to which ones are valued in the school context.

Moll, Amanti, Neff & Gonzales (1992) introduced the term ***funds of knowledge*** as a way to talk about the historically and culturally accumulated bodies of knowledge that people have access to as they navigate their daily worlds. (See Chapter 3 for a more in-depth discussion on Funds of Knowledge.) For some children, these funds of knowledge and experiences will closely match the literacy engagements that are prevalent in school settings (e.g., story reading, library trips, writing lists and other documents, drawing pictures, talking about a previous experience). Children with such practices as part of their repertoire are said to have what Bourdieu (1986) notes as cultural capital. This cultural capital are the resources at hand that children draw upon as they make sense of the texts and the literacy practices surrounding such texts. These resources may be social, linguistic, or cultural.

funds of knowledge

Are historically and culturally accumulated bodies of knowledge.

Other children may enter school without such a close alignment between what they know and do and school-based literacy practices. For children who may not have access to this type of cultural capital, it means their ways of participating may not be seen as valuable or "count" in the larger context of what it means to be in school. Knowing the latest version of a handheld game, how to text message on a cell phone, or the power strength of a Pokemon trading card usually does not count toward developing literacy knowledge. Acknowledging the funds of knowledge and cultural capital that children bring to the literacy event creates space and opportunities for children to build on what they know as they engage with unfamiliar practices around literacy development.

Literacy practices involve digital media.

It is important to consider how some literacy practices and behaviors are privileged over others, and how teachers might create more space in their curriculum for students to share their interests, passions, and resources in ways that matter. Disrupting the notion that there is one universal way of thinking about literacy (autonomous) is necessary to shift the perspective of literacy as a set of neutral skills to a perspective that literacy is socially and culturally constructed; that the materials and availability of particular kinds of texts in the classroom library matter to the students and the teachers they work with.

> ### *Creating Connections* 1.5
>
> 1. How do children's different linguistic, social, and cultural resources impact their literacy experiences in school settings?
> 2. What home experiences are made visible in classroom literacy events?

Principle #6: Literacy practices expand to include everyday texts and multimodal texts.

Children quickly learn to identify important icons such as McDonald's®, Coca-cola™, Nike®, favorite cereal brands, and cartoon characters' names such as SpongeBob SquarePants™, Mickey Mouse™, and Blue™. The early attempts often occur without explicit attention or instruction. Rather, children are immersed in print all around them, and as they progress through the grade levels they begin reading Pokemon™ and Yugio™ trading cards, Harry Potter series books, stories from reading anthologies, Eye Witness books, and surfing Internet websites for information on a hobby or interest. The notion of text expands to include materials including "everyday" materials such as advertisements, Pokemon trading cards, and posters.

Children live and operate in a world where language is not the only form of communication, but images, graphics, sound, and the nonlinear nature of such texts are also significant. "It is important to remember that the children in elementary schools today were born into a world complete with digital gizmos. To them, typewriters are almost as old-fashioned as dinosaurs. Their history is one of computerization." (Lotherington, 2004, p. 317).

The *multimodal* literacies (a combination of linguistic, visual, auditory, and spatial modes) children are exposed to, through interactive digital media, play a significant role in the ways they access and use text (both print based and visual). Before coming to school, many children will experience some sort of interactive digital media, whether it is DVD movies, electronic "educational toys" (e.g., Leapfrog®), software programs for computers, or handheld gaming devices, such as Gameboy®. The access to digital media increases as children learn to surf the Internet for information, play Internet games, download music files into their MP3 players, utilize text messaging, email, and chatrooms for communication, design BLOGs, create movies with cell phones, and other possibilities not even imagined. Even children who do not have access to home computers and other digital platforms find them at school, public libraries, and friends' and relatives' homes.

Along with the digital world, there is also an explosion of what Vasquez (2003) calls "pocket monsters" (e.g., Pokemon, Yu-Gi-Oh, DragonballZ, Digimon). These television-based cartoon characters are central to trading card games. Young children collect and trade cards. There are a wide range of icons, abbreviations, and symbols on each card that refer to characteristics and attributes of the Pokemon character. Children are quite adept at "reading" these cards and understanding the available textual information. Not only are children reading and trading cards, they are also redesigning and creating their own. Redesigned cards indicate that children are sophisticated in their interactions with these texts and digital media platforms.

In school, then, it is critically important that teachers are more aware and accepting of the multiliteracies that children bring with them. These literacy practices can be used to support reading and writing practices in school settings. Instead of writing a book report, children can create imovies™ to explore the theme of the book. They can use text messaging to talk about disruptions of grammar and conventions and when this text messaging format of writing is appropriate and acceptable.

multimodal literacy

The different ways in which meaning can be created and communicated in the world today.

Student-created trading cards.

Creating Connections **1.6**

• List some of your experiences with young children and digital media. What have you observed as they interact with these new technologies?
• Observe how children access and use technology in school settings. What do these interactions say about the ways in which digital media is viewed as a tool for learning?

The upcoming chapters in this book explore the following topics in teaching reading and writing to elementary school children: oral language, culturally relevant pedagogy, models of reading, curricular programs, emergent literacy, phonics, vocabulary, comprehension, literature discussions, assessment, inquiry and struggling readers and writers. Each of these topics (chapters) uses the six guiding principles as a framework for discussing how to effectively teach literacy.

The role of *No Child Left Behind* in literacy instruction

The models of schooling and the guiding principles provide a way to think about how literacy practices are currently enacted in classrooms and what the possibilities may be in your own classroom. Before we consider how your own vision and goals for teaching literacy play an important role in developing as an effective literacy teacher, it is necessary to address the implications of *No Child Left Behind* on literacy development in this new century.

Invitation for the classroom

Interview a small group of students about their perceptions and understandings of what reading and writing are for. Possible questions to ask include:

1. Why do people read? Write?
2. How did you learn to read? Write?
3. Who helps you with your reading? Writing?
4. What do you do when you have trouble reading text? Writing?
5. What types of things do you like to read? Write?
6. Who do you know who is a good reader? Writer?
7. How would you help someone who is having trouble reading? Writing?
8. Where do you like to read? Write?
9. How do you choose what you read? Write?
10. How often do you read, in school, at home? Write?
11. How do you feel about writing? Reading?
12. Do you like to write? Why or why not?
13. Do you like to read? Why or why not?
14. How do you decide what to write about?

Invariably, one cannot listen to the news or open a newspaper and not hear or read about *No Child Left Behind* (*NCLB*) legislation. Signed into law in 2001, NCLB is an amendment to the Elementary and Secondary Education Act of 1965. NCLB provides sweeping reform efforts in a number of areas, including a stronger emphasis on reading, particularly in the early grades; increased measures for states, school districts, and schools to be held accountable for the work being accomplished; more parental choice in selecting schools for their children; and more flexibility for states to use federal education dollars. NCLB is instrumental in setting the agenda for how teachers teach reading and how schools are evaluated and held accountable.

A goal of *No Child Left Behind* is to have children reading on grade level by the end of third grade. No one can argue that this isn't a worthwhile and laudable goal. At issue, however, is the means by which this goal is achieved. The federal government created the Reading First initiative, whereby significant amounts of money are provided to States to support scientifically based reading instruction programs for the early grades (K-3). Teachers are feeling the direct effects of NCLB as their instructional decision making is called into question in reading instruction, as well as the increased number of standardized tests required at all grade levels. What does scientifically based reading instruction mean? And what does this mean for teachers and the children they teach?

Scientifically based reading instruction and the National Reading Panel

At the center of the Reading First initiative is the idea that reading programs, professional development, and assessment are driven by what is termed ***scientifically based reading research*** (***SBRR***). This means that evidence is used to make decisions about how to best teach reading. Evidence is drawn from research that is deemed rigorous, systematic, and empirical. SBRR also implies that the research design and questions can be replicated in other contexts. For example, a research study on the effectiveness of a tutoring program on reading achievement can be conducted with another group of students and yield similar results.

scientifically based reading research (SBRR)
Involves the application of rigorous, systematic, and objective procedures to obtain reliable and valid knowledge.

The National Reading Panel, a group convened in 1997 by the federal government, was charged with the task of assessing the effectiveness of different approaches to reading instruction. They reviewed 438 studies out of nearly 100,000, published in referred journals, focused on children's reading development. These studies were mostly experimental and quasi-experimental in design. Experimental research randomly assigns participants to be placed in either the control group or the target intervention group. After a predetermined amount of time, the researcher then examines whether or not the group receiving the intervention has significant gains in reading achievement. A quasi-experimental design does not randomly assign participants, but rather places participants in groups based on various characteristics (gender, age, learning disabilities, etc.). This approach is more common in education because of the difficulties of randomizing participants in school settings. While these two designs are important, the panel eliminated a large body of research that uses a qualitative research methodology. This methodology reveals aspects of the literacy process that experimental and quasi-experimental are unable to investigate.

> ### *Creating Connections* 1.7
> Access the executive summary of the National Reading Panel Report from the website (http://www.nationalreadingpanel.org/).
>
> How does their discussion of the reading process align with or conflict with the guiding principles of this text?

The panel's review of the selected research led to the conclusion that the following areas are critical to reading instruction and development:

- **Phonemic awareness (PA):** the ability to hear sounds in various words. Instruction in phonemic awareness involves teaching children to focus on and manipulate phonemes in spoken syllables and words.

- **Phonics:** the relationship between letters of the written language and sounds in the spoken language. The primary focus of phonics instruction is to help beginning readers understand how letters are linked to sounds (phonemes) to form letter–sound correspondences and spelling patterns.

- **Fluency:** the ability to read with speed, accuracy, and proper expression. Guided oral reading and silent reading provide opportunities for students to practice fluency.

- **Vocabulary:** the words students must know to communicate effectively. Repeated use of the words and in multiple contexts supports learning.

- **Comprehension:** the ability to gain meaning from what is being read. Comprehension strategies include summarizing, monitoring, answering and generating questions, and using graphic and semantic organizers.

These five areas identified by the National Reading Panel become the core features of programs endorsed by the Reading First initiative. Problematic to this report, however, is the isolated nature by which the panel delineated and reported on the five areas—as though they are separate and discrete skills to be learned by the novice reader. The panel did not consider the dynamic and integrated nature of the reading process, nor how these features interact with each other over time. As readers construct the meaning of text, they rely not only on making sense of the words, but how these words come together to form particular ideas.

Reading First initiative

Reading First initiative

Is a federal initiative to apply scientifically based reading research and instruction in grades K–3.

The panel's report had significant implications on the ***Reading First initiative***. Public schools and school districts receiving Reading First funds must purchase reading programs that meet the requirements as determined by the States (which are invariably determined by the federal government). Commercial reading programs that qualify are comprehensive, scientifically research based, and emphasize the five previously listed components (PA, phonics, fluency, vocabulary, and comprehension). These programs have a systematic and predominant focus on phonics instruction. The Reading First initiative does not specify any commercial programs, but popular choices are *Reading Mastery* (McGraw-Hill), *Open Court* (SRA), and *Scott Foresman Reading 2004* (Scott Foresman). Chapter 5 provides a detailed explanation of prescriptive reading programs.

What impact does the NRP report, and subsequently, Reading First initiative have on classroom teachers? In schools where Reading First funding is available, teachers are required to use the prepackaged and scripted programs. As a result of funding requirements, there is very little teacher decision making regarding the most effective and meaningful ways to teach reading. The programs do not present the complexities of the reading process, or the myriad of ways in which students interact and engage with text to make meaning. In many cases, the prepackaged and scripted programs limit the choices teachers and students have when it comes to learning strategies to decode and comprehend the text, and the materials used to do such work. Moreover, NCLB and the Reading First mandates have all but discounted the guiding principles addressed earlier in the chapter, as well as what it might mean to reorganize schools toward inquiry and critical models. It is important to begin problematizing the narrow scope of literacy that is currently driving the reading and writing curriculum in most schools in the country. To do so, the next section offers a discussion on how to establish one's vision for literacy.

Creating a vision for effective literacy instruction

All teachers bring to the classroom their understandings and beliefs about literacy that influence decision making on a daily basis. As evidenced in the opening vignette, when Quantez's teacher grouped students by ability for reading instruction, there was an implicit assumption that some skills needed to be mastered before moving to the next level. Likewise, when Ms. Barwick offers her students opportunities to discuss current immigration policies through various literacy events, she has a belief that literacy practices are embedded in the lives of her students. Long before teachers enter the classroom, they have a vision or image of what teaching reading will be like. There are images of the classroom (arrangement of furniture, types of materials accessible to the students), the students (who will be in the classroom), and their own ideal classroom practices (what type of teacher will they be). These images may at times be congruent with what is actually happening in the classroom, and at times be at odds with the current context. For many teachers, their visions of the ideal classroom are unstated and implicit. Yet, when these visions become visible, teachers may develop a more defined sense of purpose (Hammerness, 2003), and ultimately, provide a literacy curriculum that is meaningful for students in the classroom.

A teacher's vision of what constitutes an ideal is personal and individual. Duffy (1998) explains that when teachers develop their own stances (visions), they also develop a "focused mindfulness" about their actions. This mindfulness is not based in someone else's vision for the future, but rather their own values and intentions for the students in their classrooms. Duffy notes that when given the opportunity to think deeply about their practice, teachers began to seek alignment between what they valued about teaching, learning, and literacy and what actions they were taking in the classroom. For example, current and recurring debates in the field of literacy instruction include "Is whole language or phonics the best way to teach reading?," or "Should writing instruction include timed writing prompts?," or "Do leveled readers support reading

> ### Creating Connections 1.8
> Create your vision of the ideal classroom engaged in literacy practices. Consider the following five questions:
> 1. What are the sights and sounds of the classroom?
> 2. What are the types of materials students are accessing?
> 3. What is the role of the teacher? The students? The curriculum?
> 4. How do these factors relate to student learning?
> 5. What is the relationship between the classroom and the kind of citizens you want to see in the twenty-first century?

development?" Questions framed this way really only allow for one particular vision to emerge. But asked differently, "Given what your vision is for students, what roles do whole language and phonics play in literacy development?," or "Given your vision for a writing curriculum, what contributions do timed writing prompts make?," or "Given what you envision for students, what role do leveled readers play in supporting students' literacy development and knowledge?" These questions allow space for teachers to construct responses that reflect their own understandings of literacy development and what they acknowledge as central to creating literate students.

In Closing

This chapter provided a foundation for thinking about literacy practices in the twenty-first century. Literacy practices are rapidly changing from print based and linear, to multimodal and digital. The definitions of reading and writing are changing along with the technologies. Children are beginning to redefine what it means to be "literate" and how to flexibly navigate the fluidity of images, words, logos, and icons that appear before them (either in print or on a screen). And while there are significant advances in our technologies and children's access to such technology, we continue to operate with outdated models of schooling. There are three models of schooling discussed in this chapter: industrial, inquiry, and critical. The industrial model remains the most common form of schooling, with an emphasis on compliance, punctuality, and accountability. Current federal policies and mandates, such as *No Child Left Behind* and *Reading First* initiatives are based in this model. The inquiry and critical models of schooling encourage students to select personally meaningful topics and issues, to use authentic texts (literature), to collaborate with others, and to consider alternative perspectives.

The guiding principles addressed in this chapter provide a framework for addressing literacy development in the twenty-first century. These six principles include:

- **Principle #1:** Literacy practices are socially and culturally constructed.
- **Principle #2:** Literacy practices are purposeful.
- **Principle #3:** Literacy practices contain ideologies and values.
- **Principle #4:** Literacy practices are learned through inquiry.
- **Principle #5:** Literacy practices invite readers and writers to use their background knowledge and cultural understandings to make sense of texts.
- **Principle #6:** Literacy practices expand to include everyday texts and multimodal texts.

These principles impact the type of curriculum, materials, and activities that teachers make available in their classrooms. Moreover, as teachers begin to consider these principles in light of their literacy curriculum, they begin to create particular visions. Envisioning a meaningful and productive literacy curriculum requires that teachers think deeply about their practice. They seek alignment between their ideologies and what they value and their instructional decisions and activities in the classroom.

Terms to Remember

autonomous model *(13)*

critical model *(9)*

funds of knowledge *(15)*

ideological model *(14)*

ideologies *(5)*

industrial model *(6)*

inquiry model *(8)*

multimodal literacy *(17)*

No Child Left Behind (NCLB) *(7)*

Reading First initiative *(20)*

scientifically based reading research
  (SBRR) *(19)*

Resources for More Information

Hall, N. (1998). Real literacy in a school setting: Five-year-olds take on the world. *Reading Teacher*, 52 (1), 8–17.

Hammerness, K. (2003). Learning to hope, or hoping to learn? The role of vision in the early professional lives of teachers. *Journal of Teacher Education*, 54 (1), 43–56.

Moss. G. (2001). Critical Pedagogy: Translation for Education that is Multicultural. *Multicultural Education*, Winter 2001.

Quigley, B. A. (1997). *Rethinking literacy education: The critical need for practice-based change*. San Francisco: Jossey-Bass Publishers.

Questions for Further Reflection

- How do you see the guiding principles described in this chapter playing out in classroom literacy programs?

- What tensions do you see between the guiding principles and literacy instruction in an industrial model?

CHAPTER 2

Oral Language Learning In and Out of the Classroom

My Heart Be Beepin': Ms Adams Learns from Angie

As a kindergarten teacher, I see a large gap in the academic abilities of my students at the beginning of each school year. Some of the children enter into my classroom with background experiences in reading and writing. They have attended daycare and/or preschool. They know how to listen during read alouds; how to write their names; and how to move from one activity to another. Other students begin the year with far fewer skills. These students struggle to write their name or even identify one letter of the alphabet. I often assume that those students who receive little parental support at home will not have the concepts I teach reinforced at home. I even become a bit frustrated by the fact that if someone would have taken some time with these students prior to beginning school, they would not be so far behind when they enter school. All of this changed, however, the year I had Angie in my classroom. I no longer make blanket assumptions about children's learning based on how they talk or the type of support they receive at home.

Angie was one of those students who did not do well on the kindergarten baseline readiness assessment and her overall classroom performance was below that of the other students in the class. Angie used African American Vernacular when she spoke. At that time, I took the position that her speech needed to be corrected if she was going to make any gains in literacy. Angie was not living with her mother, and so whenever there was sharing time in the classroom, she talked about her mother. "Ms. Adams, me and my mama be going to the mall all of the time!" In an attempt to help her learn and use Standard English, I would say, "Angie, you are supposed to say, My mama and I go to the mall all of the time, not *be* going to the mall." It would take her two or three tries before she said it correctly. And yet, "Ms. Adams, my mama and me be . . . ." was something that I heard everyday from Angie. Each time, I would model how to say the sentence in Standard English. In addition to Angie's need to develop her oral language, she also required extra help in reading and math. I referred her to the Early Intervention Program (EIP). The EIP teacher and I knew that we would have to work intensely with Angie if she was to make adequate progress during her kindergarten year.

One day during center time I observed Angie mumble under her breath as she matched letters and pictures to a book. As I headed over to her table to work one-on-one with her, Angie ran up to me and said that she made up a song and she wanted me to hear it. With a huge grin on her face, she sang the words, "My heart be beepin', my heart be beepin', my heart be beepin', all the time! I can run, I can play, I can live all day!" I realized that when she was mumbling under her breath, she was actually composing the song from the activity that she was working on at the literacy center. I was honestly surprised to hear the words that she used and how she applied the pictures and words that she was working with at that center to have meaning to her. She did this without any scaffolding or support from me or any of her classmates. I did not know that Angie had the ability to think on this level. Even though the song was grammatically incorrect, Angie demonstrated what she knew about letter sounds, rhyming, and her comprehension of the lesson that I taught on *The Heart*. I then realized that the literacy experiences from

home, in conjunction with her experiences at school, definitely allowed her to create that song. Angie helped me to see that there are a multitude of literacy experiences that students engage in at home that may not be viewed as supporting literacy learning in the classroom. Even if those experiences do not generate the knowledge that we think our students should have when they enter school, we still have to value those experiences so that we do not devalue the students.

I no longer explicitly correct Angie when she starts one of her stories about what her and her mama "be" doing. I realized how important it was for Angie to share stories about her mother and I realized how important the language was to her that she and her mom shared. It was important for me to value that. As an educator, I understand the tensions between promoting Standard English at the expense of devaluing other languages and dialects. It is my responsibility to provide opportunities for children to explore and examine these tensions. I decided that I would not constantly correct my students because, through the stories that Angie shared about her mom and the song that she composed, I came to see that there is definitely a connection between language and literacy experiences at home and how a child uses those experiences as they acquire knowledge from what is taught at school. This was truly a defining moment in my experience as an educator. I come to see that it is very important to not only meet students where they are when they enter the classroom, but draw upon what they have already experienced and to not make assumptions if they seem to be struggling in class or have low academic ability. Every child knows *something*. We must be cognizant of that fact and value every child's literacy experience regardless if it meets our expectations of what we think they should know when they enter the classroom. "My heart be beeping, My heart be beeping, My heart be beeping, all the time!" Now that song is music to my ears and is in need of no correction!

I wonder...

- What knowledge and experience does Angie bring to her literacy events?

- What does Ms. Adams's decision to accept a text (song) composed in African American Vernacular English say about her growing understanding of language?

- Beyond interviews and formal school assessments, how can teachers like Ms. Adams begin to learn about the literacy practices of their students?

Chapter Overview

Oral language development is a foundational aspect of learning to read and write. Oral language is important for building literacy skills such as phonological awareness (knowing that words are comprised of various sounds), decoding skills (mapping sounds to letters), and reading comprehension. Other oral language skills, such as development of narrative, use of talk while pretending, and vocabulary are also necessary in literacy development (Dickinson, McCabe, & Sprague, 2003). Children with strong oral language capacity do well in learning to read and write (Scarborough, 1990; Snow, Burns, & Griffen, 1998). Oral language development, along with reading and writing, are developmental processes that undergo a number of different changes as the child gains competence and skills.

In this chapter, the focus on oral language development is to provide a framework for understanding reading and writing processes. There are two broad and significant discussions in this chapter: (1) oral language use and variation and (2) oral language acquisition. With regards to oral language use and variation, many people hold assumptions about what someone says, and how it is said indicates a particular level of economic, social, or cultural status. There are many conversations in education, business, and politics around the notion of "Standard English." What is "Standard" English, and who determines what is standard? How can teachers and children come to see that language and power are intimately connected?

The other important aspect of oral language development involves language acquisition and the connections to reading and writing. There are a number of linguistic terms critical to understanding early reading and writing processes. Many teachers have a general understanding of language development and how the English language works. Yet, when introducing language concepts such as word families, word patterns, vocabulary, and spelling, there are limited explanations of why the language is structured the way it is. Offering an explanation of "just because" for a particular grammatical rule or spelling does little to support readers and writers in the classroom. This is not to say that teachers should be linguistic experts, but a basic working knowledge of the linguistic features of English is important when teaching children to read and write.

Guiding questions for this chapter include:

- How do assumptions about oral language use influence our perceptions of one's economic, social, and cultural status?
- What are the implications of language policies, such as "English only as clasroom literacy practices?"
- What strategies are most effective for working with linguistically diverse students in the classroom?
- What are Cambourne's conditions for language learning?
- How does Halliday's model of language learning influence classroom practices?
- What are language cueing systems, and how do these cueing systems impact reading and writing development?

Oral language development from a sociocritical perspective

The opening vignette highlights how children and teachers access and use oral language to understand the world around them. Angie created her own song to make sense of the story and the literacy activities in her classroom. She demonstrated how language is socially and culturally situated by using familiar language patterns from her community in a new setting, school. Children come into classrooms with a rich repertoire of language from their communities and homes. They have learned how to communicate with those around them. Five-year-old Kadin's ability to recount a personal experience of finding his pet snake in the closet after it had been missing for a week, or eight-year-old Abel's question, "Is your country safe?" when introduced to a classroom visitor demonstrates the powerful nature of language use. Children's use of language to make sense of their communities and the world they live in is ever-expanding. The following guiding assumptions about oral language development provide a framework for teachers to maximize children's learning and literacy development.

Creating Connections 2.1

Make a list of common words that you use that are relatively "new" to our lexicon. Examples may include: BLOG, fast-track, globalization, ipod, etc.

Where did these words come from?
How often do you use these words?

Language practices are dialogic and evolving

Language users are always in the process of refining their language use. Children regularly and in visible ways try out various hypotheses about language structures, word meanings, and pronunciations. Toddlers play with language, wondering if certain combinations of sounds mean anything to those around them. Is it possible to say "fa fa" in an English speaking community and have it mean anything, or is it only when the toddler says "wa wa" that something happens? Even adults continuously acquire language—learning new vocabulary, nuances of the language, and rules for using language in particular contexts. Because language use is a human phenomenon, it is constantly evolving into new forms. New words become a part of the lexicon (e.g., blog, ipod, email), while others disappear.

Language is dialogic in that it is negotiated from speaker to speaker. Bahktin (1981) talks about how language is appropriated by others,

[the word in language] is half someone else's. It becomes "one's own" only when the speaker populates it with his own intentions, his own accent, when he appropriates the word, adapting it to his own semantic and expressive intentions. . . (pp. 293–294)

When we interact with others, we build upon their words, shaping them for our own purposes. These words, then, are put out for others to borrow, shape, and reconstitute for other purposes. Seven-year-old Zamir and his friends talk nonstop about Sonic X, a cartoon series featuring a hyper-hero hedgehog (Sonic) and his archenemy, Dr. Eggman. When the boys reenact various scenes from the show, they depend on shared meanings, shared concepts, and shared modes of talking for negotiating differences in meaning and interpretation (Bruner, 1990). Children begin to appropriate particular features of oral and written language when they enter school. Literature discussion groups, whole group conversations, morning meeting time, and small group discussions all have unique discourse structures to which children have become accustomed. They learn how to respond to teachers' direct questions and peers' wonderings, as well as how to construct their own interpretations and questions. Children also learn the various features and purposes in written texts, such as to inform, question, persuade, and share. They discover how to write reports, letters, memoirs, stories, and poems, among many other genres. For example, in Ms. Barwick's third grade classroom, Sierra shares her list of "defining moments" (Bomer, 2005) that she will use to construct a memoir. These defining moments are significant and important moments that Sierra can draw upon to craft her own story. As she shares her list with her writing partners, Alfonso and Dostin are inspired to add to their own list of "defining moments."

Children learn language by interacting with others.

Alfonso's list of defining moments.

Sierra's list of defining moments.

Language practices are culturally and socially situated

People have access to a range of language practices depending on the contexts in which they are talking and writing. Learning a language is learning a culture. How people speak and write often reflects the communities to which they belong. We all use one way of talking with our friends that is different and sometimes contradictory to how we might talk with parents, grandparents, employers, ministers, or others that are in positions different than our own. Consider how a group of adolescent snowboarders engage in and interact with each other about snowboarding, tricks, and mountain conditions, as compared to these same adolescent students in a classroom setting with a teacher discussing homework assignments. As language users participate in groups and communities, they navigate different linguistic features of the language.

To **codeswitch** is to use the pattern of language that is appropriate for the time, place, audience, and purpose. For example, an adolescent might use the phrase "you chillin'?" with a group of friends, but in talking with her grandparents, she asks, "How are you doing?" There is substantial evidence that demonstrates how students and teachers of various linguistic backgrounds use codeswitching as a mechanism for participating in different settings. When teachers and students interact with each other, they present a range of linguistic features that sometimes compete, but are always engaged in an ongoing struggle to make sense of the texts and events. Sometimes codeswitching can reflect tensions and contradictions. When does one codeswitch? Who determines the appropriateness of the variety used? Why should one codeswitch? These questions bring to the surface how language practices are multifaceted and complex.

codeswitch

A linguistic term meaning to alternate between one or more languages, dialects, or registers in a single stretch of talk.

Invitation for the classroom

What Are They Saying?

Build a text set of books that features code switching or language variation, such as *Flossie and the Fox* (McKissack, 1986), *Be Boy Buzz* (hooks, 2002), *Cajun Night before Christmas* (Trosclair, 1998), and *Bruh Rabbit and Tar Baby Girl* (Hamilton, 2003). Have students consider the different language features and patterns used by the characters in the stories.

Language practices reflect power and politics

Language use is one way in which we define others and ourselves. We judge people by how they talk. We evaluate their lives, their positions, and their ideas by the way in which language is used. A newscaster documenting the devastating effects of a tornado in a rural community will interview those affected, and as viewers we make judgments on their social class and status. Similarly, we may notice and comment on how politicians use language or how professional athletes talk with reporters. We may say "He sounds like a politician" or "I have no idea what he just said." What does it mean to sound like a politician or to not understand someone even when the language is the same? Language is inclusive and exclusive. It is never neutral and as such imposes "a perspective in which things are viewed and a stance toward what we view" (Bruner, 1986, p. 121).

Creating Connections **2.2**

Conduct a search of newspaper articles, news magazines, and websites regarding U.S. language policy. What viewpoints are presented around language use?

Creating Connections 2.3

Review the English/Language Arts standards for speaking in your state. What aspects of oral language development do the standards focus on? How are issues of power reflected in the standards?

Through language we create versions or storylines of the social and natural worlds that position people in relation to power (Wilson–Keenan, Solsken, & Willett, 2001). It is readily apparent in many state departments of education (e.g., Virginia, Indiana, New Jersey) that some forms of English have more power than others. "Standard English" is the language of power in the United States. Students in grades K–12 are expected to achieve particular oral language standards, such as "speak in complete, coherent sentences," "stay on topic when speaking," and "tell an experience or creative story in a logical sequence" (Indiana: http://www.doe.state.in.us/standards/Docs-TeacherEdition/Teacher-EnglishLA-081303.pdf), or "use conventions of English, including grammar and appropriate forms of address" and "use clear, concise, organized language" (New Jersey: http://www.state.nj.us/njded/frameworks/lal/chapt2.pdf). It is also noted in Virginia that a Standards of Learning goal is for students to "develop a full command of the English language, evidenced by their use of standard English and their rich speaking and writing vocabularies" (http://www.knowledge.state.va.us/main/sol/solview.cfm?curriculum_abb=E/W). These examples highlight that a particular way of speaking (Standard English) is privileged over other variations and dialects, such as African-American Vernacular, Creole, Hawaiian pidgin, or Appalachian. In many instances, when children access and use nondominant linguistic forms, they are seen as not having the linguistic capital needed for economic and social success. Teachers will routinely ask children to restate their comments and questions in Standard English, or they may model for the students the 'correct way' of saying something. In either case, the message for students is that there is one form of language that is necessary for success in this country.

The three assumptions regarding language use and development: (1) language is evolving and dynamic; (2) language practices are culturally and socially situated; and (3) language practices reflect power and politics and are important for teachers to consider as they interact and work with children in their classrooms. These principles suggest that how children talk and what they talk about is valuable to the learning community. Recall that in the opening vignette, we can see how Ms. Adams comes to value Angie's language use as she negotiates classroom literacy events. The next section offers a discussion on language variation, attitudes, and policies that play an important role in how students respond to and participate in classroom discourse.

Variations in oral language

Language (oral and written) is the means by which teachers and students impart information, construct new understandings, represent relationships, ask questions, and reflect on what they know and understand. How language is used in the classroom and the values and attitudes speakers/listeners carry in relation to what they say/hear play an important role in how teachers and students begin to position themselves and others in the learning community. Language, not only the specific language a family speaks (Spanish, English, Cantonese), but the dialect and forms of language help define identity and mark membership in particular groups who have shared knowledge and shared meanings. A

Creating Connections 2.4

How would you complete the following statements?

It _____ (feeling, emotion, stance) when people say _____.

When I hear them say this, it makes me think they _____.

In small groups, consider how your peers responded to the statements. What attitudes, assumptions, and beliefs are apparent in the statements?

number of factors contribute to how oral language is developed and how it is perceived. Important in these discussions is knowing terminology related to language variation (in particular, *English Language Learners, registers, dialects, African American Vernacular*), attitudes related to such variations, and language policies that are in place in many districts throughout the country.

Increase of multiple languages in classroom settings

Classrooms throughout the country are in a constant state of flux when it comes to student demographics. The past 20 years or so have seen a tremendous increase of students entering school with languages other than English as their primary language. Nationally, the number of English Language Learners (ELL) increased from approximately 2 million in 1993–1994 to 3 million in 1999–2000 (Meyer, Madden, McGrath, 2004). This represents a 5.3 percent increase from 1990. Over half of these students (55%) live in California, Texas, and New York. Teachers in these states are often familiar with the linguistic differences and needs of students. In other states, such as Nebraska, Georgia, Arkansas, and Oregon, the number of English Language Learners has grown by more than 124 percent from 1990 to 2000. Latino students make up the largest group of ELL students (more than 50%). Additionally, in a survey of nearly 3 million teachers, 41 percent report that they teach students with limited English language proficiencies (NCES, 2002). The rapid increase of students with diverse language experiences and needs has left many teachers grappling with instruction and teaching practices that seem inadequate. Figure 2.1 identifies which states have increased ELL populations by growth, density, and numbers.

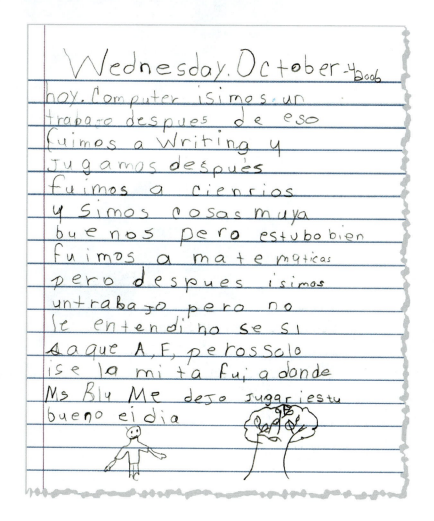

A fourth grader beginning to navigate two languages.

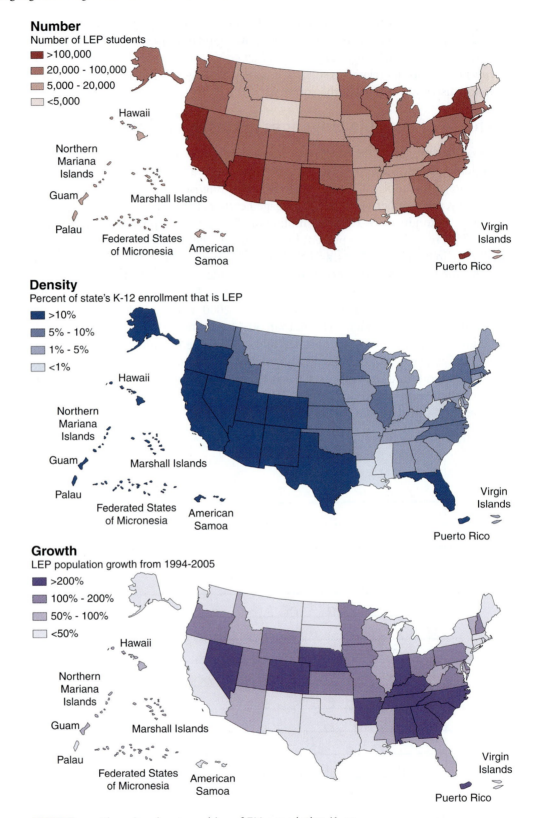

FIGURE 2.1 Changing demographics of ELL population K–12.

Source: National Clearighouse for English Language Acquisition and Language Instruction Education Programs (NCELA) (2006).

Did you know...

There are many different terms used for children who enter into classrooms speaking languages other than English.

English Language Learner (ELL) is a term used for students who first learn a language other than English in their home and community (U.S. born or immigrant) and then learn English as a new language.

Limited English Proficient (LEP) is another term that classifies children based on their language proficiency. The child may have some knowledge but is not fully proficient.

Other terms include:

nonnative English speaker, language minority student, ESL (English as a Second Language) student, ENL (English as a New Language), or *bilingual student.*

TABLE 2.1

The most widely spoken languages in the world

	Language	Approximate Number of Speakers
1.	Chinese (Mandarin)	1,075,000,000
2.	English	514,000,000
3.	Hindustani	496,000,000
4.	Spanish	425,000,000
5.	Russian	275,000,000
6.	Arabic	256,000,000
7.	Bengali	215,000,000
8.	Portuguese	194,000,000
9.	Malay-Indonesian	176,000,000
10.	French	124,000,000

Source: Ethnologue, 13th Edition,

Invitation for the classroom

Languages around the World

Read *If the World Were a Village* (Smith, 2002). Engage students in a discussion about languages used in the world. Compare the information on Table 2.1.

Additionally, collect samples of text in other languages.

1. What are the purpose and function of the text?

2. How is print placed on the page?

3. What strategies do you use to make sense of the text?

As of the 2004–05 academic year, five states reporting the highest density of ELLs in public schools (percentage of total school-age population).

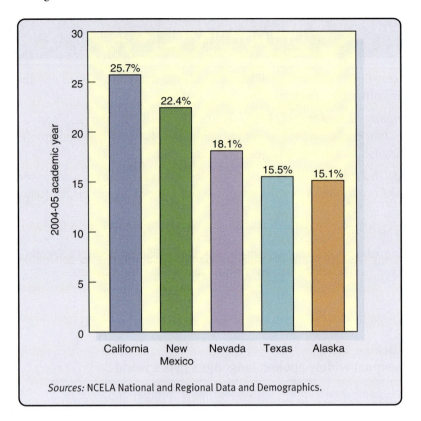

Sources: NCELA National and Regional Data and Demographics.

Linguistic variation within English: Is there a standard?

Interacting with people from different communities and countries tells us that there is quite a bit of linguistic variation even when everyone is speaking "English." While the United States does not have an official language policy indicating English is the official language, teachers, editors, writers, and other self-appointed experts serve to police correctness in language use. However, there is no single standard of correctness. Rather, there are a vast array of **registers** and **dialects** that reflect how language is socially and culturally constructed.

register

Language used for a particular purpose or in a particular setting.

dialect

A variety of language used by people in a particular geographic region.

REGISTER. Register refers to the way language is used. It is connected and identified by a social situation. A register shows what a speaker or writer is doing with language at a given moment in time. The social roles and context influence the form and function of the speech or written event. To illustrate how speakers navigate through various registers depending on the context and the purpose of the speech event, consider the well-known children's story *Bridge to Terabithia* (Paterson, 1987). In this story, Jess and Leslie are in a magic kingdom where there are rulers, kings, and queens. Kings and queens use a register that exemplifies and reflects a sense of "regalness." Jess's first interactions within this community were quite uncomfortable. He talks with Leslie using terms that are commonplace. Leslie, on the other hand, takes on the role of the queen and in doing so adopts a much more royal sounding discourse. Jess, recognizing that he needs to adopt a different register, begins to take on a more regal register used by kings and queens in the magic kingdom of Terabithia. He uses a form of language that is appropriate to the social situation. In battling the imaginary foe, Jess alters his language as he becomes more comfortable with his role in this particular community. Leslie, in her acceptance of Jess's change, reinforces the form and function of language use.

Did you know...

Dialect Myths and Reality

MYTH: A dialect is something that SOMEONE ELSE speaks.
REALITY: Everyone who speaks a language speaks some dialect of the language; it is not possible to speak a language without speaking a dialect of the language.

MYTH: Dialects always have highly noticeable features that set them apart.
REALITY: Some dialects get much more attention than others; the status of the dialect, however, is unrelated to public commentary about its special characteristics.

MYTH: Dialects result from unsuccessful attempts to speak the "correct" form of the language.
REALITY: Dialect speakers acquire their language by adopting the speech features of those around them, not by failing in their attempts to adopt standard language features.

MYTH: Dialects have no linguistic patterning in their own right; they are derivations from standard speech.
REALITY: Dialects, like all language systems, are systematic and regular; furthermore, socially disfavored dialects can be described with the same kind of precision as standard language varieties.

Source: Wolfram, W. & Schilling-Estes, N. (1998). *American English: Dialects and Variation.* Oxford: Basil Blackwell.

DIALECTS. Dialects are influenced by factors such as race, class, region, gender, and age of the language users. Linguists and social scientists estimate that there are as few as three basic dialects in the United States (Northeast, South, and Western) and as many as 24, including African American Vernacular English, Cajun, Chicano English, Pittsburghese, R-ful Southern, and Texan (Wolfram & Schilling–Estes, 1998). Depending on where one was raised or currently lives, there are distinct ways of pronouncing particular words, such as /kar/ or /rüf/, or in vocabulary, such as "pocketbooks" or "purses," "couch" or "davenport," "getting ready" or "fixin' to." Word selection also varies from generation to generation, "groovy" to "bad" to "that rocks." Regional variations are noticeable in the speaker's tone, how quickly one talks, the rhythm of speech patterns, and how long it takes to get to the central point of the discussion. People living in the northeast often talk in hurried tones and ways compared to those living in the south with a southern drawl. And while these are generalizations, a majority of people in any given region will sound more alike than different.

Dialects carry with them common assumptions and biases. This is because language is a socially constructed system of communication. In the United States, "Standard English," a dialect often portrayed as the "correct" variation, is known as the "variety of English that is generally acknowledged as the model for the speech and writing of educated speakers" (American Heritage Dictionary, 2000). Standard English is used in academic, political, and economic circles. The editors of the dictionary go on to say that "in recent years, however, the term has more often been used to distinguish the speech and writing of middle-class educated speakers from the speech of other groups and classes, which are termed *nonstandard.*" What this definition implies then is that speakers of other dialects are somehow not standard and essentially not educated. Although Standard English varies from locality to

TECHNOLOGY LINK
http://cfprod01.imt.uwm.edu/Dept/FLL/linguistics/dialect/maps.html

Dr. Vaux conducted a four-year survey study of dialectic differences in the United States. View data-embedded maps of Dr. Vaux's survey results or sort the differences by your home state.

TABLE 2.2
Contrasting Uses of Be in AAVE

Feature	AAVE	Standard English Equivalent
Habitual be	She be walking down the street.	She always walks down the street.
Future be	She be walking.	She will be walking.
Absent be	She walking.	She is walking right now.
Past be	She was walking.	She was walking.

locality (from President Kennedy's dropping of the /r/ in words like *car, power*, and *either* to President G. W. Bush's folksiness and Texan twang), there is a tendency in our schools to not discuss the distinctions or variations in people's language use, but to privilege a notion of "Standard English" over other ways of talking.

African American Vernacular or "Ebonics." One dialect often seen from a deficit perspective is *Ebonics*, or *African American Vernacular English* (AAVE). Many wonder if Ebonics is a dialect or even a language. Should teachers correct students when they use AAVE? As described by the Linguistics Society of America, African American Vernacular English (AAVE), or Ebonics, is a "systematic and rule governed" language variety spoken by many African American students. As a distinctive language variation, one of the most common distinctions is in the verb "be" (Redd & Webb, 2005; Smitherman, 1977). Drawn from work by Redd and Webb (2005), Table 2.2 reflects what an AAVE speaker might say and the equivalent Standard English form.

In addition to the use/omission of the verb be, there are other distinctions including pronunciation (e.g., *thang* for thank, *dem* for them, *mouf* for mouth, *bruvver* for brother, *wid* for with, *walkin* for walking), plural and possessive features (e.g., *three girl* for three girls and *Jamal house* for Jamal's house), and a whole host of other grammatical features.

Classroom approaches to issues of dialect. Issues related to Ebonics and learning surfaced in the mid-1990s when Oakland, California passed a resolution legitimizing Ebonics as a language variant in classroom settings. Media, politicians, and the public voiced their opposition or support for such a resolution. Those who opposed AAVE in the classrooms operated from a verbal deficit hypothesis that suggests that when a student speaks a language variation that is perceived to be nonstandard, that language is inadequate for success in schools and thus, it needs to be changed. When teachers adopt a *correctionist* perspective, they will correct or insist that the student self-correct when AAVE is used rather than Standard English (SE). For example, in Ms. Shepard's classroom, Shakeila informs the teacher that Dharma is going to be a few minutes late to class, "Ms. S, she be comin'". To this, Ms. Shepard responds, "We don't say 'she be comin.' We say 'she is coming.'" This is similar to Ms. Adams' early perspectives about language learning in the opening vignette.

On the other hand, teachers who support using AAVE in the classroom view a child's language not as a problem to be fixed but as a resource for learning. A *contrastive* approach recognizes that a child's home language is different (not deficit) in structure than what is used at school. Ms. Camponi uses students' writing to discuss differences in plurals between AAVE and Standard English. Students share sentences from their writing journals and Ms. Camponi writes them on one side of the chart paper. This column is labeled informal language. On the other side

Ebonics or AAVE

Systematic and rule governed language variety spoken by many African American students.

correctionist perspective

A perspective that attemps to correct any nonstandard language use.

contrastive perspective

A perspective that accepts nonstandard language use.

of the paper, students revise the sentences into Standard English. There are discussions about how in both cases meaning is understood. From a contrastive position, it can be argued that AAVE serves as a bridge to acquire the language variation of power. And it isn't just about Ebonics. There are many children who come into classrooms with a vast array of regional and social dialects that are different than Standard English forms (e.g., Appalachian, pidgin, Creole).

An important issue, however, remains: Competence in Standard English is critical for academic achievement and social mobility. The focus, then, for the discussion is not whether students should use Ebonics in the classroom, but rather what are the mechanisms and instructional support that will validate students' language systems and dialects, while at the same time provide meaningful interactions with Standard English. In other words, how can teachers use AAVE or other nondominant forms of English to effectively teach children to read and write in Standard English? One avenue, as demonstrated by the work in Ms. Camponi's classroom, may be to facilitate conversations around language use and to recognize that language users make choices of which dialect/register to use at any given time.

Language variation as a resource, not a deficit

Language is central in defining one's culture and identity. Students bring into the classroom a rich array of linguistic variations that often lead to creating unwarranted stereotypes. Think for a moment when you hear conversation on a subway train, listen to an interview with eyewitnesses to a tragic event, walk by a group of young adolescent boys playing basketball in the park, or listen to a couple of young mothers as they shop at a local mall. In each of these instances, you make assumptions and judgments about the person(s) intelligence, and social and financial standing in the community. Of course, there is a host of other factors that contribute to these early impressions, but language use is a dominant factor in how we view people. Language use is very situation specific; therefore, generalizations about groups of people should not be made based on their use and style of language.

Sociopolitical influences on language relate to power structures in societies. Language is power. Those in dominant political, social, and economic groups in a society are often the ones that determine the accepted variation of a particular language. In the case of English, "Standard English" is perceived as the only acceptable variation. This variation is viewed as being socially prestigious among those in power. Social institutions, such as school, try to instill a particular value of learning "Standard English" by relating it to better opportunities—politically, socially, and economically. School practices focus on eliminating other dialects rather than adding to them (Brisk, 1998). Fluency in multiple dialects (and languages) is not a valued practice in the United States unless one's first language is English and one's first dialect is Standard English (Gollnick, 2002). When children come into classrooms speaking something other than "Standard English" there is a concern that these children will not succeed in school or in *life*. A common argument heard in relation to this issue is that "they [students who do not speak Standard English] will need it in the *real world*." Well, these children are living in the real world—they are fully functioning members of their communities. What is implied in the previous statement is that other variations of English (i.e., pidgin, AAVE, Appalachian dialect, Creole) and in many cases, other languages (e.g., Spanish, Arabic, Vietnamese) are not acceptable forms of language use; that children [who use variations of standard English] will not be prepared to succeed in a world that is dominated by a particular language ideology and standard—one that is controlled by a particular group of people.

TECHNOLOGY LINK
http://www.tolerance.org/pt/index.html

Online activities for children to learn about bias in history, language, and culture. A teacher guide is also provided.

TABLE 2.3
Perceptions of Language

Language as a Deficit	Language as a Resource
Changes or deviations from the "standard" contribute to a deprivation theory. *Saying "ya'll" rather than "you all," or "he be walking" for "he is walking" is a sign that the speaker is less cognitive capable than others.*	Inviting students to consider different purposes and audiences for their language choices. *Students are encouraged to have conversations about language variation and power.*
Preventing students to access and utilize their primary language during instructional time *All instruction is in English with little accommodation, if any, for students who do not speak English.*	Acquiring multiple languages expands an individual's repertoire for effectively communicating in many situations. Multiple languages also increase cognitive flexibility. *Being able to effectively communicate with Spanish-speaking parents and English-speaking friends suggests an expansive linguistic repertoire.*
Schools remediate "disadvantages" associated with linguistic differences in race/ethnicity, class, or parenting styles. *Teachers instruct students to "speak" right and do not accept linguistic variations in students' speech patterns.*	Linguistic and cultural differences seen as "funds of knowledge" for building literacy in the classroom. *Students' knowledge and language experiences are used to support literacy learning in the classroom.*
Learning a language is based on a single developmental timetable. *Operating with the assumption that children at a particular age will learn to speak a language, and that all languages have some universal or common structures. And that these structures are learned in isolation*	Literate ways of thinking develop by actively engaging in the practices of a community of learners. Language is an integral part of the sociocultural context of the community. *Learning a language requires that learners are actively participating in the event or setting where the language is being used.*
Speakers who codeswitch are viewed as ambiguous and culturally ambivalent. This codeswitching is seen as "interference" for learning a language. *Students who use words in their primary language as they try to explain their thinking in another language are not effective in their communication. The use of another language interferes with the target language.*	Speakers who codeswitch are sensitive to a relationship between language status and context. Language code "mixing" is seen as a meaningful verbal strategy and as an indicator of bilingual development. *Students who codeswitch are focused on the content of their talk. Codeswitching suggests that a language user is adaptable.*
English-only is the communicative norm for educational and economic success. *This perspective is represented in English-only movements*	Bilingualism/biliteracy is a living, desirable, functioning mode of communication in academic work and social contexts. *This perspective is held by those who support and value multiple languages.*

Invitation for the classroom

Language Profile

Students can fill out a language profile that documents their own language variations as they shift audiences and purposes. They can also document language use of others in the community.

Speaker	Words and Phrases	Definition	Who Is the Audience?

How do I feel about the different ways people speak?

Why are some languages or dialects more highly valued than others?

Adapted from Y. Goodman, 2003.

Table 2.3 on page 38, adapted from Franquiz and Reyes (1998), highlights key tenets from two contrasting positions: (1) language as a deficit or (2) language as a resource.

It is not enough for teachers to know about Standard English grammar and use; they also need to examine their own viewpoints of language use as it relates to students' capabilities in the classroom. "Language, like ethnicity and social class, is a status predictor in the classroom, raising or lowering teachers' expectations and students' self-esteem" (Redd & Webb. 2005, p. 3). There are five principles to keep in mind when thinking about language variation and use (Y. Goodman, 2003).

• Language is neither good nor bad, neither correct nor incorrect; rather, what is considered appropriate is dependent on the context in which it is used.
• Some language use is acceptable with peers but not with members of older generations.
• Language acceptability often varies from one cultural group to another.
• Meaning is specific to the context in which language is used.
• Some vocabulary terms have the same pronunciation but different meanings depending on the context, the content of the discussion, and the participants.

These principles can shape how language use is viewed in the classrooms.

Language policies: Implications for teaching literacy

Language policies, such as "English only" have been around as long as British colonists. As early as the 1750s, there was discussion and debate regarding English versus German. Many British colonists in Pennsylvania were concerned that too many of their neighbors were speaking German. This became a political and emotional issue. Since then, there have been numerous accounts of opposition to languages other than English, particularly during the latter part of the nineteenth century, after WWI, and now as the ELL population continues to rise throughout the country. At issue in these debates are concerns of patriotism, language loyalty, assimilation, and racism. In recent times, advocates of "English-only" policies have made their positions known through state official-language referenda, local ordinances, and regulations. In some states, there are ordinances mandating Roman alphabet on signboards, forbidding public libraries to purchase non-English books, and requiring employees to use English on the job and during breaks (Baron, 2005). As recently as 2002, the Bilingual

Education Act of 1968 was replaced with the English Language Acquisition, Language Enhancement, and Academic Achievement Act. The focus shifted tremendously from accessing and utilizing a student's primary language as a bridge to academic English to preparing ELL students for rapid placement in mainstream classrooms.

Two states, California and Arizona, with others such as Massachusetts and Colorado close behind, eliminated or are planning to eliminate bilingual education from their school systems. The new laws severely limit services for English Language Learners. ELL students are temporarily placed in a separate English classroom (sheltered English) for a period of time, which is not to exceed one year. In the sheltered English classroom, students receive "survival" English skills so that they can transitioned into mainstream classrooms as quickly as possible. Schools are being asked to remove all library books in other languages, to only offer instructional materials in English, and to discourage children from using their primary languages. While "English-only" debates usually focus on eliminating languages other than English, issues related to *nonstandard* dialects, such as African American Vernacular English, should also be considered in light of implications (remember the Ebonics debate in California).

The impact of "English only" or "Standard English" on learning to read and write is consequential for many ELL learners and AAVE speakers in the classroom. Research indicates that many children who speak AAVE or languages other than English often received highly scripted phonics-only reading curriculum (Gutierrez, Asato, Santos, & Gotanda, 2002; Wolfram, Adger, & Christian, 1999). These structured programs are a one size fits all approach to literacy development. It is assumed, all students, irrespective of their language experiences and backgrounds, will map the language of the text to his or her speech patterns. For AAVE and ELL speakers this may not match with the teacher's expectations, and the lesson turns into a lesson on pronunciation rather than comprehension. "Sounding like the teacher becomes a prerequisite for students to decode text" (Chamot & O'Malley, 1994, p. 89).

Additionally, because of language differences, ELL students are often segregated in the classroom in terms of their access to particular curricular activities and materials. Language is not employed as a tool for learning but rather oral language fluency becomes the primary target of instruction (Gutierrez, Asato, Santos, & Gotanda, 2002). Moll et al. (2002) noted that ELL students in mainstream classrooms often engage in a low-level academic curriculum, where language is used largely in isolation from a student's experiences (e.g., language drills on phonemes; procedural aspects of reading; activity sheets with sight words). Additionally, ELL children are not participating in whole-class discussions, because there is a perception that one needs to know more about language rather than the content being discussed. ELL students often express frustration in not being able to remember important words in Spanish and are unable to produce the words in English (Dixon, Green, Yeager, Baker, & Franquez, 2000).

The results of such policies and subsequent instructional practices for linguistically and culturally diverse students leave little room for reading and writing to be meaningful and semantically driven. Learning to read and write is not just about acquiring the ability to decode sounds in a linear progression, but about making sense of text in meaningful ways.

In the next section, a close examination of language learning is presented as a starting point for thinking about the interrelated connections between oral language development and reading and writing.

Conditions and models for oral language acquisition

As babies grow and develop, they learn to talk. This process, one that is incredibly abstract and complex, is learned with relative ease by most children. Babies begin interacting with their environment from the moment they are born, making sense of all that is around them. Early on, babies coo and babble to indicate comfort or happiness. They might repeat single syllable sounds such as "ma ma" or "da da," which are very often interpreted by family members and friends as the words "mom" and "dad." Before age 1, babies will use one word, "up," to represent an entire thought such as "pick me up." These initial utterances are often responded to as though the baby has clearly articulated her thoughts and wishes, thereby indicating that the sounds are worthy of action and response.

As babies become toddlers they begin to use telegraphic speech, which is using one or two words to communicate whole ideas. "Daddy come," "I fall," "all gone" are common possibilities. From this point forward, children rapidly learn language. Researchers note that a child's working vocabulary goes from 20 to 50 words as a toddler to over 5000 when they enter kindergarten (Nagy, 1988). Frank Smith suggests that the number is even larger—10,000 words (1988). They do not all know the same 5000 words, but they will know most of the words their friends and families know. They will not know all of the words teachers know, but they will know words that the teacher is unfamiliar with (Smith, 1992). During this time children are learning something about hundreds of words at a rate of about one an hour while they are awake. Children in preschool and kindergarten play with language as they make up rhymes and words. They are able to talk about their actions, create stories, take turns in conversations, and ask many questions (why, how come, when). By the time children enter kindergarten, they have mastered nearly all of the complexities of language use and development. With this ability, children express their needs, thoughts, and feelings. Prior to starting first grade, Trey's mother asked Trey if he wanted to take his lunch to school or buy the school lunch. Trey responded rather quizzically, "How will I know what they have for lunch?" His mother explained that there is a menu and every morning they can read it to see what will be served that day. Trey was quite excited by this and said, "For sure I'll buy lunch on days they have artichokes."

So, how does all of this happen when formalized instruction or learning does not seem to occur between the young child and those in the immediate surroundings?

Cambourne's model of oral language development

Brian Cambourne, a noted literacy researcher, began studying how children who struggled with school-based tasks, such as reading, writing, math, and spelling, had little trouble mastering complex and sophisticated concepts outside of school, including oral language.

TECHNOLOGY LINK

http://www.child
developmentinfo.com/
development/language_
development.shtml

This site provides a list of current research on language development.

Did you know...

Children enter kindergarten with approximately 5000 words in their working vocabulary. They continue acquiring words at a rate of about 3000–4000 each year during their elementary years. This adds up to over 36,000 words by the time they finish high school.

Learning how to talk, that is, learning how to control oral language of the culture into which one has been born, is a stunning intellectual achievement of incredible complexity . . . Despite this complexity, as a learning enterprise, it is almost universally successful, extremely rapid, usually effortless, painless and furthermore, it's extremely durable. (1995, p. 183)

CAMBOURNE'S CONDITIONS FOR ORAL LANGUAGE DEVELOPMENT. Cambourne hypothesized that perhaps there were certain conditions in place when children learn to talk that could be applied to classroom settings when children learn to read and write. He identified eight conditions that are "naturally" in place as young children acquire language—*immersion, demonstration, use, feedback, responsibility, approximation, expectation*, and *engagement*. These conditions provide a powerful framework for developing and maintaining language and learning.

Cambourne's conditions of learning:

- **Immersion.** Children are surrounded by authentic uses of oral language in their homes and communities. Even though the young child is not yet able to produce accurate forms of the language, the child hears the language used in meaningful ways.
- **Demonstration.** Children live in the world. They hear how language is being used to get things done in the world, to share feelings and ideas.
- **Use.** Children have opportunities to use oral language in meaningful and authentic ways.
- **Feedback.** Children are given feedback (through meaningful response) on what they say.
- **Responsibility.** Children have ownership of using oral language to meet their needs.
- **Approximation.** Children make "best guesses" when they learn oral language. Their initial attempts to say words are often close to the actual word ("da da" for dad or daddy)
- **Expectation.** There is an expectation that children will learn to talk; therefore, they do.
- **Engagement.** Children readily participate in making sense of their environment. They use oral language to take part in the world.

These conditions work in concert with each other. Parents, caregivers, and others use language around a baby. Conversations are carried on in the presence of the young child. The first time a baby babbles or coos in ways that seem to "make sense" to others, there is a sense of accomplishment and celebration. The adult accepts the approximation and provides appropriate response and feedback. So when Roarke, at one and half years old, indicated that he wanted his bottle and said "ba ba," his mother recognized this as an approximation and responded by giving him a bottle. The parent may also provide a demonstration to the child by saying something like, "Oh, here is your bottle. Do you want your bottle?" The toddler begins to make the connection between action and language, thereby taking on responsibility and use. Learning one's first language does not occur through explicit instruction, whereby the caregiver provides a lecture on how to say a particular word. Parents and other caregivers

> ### *Creating Connections* 2.5
>
> What are your current understandings of the role of language development in learning to read and write? Share your initial thinking with classmates.

also do not provide only bits of a language (e.g., mastering the /m/ before introducing the /p/). Rather, children are immersed in all of the language, and as their needs arise they use language, take risks with structure and form, and eventually learn the best ways to put particular sounds and words together for a specific effect.

CAMBOURNE'S CONDITIONS FOR READING AND WRITING. Given that oral language is acquired through these seemingly commonplace and natural conditions in homes and communities, Cambourne pursued the notion that maybe learning written language (reading and writing) could be approached with these conditions in place. Instead of reducing the reading and writing process into discrete skills that must be mastered before other skills are introduced (which is a common approach to reading and writing development), these processes might be learned in ways that more closely mimic learning oral language. In the following chart, Table 2.4, Cambourne's conditions are considered in light of reading and writing processes.

> ### *Creating Connections* 2.6
>
> Return to your literacy timeline composed in chapter one. Which of Cambourne's conditions are apparent in your reflections of learning to read and write? For example, did you note the types of activities and/or titles that supported your early literacy development? What was it about those specific activities or titles that you remember?

TABLE 2.4
Cambourne's Conditions for Reading and Writing

Cambourne's Condition	Description	Classroom Example
Immersion	Children are surrounded by a variety of texts in the classroom.	Extensive classroom libraries; environmental print on the classroom walls; opportunities to read and write throughout the instructional day
Demonstration	Children have the opportunity to see others read and write for meaningful reasons.	The teacher actively participates in reading and writing during reader/writer workshop. The teacher shares what she is reading with students.
Use	Children have opportunities to use reading and writing to make sense of their experiences.	Throughout the instructional day, children are reading and writing a variety of texts that support their inquiries about the world (hurricanes, planets, NASCAR, horses).
Feedback	Children learn to read and write by engaging with others. Reading and writing are socially constructed events.	Author circles, literature discussions, reading and writing conferences, and partner reading are opportunities to receive response and feedback.
Approximation	Children learn to read and write by making "best guesses" as to what words say or how words are spelled.	Teachers support early readers and writers by using "best guesses" and "have a go" strategies for unfamiliar words.
Responsibility	Children assume ownership of learning to read and write for meaningful reasons.	Workshop structures encourage readers and writers to read and write texts that they find personally meaningful.
Expectation	There is an expectation that children will learn to read and write in formal school settings.	Classroom libraries stocked with texts of varying levels of difficulty encourage and support readers and writers to achieve more sophisticated moves with literacy.
Engagement	Children learn to read and write when they are involved in the process.	Classroom literacy events that meet the children's needs and interests support higher levels of engagement.

TECHNOLOGY LINK

http://www.wiu.edu/itlc/
ws/ws1/docs/
Language%20Play.pdf

This site provides a list of
picture books that contain
language play.

Halliday's model of language acquisition

While Cambourne's work helps teachers and literacy researchers consider the important role environment and interaction patterns are in learning to talk, read, and write, another theorist Michael Halliday (1975) investigated the process of learning language and how language is used. Halliday developed a three-part model: learning language, learning about language, and learning through language. Each component of the model is further explained in the following sections.

LEARNING LANGUAGE. *Learning language* is a complex, meaningful endeavor that is achieved through the interplay of a number of meaning-making processes. As children learn language, they progressively move from the immediate and concrete to the more abstract and metaphorical. Young children often name all four-legged animals "dogs" or "cats" without realizing that there are significant differences between dogs and cats. Eventually, they learn to discriminate between dogs and cats, providing the correct label when necessary. Upon entering formal schooling at about age 5, children have a fairly developed understanding of abstract concepts. This coincides with the abstract notion of learning to read and write—that meaning is reflected in the marks on the page. Additionally, learning a language progresses from merely representing a shared experience (the child and the listener have had the same experience) to representing experiences with those who are not present in the event themselves. This shift suggests that language is a dialogic activity, whereby there is an active and reflective dimension of meaning.

Halliday's work with young language learners led him to generate a series of functions that language serves. These functions, listed in the following chart (Table 2.5), are the purposes we have for engaging in meaningful linguistic acts (reading, writing, talking, and speaking) in various social contexts. Linked with the function are a number of common literacy events that highlight the particular function.

A literacy rich environment supports teachers and children's opportunities to access and utilize the various language functions. In many classrooms, the *informative* and *regulatory* functions are often over-used at the expense of the *personal* and *imaginative* functions. Galda, Cullinan, and Strickland (1993) note that the over-reliance on the informative function is problematic because this function is one of the last to develop in a child's communicative competence. To assist teachers in achieving a balance of the different language functions, teachers can use this framework to analyze their own literacy practices and events to determine if a particular function needs more attention or if some functions are over-used as suggested by Galda, Cullinan, and Strickland (1993).

Creating Connections 2.7

Observe in a classroom for a period of time during their literacy block of time. What sorts of language functions are you able to document? Do students and the teacher achieve some balance among the functions? Are there functions that dominate the talk? What do your observations say in terms of how language is used and/or learned in the classroom?

LEARNING ABOUT LANGUAGE. *Learning about language* is a component of the Halliday model that many teachers are less familiar and knowledgeable about. Language is governed by a set of rules, also known as grammar. Experiences with language tell us when sentences are not clear or when conventions are not used. Take, for example, the following three sentences. Even though each sentence has the same words, only one sentence follows a set of conventions familiar to our language.

- Charlie offered chair his to the elderly lady.
- His chair Charlie offered to the lady elderly.
- Charlie offered his chair to the elderly lady.

TABLE 2.5
Halliday's Functional Uses of Language

Halliday's Function	Description of the Function	Language Sample	Literacy Practice in Classrooms
Reveal or Assert Needs			
Instrumental	Language is used to get things done; to satisfy particular needs.	"Can I sharpen my pencil?" "Please mark your first choice for lunch"	Students indicate on a lunch form what they want to have for lunch.
Regulatory	Language is used to control others; to regulate their behavior.	"Stand in a line." "Raise your hand." "Have your materials ready."	Teachers and children create charts to indicate classroom rules and procedures.
Connect Self with Others			
Personal	Language is used to express thoughts and opinions.	"I liked when Ralph [the mouse] climbed into Keith's pocket" (in reference to the story *Mouse and the Motorcycle).*	Students participate in literature discussion groups sharing their thoughts and opinions about characters, plot, and personal connections.
Interactional	Language is used to form and maintain social relationships.	"What did you do last night?" "Do you like to read Harry Potter?"	Children engage in written conversations, pen pal letters, email notes, to develop personal relationships with others.
Create, Comprehend, and Expand Knowledge			
Heuristic	Language is used to seek knowledge; to find out information.	"How many teeth do sharks have?" "What country are you from?" "What does a category 5 hurricane mean?"	Children construct questions to pursue as part of their inquiry projects.
Informative	Language is used to convey information.	"My parents are from Vietnam." "Hurricane Katrina was a category 5 hurricane"	Children create time lines, reports, maps to demonstrate knowledge.
Imaginative	Language is used to express creative thoughts.	"Bees, bees Yellow bees Honey bees" "Once upon a time. . ."	Children write entries for a fictional character, create and perform poetry and songs, etc.

Teachers who understand how our language is structured and organized are able to more effectively teach reading and writing. When a reader comes across an unfamiliar word, a teacher knowledgeable about language systems is able to explain why the letters in the word make a particular sound or why the next word is most logically

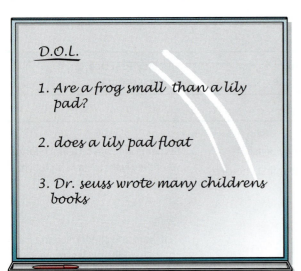

a verb given the context in which it is presented. Learning how the language works in a systematic and functional way greatly increases students' abilities to be effective and productive readers and writers. It also encourages students to take more risks with language and to use language more effectively in a variety of settings (Y. Goodman, 2003).

Studying the rules and social conventions of a language provides teachers and students with a better understanding of how language is constructed. One approach to studying the rules is through *Daily Oral Language* (*D.O.L.*). D.O.L. is usually a 10-minute activity that teachers introduce at the beginning of writing time. It is a routinized and highly scripted approach, where the teacher writes two to three sentences on the board with intentional errors in grammar, punctuation, and spelling. The sentences are part of a published series. Students are to rewrite the sentences using correct usage, spelling, and grammar. While this activity is designed to make visible and explicit grammatical rules and conventions, it does little for helping students become knowledgeable about language conventions. The sentences are not a part of the writing that students are engaged in with their journals, drafts, and other publications. Learning about language through a prescriptive, transmission approach (DOL, direct instruction of phonics, grammar, vocabulary, spelling, etc.) does not seem to transfer to the authentic writing and reading engagements that students participate in on a regular basis. Harris and Graham (1995) write, "Despite their popularity, activities that concentrate on grammar, punctuation, or usage often are not embedded in actual writing experiences and do not improve students' writing" (p. 15). This is perhaps why a student can consistently achieve high scores on spelling tests, but those same words are incorrectly spelled in other contexts, such as in writer's notebooks or in drafts for future publications. Learning about language in this way suggests that there are prerequisite skills and rules that must be mastered prior to properly using language.

A more productive approach, then, is to learn about language when using language. Readers and writers come to recognize conventions and rules by drafting their own texts and experimenting with language conventions. Writing conferences, message boards, written conversations, author sharing, and reading other people's work supports students' growth in learning about language. For example, when young writers draft personal narratives, they make decisions regarding voice (first or third person) spelling, and usage (noun and verb agreement). Writing conferences and editing are opportunities for teachers and students to discuss these decisions and the

Written conversations between third-grade classmates.

conventions of our language. As children read other people's texts, they have opportunities to wonder and question why the author selected a particular word or structure.

Bianca   and Caroline zet

How old are you? 9

what is your name? Bianca

do you go to mexico? No

why not? I don't have money.

do you have your own room? no I don't.

But I will have my own room oneday.

do you have your own room too? yes

have you ben to Califrnya? no

what book are you reading? greenegg and ham and If I finisht The book.

do you see Poccemon? no I don't like it.

when is your Birthday? October 21.

wheyer are you from? I am frome Salvador.

do you have a pet? No

A written conversation between two third-grade classmates. *(continued.)*

Alma, Leslie

February 26, 2007

how are you?
I am fine you? Iam fine to.

What is your favorite color?
My favorite color is Blue how about you? My favorite Color is blue just like you. Do you have aney pets? NO, I do not have aney pets. Do you like to play with Barbes? yes, I like to play with Barbies you. I do like to play with barbes. What do you like to play? Socer what do you like to play? Soccer just like you. Dos your mom or DaD buy you th.gs that you want? Yes, but not everything. Dos your mom l.t your jump on the bed? NO my mom does not let me jump on the bed. Do you have a brother? Yes, but he's a baby and he is 6 mouths old. What is your mom and DaD's name? Angelica and Cruz.

What is your mom and dad's name? My mom's name is Silvia and my Dad's name is Gillermo. Do you like reading and writing? yes. I do, do you? Yes, just like you. What is your brother's name? He's name is Andres.

Authentic experiences with language provide students with opportunities to examine language conventions and rules in the context of their own ideas and thoughts. Children begin to realize that language rules are not inherently right or wrong. Through conversation and discussion, children learn that language conventions are socially constructed by people who use language. We come to recognize the order in which our words appear and the conventions used to make sense of the written text. As Halliday reminds us, we learn about language because we are language users.

Invitation for the classroom

Print search, developed by Lorraine Wilson (2002), is an opportunity to assess what students understand about language conventions and rules.

1. Select a passage from a familiar text.
2. Identify various conventions and punctuation marks in the passage. Write those on one side of the column.
3. Have students write what they know about the rule or convention. In other words, why did the author choose to do what she or he did?

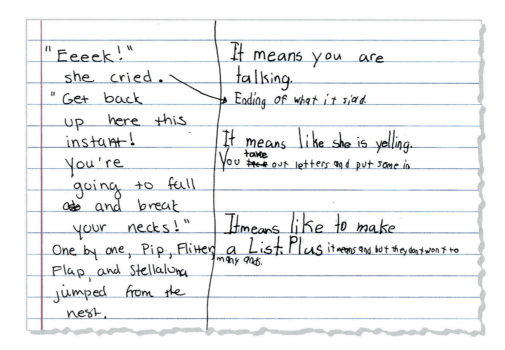

Kyleigh and Tamera's example of print search.

LEARNING THROUGH LANGUAGE. The third component of Halliday's model is *learning through language*. In this component, language is seen as the tool to explore and expand one's understanding of the world. Language processes, such as reading, writing, talking, and listening, are the ways in which children come to learn ideas and concepts as well as how to do things in the world (Mills, O'Keefe, & Jennings, 2004). For example, in literature discussion formats children take opportunities to process information, form new ideas, and share their thinking as it relates to the central themes in the text. Additional examples of learning through language include literature logs, mathematics journals, science reports, and discussions during morning meeting time. In most cases, classrooms brimming with oral and written language demonstrate how students and teachers use language to inquire, problematize, understand, act on, and critique in order to possibly make a difference in the world (Mills, O'Keefe, & Jennings, 2004).

In Ms. Crew's multi-age classroom of third, fourth, and fifth graders, the students regularly participate in a morning routine known as "What's On My Mind." Students are asked to write down issues, concerns, points of interest, or whatever is on their mind that they want to talk about with others in the classroom. The notes go into a basket, and one or two are selected for whole class discussion. In some cases, the discussion proves to be satisfactory and the issue is no longer of concern. Other issues spark conversation and debate. These topics often move into inquiry and focus studies. On one particular day, Jeremy was interested in talking about a sign he saw posted between two buildings. His note said, "Why can't we skateboard in the alley?" When his note was selected, Jeremy proceeded to share with the class the sign that he saw (No skateboarding or bike riding in the alley) and why he thought he should be able to ride his skateboard in this particular place. Some of the students agreed with Jeremy that this particular alley was a great place to try new tricks, while others seemed to sympathize with the owners of the buildings that they might not want the noise that skateboarding causes or they did not want anyone to get hurt. The students talked back and forth generating a list of possible reasons why this sign was posted. As result of the conversation, Jeremy decided to spend some time during writer's workshop drafting a letter to the building owners asking why they did not allow skateboarding in their alley. Through all of this, oral and written language was used to explore and expand understandings of the world.

Children use language to make sense of the world.

Halliday's work established a way of thinking about language development that draws upon not only the aspects of actually *learning language* and *learning about language*, but also how learners *learn through language*. This work is important in recognizing that in order for children to become competent oral and written language users, they must have opportunities to use language in meaningful and authentic ways.

Figure 2.2 (adapted from Kathy Short, 1999) illustrates how various classroom literacy events exemplify Halliday's model of language acquisition.

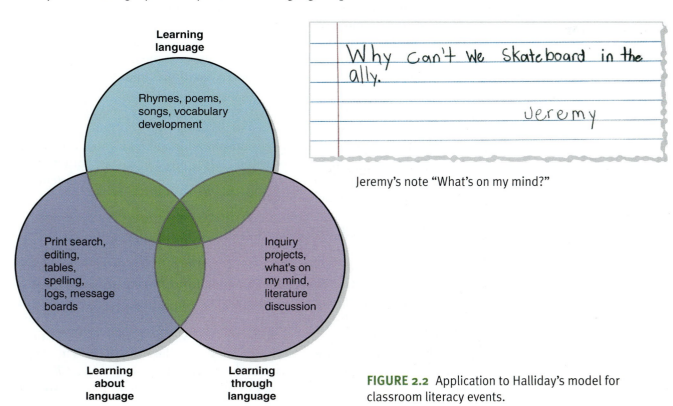

Jeremy's note "What's on my mind?"

FIGURE 2.2 Application to Halliday's model for classroom literacy events.

Language cueing systems that support reading and writing development

While Cambourne and Halliday established broad understandings of how children acquire and use oral and written language, Kenneth Goodman a psycholinguist, established a view of the reading process that involved a close look at the systems of oral language that make communication possible. Known as the psycholinguistic nature of the reading process, Goodman (1963) argued that readers bring to the text their knowledge of language (including structure, intonation, and vocabulary), their experiential background, and a conceptual framework as they strive to make meaning of the text. Goodman and Goodman (2004) write "reading is not simply knowing sounds, words, sentences and the abstract parts of language . . . reading, like listening, [reading] consists of processing language and constructing meaning" (p. 628). Readers process language through four *cueing systems*: *graphophonemic*, *pragmatic*, *semantic*, and *syntactic*. Readers access these interrelated cueing systems to varying degrees as they predict, make inferences, confirm hypotheses, and construct meaningful text.

cueing systems

Are sets of cues or clues built into the structure and patterns of the language.

Knowing how readers and writers make use of cueing systems is essential to providing meaningful and effective literacy instruction at any grade level. When readers come to unfamiliar words or are struggling with comprehension, it is helpful to know which cueing system they are focusing on. With this information, the teacher can then provide strategies that will contribute to their literacy development. Chapter 5 offers an expanded discussion of the cueing systems in relation to reading curriculum, and Chapter 10 offers assessments that attend to the different cueing systems.

Graphophonemic: Sounds and symbols

Every language makes use of a set of symbols, such as sounds and letters, to construct spoken and written words. The graphophonemic cueing system pays particular attention to the sounds and symbols of language. Babies begin to attend to sounds of the language early on, noticing changes in intonation as adult speakers ask questions or make statements. They learn to recognize and use only those sounds that are particular to the language or languages they hear. Over time, children test out various hypotheses about sounds, how sounds work together, and the results or implications of uttering such combinations. As children experiment with the language, they come to understand how languages are nuanced in particular ways. As noted by Halliday and Cambourne, much of this learning is unconscious and incidental. Parents and caregivers rarely provide explicit instruction on learning a language. Rather, by using the language in authentic and purposeful ways, children become competent language users in their homes and communities.

PHONEMES AND PHONEMIC AWARENESS. With the publication of the National Reading Panel's report *Teaching Children to Read* (2000), there has been increased emphasis in policy and early reading programs on the graphophonemic cueing system. The National Reading Panel identified *phonemic awareness* as a critical precursor to learning to read and preventing reading difficulties. According to the National Reading Panel there were a number of correlational studies that identified phonemic awareness and letter knowledge as two of the best predictors of how well children will learn to read during their first 2 years in school. Given the prominence of this report and the resulting legislation (*No Child Left Behind, Reading First Initiative*), it is essential for teachers to have a working knowledge of linguistic terms related to learning to read. Phoneme, phonemic awareness, phonics, and phonetics are the most commonly used terms in the graphophonemic cueing system. A ***phoneme*** is the smallest unit of sound in a language. In English, there are approximately 42 phonemes: 20 vowel sounds and 24 consonants. The following chart (Table 2.6) identifies phonemes in the English language.

phoneme
Is the smallest unit of sound in the language.

TABLE 2.6
Phonemes in the English language

Phoneme	Spelling(s) and Example Words	Phoneme	Spelling(s) and Example Words
/A/	a (table), a_e (bake), ai (train), ay (say)	/s/	s (say), c[e, i, y] (cent)
/a/	a (flat)	/t/	t (time)
/b/	b (ball)	/U/	u (future), u_e (use), ew (few)
/k/	c (cake), k (key), ck (back)	/u/	u (thumb), a (about), e (loaded), o (wagon)
/d/	d (door)	/v/	v (voice)
/E/	e (me), ee (feet), ea (leap), y (baby)	/w/	w (wash)
/e/	e (pet), ea (head)	/ks/ or /gz/	x (box, exam)
/f/	f (fix), ph (phone)	/y/	y (yes)
/g/	g (gas)	/z/	z (zoo), s (nose)
/h/	h (hot)	/OO/	oo (boot), u (truth), u_e (rude), ew (chew)
/I/	i (I), i_e (bite), igh (light), y (sky)	/oo/	oo (book), u (put)
/i/	i (sit)	/oi/	oi (soil), oy (toy)
/j/	j (jet), dge (edge), g[e, i, y] (gem)	/ou/	ou (out), ow (cow)
/l/	l (lamp)	/aw/	aw (saw), au (caught), a[l] (tall)
/m/	m (my)	/ar/	ar (car)
/n/	n (no), kn (knock)	/sh/	sh (ship), ti (nation), ci (special)
/O/	o (okay), o_e (bone), oa (soap), ow (low)	/hw/	wh (white)
/o/	o (hot)	/ch/	ch (chest), tch (catch)
/p/	p (pie)	/th/ or /th/	th (thick, this)
/kw/	qu (quick)	/ng	ng (sing), n (think)
/r/	r (road), wr (wrong), er (her), ir (sir), ur (fur)	/zh/	s (measure)

Each language has its own set of phonemes and the rules that govern which combinations are permitted and which are not. In English, there are combinations of consonants that do not include intervening vowels, such as /str/, /fl/, and /dr/. There are also rules that govern where particular consonant blends and clusters may appear in words. There are no words that begin with the consonant cluster /mp/ but plenty of words that have this cluster in the final position, including dump, lump, and cramp.

A phoneme may also be identified by the virtue that a change in sound changes the meaning of the word, so /sit/ is a different word than /sEt/ because the vowel sounds are different, as well as /tip/ is a different word than /dip/ because the /t/ and the /d/ produce different meanings for the word. This knowledge is important because speakers pronounce words that are seemingly the same and yet the phoneme indicates a difference in meaning. For example, a child raised in the southern states may say *pen* and *pin* with no distinction, or a child with Spanish as a first language may substitute the sound /b/ for /v/ in the word *very* because in Spanish there is no distinction between the /b/ and /v/. The impact of these differences is visible when children begin to pronounce and/or spell various words.

phonemic awareness

To consciously attend to sounds in the language.

Phonemic awareness is the ability to consciously attend to sounds in the language. Children who are phonemically aware recognize that the word *dog* has three distinct sounds /d/ /o/ /g/, while the word *happy* has four distinct sounds /h/ /a/ /p/ /E/. They would also note the different sounds in *map* and *tap*. Phonemic awareness is not an issue of one-to-one correspondence of letters to sounds. It merely is the awareness that words are comprised of sounds.

PHONETICS AND PHONICS. Studying how we articulate and segment various phonemes is *phonetics*. Speech and language specialists will have a thorough understanding of how sounds are constructed and articulated. In early primary

phonetics

Studying how we articulate and segment various phonemes.

Invitation for the classroom

Phonemic Awareness: Words Are Made up of Sounds

Read *The Hungry Thing*, by Jan Slepian and Ann Seidler (1991) to a group of young children. Each time the hungry thing asks for something to eat, have the children try to figure out what he wants (e.g., schmancakes, fancakes, pancakes; feetloaf, beetloaf, meatloaf). Encourage children to make predictions as you read the book. The charm of this book is that the listener plays with language.

After reading the book, pull out a lunchbag and announce how hungry you are. Look into the bag and tell the children what you have for lunch today. "Ah! Mogurt! I love mogurt!" Encourage the children to guess what mogurt is. Once they have figured out that mogurt is yogurt, take it out of the bag to show them and ask them how they knew. Repeat this with three or four other food items you have in the lunchbag.

Next, provide the children with paperbags, paper, and markers (or magazines with photographs of food) so they can create their own lunchbags full of food. After they draw or select and cut out their favorite foods and put them in the bag, have each child sit with a partner and provide "clues" about what his or her bag contains. "I have a piece of nizza." The partner's task is to determine what "nizza" is.

You may also create a center with plastic foods and lunchbags. Children will play with these items, retelling the story and creating rhymes as they have their peers guess what they have in their bags. A copy of the book should be available at the center.

grades teachers often focus on **onsets** and **rimes**. An onset precedes the vowel and can include up to three consonants, while the rime is the vowel and all succeeding consonants.

In English, all spoken words have rimes, but not all words have onsets. Table 2.7 illustrates a few onset and rime combinations.

Teachers also work with children on articulating syllables. A *syllable*, which is larger than a phoneme, is made up of a minimum of a vowel and associated consonants. The number of syllables is equal to the number of articulated vowel sounds, so the word "mat" has one syllable, while the word "matter" has two (mat-ter). To help children distinguish between monosyllabic and polysyllabic words, teachers often ask children to tap or clap once for each syllable identified.

Phonics is the association between letter and sounds. It is also an approach to reading instruction. The focus is on mapping letters to sounds. When a young reader comes across the word dog, she recognizes that the symbol "d" makes a /d/ sound, that "o" makes a /o/ sound, and that "g" makes a /g/ sound. As the young reader sounds out the individual letters, she comes up with the word "dog." Effective reading teachers are knowledgeable about phonemes, phonemic awareness, and phonics as they relate to reading development. Chapters 6 and 7 detail a number of instructional strategies to facilitate young children's understandings of sounds and letters.

Semantics: The meaning of words

The semantic cueing system focuses on the *what*, or the content of the language. When faced with unfamiliar words, teachers encourage readers to consider the context in which the word is being used, as well as the surrounding words in which the unfamiliar word appears. Word meanings depend on a system of semantic relationships that organize the world in particular ways, and not in others. For example, the word "run" has approximately 30 definitions (http://www.m-w.com/dictionary/run). Notice how the word "running" has different meanings based on the other words in the sentence:

- The boy is *running* down the street.
- She is *running* for a seat in the next election.

onsets

Part of the single syllable word that precedes the vowel.

rimes

Part of the single syllable word that includes the vowel and all succeeding consonants.

phonics

Association between letter and sounds.

TABLE 2.7
Onsets and Rimes

Word	Onset	Rime
Big	B	ig
At		At
Kite	K	ite
In		In
Red	R	ed
Sound	S	ound
Best	B	est
Black	Bl	ack
String	Str	ing

Invitation for the classroom

Playing with Sounds in Language

More accomplished readers also enjoy playing with language. Alliteration is one possibility. Alliteration is the repetition of beginning consonant sounds in phrases and sentences (e.g., do or die; safe and sound; now or never).

1. Read a story that demonstrates alliteration such as *The Worrywarts* by Pamela Edwards Duncan (Harper Collins, 2003).
2. Discuss what students notice in the text, that certain sounds are repeated over and over in the beginning of words.
3. Have student create their own alliterations to share with the class. Students may also begin to create tongue twisters.

morpheme

Smallest linguistic unit that carries meaning.

Words can also carry different meanings because of the morphemes in a word. A **morpheme** is the smallest linguistic unit that carries meaning. A morpheme may be considered *free,* such as the words "dog," "walk," and "fast." Or the morpheme may be *bound*, meaning that it needs to be attached to another morpheme. Suffixes and prefixes such as -ed, -ing, -s, pre-, and dis- are bound morphemes because they change the meaning of the word. For example, the word "dogs" has two morphemes (dog + s [plural]), "teacher" also has two (teach + er [one who does]), while the word "pretend" has only one. "Pre" is not a bound morpheme in this case because it does not alter the meaning of the root word. When children come to an unfamiliar word, they may search for words they know inside the word. It is important to note that many of these words are not morphologically connected because the new words are not connected in meaning to the old word (e.g., mat inside of matter; rag inside of fragrant; play inside of display). Teachers' knowledge of free and bound morphemes is particularly helpful in understanding children's miscues when using English in speaking, reading, and writing.

Additionally, vocabulary knowledge supports children as they use words in varied contexts and for multiple purposes (Richgels, 2004). Blachowicz and Fisher (2005) comment that learners move from not knowing a word, to being somewhat acquainted with it, to attaining a deeper and richer knowledge of how to flexibly use the word in different ways. Nagy and Scott (2001) suggest that adequate instruction in vocabulary development should go beyond a "diet of synonyms and short glossary definitions. Chapters 7 and 8 present a number of invitations that highlight vocabulary work.

Syntactics: The structure of language

syntax

The study of the rules or "patterned relations" that govern the way words combine.

Syntax is the study of the systematic ways in which words and sentences are organized and related to one another. The syntax reveals how words relate to one another within a sentence or paragraph. This cueing system is very similar to Halliday's notion of learning about language. Readers rely on their understanding of the language's grammar to know the likelihood of a particular word type being the next word in a sentence. When a reader comes to the sentence, "Wow, Tony just won a wonderful *ribbon* for being first in the competition," the reader is anticipating a "something" in the place where ribbon is located. If on the other hand, the reader says, "Wow, Tony just won a wonderful *red* for being first in the competition," we know that red is not the appropriate word because we were anticipating a noun, not an adjective or descriptor word. This knowledge is based on our intuitive understanding of how the English language is structured.

orthography

The study of how language is organized in written text.

etymology

The study of word origins.

In addition to sounds and meaning, there are other aspects of language that are important to know. *Orthography* is the way in which language is organized in a written text. Aspects, such as spelling, punctuation, and capitalization are included in this system. *Etymology* is the study of word origins. The English language is comprised of many words that are borrowed from all over the world (e.g., Greek, Latin, Hindi, Nordic). Teachers and students access this knowledge when working with base or root words, prefixes, and suffixes. Many of the words in the English language are derived from Latin and Greek roots. Knowing the history of a word is important when it comes to vocabulary development. Recognizing the **root word** helps a reader learn words that are in the same word family. For example, when a reader comes across the unfamiliar word *solarium,* she may know that this word has as its base, sol, which means sun. This knowledge helps the reader to figure out that solarium has something to do with the sun.

Affixes are linguistic elements that are added to words that change the meaning of the word. Prefixes and suffixes are used to generate a number of new words. Common prefixes include re-, dis-, un-, pre, while common suffixes include -ly, -able, -less, and -ful. An effective approach to teaching affixes and suffixes is to have students work with the unfamiliar words in context. They define what the prefix means, create whole meaningful sentences, and then define the word within the sentence. For example, a reader comes across the word "connected" and knows that "con" means together. The reader creates the following sentences, "The TV and DVD player are not *connected* to cable." My *connection* to the story is not very strong." Through discussion, the students and teacher create definitions for the word[s].

affixes

Linguistic elements that are added to words to change the meaning.

Pragmatics: Language in use

Pragmatic conventions address *why* and *how* a person communicates. Young language learners are figuring out who can say or write what to whom. They begin to recognize that children do not say the same things as adults; they learn rules and conventions in their homes and communities about how children interact with peers and with adults. They learn there are some words adults use that children do not. Pragmatic conventions also are concerned with the purpose of the language—where, when, and how it is constructed. The social context of language includes power relations, distance, function, and communicative style. As noted earlier, the same speaker will speak differently when giving an oral book report as compared to talking in the lunch room, or participating in a literature discussion. In writing, students learn to navigate particular features of text. To illustrate, when Caleb's first grade teacher experienced a death in her family, he wrote a sympathy card. Caleb appropriated common sympathy card discourse as his own to express his thoughts. Hymes (1972) noted that people use language flexibly depending on the range of intentions and communities in which it is used.

Building one's foundational knowledge in the area of language use and development raises language to a conscious level. Learning and studying the systems of language in more public ways enable teachers and students to be in control of their language use. As a result of this growing awareness of how language works, students and teachers become more effective language users and ultimately more effective readers and writers.

 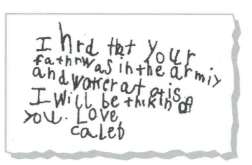

Caleb's sympathy card.
Dear Mrs. Kern I am sorry that your father died. Love Caleb.
I heard that your father was in the army and worked at Otis. I will be thinking of you.
Love Caleb

In Closing

Classrooms are linguistically diverse places. Children bring their languages and dialects into the classroom. In order for teachers to provide productive and effective learning environments for literacy development, it is important to understand how beliefs and assumptions about language impact the reading and writing curriculum. As noted throughout the chapter, language is dynamic—it changes as language users engage and interact with each other.

This chapter focused on two broad areas of language use and development. One area is how languages are perceived in classroom contexts and how teachers should be sensitive to how language can be used to position people in particular ways. Some languages and variations hold more power and prestige than others. Engaging children in conversations around language use will support their growing understandings of why particular forms of language are used and mandated in classroom settings.

Additionally, this chapter offered discussion on language acquisition. Three models were presented to provide a framework for considering how children learn language and the implications for reading and writing. Cambourne's model encourages teachers to pay close attention to the various conditions that are present in classrooms that support literacy development. Halliday's model outlines three aspects of language development that are critical to not only learning language but using language in productive ways. And Goodman's work with the cueing systems provides teachers with a more comprehensive view of the linguistic nature of reading and writing.

Terms to Remember

African American Vernacular *(35)*

affixes *(55)*

codeswitch *(29)*

contrastive perspective *(36)*

correctionist perspective *(36)*

cueing systems (graphophonemic, syntactic, semantic, pragmatic) *(50)*

dialect *(34)*

Ebonics *(36)*

etymology *(54)*

morpheme *(54)*

onset *(53)*

orthography *(54)*

phoneme *(51)*

phonemic awareness *(52)*

phonetics *(52)*

phonics *(53)*

register *(34)*

rime *(53)*

syntax *(54)*

Resources for More Information

Adger, C. T., Snow, C., Christian, D. (2002). *What teachers need to know about language* (Eds.), Washington, DC: Center for Applied Linguistics.

Goodman, Y. (2003). *Valuing language study: Inquiry into language for elementary and middle schools.* Urbana, IL: National Council of Teachers of English.

Horng, E. L., Ruiz, R., Garcia, E., McCarty, T. L. (2002). 'Sounding American': The consequences of new reforms on English language learners. *Reading Research Quarterly*, 37 (3), 328–243.

Mills, H., O'keefe, T. & Jennings, L. B. (2004). *Looking closely and listening carefully: Learning literacy through inquiry.* Urbana, IL: National Council of Teachers.

Redd, T. M. & Webb, K. S. (2005). *A teacher's introduction to African American English: What a writing teacher should know.* Urbana, TL: National Council of Teachers of English.

Short, K. (1999). *The Search for 'Balance' in a literature-rich curriculum.* Theory Into Practice, 38(3), pp.130–137.

Questions for Further Reflection

- As you reflect upon the linguistic variation in your community, what decisions will you make regarding classroom discourse practices?

- How do the models around language acquisition help you make sense of the connection between oral language development and reading and writing?

- Return to the opening vignette and consider the perspectives or beliefs that the teacher drew upon to facilitate language development and reading in her classroom.

Getting to Know Students: Developing Culturally Relevant Practices for Reading and Writing

Ms. Garrity Learns from Bianca

"Miss Garrity, when we eat lunch?" "Miss Garrity, when we have centers?" If she wasn't asking me questions, then she was asking the person at the table next to her or the child walking by to sharpen a pencil. Bianca, a bright, inquisitive learner was learning how to navigate two languages and two cultures.

Bianca was returning to my school for the second time. She originally started kindergarten the year before in another teacher's class, only to leave for Mexico because of a family emergency. Bianca returned months later and re-enrolled into kindergarten. And at the beginning of the following school year, she entered my first grade classroom. I remembered her from the year before and was looking forward to having her in my room. I wanted to learn more about Mexico and her culture.

On the first day of school, I decided to sit Bianca next to another child from Mexico named Rosa. At that time, Bianca and Rosa were the only two Hispanic children in my classroom. I knew that Rosa could not speak or understand English. Bianca, on the other hand, was able to speak and understand both English and Spanish. I thought she could possibly use her cultural knowledge and experiences to help Rosa feel more comfortable. Maybe she could explain assignments and procedures to Rosa in Spanish. I also had a picture in my mind of the two of them becoming best friends over conversations about Mexico and their similar family backgrounds.

Unfortunately, I was wrong. Bianca hardly talked to Rosa at all. Rosa would just sit there staring at her paper. I would say, "Bianca, can you tell Rosa in Spanish to draw a picture of herself?" Bianca would answer, "I don't know how to say it." I would answer, "Well, can you say the word 'picture' for me in Spanish?" Her answer was always, "I don't remember how."

There was similar resistance from Bianca anytime I asked her to tell me anything about her culture. While reading *Gathering the Sun* (Ada, 2001), a book of alphabet poetry in Spanish and English, where each letter represents a Spanish word, I asked Bianca, "Do you remember seeing anything like this when you were in Mexico?" She answered, "No." No matter how hard I tried, I could not bring out what Louis Moll and his collaguéas (1992) refer to as Bianca's "funds on knowledge." I knew she had a rich knowledge about both the Spanish language and about the Mexican culture, but I could not get her to share any of it with me or the class. It wasn't that she was a quiet child afraid to open up. She had plenty to say about most things. However, in response to questions about her culture, she said nothing.

I finally called Bianca's mother in for a conference. I felt that Bianca was abandoning her culture and I didn't know what to do. This conference was invaluable as I learned about

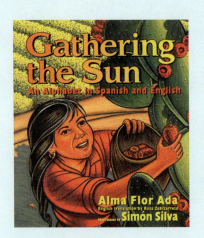

Bianca and how to draw out her strengths and cultural knowledge.

Bianca's mother, Mrs. Rosales, told me that she, too, was having trouble with Bianca. She said that she didn't understand it because Bianca never wanted to speak Spanish at home. Due to her daughter's dislike of the Spanish language, she was trying to speak only English around Bianca. Mrs. Rosales also told me that she felt it was important for Bianca to learn English so that she could "fit in" with the other students at school and understand her assignments at school. She then explained that Bianca did not think fondly of Mexico because her father had stayed behind and Bianca didn't understand why. I explained to Mrs. Rosales that it was very important for Bianca to continue to use Spanish at home and in the classroom; that the other students and I could learn from Bianca's knowledge and experiences if we could just get her to share them with us. I knew that unless Bianca valued her knowledge and knew that others valued it, too, she was never going to want to share it or remember it.

In addition to her knowledge of the Mexican culture and Spanish, I learned from Mrs. Rosales that Bianca had many responsibilities at home. She was expected to help her mother with her two younger brothers and to clean their rooms. Learning this information about Bianca really helped me to understand more about Bianca's home-life and background experiences. I felt that her knowledge of organizing could be brought into the classroom. I began to ask her to be in charge of organizing the writing center, straightening the library books, and clearing the art center. Bianca demonstrated leadership and skill in organizing and participating in these classroom jobs. She took pride in being able to do it so well. Other students noticed her new responsibilities and before long they all wanted to help and be involved.

I made a conscious effort to include more stories and pictures that highlighted places and people in Mexico during reading and writing time. My calendar area, which had a calendar, weather, lunch count, and other daily markers, reflected both English and Spanish words. All of my students were learning more about Mexico as I continued to encourage Bianca and Rosa to share their own knowledge and experiences. I brought in my own photographs and

I wonder...

- In what ways does Ms. Garrity demonstrate to Bianca and the other students in her class that multiple languages are valued and important?

- What do Ms. Garrity's experiences suggest about the relationship between texts and students' cultural lives?

- What strategies does Ms. Garrity use to foster Bianca's understandings of text and to share her knowledge and experiences?

stories of visiting Mexico. This small change in the classroom made a big difference for Bianca. She began participating more in the learning centers and other activities. After sharing my photographs, I noticed that Bianca started to open up a little more about her knowledge and experiences. She started to help me pronounce Spanish words correctly during calendar time as the rest of the students repeated. She also started to talk about her visits and experiences in Mexico a little bit more.

On one occasion in particular, students were asked to put a set of picture cards in chronological order and then create a story based on the pictures. I gave Bianca a set of cards that reflected a group of children hitting a piñata at a party. I hoped that Bianca would have some knowledge of the piñata and be able to put the cards in chronological order. I will admit that as teachers, we must be careful not to over-generalize when teaching about cultural traditions. I know that not all Mexican children grew up having piñatas at their birthday parties. Fortunately for me, Bianca said, "I know that! That's a piñata!" Her story reflected not only her ability to accurately sequence the pictures (which was the objective), but also demonstrated her rich cultural knowledge and experiences.

Bianca taught me a lot that year. As she moves on to the second grade and I on to another school and different grade, I hope that her new teacher will see the value and importance of her cultural knowledge and experiences. I want her future teachers to notice that she is full of knowledge and skills that they and their students can learn from. Most of all, I hope that Bianca will no longer be hesitant to share who she is and that she will celebrate her bilingual knowledge and life skills as she confidently and proficiently navigates two languages and two cultures.

Chapter Overview

Teachers know quite a bit about their students as the school year goes by. They learn about students' academic strengths and weaknesses, cultural experiences and differences, and personality traits and behavior. Teachers gain this information through many avenues. They observe how students interact with those in the classroom. They document students' conceptual understandings that reflect academic strengths and weaknesses. Teachers hold parent conferences where they often learn more about the student's home environment and experiences. By the end of the school year, teachers know their students quite well as they say good-bye; only to start the cycle over at the beginning of the next school year.

Understanding the experiences and knowledge that children bring into the classroom enables teachers to appropriately design and implement a reading and writing curriculum that will best meet the individual and varied needs of the students in the class. This chapter provides essential knowledge to benefit a teacher's instructional decision-making processes. Guiding questions explored in this chapter include:

- How can teachers connect experiences that children have in neighborhoods and communities to school-based experiences and texts?
- What is meant by culturally relevant pedagogy?
- Why is it important to conduct early informal assessments around reading and writing?
- Why is kidwatching a critical practice for teachers to use?
- What are some strategies for assessing reading attitudes and interests?

Examining cultural diversity in classroom settings

...student's lives are not 'background' to what occurs in schools...some children may appear 'ready' for school because they come with a selective repertoire of social and communicative practices...In contrast, other children may appear 'unready' for school literacy learning because their participative repertoires are different from those required for literacy lessons. (Comber, 2000, p. 40)

Teachers and educational researchers often talk about the importance of knowing children's background experiences when introducing new ideas or concepts in a story. The connections students draw between their knowledge and experiences and what is being presented in the story or piece of informational text facilitates the comprehension process. But what do we mean by background? Are there *particular,* or as Barbara Comber states, *selective*, practices that are valued and recognized in the classroom context? And at the same time, are there practices that are dismissed and not recognized as contributing to students' engagement and participation in school?

Students bring to the classroom and their learning a vast array of linguistic knowledge, cultural experiences, values, and assumptions. These experiences play a critical role in establishing an effective and meaningful literacy curriculum. Differences have an impact on how students respond to a reading and writing curriculum and corresponding instructional decisions.

> ### Creating Connections 3.1
> What experiences and knowledge do you have about racial, ethnic, and economic groups that are different than yours? Why might it be important to explore and learn more about students' cultures, families, and communities when they differ from yours?
> Use your blog to share your thinking.

The divide between the teacher's culture and students' cultures

There is an ever-widening divide between the teacher's background, culture, and experiences and the students' in the classroom. Recent reports from the National Education Association document that the teaching workforce in the United States continues to represent a largely white, female, and middle-aged group. In 2001, 80 percent of the teaching force was Caucasian. More than 40 percent of schools across America have no teachers of color on staff (NEA, 2002). Recent trends indicate that only eight percent of the teaching force is African American, and 6 percent is Hispanic (see Figure 3.1). These percentages are in stark contrast to the growing numbers of students of color. It is projected that by 2050, 57 percent of the student population in the United States will be comprised of African American, Latino/a, and Asian Americans (U.S. Department of Commerce, 1996). However, large school districts tend to reflect more teacher diversity, with Black/African American teachers and Asian teachers representing 18 percent of the teacher workforce in such districts. Teachers of Hispanic origin were also more likely to be in larger districts (9 %).

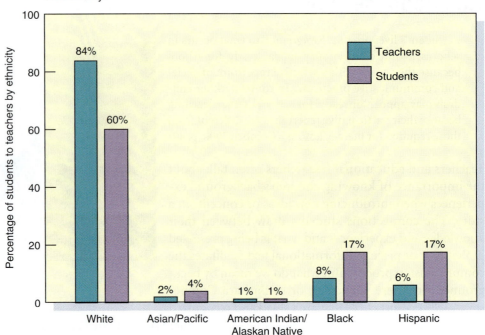

Minority Teacher Shortage
Close to 40 percent of K-12 students are non-white, but the ratio of minority teachers lags considerably.

FIGURE 3.1 Minority teacher shortage.
Source: US Department of Education National Center for Educational Statistics (2002).

Recall the discussion in Chapter 2 on language variation and diversity in classroom settings. National demographics and statistics indicate that the growth in the English Language Learner (ELL) student population is not evenly distributed across the geographic regions (West, South, Midwest, Northeast). All but the Northeast region have shown an increase in ELL students in public schools. In urban, suburban, and rural schools throughout the country it is common to have ELL students in classrooms where the teacher is not fluent in the represented language(s). A recent statistic indicates that more than 50 percent of the teachers in the United States work with and teach students that speak languages other than English as their primary language and that only 20 percent of them believe they are qualified to do so. In one urban third grade in the Southeast, there were children from five different countries (Honduras, Mexico, Russia, Vietnam, and China). Two of the students had just moved to the United States, the others had completed at least second grade at the school. All of the students' parents were first generation immigrants. And yet, the teacher is monolingual. What strategies can she use to provide students with an environment that recognizes their diverse linguistic and cultural experiences?

Recognizing differences within English Language Learners

Understanding that children do not all have the same linguistic backgrounds, home experiences, or educational histories is an important consideration. There is a tendency to group students together as though their experiences and knowledge are the same. This is often the case with English Language Learners. In many cases, ELL students are grouped together as though they have similar backgrounds, when the only common factor is that they are learning English. This is particularly the case with

TECHNOLOGY LINK

www.baby-names-meaning.com.

This site includes an index with first and last names in alphabetical order and a briefly stated name meaning and can be used along with children's own research with their families on their name origins.

www.kbyu.org/capturingpast/
and
www.ancestry.com/library/view/columns/tips/66.asp.

These sites offer detailed suggestions and checklists for helping children conduct an oral history interview with an older family member.

Spanish-speaking students. One student may be from a rural community in Honduras, while another is from a border town near Texas, and still another is from a large metropolitan city in Ecuador. All three students may be provided the same instruction without much consideration of their previous experiences.

In addition to knowing what part of the world a student is from, other factors to consider include the age in which a student is exposed to English, the quality and quantity of this exposure, their language learning aptitude, and whether the primary language is Latin based (Jimenez, 2004). ELL students whose primary language is Latin based will in all likelihood more easily recognize English words with similar Latin derivations, while those with different language backgrounds such as Mandarin, Farsi, or Russian do not have this advantage. Some students are only able to speak their primary language. And some African languages do not have a written form, making this sort of transfer difficult if not impossible.

Educational histories are also an important distinction to make among students. Some may have little or no schooling because of lack of teachers in rural communities, family poverty, or frequent mobility. Others may have fragmented schooling experiences where they may have a number of different placements in one year or over several years. The placements are rarely cohesive. This fragmented schooling results in some instruction being missed and other instruction being duplicated. And others will have comprehensive schooling in home countries. All of these factors must be taken into consideration for teachers to effectively support students in the classroom.

Learning about home and community practices

Along with developing a knowledge base about the students' cultural and linguistic resources, it is helpful to learn about the home and community literacy practices with

Creating Connections **3.2**

How do you think about students' funds of knowledge without falling into stereotypes about cultural practices?
How might you move away from assumptions about what may or may not go on in households?

which students are familiar. Teachers may wonder about the types of texts that parents, caregivers, and community members read and have access to, and the various purposes held for such reading events. Considering the role of home and community practices begins to open up space for talking about how literacy is used and valued in different communities. Recall the guiding assumptions from Chapter 1 that suggest literacy practices reflect the work in the community; that people engage in literacy when there are purposes to serve; that some literacy practices are valued more than others; and that literacy events take place inside social contexts.

The cultural and linguistic diversity in most classrooms contributes to teachers' growing knowledge about which students are in the classroom. Developing curriculum that draws upon the students' lives should also include thinking about the resources and knowledge that families use to navigate their daily lives. For example, in the opening vignette Ms. Garrity uses her

Children learn many skills from family and community members.

knowledge about Bianca's home practices to invite Bianca to take on the classroom responsibility of organizing the writing center. As a result, Bianca began to take on more responsibilities in the classroom.

funds of knowledge

Historically accumulated resources, knowledge, and competencies that families and community members have.

FUNDS OF KNOWLEDGE.   Louis Moll, Cathy Amanti, Deborah Neff, and Norma Gonzalez (1992) developed the concept of ***funds of knowledge*** to talk about the knowledge, resources, and competencies that families and community members have, and that it is through life experiences that people come to have this knowledge. This knowledge is representative of a broad set of activities that are important to maintaining households and communities. They are developed in social networks, from parents to children, siblings to siblings, neighbors to neighbors. Take, for example, a yard sale happening in a neighborhood. What are the types of activities associated with the yard sale? There will probably be marketing skills

Invitation for the classroom

Learning from Parents

Possible questions to ask during parent interviews:

- What are some of your child's interests and hobbies that she or he likes to do at home?
- What are some of the ways in which your child helps at home? What are some of his or her responsibilities?
- What do you want me to know about your child?
- How do your child's experiences in school differ from your own?
- What are some things that your child has experience with? Do you think she or he would be willing to share this with others in our class?
- Are there some talents and/or knowledge that you would you like to share with your child's classmates?

(making signs to advertise the yard sale; displaying the goods); economics (what is a reasonable price for this used good? bargaining techniques); interaction skills (older siblings caring for younger siblings); language use (maybe there are multiple languages in place); and selling handmade items (indicating sewing, knitting, crocheting skills, etc.). All of these knowledges are distributed across the social networks of the community. Take another household event, such as cooking. There are a number of skills involved, from measuring to knowing how ingredients interact when combined, and more. Very often these funds of knowledge are shared across families and generations.

Moll et al.'s work on funds of knowledge is helpful in thinking about the richness and diversity that children bring to the classroom. Classroom practices are greatly enhanced when teachers know more about their students and the households in which they live. As teachers begin to learn more about their students, through interviews, surveys, questionnaires, and observations, they are able to link home and community practices with those in the classroom. In 1995, researchers Gonzalez, Moll, Tenery, Rivera, Rendon, and Gonzales drew upon ethnography and anthropology by asking teachers to make home visits and record through interviews and observations the various practices occurring in the household. While many teachers make home visits, the difference was that these teachers were there to learn about the student and the family, rather than provide information about "how to succeed in school." In doing so, the curriculum becomes one that is relevant and meaningful to the lives of students.

Learning about the various funds of knowledge that students possess enables teachers to get to know the child as a "whole" person because of the multiple activities that the child and family members are involved in. This is a departure from the more narrow view of the child, whereby the teacher knows the child as merely a "student."

Creating Connections 3.3

Read *Just Juice* by Karen Hesse (Scholastic, 1999)

When many of us think about cultural diversity, we often refer to students' ethnic heritage and background. Karen Hesse, a children's author and young adult novelist, invites readers to consider diversity in terms of regions of the United States and the cultural heritage that regions afford. *Just Juice* is the story of a family living on the outskirts of a small town in the Appalachian region of the country. Juice is one of six children. She is in the fourth grade and struggles considerably with reading. She often chooses not to attend school and prefers to be at home spending time with her father in the workshop/shed. The story relates struggles this family faces in living day to day. Readers come to know that Juice's father does not read and has neglected to pay property taxes to keep the house. Juice devises a way for the family to make money, and in the end she is responsible for helping her mother deliver her baby.

Create a virtual backpack for Juice. What are the types of resources, knowledge, and skills Juice has? Which of these are valued for school practices? Which are not valued?

VIRTUAL SCHOOL BAGS. Along the lines of Luis Moll's work is the notion of a *virtual school bag*. Coined by Pat Thomson (2002) in Australia, virtual school bags are full of things [knowledges, skills, ways of being] that children already learned at home, with their friends, and from the world in which they live. Imagine a virtual backpack that students bring to class. Inside this virtual backpack students carry with them a number of practices, resources, skills, knowledge, values, and assumptions about learning, teaching, and life. Some of these will be accessed and celebrated in classroom experiences; others will be hidden from teachers and classmates. Knowledge and resources recognized and accessed in classroom settings typically resemble common school-based practices.

To illustrate, consider Than, an eight-year-old Cambodian student who lives with his parents, siblings, and grandmother. Than's family moved to the United States, looking for better opportunities for the children. They opened a local Cambodian restaurant and spend every day and evening working. Than goes to the restaurant after school where he is expected to help when the dinner crowd starts

virtual school bags

A concept whereby a teacher considers the knowledges, skills and ways of being that children carry with them in a virtual back pack.

Did you know...

Gloria Ladson-Billings has written extensively about culturally relevant pedagogy and teacher quality. The following resources may be helpful in learning more.

- An interview with Gloria Ladson-Billings: http://www.rethinkingschools.org/archive/20_02/glor202.shtml.
- Ladson-Billings, G. (2001). *Crossing over to Canaan: The journey of new teachers in diverse classrooms*. San Francisco: Jossey Bass.
- Ladson-Billings, G (1995). Toward a theory of culturally relevant pedagogy. *American Education Research Journal*, 35, 465–491.
- Ladson-Billings, G. (1994). *The Dreamkeepers: Successful Teachers of African American Children*. San Francisco: Jossey Bass.

Creating Connections 3.4

Think about a child you know in a classroom. How might you answer the following questions?

- Describe the school's neighborhood.
- Create a list of questions for an interview or survey that aims to identify interests, skills, resources that the student accesses at home.
- Consider the child in school. What would you say about this child?
- What are some lingering questions to ask?

TECHNOLOGY LINK

http://www.learner.org/channel/libraries/readingk2/thalia/index.html#

Watch the Annenberg Video on Demand about Thalia learning to read in a bilingual kindergarten class taught by Mr. St. Clair. Also watch how Mr. St. Clair communicates Thalia's progress with Thalia's mother.

to arrive. Than clears tables, takes to-go orders over the phone, and rings up customers' bills. When he has a chance, Than is drawing. He particularly likes to draw comic book characters. Than's ability to converse in two languages, make change, draw, and interact with many people are the experiences and knowledges he brings to the classroom. Sometimes these will be recognized in the classroom; most often they won't.

Alex is an 11-year old whose mother manages a clothing store in a local mall. Alex knows quite a bit about the clothing and accessories sold in the store. She understands the difference between buyer's price and retail. Alex also has learned some of her mom's entrepreneurial skills and started selling surfing stickers at school (with permission). Alex's understandings of what is popular in terms of the clothing industry will be a resource that may be identified by her peers, but probably less so by her teachers. The two brief examples suggest that children come to school with virtual backpacks full of talents, skills, knowledge, and resources.

Inviting the "whole" student into the classroom requires that teachers tap into students' lives by creating a curriculum that enables students to bring their resources, skills, and knowledges to the learning event. One possibility is to provide a culturally relevant curriculum and to teach from a culturally relevant perspective.

Teaching from a culturally relevant perspective

culturally relevant pedagogy

Teaching into the academic and social needs of culturally and linguistically diverse students.

Culture is not something to teach. Culture is the way in which we respond, think, believe, feel, act, and learn. Many of you may remember participating in festivities that highlight food, music, dance, heroes, and crafts as ways to "understand" and "know" a particular culture or ethnic group. These experiences, while inviting and welcoming, merely touch the surface of what is meant by culture and culturally relevant teaching. **Culturally relevant pedagogy**, as described by a number of theorists and researchers, is meeting the academic and social needs of culturally and linguistically diverse students (Gay, 2000 ; Howard, 2001; Ladson-Billings, 1995). Culturally relevant teaching is the "kind of teaching that is designed not merely to fit the school culture to the students' culture but also to use student culture as the basis for helping students understand themselves and others, structure interactions, and conceptualize knowledge" (Ladson-Billings, 2001, p. 314). As with language diversity, it is important to recognize culture as a resource for learning in school settings. How one goes about meeting these needs is determined by the teacher's willingness to not only learn who their students are, but also who they themselves are as cultural beings (Pransky & Bailey, 2002).

Villegas and Lucas (2002) have identified six characteristics of what it means to teach from a culturally responsive perspective.

In addition to these characteristics, Irvine and Armento (2001) suggest that teachers

- provide and use meaningful learning materials;
- create environments inclusive of cultures, customs, and traditions that are different from their own; and
- include lessons that assist students in making meaningful connections between their lives and school-related experiences

> ### Characteristics of Culturally Responsive Pedagogy (Villegas & Lucas, 2002)
>
> 1. Teachers recognize that the ways people perceive the world, interact with one another, and approach learning, among other things, are deeply influenced by such factors as race/ethnicity, social class, and language. This understanding enables teachers to cross the cultural boundaries that separate them from their students.
> 2. Teachers have affirming views of students from diverse backgrounds, seeing resources for learning in all students rather than viewing differences as problems to be solved.
> 3. Teachers have a sense that they are both responsible and capable of bringing about educational change that will make schooling more responsive to students of diverse backgrounds.
> 4. Teachers are familiar with their students' prior knowledges and beliefs, derived from both personal and cultural experiences.
> 5. Teacher see learning as an active process by which learners give meaning to new information.
> 6. Teachers design instruction that builds on what students already know while stretching them beyond the familiar.

Teachers that implement these guiding tenets into their teaching offer students an engaging and enriching curriculum. By supporting linguistically diverse students in the meaning making process; by documenting students' home and community literacy practices to further expand notions of what it means to be literate; and by establishing interaction patterns with students that challenge transmission models of teaching, teachers can begin to broaden their own understandings of what it means to offer culturally relevant pedagogy.

Supporting linguistically diverse learners in reading and writing

Teaching reading and writing to linguistically diverse students is complex and challenging. "Linguistic diversity includes the total range of structures and functions of languages and dialects found in authentic communicative situations in our schools and wider communities" (Barnitz, 1997, p. 264). Research suggests

> ### *Creating Connections 3.5*
> What are the ways in which Ms. Garrity in the opening vignette met the characteristics and standards listed by Villegas, Lucas, Irvine, and Armento for developing culturally relevant pedagogy?

that when ELL children are literate in their primary language they bring that knowledge to learning English. They already know that reading should make sense and that they can utilize similar strategies for reading in English as they can when reading in their primary language. While it is certainly desired that students are able to access their primary language during instruction, the reality is that there are limited numbers of teachers able to teach in students' primary languages. In fact, according to the National Center on

Educational Statistics (NCELA, 2002), only about 12.5 percent of the teaching force has received eight or more hours of training in working with ELL students in the classroom. In most classrooms, ELL students are learning alongside their English-speaking peers. In a similar vein, students who speak African American Vernacular English (AAVE) should have opportunities to capitalize on their knowledge of AAVE patterns to use as a bridge to more standard forms of English.

There are a number of effective strategies and core principles to support linguistically diverse students' language and literacy development. These strategies identified in the next section are based on the work of Sarah Huddleson (1984) and David and Yvonne Freeman (2000).

CONNECT STUDENTS' BACKGROUND KNOWLEDGE AND PERSONAL EXPERIENCES TO LITERACY EVENTS.
Effective literacy teachers implement this principle for all learners, but for linguistically diverse students it is even more critical. Students bring to classroom literacy events a range of experiences and knowledge. English Language Learners sometimes lack the background needed to make sense of much of the texts available in classrooms. Authors often assume that readers share certain cultural knowledge, history, and customs. For ELL students, this background is not the same. While there are many ELL students who are able to read the text, the issue is not necessarily vocabulary, but rather overall meaning making (i.e., multiple meanings of words, idioms, and figurative language).

Incorporating multicultural texts that use a variety of styles, voices, and languages enables students to draw upon their own experiences. *Multicultural texts* honor the diverse cultures and language communities of which students are a part. Such texts can connect people of different backgrounds and become the starting place for deeper examination and discussion of experiences. Figure 3.2 identifies authors from various ethnic and cultural backgrounds that write children's literature.

Teachers implement literature discussions and interactive journals (sometimes known as dialogue journals) to extend the conversation around multicultural texts. Literature discussions offer opportunities for students to share aspects of the text that are personally meaningful, thereby increasing engagement in the text. Teachers may also invite students to share experiences prior to reading the text so that connections to the text may be facilitated when they are reading.

Interactive journals are writing events that support diverse learners by encouraging them to write about their own experiences. Students and teachers write back and forth sharing ideas and experiences. This creates space in the curriculum for students' interests and concerns. The interactive journal is not a venue for correction of language use. Rather, the teacher accepts the writing that is provided and models appropriate language use by making comments and asking questions. The interactive journal provides an authentic context for communication. Literature discussions and interactive journals bring to the foreground students' background experiences and lives.

---

multicultural texts

Picture books and young adult novels that portray and honor diverse languages and cultures.

A Sampling of Multicultural Titles to Use with Children

All the Colors We Are: Todos los Colores de Nuestra Piel/The Story of How We Get Our Skin Color by Katie Kissinger (Redleaf Press, 1994). This story provides straightforward information for children, teachers, and parents that answers the often asked and hard to answer questions about how we get our skin color. All The Colors We Are, through a positive exploration and celebration of skin color differences, takes the power out of the prevailing color bias.

Whoever You Are by Mem Fox (Voyager, 2001) demonstrates how every day all over the world, children are laughing and crying, playing and learning, eating and sleeping. They may not look the same. They may not speak the same language. Their lives may be quite different. But on the inside, they are all alike.

The Colors of Us by Karen Katz (Holt, 1999) is the story of Lena and her mother as they walk through the neighborhood, noticing all the different shades of brown of friends and relatives. Their skin colors are compared to honey, peanut butter, pizza crust, ginger, peaches, chocolate, and more, conjuring up delicious and beautiful comparisons for every tint.

---

interactive journals

Teachers and students write to each other in a journal. They ask questions, share experiences, and record ideas.

FIGURE 3.2 Multicultural authors

	Authors		
African American Children's Literature	Lucille Clifton Jeanette Caines Sharon Bell Marthis Camille Yarbrough Mildred Taylor Emily Moore	Brenda Wilkinson Rosa Guy Mildred Walter John Steptoe Joyce Hansen Joyce Carol Thomas	Eloise Greenfield Patricia McKissack Walter Dean Myers Rita Garcia-Williams Angela Johnson
Asian American Children's Literature	Yoshiko Uchida Allen Say Laurence Yed Jeanette Eaton Me Li	Ed Young Paul Yee Arthur Bowie Chrisman Elizabeth Seeger Rhoda Blumberg	Tao Yashima Tuan Ch'eng Shih Elizabeth Forman Lewis Mildred Batchelder
Native American Children's Literature	Virginia Driving Hawk Sneve Jamke Highwater William Apes Charles Eastman Sharon CreechJean	John Bierhorst Byrd Baylor John Rollin Ridge Elias Boudinot Craighead George	Te Ata Gerald McDermott David Cusick Lois Lenski
Latino American Children's Literature	Pura Belpre Piri Thomas Joseph Krumgold Elizabeth Borton	Carmen Lomas Garza Gary Soto Francis Kalnay Scott O'Dell	Nicholasa Mohr Ann Nolan Clark Jack Schaefer Maia Wojciechowska

Source: Callins, T. (2004) Culturally Responsive Literacy Instruction National Center for Culturally Responsive Education Systems (NCCREST). U.S. Department of Education, Office of Special Programs.

CREATE OPPORTUNITIES FOR STUDENTS TO MEANINGFULLY AND AUTHENTI-CALLY APPLY ORAL LANGUAGE SKILLS. When linguistically diverse students have opportunities to collaborate with others in meaningful contexts, there is increased communication and interaction among those in the classroom. Fostering oral language in the classroom environment is essential for linguistically diverse students to flourish. ELL students learn English by interacting with others in environments that use language to achieve particular purposes. These purposes include

- using language to question;
- making understandings more precise;
- making understandings more retrievable;
- reinterpreting past experiences; and
- moving beyond personal experiences.

In classrooms where language is viewed as a resource, there are a number of different ways to encourage oral language development: small group discussions, brainstorming, choral reading, dramatic play, debates, storytelling, partner reading, language experience stories, and read aloud. These events support students' evolving understandings of language variation and use. Engaging students in literacy activities that make explicit use of home languages helps to affirm the relationships between home, community, school, language, and identity. Students begin to discern the similarities and differences among home and school languages.

Sample of Titles That Are Published in Multiple Languages

Brown Bear, Brown Bear, What Do You See? Oso Pardo, Oso Pardo, Que Ves Ahi? By Bill Martin Jr. (Henry Holt and Company, 1995). Translation by Teresa Mlawer (1998).

If You Give a Mouse a Cookie: Si Le Das Una Gallentita a Un Raton. By L. J. Numeroff (HarperCollins, 1985). Translation by Teresa Mlawer (1995).

El Capitan Calzoncillos: Captain Underpants. By Dav Pilkey (Scholastic, 1999). Translation by Ediciones Salamandra.

No Fair to Tigers: No Es Justo Para Los Tigres. By Eric Hoffman (Redleaf Press, 1999).

TECHNOLOGY LINK

http://www.childrenslibrary.org/

Access digital copies of children's books from all over the world written in their original languages.

ENCOURAGE STUDENTS' PRIMARY LANGUAGE AND/OR CODE SWITCHING DURING LITERACY EVENTS. It is important for linguistically diverse students to use a language they feel most comfortable with during reading and writing events. By having the choice, students may remember more of what they learned. Allowing students to move between languages helps them become more linguistically savvy; they may choose to try English or standard variations knowing that they can return to their primary language at any time. Students with such flexibility extend and develop their linguistic repertoire by using a language variety that is appropriate to the time, place, audience, and purpose. "Primary language support is a validation of the child's language and culture, which facilitates self-esteem to be maintained, stress to be reduced, and education to be a positive experience as access to the core curriculum is provided" (Necochea & Cline, 2000).

Literacy events, such as literature discussions and writing, are opportunities for students to take risks in language development. They can convey their thoughts and ideas using their primary language without interference of a "correction" to English usage. Students are more at ease interacting with others and discussing the themes in the texts, thereby expanding their knowledge and understanding. Literature discussions also enhance vocabulary development because the unfamiliar terms are presented in the context of the conversation.

A writing journal is another avenue for linguistically diverse learners to experiment and explore language. Students can navigate between languages as they write. If students are able to write words in a primary language that they have not yet learned in English, they are able to express more complex ideas. Having choice and freedom to experiment with different symbols associated with different languages supports language growth and development. For example, in Ms. Fisher's classroom, Luis Felipe navigates between English and Spanish as he lists ideas to write about. For teachers not familiar with students' primary languages, parent or community volunteers may be helpful in reading students' work.

CONTEXTUALIZE INSTRUCTION OF LANGUAGE THROUGH AUTHENTIC LITERATURE. Using authentic pieces of literature for instruction provides greater opportunities to learn language, as well as learn about language. Students are introduced to new vocabulary, language patterns, nuances in the language, and structural features of the language. Authentic literature facilitates oral and written language acquisition. Students can employ various mapping strategies as they navigate their ways

Luis Felipe's list of possible writing topics.

through unfamiliar texts. Generating story maps supports comprehension and composing as students work with a range of texts, both familiar and unfamiliar.

The core understandings around linguistic diversity in the classroom provide teachers with a framework to create and establish a literacy curriculum that meets the needs of all of their students. Based on these core principles, Freeman and Freeman (2000) pose a number of key questions that teachers can ask as they plan and monitor their own literacy curriculum.

- Is there an attempt to draw upon students' background knowledge and experiences? Are students given choices?
- Are students' primary languages and cultures valued, respected, and developed?
- Are students involved in activities that develop their self-esteem and provide them with opportunities to succeed?
- Do students read and write, as well as speak and listen during learning activities?
- Is instruction organized around "big" ideas?
- Are students involved in authentic reading and writing activities?
- Is the content meaningful? Does it serve a purpose for the learners?
- Do students have opportunities to work collaboratively?

Questions such as these provide teachers with a way of reflecting on their own classrooms and the types of activities and events that are implemented. In the next section, the focus switches to documenting events and practices that occur in the home and community.

DOCUMENTING STUDENTS' HOME AND COMMUNITY LITERACY PRACTICES. "In their lives outside of school, children are constantly creating and recreating literacy practices that are meaningful to them" (Burnett & Myers, 2002, p. 56). They compose instant text messages, create Pokemon cards, respond to television, read pop culture magazines, read billboards and other advertisements, play video games, write notes to each other, among many other events. Yet, when asked about literacy events, students often respond

---

Sample of Children's Titles That Have Two Languages in the Story

My House/Mi Casa: A Book in Two Languages by Rebecca Emberly (Little, Brown and Company, 1999).

Picture dictionary in English and Spanish. Labels items from parts of a house as well as items commonly found inside a house.

Arroz con Leche: Popular Songs and Rhymes from Latin America by Lulu Delacre (Scholastic, 1991).

Side-by-side text with songs and rhymes from Latin America. In the back is music for each of the songs.

Aekyung's Dream by Min Paek (Children's Book Press, 1988).

Aekyung, a young Korean girl, wakes up unhappy every morning since she moved to America six months before. She dislikes school because the kids tease her and she has a hard time understanding English. When her Aunt Kim returns from Korea with presents, she reminds Aekyung about the great King Sejong, who helped create the Korean alphabet. His strength and wisdom motivate her to work hard in school and ignore the insults. Eventually, the other children realize how special she is and she teaches them about King Sejong.

Going Home, Coming Home / Ve Nha, Tham Que Huong by Truong Tran (Children's Book Press, 2003).

A young girl visits her grandmother in Vietnam, where her parents were born, and learns that she can call two places home.

Calavera Abecedario: A Day of the Dead Alphabet Book by Jeannette Winter (Voyager Books, 2006).

Don Pedro and his family make skeletons for el Dia de los Muertos celebration in Mexico City. When the papier-mache Calaveras go to market on fiesta day, each skeleton acts out a letter of the alphabet.

TECHNOLOGY LINK

http://www.multicultural-childrenslit.com/

Dr. Robert Smith of Towson University in Maryland maintains this annotated bibliography of multicultural books appropriate for grades kindergarten through sixth.

Creating Connections 3.6

Classrooms often have libraries as part of their reading/writing centers. Notice the titles in the library.

- How well does the classroom library represent the diversity of ethnic and cultural backgrounds of the students? What titles might you suggest for the library?
- What about the school library and media center? How well does the school library represent the multiple cultures and backgrounds of the students at the school? What suggestions might you make to the school librarian to better reflect the school's ethnic and cultural diversity?

Invitation for the classroom

Literacy Dig

We are surrounded by words. Literacy digs, much like archeology digs, ask us to search our enviroiments for items and materials we read on regular basis.

- Ask children to conduct their own literacy dig.
- Have children collect examples of literacy in their homes and communities.
- How might these examples be categorized? For what purposes do they serve?

with more school-based practices such as reading [a particular basal anthology], writing stories and journals, and reading directions for school assignments. These school-based literacy practices seem to dominate how students conceptualize literacy in their lives. Teachers also view literacy events and practices in much the same way. Teachers rarely value literacy practices that do not align with more traditional, school-based forms of reading and writing. Cook (2005) suggests that many teachers operate with a view of home and community literacy practice that is quite narrow—that of a parent and a child snuggled up together reading a text. In reality, there are many different ways in which children interact with texts in their home and community environments (i.e., reading ads, writing grocery lists, reading phone messages).

A recent study by Burnett and Myers (2002) noted that children's literacy practices at home are framed around relationships, values, and interests. Students accessed and utilized texts to organize and maintain relationships, to organize life, as a vehicle for learning, reflection of identity, and private pleasure. How similar and/or different are these uses compared to school-based practices? Based on their findings, Burnett and Myers suggest the following questions to further the notion that literacy practices must be relevant and meaningful to students' lives.

- How often do children use literacy in the context of establishing and maintaining relationships, with peers in the classroom or different-aged pairings?
- How often do teachers provide opportunities for children to use literacy as an organizational tool for their own learning?
- How often do teachers allow children to take responsibility for their own learning?
- How often do teachers validate and recognize students' interests and passions?
- How often do teachers enable children to read and write for pleasure without judgment or evaluation?

Establishing culturally relevant interaction patterns in literacy events

Culturally relevant pedagogy considers students' linguistic resources, uses materials that reflect the content of students' lives, and draws upon home and community interaction patterns that are central to students' learning and relationships in and outside of school (Hefflin, 2002). Figure 3.3 highlights aspects of culturally relevant teaching. The materials should accurately and authentically represent the culture, cultural knowledge, and background students know and live (Bullivant, 1989). The learning environments should include customs and traditions that are different from the teacher's. Students should be encouraged to make meaningful connections between their lives and school experiences. The goal of culturally relevant teaching is to heighten students' academic performance by providing materials that encourage students to use what they know to acquire new knowledge, skills, and dispositions (Hefflin, 2002).

To illustrate how culturally relevant pedagogy may take place in the classroom, consider a common literacy event, such as the read aloud. For many teachers a read-aloud experience is an opportunity for children to listen to language, make personal and world connections, raise questions, and develop listening skills (*goals of the reading event*). The materials used for this event vary in genres and styles (*materials and texts*).

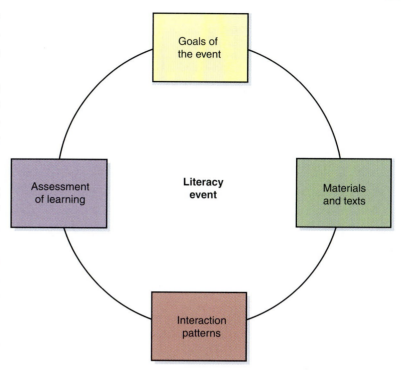

FIGURE 3.3 Aspects of a culturally relevant teaching as related to a literacy event.

The interaction and participation patterns differ from teacher to teacher, but in general many teachers request that students sit in a group on the floor (*interaction patterns*). Often, there are expectations for students to sit quietly and focus their attention on the text being read. Some teachers invite students to interact with the text, discussing ideas throughout the story; others prefer that students share their thinking following the story. Students' learning is often assessed by their ability to answer questions drawn from the text (*assessment of learning*).

Read-aloud events, while seemingly neutral and culture free, are imbued with many cultural assumptions about how teaching and learning take place. Shirley Brice Heath's (1983) work on three communities in the Piedmont Region of the Carolinas and Katherine Au's (1980; 1983) work in Hawaii demonstrate that teachers' beliefs about cultural diversity shape the way in which the reading event takes place. The goals, texts, interaction patterns and ways of assessing learning are central. To highlight how assumptions play out, the following two examples reflect different ways of orchestrating and implementing a read aloud event in the classroom.

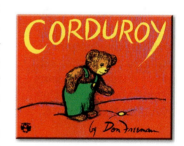

READ ALOUD FROM A TEACHER-CENTERED PERSPECTIVE. Ms. Steel is a first grade teacher in an urban city school. Over 90 percent of her students are African American. The remaining 10 percent are students of varied cultural backgrounds (Korean, Pakistani, and Ecuadoran). She selected *Corduroy* (Freeman, 1968) for this read aloud because of the central theme: acceptance and friendship. Corduroy is a stuffed teddy bear that has many adventures

Creating Connections 3.7

To learn more about interaction patterns in diverse communities and the impact in classrooms settings read:

- *Ways with Words* (Heath, 1983). Heath's work exemplifies that parent–child and community–child interaction patterns do not necessarily mimic those interaction patterns found in school settings. Not all children experience a flurry of rhetorical questions after reading a children's story, or have the familiar bedtime reading experience.

- Kathryn Au (1980; 1983) discovered that students are familiar with a story-telling pattern known as "talk story" but are not familiar with the ways in which teachers asked questions.

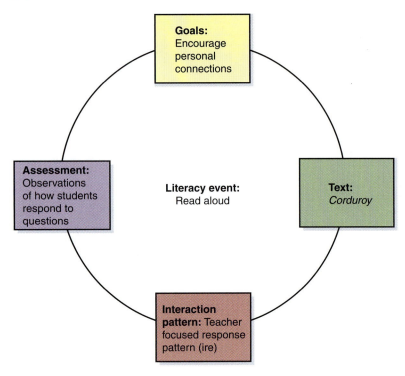

FIGURE 3.4 Teacher-centered read aloud.

at night when the department store closes. He rides the escalator, pulls buttons off of a mattress, and knocks over lamps. The next day, a little girl, Lisa, purchases Corduroy with money she has saved. Corduroy decides that this must be home and Lisa must be his friend. Ms. Steel requests that students sit on the floor in front of her while she reads the book. She also wants students to focus their eyes on the text. Students are expected to listen to the entire story before engaging in any discussion. Following the reading, Ms. Steel asks a series of questions that reflect events and characters from the story. A question or two invites students to make personal connections, but the majority of questions are more literal in nature. (e.g., How did Corduroy feel when Lisa took him home?) Because Ms. Steel believes that learning best occurs when students are quiet and focused, she reminds students to raise their hands when they want to talk. Ms. Steel determines who talks by selecting only students with their hands raised. This interaction pattern is known as ***initiate-respond-evaluate (IRE).*** Given the nature of her questions, she is able to quickly assess whether or not students accurately understood the story. In this instance, learning is seen from a more individual perspective and the interaction patterns are between the teacher and student, not among students.

READ ALOUD FROM A STUDENT-CENTERED PERSPECTIVE. In another classroom, Ms. Jacobs has similar goals for her students. She wants them to make personal and world connections to the text. Ms Jacobs teaches first grade in an urban school where the students are more ethnically mixed: 48 percent African American, 29 percent Latino/a, 14 percent Caucasian, and 3 percent other. She begins by inviting students to talk with each other about what they know about their own neighborhoods. "What do you see when you come to school?" is an opening question. Ms. Jacobs has students share their comments with each other and with her. She does not require students to raise their hands, but to be respectful of when others are talking and to try and wait until the person is finished. Ms. Jacobs then reads *Something Beautiful* (Wyeth, 1998). This is the story of an African American girl who lives in an inner city apartment with graffiti and trash littering her courtyard. She searches for something beautiful and asks various neighbors. In the end, she creates her own something beautiful by cleaning up her own courtyard and beautifying her neighborhood. As Ms. Jacobs and students talk about the text, there is explicit attention paid to the connections students are able to make between events in the story and their own neighborhoods. There were no predetermined questions asked by Ms. Jacobs. Rather she invited students to think about the text and to ask their own questions. Students worked in pairs to discuss the story. Throughout the read-aloud event, Ms. Jacobs observes how student pairs interact and the connections they make to the text.

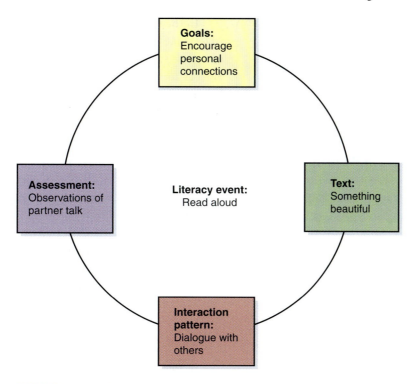

FIGURE 3.5 Student-centered read aloud.

The following chart provides a summary of two reading events.

	Teacher centered	Student centered
Goal	Personal connections to the story	Personal connections to the story
Materials	*Corduroy* by Don Freeman (1968)	*Something Beautiful* by Sharon Wyeth (1998);
Interaction Patterns	Teacher centered (IRE)	Conversational, student-centered
Assessments	Observations of how students respond to teacher questions	Observations of partner talk

The differences in these two read-aloud examples highlight the importance of paying attention to the ways in which culture can and does impact learning. In any instructional event, there is great potential for **cultural mismatch** to occur—to view students from a deficit perspective. A deficit viewpoint assumes that students come to school culturally deprived because of some deficiency in the students' homes or communities. Based on the two reading-aloud events described above, the teacher in the first event may view her culturally and ethnically diverse students as difficult or disengaged if they are unable to sit and *listen quietly* to the story being read. The bounded nature of the questions (based only on the text) provides Ms. Steel with information regarding students' capacity to recall information. What she may be missing is that these students may be operating with a different set of expectations and assumptions about learning. Some communities use different interaction patterns (call/response, talk story) that are quite different than the initiate-respond-evaluate (I-R-E) structure of school discourse.

cultural mismatch

To view students from a deficit perspective based on cultural and/or linguistic differences.

Creating Connections 3.8

Conduct a read-aloud event with a small group of children. Consider the goals and materials for the event. Notice the interaction patterns that you and the students engage in. What assessments will you use to determine effectiveness of the read-aloud event?

Share your experiences with a classmate.

In the second example, Ms. Jacobs recognizes that learning is a social event and encourages students to share their thinking in a variety of ways. Students participate by dialoguing with each other and the teacher. The questions draw upon their own experiences. In doing so, she invites students to share and reflect upon personal and world connections. Ms. Jacobs works to understand all the ways in which meaning is constructed. She aims to develop a *cultural match* among the students and the literacy event.

Developing curriculum that is culturally relevant and meaningful is essential in becoming and effective teacher. How teachers begin to do this is the topic of the next section—early assessments. These early assessments, informal in nature, are often conducted in the first couple of weeks as possible information in who the students are in the classroom, and their interests. They are the starting points for productive curriculum.

Using early assessment to know your students

Teachers begin each year with some information about their students. There may be cumulative records indicating grades, test scores, abilities, and challenges; stories from previous teachers; or knowledge based on having older siblings in previous years. This type of preview information, while helpful in some instances, does not provide the teacher with enough information about a student's strengths in literacy development. At the beginning of the year, there are a number of questions teachers have about the students in their classroom:

- What experiences with reading and writing do my students bring?
- Do my students have favorite authors? Do they like to read books that are in a series?
- What interests do my students have for writing? What genres do they like to write in?
- What do my students think reading and writing are for? What is their perception of literacy?
- Are my students excited to read and write? Or do they see it as a chore?
- What are some home and community literacy practices my students engage in?

Notice that these questions focus on students' interests, preferred genres, and ways of thinking about literacy. They are not questions that attend to the particular ability or skill level of a reader or writer. These questions focus on building community in the classroom. In the first few weeks of the school year, it is important to let students demonstrate what they know, what they value, what they are confident and competent in, not what they don't know, understand, or feel insecure about. Creating an effective and meaningful literacy curriculum for students should not be based on a deficit view that is focused on "repairing weakness" (Ayers, 2004, p. 57). Rather, students should be able to begin a school year celebrating all that they know and sharing with the teacher what they want to know more about.

Kidwatching

Kidwatching, just as the term implies, is the process of closely observing children's learning processes as they occur in various settings (e.g., in the classroom with whole group instruction, individual work, small group and partner work; on the playground, in the cafeteria and in the library). It is learning about children by watching how they learn (Y. Goodman, 1978). How individual children respond to various tasks, texts, and each other can signal to the teacher ways to plan curriculum that will best meet the needs of the students. When a reader struggles to make sense of text, a teacher using kidwatching strategies will pay close attention to how the reader approaches the task, the level of enthusiasm for reading, the types of miscues or errors made, and what sorts of strategies the reader employs to make the text more comprehensible.

To illustrate how kidwatching notes enable teachers to make informed decisions, notice how Ms. White observes and records the actions and behaviors of one reader in her class. Ms White's fifth graders have a daily time period when they read texts selected from the class library, school library, or brought from home. These selections often reflect their current interests. Students are asked to have two to three texts available to them at all times, so that if they finish one text, another one can be quickly started; or if a particular text is not engaging, another choice is available. One morning, early in the school year, Ms. White spent a few minutes observing students as they read. She quickly noticed Jacob; he was not using his time to read. He was at the classroom library thumbing through text after text. Jacob was not reading any of these texts; rather he was merely turning the pages. Ms. White decided to document his actions by recording her observation.

> Name ___Jacob___
> August 28: Jacob spent most of the independent reading time flipping through books in the class library. He didn't seem to be looking for any book in particular, but rather seemed to be focused on "looking busy." I wonder what sorts of interests and hobbies Jacob has?

Later that same week, Ms. White decided to pair students together to share what they had been reading and what some of their interests were. As she circulated around the classroom, Ms. White overheard Jacob complaining that he hated reading and that there was nothing interesting to read. Ms. White again recorded this information.

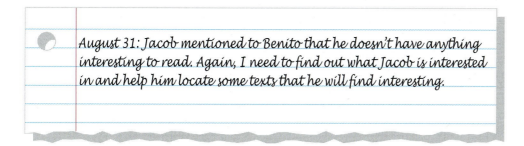

> August 31: Jacob mentioned to Benito that he doesn't have anything interesting to read. Again, I need to find out what Jacob is interested in and help him locate some texts that he will find interesting.

Ms. White decided that in order to learn about Jacob's interests she needed to conduct a brief interest inventory. She asked all of her students in the class the following questions:

1. What do you like to do when you are not in school?
2. What topics do you like to read about?
3. What activities and lessons do you do after school?
4. Who is your favorite author?
5. What types of books do you like to read?
6. What do you know a lot about (e. g., remote control cars, baseball, Hello Kitty characters, Civil War, skateboarding, music groups)?

Jacob's response to the questions

1. What do you like to do when you are not in school?
   Play soccer, watch TV, play on the computer

2. What do you like to read about?
   Nothing

3. What activities and lessons do you go to after school?
   Soccer practice

4. Who is your favorite author?
   Gary Paulson

5. What types of books do you like to read?
   Harry Potter and Lemonyskicket

6. What do you know a lot about (e. g., remote control cars, baseball, NASCAR, Hello Kitty characters, American Girls, Civil War, skateboarding, music groups, etc.)
   Soccer

This small bit of information is important to Ms. White. While Jacob does not provide extended responses to her questions, Ms. White learns that Jacob reads mostly because it is expected in school. Jacob probably wrote the responses of Gary Paulson, Harry Potter, and Lemonysnicket because that is what he thinks is 'appropriate' or 'expected'. Jacob has not yet discovered that reading is a pleasurable activity that he can learn from. With this information, Ms. White decided to bring in a few titles that focus on soccer such as *Soccer* (Dorling Kindersay, 2000), *Soccer Duel* (Christopher, 2000), *Lives of the Athletes: Thrills, Spills (and What the Neighbors Thought)* (Krull, 1997), and a biography on David Beckham from an internet site (http://www.kidzworld.com/site/p451.htm). She placed these in the library and informed Jacob that there were a few new books and articles on soccer in the library that he may be interested in. The following day during independent reading, Ms. White noticed that Jacob was reading the biography on David Beckham. She added this comment to her previous notes:

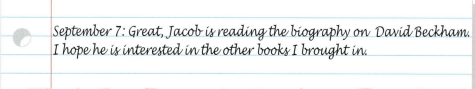

September 7: Great, Jacob is reading the biography on David Beckham. I hope he is interested in the other books I brought in.

Jacob's interest in soccer is the catalyst for reading. Ms. White's kid-watching notes over a few days enabled her to identify texts that she thought Jacob would respond to. Ms. White also talked with the school librarian/media specialist for additional titles. In doing so, she provided materials and texts that were engaging and interesting for Jacob to read.

Kidwatching is a way for teachers to closely observe and document the actions and behaviors that students exhibit in class. Each teacher develops his or her own "system" for collecting, managing, and analyzing these anecdotal notes and reflective comments. Some teachers have notebooks, in which one page is for each child. Others utilize clipboards and sticky notes. The sticky notes are then collected in file folders under each child's name. No matter what system or process a teacher develops, it is important that the notes are reflected upon. Creating and collecting the information are not of much value in and of themselves. Teachers need to step back and reflect on the collected notes to more effectively build curriculum that is meaningful and relevant to students.

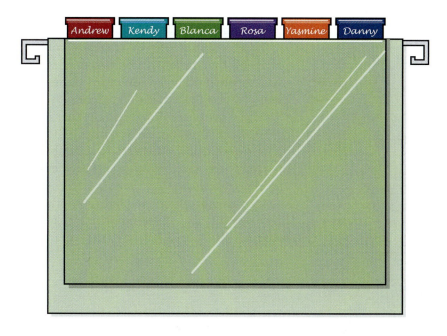

Invitation for the classroom

Elementary Reading Attitude Survey

Access the Elementary Reading Attitude Survey by McKenna and Kear (www.reading.org/library/retrieve.cfm?D=10.1598/RT.43.8.3&F=RT-43-8-McKenna.pdf). Administer the survey to a group of children in a classroom.
What are your results? What decisions can you make as a result of the survey?

Attitudes and interest in reading and writing

There are many resources and strategies, ways in which teachers can employ kidwatching strategies early in the school year to get to know the readers in their class. In addition to the kidwatching or anecdotal notes that Ms. White used to identify Jacob's lack of interest in reading, and then her subsequent use of a short interest inventory to better know students' interests and hobbies in her class, teachers may also use attitude questionnaires, observational checklists, and interviews.

ATTITUDE QUESTIONNAIRES AND SURVEYS. A popular attitude questionnaire is known as the Elementary Reading Attitude Survey (McKenna & Kear, 1990). This survey utilizes four poses of the cartoon cat Garfield (from happy to sad) that students select from as they read the corresponding questions. Teachers can administer the survey to the whole class and gain an overall impression about students' attitudes toward reading both recreational text and academic text. The Garfield survey is quite beneficial and appropriate for younger children.

Other surveys, such as the one listed in Figure 3.6 are appropriate for children in middle and upper grades.

In addition to surveys that are completed by the students, teachers may also want to elicit information from parents. Figure 3.7 is an example of a parent survey.

The surveys are designed to gather information about the views students hold about reading, how often they read for their own purposes, and the reading engagements and experiences they have at home. Teachers can use this information to plan appropriate literacy events and experiences in the classroom.

Name _____

1. If I could read anything, I would read about _____

2. My favorite book is _____

3. My favorite author is _____

4. The illustrator I like best is _____

5. My favorite website is _____

6. My favorite part of the newspaper is _____

7. The best time to read is _____

8. I want to know more about _____

9. I read for _____ minutes every night.

10. I watch _____ minutes of TV every night. Name three of your favorite television shows.

FIGURE 3.6 Student attitude survey.

Name _____

Parent Survey

1. My child likes to read the following materials:

comic books _____   library books _____

cereal boxes _____   TV guide _____

comics page _____   sports page _____

Kids page _____   email messages _____

Websites _____   magazines _____

Bible or other religious materials _____

Menus _____   Baseball/Pokemon/Digimon cards _____

Other_____

2. Have you noticed your child experiencing any reading difficulties or problems?

3. What are some of your child's favorite books/authors?

4. How often does your child read at home?

FIGURE 3.7 Parent survey.

Interview Questions

- What should your friends and other kids know about you as a reader?
- Who do you like to read with?
- What are some things you read at home?
- What sorts of books or authors do you like to read?
- How many books did you read over the summer?
- What is your favorite book?
- What do you want to learn this year?
- What do you think it means to be a good reader?
- Where do you like to read?

FIGURE 3.8 Interview questions for Blake and Lukas.

1 i Like To Read STORY As booKs.
2 MY moм Reads with me
3 booKS
4 Dr. suessanchapr books
5 60
6 super Diaper bodY
7 Smarteset kib in the World.
8 be focused and looK oniT
9 ot home at falhiLX Read
10
11
12
13
14 LUKAS

1 I like to read yu-Gi-ohmagazine
2 timmy reading buddy
3 super biaer baby
4 Chapter books
5 two
6 Super biaper baby
7 to be the smatest kid in school
8 to be focused on try your hardest
9 at my house anfamily read

Blake

FIGURE 3.9 Blake's and Lukas's responses to interview questions.

Interviews

Interviews are an important source of information as teachers begin to create profiles of the readers in their classrooms. Interviews may be conducted between the teacher and the student or between classmates. Having students interview each other in the first few weeks of school not only reveals information about each student as a reader, but also begins to a build a learning community where common interests may be shared. In Ms. Karlsson's classroom, two of her second graders interviewed each other to find out what sorts of texts they each read and where their favorite reading spots were (Figure 3.8).

Lukas and Blake interviewed each other and wrote down their responses to share with the larger group. As is typical with young children, they built upon each other's answers and in some cases had very similar responses.

Ms. Karlsson then asked her students to come together and share what they learned from each other. Lukas and Blake decided that they would like to read what each other is reading. Later that week during independent reading time, Lukas and Blake were busy looking at Blake's *Yu-Gi-O* magazine, commenting on the different characters and talking about which cards they each had.

This information can be used as teachers establish classroom libraries, help students select books in the school library, and to begin thinking about possible inquiries and focus studies.

Assessments that focus on students' abilities and challenges in reading and writing are more fully addressed in Chapter 10. These assessments include miscue analysis, reading conferences, running records, and other more formal measures. Teachers use such assessments throughout the year as they begin to work more specifically on reading and writing strategies.

> ### Creating Connections 3.8
> What are some of your reading interests?
> How might you share this information with students?

In Closing

The focus of this chapter, culturally relevant pedagogy and initial assessments, supports the guiding assumptions that literacy practices are purposeful and embedded in larger *social goals*, and that readers and writers access their "*funds of knowledge*" as they participate in literacy events. Developing culturally relevant practices invites teachers and students to consider the multiple ways in which learning occurs. Children are able to draw upon their lived experiences and knowledge to make sense of the literacy events and practices in the classroom. In order for teachers to learn about their students' strengths and interests, a number of initial assessments can be used. These initial assessments, such as interest inventories and surveys, along with anecdotal kidwatching notes provide a place for teachers to consider what might be the next best step in developing readers and writers in the classroom.

Terms to Remember

Culturally relevant pedagogy *(66)*

Cultural mismatch *(75)*

Funds of knowledge *(64)*

Initiate-respond-evaluate (IRE) *(74)*

Interactive journals *(68)*

Kidwatching *(77)*

Multicultural texts *(68)*

Virtual school bags *(65)*

Resources for More Information

Burnett, C., & Myers, J. (2002) "Beyond the frame": Exploring children's literacy practices. *Reading,* 36(2), 56–62.

Comber, B. (2000) What really counts in early literacy lessons, *Language Arts,* 78(1) 39–49.

Jimenez, R. T. (2004) More equitable literacy assessments for Latino students. *Reading Teacher* 57(6), 576–578.

Moll, L., Amanti, C., Neff, D., & González, N. (1992) Funds of knowledge for teaching: Using a qualitative approach to connect homes and classrooms. *Theory into Practice* 31(2) 132–141.

National Center for Culturally Responsive Educational Systems (www.nccrest.org).

Questions for Further Reflection

- As you reflect upon the key issues in this chapter, what role do you see culturally relevant pedagogy playing in how you develop and implement your literacy instruction?

- What resources might you access to help you gain knowledge and insights about your students' cultures, backgrounds, reading interests, and strategies?

CHAPTER 4

Theories of Literacy Development

Lev Vygotsky

Jean Piaget

A classmate in my teacher education program, Samantha (Sam), and I often carpool to our field experience site together. During our half-hour car rides through the city, we often discussed the courses we were required to take and how they were going for us. One day, we compared courses that were very helpful versus the courses we felt were less helpful. I told Sam that I didn't think there were enough theory-based courses in our teacher education program. This got a strong reaction out of Sam. Although the two of us agreed on many aspects regarding our teacher education program, this was apparently not going to be one of them.

Sam questioned how theory-based courses could be helpful to learning how to teach. She thought that there was already too much theory taught in our courses and not enough practical information. She wasn't convinced that theory-based courses were necessary. "What we really need," Sam said, "are more opportunities to learn what to do with kids. What if I have a struggling reader in my class? I want to know a few different activities to do with the student, so that he or she will learn how to read." I, on the other hand, felt that having a solid understanding of different theories would help us as pre-service and novice teachers make more sense of all the different positions and arguments that experienced teachers, researchers, and politicians have. I suggested to Sam that without knowledge of the theories that teaching methods and materials are based on, it would be difficult for us to understand and explain the reasons behind the various methods we use in the classroom. What if, while teaching, we find that a method we are using with our students is not working? How can we begin to understand why the method failed if we don't have theory-based knowledge to draw from? How do we begin to explain why we teach the way that we do when asked by parents and administrators? We continued to talk back and forth, trying to understand the role of theory in all of this. Like Sam, I wanted to be well equipped with strategies and activities, but I also wanted to make sure that my teaching was grounded in theories that were aligned with my own ideological perspectives about how children learn.

Following my conversation with Sam, I began to reflect on the various theorists that have influenced the way I think about teaching, learning, and literacy. Developmental theorists, such as Jean Piaget and Lev Vygotsky explored how children construct knowledge. Piaget identified various stages of children's development, while Vygotsky examined the influences of social and cultural factors on children's knowledge construction and cognitive development. Despite their differences, Piaget and Vygotsky agreed that biological and environmental factors play an equally important role in children's development and that children are active in the construction of their own knowledge.

Another theorist who had a tremendous influence on my thinking is John Dewey. Dewey emphasized the importance of experience on children's development. Dewey perceived growth and learning as ongoing processes that extend beyond classroom experiences. Like Vygotsky, Dewey believed construction and reconstruction of knowledge to be essential to people's understanding of society and of themselves, and not a process that only children undergo. Dewey (1990) also suggested that children should be encouraged to contribute to the curriculum. In fact, children's contributions should be evident in classroom situations and in the classroom environment. Lillian Katz, who is an influential scholar in the field of early childhood education and whose work is very much in line with Dewey's theories, argued that too often in our classrooms, young children are asked to engage in mindless tasks such as coloring, tracing lines, and filling in workbooks, that do not challenge children's cognitive development (Katz & Chard, 1989). Instead, children should be encouraged to interact with their environment, content, and people around them in ways that are personally meaningful.

John Dewey

All of the theorists mentioned primarily emphasized a progressive, child-centered approach to teaching children, where the interests of the learner are emphasized, real life experiences are valued, individual children are viewed as important, and the learning process is just as critical as the outcome. Although I support the child-centered approach, other theorists with a more critical slant have influenced my perspectives on teaching, including Paolo Freire and James Banks. Paolo Freire (1970) uses the metaphor of the banking system to describe the traditional classroom. In describing this approach, the teacher is often seen as the depositor of knowledge whereas students are perceived as the depositories of that knowledge; they are expected to receive, memorize, and regurgitate information that they are given. Freire (1970) stated that through this method, teachers are assuming students have no prior knowledge of what is being taught nor do students have the capability to question what is being taught. In this way, students become oppressed while teachers become the oppressors, most certainly without realizing it. As children continue storing their deposits, they become increasingly incapable of developing critical consciousness, which in turn may result in simplistic ways of viewing the world unless they are exposed to critical consciousness later on. James Banks (2004) adds

I wonder...

- What connections does Ms Yang Herr see between theory and practice?

- How do you see theory playing out in your own teaching practice?

- What learning theories are you familiar with?

to Freire's argument by stating that teachers and schools that value bettering society must see the important role of multicultural education in our schools as a means to obtaining a democratic and diverse society.

Knowing these different theorists and their perspectives helps me envision a classroom in which each student's experiences are valued and that these experiences are connected to new concepts and insights in meaningful and powerful ways. I also see myself more as a facilitator of children's knowledge rather than someone who applies the banking method and deposits information into a student's head. I realized that my ideas about teaching aligned with aspects of progressive and critical theories, that I can articulate my teaching perspectives as belonging to these schools of thought. Theory informs practice just as practice can inform theory. The knowledge of both contributes to my growth and to how I view teaching and learning.

As preservice and in-service teachers, we all desire to become *good* teachers, but unless we are knowledgeable of and challenged to reflect on how different theorists define good teaching, we are left to simply accept as best practice the teaching methods that are taught to us. What we learn in our teacher education programs may be representative of good teaching methods, but we should be prepared to intellectually critique those methods.

Chapter Overview

Inquiries in how children learn to read are ones that continue to fuel questions and disagreements in research arenas, teacher education programs, political debates, school board meetings, and in faculty lounges at local schools. Do children learn to read by using books with highly regulated and decodable words? Should children first identify sounds (phonemic awareness) and map those sounds onto various letters and eventually words (phonics)? Or should children be exposed to whole texts that offer authentic uses of language and through immersion and demonstrations begin to make sense of the text? How one answers these questions depends on which theories of learning and the reading process one ascribes to. These theories then, lead to particular kinds of curriculum and activities in the classroom.

Politicians, legislators, curriculum publishers, and district administrators often present the illusion that teaching children to read is really quite simple. Teachers only need to implement the prescribed curriculum and children will learn to read. Missing in this equation is a discussion of the theory or theories that the curriculum is based on. This is the stance that Samantha in the opening vignette assumed. She wanted to know activities rather than theory. What Ms Yang Herr points out, however, is that it is important to know theory and the connections to curriculum. When teachers understand theory, they are able to create a literacy curriculum that reflects what they believe about teaching, learning, and literacy. Experienced teachers know that the debate is not really about teaching reading. It is about how children learn.

This chapter focuses on developing a knowledge base about the reading process. Beliefs about the reading process and how children learn to read have a direct impact on reading models, curricula, and the texts made available in the classroom. Included in this chapter are different theories and perspectives about the reading process. These theories inform the instructional decisions that teachers make on a daily basis. Guiding questions include:

- How does theory link with reading models?
- What is a cognitive pyschologist model of reading?
- How does a psycholinguistics model of reading differ from a stage model?
- What are the contributions of a transactional model of reading?
- What is a critical model of reading?

What does theory have to do with curriculum building?

Chapter 1 established the relationship between ideological stances about teaching and learning and various models of schooling. The connection between what one believes and how schools are organized can be further narrowed to think about the relationship between reading theories, curriculum, and classroom practices. Take, for example, a teacher who believes that learning to read and write is a social endeavor. As part of her literacy curriculum, she invites children to participate in literature discussions. This teacher also believes that children learn when their interests are addressed. She then considers texts and materials for the literature discussions that reflect students' interests (e.g., *American Girls,* NASCAR, horses).

> ## Creating Connections 4.1
>
> Consider the numerous classrooms you have observed. Select one teacher and address these questions:
>
> 1. What did the classroom arrangement look like? How were desks and chairs arranged—in small groups and work centers, or in rows with desks all facing one direction?
>
> 2. What types of texts were available for students to read—basal readers, leveled readers, children's literature, trade books, or a combination?
>
> 3. What kinds of engagements and activities were offered?
>
> Given your findings, what assumptions can you make about how the teacher views learning to read and write?

Building curriculum is dynamic and responsive; it is about putting beliefs into action. Curriculum is not a set of unchanging mandates, but rather an organizational device that helps teachers think about their classrooms and the practices that operate in their classrooms (Short & Burke, 1991; Short, Harste, w/Burke, 1996). Curriculum should be in a constant state of flux to meet the needs of the students in particular classroom situations (Mills & Clyde, 1990).

While it is tempting to match particular beliefs and theories to curricula and activities, it is not usually that simple. In some cases, there may be a disconnect between what one believes about how children learn to read and write and the type of curriculum implemented in the classroom. A teacher may believe that reading is about meaning making, but use a curriculum that emphasizes word identification and phonics at the expense of constructing meaning. This disconnect often happens when there are external pressures from district, state, and federal mandates. In recent years pressure to achieve *AYP* (*adequate yearly progress*) and state standards has left little room for teachers to consider their own theoretical positions in relation to teaching reading and writing. Given particular mandates, teachers, particularly beginning teachers, often find themselves implementing curriculum without much consideration of the underlying theories. Because curriculum is based on theory, it is important to be familiar with different theories of how children learn to read and write. The following questions may serve as a starting point for linking theory to curriculum building.

Uncovering your beliefs about teaching and instruction

- What constitutes good teaching? And good teaching of reading?
- What environments support literacy learning?
- What knowledge and experiences are most valued?

FIGURE 4.1 Theory is a foundation for classroom instruction.

Focusing on these questions begins to challenge traditional ways of thinking about theory, curriculum, and classroom practices as static and unchanging entities. The next section profiles four beginning teachers as they make decisions regarding classroom instruction. The connections between theory, models, curriculum, and practices are made visible as each teacher considers instructional practices in light of what is believed about literacy and learning.

Four classroom portraits and four theories of literacy development

Creating Connections 4.2

Access a local school district's website. What statements are being made around literacy development?
What impressions do you have as a result of reading the website?
Share your thinking with classmates.

In this section, you will meet four elementary school teachers who have different approaches to learning and literacy development. The four teachers, Ms. Teal, Ms. Battle, Mr. Ruby, and Ms. Fuller, are new to the profession, all having less than three years of experience. As the descriptions of their classrooms unfold, consider how each teacher might respond to the questions listed in "Uncovering Your Beliefs About Teaching and Instruction" from the previous section. How do these teachers position literacy in their classrooms?

- *Ms. Robyn Teal's classroom:* Learning to read means focusing on skills.
- *Ms. Sharonda Battle's classroom:* Learning to read means understanding the meaning of words.
- *Mr. Thomas Ruby's classroom:* Learning to read means learning how to bring meaning to a text and how to get meaning from a text.
- *Ms. Pauline Fuller's classroom:* Learning to read means critically examining the text.

To examine the links between theory and curriculum building, three aspects of the classroom are presented: physical environment (including layout of the furniture and texts); grouping structures (whole class and small groups); and the affective environment (tone and atmosphere in the classroom). These aspects begin to uncover a theory of reading, which leads to a particular reading model and ultimately curriculum building and activities.

Robyn Teal's classroom: Learning to read means focusing on skills

Robyn Teal is in her second year of teaching. Ms. Teal was very excited to accept the fourth grade teaching position at Wilson Elementary School. She is enthusiastic and wants to make a difference in students' lives. She had preferred working with older students during her teacher education program. She has 24 students, five of which are English Language Learners (ELL). Four speak Spanish as their primary language and one speaks Vietnamese. These students have been in the United States anywhere from one to three years. Given recent policies in the district regarding English only, the ELL students spend 20–30 minutes each day with the English as a Second or

Other Language (ESOL) teacher. There is no additional support in her classroom. All instruction and materials in Ms. Teal's classroom are in English.

Ms. Teal works with two other fourth grade teachers who have many years of experience. They meet weekly to discuss curriculum. The students at Wilson Elementary School struggle to do well on state mandated standardized tests. Because of these pressures, there is an expectation that Ms. Teal will provide her students with the same curriculum as the other teachers provide their students. The two other fourth grade teachers operate with an industrial perspective of learning (as does the school). As noted in Chapter 1, this perspective means that all of the students are expected to complete the prescribed curriculum at a predetermined pace. Ms. Teal feels that she has little freedom to go beyond the predetermined structure. She wants to do well in teaching and is concerned that her students will not achieve the established benchmarks for her state. She accepts the curriculum as it is offered to her, with little challenge or disagreement.

An observer walking into Ms. Teal's classroom will notice the walls are filled with a variety of texts (procedural/rule charts, motivational posters, an entire wall devoted to a word wall, student work with corresponding state standards, etc.). A majority of the text on the walls is commercially produced. During the instructional day, students do not seem to pay much attention to the texts on the walls. They are on static display. There is a classroom library in the corner of the room, but it is not organized in any fashion. The books reflect an early career teacher's collection. There are some, but the collection is not extensive. Students rarely use the library other than when they need a book during DEAR (Drop Everything and Read) time. During this time, students peruse the shelves but do not to seem to be engaged with the texts. A common interest in this classroom is the local professional basketball team. Ms. Teal does not have any texts that relate to basketball.

Students' desks are arranged in a "U" formation and Ms. Teal's desk is in the far corner of the room. The majority of learning activities are individual in nature (skill-based worksheets, outlining, journal writing), so there are few opportunities for students to work collaboratively. Ms. Teal reminds students that reading and writing are quiet practices, and there should be no talking.

Reading and writing in this class are not integrated processes. During the 45 minutes each day when reading is taught, students read selections from a basal anthology or a chapter book that the whole class is working on. Students are divided into groups (mostly ability) and work with Ms. Teal in a reading group for 15–20 minutes at a time. In these groups, students discuss preselected vocabulary words and predict what the book or chapter is going to be about. At this time, students are reading *Tales of a Fourth Grade Nothing* (Blume, 1972). In this story, Peter, who is nine years old, resents having to be cooperative and polite while Fudge, his three-year-old brother, gets away with having temper tantrums, making messes, and performing crazy antics. Individual students are asked to read aloud sections of the chapter. After students read aloud, they answer a series of comprehension questions that correspond to a particular chapter in the book. The questions focus on literal details in the story. During the reading group conversations, there is little discussion of how the text is relevant to the lives and experiences of the children in the classroom. Vocabulary words are introduced (e.g., transportation, pollution, committee,

> **Comprehension questions for Tales of a Fourth Grade Nothing**
>
> 1. What does Peter win at Jimmy's birthday party?
> 2. How does Henry's mom feel when he brings home his prize?
> 3. What is the biggest problem in Peter's life?
> 4. Describe how Peter felt when Mr. Yarby made such a fuss over Fudge.
> 5. What does Fudge do to embarrass Peter? List and describe at least three things.

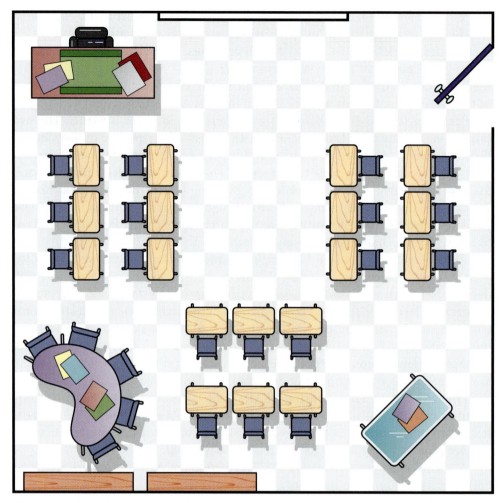

Ms. Teal's classroom arrangement.

monorail, and illustration). Based on their test scores, the five English Language Learners are placed in the lowest reading group. Students not working with Ms. Teal are expected to complete various worksheets and then read silently. There is additional time after lunch to engage in self-sustained silent reading (DEAR time). Ms. Teal uses this time to prepare for the afternoon activities and lessons.

Writing is not integrated into the instruction time set aside for reading. The students work from spelling and language arts textbooks and respond to writing prompts provided by Ms. Teal. These writing samples are placed in writing folders. Occasionally, students have opportunities to write their own stories. Final drafts are placed in their writing folders to be taken home at the end of the grading period.

Robyn Teal's classroom illustrates a particular orientation to literacy development. She approaches literacy as an individual endeavor. Reading and writing are silent acts and there is little encouragement for students to develop shared and negotiated understandings. Reading and writing are skills to be learned. The perspective in this classroom is that students learn best by practicing discrete skills until mastery occurs. In order for students to master particular skills, there is little choice in the types of texts they read or how learning occurs. Ms. Teal works from the premise that all students should have the same experience; therefore, she does not differentiate her instruction or learning engagements. Based on a small glimpse into Robyn Teal's classroom, we might say that teaching reading involves learning skills in a predetermined and prescribed fashion.

BOTTOM-UP THEORY OF LITERACY DEVELOPMENT. Robyn Teal's classroom is based on a cognitive psychologist or "bottom-up" theory of literacy learning. A ***bottom-up theory*** views learning to read as a series of small, discrete steps, from simple to more complex (from the bottom up!). This theory of learning has a building block mindset, where learners build upon their knowledge starting from the smallest piece of language and working up toward meaning. A bottom-up theory toward literacy development gained popularity in the latter half of the twentieth century with Jeanne Chall's (1967) book, *Learning to Read: The Great Debate* and LaBerg and Samuels' (1974) work on automaticity. LaBerg and Samuels discuss the capacity of the human mind to process information. They saw decoding and comprehending as two separate mental tasks. Readers need to recognize words *automatically* and to assign meanings to words *automatically*. If one of those tasks required more attention, the student would not be able to fully attend to comprehending the text. In this theory, it becomes critical to master one of these processes (most likely word analysis) so that the mind can attend to the other process (comprehension).

A cognitive psychologist theory of reading is one that emphasizes awareness and control over word learning. Cognitive psychologists view the alphabetic nature of the written language to be central in learning to read. Students read texts that make the alphabet system transparent and this is usually accomplished by controlling the vocabulary that the student is exposed to. Students read texts and engage in activities that focus on the development of spelling—sound knowledge, either through synthetic and analytic phonics. Synthetic phonics emphasizes letter-by-letter phonological decoding, while analytic phonics is the process of identifying unknown words with analogies to onsets and rimes. These two approaches to phonics are further explained in Chapter 7.

A bottom-up theory to literacy learning also has roots in behaviorism. Behaviorists believe that learning is best accomplished through practice and rewards. Students are presented with very specific "stimuli" such as textbooks, worksheets, flashcards, and other materials that break the reading process down into discrete skills. These materials often represent consistency in language patterns and rules. Students repeatedly practice the parts of a complex process until they reach a level of automaticity. Bottom-up theories work quite well for the decoding aspect of the reading process, which is being able to accurately map letters to sounds for word identification. However, there is more to reading than decoding. Bottom-up theories do not consider the reader's background and prior experiences, nor do readers have a sense of the larger picture of why people learn to read.

SKILLS MODEL. A skills model for curriculum is one that many of us are familiar with. When schools are portrayed in the movies and on television, there is often the image of the teacher standing at the front of the room, children in desks (in rows) passively receiving the information, raising their hand to answer a question, and everyone on the same page of the reading book. In a skills model, the *basics*, which typically include sequential reading skills and a heavy focus on decoding, are the most valued components of the reading process.

A teacher like Ms. Teal, who ascribes to a bottom-up theory of literacy learning, will most likely use a ***skills-based approach*** to literacy development. Because Ms. Teal is a fourth grade teacher, she does not spend as much time on phonics as she

---

cognitive psychologist or bottom-up theory

Learning to read is based on a series of small discrete steps from the simplest to the most complex.

> ### *Creating Connections 4.3*
> Imagine learning something outside of school (cooking, a sport, car mechanics, guitar). What would the process look like if a bottom-up theory to learning were used?

---

skills-based approach

Instructional materials and pedagogy that focus on discrete skills in learning to read.

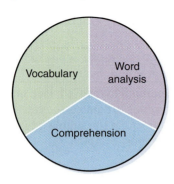

FIGURE 4.2 Skills-based approach to literacy.

phonics-first approach
_____

Instructional materials and pedagogy that focuses on letters and sounds as the primary component of learning to read.

would if she were teaching in the primary grades. For her, the components of the reading process have equal weight in her reading lessons. The three significant areas of reading instruction are word analysis, vocabulary, and comprehension (see Figure 4.2). Reading ability is seen as skill + skill + skill. While the overall structure of the reading program has students accessing all three of these components, the identified skill to be learned is taught in a self-contained lesson and then the reader must apply the skill to the reading selection.

The emphasis is on mastering particular skills during the reading process. Teachers working with beginning readers will focus on subskills first (letters and sounds). This is often known as the ***phonics-first approach***. After students learn to identify various letters and sounds, they progress to learning whole words; then reading those words in sentences and paragraphs.

Guiding assumptions of a skills model include:

- Reading proceeds from the bottom up, whereby skills are arranged in a hierarchy from smaller to larger.
- Reading skills are taught and assessed sequentially and in isolation.
- Fluency, being able to read without hesitation and in a fluid manner, is an important aspect of the reading process.
- Meaning is a residual outcome of the process.
- Teachers provide direct instruction of skills.

> ### *Creating Connections 4.4*
>
> What experiences have you had with basal reading and worksheets? Did you put forth your best effort and creativity?

ANOTHER GLIMPSE INTO MS. TEAL'S CLASSROOM. Taking a second look in Ms. Teal's room on another day reveals that Ms. Teal also uses her basal anthology to teach reading. Ms. Teal uses a basal program that equally attends to comprehension, word analysis, and vocabulary. Basal reading materials are the most common commercially produced materials in elementary classrooms in the United States. Each week, students learn new vocabulary words from a story, read the selected story, work on a reading skill (e.g., prediction, summarizing, main idea, compare/contrast), and answer comprehension questions following the story. One story focused on ranching and what it might be like to live on a ranch in 1900 and in 2000. Students were asked to think about the differences in the two diary entries and record notes on these differences. The focusing question was "How has life on a ranch changed in 100 years?" After students complete this story and the other six stories in this "unit," they are tested on how well they retained the skills learned in those stories. The con-

---

Bottom-up Theory and Skills Model: Advantages and Disadvantages

What a Bottom-up Theory and Skills Approach Offers	What a Bottom-up Theory and Skills Approach Lacks
• There is a predetermined series of skills. • Scope and sequence of skills are taught. • Complete sets of materials are provided. • There are clear expectations for success. • A teacher's edition lays out all lessons and activities. • Focus is on fluency and decoding.	• There is minimal attention to individual needs and interests of readers and writers. • There is very little emphasis on differentiating among students. • Creativity is limited because there is a predetermined way to respond. • Skills are not taught in context.

nection between these skills and standardized tests make the basal reading materials popular in classroom literacy instruction. Figure 4.3 offers a flowchart for the bottom up theory of basal programs.

Ms. Sharonda Battle's classroom: Learning to read means understanding the meaning of words

Ms. Sharonda Battle is also a new teacher with less than three years of experience. She has looked forward to her teaching career for a long time and is excited to finally achieve her goals. Ms. Battle's school is located in a low socioeconomic area of a major metropolitan city. Ms. Battle graduated from her teacher education program with an interest in teaching young children. She completed her student teaching in fifth grade, but was really interested in teaching kindergarten. Ms. Battle interviewed at a school known for progressive pedagogy. During her interview, she shared a portfolio of work she had completed during her teacher education program. Some of the artifacts in the portfolio included reading conferences with students, a sample focus study on maps, a miscue analysis completed with a student she tutored, and writing samples from students in the fifth grade classroom. Ms. Battle accepted a third grade position, and was looking forward to implementing theme cycles with the students. *Theme cycles* are units of study that can be either teacher or student initiated. Animals, environment, and life cycle are examples of possible theme cycles that Ms. Battle will implement.

Ms. Battle is in a grade level team of four teachers. She works closely with one other third grade teacher who has five years of experience. These two teachers plan their curriculum based on the interests and needs of the children. Unlike Ms. Teal in the earlier portrait, Ms. Battle is flexible in how she provides instruction. While there are pressures to achieve benchmarks and district and state standards, the administration draws upon the teachers' expertise and knowledge to accomplish those goals.

Walking into Ms. Battle's third grade classroom, an observer will immediately notice differences between this classroom and Ms. Teal's. Texts of all kinds are on the walls and shelves. Student-produced work is visible throughout the classroom. There are displays of finished products, in-progress student thinking (charts, webs, timelines), and student-created labels and procedural information (rules, instructions). Almost half of the students in this classroom speak languages other than English as their primary language. Ms. Battle supports these English Language Learners by displaying texts in their primary language. There are multi-language texts in the classroom library, as well as labels on the walls. Students have access to a variety of writing materials and texts. A writing center includes assorted paper and writing tools. The classroom library is a focal point in the room, with tubs, bins, and shelves of books of different genres, text complexity, languages, and subjects. Like many beginning teachers, Ms. Battle has not had the time or resources to build the kind of classroom library she wants. To meet her curricular needs, she regularly borrows books from the school library and local community library.

Students work in small groups, and their desks are arranged to facilitate conversations (e.g., four desks pushed together). There is quite a bit of movement in the classroom as students participate in a variety of groups depending on the project and the work. Students come together in the library area for whole class discussions. Whole class discussions often become the time for students to discuss current issues and events. Students in this classroom have developed procedures for participating in large group conversations. For example, they listen closely when a classmate is talking, ask questions if they are unsure of a comment, and know how to offer their own opinions and ideas without talking over each other.

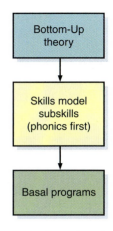

FIGURE 4.3 Flowchart for bottom-up theory.

There is a two-hour block that has been set aside for reading and writing in-struction each morning. Students work seamlessly between the two as they read and write a variety of texts. As a primary focus for instruction, Ms. Battle introduces a number of different reading strategies to her students. Each day she conducts read-ing conferences, so that each student meets with her at least once a week. In these reading conferences, she has students read aloud a text that they have selected. She wants students to feel comfortable with their oral fluency. Ms. Battle asks students to talk about what they are reading, as well as to talk about the different strategies they use to make sense of the text. As students share, Ms. Battle records the infor-mation on a reading conference form. This information is used to plan her mini-lessons around reading strategies. Sometimes the mini-lesson is for the whole class, and other times she brings together small groups of students to work intensely on a particular strategy. In addition to the strategy work, students also participate in literature discussions and read alouds. Ms. Battle selects titles that students indicate on their interest inventories as being of high interest.

Students also engage in sustained silent reading, whereby they select the books and texts they want to read. Ms. Battle has put together a number of different text sets on various topics and issues. Text sets are collections of materials around a particular is-sue or topic. Because of the recent hurricanes in the Southeast, Ms. Battle has gathered a number of different texts about hurricanes. In this text set there are newspaper arti-cles, stories from news magazines, Internet print outs, and informational picture books.

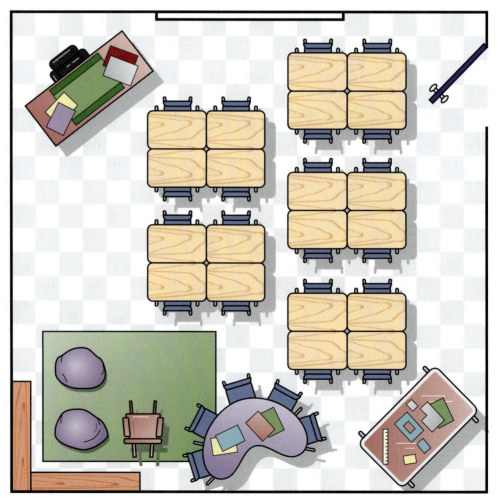

Arrangement of Ms Batte's classroom.

Students access these text sets as part of their sustained silent reading time. Students are expected to read and record their impressions and wonderings. This self-sustained silent reading time occurs during the literacy block when students are not participating in mini-lessons or reading conferences. There is quite a bit of responsibility on the students to manage their own reading schedules. If students experience difficulty in managing their own reading schedules, Ms. Battle will intervene. Her long-term goal for the students is for students to have ownership of their literacy development.

From this brief description of Ms. Battle's classroom and some of her teaching structures, it is apparent that Ms. Battle considers reading as a tool for understanding larger issues in the world. She offers students opportunities to choose their texts, as well as read multiple texts on the same issue or genre. Ms. Battle believes in the socially situated nature of learning, where new understandings emerge as a result of the collaboration and dialogue that occur—the social interaction. Ms. Battle also provides students with opportunities to be responsible for their own learning—what texts they want to read, how much the group will work through in the week, and ways of presenting the information. In Ms. Battle's classroom, teaching reading is about engaging students in their quest for learning.

Teacher–Student Reading Conference Form

Name _____   Date _____

Text title _____

Type of text (picture book, chapter book, magazine, etc.)
_____

Points discussed?

Strategies used?

Recommendations?

Next steps?

Date of next conference _____

Additional comments

Ms Battle's reading conference form.

Reading is not the focus of the event, but rather it is a way to understand a particular idea of concept.

TOP-DOWN THEORY OF LITERACY DEVELOPMENT.

psycholinguistics or top-down theory

Meaning is central to the reading process. The emphasis moves from meaning to letters/sounds.

TOP-DOWN THEORY OF LITERACY DEVELOPMENT. On the other end of the spectrum from bottom-up theory is the ***psycholinguistics*** or ***top-down theory*** of literacy learning. This theory brings together two fields, psychology and linguistics, to determine how literacy practices are learned. K. Goodman (1968, 1986), a renowned leader in this theory, determined that meaning is what is most salient in the reading process. Readers do not engage with a text if they do not make sense of the text. Because the emphasis moves from the larger piece of the process (meaning) to the smaller pieces (letters/sounds), this is known as top-down theory of reading. In a top-down theory of reading, language is processed from the whole to the parts, so the axiom, "the whole is greater than the sum of its parts" is quite appropriate.

A top-down theory of literacy advocates for a student-centered approach to literacy learning. There is an emphasis on integrating students' needs and interests into the curriculum, as seen in Chapter 1 with the inquiry model of schooling. Students are actively involved in what they read, write, and learn. A top-down theory ascribes to a progressive ideology that supports learners as knowledgeable beings able to construct meaning from texts. Reading is viewed as an intellectual process where access to background knowledge plays a critical role in reading to learn.

whole language model

Reading is seen as an all-encompassing act involving the 4 cueing systems graphophonemic, syntactic, semantic, and pragmatic.

WHOLE LANGUAGE MODEL OF LITERACY DEVELOPMENT. Reflecting the elements of a top-down theory of literacy development is the ***whole language model*** (Edelsky, Altwerger, & Flores, 1991; Goodman, 1986, 1989; Short, Harste, & w/Burke, 1996; Watson, 1989; Weaver, 1990). Whole language is a set of beliefs, not a method. The Whole Language Umbrella, an international conference under the auspices of National Council of Teachers of English (NCTE), operates with a number of guiding principles that value learning in a meaningful context. At the heart of these principles is the notion that language use is purposeful and authentic. Reading, writing, listening, and speaking are interrelated and used in authentic means to accomplish the work. In Ms. Battle's classroom, a group of students are learning about hurricanes by reading a number of different texts. As they work in small groups, they read materials, write notes, listen to others, and share their own thinking. Whole language teachers immerse children in reading and writing events. Whole language teachers also:

- Value all learners, regardless of their intellectual or linguistic abilities and regardless of their sociocultural or ethnic backgrounds.
- Recognize that an individual learner's knowledge is constructed through reflection as well as interaction, collaboration, and transaction with others.
- Understand that learning involves risk taking, as well as hypothesis forming and testing within a community.
- Know that students learn the subsystems of language, (phonics, syntax, punctuation) as they use language in meaningful contexts.
- Understand that assessment informs teaching. Assessment involves talking with children, listening to them read, reading their writing, observing them at work, and observing their work over time.
- Recognize that teachers are professionals who take responsibility for their learning by observing students closely, by learning from each other, and by engaging in on-going professional development.

TECHNOLOGY LINK

http://www.ncte.org/groups/wlu/who/107138.htm.

Access the Whole Language Umbrella and the organization's beliefs for more information.

Whole language teachers know that readers and writers access and use a number of different cues as they engage with texts. Recall the discussion in Chapter 2 on the language cueing systems—graphophonemic, semantic, syntactic, and pragmatic. Each of these cueing systems plays a critical role in the reading process. Whole language teachers often support readers and writers by determining which cueing systems are being used and which ones could be further examined. For example, when Ms. Battle conducts the reading conferences, she pays particular attention to how students make sense of the text. She notes the strategy a reader uses (e.g., look for word patterns) and if needed, will introduce other strategies (e.g., using context, skipping the word) that can also be useful to the reader. Because the cueing systems work in concert with each other, the whole language model is best represented by a series of concentric circles, whereby the reading moment is represented in the "piece of the pie" (see Figures 4.4 and 4.5).

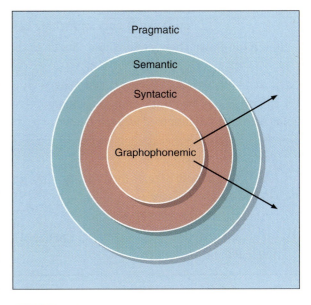

FIGURE 4.4 Whole language model of literacy development.

ANOTHER GLIMPSE INTO MS. BATTLE'S CLASSROOM.

Ms. Battle's classroom is typical of other classrooms where a whole language model for literacy is in place. Children learn to read in environments that are print rich, and with texts that offer an authentic use of vocabulary. Ms. Battle provides many opportunities for students to engage with whole, authentic texts. The students interested in hurricanes have access to books, magazines, and other texts that reflect different genres and levels of difficulty. They focus their attention on finding information about hurricanes to share with classmates. Ms. Battle's students are interested in learning why hurricanes have names. Justin, a member of the group, reads, "Names repeat every six years. But if a storm is particularly violent, its name may be taken off the list" (from a passage in *Hurricanes: Earth's Mightiest Storms*, Lauber, 1996). He is unsure of the word "violent." He pauses and thinks about what he knows about hurricanes and what to expect in the sentence. He also accesses his knowledge of letters and sounds. In the end, he reads the word "violent" and talks about how it means strong or fierce.

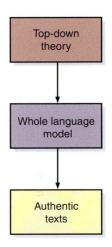

FIGURE 4.5 Flow chart for top-down theory.

Mr. Thomas Ruby's classroom: Learning to read means learning how to respond to a text

Mr. Thomas Ruby is in his first year of teaching. He is a warm and caring individual. Mr. Ruby completed his student teaching at the school where he now teaches, so he was very familiar with many of the teachers and their approaches to literacy. The neighborhood that the school is located in is one that is transitional, with a number of homes and businesses experiencing urban renewal. There is quite a bit of diversity (socioeconomically, culturally, and linguistically) reflected in the school and in Mr. Ruby's third grade classroom. He has students from Bangladesh, China, Ecuador, and Mexico. Because the students are not recent arrivals, they receive instruction in English.

Mr. Ruby's classroom environment is similar to Ms. Battle's. There are a number of texts (both commercially produced and classroom produced) on the walls and shelves. Mr. Ruby has been collecting texts for a few years and has an extensive

---

Top-Down Theory and Whole Language Model: Advantages and Disadvantages

What a Top-Down Theory and Whole Language Offers

- There is abundant attention to individual needs and interests as readers and writers.
- Opportunities for creativity because there is no one predetermined way to respond.
- Opportunities to access cueing systems that are meaningful.
- Access to a variety of texts for a variety of purposes.
- Engagement with texts that more closely mirror experiences outside of school.
- Language systems (reading, writing, speaking, and listening) are interrelated.

What a Top-Down Theory and Whole Language Lacks

- Explicit and systematic focus on a particular skill.
- Prescribed or predetermined sequence of lessons or events.
- Predetermined assessments.
- There is minimal attention to social and critical issues.

---

library corner with bins of texts of all kinds. He canvasses libraries and used book stores for additional texts, as well as encourages students to bring in their own books and reading materials to share with the class. The library corner is designed to resemble a comfortable reading nook. There is a structure with stairs that the students can climb upon or sit under to read. There is an overstuffed couch with a number of pillows. Additionally, Mr. Ruby has acquired a couple of reading lamps to soften the glare from the fluorescent lights. Plants and a fish tank also occupy this space, giving it a feeling of calmness.

Students in Mr. Ruby's class have access to books throughout the day. Students have a two-hour literacy block each morning. During this time, they engage in literature discussions, writing, and reading. They work individually or in small groups, depending on the task. Choice is an essential characteristic in Mr. Ruby's classroom. Students can choose their reading materials and if they want to read alone or with a partner. An observer in Mr. Ruby's classroom will notice that he seamlessly moves around to different literature discussions. He joins these small group conversations and pushes readers to consider new concepts and to work on reading strategies for more productive reading. Mr. Ruby encourages them to think beyond a surface understanding and to consider the theme of the story.

Students self-select the texts they want to read. At this time, the literature discussion groups are reading a text set on Martin Luther King [*I've Seen the Promised Land: The Life of Dr. Martin Luther King, Jr.* (Myers, 2004); *My Brother Martin: A Sister Remembers Growing Up with the Rev. Dr. Martin Luther King, Jr.* (Farris, 2003); *Martin's Big Words: The Life of Dr. Martin Luther King, Jr.* (Rappaport, 2001)], a text set on pirates [*Pirates* (Matthews, 2006); *Everything I Know About Pirates* (Lichtenheld, 2000); *How I Became a Pirate* (Long, 2006)] and a text set on fractured fairy tales [*Once upon a Fairy Tale: Four Favorite Stories* (Starbright Foundation, 2001); *The Wolf's Story: What Really Happened to Little Red Riding Hood* (Forward, 2005); and *Three Spinning Fairies* (Ernst, 2002)].

An expectation in Mr. Ruby's classroom is that students will complete a reading journal for the texts they read. Mr. Ruby uses the reading journals to assess the students' understandings of the texts they read. He monitors the types of connections students make to the texts, whether they are connections in the text, to another text, or to life experiences they have had.

The reading journals are springboards for students' writing. The students keep writers' notebooks where they record daily observations, ideas, things to remember, and issues to pursue. In many of the students' notebooks are connections and ideas related to the readings they are doing in class. Chad's fascination with owls was evident in both his reading journal and in the writer's notebook. He was reading an expository/nonfiction text on the habitat and life cycle of owls. His journal recorded facts about different types of owls. His writer's notebook documents a time when he saw an owl in the eaves of his garage. The notebook also contains the first few lines of a story that he is writing about owls.

Students in this classroom are expected to share their thinking with others in the classroom. Sometimes this occurs as more formal presentations; but most often students share their learning in small groups. Students form literature discussion groups in which they read and respond to a common text. They note various connections they have with the text and think about how these connections fit together. Occasionally, students form groups in which everyone is reading a different text. In these groups, students highlight and share particularly interesting and engaging aspects of their story.

The group reading fairy tales has created charts that differentiate character traits. These charts will be used when they present their work to the other students. During these small group literature discussions, students challenge each other and negotiate their understandings of the text.

Mr. Ruby's understandings of literacy are similar to Ms. Battle's—he also views reading and writing as tools for learning. However, Mr. Ruby's classroom invites children into the reading process by acknowledging their current interests, supporting the connections that these readers make, and encouraging them to share those interpretations and connections with others. Reading and writing are socially constructed endeavors. In Mr. Ruby's classroom, teaching reading is about making connections and interpreting texts in ways that are meaningful for the reading. Reading then provides opportunities for students to access their background experiences and knowledge as they make sense of the text. Enjoyment of the reading process is prioritized over gathering facts or details in what is read.

TRANSACTIONAL THEORY OF READING. While top-down and bottom-up theories of reading dominate the "reading war" conversations among various stakeholders (ie., media, politicians, public), there is another theory that contributes to understanding how readers come to make meaning of text. A *transactional* *theory* takes into consideration the reader's intentions, purposes, and the situational context of the reading event (Rosenblatt, 1978). When a reader encounters a text, a transaction occurs, meaning that there is a negotiation between the reader and the text. It is a shared journey between readers and texts (see Figure 4.6). A reader's background experiences and knowledge contribute to this transaction, so that no two readers read the text in exactly the same way. To illustrate, a group of third graders in Mr. Ruby's class read *Charlotte's Web* (White, 1952) and completed a reading log of words they didn't know, a summary of the chapter, and how they felt about the chapter. After reading the first chapter where Fern asks to keep Wilbur, Shariha writes for his summary and feelings section, "I think her dad was very nice to let her keep Wilbur. Fern gets to keep [the] pig and take care of it. Her brother wants a pig too, but early risers only get one. I like this chapter because it was exciting." Peter writes, "Fern wakes up early and has a fit about how her dad is going to kill a pig. I don't like this chapter because it was weird she just had a fit and she got a pet." And Melvin writes, "Fern begs [her] father not to kill the pig and instead gets it. And then gives it milk and then names it Wilbur. So far I think the story is okay. And it isn't like the movie at all. And I didn't know that Fern was eight." These examples suggest that readers bring to the reading event their own sense of what is salient in the story as well as how well they like the events in the story.

Rosenblatt also determined that readers attend to different aspects of the text depending on their purposes for reading (1978). These purposes, or stances, vary from an informational stance (efferent) to a pleasure-seeking stance (aesthetic). Stances influence what the reader will retain from the reading event, whether it is information to be stored for later, or an emotion or impression that lingers on. (See Chapter 10 for a more extended discussion on efferent and aesthetic stances.)

Transactional theory considers responding to a text as an active process of thinking, talking, and writing. The interpretation of a text is a social activity in an environment where ideas are shared and negotiated. Readers enter into the reading event with cultural knowledge and assumptions, experiences, world knowledge, and awareness of literary conventions. As demonstrated with the third grade readers around *Charlotte's Web*, each reader responded to the text based on experiences they have had (what it means to "have a fit," seeing the movie); and how to use appropriate language (I like/ I didn't like) in a Reading Response Log genre. Langer (1995) talks about these as "envisionments." She suggests that envisionments are

> . . .text worlds in the mind and they differ from individual to individual. They are a function of one's personal and cultural experiences, one's relationship to the current experience, what one knows, how one feels, and what one is after. Envisionments are dynamic sets of related ideas, images, questions, disagreements, anticipations, arguments, and hunches that fill the mind during every reading [event]. . . .(p. 9)

Reprinted by permission of the Publisher. From Judith A Langer, Envisioning Literature: Literary Understanding and Literature Instruction, New York: Teachers College Press, (c) 1995 by teachers College, Columbia University. All rights reserved.

Classrooms that foster a transactional view of reading invite learners and teachers to appropriate ideas and images from the text into their own thinking. For example, ten-year-old Rebecca may not have realized that there was a women's movement prior to the 1960s woman's liberation movement. But upon reading about Susan B. Anthony in *Susan B. Anthony: A Photo-Illustrated Biography* (Davies,

---

Creating Connections 4.5

Make a list of your current reading. Which texts are you reading with an efferent stance? Which are you reading from an aesthetic stance?

1998), she added this knowledge and the idea of the long history of women's rights in this country. There is space in text-related conversations to share responses and interpretations. Rebecca shares her new understandings in her literature response journal as well as with a reading partner. In doing so, her interpretations become more sophisticated and complex.

READER RESPONSE MODEL.   Students construct meanings of text by linking ideas and creating connections among and between texts and the world around them. These meanings are links to past experiences, conversations, situations, and texts. The meanings we construct continuously change in light of past and evolving understandings. Hartman's (1992; 1995) discussion of ***intertextuality***, the process of constructing links between texts and our ideas and experiences, suggests that there are connections that are based in the text itself; connections to other texts; and connections to outside or world knowledge. These connections support the reader's meaning making process. In recent years, there has been a push in literature discussions for young readers to make their connections more explicit. One strategy that has been particularly helpful is the ***text to text***, ***text to self***, and ***text to world*** connections (Harvey & Goudivas, 2000). These connections enable readers to better comprehend the text being read. Readers may also connect to literary elements and features, different genres, and different authors.

intertextuality

The process of constructing links between text and one's experiences to other texts, or to outside knowledge.

text to text

Connection is to another piece of text.

text to self

Connection is based on personal experience.

text to world

Connection is to a larger world on social events or issues.

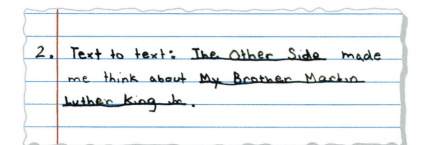

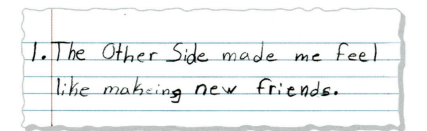

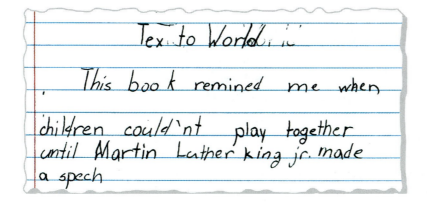

TECHNOLOGY LINK

http://www.education.miami.edu/ep/Rosenblatt/

Read an interview with Louise Rosenblatt conducted in 1999 at the University of Miami.

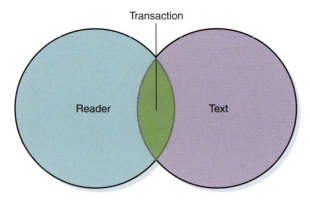

FIGURE 4.6 Transactional model of reading.

reader response model

Readers transact with the text, creating new understandings based on prior experiences.

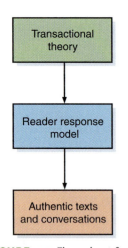

FIGURE 4.7 Flow chart for transactional theory.

In some cases, the connections students make seem tangential to the conversation or focus of the discussion. These connections are not always tangential, and it is important for the teacher to ask the student to further explain what is meant by the comment. This will help alleviate any concerns that students are purposefully off track and may also illuminate thoughtful connections and insights not readily apparent to the teacher.

As with the whole language model of reading, a ***reader response model*** is most effective with texts that are conceptually strong and use authentic vocabulary and language. Books that address socially significant issues, experiences, and events that are conceptually rich and allow the reader to make personal and meaningful connections.

ANOTHER GLIMPSE INTO MR. RUBY'S CLASSROOM. Returning to Mr. Ruby's classroom, it is possible to envision a reader response model because of all the work around authentic pieces of literature. Figure 4.7 highlights the path from transactional theory to authentic texts. Students in this classroom read a number of different texts throughout the year, including a number of titles in the *Encyclopedia Brown* series (Sobol), *Ramona Quimby, Age 8* (Beverly Cleary, 1992), *Sarah, Plain and Tall* (MacLachlan, 1985), and *Shiloh* (Naylor, 1992). These books are common core selections in many school districts. Mr. Ruby also introduces a number of other titles that he thinks may be of interest to the students. He encourages students to bring in their own selections to share with others. At the beginning of the year, Mr. Ruby conducted an interest inventory to gain a sense of what this group of students would like to read. A group of girls was interested in reading some of the stories, from the *American Girl* series. Mr. Ruby gathered some of the stories and the girls created a system so that they could all have an opportunity to read. They eagerly talked about the characters and how different their lives are from the characters. These conversations were reflected in their writing notebooks, and two of the girls decided to write a story about one of the characters, Felicity. They collaborated on the story and eventually published the story for the class library.

Transactional Theory and Reader Response Model: Advantages and Disadvantages

What Transactional Theory and Reader Response Offers	What Transactional Theory and Reader Response Is Lacking
• Readers construct meaning of text by accessing prior knowledge and experiences.	• There is not a systematic or explicit curriculum to follow.
• Readers transact with a variety of texts.	• There is little if any attention to decoding strategies.
• Interpretations may vary from reader to reader.	• All interpretations are accepted with equal validity.
• Readers recognize there are many different purposes for reading.	• There are no predetermined assessments.
• Readers have an opportunity to construct alternative interpretations of text.	

Ms. Pauline Fuller's classroom: Learning to read means critically examining the text

Ms. Pauline Fuller is in her second year of teaching. She has a vibrant energy that infuses her classroom with excitement. Ms. Fuller lives and works in a community that is experiencing urban renewal. Similar to the students in Mr. Ruby's class, her students reflect the diversity of the city. Ms. Fuller was thrilled to accept a position teaching first grade in an ethnically and linguistically diverse neighborhood. She has 22 first grade students, of which only 13 attended kindergarten at the school. Five students are recent arrivals to the United States from different rural communities in Mexico.

Ms. Fuller established an environment that supports an authentic use of literacy. The walls are primarily covered with student-made materials that reflect everything from rules and procedures in the class to student artifacts. One large bulletin board area houses the audit trail (sometimes called learning trail or learning wall). An *audit* or *learning trail* is a dynamic and interactive space that documents the connections and understandings students construct in their reading, writing, and discussions. On this wall is a photocopy of the text *Going Home* (Bunting, 1998), a series of questions that were raised while reading the text and artifacts that signify and represent the conversations. The discussions have prompted students to begin exploring their own neighborhoods, considering what it means to call someplace home, and thinking about travel between two countries. The connections are linked to the text by a piece of string.

As in Mr. Ruby and Ms. Battle's classrooms, there is a well-stocked library. However, upon closer inspection of the titles, there are a greater number of texts that exemplify critical texts. "These texts invite conversations about fairness and justice; they encourage children to ask why some groups of people are positioned as 'others' " (Leland, Harste, Ociepka, Lewison, & Vasquez, 1999). Additional characteristics of these books include:

- They don't make difference invisible, but rather explore what differences *make a difference;*
- They enrich our understanding of history and life by giving voice to those who traditionally have been silenced or marginalized;

- They show how people can begin to take action on important social issues;
- They explore dominant systems of meaning that operate in our society to position people and groups of people;
- They don't provide "happily ever after" endings for complex social problems.

Students actively engage with these texts, asking questions of the text and of themselves as readers. They want to know more about the issues presented in the texts. Many of the students are currently working on projects that reflect their inquiry questions.

Writing in this class is integrated with reading, as in Ms. Battle's and Mr. Ruby's classrooms. The students in this class use their writer's notebooks to reflect upon their daily observations. The notebooks take on a more critical stance as students begin to address socially significant issues in their writing. In connection to *Going Home,* many of the students draw pictures and write about their own neighborhoods. In Lourdres's notebook, she has recorded an entry that shows the differences between her home in the United States and her home in Mexico. Lourdres was born in Mexico and moved to the United States a few months ago. She primarily writes in Spanish. Next to Lourdres, Marianna is creating a map of her home in the United States. In these two examples the students have ownership of their writing and are exploring issues that are socially significant to their lives. In future discussions of living spaces, Ms. Fuller and the students will consider issues related to the neighborhood they live in and how it is changing.

Ms. Fuller provides her students with opportunities to challenge the text—to question and wonder why things are the way they are. Ms. Fuller does not see herself as a transmitter of knowledge. Rather, she encourages her students to consider alternative perspectives and to read texts that invite conversations. Reading and writing in this classroom are seen as avenues for critique and transformation. An observer in Ms. Fuller's classroom might say that students are empowered to move literacy beyond text and into social action.

critical theory

Invites teachers and students to problematize and question current beliefs on practices.

CRITICAL THEORIES AND CRITICAL LITERACY. *Critical theories* in teaching children to read invite teachers and students to consider the varied ways literacy practices matter to the participants and their place in the world. As discussed in Chapter 1 in the critical model of schooling, literacy is seen as a social practice, not simply a technical skill (Comber, 2000; Luke & Freebody, 1999; Street, 1995). Language and literacy are not neutral acts, but rather are situated in personal, social, historical, and political relationships. There is an emphasis on the context in which the texts are created and contested. Students' interests and purposes serve as the foundation for what occurs in the classroom.

Critical literacy theories encourage teachers and students to question texts—to wonder who or what is missing, address issues of power, and consider alternative stances or ways to interact with the text. Comber (2001) notes that when teachers and students engage with critical literacy they will ask questions related to "language and power, people and lifestyles, morality and ethics, and who is advantaged by the way things are and who is disadvantaged" (p. 271).

Lewison, Flint, & VanSluys (2002) argue that critical literacy encompasses four dimensions:

- **Disrupting the commonplace:** seeing the "everyday" through new lenses.
- **Interrogating multiple perspectives:** imagining what it might be like to stand in the shoes of others.

TECHNOLOGY LINK

http://www.clippodcast.com/

This link is to CLIP (Critical Literacy in Practice) Podcast. There are many topics covered in the podcasts, ranging from bullying and racism to music and petitions. The podcasts are narrated by Vivian Vasquez.

- **Focusing on sociopolitical issues:** moving beyond the personal to consider the sociopolitical systems we all belong to.
- **Taking social action:** informed action against oppression and injustices in the world.

As teachers and students engage with critical literacy practices, these dimensions play out in an integrated fashion; they do not operate in isolation. From a critical perspective, being literate is more than the ability to decode and comprehend. It is being able to analyze and question the way things are. Readers in the twenty-first century need to know how to read for their own purposes as well as for the purposes that are defined by the context in which they operate.

FOUR-RESOURCE MODEL. The *four-resource model* by Luke and Freebody (1997), based on critical theories, is one model that teachers may use in their literacy curriculum. This model involves four sets of practices: *code breaker, text participant, text user,* and *critical practices.* Readers draw upon these resources (or practices) as they engage with texts on an everyday basis. Each of these practices is necessary, but none in and of itself is sufficient to develop literate persons. Luke and Freebody note that these practices are not discrete; nor are they learned in a hierarchical sequence. The practices are inclusive.

> **four-resource model**
> A comprehensive view of reading that includes code breaking of text participant, text user, and critical practices.

In order to read proficiently and effectively, readers need to develop their repertoire of practices for interacting with texts.

Code breaking: This practice involves breaking the code of written text by knowing about and using the relationship of spoken sounds to the graphic system. The reader is inside the text unlocking the mysteries of the print to access the meaning. Within the code breaking practice, readers:

- Recognize and use the alphabet.
- Recognize letter/sound relationships; patterns in words.
- Spell accurately.
- Recognize and use grammar and vocabulary.

Text Participant: The text participant practice involves understanding and composing meaningful written, visual, and spoken texts. The emphasis is on comprehending texts based on prior knowledge and experiences. Text participation occurs throughout the reading of the text, not just when we are finished with the text. While engaged with text participation, readers:

- Draw upon prior knowledge and experiences.
- Compare their experiences with those in the text.
- Interpret text using literal and inferential meanings.
- Understand that texts are constructed to make meaning.

Text User: The text user practice entails knowing about the purpose and form of texts. A text user has some purpose for reading and to make use of the reading. Involved in this practice, a reader:

- Understands that different cultural and social contexts shape the text.
- Uses appropriate text(s) for a particular purpose.
- Recognizes that each text type has particular features.

Critical Practices: The critical practice encourages readers to analyze the text from a social–critical perspective. The emphasis in this practice is to understand that texts are not neutral but represent a particular point of view. Attending to this practice, readers:

- Recognize that the author has a purpose for creating a text.
- Recognize opinions, bias, and points of view in a text.
- Understand how texts are crafted according to the viewpoints of the author.
- Identify how texts influence readers' understandings.

> **Creating Connections 4.6**
>
> In your own reading lives, when have you had opportunities to read from a critical practice perspective?

The four practices presented in this model are available for readers to use and orchestrate in a variety of ways, depending on the contexts and purposes for the texts. The four resource model and, ultimately, critical literacy encourages readers "to become life long learners, effective communicators and citizens who actively contribute to building a more equitable and socially just world" (Comber, 2001, cited in Vasquez, 2003). Figure 4.8 highlights the features of each practice by asking a series of questions.

FIGURE 4.8 Four Resource model for literacy.

Code Breaking Practices

Developing your resources as code breakers:

- How do I crack this code?
- How does it work?
- What are the patterns and conventions of the text/language?
- How do the sounds and the marks relate, singly, and in combination?

Focusing areas:
Alphabetic awareness, phonemic awareness, spelling, word building, conventions or mechanics of text/sentence structure.

Text-Meaning Practices

Developing your resources as text participant:

- How do the ideas represented in the text string together?
- What cultural resources can be brought to bear on this text?
- What are the cultural meanings and possible readings that can be constructed from this text?

Focusing areas:
Drawing on own experiences, comparing own experiences with text, understanding how a text works, active participation to gain meaning from texts and illustrations

Pragmatic/Text Users

Developing your resources as text user:

- How do the uses of this text shape its composition?
- What do I do with this text, here and now? What will others do with it?
- What are my options and alternatives?

Focusing areas:
Using texts in different ways both in and out of school, knowing what is expected at school, real purposes for texts, using a variety of texts appropriately

Critical Practices

Developing your resources as text analyst and critic:

- What kind of person, with what interests and values could both write and read this naively and unproblematically?
- What is this text trying to do to me? In whose interests?
- Which positions, voices, and interests are at play? Which are silent and absent?

Focusing areas:
Recognizing texts are not neutral, understanding that texts represent particular views, understanding that texts influence people's ideas, challenging/questioning texts

Source: Luke, A. & Freebody, P. (1997). "Shaping the social practices of reading." In S. Muspratt, A. Luke, and P. Freebody (Eds). *Constructing critical literacies.* Catskill, NJ: Hampton Press, 185–223.

HALLIDAY +. Another model that teachers may organize their instruction around is the ***Halliday + model*** (Egawa & Harste, 2001). This model extends the work of M. A. K. Halliday (1975), who first articulated a framework of learning language. Recall from Chapter 2 that Halliday's model is comprised of "learning language," "learning about language," and "learning through language."

- **Learning language** is using language to engage in meaning making. Children gain insights into the functions and purposes of language by using oral and written language in authentic contexts (e.g., read alouds, morning meetings, discussions, etc.)

- **Learning about language** involves learning how language is constructed—its functions and conventions. Children learn about letter–sound relationships and word order as they add to their knowledge of punctuation, spelling, and grammar (reading and writing conferences, mini-lessons, journal writing)

- **Learning through language** is learning more about the world through reading, writing, and talking. Children engage in learning events that provide opportunities to reflect on what they know as well as generate new knowledge (inquiry projects, literature discussions and response logs, writer's notebooks).

Egawa and Harste add a fourth component to this model:

- **Learning to Use Language to Critique** enables language users to question the way things are, how they got that way, and how they might be changed to create democratic practices. Children analyze language use as they challenge and problematize texts (e.g., critical conversations, social action projects).

As Ms. Fuller and her students engage with texts related to living spaces, neighborhoods, and community, they begin to develop their own critical lens. In this classroom, students work toward problematizing the status quo and asking questions that do not have simple answers.

ANOTHER GLIMPSE INTO MS. FULLER'S CLASSROOM. The students in Ms. Fuller's first grade classroom are busy talking, reading, and writing. Figure 4.9 offers the pathway from critical theory to critical literacy texts. One of the tubs of books has titles that address racial discrimination and segregation. The students have listened to Ms. Fuller read *White Socks Only* (Coleman, 1999), *Sister Anne's Hands* (Lorbiecki, 1998), *Freedom Summer* (Wiles, 2001), and *The Other Side*

Halliday + model

Extends the Halliday model (learning language, learning about language, and learning through language) to include learning to use language to critique.

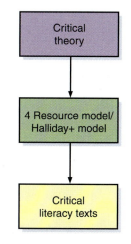

FIGURE 4.9 Flow chart for critical theory.

Critical Theory and Four Resource Model: Advantages and Disadvantages	
What Critical Literacy and the Four-Resource Model Offers	**What Critical Literacy and the Four-Resource Model Is Lacking**
• Reading and writing are considered complex processes.	• There is not a systematic or explicit curriculum to follow.
• Readers and writers engage with texts that are meaningful and authentic.	• Issues may be lacking or difficult to address in the classroom.
• Readers and writers are encouraged to consider multiple perspectives.	• It is sometimes difficult to find critical literacy texts for classroom libraries.
• Readers and writers are encouraged to challenge dominant perspectives and ask questions.	
• Literacy is seen as a social process.	

(Woodson, 2001). They have written on post-it notes questions they have after hearing the stories. The questions are used as springboards for morning meeting time. Students are actively engaged in these conversations wondering if discrimination still happens. Marcus writes in his notebook, "Does John Henry [from *Freedom Summer*] ever get to go into the store?" And Rachel writes, "How come they can't play together when they live next door to each other?" in response to listening to *The Other Side.* These initial questions link to other questions and texts about exclusion. Later in the year, students think about the differences in what boys and girls like to do on the playground. They talk about games on the playground that are "boys only" or "girls only." They read other texts such as *Oliver Button is a Sissy* (dePaola, 1979) and *Paperbag Princess* (Munch, 1992). The students discover that there are times when they want to cross those perceived gender lines and that they begin to create opportunities for all students to play. Ms. Fuller continues to encourage her students to problematize the text, to consider multiple perspectives, and to take social action on critical issues.

Looking across the four reading models

The decisions teachers make on a daily basis regarding literacy instruction are based on a particular perspective, or theory. A theory of literacy learning involves a set of beliefs or principles that guides actions and decisions about how children become proficient readers and writers. As demonstrated by the four teacher portraits in this chapter, teachers operate with a variety of belief systems that impact their literacy practices, events, and curriculum. These beliefs are often developed as a result of what they have experienced as readers and writers, their teacher education programs, the schools in which they work, and the ways in which literacy is defined by the larger social context. Theories about literacy learning and, in particular, reading can be placed into four major categories: bottom-up; top-down; transactional; and critical. Each of these theories is linked to a particular model of literacy learning and ultimately, particular instructional choices and materials.

Summary of Reading Models

Theory	Model	Literacy Events and Materials in Classroom Settings
Behaviorism/Bottom-Up	Skills-based	Ability-based reading groups; direct instruction of skills; basal anthologies; leveled texts; skill worksheets
Pyscholinguistics/Top-Down	Whole language	Groups formed based on interests; reading conferences; mini-lessons; authentic texts; range of reading levels
Transactional	Reader response	Groups formed based on interest; authentic uses and purposes for reading; connections to own life and experiences
Critical	Four-resource and Halliday +	Groups formed based on interests; authentic purposes; authentic texts, critical lens on issues

Teachers implement a reading curriculum that accounts for their working knowledge of how children learn and process information. They offer literacy experiences that are influenced by this theory. Students construct their own definitions of what it means to read based on the curriculum and materials they work with; and they develop their knowledge of various reading strategies that complement their own understandings of the reading process. The process is recursive, meaning that the ways students respond to the curriculum feed back into teachers' understandings of literacy learning. Figure 4.10 illustrates this idea.

Creating Connections 4.7

Return to your Literacy Timeline from Chapter 1.
What models of reading were evident in your history? What examples can you draw upon that demonstrates the model?

Share these new insights with classmates.

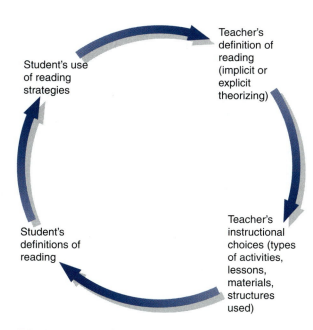

Teacher's definition of reading (implicit or explicit theorizing)

Teacher's instructional choices (types of activities, lessons, materials, structures used)

Student's definitions of reading

Student's use of reading strategies

FIGURE 4.10 Implementing a reading curriculum is a recursive process.

Invitation for the classroom

Return to the interviews conducted in Chapter 1. Ask students to work with you in categorizing their reading and writing experiences into the various reading theories and curriculum. What are students noticing about how they are learning to read and write?

In Closing

The focus for this chapter was to provide you with a knowledge base of four different theoretical approaches to literacy development. The first portrait centered on a bottom-up theory with skills model of instruction. In this portrait, Ms. Teal works from a predetermined curriculum that has been purchased by the school system. This portrait reflects what is most typical in many classrooms throughout the United States. There was more pressure on Ms. Teal to achieve on state sanctioned standardized tests and meet adequate yearly progress. In Ms. Battle's classroom, you were introduced to a top-down perspective that encompasses a whole language model for instruction. Ms. Battle pays close attention to how her students are making sense of the text, the cueing systems that are at play, and how she may support them in improving their practice. Next was Mr. Ruby's classroom. His theory, transactional (Rosenblatt, 1938/78) and the reading model of reader response suggests that readers make meaning and transact with the text based on their own experiences and knowledge. Finally, the critical perspectives and subsequently the four-resource model and Halliday+ demonstrate the powerful nature of literacy. Exposure to significant issues in our country and world is important to developing life-long learners and responsible citizens. By reading across the four portraits, you now have some background on theory and are able to link theory with practice. You have a more complete understanding of the array of curricular materials available to you and how they support or hinder the reading process.

Terms to Remember

Cognitive psychologist
    or bottom-up theory *(91)*

Critical theory *(104)*

Four-resource model *(105)*

Halliday + model *(107)*

Intertextuality *(101)*

Pyscholinguistics theory *(96)*

Phonics-first approach *(92)*

Reader response model *(102)*

Skills-based approach *(91)*

Text to self *(101)*

Text to text *(101)*

Text to world *(101)*

Top-down theory *(96)*

Transactional theory *(100)*

Whole language model *(96)*

Resources for More Information

Chall, J. (1967). *Learning to Read: The Great Debate: An inquiry into the science, art, and ideology of old and new methods of teaching children to read, 1910–1965.* New York: McGraw-Hill,

Goodman, K. S. (1986). *What's whole in whole language?* Portsmouth, NH: Heinemann.

Lewison, M., Flint, A. S. & Van Sluys, K. (2002). Taking on critical literacy: The journey of newcomers and novices. *Language Arts, 79* (5), 382–392.

Luke, A., & Freebody, P. (1997). Shaping the social practices of reading. In S. Muspratt, A. Luke, and P. Freebody (Eds). *Constructing critical literacies.* Catskill, NJ: Hampton Press, pp.185–223.

Rosenblatt, L. (1978). *The reader, the text, the poem: The transactional theory of the literary work.* Carbondale, IL: Southern Illinois University Press.

Short, K. G., Harste, J. C., & Burke, C. (1996). *Creating classrooms for authors and inquirers.* Portsmouth, NH: Heinemann.

Questions for Further Reflection

- What were your beliefs about teaching reading before you read this chapter?

- What do you now understand about literacy learning and development and instructional choices?

- Which theory or theories might you ascribe to as you develop your own teaching beliefs and practices?

CHAPTER 5

Literacy Programs and Approaches

Ms. Binns Rethinks Sustained, Silent Reading Time

I designate Fridays as a time to take stock of what we did during the week, as well as provide extended time to engage in independent reading time. My school has articulated a school-wide goal of having all students read at least 25 books over the course of the school year. For many of my sixth grade students who struggle with reading, this seems like a daunting goal. Because they have not experienced success with reading, most of them are reluctant to engage with any sort of event that involves reading. So, having even more time on Fridays to do something many of them do not like is a big challenge. A challenge I'm willing to persevere with because I know that when students have prolonged opportunities to engage with meaningful and relevant texts they become more accomplished readers and writers. Two significant things happened one Friday morning that changed the way I view this particular event, the school-wide initiative, and how reading and writing are not silent activities. Prior to explaining what happened, I believe it is necessary to provide a framework for how I initially viewed independent reading time. Like many of my colleagues, I implement SSR (sustained silent reading) during the instructional day. During this time, students select a book to read. The books they select usually come from the school or classroom library. I've worked with my students on selecting books that are appropriate to their reading level. I try to have a variety of books on the shelves, but my students tend to flip through them as though they are not interested. Occasionally, I bring in some titles that grab their attention, but for the most part the books are seen as something they "have to" engage with. The other important aspect is that this is a SILENT time in the classroom. Students are to spend their time reading, not talking. So, what happened on one particular Friday that has me rethinking sustained silent reading?

One Friday early in the school year seemed like a huge disaster. We were in the school library that morning because of an assembly and scheduling issues. I decided to have the sustained silent reading time in the library. The first thing I noticed was that my students did not choose books, but rather magazines (e.g., *Time for Kids*, *Skateboarder Magazine*, *National Geographic for Kids, Sports Illustrated for Kids,* and *Kids Castle*). I questioned the amount of "reading" that was taking place as they perused these magazines. Additionally, their excitement in reading these magazines was infectious, because before I knew it, they were not reading SILENTLY, but rather talking with each other, sharing what they just read and in some cases reading to each other. From an outsider's perspective, this sustained silent reading time was not going as planned. Students were not working toward the school initiative of 25 books and they were talking with each other, which can sometimes be construed as "being off task."

However, what I did know was that my students who rarely exhibit enthusiasm for reading were actually excited to share what they were learning. One student, sitting with a group of boys, called me over to the table. As I approached the table, he was showing the other boys pictures in his magazine. He pointed to one of the pictures and asked me. . ., "Ms. Binns, do you know what that is?" I said, "An airplane." He then asked me,

"How big do you think it is?" I replied, "Really big." He said, "Actually, Ms. Binns, it's a model airplane. The army makes model airplanes, tests them out, and if they work, they will make bigger airplanes that look just like the model airplanes." He then proceeded to show me that you could tell the airplane was actually small by comparing it to other objects in the picture. This student not only continued to read about the model airplanes for the rest of our time in the library, but as we headed to lunch shared more about the airplanes.

In another instance that morning, I "caught" students sharing their Japanese anime drawings with each other. I know that these students love Japanese anime and manga. They were discussing and pointing to pictures in Japanese anime magazines. They were reading the captions. While I did tell the students to get back "on task" with their reading, I later asked them to show me their drawings. Their enthusiasm reminded me that it is essential that these students perceive reading and writing as enjoyable activities. I can build upon students' interests in this area to make connections to other reading events and experiences. Perhaps after reading the magazines, they could work collaboratively to create Japanese anime picture illustrations of scenes in the book.

Although these students may not have accomplished my literacy goal for them—to silently read a book—I believe that they accomplished far more by creating their own purposes for reading. First, they used both words and pictures to make meaning from the text. Second, they demonstrated their comprehension by sharing with others what they were reading and what they knew about the topic (airplanes, Japanese anime).

Finally, yet unintentionally, these students helped me as a teacher. I became more familiar with their interests in airplanes and Japanese anime as a genre. I can use this information when considering texts for the classroom library and when we engage in inquiry projects throughout the school year.

I wonder...

● What does Ms. Binns come to know about her students as a result of providing space for conversation and choices during sustained silent reading time?

● What guiding principles from chapter 1 does Ms. Binn embrace as she works with her struggling sixth grade readers?

● How does Ms. Binns reconcile her goals for literacy with those of her students?

Sustained silent reading has taken on a whole new look in my classroom. As I reflect on what happened in the library, what I initially perceived as a failure is actually a success. Students are reading a variety of texts, including novels, reference materials, picture books, websites, and comic books. They are sharing and working with each other during this time. It is no longer silent, but there is a hum and buzz that indicates to me that these students are actively engaged in reading and learning. I learned about students' interests beyond traditional school parameters. As a teacher, I want to make reading purposeful and meaningful for my students. I had a purpose for the silent reading time—to help students achieve their 25-book goal. However, my students found other purposes, and I would argue more important purposes, for their reading. By knowing "what counts" as important to my student, I can better create literacy events and experiences that will help them see reading as something that is meaningful in their lives.

Chapter Overview

Ms. Binns's insights into how her sustained silent reading structure was redefined by the students are important as we consider the curricular decisions teachers enact on a daily basis. Her initial purposes, to have students read independently and for long periods of time, were not sufficient to engage her students. She found that they continued to be reluctant and disengaged. However, when Ms. Binns focused more on how they were interacting with texts and when she responded to their interests, she discovered that they had a lot to share with each other and with her.

Classroom literacy events are very often defined by the reading program that is implemented at a particular school or within a particular district. In Ms. Binns's school, the 25-book campaign was a part of *America's Choice,* a standards-based reform effort designed to increase achievement performance on state and local assessments. Ms. Binns used her sustained silent reading structure as an avenue for her students to achieve the 25-book goal. The goal was not one that Ms Binns and her students created, but one that was articulated for all students in the school.

Most prescriptive literacy programs are school-wide initiatives. Usually a school system will adopt a program to be implemented in all grade levels at a school. The programs lay out the sequence of skills to be addressed and provide all the instructional materials and assessments needed to achieve the skills. Some administrators expect teachers to adhere closely to the literacy program as it is presented. In other schools, teachers have more flexibility in how they use the prescribed materials. In either case, teachers often find themselves implementing reading and writing programs because it is a school mandate, not because it is the most effective approach for the students they are working with. There is little professional decision making on the part of the teachers. For teachers who have options in the literacy curricula they offer, an alternative is a reading and writing workshop. This alternative to prescriptive literacy programs is designed for teachers to make their own instructional decisions for teaching reading and writing.

This chapter focuses on the most common curricular programs for elementary literacy development over the last four decades. There have been significant shifts in what researchers and policy makers advocate as effective literacy practice. As a result, literacy programs and curricula greatly vary. Guiding questions for this chapter include:

- What has contributed to the shifts in reading and writing curriculum?
- What prescriptive literacy materials are common in elementary schools?
- In what ways do these materials align with the core understandings addressed in Chapter 1?
- How might a reading and writing workshop approach to literacy development better serve the needs of individual students, as they become accomplished readers and writers?

Four decades of change in reading and writing curriculum

The last 40 years have witnessed large shifts in reading and writing curriculum and instruction. These shifts reflect ideologies and beliefs about learning, teaching, and reading; policies and mandates in the federal government; and sentiment about how well students are doing in comparison to other developed countries. Shifts also occur because different goals for reading instruction are emphasized.

Skills: Grammar, decoding, and drills

In the 1960s and early-to-mid–1970s the country was responding to concerns that Russia's launching of Sputnik, the first unmanned rocket in space, threatened national security. Additionally, Rudolf Flesch's book *Why Johnny Can't Read* (1957) argued that the American education system was not adequately preparing students and that we were falling behind international rivals. Jeanne Chall's *Learning to Read: The Great Debate* (1967) concludes that "a code emphasis method of reading, based on phonics, produced better results than a meaning-emphasis approach" (Kantrowitz & Hammill, 1990). As a result of the public's concerns and educators' reaction to these studies and books, reading instruction and materials began to emphasize decoding, while writing instruction focused on grammar, conventions, and mechanics. Students acquired skills through direct instruction and drills. Reading and writing development were based on a skills model, where teachers taught every skill a student might need. When students had mastered enough skills they were accomplished readers and writers. The skills model for literacy instruction was highlighted in Chapter 1 in the discussion of the industrial model of schooling section, as well as in Chapter 4 in Ms. Teal's vignette.

Students learned to read and write through phonics-oriented reading anthologies and grammar textbooks. Stories in the reading anthologies were written especially for the series. There was increased focus on decoding words, and this was accomplished by controlling new words through phonics patterns. In writing, students learned rules and conventions by copying sentences from grammar textbooks and writing structured essays. Reading and writing were not integrated processes, and therefore were taught as separate disciplines.

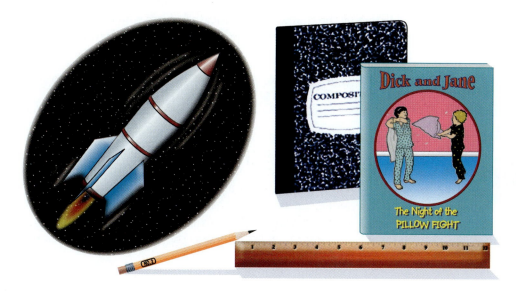

Whole language: Authentic texts and meaning making

In the late 1970s through the mid-1990s, there was a shift in the way in which reading and writing were taught. Progressive ideology, described in Chapter 1, and profiled in Chapter 4 with Ms Battle's and Mr. Ruby's classrooms, influenced how reading and writing were approached. Teachers began demanding more authentic sources for reading and writing. They wanted to take on a larger decision making role as they considered materials appropriate for literacy instruction in their classrooms. Reading and writing instruction started to include authentic, connected texts as the primary materials. In the early 1990s, literature-based reading textbooks were developed, whereby the selections first appeared as a trade book and then revised for the basal. There was also an emphasis on predictability of text structure, quality of design, and less control of vocabulary. The stories included rhymes, rhythms, and patterns. Students were not taught individual skills to be added up later. The focus was on meaning making. Students were taught how to access the four language cueing systems (graphophonemic, semantic, syntactic, and pragmatic) to make sense of unfamiliar text. They were also encouraged to draw upon their own prior experiences and background knowledge to derive meaning from the text.

The balanced approach to literacy development

Another shift occurred in the mid-1990s through the early years of the new century. A large part of this shift was due in part to what was perceived as California's plummeting scores on state level National Assessment of Educational Progress (NAEP) tests in 1992 and 1994. Many attributed the decline in reading scores to the state's 1987 implementation of a literature-based reading framework that was holistic in nature. It seemed that whole language was the scapegoat. The pendulum moved away from whole language to what was named a *balanced approach*. The balanced approach was seen as taking a little bit from phonics and a little bit from whole language. While this may seem to be an effective compromise, it meant different things to different people; some advocated students starting with phonics and skills and graduating to whole language. Others wanted to explicitly teach phonics while at the same time provide opportunities for students to read connected, authentic literature. In many districts, what ended up happening was that teachers were expected to add a half hour of phonics instruction to what they were already doing, thereby adding more to an already packed reading and writing curriculum.

Publishers, sensitive to the demands of educators, were quick to market the term "balanced approach" in hopes of reframing their materials in a new light. Many

TECHNOLOGY LINK

http://nces.ed.gov/nation-sreportcard/states/

Visit the site of the National Assessment of Educational Progress and check out your state's profile on how well students and schools performed on reading and math.

Did you know. . .

The National Assessment of Educational Progress (NAEP), also known as "the Nation's Report Card," is a national assessment given every two years to students in grades 4, 8, and 12. Between 1992 and 2005 there was no significant change in the percentage of fourth-graders performing at or above *Basic*, but the percentage performing at or above *Proficient* increased during this time. The percentage of eighth-graders performing at or above *Basic* was higher in 2005 (73%) than in 1992 (69%), but there was no significant change in the percentage scoring at or above *Proficient* between these same years.

of the reading curricula and programs in the late 1990s returned to a more systematic approach to decoding. Publishers began including "little books" as a supplemental source of reading instruction. Little books are eight to twelve pages in length and are designed to provide practice by combining control of vocabulary and spelling patterns with predictable language patterns (Hoffman, Roser, Salas, Patterson, & Pennington, 2000). There is very little substantive content in these books.

Prescriptive reading programs and materials: Connections to "scientifically based reading research"

And now in the first decade of the twenty-first century, the pendulum has once again shifted. There is a proliferation of commercially produced reading programs and materials used in classroom literacy events. This recent explosion is in part due to what is perceived as continued failure among students in literacy development; a growing distrust of teachers to make informed decisions about curriculum, materials, and literacy events; the National Reading Panel's call for reading methods to be "scientifically based," "reliable" and "replicable"; and *Reading First* criteria for state funding for materials and professional development. The National Reading Panel's five pillars of reading instruction—phonemic awareness, phonics, fluency, vocabulary, and comprehension—are promoted as the essential aspects of reading instruction. Schools that receive federal money through a *Reading First* grant are required to select reading programs that specifically address these five key early reading skills. The grant also specifies that teachers' classroom instructional decisions must be informed by scientifically based reading research.

Publishers responded to the National Panel's call and realigned their materials to highlight the key components and to suggest that their materials are based on scientifically based reading research. Note how many of the publishing companies have appropriated the language from No Child Left Behind and the National Reading Panel as they describe their reading product.

- **Reading Street** by Scott Foresman
  (http://www.pearsoned.com/pr_2006/022806.htm)

  The first reading program to align with the *No Child Left Behind Act*. . . Solidly anchored in the most current scientific research, *Reading Street* prioritizes skill instruction at each grade level, so teachers can focus on the right skill, at the right time, for every student. These priority skills are proven to be indicators of reading success identified by the National Reading Panel—*phonemic awareness; phonics; fluency; vocabulary;* and *text comprehension.*

- **Trophies** by Harcourt Brace (https://jstore.harcourtschool.com/marketplace/index.html)

  A research-based, developmental reading/language arts program. *Explicit phonics instruction;* direct reading instruction; guided reading strategies; *phonemic awareness instruction;* systematic, intervention strategies; integrated language arts components; and state-of-the-art assessment tools ensure every student successfully learns to read.

- **Rigby Literacy** (www.rigby.com)

  A comprehensive literacy program offering opportunities for modeled, shared, interactive, guided, and independent reading and writing. With enhanced focus on National Reading Panel guidelines addressing *phonemic awareness, phonics, vocabulary, comprehension, and fluency, Rigby Literacy* can be used as a core or supplemental program within any K-5 classroom.

- **Sing, Spell, Read & Write** (www.pearsonlearning.com)

  A multisensory, phonics-based reading program that *supports all five key components of reading instruction called for by the Reading First Initiative.* The program utilizes carefully sequenced systematic, explicit phonics instructional strategies to build fluent, independent readers. It integrates the most current research on brain function, language acquisition, and reading to quickly and effectively reach all types of learners.

- **Breakthrough to Literacy** (www.wrightgroup.com)

  A comprehensive PreK-3 program designed to build on the predictors of reading success: *phonemic awareness, alphabet knowledge, oral vocabulary, and word recognition skills.* Backed by over 20 years of scientific research conducted initially at the University of Iowa, the *Breakthrough to Literacy* model clearly supports the recommendations of the National Reading Panel Report and No Child Left Behind legislation.

- **Houghton Mifflin Reading** (www.eduplace.com)

  With evidence of effectiveness, based on *scientific research, Houghton Mifflin Reading* is proven to work, based on research that meets the criteria of the No Child Left Behind and Reading First legislation. With built-in resources for meeting individual needs—including hundreds of leveled books, resources for English language learners, and powerful intervention programs—*Houghton Mifflin Reading* ensures that no child is left behind.

These prescriptive programs, among others, provide little flexibility in how to approach reading instruction. They use explicit and systematic phonics instruction as a central piece in early reading instruction. They are skills driven with a 'one size fits all' perspective on reading, teaching, and learning. These commercially produced materials and programs suggest that *only* when utilizing these materials will a teacher be able to effectively teach reading and writing.

Where will the pendulum swing next? Recognizing the number of shortcomings with prescriptive reading programs and the emphasis on accountability and standards, it is hopeful that the shift may result in a critical literacy curriculum that encourages students to read and write to make a difference in the world. The reading materials will expand to include not only conventional materials, but also technology-based text such as websites and blogs. Students will have opportunities to engage in literacy events through a reader/writer workshop model.

As we consider the future for reading and writing instruction, it is important to take note of current practices and materials. The next section offers a detailed discussion of basal reading programs, which are the most common reading materials in the country. There are similarities and differences among the features in basal reading programs; some basals are more literature oriented while others are more phonics oriented. Teachers also structure and use these materials in varying degrees, anywhere from as the central focus of the instruction to ancillary and supplemental. Richard Allington (1993) categorized these curricular structures as *basal program, basal + books, books + basal,* and *books.*

> ### Creating Connections 5.1
>
> Interview classroom teachers and/or reading specialists with different years of experience about how their practices and curriculum have changed over the years. Share these experiences with others through your blog.

Basal readers: The most familiar reading material in the classroom

Walk into most classrooms and you will most likely see a ***basal reading series*** as the core material for a reading curriculum. A basal reading program is a comprehensive set of materials from kindergarten through eighth grade. The materials include a series of readers or anthologies (student textbooks), workbooks, supplementary reading materials, and teacher's manuals that gradually increase in difficulty. Recalling information presented in Chapter 4, Ms. Teal, along with her grade level colleagues, implemented a basal reading program as the core reading program for fourth grade. Ms. Teal is not alone in her use. Basal reading materials have been in classrooms for over 70 years.

basal reading series

A comprehensive set of materials designed for the purpose of teaching reading.

Basals are commercially produced materials that align with a prescriptive approach or skills model to literacy development. There is a predetermined order in which reading strategies and skills are introduced and taught. Most basal reading programs provide teachers with a scope and sequence chart, which is essentially a road map for using the program (what skills and when). Scott Foresman, McGraw-Hill, Houghton Mifflin, Scholastic, and Harcourt Brace are the five most common publishers of basal reader used in school systems and districts.

Common characteristics and features

Basal reading programs have common characteristics and features across the materials. Typically, students have one reading anthology for the school year. The reading textbook is typically segmented into units and each unit is themed with a collection of published short stories, poems, excerpts of longer narratives, and original works. Themes include such concepts as journeys, amazing animals, heroes, and celebrating traditions. At the end of each story, there are comprehension questions for students to answer, as well as follow-up activities.

Many publishers supplement the reading anthology with collections of leveled books. These texts are often used for guided reading groups (see upcoming section for a discussion on guided reading groups). Proponents of leveled texts suggest that by leveling texts, teachers and students are able to better match reading ability and text

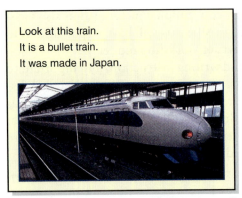

Look at this train.
It is a bullet train.
It was made in Japan.

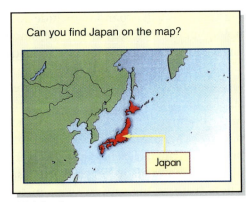

Can you find Japan on the map?

Japan

FIGURE 5.1 An example of a leveled text (from Wright Group,
http://www.wrightgroup.com/download/lit/trains_spread.pdf).

difficulty. This helps prevent frustration in selecting texts that are beyond what the reader can read comfortably. To determine a reader's level, teachers have students read the text aloud to determine oral reading proficiency. If the reader can read the text with 95% accuracy, the text is at the student's independent reading level.

Brabham and Villume (2002) note there are three different ways that texts are leveled. One approach is to take a formulaic view, in which texts are leveled based on a readability formula. Another approach is a comprehensive view which takes into consideration a number of factors, including text and print features, vocabulary, sentence length and complexity, content, and text structure. This type of leveling is a result of the work of Reading Recovery, an intervention program designed for struggling early readers. A third approach to leveling texts is a phonics view that builds on students' developing understandings of letter–sound relationships. There are consistent letter–sound patterns in words. Illustrations are minimal because the goal is to maximize attention on word analysis. These different text progression criteria also result in different ways of reporting the information. Some publishers note the general grade level (e.g., 3); others offer a more refined level (e.g., 3.4), and some depart from grade levels and use letters or numbers (e.g., A-F, or 1-20).

Samples of pages from a teacher manual for a basal reading series.

In addition to the reading anthology and leveled texts, each student receives a student workbook focused on skill development.

The teacher's manual in a basal program is highly scripted, with detailed lesson plans for each story. The manual has instructions on how to plan lessons, what skills and strategies to focus on and how to best coordinate them, as well as how to assess student progress. There are activities to complete prior to reading the story, questions to ask while reading the story (with suggested answers), and follow-up activities after reading the story.

Publishers often include ancillary materials such as big books, blackline masters, kits with magnetic letters and word cards, wall charts, CDs, and assessment materials (running records, placement evaluations, inventories). In some programs, such as Scholastic's *Literacy Place*, **trade books** are also included. Trade books are those selections that one can usually find in a bookstore. In trade books the vocabulary is not controlled; the topics are wide reaching; and they usually maintain high interest in students.

trade books

Books that are not designed to specifically teach reading. Generally trade books are found in libraries and bookstores.

Differences among basal programs

While the surface features and components of basal reading programs are similar, there are differences in how basal programs address reading. As mentioned in the discussion on the shifts in reading curriculum, some basal series emphasize exposure to authentic pieces of children's literature, referred to as **literature-based basals**, while other series emphasize early and automatic decoding skills. The differing perspectives are reflected in the content and structure of the lessons and stories that are provided to the children.

LITERATURE-BASED BASALS. A literature-based basal program incorporates contemporary and classic children's literature in the student anthologies. Students are introduced to vocabulary development, comprehension, and phonic skills from the beginning, rather than waiting until decoding and word identification skills have been mastered (as in the phonics-oriented approaches). For example, Scholastic's *Literacy Place* is a literature-based reading program that does not sacrifice meaning over decoding. Students work on decoding skills and fluency as they read authentic literature selections. Vocabulary and comprehension are addressed before, during, and after reading. Reading and writing are integrated throughout the curriculum. McCarthy and Hoffman (1995) noted in their analysis of two literature-based basals published in 1987 and 1993, that the 1993 edition "offered reduced vocabulary control, minimal adaptations [of authentic children's literature], more diversity of genre, more engaging literary quality, more predictable texts, and increased decoding demands" (p. 73) than did the 1987 edition.

literature-based basal

Incorporates contemporary and classic literature in student anthologies. Vocabulary, comprehension and phonics skills are introduced in the beginning.

phonics-oriented basal

Provides explicit and systematic instruction in phonics. Stories are designed to teach letter-sound correspondence.

PHONICS-ORIENTED BASALS. Basal programs that emphasize phonics (**phonics-oriented basals**) are designed to have students "crack the code" by mastering the letters of the alphabet and the 40+ sounds that those letters represent. Much of the instructional time is devoted to having students "sound out" words. Learning letters and sounds are a prerequisite to reading words. The types of texts students are exposed to in phonics-oriented programs are

Pap gets a pan.
Pap gets in a pan.

7

Nan and Pap are in a pan.

8

FIGURE 5.2 A sample page of decodable text.

decodable text

A part of phonics-oriented basal programs that starts with the smallest units of language and progresses upwards to more meaningful units.

known as decodable texts. ***Decodable texts*** start with the smallest units of language and progress to more meaningful units. The previous page shows an example of a decodable text (www.readinga-z.com). Notice the phonetically controlled text.

Two popular phonics-oriented programs in many districts, particularly in poor urban school systems, are *Reading Mastery* (published by SRA/McGraw-Hill) and *Open Court* (also published by McGraw-Hill). *Reading Mastery* and *Open Court* are two programs among many that meet the criteria of the Reading First federal grant money. Because poor urban districts must rely heavily on federal support for their programs, they are more likely to adopt an "approved program" to ensure continued funding (Jordan, 2005).

Reading Mastery and *Open Court* provide explicit instruction in oral language, phonemic awareness, and phonics. These components of the reading process are seen as the starting point. Likewise, Reading A–Z is a systematic phonics program, meeting the same guidelines as *Reading Mastery* and *Open Court*. The publishers of *Open Court* suggest that early, explicit, and systematic phonics instruction is the key to effective reading (http://www.sraonline.com). They note that early means in preschool or kindergarten, that explicit means teaching skills directly and not having students discover the skills on their own, and that systematic implies there is a prescribed plan in place that builds on previously learned skills.

Recent criticism of such phonics-based basal reading programs suggests that the lessons become ritualized (Jordan, 2005). Children participate in repetitive reading lessons in which they recite and chant to the teacher's commands. Students often answer with one-word responses. Speed and accuracy are at the core of the programs, impressing upon the students the need to stay on task.

> ### Creating Connection 5.2
>
> Gather a few titles of decodable texts as well as leveled texts. What are the distinguishing characteristics of these texts?

Classroom organizational structures when using basal materials

There are a number of different ways in which teachers organize their instructional time when using basal reading series. As noted, Richard Allington (1993) identified four common structures. Of course, as with anything, there is always great variation in the degree to which teachers use the materials, but these classifications may be helpful as you consider what you have observed in classrooms.

- **Basal Curriculum.** In this structure the teacher uses the basal reading series as the core materials for reading instruction. The majority of the lessons are drawn from the teacher's manual and often include skill sheets, composition activities, and spelling and editing lessons. Many of the classrooms have classroom libraries and literature kits, but tradebooks are used almost exclusively during independent reading time (*Sustained Silent Reading* or *Drop Everything and Read*). Teachers also read aloud to children from tradebooks.

- **Basal + Books Curriculum.** Teachers implementing this organizational structure use the basal reading series as the base for their program. However, tradebooks are incorporated into instruction and are typically linked to the reading anthology themes or stories. In some classrooms, the teacher may teach from the basal series two or three days a week and tradebooks the remaining days incorporating art, music, dramatic enactments, reader's theater. In this structure the teacher is more selective about which skills and lessons are most appropriate for the students and eliminates the rest of the suggested activities.

- **Books + Basal Curriculum**. In this structure, tradebooks drive the instruction, usually through a thematic approach. Strategy lessons are developed from the tradebook selections. The basal reading series is used occasionally. Teachers rarely have students read all of the stories or complete all of the lessons. The basal is used as an anthology, with teachers picking and choosing stories based on the theme or genre. The basal is seen as a source for focused skill and strategy lessons.

- **Book Curriculum**. This structure relies on tradebooks as the core material for reading instruction (see *Reading and Writing Workshop Approach for Literacy Development* section for more information). Commercial reading materials are rarely used. Reading strategy lessons are developed from the tradebook materials. Thematic curriculum organization and special attention to genre are often hallmarks of this approach. Composing, art, music, and dramatic enactments are linked to the literature that students are reading.

There are teachers whose classrooms represent all four of these organizational patterns; the most common and/or popular are the basal curriculum and basal + books curriculum. Because the basal curriculum is the most common it is important to further detail a basal reading lesson plan, as well as how a teacher may organize literacy centers for those times when students are not working with the teacher. Following that discussion, the focus switches to a discussion of guided reading formats and how they are similar and different than traditional basal lessons. And then, a reading and writing workshop approach is presented as a possibility for classroom instruction.

Organizing daily instruction when using reading anthologies and leveled texts

Most teachers using a basal program for their reading instruction will work with groups of students daily in 20- to 30-minute blocks of time. When using commercial materials, teachers can choose to either work with children in traditional basal lesson formats or they may work with children in ***guided reading groups*** [see next section for complete details on guided reading].

guided reading group
Flexible reading groups based on students' needs. Leveled texts are commonly used.

READING ANTHOLOGY LESSON. With a reading anthology, the format of the lesson follows a modified ***DR-TA format*** (Directed Reading–Thinking Activity) developed by Russell Stauffer over 30 years ago (1969). The components of a basal reading lesson include:

DR-TA format
Directed reading thinking activity to promote comprehension.

- ***Activate prior knowledge and background experience***. Teachers initiate discussion of central ideas or concepts covered in the story. In some instances, unfamiliar words are introduced and there is some discussion of how they are used in the context of the story. This sequence is designed for the stories that appear in the reading anthology.

- ***Skill lesson***. Skill lessons focus on phonics, vocabulary, or comprehension skills. This helps to prepare the student to read the selected story.

- ***Preview and predict***. Teachers often have students read the title and engage

> **Basal Anthology**
>
> Teacher monitors for application of strategies.
> - *Materials*: reading anthology for the selected grade level
> - *Choice*: teacher's choice
> - *Grouping*: small group designated by ability
> - *Purpose*: to practice application of specific strategies/skills in highly focused manner; to provide opportunity for teacher-monitoring of application of skills and strategies
>
> Readers benefit when they read materials with which they can practice what they have learned.

TECHNOLOGY LINK
http://www.learner.org/re-sources/series162.html?pop=yes&vodid=482369&pid=1730#
Select #7 Connecting Skills to Text (part of the Teaching Reading K-2 video series from www.learner.org) In this short video segment (enter the video at 6 minutes and 14 seconds), Charmon Evans conducts a guided reading lesson with her first grade students.

in picture walks, previewing the illustrations. Students are encouraged to predict what they think the story will be about based on what they learn from the title and illustrations. Their background knowledge may also come into play.

- *Set the purpose*. The teacher invites students to consider their purposes for reading the story.

- *Read the selection*. Teachers often have students read portions of the text, either silently or in round robin fashion. In the primary grades, teachers use this opportunity to assess word decoding strategies and fluency.

- *Confirm predictions*. Following the reading, students return to their earlier predictions to confirm their accuracy.

- *Comprehension questions*. Teachers ask a series of comprehension questions. The predetermined questions tend to be at a literal level, so students are able to locate information in the text. There are relatively few inference-type or higher-level thinking questions. Students generally do not have to extend themselves beyond the text.

- *Skill instruction and practice*. Students practice strategies (e.g., main idea, sequencing, summarizing) related to reading development. Most of this work is accomplished in the reading workbooks and worksheets.

- *Enrichment projects*. Students have opportunities to engage in creative projects that synthesize the learning that has occurred during the unit.

GUIDED READING GROUP LESSON. An alternative instructional structure is the *guided reading group* format (Fountas & Pinell, 1996). Guiding reading has become a well-known instructional format for all readers in a classroom. The purpose for guiding reading groups is to meet the varying instructional needs of all of the students; to support children as they read more and more difficult text; to encourage children to use problem-solving strategies for figuring out unfamiliar words, and to understand concepts and themes of the books (Iaquinta, 2006).

Unlike the traditional basal reading groups where the grouping structures are static and virtually unchanging, guided reading groups are designed to be dynamic and flexible. Teachers regularly change the group composition to accommodate the different learning paths of the children. Teachers base these grouping decisions on the individual needs of the students, running records and other forms of assessment.

A goal in a guided reading lesson is to support students as they read leveled texts that are generally more challenging than those they can read on their own. Every guided reading lesson is different because each group of readers has different strengths and needs. During a guided reading lesson, the teacher will introduce the story, provide word meanings, and ask students to read the text softly or silently to themselves. As students read, the teacher observes and notes the individual reading needs and behaviors of each student. After reading, the teacher and students discuss the meaning of the story as well as engage in reading strategy work, including phonics and word work. The chart on page 125 summarizes the teacher's role when implementing guided reading lessons in the classroom (adapted from Iaquinta, 2006).

Guided Reading

Teacher monitors for application of strategies.

- *Materials*: leveled texts with various designations
- *Choice*: teacher's choice
- *Grouping*: small group designated by ability
- *Purpose*: to meet the varying instructional needs of all readers; to provide an opportunity for teacher-monitoring of application of skills and strategies as readers work with leveled texts that are slightly more challenging

Readers benefit when they read materials with which they can practice what they have learned.

Before a Guided Reading Lesson	Teacher's Role
Select a text	Teacher selects texts that will provide opportunities for students to extend their reading processing strategies and skills.
Introduce a text	Teacher introduces the text by helping readers attend to all sources of information (title, author, visual cues). Selected key words are introduced as are key concepts.

During a Guided Reading Lesson	
	Teacher asks readers to begin reading the story aloud. As they do so, the teacher "listens in" and takes notes on how the student is processing the text. The teacher notices how readers:
	• use letter/sound knowledge to notice mismatches.
	• use letter/sound knowledge to know how words begin.
	• use letter/sound knowledge to solve unfamiliar words.
	The teacher may also provide a quick comment about the text.

After Reading	
Discussing and revising	The teacher talks with the students and encourages dialogue.
Processing strategies	The teacher invites students to make personal responses.
Extend the meaning	The teacher assesses students' understandings of what they have read.

When students are not meeting with the teacher, they work independently at various literacy centers around the room. The centers are linked to the stories being read in the basal reading series and focus on a variety of skills. Centers may include:

- **Word work center**: Students work with high-frequency words and letter/sound patterns.
- **Vocabulary center**: Words from the corresponding stories are written on word cards. Students sort the words into categories and work on definitions.
- **Listening center**: Students listen to a story on tape and complete a response sheet.
- **Comprehension center**: Students complete activities that relate to comprehension skills.
- **Writing center**: Students complete writing tasks that are related to the story.

Other centers can be created depending on the needs of the students and the direction of the reading program (see chart of weekly schedule).

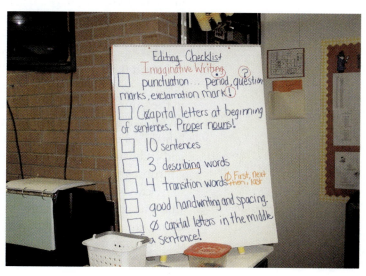

Chart of weekly schedule where a commercial reading program is used. Three groups meet daily with the teacher.

TEACHER	Monday	Tuesday	Wednesday	Thursday	Friday
9:00-9:30	A	B	C	A	B
9:30-10:00	B	C	A	B	C
10:00-10:30	C	A	B	C	A

INDEPENDENT SKILLS	Monday	Tuesday	Wednesday	Thursday	Friday
9:00-9:30	C	A	B	C	A
9:30-10:00	A	B	C	A	B
10:00-10:30	B	C	A	B	C

CENTERS	Monday	Tuesday	Wednesday	Thursday	Friday
9:00-9:30	B (writing)	C (listen)	A (word work)	B (vocab)	C (vocab)
9:30-10:00	C (word work)	A (ind. reading)	B (listen)	C (ind. reading)	A (listen)
10:00-10:30	A (vocab)	B (word work)	C (writing)	A (writing)	B (ind. reading)

Concerns with prescriptive approaches

While commercially produced reading series are quite prevalent in classrooms throughout the country, there are a number of issues to be considered. Basal reading series (both literature- and phonics-based) hold a view of reading that is technical—a series of component skills that unite in the end to form a mechanical process. This assumption is not supported by other, more complex views of the reading process. There is little thought about the complexities of the reading process and what it might take to become a thoughtful and responsive reader. Reading is more than decoding—it involves critique and inquiry.

One size does not fit all.

Prescriptive approaches may also discourage teachers from learning how to best address individual student's needs. The programs often require that the teachers present the lessons in predetermined sequence. This sequence begins with sounds and letters (phonemic awareness and phonics) and works toward the notion of reading to learn (comprehension and critical thinking). Only when students have essentially mastered the lower-level skills through daily assignments and monitoring can they progress to the next skill. The programs are designed so that all students move along in the same sequence and pursue the same knowledge. However, students have individual learning needs and styles and may end up lagging "behind" or being "ahead" of where they are supposed to be. The teacher's manual offers remediation and extension activities, but these are often afterthoughts as the "regular" activities consume much of the instructional time.

However, perhaps the most salient concern is that prescriptive reading series devalue teachers' professional judgment. Highly scripted programs, such as *Open Court* and *Reading Mastery,* do not allow teachers to make informed decisions based on the current needs of their students. The pressure for teachers to remain on target with the program and to cover the curriculum results in fewer opportunities to take advantage of the teachable moment, the wondering, and the questions that surface as a result of reading and discussing. When texts are engaging and promote critical thinking, students need to have time for dialogue and for asking questions; they need time to reevaluate their responses and rethink their positions. This is only possible when the teacher is able to make informed decisions about curriculum and what will best serve the needs of the students.

The lack of additional support or alternatives

On a related note, it may seem that commercially produced programs are all that are available, particularly to new teachers. It's not uncommon for new teachers to have questions about alternatives to basal anthologies and leveled readers:

- If I don't use a basal, what will I do?
- How do I know what reading skill or strategy to teach if I don't follow the teacher's manual?
- I'm not that familiar with the reading process. Aren't there certain skills kids need to know?
- What if everyone else at the school is using (a particular program)? Shouldn't I use it too?
- My school has a "book room" that houses the leveled readers that I'm expected to use. What would I use instead?

New teachers know that teaching reading is complex. There are many factors to consider: children's abilities and development; types of materials; strategies to teach; and ways to assess. Additionally, teachers need to think about the school climate and context in which they work. What support do teachers have when trying something that is not *traditional* or *status quo?* How do teachers at the school begin professional conversations about teaching, learning, and literacy development? What artifacts and teaching styles are privileged over others? These last questions are ones that you may want to reflect upon as you consider the school climate and context. You want to be a part of a school community that values your understandings and knowledge about literacy development and learning.

So what do you know about teaching children to read and write? Well, from the first four chapters, you discovered a set of guiding principles that can serve as a foundation for your literacy program. You learned that children come into classrooms with a range of literacy practices and experiences. You examined how these differences support a culturally responsive pedagogy that honors and validates home and community experiences children bring to the classroom. You also learned about kidwatching and ways to begin informally assessing where students are in their development and understandings of the reading process. In the fourth chapter, you learned about the different reading models and what classrooms may look like when the model is implemented. While some of this information may be covered in prescriptive programs and reform models, it is usually not evident in the lesson or strategy work. And yet, it is this foundational knowledge that will support your decisions as you plan curriculum to effectively teach into the needs of your students and not beside them with no relevance to their lives.

Given the current climate in reading instruction, is it even possible to consider alternatives to prescriptive programs and mandates? How might beginning teachers offer a reading and writing curriculum that is not one size fits all but rather tailored to meet the specific needs of the students? A reader and writer workshop

Creating Connections 5.3

List your own questions and concerns around prescriptive programs, as well as what it might mean to offer a reader/writer workshop. Share your concerns with classmates. What general themes emerge from your questions?

model as profiled in Mr. Ruby's and Ms. Fuller's classrooms (Chapter 4) is one particular model that begins to address the individual needs of students in meaningful and authentic ways.

The reader/writer workshop approach for literacy development

We have always known that there are tremendous individual differences in literacy learning, and yet we persist in offering grade-level, textbook-centered instruction. When the children do not thrive in these environments, we create low reading groups, remedial programs, and pull-out programs. LD, MD, LEP, ED—the letters proliferate, and the children suffer. It's time we stop trying to fix the children and start fixing the schools that fail them. Traditional organizational patterns for reading instruction have trapped caring teachers and children in a system that creates disability (Roller, 1996, p. 138)

If published programs have a legacy of standardizing curriculum and not attending to students' needs, what choices do teachers and students have for more meaningful and effective literacy curricula? A ***reader/writer workshop approach*** is one way to teach reading and writing that acknowledges the variability that children bring into the classroom. It is a process-oriented approach to literacy development that embodies many of the guiding principles addressed in Chapter 1. Similar to an art studio where artists learn their craft by doing it, in reader/writer workshop settings, children learn to read and write by reading and writing. This approach to teaching reading and writing reflects the complex and dynamic nature of literacy development.

reader/writer workshop approach

Structure for teaching reading and writing that individualizes instruction.

Designing a literacy-rich reader/writer workshop

Literacy-rich elementary classrooms are loaded with text materials that support literacy development. Books of all kinds (e.g., different genres, lengths, and complexity), magazines, brochures, charts and maps, songs, websites, CDs and other texts are ideal resources for reading and writing workshops. *[Guiding Principle 6 (from chapter one): Literacy practices expand to include everyday and multimodal texts.]*

In literacy-rich classrooms:

- The classroom library is central to the room.
- There is an abundance of text on bulletin boards and walls (e.g., labeling of artifacts, name cards, alphabet cards; signs, children's drawings and stories, and more).
- There are reading corners and nooks, writing tables, inquiry, drama and play centers.
- Teachers make conscious decisions about the types of stories on their shelves, making connections across science, math, social studies, and other content domains.

text sets

Collections of books and other materials that are organized around a particular theme or concept.

In the end, an environment such as this is the first step to developing "literate thinkers that shape decisions of tomorrow" (Langer, 1995, p. 1).

The literacy-rich classroom should also have reading materials that range in difficulty, genre, and topic. ***Text sets*** are collections of books and other texts [poems, artworks, songs, web pages, brochures, instructions, pop cultural artifacts (Pokemon cards), etc.] organized around a particular theme or concept (alphabet books, variations of Cinderella stories or Little Red Riding Hood, Holocaust, memories, Martin Luther King, Jr., stories with circular structures, and many more). The variation in the text set enables readers of all abilities to successfully engage with the topic and material. Students will have opportunities to learn new information and contribute to the ongoing discussions. The varied texts also provide multiple perspectives on an issue, which encourages students to take a critical stance and deepen their understandings.

When readers have multiple texts on a single theme or topic, they are better able to see patterns within texts and make important connections between the texts and the outside world. Miranda, a kindergartener, looks through a set of Eric Carle books and wonders if the caterpillar in *The Very Hungry Caterpillar* (1979) will be in *The Grouchy Ladybug* (1996). This wondering, made to no one in particular, illustrates that Miranda is starting to think about how characters (in this case, insects) might appear in other places. She also comments that she has seen both ladybugs and caterpillars at home in her backyard. According to Laura Robb (2002), "Multiple texts enable teachers to offer students books they can read, improve students' application of reading–thinking strategies, build confidence, and develop the motivation to learn."

> ### Creating Connections 5.4
> Create a text set that will be used in a classroom. What criteria are you using to build your text set? Share your text set with your classmates.

Organizing a reader/writer workshop

Once a literacy-rich classroom is established, teachers can then decide the best ways to structure and organize workshop time so that children can get the most out of their reading and writing experiences.

Resources for Putting Together Text Sets

- *The Best in Children's Nonfiction: Reading, Writing, and Teaching Orbis Pictus Award Books.* (2001). M. Zarnowski, R.H. Kerper, & J.M. Jenson (Eds.). Urbana, IL: National Council of Teachers of English.
This book includes a history of the Orbis Pictus Award, chapters where award-winning authors discuss their work, and an annotated bibliography of winners, honor books, and other recommended titles.

- *The Horn Book Guide* is published by The Horn Book. (The Horn Book, Inc., 56 Roland Street, Suite 200, Boston, MA 02129).
The guide is a biannual publication that organizes books by genre, age, and subject. Reviewers rate books from 1 to 6, with ratings of 1 and 2 being the best.

- *Making Facts Come Alive: Choosing Quality Nonfiction Literature K–8.* (1998). R. A. Bamford & J. V. Kristo (Eds.). Norwood, MA: Christopher-Gordon.
With chapters written by respected, well-known educators, this resource contains teaching ideas and a wealth of excellent nonfiction titles for math, science, English, and social studies.

- *Adventuring with Books: A Booklist for Pre-k–Grade 6: 13th Edition (2002). A. McClure & J.V. Kristo (Eds). Urbana, IL: National Council of Teachers of English.*
This book has descriptions of more than 850 engaging texts suitable for student use in background research, unit study, or pleasure reading. This booklist also introduces readers to recent literature that celebrates African American, Asian and Pacific Island, Hispanic American, and indigenous cultures.

- http://www.nea.org/readacross/resources/50multibooks.html
This list of must-have multicultural books was compiled by the Cooperative Children's Book Center, School of Education, University of Wisconsin-Madison.

SPACES AND PLACES IN THE CLASSROOM TO SUP-PORT LITERACY DEVELOPMENT. Three essential areas in a classroom using the reader/writer workshop approach are *writing centers, reading centers,* and the *classroom library.* The writing center houses a number of writing materials, including paper, pens, pencils, markers, envelopes, clipboards, sticky notes, bins, folders, and stamps.

Reading centers, the second area, can be organized around the:

- Kind of book (ABC, pattern, wordless, circular, multiple points of view, conversation)
- Genre of text (nonfiction, poetry, fairy tales, mystery, memoir, biography, historical fiction)
- Umbrella topic (favorite author, topic of study, series books)
- Reading goal (read aloud, books that teach, help with writing, connections among books, fluency, intonation)

The third area in a classroom devoted to the reader/writer workshop approach is the classroom library. The International Reading Association recommends providing at least seven books per student. The library should reflect a range of texts, such as wordless books, picture books, young adult novels, magazines, reference materials, comic books, web pages, and other sources of printed materials. Creating an inviting library might include open book racks to display books, comfortable seating areas with pillows and cushions, and even plants and soft lighting.

TECHNOLOGY LINK

http://content.scholastic.com/browse/article.jsp?id=4456

Photographs and tips for organizing classroom libraries.

Creating Connections 5.5

Visit a classroom and note the following information.

1. Approximately how many books are in the *classroom library*?

2. How many students are in the class?

3. What types of books are currently featured in the *classroom library?* Check all that apply.

   ( ) a.   Fiction

   ( ) b.   Nonfiction

   ( ) c.   Poetry

   ( ) d.   Biography / Autobiography

   ( ) e.   Reference books

   ( ) f.   Fairytales Folklore/Myths

   ( ) g.   Mysteries

   ( ) h.   Drama

   ( ) i.   Fantasy/Science Fiction

   ( ) j.   Other

4. How much of the *classroom library* consists of nonfiction?

   ( ) a.   Less than 20 percent

   ( ) b.   20 to 39 percent

   ( ) c.   40 percent or more

5. How are the books displayed and arranged? Check all that apply. The books are:

( ) a. stacked on shelves, ordered alphabetically and/or by genre

( ) b. stored in labeled bins, arranged by author or genre

( ) c. displayed on racks or wedges (so that some covers face out)

( ) d. easily accessible to children

( ) e. promoted through posters, print-rich displays, and more

6. What kinds of areas are provided where children can read independently? Check all that apply.

( ) a. Floor space

( ) b. A couch, chairs, or beanbag chairs

( ) c. Carpeted areas

( ) d. Other private nooks

7. How do students independently find books in the *library* that are the right match for their reading levels? Check all that apply.

( ) a. Reading levels are clearly labeled or color-coded on each book.

( ) b. Books are placed in bins or shelves according to reading level

( ) c. The students don't select their own books by reading-level; teachers help them pick the right books

( ) d. The books are not organized by reading level.

8. How much time is set aside for independent reading per day? Check one.

( ) a. Under 20 minutes

( ) b. 20 to 40 minutes

( ) c. 40 minutes to 1 hour

( ) d. More than 1 hour

9. Do you agree or disagree with this statement? The *library* reflects the multicultural nature of American society, featuring authors from different cultures/countries and containing a wide range of multicultural subject matter.

( ) a. Strongly agree

( ) b. Agree

( ) c. Disagree

( ) d. Strongly disagree

(Questionnaire adapted from Does Your Classroom Library Stack Up?, Instructor, Aug. 2004, Vol. 114, Issue 1.)

Neuman (2001) suggests that the classroom library be comprised of a core collection and a revolving collection. The core collection is made up of books and materials that remain in the library all year, much like the permanent collection at a local library. The revolving collection, rotated every few weeks, is linked to current student interests, topics in the local community, as well as thematic units in the classroom. The revolving collection increases students' engagement and interests in reading by bringing new titles into the library on a regular basis.

In addition to housing the materials for a reader/writer workshop, the classroom library may significantly improve students' reading abilities by increasing contact time with actual texts. Providing students with opportunities to organize the library is one strategy for connecting them with texts. There are a number of ways that students can classify the books—author, genre, topic, or reading difficulty. This classroom job may be shared across class members throughout the school year.

Invitation for the classroom

Book Reviews

Invite students to select and review a book from the classroom library. This selection may be from either the core collection or the rotating collection.

Display the selected books on the chalkboard ledge. Have the reviewers: (a) note the title and author; (b) skim the book, noticing special features or illustrations; (c) read the book jacket for a summary; (d) determine the genre; and (e) indicate if they are interested in reading the book and why.

As reviewers present the information, other students note in their reading notebooks if they might also be interested in the book. These personal lists can be used when students are searching for a book to read during independent reading time.

FLEXIBLE READING GROUPS. In the 1920s, reading instruction emphasized an approach referred to as three-group instruction. This approach was based on reading abilities (low, middle, and high) and often resulted in differentiated instruction that did not benefit struggling readers. Instruction in the lower-reading group revolved around word identification and low levels of comprehension. For readers in this group, they did not have the more capable peer (Vygotsky, 1978) to draw upon as a model of what an effective and efficient reader does. In addition, readers designated to the lowest reading group often develop little self-confidence about reading, which in turn, results in having more difficulties with the reading process.

Flexible grouping

Children are placed in groups based on common interests, strengths, or needs.

Flexible grouping offers an alternative to ability grouping. Teachers can be flexible when placing children in reading groups. Rather than placing children in groups based on their reading ability, teachers group students together to work on a specific strategy or skill, or common interests and strengths. Recognizing and building on these strengths and challenges enables teachers to more effectively meet the needs of children. Flexible reading groups are a unique opportunity for teachers to kidwatch—that is, to observe how children learn and address any difficulties they encounter.

Structure of a reader/writer workshop

The premise of a reader/writer workshop is that the classroom environment resembles a workshop setting—one that encourages flexibility as students work individually and collaboratively as they engage in various reading and writing events. Students actively read, write, respond, and discuss texts with others, rather than work in isolation to complete skill worksheets (*Guiding Principle 1: Literacy is socially and culturally constructed and situated and Guiding Principle 2: Literacy practices are purposeful and embedded in larger social goals*). Reader/writer workshops often take place in blocks of time (usually 75 minutes to 120 minutes, depending on how the school day is organized). There is a seamless transition between reading and writing events and activities. Reader/writer workshops are generally structured to include the following events and instructional opportunities:

- Mini-lessons that focus on reading and writing strategies
- Reading and response (including independent reading, shared reading, and literature discussions)
- Writing and response (including author's circles, editing work, author's chairs)

- Reading and writing conferences
- Status of the class
- Sharing time

These particular events are central to reader/writer workshops. There is flexibility as students move in and out of these events. This movement is not synonymous with chaos or disarray. Teachers should establish a routine that maximizes students' learning and engagement with texts. Students are more productive in reader/writer workshop settings when they have a sense of the activities and events that they are expected to participate in.

Sample schedule for reader/writer workshop for third grade Week of November 1–5

Monday	Tuesday	Wednesday	Thursday	Friday
Status of the Class Mini-lesson (reading) Judy Moody Lit. Disc.	Mini-lesson (reading) Ralph S Mouse Lit. Disc.	Mini-lesson (writing) Judy Moody Lit. Disc.	Mini-lesson (writing) Ralph S Mouse Lit. Disc.	Status of the Class
Options: *independent reading *independent writing *author's circle *partner reading	Options: *independent reading *independent writing *author's circle *partner reading	Options: *independent reading *independent writing *author's circle *partner reading	Options: *independent reading *independent writing *author's circle *partner reading	Options: *independent reading *independent writing *author's circle *partner reading
**Conferences: Erin Madeline Quantez Patrick Jessica C Book reviews	Conferences: Frank Dharma Marla Javon Leslie Book reviews	Conferences: Barret Lakiesha Zoe Jessica P Rohi Author's Chair	Conferences: Autumn Katherine Gilberto Zamir Author's Chair	Conferences: Andrew Charlie Jenna Urial Author's Chair

** In the beginning, students' names will be listed by the teacher. Once students understand and are comfortable with this process, students will determine when they want to meet with the teacher, recognizing that they have to meet with the teacher at least once during the week.

MINI-LESSONS. A significant feature of the reader/writer workshop is the ***mini-lesson***. Mini-lessons are short, instructional sessions where reading and writing strategies are discussed and demonstrated. The goal for mini-lessons is to teach *into* students' intentions. What are the best next steps for students as they become confident and accomplished readers and writers? This question is what is often most intimidating to teachers about reader/writer workshop formats. Teachers often feel as though they are not as knowledgeable or prepared to determine a student's progression or pathway in reading. However, by having students consider their own goals for becoming accomplished readers, they can often tell the teacher what they want to work on next, whether it is to read more smoothly (fluently), read harder books (developing stamina and capacity for reading), learn how to pick "just right" books, or what to do when presented with an unfamiliar word. Teachers may also draw from scope and sequence charts found in basal materials for topic ideas and suggestions. For example, in Ms. Sasser's third grade classroom, she requests students complete a goal setting sheet each week. From these goals, Ms. Sasser

mini-lesson

Short, focused instructional session where strategies are introduced and discussed.

identifies reading strategies that become the focus of her mini-lessons. One particular week, she noticed that a number of her students commented that they were trying to figure out what the term "setting" means. In her mini-lessons for the week, Ms. Sasser reads a number of passages that exemplify an author's use of setting, including Gary Paulsen's *Hachet* (1996); Cynthia Rylant's (1993) *When I Was Young in the Mountains,* and EB White's (1952) *Charlotte's Web.* In their discussions Ms. Sasser asks students to think about how the setting influences what they visualize in their minds. She also invites them to take note of the setting in the stories they are currently reading. Later that day when students come together for sharing time, they are encouraged to share anything they noticed about the mini-lesson topic, which was setting. In doing this, Ms. Sasser reinforces the mini-lesson, as well as provides students with opportunities to explore literary elements in a meaningful way.

As the name indicates, mini-lessons are just that—brief opportunities to focus students' attention on *one* particular reading strategy, procedure, or literary element. The teacher may want to ask himself or herself, "What is the one thing I can suggest or demonstrate that might help the most?" Additionally, the mini-lesson creates an opportunity to explore an issue, a model, a technique, or to reinforce a strategy for the whole class. Effective mini-lessons often incorporate a piece of literature or other text, so that the teacher can demonstrate and model the strategy, rather than just explain the strategy.

INDEPENDENT READING AND LITERATURE DISCUSSIONS. A majority of the time in a reader/writer workshop is devoted to reading and responding. This instructional

---

Reading Conference and Goal Sheet

Name: _____ Date _____

Begin time _____ End time _____

Bring to your conference a book you are currently reading or working with

Title _____

Is this book too easy, just right, or challenging? How do you know?

Tell me what this book is about so far.

What are your reading plans with this book? How much time will you
need to complete the book? What will you do after you finish this
book?

What are your goals for reading? Possible areas to consider include:
• Rereading when meaning is unclear, when something doesn't make sense
• Think about what you are reading and what is happening
• Make sure you can decode and understand almost all of the words in a book
• Think about why characters act and behave as they do
• Make connections to your own life
• Try reading in another genre
• Extend the amount of time you read daily
• Learn different parts of stories (e.g., main idea, setting, plot, conclusion)
• Learn new strategies for decoding unfamiliar words

My goals:

time includes independent reading and literature discussions. ***Independent reading***, also known as ***sustained silent reading (SSR)***, is an opportunity for students to read texts they are highly interested in and motivated by. Choice is essential. For some children, it may be a particular author they like (e.g., Cleary, Creech, Fleishman, Paulson, Henkes), or a particular genre (e.g., mystery, joke books, science fiction, comic books, historical fiction). Classroom libraries, school libraries, and home collections provide students with access to these materials. Classroom libraries are particularly important in supporting a reader/writer workshop.

Students may also read the texts that have been selected for the literature discussion groups. While students read these selections, there are opportunities for them to respond in literature response journals (*Guiding Principle 3: Readers and writers access their 'funds of knowledge' and 'cultural capital' to make sense of texts*).

independent reading/ sustained silent reading

A time during the reader/writer workshop where students read selections of their own choosing.

Justine's Reading Log

Title Charlotte's Web

Author E.B. White

Date 3/31/98

Pages 1-7

Vocabulary hoghouse

Summary/Feelings Fren saved a pig "and she got to cepe him. Fren saved a pig I thout it was brave. If it were my disen I would have whated longer to see how the runt did befor I killed it.

Date April 3d

Pages 7-12

Vocabulary Sopping.

Summary/Feelings Willber was soled to the Zuckermans. I thout it was sad for Furn because she rilly loved him very much. I could tell because it said in the book that Fern loved everything about Wilber!

Date April 9th

Pages 13-24

Vocabulary Slopps.

Summary/Feelings I would have ran and ran happy to be free! Wilber ran away and got capshered agen. this is like when my bunny got away and we cot him agen because he would not go out of his cog for a day

These journals provide the thinking space for students to make connections (text to text, text to self, text to world), ask questions, and record new understandings. The goal for the literature response journals is to record thinking while reading. It is common for teachers to mandate a particular structure for the literature response log, but the quality of the response may be reduced because students begin to focus on the structure (summary, unfamiliar words) rather than what the reader found to be most interesting to write about.

During this time students can also meet in their literature discussion groups to share interpretations, reflections, and wonderings. Depending on how the time is organized, there may be multiple literature discussions occurring. The teacher will often meet with one of the discussion groups, listening to how students respond to the story. This may also be a time for teachers to observe how students interact with each other, listen to alternative points of view, and contribute to the discussion. Teachers use their own methods for collecting and filing such information for future reference and assessment.

authoring cycle

A model for writing development that highlights the transactional nature between reading and writing.

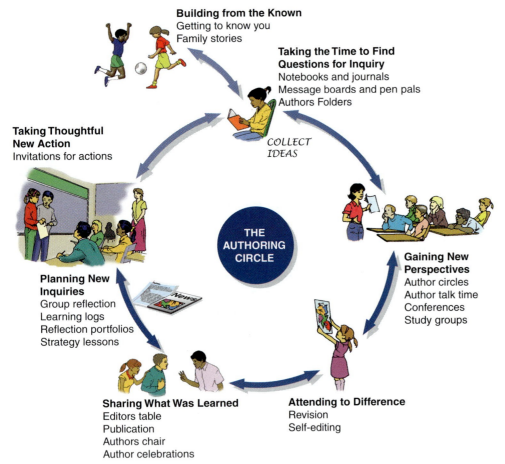

Building from the Known
Getting to know you
Family stories

Taking the Time to Find Questions for Inquiry
Notebooks and journals
Message boards and pen pals
Authors Folders

COLLECT IDEAS

THE AUTHORING CIRCLE

Taking Thoughtful New Action
Invitations for actions

Planning New Inquiries
Group reflection
Learning logs
Reflection portfolios
Strategy lessons

Gaining New Perspectives
Author circles
Author talk time
Conferences
Study groups

Sharing What Was Learned
Editors table
Publication
Authors chair
Author celebrations

Attending to Difference
Revision
Self-editing

FIGURE 5.3 Authoring cycle.

WRITING AND RESPONDING. While some students participate in independent reading or literature discussion groups, others may be working on their own writing. During this time, students may decide to take a piece they are drafting and move it through the *authoring cycle* to publication. The authoring cycle developed by Short, Harste, and Burke (1996) incorporates many ideas from the early writing process approach (Calkins, 1983 1986; Graves, 1982) but recognizes that writing is a more recursive process—that the process does not end with a published piece. Rather, new ideas or goals are developed as a result of writing. Figure 5.3 illustrates the recursive nature of the authoring cycle.

Inside this block of time in the reader/writer workshop, students may work on:

- Writing about their experiences (beginning with the known)
- Uninterrupted reading and writing
- Writing to gain new perspectives
- Editing and self-reflection

Beginning with the known invites students to draft from their own experiences. Students often worry that they do not have "anything to write about" yet they have lived entire lives of experience. Much like authors, students should be encouraged to keep a writer's notebook (Bomer & Bomer, 2001) where they can record observations, daily life, snippets of conversations, interesting words, wonderings, lists, maps, and artifacts. After collecting some of these initial ideas, students are asked to consider one of them as a longer piece. In doing so, students move into the *uninterrupted writing* segment. Here is where students begin to write their ideas and thoughts. This segment occupies a large portion of the writing and responding time.

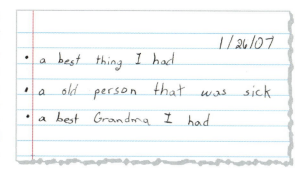

As students draft and write, they meet in author circles to discuss current rough draft thinking. **Author circles** are venues of three to four students to share their less polished writing and thinking. Often authors will ask their audience members to help with a particular area in the writing (e.g., interesting leads, character development, setting, sequence of events). Immediate feedback is important as the author considers which revisions to make. The author circles exemplify how authors *gain new perspectives* on their drafts.

author circles

Strategy designed to facilitate children sharing works in progress.

Following the author's circle, students continue to *draft*, *edit*, and *reflect* on their piece. They may edit their piece using an editing checklist that the class has helped to create. They may meet with others to share new possibilities for their writing. In all of this, students are writing and responding to various pieces of work.

There is plenty of activity during the reader/writer and responding time. Students are working on their own or

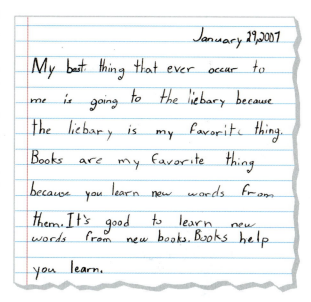

Examples of writers' notebooks.

meeting with others to push new understandings and interpretations. Because there is no predetermined activity or set of skill lessons for the students to complete, the most difficult aspect is classroom management and organization. There are a number of structures that teachers and students may negotiate to accomplish a particular goal. For example, the chart below is displayed in Ms. Webster's classroom. Students refer to the chart on a regular basis, as they move seamlessly between reading, writing, and responding. Ms. Webster has also developed organizational tools as journals to help her manage the discussion groups and students' writing progress.

READING AND WRITING CONFERENCES. While students are actively engaged in independent reading and writing or literature discussion groups, teachers work individually with students in reading and writing conferences. These conferences are opportunities for teachers to assess students' strengths as well as determine what areas may need more support (Gill, 2000; Rhodes & Dudley-Marling, 1996). Teachers usually meet with two to three students a day. The results of these conferences are used to develop mini-lessons.

miscue analysis

An assessment that documents the miscues a reader makes while reading aloud.

In reading conferences, students typically read from both a familiar text (usually self-selected) and a less-familiar text (usually selected by the teacher). As the student reads the more familiar text, the teacher monitors the student's fluency and comprehension. Occasionally, less familiar texts may be used to conduct a running record and/or miscue analysis. *Miscue analysis* is an assessment tool that documents the number of miscues a student makes as she or he reads aloud, as well as how well the student retells the story (see Chapter 9 for more information on miscue analysis). Reading conferences may include discussions about students' strengths and abilities with reading strategies, what the student wants to work on (in terms of strategies and goals), and why particular books were selected.

status of the class

An organizational technique to keep track of student progress.

Writing conferences are very similar to reading conferences. Teachers address a particular writing strategy, share reactions to a student's piece of writing, or ask students to identify areas they may need support with. Writing conferences offer opportunities for students to reflect on their work as they progress through the authoring cycle.

Check Your Progress

- ☐ Complete any missing homework
- ☐ Book Club
  - ☐ read agreed pages
  - ☐ respond to reading journal
  - ☐ find one or two points for discussion
- ☐ Writing
  - ☐ write in journal
  - ☐ work on publishing a piece
- ☐ Book Club Discussion
  - ☐ bring journal
- ☐ Project Work
  - ☐ plan
  - ☐ work on project

STATUS OF THE CLASS. Coined by Lucy Calkins (1986), *status of the class* is an organizational technique to manage all the places students are with their reading and writing. Some teachers have a status-of-the-class check every day to determine what students will be working on during workshop time. Other teachers have a status-of-the-class check a couple of times a week. Status of the class is designed to keep track and account for all the work students are engaged in during reader/writer workshop time.

SHARING. At the completion of each day of reader/writer workshop, there should be

JOURNALS   JOURNALS   JOURNALS   JOURNALS

time devoted to sharing work. Teachers and students can determine the types of materials and processes to be shared in reading and writing. Having students share their literature discussion talk or book reviews are good opportunities for students to hear about other texts they may want to read. Students can also share their writing as they continue to progress through the authoring cycle. Teachers may ask students to share their progress in trying out a mini-lesson strategy. In these sharing episodes, the goal is to make explicit the thoughtful and hard work the students have engaged in over a period of time. It also makes visible the ways students interact with texts and the range of interpretations that are available.

Summary of teaching structures for reader/writer workshops

The teaching structures that make up the reading workshop offer explicit and focused attention on code-breaking practices, text-meaning practices, text-use practices, and critical practices. Students engage with texts from multiple vantage points and come to see that reading is more than

Name: _____ Date: _____

Book Title: _____

BOOK CELEBRATION PLAN!

For my book celebration project I will create a(n): _____

_____

I think this project is a good one because _____

_____

I will be working with _____

Book pages I will use	Quotes from that page

Why is this an important part of the story?_____

_____

On the back of this sheet, draw a sketch of your project

Literature discussion form for students to complete.

Invitation for the classroom

Reading Conference Form (narrative)

Conduct a reading conference with a student. Consider the following questions as possible directions to pursue in the conference.

Name _____
Title _____
Author _____
Number of pages _____

1. Tell what the story is about in three or four sentences.
2. Tell what part of the story you liked best and why it kept your interest.
3. Read aloud a favorite part of the book (paragraph or page) and tell why you chose it.
4. What is something you learned in reading this book?
5. What are some new or interesting words you learned in this book?
6. Were there any parts that were confusing? If so, what made them confusing?
7. What strategies did you use to pick out this book?
8. What strategies helped you read this book (think about the mini-lesson strategies we have talked about)?
9. What are some of the feelings you had while reading this book?
10. Name something in this book that reminds you of your own life.
11. Would you recommend this book to another person?

Invitation for the classroom

Reading Conference Form (informational)

Name _____

Title _____   Topic _____

Author _____

Number of pages _____

1. Tell what the story is about in three or four sentences.
2. Tell what you think is the author's reason for writing this book.
3. Read aloud a favorite part of the book (paragraph or page) and tell why you chose it.
4. What is something you learned from reading this book that you didn't know before?
5. What are some new or interesting words you learned in this book?
6. Did the book have a lot of pictures, charts, graphs, or diagrams? Tell how any of these things helped you understand the book.
7. What strategies did you use to pick out this book?
8. What strategies helped you read this book (think about the mini-lesson strategies we have talked about)?
9. What other books have you read on this topic?
10. Name some things from your own life that you thought about as you read this book.

deconstructing the sounds in a word, locating rhyming words, or retelling their own stories. Reading is all of these aspects of word analysis, comprehension, and more. The reading workshop provides readers and writers with literacy experiences that cut across many purposes and genres.

Invitation for the classroom

Writing Conference

Conduct a writing conference with a young writer. Note the various writing strategies the child uses, as well as what you can offer to lift the work a child does to a new level.

Child's Name: _____

Date	Research / Compliment	Teaching Point	What Is next?
	What strategies did I notice the child using independently?	*What strategy did I teach the child in today's conference? What literature connection did I use?*	*What strategies could I teach the child in the future?*

Summary of Teaching Structures in Reading and Writing Workshops

Reading Aloud
Teacher models reading process, students listen and respond.
Materials: Storybooks, content materials, poetry
Choice: Usually teacher's choice
Grouping: Usually whole group
Purpose: To stretch students beyond their reading levels
To expose students to varied forms of text
To enlist varied forms of response
To study genres, literary devices, writer's craft
Readers benefit from listening, responding, and expanding their knowledge, vocabulary, and concepts.

Shared Reading
Teacher leads, students participate.
Materials: Enlarged texts visible to students (big books)
Choice: Usually teacher's choice
Grouping: Whole group or small group
Purpose: To teach concepts about print and print conventions
To analyze textual features; word study
To teach comprehension and interpretation
To enlist varied forms of response
Readers benefit from highly visible demonstrations of the reading process. Concepts and conventions of print are made very accessible for them. Examination of textual features (letters, word parts) helps develop an understanding of alphabetic principle and the nature of written language.

Mini-Lesson
Teacher invites students to consider a new strategy.
Materials: Text that modestly challenges the reader; can also be a new text
Choice: Usually teacher's choice
Grouping: Small group
Purpose: To introduce and practice a particular strategy that will move the readers forward in becoming effective and efficient readers
Beginning readers benefit when they see the reading strategy modeled by the teacher and then have opportunities to practice.

Literature Discussion
Teacher invites children to respond to text in meaningful ways.
Materials: Text that modestly challenges the reader; has significant issues to discuss
Choice: Varies depending on the goals
Grouping: Small group
Purpose: To invite students to discuss texts that offer multiple perspectives, challenge the status quo, consider voices not present in the text, to take social action.
Readers benefit by connecting texts to the purpose of reading—to find out information about themselves and the world in which they live.

Independent Reading and Writing
Teacher provides time for students to read a self-selected text or to compose self-selected text.
Materials: Text that is self-selected by the reader; should be comfortable for the reader
Choice: Varies depending on the goals
Grouping: Individual
Purpose: To provide opportunities for readers to practice reading strategies as well as immerse themselves into a text
Beginning readers benefit by self-selecting the text and reading for the pleasure of reading.

Reading and Writing Conferences
Teacher meets with individual children to discuss reading and writing strategies and progress.
Materials: Text may be self-selected by the reader; should be comfortable for the reader
Choice: Varies depending on the goals
Grouping: Individual
Purpose: To provide opportunities for readers to demonstrate their reading strategies and to share reading goals
Readers benefit by having teachers pay close attention to the strategies they are using to code break and make meaning of text.

In Closing

This chapter addressed different curricular structures and materials for effectively teaching reading and writing. Along with shifts in models of schooling and reading theories, there are also shifts in reading curricula. There have been four significant shifts, from prescriptive programs to reader response and authentic children's literature, to a "balanced" approach, and then back to prescriptive programs. Given the current political climate of No Child Left Behind and Reading First, publishers developed and repackaged their materials to match the language of the National Reading Panel's report. Many commercially produced programs suggest that their materials address the five key components of reading: (1) phonemic awareness, (2) phonics, (3) comprehension, (4) vocabulary, and (5) fluency.

There are a number of possibilities that teachers may consider as they begin to plan their literacy curriculum. Currently, the most common reading curriculum in classrooms is the basal reading series. These are comprehensive programs that include a number of different materials (anthologies, kits, word cards, leveled texts, etc.). Prescriptive programs, such as the basal, limit teachers' professional decision making because there are fewer opportunities to take advantage of the teachable moment. There is pressure to cover the curriculum and remain on target.

Reader/writer workshops invite teachers and children into a different possibility—one that takes advantage of children's excitement for learning. The workshop structure accommodates a wide range of differences in literacy development. There are three key variables in reader/writer workshops: (1) time, (2) choice, and (3) groups. Children spend their time reading and writing in a number of different structures, from independent reading and literature discussions to writing conferences and author's chair. In reader/writer workshops children have opportunities to read a variety of texts. They read and write about topics that they are interested in. A reader/writer workshop structure takes advantage of children's motivation and how to harness it for learning literacy.

Terms to Remember

Author circles *(137)*

Authoring cycle *(136)*

Basal reading series *(119)*

Decodable text *(122)*

DR-TA format *(123)*

Flexible grouping *(132)*

Guided reading group *(123)*

Independent reading/sustained silent reading *(135)*

Literature-based basal *(121)*

Mini-lesson *(133)*

Miscue analysis *(138)*

Phonics-oriented basals *(121)*

Status of the class *(138)*

Reader/writer workshop approach *(128)*

Text sets *(128)*

Trade books *(121)*

Resources for More Information

Brabham, E., & Villaume, S. (2002). Leveled texts: The good news and the bad news. *The Reading Teacher*, (55), 5, 483–441.

Chall, J. (1967). Learning to read: The great debate. An inquiry into the science, art, and ideology of old and new methods of teaching children to read, 1910-1965 New York, McGraw-Hill.

Gill, S. R. (2000). Reading with Amy: Teaching and learning through reading conferences. *Reading Teacher*, 53(6), 500–510.

Hoffman, J. V., Roser, N., Salas, R., Patterson, B., & Pennington, J. (2000). Text leveling and little books in first grade reading. Report # 1–010. Center for the Improvement of Early Reading Achievement, Ann Arbor, MI.

Jordan, N. (2005). *Basal readers and reading as socialization: What are children learning? Language Arts*, 82 (3), 204–213.

Neuman, S. (2001). *Access for all: Closing the book gap for children in early education*. Newark, DE: International Reading Association.

Short, K. G., Harste, J. C., & Burke, C. (1988). *Creating classrooms for authors: The reading-writing connection*. Portsmouth, NH: Heinemann.

Questions for Further Reflection

- Examine a school district's materials addressing the reading and writing curriculum in their schools. After reading this chapter, what questions do you have for a district level curriculum specialist about their selected programs and approaches?

- Considering the complexity of a reader/writer workshop model for literacy instruction, what aspects do you feel most comfortable with and on which aspects do you want more information?

- Review of basal materials. Consider the following points as you review the materials: (a) Locate the statement of philosophy and approach regarding reading. What does this statement mean to you?; (b) What do you notice about the annotations for the teacher in the lesson plans?; and (c) Find entries that are children's literature selections. What adaptations are made to these selections: Vocabulary, length, sentence complexity?

Entering into the Literacy Landscape: Emergent Readers and Writers

Kadin Reads at Home

Kadin, an active four-year-old boy, sits on a couch in his family's living room with two of his favorite picture books—Dr. Suess's *Hop on Pop* (1963), and *Bubblegum, Bubblegum* (Wheeler, 2004). He regularly requests *Hop on Pop* to be read when going to sleep. He received *Bubblegum Bubblegum* as a gift for his fourth birthday. Kadin has been exposed to books and reading since he was a baby. His mother reads to him nightly and his grandmother routinely takes him to the local library for story time. Kadin attends a preschool at a local community center three mornings a week. The preschool setting is rich in literacy events. On the walls are alphabet charts, large reproductions of poems and nursery rhymes, and children's work. The teacher reads at least one to two stories to the children each morning. At home, Kadin observes and participates in a number of literacy events. He watches his sisters, who are in middle school, complete homework and text message friends on the computer. He also watches his mother use the computer for business and to touch base with family and friends. Kadin's father loves to cook and regularly involves Kadin in making meals and reading recipes. Kadin is growing up in a family where literacy practices are plentiful.

Kadin opens *Hop on Pop*, turns to the first page and begins reading the story. As he reads each page there is a rhythm to his talking. He uses his finger to track the words, and as he turns each page Kadin quickly checks the illustrations. In doing so, he confirms that what he is going to say matches the picture. About halfway through the story, Kadin decides to use inflection in his voice. When he reaches the line that says "we all are tall," Kadin changes his voice to be very deep and when he reads "we all are small," his voice changes to be high. As Kadin nears the end of this book, he comes across words that he can't remember. He asks his mom for help, "Mommy, what does this say?" His mom replies "You know those words. They are jump bump." Kadin looks at the words, uses the pictures to support his hypothesis and says, "jump" in a very quiet tone. He has lost some of his confidence in knowing what the text says. When Kadin reaches the end of the book, he grandly closes the book and says, "the end."

In the next reading event, Kadin takes up *Bubblegum Bubblegum*. In this book, a series of animals, from a frog to a shrew, a goose, and a crow all find themselves stuck in the gob of bubble gum in the road. A truck comes by, creates a bubble, and the animals are free. The story has a repeatable refrain, "chewy-gooey icky-sticky mess" that

is said each time an animal is stuck. There is also a rhythmic quality to the text as each animal is described and eventually stuck in the mess. The language in this text is more sophisticated than that of *Hop on Pop*. Unlike his interaction patterns with *Hop on Pop*, when Kadin opens this book he spends a long time looking at the pictures. He turns a number of pages before he says anything. It is almost as though he is doing a picture walk, where he is getting a sense of the story before he commits himself to saying any words. When Kadin does begin to read, he starts off very quietly and improvises what he says. He begins to invent words that he thinks match the pictures in the story. When he sees the second page with the frog stuck in the gum, he remembers the refrain and says, "chewy-gooey icky-sticky mess." As Kadin continues to read this text, there is less attention paid to the words on the page and more attention given to the illustrations. He uses the illustrations to craft his own rendition of the story.

These two reading events signal that Kadin has had many experiences at home and in the local library listening to stories, as well as observing how people interact with text. He knows how to handle a book, which direction to read, and how stories have a particular rhythm to them. There were distinct differences in how Kadin responded to each of the stories. He was very familiar with *Hop on Pop,* and less familiar with *Bubblegum, Bubblegum*. Additionally, as Kadin grew in his confidence around reading, he relied less on the pictures to support his understandings. He also began tracking the text with his finger which is something he did not do with *Bubblegum, Bubblegum*.

The differences in how Kadin responded to each story indicate the important role repeated readings play in young children's literacy lives. Additionally, the role of predictable and rhythmic language supported Kadin as he hypothesized about what would make sense in the text.

I Wonder. . .

- What does Kadin know about the reading process?

- What textual features in these stories contribute to Kadin's reading process?

- What does Kadin know about story structure? How does he demonstrate this knowledge?

Chapter Overview

Young children bring a multitude of personal experiences from home and community settings (e.g., preschools, day-cares, libraries, etc.) as they begin to understand the world of print. They learn what print is, how it works, and why it is used. Kadin's interactions with *Hop on Pop* and *Bubblegum, Bubblegum* illustrate that these early "hands on" experiences with text contribute to literacy development. His budding literacy-like behavior (pretend reading of *Bubblegum*) suggests that he is engaging in the early intellectual work of reading and writing.

Becoming literate is a developmental process that begins early in a child's life through interactions with family members and caregivers in a variety of settings. The National Association of Early Childhood Education and the International Reading Association note that when teachers, daycare providers, and caregivers support early literacy practices in school and home settings, they are helping young children foster and sustain their interest and enjoyment for reading and writing (NAECY, 1998). Teachers and caregivers can facilitate these early literacy practices in many ways as children enter the literacy landscape. This chapter focuses on the literacy practice for children prior to entering formal school experiences, most notably kindergarten, and addresses the following questions:

- What is the difference between a reading readiness perspective and an emergent literacy perspective toward literacy learning?
- What are the dimensions of emergent literacy knowledge?
- How do environmental print and technology support early literacy development?
- What are some strategies and invitations to facilitate emergent literacy knowledge?

Historical beginnings of emergent literacy

Over the years, researchers have developed theories for when and how a child learns to read and write. When do children realize that symbols on a page actually hold meaning? How do children access and mediate written text for their own purposes? Some theorists focused on children's maturation levels and concluded that children learn to read when they were ready. Other theorists, recognizing the complexity of the reading process, believed that readiness was influenced by instruction. From this perspective, prereading instruction (e.g., knows the alphabet and numbers; understands directionality; and distinguishes print from other graphic forms) was critical to the reading process. More recently, researchers and theorists have begun to consider how young children's understandings of print develop before they receive formal instruction in how to read and write (Clay, 1967; Harste, Burke, & Woodward, 1982; Teale & Sulzby, 1986; Goodman, 1990). Termed "emergent literacy," this perspective acknowledges children's literacy behaviors but indicates a difference from conventional reading.

To appreciate evolving understandings of emergent literacy, it is important to consider the history of emergent literacy learning in the twentieth century. Similar to models of schooling (Chapter 1) and models of literacy development (Chapter 4), how researchers, educators, and the public viewed early literacy was based on philosophical views of learning, as well as what was occurring politically and socially in the country.

Reading readiness

Throughout most of the twentieth century, a ***reading readiness*** perspective dominated the way in which educators understood young children's literacy development. Preschool and kindergarten teachers believed a foundation for formal reading instruction was necessary. There were two different views on how children became prepared for such instruction. One pathway was the ***maturation view***, where a child's mental age was a determining factor in whether or not formal reading instruction should take place. A well-known study by Morphett and Washburne (1931) concludes that children between ages 6 and 7 were ready for reading instruction. The focus was on biological factors, or neural ripeness, rather than cognitive and/or social factors. Arthur Gesell, a developmental psychologist in the 1940s, promoted this maturation view by suggesting that educators should "wait and see" where the child was in terms of development and that instruction should be postponed until the child naturally possessed some prerequisite skills. With this particular view of literacy development, preschool and kindergarten teachers did not offer any reading instruction, but rather informed the first grade teacher which children had passed the readiness threshold and which children needed more time.

A second pathway, introduced because of concerns with American education and the performance of children from low socioeconomic levels, was the ***experience view***. This perspective was based on the work of cognitive psychologists and focused on getting children ready to read, rather than sitting back and waiting. Researchers suggested that there were certain prerequisite skills to learn before learning to read. Readiness programs in preschools and kindergartens included activities to develop auditory discrimination and memory, as well as visual discrimination and memory. Instruction featured incremental steps to learning and drill and practice routines. There was very little, if any, consideration given to the social and cultural contexts in which children were acquiring these prerequisites for reading and writing. What became an important issue was that some children experienced these readiness skills (those that are closely aligned with conventional school practices) as part of their home and community practices, while other children had different experiences around texts.

For example, when four-year-old Justin entered preschool, he did not bring with him experiences around books and writing that promote school-like literacy behaviors. Justin was not read to at home or taken to the local library. He was also not familiar with crayons, markers, and other writing tools. Justin was unsure of how to participate in shared reading events, or how to use a crayon to write his name. He spent a large part of his day on the porch playing with cousins and neighbors. They invented songs, rhymes, and games, while the adults in his life discussed the ongoings of daily life. Justin regularly participated in church activities: singing, listening, and memorizing biblical stories and scriptures. Justin's experiences at home and at church were not recognized in the classroom as contributing to literacy knowledge because they did not mimic conventional literacy activities. His preschool teacher assumed that because Justin was not familiar with early literacy concepts and behaviors, he was lacking in literacy knowledge and that he was "at risk" for failing in the early grades.

His preschool teacher, operating from an experience view of readiness, provided Justin with instructional materials that focused on learning prerequisite skills. These skills include print awareness (identifying letters of the alphabet; distinguishing between letters and other random marks); linguistic awareness (knowledge of particular sounds, rhyming attributes); directionality concepts (up, down, top, bottom, inside, outside, etc); knowledge of colors, numbers (up to 20), and same/different (which one of these is not like the other). Sensorimotor skills (crawling, hopping, skipping) were also believed to contribute to literacy development. Justin's teacher offered a literacy

reading readiness
A perspective that believes that children need to be taught a series of prerequisite skills prior to reading and writing.

maturation view
Mental age is a determining factor in whether formal reading instruction should begin (nature).

experience view
Children need to experience prerequisite skills to accelerate readiness (nature).

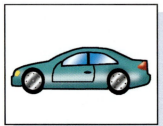

FIGURE 6.1 These pictures are of a fish, car, boy, apple. Which one is a car? Find car. Circle the car.

Source: Getting Ready to Read screening tool (http://www.getreadytoread.org).

emergent literacy

A perspective that focuses on the informal learning of literacy in home, preschool, or kindergarten settings.

curriculum that was skills oriented. Justin needed to learn these skills first before engaging in formal reading lessons. Justin, and children like Justin, were not formally taught to read and write until they had mastered many of these skills. Figure 6.1 is an example of readiness items on a worksheet that Justin may have encountered in his preschool experience.

The readiness perspective on early literacy learning and development has spilled over into *Head Start* (a federally funded initiative), *Jump Start* (a national nonprofit organization), and *Sesame Street* (a nationally televised program). These initiatives and programs are designed to increase school readiness in children that come from economically disadvantaged communities. There was a boundary between "prereading" that children engage in at home and other settings and "real" reading that children were taught in school (Whitehurst & Lonigan, 1998). A readiness perspective viewed reading and writing as independent of each other, with writing taking a back seat. The belief was that children need formal instruction in reading prior to learning how to write.

Emergent literacy

By the 1980s, researchers and educators challenged many of the tenets of a reading readiness perspective, most notably, the idea that general cognitive skills transfer to reading skills. This shift in early literacy development coincided with the work that whole language advocates were promoting about literacy development in general. An **emergent literacy** perspective recognizes and appreciates children's encounters with print. It is often viewed as a precursor to conventional reading and writing. Researchers began to consider how children interact with the learning environment, noting that children who experienced reading, even informally, were gaining reading skills (Harste, Burke, & Woodward, 1982; Mason & Allen, 1986; Schweiker & Schweiker, 1993). Many of these early studies shared the following perspectives as detailed by Mason and Sinha (1992):

- Literacy emerges before children are formally taught to read.
- Literacy is defined to encompass the whole act of reading, not merely decoding.
- The child's point of view and active involvement with emerging literacy constructs is featured.
- The social setting for literacy instruction is not ignored.

Teale and Sulzy (1986) suggest that it is not reasonable to point to a time in a child's life when literacy begins. Literacy learning is on a developmental continuum that begins early in life. Piaget (1959) and Vygotsky (1978) add to the discussion by describing children not as passive recipients waiting for knowledge, but rather active meaning makers. Children hypothesize and take risks with what they know about oral and written language. An emergent literacy perspective has changed the view of literacy development and what it means for a young child to be a literacy user:

All children have some knowledge about literacy as a cultural form, and they have attitudes and beliefs about literacy as a result of their developing concepts about literacy. They know the functions that written language serves, and they know who may participate in its use. Children know what reading is and in what kinds of materials reading can occur. They know who reads, where people read, what different people use reading for, and who can and cannot read. Children know what writing is and what kinds of forms writing takes. They know who writes, what people write, and what people use writing for. (Y. Goodman, 1990, p. 116)

Children develop this early reading and writing knowledge concurrently and interdependently. They are immersed in oral and written language events in their daily lives. Young children sing songs, invent rhymes, ask questions, tell stories, participate in conversations, and engage in a host of other language-based activities. By interacting with those in their surroundings, children develop listening skills, comprehension, vocabulary, and language facility. Literacy is developed within the framework of real-life activities, in order to "get things done." These instances keep language and its complexity intact—children are working with whole words, written messages, and storybooks instead of activities focused on individual letters, sounds, or letter–sound relationships (Clay, 1998).

Creating Connections 6.1

http://www.jstart.org/   http://www.acf.hhs.gov/programs/hsb/

Take a look at the websites for government and nonprofit agencies focused on emergent literacy (e.g., *Headstart and Jumpstart*). How do the various agencies talk about early literacy development? What are some of their key points? What types of activities do they encourage adult caregivers/parents and children to engage in?

Home and community contexts play a central role in the literacy development of young children. For most children, emergent literacy knowledge is learned in the context of others and is influenced by the social and cultural surroundings in which the child is raised. These surroundings may include activities such as watching television and movies, playing videogames, storybook reading, conversations with others, singing, and participating in everyday activities of the home and community. Returning to Justin's experiences of attending church services during which he listens to the pastor, sings, and learns to repeat various scriptures, a sociocultural emergent perspective acknowledges that these experiences, values, and ways with words count as literacy learning. Early childhood teachers should consider ways to "connect what happens inside the classroom to what happens outside so that literacy can become a meaningful tool for addressing the issues in students' lives" (Auerbach, 1989, p.166).

Most early childhood teachers, researchers, curriculum publishers, and policy makers view preschool and kindergarten literacy development through an emergent literacy lens. However, current political contexts and pressures from No Child Left Behind have reintroduced a readiness perspective in early literacy classrooms. Documents such as *Eager to Learn* (National Academy of Sciences, 2000) and *Starting out Right: A Guide to Promoting Children's Reading Success* (Burns, Griffin, & Snow, 1999) have begun to influence many preschool classrooms. While both documents acknowledge that the research has moved beyond a strict adherence to a readiness perspective, the discussion focuses mostly on the acquisition of skills and knowledge to develop competence (e.g, phonological awareness, letter naming, conventions of print, listening, and oral language development). Noted in the reports is the correlation between home literacy environments and later literacy achievement. Again, there is an assumption that children do not have a rich repertoire of experiences to bring to the literacy event and that it is important that they learn a set of basic skills before they are able to read. The child's previous experiences, participation in daily routines, and developmental levels are ignored (Dantas, 1999).

TECHNOLOGY LINK

http://www.ncrel.org/sdrs/areas/issues/content/cntareas/reading/li100.htm

Critical Issue: Addressing the Literacy Needs of Emergent and Early Readers

In partnership with NCREL (North Central Regional Educational Laboratory), this site produced by Learning Associates provides extended discussion on emergent literacy, actions to take in preschool settings, and teaching cases that profile developmentally appropriate curriculum

Readiness Perspective	Emergent Literacy Perspective
Learning to read and write begins after children have acquired a set of prerequisite skills, usually at age 5 or 6.	Learning to read and write begins very early in a child's life.
Reading, writing, and oral language develop sequentially.	Reading, writing, and oral language develop concurrently.
Children learn written language by completing workbook activities.	Children learn written language through active engagement in their communities.
Children's acquisition of literacy can be prescribed through a scope and sequence chart that assumes one path to literacy.	Children become literate at different rates and through different paths.

Oral language learning: What it means for emergent reading and writing practices

Children's comprehension of written language depends in large part upon their effective use and understanding of oral language. Young children learn oral language by participating in the linguistic environment around them. It does not happen in a vacuum. Very young children imitate the sounds they hear and develop their own word/sound (ba-ba) when they can not yet say the conventional word (bottle). They are flooded with new experiences and words. Young children selectively attend to situations that have meaning for them at the moment. Initially, children learn words that help them acquire the things they need. As they begin to create utterances, those around them (most often parents, family members, and caregivers) put meaning into these sounds. Many of us have experienced young children's attempts as they navigate how to most effectively use oral language. We have heard young children say "stop-ped" "runned" "buyed" and while not conventional, we eagerly respond to these attempts. These utterances and their uses are evidence that young children work hard to figure out the systems that operate in their language.

As discussed in detail in Chapter 2, Halliday's (1975) research noted that children learn language as they learn other concepts (e.g., how to live in the world). Young children take risks with language. They play with familiar words, explore new meanings, and test uses of language in different contexts. Parents and caretakers do not set out to teach their children language, but rather to teach them how to navigate their interactions with the world. In the process, language is learned.

Marie Clay, an educator and researcher from New Zealand notes:

> Language is a gateway to new concepts, a means of sorting out confusions, a way of interacting with people, or to get help, a way of testing out what one knows. It enters into every activity we can envisage. It is the source of much pleasure for the child and the adult. It is a pervasive, persuasive, perpetual foundation of learning—and there is no equipment that will give children the interactive experiences that will power their progress. (1998, p.11)

Children's oral language development increases when adults and more experienced peers provide oral language in authentic contexts; when young children have opportunities to engage with meaningful language; and when those in the immediate context provide feedback and response. Cambourne's conditions for oral language development remind us that young language users are rewarded for their approximations and attempts (see chapter 2 for an in-depth discussion of his conditions). When Kevin, age 2, asks to "sweep the leaves," he is handed a rake and begins to help his parents rake the front lawn. Kevin's environment for language learning is one that is accepting, responding, and supporting (Lindfors, 1999). He is viewed as a participating member in conversations. Responding to Kevin's language skills provides him with the support he needs to further enhance his abilities in language use.

Conditions for developing oral language skills

Children learn language through implicit and explicit instruction (Brabham & Villaume, 2002). They learn both the form and the function to create meaningful communication and to make sense of the world around them. Children learn the linguistic rules of how their language works; they also learn the communicative rules of how to use their language (learning when to talk, who can say what, how to participate in conversations, etc.).

D. Strickland (2001) suggests that young children's oral language development thrives when:

- The atmosphere surrounding oral language development is warm and rewarding.
- Language development occurs in a social, child-centered context.
- The context for language and conceptual development is meaningful.
- Children are presented with the entire language system at once.

The classroom setting plays an important role in supporting oral language development. A print-rich environment, including displays of children's work, sign-in sheets and schedules, language experience activities, and co-authored stories encourage children to socially interact as well as see print for functional purposes. Areas of the classroom set up for retellings of favorite stories also enhance oral language development. Flannel boards, dress-up areas, puppets, and listening centers all help children experiment and explore stories repeatedly. These opportunities to create and retell versions of stories enable children to participate in a way that makes sense to them. Additionally, establishing routines and rituals (e.g., singing a particular song at the end of the day; providing share time after lunch; or reading a morning poem) provide children with nonthreatening, predictable environments where they can express themselves in a comfortable manner.

Creating Connections 6.2

Interview three different preschool or daycare teachers in public and private settings about their emergent literacy beliefs and practices. Include in the interview questions on how they define literacy and how they engage children in literacy practices. Also discuss the types of literacy materials available in the classroom.

What do these differences mean for how young children are constructed as literacy users?

Share your findings with classmates through your blog.

Halliday's Eight Conditions for Language Learning

- **Immersion:** Being saturated with language; constantly being enveloped in language.
- **Demonstration:** The ability to observe more knowledgeable others model language use.
- **Expectation:** Messages the young child receives that she is capable of learning language.
- **Approximation:** Taking a best guess at the conventional form.
- **Responsibility:** Ability to make decisions about what will be paid attention to; what will be learned.
- **Response:** Receiving feedback in relation to using developing language skills and behaviors.
- **Employment:** Opportunities for use and practice.
- **Engagement:** Active participation and attention.

Sharing time supports oral language development.

Conditions to support young English Language Learners in preschool settings

In preschool settings, young ELL students are working to fully develop their primary language as well as acquire English. It is important to recognize that for children under age 5, many aspects of their primary language are not fully developed. Children many not know particular vocabulary words, sentence structures, or other language features in their primary language, and so merely translating a word may not necessarily support their English language development (Coltrane, 2003).

Preschool settings should be nurturing and enriching learning environments. For young ELL this often means building collaborations with parents and community members. These collaborations include inviting volunteers into the classroom, raising awareness with parents about the importance of supporting primary languages at home, and family literacy programs. Additionally, tapping into the funds of knowledge and literacy practices (i.e., storytelling routines, types of materials read, topics of discussion) that parents and children bring to the classroom can be a basis for instruction. Teachers can gather this information through conversations with parents and caregivers, visiting the child's home, and eliciting the help of community members who know children's home cultures. These collaborations help to develop and maintain children's primary languages so that they can communicate with parents and extended family members.

In addition to the support that family and community members provide as they work in collaboration with preschools and other early literacy environments, there are a number of other key points to consider in working with young ELL students. These points are similar to effective practices with non-ELL students. According to the Center for Child and Family Studies (CCFS):

- Children benefit when teachers understand and incorporate cultural differences into language use within their daily routine.
- Successful practices promote shared experiences in which language is used as a meaningful tool to communicate interests, ideas, and emotions.
- Language development and learning are promoted when preschool teachers and children creatively and interactively use language.
- Experimenting with the use, form, purpose, and intent of both the first and second language leads to growth in the acquisition of the second language.
- Continued use and development of the child's home language will benefit the child as he or she acquires English.
- Code switching is a normal part of language development for many bilingual children.
- Engaging in multiple literacy practices, such as reading books, singing songs, and reciting poetry, is part of the daily life of most families.
- Offering a variety of opportunities for children to explore written materials and their meanings as well as the sounds of spoken language through rhyme and al-

literation builds the language and literacy skills of preschool English Learners.

These principles support and foster an environment that respects the linguistic and cultural diversity that is rapidly growing in preschool settings (www.edgateway.net/pel/pdf/principles.pdf).

Dimensions of Emergent Literacy

Emergent literacy knowledge involves speaking, reading, and writing practices that young children engage in as they acquire more competence with conventional print. Three major areas of literacy acquisition include *concepts of text, concepts of words*, and *concepts of letters and sounds*. The National Early Literacy Panel (Strickland & Shanahan, 2004) further delineated oral language development, print knowledge, alphabet knowledge, phonological/phonemic awareness, and inventive spelling as essential to developing the dimensions of emergent literacy. These interrelated components were identified in the International Reading Association and National Association for Education of Young Children literacy plan developed in 1998. Consisting of five phases, the plan addresses student literacy needs from preschool to third grade. This chapter

---

Invitation for the classroom

Exploring language through poetry

The following list of poetry books supports children as they play with and enjoy the sounds and images of language. Books reviewed include collections of contemporary and traditional poetry, traditional folk songs, chants, jump rope rhymes, and Spanish and English versions of poems. Many that offer simple rhymes or repeated patterns will appeal to children.

- *A Small Child's Book of Cozy Poems*. New York: Scholastic (1999).
- *Frog went a-courting: A Musical Play in Six Acts*. Dominic Catalano (1998). Honesdale, PA: Boyds Mills Press.
- *From the Bellybutton of the Moon and Other Summer Poems: Del Ombligo de la Luna y Otros Poemas de Verano*. Francisco Alarcón (1998). San Francisco, CA: Children's Book Press.
- *I Scream, You Scream: A Feast of Food Rhymes*. Lillian Morrison (1997). Little Rock, AK: House Pub.
- *Lemonade Sun and Other Summer Poems*. Rebecca Dotlich (1998). Honesdale, PA: Boyds Mills Press.
- *Old Macdonald (2005)*. Worthington, OH: Brighter minds Children's Pub.
- *Snow, Snow: Winter Poems for Children*. Jane Yolan (1998). Honesdale, PA: Wordsong.
- *Tea Party Today: Poems to Sip and Savor*. Eileen Spinell: (1999). Honesdale, PA: Wordsong.
- *The Purchase of Small Secrets: Poems*. David Harrison (1998). Honesdale, PA: Wordsong.
- *Under the Breadfruit Tree: Island Poems*. Monica Gunning (1998). Honesdale, PA: Wordsong.
- *Walking on the Boundaries of Change: Poems of Transition*. Sara Holbrook (1998). Honesdale, PA: Boyds Mills Press.
- *Words with Wrinkled Knees: Animal Poems*. Barbara Esbensen (1998). Honesdale, PA: Wordsong/Boyds Mills Press.

highlights Phase 1: Awareness and Exploration. The remaining phases (Phase 2: Experimental Reading and Writing; Phase 3: Early Reading and Writing; Phase 4: Transitional Reading and Writing; and Phase 5: Independent and Productive Reading and Writing) are addressed in Chapters 7 and 8. Table 6.1 highlights the literacy goals for preschool children.

Preschool teachers and caregivers in home and community settings can use this information as a way to plan literacy experiences for children. In doing so, educators and caregivers provide opportunities for children to view literacy as a socially constructed practice; to be risk takers and hypothesize about language use; and to experience multiple and meaningful ways to engage with language.

<table>
<tr><td>**TECHNOLOGY LINK**
http://www.literacy.uconn.edu/earlit.htm

The Literacy Web is designed to promote the use of the Internet as a tool to assist classroom teachers in their search for best practices in literacy instruction, including the new literacies of Internet technologies.</td></tr>
</table>

Concepts of texts

Young children begin to understand various aspects of literature by listening to, telling, and acting out stories. They borrow story language in their conversations and play. For example, in the house center of a local preschool classroom, two three-year-olds are deciding who will be the "mommy" and who will be the "daddy."

Ashley: Well, once upon a time I was the mommy.
Markita: Let's pretend you are the mommy. I'm the daddy and we need a baby. Baby is sick and we need to give him medicine
Ashley: Let's go to the hospital. Here's your medicine, baby.

TABLE 6.1
Planning Emergent Literacy Experiences for Children
In preschools, day care centers, and at home, children explore their environment and build the foundations for learning to read and write

Young children enjoy:	Teachers can promote literacy by:	Examples of literacy engagements include:
• listening to and discussing storybooks	• sharing books with children, including Big Books • modeling reading behaviors	• reading aloud • visiting the library • storytelling
• understanding that print carries a message	• establishing a literacy-rich environment	• reading aloud • responding to message boards • working at writing centers
• engaging in reading and writing attempts by using known letters or approximations of letters to represent written language like their name and phrases such as "I love you"	• rereading favorite stories • reading predictable stories • encouraging children to experiment with writing	• reading independently • working at writing centers • responding to message boards • writing in journals
• identifying labels and signs in their environment	• incorporating literacy-related activities in play centers	• engaging with peers at play centers • interacting with environmental print and signs • creating name cards
• participating in rhyming games	• engaging children in language games	• reading poems • singing songs
• identifying some letters and making letter–sound matches	• talking about letters by name and sounds • singing the alphabet song	• using magnetic letters • using alphabet charts

Source: Learning to Read and Write: Developmentally appropropriate practices for young children. Joint position statement of the International Reading Association and the National Assocation for the Education of young children (1998).

In another example, Callum, age 4 and wearing a black cape, emerges from the family room. When asked about being Superman, he replies, "I'm not Superman. I'm Batman Kid. Batman Kid has a cape but no mask. And if you hear the 'dun-da-dun-da' [Superman music], it is Batman Kid."

These brief encounters suggest that children engaged in storytelling and reenactments are extending their understandings of literature. Vivian Paley (1981, 1992, 1997) writes extensively about the role of a storytelling curriculum to support literacy development. In a storytelling curriculum, children participate in dictation and dramatization. Dictation is usually the first step, and in this a child will dictate his or her story to a teacher, who acts as a scribe, editor, and initial audience. All topics, imaginative and otherwise, are accepted. After the story is told, the teacher rereads the story and asks for any clarification or revision. Following the dictation, children move into dramatization, whereby they select classmates to play various parts from the list of classmates waiting for a turn in a story.

Dramatization is a one-time through, no-rehearsal event. The teacher will read the dictated story aloud, and as she does so, the children step into their roles. There are relatively few expectations of the dramatic performance. The overall focus for the dramatization is to support children as they further develop their understandings of language, print, and narrative. They gain knowledge of narrative form—how stories work, where stories come from, what stories are composed of, sequencing, plot development, characterization, writing process, authorial intention, and use of imagination (Cooper, 2005).

Along with a storytelling curriculum, interactions with storybooks also promote concepts of texts. Megan, age 4, is sitting at the kitchen table while her mother prepares lunch. As she waits, she opens Jan Pienkowski's book, *Dinnertime* (1981), and turns

Did you know. . .

Vivian Paley has written extensively about culturally relevant pedagogy and teacher quality. The following resources may be helpful in learning more.

- Paley, V. G. (1981) *Wally's Stories: Conversations in the Kindergarten*. Cambridge, MA: Harvard University Press.
- Paley, V. G. (1990) *The Boy Who Would Be a Helicopter: The Uses of Storytelling in the Classroom*. Cambridge, MA: Harvard University Press.
- Paley, V. G. (1992) *You Can't Say You Can't Play*. Cambridge, MA: Harvard University Press.
- Paley, V. G. (1997) *The Girl with the Brown Crayon*. Cambridge, MA: Harvard University Press.
- Paley, V. G. (2004) *A Child's Work: The Importance of Fantasy Play*. Chicago. IL: University of Chicago Press.

Invitation for the classroom

Using Puppets to Retell Stories

Select a familiar story and have children use puppets, toys, and other props to dramatize or retell the story, using the dialogue of different characters.

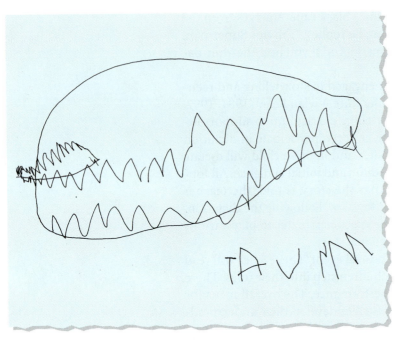

Megan's picture of the shark.

each page. An adult neighbor sitting next to her started to read the story. At the end of each page, Megan turned the page. She didn't say anything but touched each animal as it "popped out" of the page. This is a pop-up book that has vivid animal heads with very big mouths. The story begins with a frog eating flies, and as each page is turned a larger animal (vulture, tiger, crocodile, shark) eats the animal before it (e.g., vulture eats frog, tiger eats vulture). The story is patterned after *There Was an Old Lady Who Swallowed a Fly* (Taback, 1997). When Megan came to the last page, the shark, she promptly closed the book, turned it over, and opened it again. The second time around she started to talk as though she was reading the story to herself. She was not reading the actual words in the story, but rather creating a story that seemed to fit the pictures. When asked what she was doing, she said she was "telling the book."

In this brief moment around text interactions, Megan demonstrated some knowledge of *concepts about print* (Clay, 2000). Similar to Kadin's actions in the opening vignette, she turned each page in the right direction. She knew how to open the book and hold it in the appropriate direction. Megan also looked carefully at each page and touched the animal's popped out mouth while the text was being read.

Megan has emerging understandings that print is everywhere around her and that it provides a function. Through her interactions with this book, *Dinnertime*, and an array of other texts, she is developing an awareness that print serves to get ideas, explain, entertain, and comfort (National Academy of Sciences, 2000). Her attempt to respond to the text also confirms that she considers written language to mean something.

Concepts of words

Concepts of words develop around the same time as concepts of texts. Children engaged in storybook reading, storytelling (dictation), and other such events begin to connect objects and names of things to printed words. Early on they believe that each printed word is a complete utterance. They also work under the premise that written language makes sense. For example, when Harste, Burke, and Woodward (1982) asked children to "read" printed labels in and out of context, their responses

Invitation for the classroom

Monthly Memory Poster

Monthly memory posters are expressions of children's language and literacy development.

Decide with children what to include in the poster. Annotated photographs of classroom experiences, samples of children's writings and drawings, favorite poems, songs, rhymes, and/or pictures of special guests may be included.

Invitation for the classroom

Developing text awareness

Read a favorite children's story that has some complexity in the events. Stories such as *Chrysanthemum* (Henkes, 1996) *or Julius, the Baby of the World* (Henkes, 1990) are two good examples.

Engage children in a discussion of the story by asking open-ended questions. Children will need to explain and describe the events.

Follow-up questions encourage students to elaborate on initial ideas.

indicated that they were working toward sense making. One young child when presented with *Crest* said "brush teeth."

Children soon begin to recognize favorite words, such as their name and local fast food restaurants (e.g., *McDonalds, Taco Bell, Wendy's,* and *Burger King).* They may know that letters are used to make up words, but have no idea which letters to select. So when given the opportunity to create words, young children may have a long string of letters to represent one idea or word.

Concept of words also has to do with understanding the form and function of print. Children gain insights into: (a) differences between graphic displays of words and nonwords; (b) knowing that print corresponds to speech, word by word; (c) understanding the function of empty space in establishing word boundaries; and (d) understanding that we read from left to right and top to bottom. Meaningful interactions with storybooks and texts support children's development.

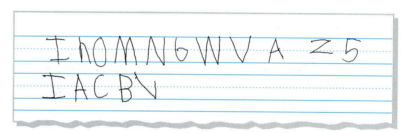

Four-year-old handwriting representing the word *Halloween.*

Concepts of letters and sounds

Concept of letters and sounds is probably the dimension that most people associate with emergent literacy knowledge and development. Two areas are of particular importance: alphabet knowledge and phonemic awareness.

ALPHABET KNOWLEDGE. Alphabet knowledge, specifically being able identify letters, is regularly thought of as a component of emergent reading. Research in the 1960s (Bond & Dyskstra; Chall) and later in the early 1990s (Adams) suggested "the best predictor of student's year-end reading achievement was their entering ability to recognize and name upper and lowercase letters" (p. 43). This notion that letter naming is a strong predictor of early reading achievement is emphasized in the federal government's *Early Reading First* initiative. Alphabet knowledge is listed as one of the four key components that should be the focus of instruction in preschools and other early learning environments. Alphabet knowledge includes:

- recognizing and naming letters,
- recognizing beginning letters in familiar words (especially the first letter in their name), and
- recognizing both capital and lowercase letters.

PHONEMIC AWARENESS. Since the National Reading Panel report in 2000, there has been extensive interest and attention on phonemic awareness in emergent reading. Similar to alphabet knowledge, there are a number of studies that suggest phonemic awareness is an important factor in learning to read (National Reading Panel, 2000; Snow, et al., 1998). While it is certainly a factor in learning to read, it is not the only aspect of emergent literacy. Recall from Chapter 2

Invitation for the classroom

Build Children's Alphabet Knowledge

There are a number of ways in which preschool and day care teachers and parents can support the young reader in learning letter names. In the classroom there should be an alphabet on display at children's eye level, along with alphabet cards, large paper or foam letters, magnetic letters, materials to make letters (string, straws, play dough, pipe cleaners, paper, crayons, etc.), and alphabet books.

- As young children begin to explore the alphabet letters, teachers and other caregivers can encourage children to notice letters in their environment and surroundings. (What letters do you see in the word FEDEX? MCDONALDS? TACOBELL? KINKOS?)
- Have children rearrange magnetic alphabet letters or alphabet tiles to create their names and words that they know.
- Ask children to press particular letters on a keyboard and say the letter as it is displayed on the computer monitor.
- Encourage children to create various letters and words using tactile materials (pipe cleaners, yarn, sand), as well as paper and pencil/crayons.
- Sing and read alphabet songs and books regularly.

Invitation for classroom

Who Naps in *The Napping House*

Read the story *The Napping House* (Wood, 1984). After children are familiar with the story, ask them to list all the people and animals who were napping in the bed (flea, mouse, cat, dog, child, granny). Write these words on index cards, emphasizing the first letter of the word (e.g., **c**at, **f**lea, **g**ranny). Each child should have two to four cards. Next, write the letter on the white board or chalk board and ask students to name the letter and see if they have a word that starts with that letter.

that phonemic awareness is the ability to hear the distinct sounds in words. It is not the ability to know which letter makes which sound. Children who have developed phonemic awareness are able to recognize that there are a particular number of sounds in a given word (e.g., *dog* has three sounds; *baby* has four distinct sounds; and *ice* has two sounds). Phonemic awareness also involves noticing that words can begin with the same sound—that *tiger, toy*, and *Tennesha* all begin with the sound of /t/, and that words can rhyme (*cat, fat, mat, rat*).

Invitation for the classroom

Enhancing Children's Phonemic Awareness

Phonological awareness involves language play. In preschool and home settings, teachers and other caregivers can encourage young children to begin attending to the notion that words are comprised of different sounds. Through language play activities, such as rhyming games, poetry, and reading, children can begin to recognize common sounds at the beginning of words, isolate beginning sounds, and generate rhyming words.

- Choose books to read aloud that focus on rhyming and alliteration.
- Invite children to sing familiar songs and nursery rhymes.
- Ask children to make up new verses of familiar songs or rhymes by changing beginning sounds in words.
- Play word games with children and when possible, use children's names in the games.

Invitation for the classroom

Sorting Pictures by Initial Sounds or by Rime

Create picture cards of the following: bat, hat, cat, rat; can, fan, man, pan; snail, tail, pail, whale; cake, rake, snake; hen, men, ten, pen; car, jar, star; string, ring, wing; clock, rock, sock.

Have children sort the pictures according to initial sound or by the rime.

Assessing the dimensions of emergent literacy

Marie Clay developed the *Concepts about Print* assessment tool (C.A.P) to help preschool and early primary teachers understand young children's awareness of literacy concepts. This tool assesses what young readers know about how printed language works on the page. The concepts include:

- Book orientation skills
- Print and directionality
- Letter and word concepts
- Advanced print concepts (position and sequence)

Table 6.2 contains the individual print concepts and what teachers may say to assess children's understanding of these concepts.

Texts that a teacher may want to use when working with young readers on concepts of print should have print and illustrations on a single page or two consecutive pages; multiple lines of text on a single page, and a variety of punctuation marks (if addressing punctuation knowledge). The text should also reflect a child's interest.

Invitation for the classroom

A Hunting We Will Go

Teach children to sing the song, "A Hunting We Will Go"

> Oh, a hunting we will go, a hunting we will go.
> We'll take a little **fox** and put it in a **box** and then we'll let it go.

Ask children to identify the two words that sound the same (fox and box). Continue by singing the next phrase,

> We'll take a little **whale** and put it in a **pail** and then we'll let it go.
> We'll take a little **frog** and put it on a **log** and then we'll let it go.
> We'll take a little **fish** and put it on a **dish** and then we'll let it go.

Ask children to identify the rhyming words in these phrases.

Have students sing the song several more times.

Ask children to brainstorm other animals that can be used in the song. Ask them to think of words that rhyme with each animal.

> Dog: log, fog
> Bear: chair, hair, stair
> Cat: mat, fat, rat
> Seal: eel, meal, deal

Children can then create their own phrases for the song and add them to the original verse.

TABLE 6.2

Concepts about Print (CAP) Assessment Tool

	Print Concept	Teacher Asks Student to
1	Front cover	Show me the front of this book.
2	Back cover	Show me the back of the book.
3	Title	Show me where the name of the story is.
4	Print carry messages	Show me where the words of the story are.
5	Beginning of the story	Show me with your finger where I start reading.
6	Left to right; top to bottom	Show me with your finger which way I go as I read the page.
7	Return sweep	Where do I go then?
8	One to one matching	You point to the words as I read the story.
9	First word	Show me the first word on this page.
10	Last word	Show me the last word on this page.
11	Word	Point to one word on the page; now two words.
12	First letter in a word	Point to the first letter in this word.
13	Last letter in a word	Point to the last letter in this word.
14	One letter/two letters	Point to one letter in this word; point to two letters in the word.
15	Letter names	Show me three letters on this page, and tell me the names of the letters.
16	Capital letter	With your finger, show me a capital letter on this page.
17	Small letter	With your finger, show me a small letter on this page.
*18	Period	What is this called? Or what is this for?
19	Question mark	What is this called? Or what is this for?
20	Exclamation mark	What is this called? Or what is this for?
21	Quotation mark	What is this called? Or what is this for?
22	Comma	What is this called? Or what is this for?

* The last few concepts (18–22) may not be attended to until well into kindergarten or even first grade for some students.

The C.A.P assessment tool provides teachers with some starting points for instruction. It may be used to establish what children know about written literacy practices, and what instruction to offer. Remember that children come into literacy practices from different vantage points. These individual differences are often related to social and cultural factors that expand or limit opportunities.

Emergent writing

One afternoon, three-year-old Andrea is in the kitchen with her grandmother, Sharon. Sharon is busy cleaning out the pantry. At one point, Sharon says, "Andrea, I wish you were old enough to write grandma's grocery list." Andrea responds, "Why, grandma?" Sharon then says, "Because I need to remember to get toothpicks for grandpa." Andrea leaves the kitchen and comes back a few minutes later with a "2" on a sheet of paper and asks, "how do you write picks."

In this exchange Andrea is participating in a writing event that is socially and culturally situated. She has internalized what it means to "write a grocery list" and the purpose of the grocery list. Andrea has also demonstrated how young children generate new hypotheses for how to represent ideas and concepts. She navigated between her own personal constructions (invention—writing "2" for "tooth") and what society has agreed upon as social uses of literacy (convention—creating a list to remember items) (Whitmore, Martens, Goodman, & Owocki, 2004).

Inventing and refining written language forms

Long before formal instruction in writing, children begin to make sense of the literacy environment around them (billboards, TV, posters, books, toys, road signs, etc.). They begin to connect icons and symbols with meaning. Young children observe and note how family and community members use written text to get things accomplished in the world. Just as Max in *Bunnycakes* (Wells,

Children's Book Titles That May Be Used for CAP Assessment:

- Allen, Pamela (1983). *Who Sank the Boat*? New York: Coward-McCann.
- Anholt, Catherine and Laurence (1995). *Here Come the Babies*. Cambridge, MA: Candlewick Press.
- Barrett, Judi (2006). *Animals Should Definitely Not Wear Clothing*. New York: Aladdin Paperbacks.
- Brett, Jan (1989). *The Mitten*. New York: Putnam.
- Carle, Eric (1988). *Have You Seen My Cat?* New York: Philomel Books.
- Carle, Eric (1994). *The Very Hungry Caterpillar*. New York, NY: Philomel Books.
- Fox, Mem (1988). *Hattie and the Fox*. New York: Bradbury Press, 1988.
- George, Jean Craighead (1997). *Look to the North: A Wolf Pup Diary*. New York: HarperCollins.
- Heller, Ruth (1981). *Chickens Aren't the Only Ones*. New York: Grosset & Dunlap.
- Hirst, Robin and Sally (1990). *My Place in Space*. New York: Orchard Books.
- Hughes, Shirley (1982). *Alfie Gets in First*. New York: Lothrop, Lee & Shepard Books.
- Hutchins, Pat (1986). *The Doorbell Rang*. New York: Greenwillow Books.
- Joose, Barbara M. (2000). *Mama, Do You Love Me?* San Francisco: Chronicle Books.
- Koller, Jackie French (1999). *One Monkey Too Many*. San Diego: Harcourt Brace.
- Lillie, Patricia (1993). *When This Box Is Full*. New York: Greenwillow Books.
- Neitzel, Shirley (1989). *The Jacket I Wear in the Snow*. New York: Greenwillow Books.
- Numeroff, Laura J (1991). *If You Give a Moose a Muffin*. New York: HarperCollins.
- Waddell, Martin (1992). *Owl Babies*. Cambridge, MA: Candlewick Press.
- Wells, Rosemary (1997). *Noisy Nora*. New York: Dial Books for Young Readers.
- Wood, Don and Audrey (1984). *The Napping House*. San Diego: Harcourt Brace Jovanovich.

Creating Connections 6.3

Read *Bunnycakes* by Rosemary Wells (1992). In this story, Max uses his knowledge of written language to convey his message to the grocer.

In small groups, consider how Max's interactions with text align with an emergent perspective of literacy development.

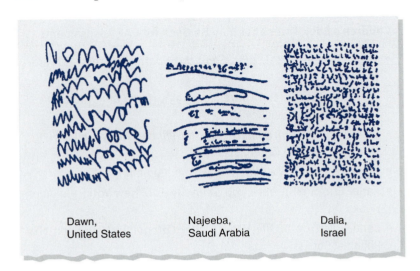

Dawn,
United States

Najeeba,
Saudi Arabia

Dalia,
Israel

Writing sample from Harste,
Burke, and Woodward.

1992) noticed and observed how Ruby, his older sister, was successful in writing her grocery list for the birthday cake, and subsequently represented his wish for red-hot marshmallow squirters, young writers integrate their knowledge of language and the world, and hypothesize how written language works.

Harste, Burke, and Woodward (1994) asked four-year-olds to write a story and to read what they had written. The children understood that language is functional and purposeful. Their writing also reflected the print environment in which they lived.

Young writers are problem-solvers and hypothesizers, as they represent meaning on paper. They consider the visual aspects of writing as they create letters and letter-like formations. There is a growing awareness about directionality, letter forms, common letter patterns, and spacing (Clay, 1975). Young writers also consider the symbolic nature of writing. They come to understand that letters represent specific sounds. Hypotheses are applied and reapplied as they become more sophisticated in their understandings of how individual letters are grouped to form words.

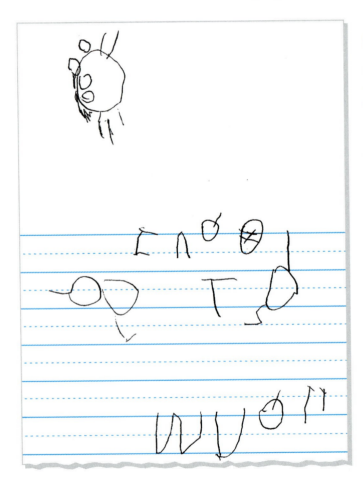

Random Marks.

Emergent spelling

In the last few decades, researchers and teachers discovered that spelling is developmental as young writers work toward more conventional forms in their writing (Bissex, 1980; Read, 1971; Temple, Nathan, Burris, & Temple, 1993). Temple, et al. along with Gentry (1982) and Bear and Templeton (1998) identified stages of spelling development. There are differences in how the stages are labeled. This chapter uses the terminology put forth by Temple and colleagues. Young children often exhibit the first two stages in preschool and home settings. The three final stages are usually apparent when children are in kindergarten and first grade.

RANDOM MARKS.   It is tempting to not give much notice to this early stage of writing development. There is not much to comment on in terms of convention or accuracy. However, just as babies learn to talk by voicing initial sounds, young writers begin their writing journey by experimenting with what happens when paper and pencil/crayon are brought together. These early marks do not appear to signify any particular intent. Later these scribbles and random marks become more purposeful as children begin to connect meaning to these marks.

tca

Prephonemic.

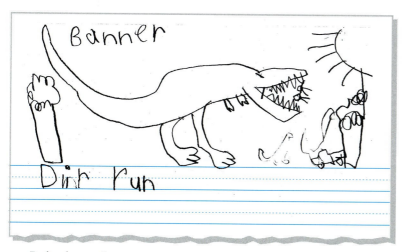

Banner

Dinr run

Early phonemic.

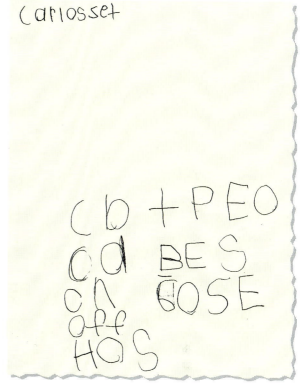

Prephonemic.

PREPHONEMIC. This stage of writing development is often characterized by a string of random letters that do not signify any known words. Often the string is in all capital letters. The young writer does not connect particular letters with sounds, but the letters represent complete thoughts and ideas to the young writer.

EARLY PHONEMIC. In this stage of spelling development, children begin to use letters to represent sounds in particular words. Words are usually comprised of one or two consonants (usually the beginning and ending sounds). In some cases there are three to six letters in the word and sometimes the same letters are rearranged to mean other words.

LETTER-NAMING. Children in this stage of spelling development usually include one or more vowels to the words they are writing. The addition of vowels indicates that children are beginning to discover that words include both consonants and vowels and that these phonemes progress from left to right in sequence.

Letter name.

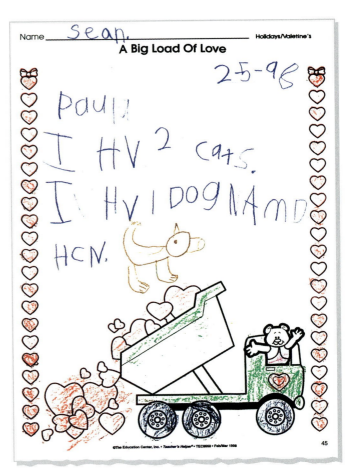

Transitional.

TRANSITIONAL. This is the final stage of spelling development. The child is able to accurately spell a majority of words, with a mixture of phonetic and conventional spellings. In this stage, young writers often over-generalize spelling pattern rules (e.g., *ed* as a past tense ending for all words; omitting the final *e* in words with a silent e ending).

These examples indicate a progression of spelling development. For many people, parents and teachers alike, prephonemic, early phonemic, and letter-naming stages have what is more commonly known as *inventive spelling*. "Children use their knowledge of English symbols and letters to 'invent' spellings for words they do not know how to spell. These spellings provide a window into children's growing comprehension of written language's organizational principles" (Griffith & Leavell, 1995, p. 84). Children are constantly hypothesizing about written language. They reorganize and refine their theories and apply this information about words in different ways. Their attempts at spelling conventional forms suggest that they are seeking to understand how words work. For additional discussions of inventive spelling and students' understandings of phonics and letter knowledge, see Chapter 7 and Chapter 9.

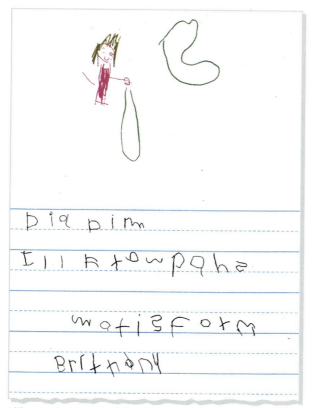

piq pim

Ill A tow pqha

watisform

Brithany

I like to play house. What is your cat's name?

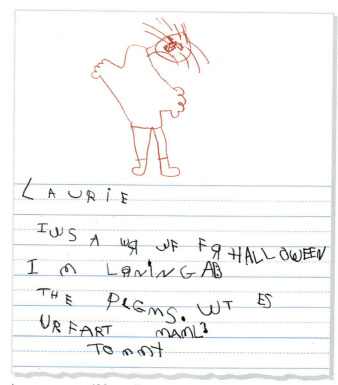

L A U R i E

I w S A w R uF Fq HALLOWEEN

I m LqniNGAB

THE PLGmS. WT ES

URFART manl?

Tommy

I was a werewolf for Halloween. I am learning about the Pilgrims. What is your favorite animal

4-21-98

Dear Mondy,

I liketo RID

MY BIK. C you

CN.

Ashley

Pen pal letters. I like to ride my bike. See you soon.

Ashley
    The weather is warming
up so we can start riding
bikes. I am so excited to
meet you next week. We have
been talking for such a long

time. I am very excited!
I hope that you have
a great week. I'll see you
soon. Your friend,
        Mandy

TMC 1900 © 1997 Teacher Created Materials

Emergent writing and meaning making

In addition to inventing spelling and learning about written language forms, emergent writers also begin to consider the purposes that written texts serve. Lists, stories, letters, and messages all carry different communicative purposes. As young writers interact with various genres and types of writing, they begin to approximate the conventions of the genre. For example, Brittney, Tommy, and Ashley received pen pal letters from students at a local college. The letters were read to them. One feature of a pen pal letter is the question. The letters contained many questions about pets, siblings, favorite colors, and so on. These young writers, responding to the pen pals, answered the questions and in some cases also asked their own questions. These approximations to conventional genre forms help children understand the communicative functions and formats of a variety of texts from early on in their literacy development (Chapman, 1994; Newkirk, 1989; Zecker, 1999). The pen pal letters involved children in the features of personal letters, and how genres of texts are used for communicative purposes.

Literacy and technology in early literacy settings

Young children interact with handheld devices that "sing and talk," books that play songs and sounds, and websites and software that "read" the words as the cursor moves across the screen. These practices are constantly changing as technology advances. New technology raises question such as:

- Do these materials support literacy learning, or do children only focus on the animation?
- Do young children develop vocabulary and build storybook language from hearing the words read to them, along with seeing the printed text?
- Are software programs for early readers nothing more than high-tech worksheets?

Concepts of screen

concepts of screen

An assessment to determine children's understandings of digital media.

Turbill (2001) identified the notion of ***concepts of screen***, when referring to technology literacy, as complementary to Clay's *concepts about print* for written language. (See Figure 6.2). Just as young readers begin to learn letters, sounds, and other concepts of print when learning to read, they learn to navigate electronic books and websites in similar ways.

As children engage with their favorite electronic books or websites, they begin to access the animation to support their meaning making and, as Turbill discovered, create more complex story lines. Similar to the role of illustrations in books, children use visual animations on the computer screen to construct understandings. For example, when Hayden interacted with *Tortoise and the Hare* (Living Books/Broderbund, 1993) he clicked on the Hare's newspaper, which caused the Hare to run out of his house, grab the paper, quickly read it, yell "Oh, no!", crumple up the paper, throw it down, and run back into his house. Hayden next clicked on the crumpled paper, and the Tortoise called to Hare, "Hey Hare, didn't you forget something?" These additional animations enabled Hayden to make sense of the character's motivations and actions.

Young children access digital media to support emergent literacy development.

Child's name: _____   **Date:**

Skills		Not yet	Can do with help	Beginning to do on own	Can do on own
Mouse	Move mouse with one hand Use index finger on left side of mouse Match mouse and cursor Use mouse to click in right place Use double–click to open icons Use click and drag				
Programs	Turn on computer Locate appropriate program on desktop Open program Close program				
Navigation	Recognize basic icons and their functions Cross to close Next page Next activity				
Directionality	Scroll Knows how to move to an activity				

Computer at Home	Yes	No
Programs child uses at home		

Confidence	Seems frightened of computer	Prepared to observe others and try	Quite confident	Very confident

Any other points of interest that you've noticed (e.g., helping others, very interested in activity).

FIGURE 6.2 Concepts of Screen Checklist (Turbill, 2001).

Electronic/talking books

talking books

Multimedia products that incorporate text, sound, and images to tell the story.

TECHNOLOGY LINK

http://www.kidsmartear-lylearning.org/EN/index.html

Kidsmart is a resource for teachers and parents to effectively use and integrate technology computers into the curriculum. The site offers strategies for computer use, teaching tips, and promising practices.

Talking books or electronic books, multimedia products in CD form, are common in early childhood settings. They employ a number of interactive and multimedia features such as animation, sound effects, music, and highlighted texts. Characters can come to life, passages are read and reread, and illustrations have special effects that produce visual and auditory responses. Labbo and Kuhn (2000) identify two categories of talking books: *considerate* and *inconsiderate*. Considerate talking books, software, and websites have animation that is integral to and supports the story, whereas inconsiderate materials have interactive features that disrupt the telling of the story. These interactive features do not contribute to the story line. Some talking books are designed to support children's reading abilities (Chera & Wood, 2003). For example, children may hear all of the text read, or individual words, or in some cases hear the word being sounded out (e.g., b-at). There may also be corresponding activities that emphasize various phonic features, such as rhymes and word families. Most electronic books have icons or animate particular features to signify an activity that the child can click on.

Labbo (2000) identified nine ways to support young children's interactions with electronic books:

- *Listen to the story*. Children should have opportunities to listen to, react to, and enjoy the story and multimedia features.
- *Read along with the story*. After multiple readings/viewings of the talking book, children can begin to read along with the digital text.
- *Echo read the story*. Children can read the text after the text has been read on the screen.
- *Look for familiar letters or words*. Children can begin to identify familiar letters or words that appear on the screen. They can have immediate feedback by listening to the word(s) being pronounced by the computer.
- *Select words with the same sound*. Talking books offer opportunities for children to develop phonemic awareness by identifying words with the same sound. They can scan the screen for particular letter–sound configurations.
- *Selecting rhyming words*. Similar to the work of identifying words with the same sound, children can focus on and highlight words on the computer screen that follow a particular word family (-at, -an, -ed, etc.)
- *Compare book and screen versions*. Children can compare book and screen versions of the story. In doing so, they notice differences in formatting, and text and illustration arrangements that may lead to more complex understandings of reading.
- *Talk about special effects and how screens work together*. Children should be invited to talk about the special features of digital texts. They can make inferences and connections throughout the story as links are pursued. These conversations are similar to considerations about illustrations in printed books.
- *Tell about similar stories*. Children can make connections to other stories they are familiar with, thereby supporting meaning making.

Children are highly engaged with many of these features, particularly the visual images and animation. Talking books are a great resource to incorporate into literacy learning events in preschools, daycare settings, and homes to encourage emergent literacy learning.

Literacy events and practices: Promoting emergent reading and writing

Preschool settings regularly include teachers and children reciting nursery rhymes, singing, storytelling, and story reading. The focus on literacy learning in these preschools has increased the prominence of these activities. Classroom libraries in preschools promote access to environmental print, writing centers, storybook reading, and play areas that foster and promote literacy learning.

> ### *Creating Connections 6.4*
> **Reviewing Software**
> Review software that is designed for young children. Consider these aspects when reviewing the materials:
> - Does the software encourage exploration, imagination, and problem solving?
> - Does the software reflect and build on what children already know?
> - Does the software maintain a child's interest?
> - Does the software involve many senses and include sound, music, and voice?
> - Is the software open-ended, with the child in control of the pace and the path?
> - Can children work the software on their own?

Noticing environmental print

Environmental print, the text found in the natural environment of children, plays an important role in developing children's knowledge about what literacy is and what it does (Miller, 1998). Environmental print includes billboards, store signs, street signs, labels, posters, and boxes. As active meaning makers, children make reasonable guesses as to what the various symbols and icons represent. They notice that these symbols and icons (print) are all around them, on boxes, newspaper, television, and clothing. Young children also begin to notice that adults use text in different ways.

environmental print

Text found in the environment (signs, posters, billboards, boxes).

Trey, sitting on his mother's lap at the computer, moves the mouse to icons that he recognizes. He knows to click on *Disney's Playhouse* to access different games and activities from some of his favorite Disney characters, like JoJo. In one activity, Trey is asked to match colors of sponges to pies thrown on the wall. Each correct match is recorded. When two-year-old Bethany passes by a local favorite fast food restaurant, she makes sense of the "golden arches." She doesn't recognize the arches as the letter "m," but rather that the arches represent to her a place to eat. These initial approximations and connections are the beginning steps into literacy. Researchers (Goodman & Altwerger, 1981, McGee & Purcell-Gates, 1997; McGee & Richgels 1996) noted, however, that for many young children, their recognition of the various words (e.g., cereal and soft drink names, signs) was significantly reduced when the word was presented without much contextual information (showing the child the word with the packaging or showing the word on a clean sheet of paper). This may indicate that children understand that print gives a message, even though they do not know what the print says (Kuby, Goodstadt-Killoran, Aldridge, & Kirkland, 1999).

Children come into the preschool and day care settings having discovered quite a bit about how language works in various settings. In the classroom, early childhood teachers can expand on young children's awareness and noticings of environmental print. They can use the print on items, such as Kleenex®, to point out various letters in context. Children can be encouraged to bring in items that have words to share during morning meeting or community circle time, such as cereal boxes, words on t-shirts, or paper products from fast food restaurants (i.e., cups, menus). This provides an opportunity to demonstrate how text is used in meaningful ways.

There are two significant benefits of using environmental print in the classroom. One benefit is that it begins to connect home and school literacy practices. When children bring in and share items that are a part of their home and community environments, teachers are able to foster connections and build background knowledge. Another benefit is that young children gain confidence in their literacy knowledge by recognizing logos and symbols. Experiencing success in identifying environmental print boosts children's self-esteem, and they begin to see themselves as readers.

Writing centers

Writing centers are becoming more prominent in preschools and day care settings. Early childhood teachers and researchers note that having such an area in the classroom promotes emergent writers' explorations with written text. The writing center provides opportunities for young children to think about themselves as writers. They will produce a variety of writing from random marks, to letter-like forms, invented and conventional spellings. The writing center is equipped with writing tools and materials to support the young writers' endeavors to make meaning on paper.

Storybook reading

Perhaps one of the most common and frequent experiences that young children have with literacy is *storybook reading*. Storybook reading remains a central piece in emergent literacy because it is well documented that children who learn to read prior to formal instruction have been read to regularly by parents and other adults (Durkin, 1966; Sulzby & Teale, 1991). Storybook reading takes place in a number of settings, from bedtime rituals, to day care centers and preschools, to local library story hours. This literacy event is particularly powerful because it provides an authentic, meaningful, and interesting context for young children as they acquire literacy knowledge. During storybook reading, young children learn how to use books—how to move from front to back, left to right. They also learn about language—new vocabulary words, new meanings, and new forms. From a review of research, Sulzy and Teale (1991) describe four literacy knowledge areas that storybook reading facilitates:

Writing Center Materials

- Variety of paper
Examples: lined, unlined, colored, white, paper stapled together as a book, memo pads, notebooks, envelopes

- Lists of the children's names

- Chalk and chalkboards

- Magnetic board and letters

- Flannel board

- Letter tiles and blocks

- Alphabet chart

- Letter and picture stamps and ink pads

- Writing tools
Examples: pencils, colored pencils, markers, crayons, chalk, magnetic boards and letters, letter stamps, inkpads

- Hole punch and yarn or ribbon for binding "books" made with hole-punch pages

- Stapler

- Glue, paste, and tape

- Scissors

- Pencil sharpener

- Book of wallpaper samples for making covers for homemade "books"

- Old magazines, catalogs, pictures, and postcards

---

storybook reading

A literacy event that usually involves an adult or older child reading to a younger child.

- Labeling and commenting on items in illustrations
- Weaving an oral recount of the pictures
- Creating a story with appropriate rhythm and word order of written language
- Attending to and decoding written text

To illustrate the ways in which these four aspects of storybook reading occur, consider how Tiana, age 4, listens to *Bunny Party* (Wells, 2003) during an afternoon at her day care center. In the story, Ruby invites a number of her stuffed animals and dolls as guests, to Grandma's birthday party. Max wants to bring his own guests and while Ruby isn't looking, sits them at the table as well. Throughout the book there are a number of opportunities to count the guests and place settings. As Tiana listens to the story, she is asked to count along with Ruby. Tiana also identifies the various guests, on the page, such as Mr. and Mrs. Quack and Ear Splitting Siren. Tiana's interaction with this text is a common experience in her life. She regularly identifies and labels items on the pages. On many occasions, Tiana recounts a slightly different version than what is on the page. Her experiences with text, including this event, are scaffolded opportunities to engage with printed text.

The scaffolded routines that adults (mostly parents and preschool teachers) provide during storybook reading play an invaluable role in supporting literacy development and knowledge for young readers. As part of this scaffolding, adults often:

- Ask open-ended questions
- Follow children's responses with additional questions
- Repeat and expand on what children say
- Offer praise and encouragement when children participate
- Incorporate verbal and nonverbal (pointing and tracking) references to print
- Follow children's interests

These strategies for interacting with texts encourage children's active participation in storybook reading. Young readers are exposed to explicit guidance of emergent literacy knowledge in highly contextualized, familiar, and meaningful contexts.

Storybook reading as a cultural practice

While there is considerable value in storybook reading for emergent literacy users, it is important to comment on storybook reading as a cultural practice. Storybook reading is a social process that is scaffolded by the parent and the family in ways that reflect particular cultural orientations (Gallas, 1997). This literacy practice, and the corresponding research that documents its effectiveness, usually occur in middle-class homes (Heath, 1983; Purcell-Gates, 1995; Anderson, 1995). Educators have taken these experiences and replicated them in school settings. Yet, for many children, storybook reading is virtually a nonexistent activity in the home. It is a literacy event that only happens in school settings. This does not mean that children who do not have storybook reading as a cultural practice are deficient. There are many other literacy events (reading religious texts, paying bills, reading labels, watching *Sesame Street*, writing notes and shopping lists, etc.) that they observe and participate in.

Preschool teachers working with children that have limited storybook reading in their repertoire of experiences should recognize and value these other literacies. Teachers can connect these experiences to the stories selected for read aloud, as well as encourage children to interact with the text through conversations, discussions, puppets, and flannel storyboards.

Creating Connections 6.5

What experiences do you have reading aloud to young children? What observations have you made as they interact with text?

Share your insights with classmates.

Sociodramatic play settings

Preschool settings often have corners of the room set up to encourage imaginative play. These play centers include grocery stores, post offices, restaurants, veterinary offices, stores, and kitchens. When the centers are infused with literacy-related props, this play can enrich young children's understandings of the functional uses of literacy. Neuman and Roskos (1990) suggest that literacy-rich play centers can make a difference in young children's literacy behaviors and understandings. These centers can become important contexts for exploration and discovery of how literacy functions in everyday experiences. Play activity creates a variety of opportunities (explicit and implicit) for children to use oral and written language as they see it practiced in daily contexts (Roskos & Christie, 2000).

Literacy-enriched play centers include a number of props that provide a frame of reference and concrete cues for how literacy functions in that particular setting. (See Table 6.4 for a list of possible props.) For example, Kadin's preschool classroom has an office center complete with office materials (paper, pencils, note cards, file folders, paperclips, tape, post-it notes, telephone, store catalogues, computer, and printer). The children in this class play in the office center as they recreate and imagine the types of jobs their parents and others have. Kadin and Josh are busy one morning creating sale signs and lists for the pretend clothes and shoes that are on sale, as well as ordering clothes from a catalogue. (Kadin's mother is a district manager for a clothing store.) Kadin answered the phone and told his playmate that the store was not open— that they had to count all the clothes (take inventory). This small incident, which lasted a brief five minutes during the morning routine, suggests that Kadin and Josh were able to use literacy to achieve their desired outcomes.

With access to literacy props and with occasional encouragement from adults in the classroom, children in Kadin's preschool explore authentic reasons for reading and writing, while learning the conventions and forms that compose written language. They begin to uncover the mysteries of printed language. Young children draw upon their own background knowledge and experiences to make sense of literacy knowledge in individual ways (Rybczynski & Troy, 1995). Neuman and Roskos (1991) identified a number of props that may be included in play centers in preschool classrooms.

Language experience approach stories (LEA) and digital language experience approach (D-LEA)

The ***Language Experience Approach (LEA)***, a strategy described by Van Allen (1976) and Stauffer (1980), provides young literacy users with relevant opportunities to develop literacy knowledge. A language experience approach allows children to tell their stories and have someone write those stories for them. Then the child will be able to read his or her own work. LEA stories can be from children's own experiences or recounts of classroom events, such as a field trip or special event. In most early childhood classrooms, the teacher selects an event, idea, object, or piece of literature to use as a springboard for the story. The child talks and draws about the event or idea. The teacher writes the student's dictation and rereads the sen-

Language Experience Approach

A strategy whereby the teacher writes the story as a child tells it. The story is then read by the teacher and child.

TABLE 6.4
Props for Literacy-Enriched Play Centers

Play Center	Literacy Props
Kitchen/Grocery Store	Cookbooks
	Blank recipe cards
	Refrigerator magnets
	Grocery store ads and flyers
	Coupons
	Message board
	Old calendars
	Labels
	Recipes
	Play money
Office	Post-it notes
	Clipboards
	Stapler/scissors (used with adult presence)
	Clips
	Printer paper
	Various labels
	Note cards
	Business cards
	Appointment books/calendars
	File folders
	Message pads
	Play money
	Signs (open/closed)
Post office	Stationery
	Stamp pads, stamps, stickers
	Envelopes
	Note cards
	Mailbox
	Mailing forms
	Tote bag
	Labels
	Paper clips
	Signs (open/closed)

Source: Adapted from Neuman & Roskos, 1991.

tences to make sure the idea is captured accurately. The teacher then reads the story aloud, and the student reads alongside the teacher. Then the student reads the story by herself. There may be follow-up to the language experience story, such as identifying particular words or phrases or drawing pictures to accompany the text.

Ms. Thea, a bilingual preschool teacher, asks the nine children (six of them are primarily Spanish speakers) to think about all the activities they do while in school. The children talked about the morning routine of changing the calendar dates, making puppets, learning to count, painting, playing, and going to the zoo. Ms. Thea typed out what each child said. Each child was then asked to draw a picture to go with the sentence. After the children drew their pictures, she put the pages together as a class book and made it available for the children in the class library. See Figure 6.3 for sample class pages.

In a ***Digital Language Experience Approach (D-LEA)***, students and teachers use digital pictures and writing software to compose digital language

Digital Language Experience Approach

Children use digital media to compose language experience stories.

Trabajamos letres.

We learn reading.

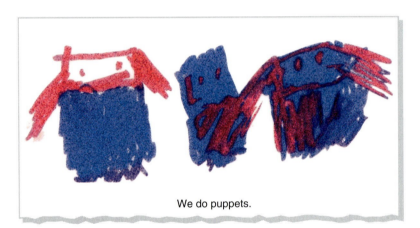

We do puppets.

Hacemos el calendario.

FIGURE 6.3 Sample pages from class book.

experience stories. Using digital cameras allows children to take photographs of significant items, experiences, or places at the school or other common setting. These photographs serve as memory links to a child's experience, as well as catalysts for descriptive language. With publishing software, children can manipulate the digital images and write and revise on the spot. The digital books are easy to share across children and classrooms. Children love to see photographs of themselves and their friends. As the photographs are shared, children can create their own stories to be composed on the computer. These multimedia interactions encourage children to develop multiple modalities for communicating.

Language experience stories are a bridge to more formal experiences with literacy. Children begin to learn that what they experience can be verbalized, written down, and read by others and themselves. As children become more comfortable with LEA and D-LEA stories, they are encouraged to write in journals about their shared experiences. These independent writing events (journals, LEA stories, and so on) demonstrate children's understandings of these writing process, as well as their knowledge and experiences.

Invitation for the classroom

Creating a D-LEA

Labbo, Eakle, and Montero (2002) offer a series of steps to take when creating D-LEA stories.

Setting up the Experience

1. The teacher or the teacher and student(s) together select a stimulus experience (teacher offers suggestions, scouts out a location, discusses expectations for students, gathers materials, decides the duration of the activity, etc.).

2. Teacher and students make decisions about picture taking:
   - Who will direct photographing (when and which activities).
   - The type of photographs that will be taken (candid or posed).
   - The number of photographs to be taken.

Photographing the Experience

3. Children engage in the stimulus activity.

4. Teacher photographs children engaging in the stimulus activity, using a digital camera.

Composing a Multimedia Story or Photo Essay

5. Children use digital photographs to prepare for composing by
   - Importing photos into creativity software.
   - Viewing photographs and recalling the stimulus experience.
   - Discussing and selecting photographs that may best tell the story.
   - Arranging photographs in sequence or story board.

6. Children compose a story about the stimulus experience:
   - Teacher types student dictation for each photograph (or student types with teacher support).
   - Teacher (or computer voice synthesizer, if available) reads the text.
   - Children decide if ideas are stated appropriately; if not, revisions are made on screen and on the spot.
   - As an optional extension, children include media effects to enhance the story (music, sound effects, animation).
   - Children may record their voices reading the story.

Engaging in Follow-up Activities

7. Children interact with the story for additional literacy learning:
   - Multimedia interactions—children may read chorally with the multimedia story on screen, echo read, listen to the story read aloud by different voice synthesizer characters, etc.
   - Teacher may make print-outs for each student to encourage reading at the word level and to promote fluency.
   - Stories may be saved on the computer or in print form as student or class sets of stories for review or as reading practice materials.

In Closing

Young children actively construct meaning as they encounter and participate in literacy events and experiences. The past 50 years or so has seen a significant shift in how educators and researchers think about literacy development for the very young. While policies and federal mandates (*Early Reading First*) continue to emphasize a readiness perspective in learning to read and write, most preschool and childcare teachers recognize that children are learning literate behaviors without formal instruction. The literacy environment in the home, preschool, or childcare setting plays a significant role in the ways in which young children access literacy.

This chapter identified key aspects of literacy development that are essential to supporting reading and writing in the early years. Early literacy knowledge includes oral language development, print knowledge, alphabet knowledge, phonological/phonemic awareness, and inventive spelling. Through language play, writing centers, and socio-dramatic play centers, children experience literacy practices and events in authentic and meaningful ways. They come to realize how literacy is used in different settings as well as how they might make sense of written language.

Additionally, this chapter addressed the increasing role that electronic media and technology play in early literacy development. Turbill's "Concepts of Screen" was discussed as one avenue for better understanding the knowledge that young children have in relation to using technology, namely computers. Characteristics of talking books were noted, as well as how to best incorporate technology into the early childhood setting.

Terms to Remember

Concepts about print *(156)*

Concepts of screen *(166)*

Concepts of words *(156)*

Digital Language Experience
    Approach *(173)*

Emergent literacy *(148)*

Environmental print *(169)*

Experience view *(147)*

Language Experience Approach *(172)*

Maturation view *(147)*

Reading readiness *(147)*

Storybook reading *(170)*

Talking books *(168)*

Resources for More Information

Bear, D. R., & Barone, D. (1998). *Developing literacy: An integrated approach to assessment and instruction.* Boston: Houghton Mifflin Co.

Burns, Griffin, & Snow (1999). *Starting out right: A guide to promoting children's reading success.*

Harste, J. C., Woodward, V. A., & Burke, C. L. (1984). Language stories & literacy lessons. Portsmouth, NH: Heinemann Educational Books.

McGee, L. M., & Richgels, D. J. (1996). *Literacy's beginnings: Supporting young readers and writers.* Boston: Allyn and Bacon.

Labbo, L. D., Eakle, A. J., & Montero, M. K. (May, 2002). Digital language experience approach: Using digital photographs and software as a language experience approach innovation. *Reading Online,* 5(8). Available http://www.reading online.org/electronic/elec_index.asp?HREF=labbo2/index.html.

Whitmore, K. F., P. Martens, Y. Goodman, & G. Owocki. 2005. Remembering critical lessons in early literacy research: Developing literacy in young children. *Language Arts* 82: 296–307.

Questions for Further Reflection

- As you reflect on the language and literacy stories presented throughout the chapter, what decisions will you make in setting up a preschool environment?

- In what ways do the theories underlying an emergent literacy perspective align with the guiding principles in Chapter 1?

Beginning Readers and Writers

Ms. Simon's Class Reads *There Was an Old Lady Who Swallowed a Fly*

"Ms. Simon! Is a horse! The old lady, she swallow da horse and ehhh, she die!," kindergarten student and English Language Learner (ELL) Jose tells me with wide eyes as we walk toward two horses standing in a grassy field behind our school. As Jose and six other ELL kindergarten students gaze at the horses, they begin to recount the story we had been reading in class for the past two weeks, *There Was An Old Lady Who Swallowed a Fly* by Sims Talback (1997).

For an observer watching this short interaction between a teacher and a kindergarten student in the beginning stages of English proficiency, they might think that this student is merely repeating short phrases and using fragmented English. What this observer might fail to see, however, is the tremendous strides each student has made since beginning kindergarten. Not only have the students become more proficient in English, they also learned to make connections between what they learned in the classroom—in this case, the Sims Talback tale—and what they experienced in real life.

For the past two weeks, my students listened to, read along with me, and enjoyed the highly predictable and patterned text in *There Was An Old Lady Who Swallowed a Fly*. I introduced the story by reading it as a read aloud to the class. We laughed and enjoyed the antics of the old lady as she swallowed various animals.

I then reintroduced the story to a small group during a shared reading event. Children gathered around the big book version, and as I read, they quickly caught on to the phrase, "I don't know why she swallowed a fly, perhaps she'll die." To help students make sense of the words, we revisited this phrase and I asked students pick out the words that rhymed. Several students shouted, "fly, why!" I asked them to clap when they said the words "fly" and "why" so that they would have a physical response to the rhyming patterns of these words. Children learn through various modalities, so a physical response can help them process the new words. I then wrote the two words on cards, placed the cards on our hanging word chart, and re-read them. Focusing on rhyming words helps beginning readers to notice word patterns. Awareness of word patterns helps beginning readers decode new words. Next, I asked the students if they could think of any words that rhyme with *fly* and *why*. Laura shouted, "die!," which I added to the chart. We talked about how *fly, die*, and *why* rhyme, but that not all

rhyming words have the same ending letters. The students then started to create nonsense words that rhymed with why, die, and fly. By the end of our exploration, we added "tie," "try," and "my" to our list of words on the hanging chart. With the students more comfortable with rhyming, I continued to read the story with students finding other words that rhymed. As part of our shared reading for the day, students also searched the classroom looking for words that rhymed with those on the hanging chart.

Following the shared reading event, students continued to work with the story in their writing journals. In doing so, I observed the multiple ways the students demonstrated their knowledge of language. Some students drew pictures of the old lady and the animals; others constructed their own short phrases and sentences about favorite parts of the story; while others retold the entire story. Students used words from the hanging word chart, the word wall, picture dictionaries, the book, as well as how they thought words were spelled. Laura, for example, is comfortable with reading and writing. She wrote, "I Like spider, fly, bird, cat, dog, cow, horse," and drew pictures of the animals listed. Marco wrote, "There was a old lady who swallowed a fly" and drew a detailed picture of an old lady. Other students wrote one or two words for their stories. Carlos drew a horse and a fly, and wrote "Hors" for his story.

The next day, these students shared their work with each other using a microphone in the Sharing Chair. The Sharing Chair provides opportunities for students to work on oral language development. When sharing, they expanded upon their writing, explaining their pictures and often retelling the story.

The culminating activity involved students using art to demonstrate their understanding of the story. They created an old lady with a Ziploc bag for a stomach and drew,

I wonder. . .

- In what ways has this teacher demonstrated to students that literacy is a socially constructed event?

- What literacy events does Ms. Simon use to promote reading and writing skills?

- How does a reading book such as *There Was an Old Lady Who Swallowed a Fly,* writing in notebooks, and sharing oral retellings of the stories, promote meaningful reading experiences for students?

- How do books with predictable patterns in language (e.g, "There was an old lady who swallowed a fly, perhaps she'll die") support beginning readers?

- Are there personal experiences and memories that you recall that are similar to Ms. Simon's teaching? Why do you think you recall these particular moments?

179

Carlos' response (Horse)

Laura's response (I like spider, fly, bird, cat, dog, cow, horse)

cut out, and added each animal that she ate as they retold the story. This activity helped these beginning readers and writers practice new vocabulary, show knowledge of story sequencing, and, above all, enjoy the story.

Now standing outside in the early morning cold, I look at Jose and the other students' excited faces as they retell the story with a genuine horse in front of them, and realize that this experience connects text with real life. Through their retellings, writing samples, drawings, and connections made as we view the horses in front of us, I am able to glean insights into what my next steps might be for each student. I use my kidwatching observations and notes as assessment tools. And when we go back inside, the students ask again, as they do every day, "Ms. Simon, can we read the Old Lady?, Please! Please!" What more can you ask as a teacher of reading and literacy?

Chapter Overview

Early primary classrooms are full of literacy events and activities—read alouds, shared reading, working with words, journal writing—that demonstrate literacy as a socially constructed enterprise. As illustrated in Ms. Simon's classroom, children learn to read and write when they interact with texts and each other. With attention on beginning reading playing a significant role in our educational policy and practices (e.g., No Child Left Behind, National Reading Panel, Early Reading First), it is important that teachers know and become comfortable with the strategies and techniques for promoting literacy in young children. Guiding questions for this chapter include:

- What are some important concepts of beginning literacy development and instruction?
- How do reading practices, such as code breaking, text meaning, text use, and critical practices serve as a foundation of an effective literacy program in early primary grades?
- How do you set up a reader/writer workshop in primary grade classrooms?
- How do instructional decision making and strategies link to academic standards?

Guiding principles to promote beginning reading and writing

Children enter primary grades with an array of reading and writing experiences. Some children begin kindergarten with a number of early literacy experiences and understandings, such as how to hold a book, listen to stories, write their names, and recognize letters. Others are learning these skills for the first time. Teachers in early primary classrooms should not only be sensitive to such individual differences in their students, but should also know how to foster literacy development in all of their students. In 1998, a joint position statement put forth by the International Reading Association (IRA) and National Association for the Education of Young Children (NAEYC) recognizes the individual nature of children's development in learning to read:

> Knowledge of the forms and functions of print serves as a foundation from which children become increasingly sensitive to letter shapes, names, sounds, and words. However, not all children typically come to kindergarten with similar levels of knowledge about printed language. Estimating where each child is developmentally and building on that base, a key feature of all good teaching, is particularly important for the kindergarten teacher. Instruction will need to be adapted to account for children's differences. . . .(1998, p. 203)

So how do teachers effectively account for children's differences and promote literacy development in all students? In what ways does Ms. Simon, the teacher in the opening vignette, respond to the different academic and linguistic needs of students, such as Jose, Marco, and Carlos? How is she able to orchestrate her literacy program so that meaning is made not only in the context of the story, but also outside the classroom walls? Many primary teachers promote reading and writing by following the literacy plan developed by the IRA and NAEYC. The three phases most applicable for early literacy classrooms are Phase 2: Experimental reading and writing; Phase 3: Early reading and writing; and Phase 4: Transitional reading and writing (see pages 182–183).

In primary grades (kindergarten, first, and second) children are ready to extend their literacy knowledge. Teachers can use the information contained in these phases to develop their own plans and goals for what they want to accomplish in the classroom. To do this, Teale and Yokota (2000) recomend that teachers:

- Provide learning opportunities that accommodate the wide range of experiences children bring to the classroom.
- Emphasize comprehension instruction from the beginning, not only after children have learned to decode written text.
- Teach a multifaceted word study program—vocabulary development, decoding, sight word recognition, and spelling.
- Emphasize writing as an integral part of the reading process.
- Recognize that fluency contributes to becoming a capable reader by supporting reading comprehension.
- Use authentic text, such as extended fiction picture books, informational books, magazines, and other appropriate texts.

Phase 2: Experimental Reading and Writing

In **kindergarten**, children develop basic concepts of print and begin to engage in and experiment with reading and writing.

Kindergartners Enjoy:	To Promote Literacy, Teachers Can:	Examples of Literacy Engagements for the Classroom:
• Being read to	• Read interesting and conceptually rich stories	• Read aloud
• Using descriptive language to explain and explore	• Encourage children to talk about life experiences and reading and writing experiences	• Literature discussion
• Recognizing letters and letter–sound matches	• Provide many opportunities for children to explore and identify sound–symbol relationships in meaningful contexts	• Shared reading events • Guided reading • Independent reading
• Showing familiarity with rhyming and beginning sounds	• Help children to segment spoken words into individual sounds and blend the sounds into whole words	• Read poems • Sing songs
• Understanding left-to-right and top-to bottom-orientation and familiar concepts of print	• Create a literacy-rich environment for children to engage independently in reading and writing	• Shared reading events • Independent reading
• Matching spoken words with written words	• Provide daily opportunities for children to write and read	• Shared reading • Writing
• Beginning to write letters of the alphabet and some high frequency words	• Help children build a sight vocabulary	• Guided reading • Writing

Phase 3: Early Reading and Writing

In the **first grade**, children begin to read simple stories and can write about a topic that is meaningful to them.

First Graders Enjoy	To Promote Literacy, Teachers Can:	Examples of Literacy Engagements for the Classroom
• Reading and retelling stories	• Give children opportunities for independent reading and writing practice	• Independent reading
• Using strategies (rereading, predicting, questioning, contextualizing) when comprehension breaks down	• Offer and demonstrate strategies to use when a child does not understand	• Mini-lessons • Guided reading
• Reading out loud with reasonable fluency	• Support the development of vocabulary by reading daily to the children, transcribing their language, and selecting materials that expand children's knowledge and language development	• Read aloud • Independent reading

• Using letter–sound associations, word parts, and context to identify new words	• Model strategies and provide practice for identifying unknown words	• Shared reading • Guided reading
• Identifying an increasing number of words by sight	• Help children build lists of commonly used words from their writing and reading	• Guided reading • Writing
• Sounding out and representing all substantial sounds in spelling a word	• Introduce new words and teach strategies for learning to spell	• Mini-lessons • Writing
• Writing about topics that are personally meaningful	• Read, write, and discuss a range of different text types (poems, informational books)	• Writing • Literature discussion

Phase 4: Transitional Reading and Writing

In **second grade**, children begin to read more fluently and write various text forms using simple and more complex sentences.

Second Graders	To Promote Literacy, Teachers Can:	Examples of Literacy Engagements for the Classroom
• Read with greater fluency	• Ensure that children read a range of texts for a variety of purposes	• Independent reading • Choral reading • Reader's theater
• Use strategies more efficiently (rereading, questioning, and so on) when comprehension breaks down	• Ensure that children read a range of texts for a variety of purposes • Create a climate that fosters analytic, evaluative, and reflective thinking	• Mini-lessons • Reading conferences • Literature discussion • Response logs
• Identify an increasing number of words by sight	• Create a climate that fosters analytic, evaluative, and reflective thinking	• Mini-lessons • Reading conferences
• Use word identification strategies with greater facility to unlock unknown words	• Create a climate that fosters analytic, evaluative, and reflective thinking	• Mini-lessons • Reading conferences
• Write about a range of topics to suit different audiences	• Teach children to write in multiple forms (stories, information, poems)	• Writer's workshop • Mini-lessons • Writing conferences
• Use common letter patterns and critical features to spell words	• Teach strategies for spelling new and difficult words	• Writer's workshop • Mini-lessons • Writing conferences
• Punctuate simple sentences correctly and proofread their own work	• Teach revising, editing, and proofreading skills	• Writer's workshop
• Spend time reading daily and use reading to research topics	• Model enjoyment of reading • Support a child's interest with reading materials and references	• Read aloud • Independent reading • Literature discussions • Focus studies

Exploring beginning reading through the four-resource model

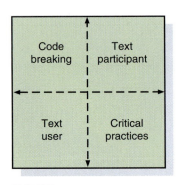

FIGURE 7.1 Four-resource model.

Young children learn to read using the four practices identified in Luke and Freebody's (1997) four-resource model—code breaking, text meaning, text use, and critical practices. The integrated nature of these practices is illustrated in Figure 7.1. The dotted line between the practices indicates that readers move in and out of the practices as they learn to read in a productive and efficient manner.

To effectively discuss the four-resource model of reading for beginning readers, each practice is described with a number of strategies and invitations that illustrate the practice. The code-breaking practice is highlighted in this chapter. Beginning readers often spend a greater amount of time on code breaking than do more accomplished readers. This is not to say, however, that a beginning reading program should only focus on code breaking. Rather, a beginning reading program must incorporate all four reading practices in order for children to become proficient readers.

Code breaking to exemplify how words work

code breaking practice

The focus is on the letter–sound relationship and the structure of words.

The **code breaking practice** involves recognizing and using the alphabet, sounds in words, spelling, and conventions and patterns of sentence structure and text. When a beginning reader is faced with an unfamiliar word, he or she will need to "break" its code. In code breaking, the nature and structure of a word is studied. For example, readers can attend to the beginning sounds or ending sounds. Accurately decoding words with some level of automaticity and fluency plays an important role in the reading process.

prescriptive approach

An approach to literacy instruction that teaches code breaking and other skills through an explicit and systematic manner with controlled texts.

The best way to teach code-breaking practices remains a topic of discussion. As discussed in previous chapters (namely Chapters 4 and 5), there are essentially two competing perspectives: the prescriptive approach and the integrated approach. The **prescriptive approach** requires that teachers teach code breaking skills in an intensive and systematic manner. Very often this requires a commercially produced reading program that uses materials designed specifically to teach decoding skills. Beginning readers hone their code-breaking skills by reading text that has a limited number of letter–sound configurations (mostly single syllable words like *Peg, Meg, mop, top*) and completing worksheets that focus on a particular letter or group of letters. Explicit instruction in phonics is a part of the prescriptive approach to teaching reading.

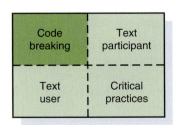

In contrast, an ***integrated approach*** teaches code breaking through a less systematic and explicit focus. Rather than using text with a limited and controlled vocabulary, teachers use authentic pieces of literature, such as *Brown Bear, Brown Bear* (Martin, 1992), *Dinnertime* (Pieńkowski, 1981) or *In the Tall, Tall, Grass* (Fleming, 1991). These texts not only have a predicable language pattern to support beginning readers, but there is a richness and authenticity in the language. During shared reading events and strategy lessons in a reader/writer workshop, the teacher encourages students to notice and observe language and word structures and patterns as they occur in the text.

integrated approach

Code breaking is taught by using authentic pieces of literature.

As Table 7.1 illustrates, Dahl, Scharer, Lawson, and Grogan (2001) show differences between code-breaking strategies taught in a more traditional, isolated fashion (the prescriptive approach) and code breaking strategies taught in context (the integrated approach).

After a year in kindergarten, most children can generate rhymes, identify syllables, and segment words into syllables (Stanovich, Cunningham, & Cramer, 1984; Yopp, 1988). By the end of first grade, most children can count and segment, delete or change phonemes at the beginning of one-, two-, or three-phoneme words (Pratt & Brady, 1988). To facilitate this understanding of code breaking, teachers often incorporate language play and rhymes, word families, alphabet knowledge, and high-frequency words into their reading curriculum.

TABLE 7.1

Comparing Code Breaking Strategies

Code Breaking from a Traditional View (prescriptive approach)	Code Breaking in Context (integrated approach)
Code breaking is taught as practice in isolation. It is a stand-alone part of the curriculum.	Code breaking instruction is integrated into the larger reading program. Children do not learn to break the code as an end goal, but rather instruction is embedded within ongoing literacy events.
Code breaking is seen as a prerequisite to reading and writing.	Code breaking knowledge is not seen as a prerequisite to reading and writing but as an instrumental component of the process.
Systematic instruction presents all letter–sound relations in a preset sequence.	Code breaking instruction involves teacher decision making. Instruction is based on the student learning and developmental needs.
Learning to code break relates to the sequence of skills taught by the teacher.	Learning to code break comes from instruction and independent exploration.

Source: Dahl, Scharer, Lawson, and Grogan (2001). Rethinking phonics: Making the best teaching decisions. Portsmouth, NH: Heinemann.

TECHNOLOGY LINK

http://teacher.scholastic.
com/products/instructor/
Octo4_oldlady.htm

Hannah Trieweilery pro-
vides teachers with new
ideas in using the rhyme
"There was an old lady. . ."
to teach early readers.
There is also a list of alternative versions of the
rhyme, such as *There Was
an Old Lady Who Swal-
lowed a Pie* and *There Was
an Old Lady Who Swal-
lowed a Trout.*

phonemic blending

Ability to articulate the
sounds of the word
together.

phonemic segmentation

Ability to segment a word
into the individual sounds
or phonemes.

LANGUAGE PLAY AND RHYMES.   Language play emphasizes a sense of playfulness about language. When children make up words and sing silly rhymes, they are experimenting with different sounds. As they isolate and blend sounds they discover which sounds, when combined, create nonsense words, and which sounds, when combined create known words. Ms. Simon used language play as part of her instructional activities for *There Was an Old Lady Who Swallowed a Fly.* She invited her students to construct words and nonsense words that rhyme with some of the words in the text. Language play supported her English Language Learners, as well as those students who have English as their primary language. Poems, rhymes, and songs offer perfect opportunities for beginning readers to play with language.

In Ms. Harvey's kindergarten and first grade classroom, her students were busy listening to the rhythm of language and sound patterns in poems from *A Rumpus of Rhymes* (Katz, 2001). As the children listened to the phrase "Bebop beetles boogie to the beat" from the poem "Summer Jazz," they discovered how alliteration contributes to the rhythm and sound of the poem. Ms. Harvey asked these beginning readers what they noticed about the words in that particular refrain. Shanequa commented, "B's. The words all have b's." Ms. Harvey then asked, "Where do we see all the b's"? Monique, with her hand raised wildly, shouts out "at the beginning!" Ms. Harvey confirmed that almost all the words in the phrase begin with the letter "b," but that not all of them do. She continued by asking Ryan to circle all the words in the phrase that start with the letter "b." Ryan accurately circled all the "b" words. The conversation then moved to talking about why the poet did this, and how the poem has a rhythmic style to it.

Blending and *segmenting* are two other aspects that are important to consider when working with code breaking practices in primary grades. **Phonemic blending** is being able to articulate the sounds of a word together in order as in spoken language (Ericson & Juliebo, 1998). For example, the teacher may ask children to listen carefully to a list of words she says slowly and deliberately. Each word is elongated (e.g., c-ar, f-ish, s-eal). Children put the sounds together to say the word (car, fish, seal).

Phonemic segmentation is the ability to segment or break up words into individual sounds. Teachers will have children elongate the word so that they can hear all of the sounds in a particular word. When children first begin to study words, they will often represent words by using a single letter in their writing. As children become more acquainted with isolating and blending sounds in words, they begin to recognize that many words—*cat, bat, mat, rat, sat,* and *fat,* for example—have a number of the same sounds in the same location. This awareness supports the child's development toward greater competency in code breaking skills.

In another kindergarten classroom, Ms. Patterson has just finished reading *Rub-a-Dub Sub* (Ashman, 2003). This is a rhyming book that showcases various sea creatures. Ms. Patterson asks her students to consider what they noticed about word patterns and sound relationships after reading this text.

Young students engaged in code breaking practices.

- How are the words *pink* and *ink* different?
- What word did you hear that rhymes with *seal*?
- What sound is added to *eel* to make it *seal*?
- What word did you hear that rhymes with *blimp*?
- How are *claw* and *jaw* alike? How are they different?

These questions focus the children's attention on the individual phonemes, as well as onsets and rimes.

WORD FAMILIES. *Word families* are words that share the same rime pattern (vowel + ending sound sequence). Word families enable beginning readers to recognize and decode a large number of words because the only change is the initial onset (letters that precede the vowel). It is possible to construct nearly 500 words by using the 37 most common rime patterns.

word families
Words that share the same rime pattern.

Invitation for the classroom

Picture Puzzles to Develop Blending and Segmenting

Create a number of different picture puzzles by cutting the picture into the requisite number of syllables of the object in the picture (e.g., highchair—two pieces, carrot—two pieces, elephant—three pieces).

Ask students to say each syllable while they point to each part of the picture (segmenting) and then blend the syllables as they put together the puzzle (blending).

This invitation can also be used when introducing sound segmentation and blending. Cut a picture of a dog in three pieces and have the children practice segmenting and blending the sounds d-o-g- as they put together the puzzle.

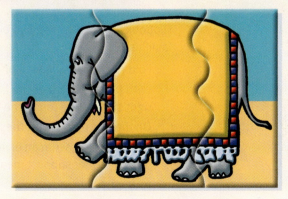

Mia's list of words for the -ice rime pattern.

TABLE 7.2
Most Common Rime Patterns in the English Language

-ack	-ank	-est	-ill	-ock	-ump
-ain	-ap	-ell	-in	-oke	-unk
-ake	-ash	-est	-ine	-op	
-ale	-at	-ice	-ing	-ot	
-all	-ate	-ick	-ink	-ore	
-ame	-aw	-ide	-ip	-uck	
-an	-ay	-ight	-ir	-ug	

When young children engage in language play, they often manipulate onset and rimes. For example, when second grader Mia writes a list of words with the rime pattern "ice," she creates the list shown on the left.

From this list, she may then begin to think about words that sound like *ice* but are in fact spelled differently, like her friend's name *Bryce*. Other words are a bit trickier for Mia to understand because the rime pattern sounds similar but does not use the same letters, such as -ite in the word bite and -ight in the word *fight*.

ALPHABET KNOWLEDGE. Many children enter kindergarten able to recognize and name letters of the alphabet; most often the letters are in their name. Some children, depending on the amount of reading experience they have had prior to kindergarten, will recognize even more letters. Developing alphabetic knowledge is a necessary component to successful early reading development (Chall, 1967; Adams, 1990).

To provide students with opportunities to work with the alphabet, Ms. Doran, an experienced kindergarten teacher, asks her students to sign an attendance book each morning as they enter the classroom. While studying her students' attendance booklet, she notices a range of ability. At the beginning of the school year, Emanuel's and Esau's attempts at recording their names are different than Judaius'. Emanuel's and Easu's letter formations are quite clear and they include many, if not all, of the letters, while Judaius progresses from unclear marks on the page to the eventual writing of his name.

Invitation for the classroom

Flipbooks

Flipbooks are another way of focusing students' attention on rime patterns and word families.

- Fold two to three sheets of paper in half.
- With the exception of the last page, cut the pages in the middle and across the right side (at the top of the fold).
- On the last page, write the rime to be used on the right side of the paper.
- On each sheet, write an onset to compliment the rime. Draw a corresponding picture to further support meaning making.
- As beginning readers flip through the book, they will see a word family.

The flipbooks serve as additional support for students learning about language patterns and structures.

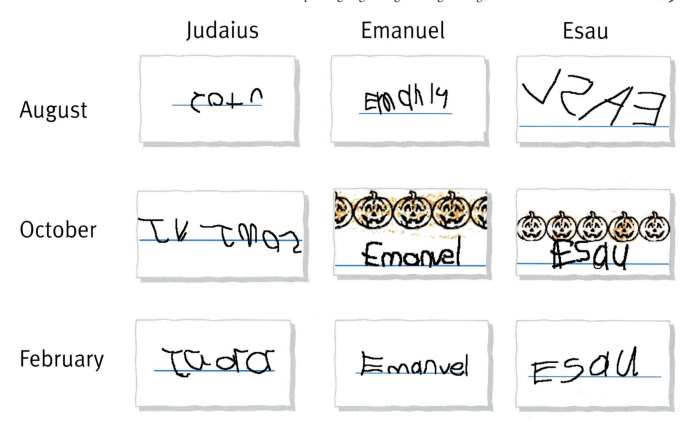

The attendance booklet enables the teacher to gauge students' understanding of the alphabet and see whether that knowledge is expanding. While a relatively insignificant task, this literacy event contextualizes students' emerging knowledge of the alphabet. There is purpose for the students writing their names as part of record keeping for the class. Students continue to develop their alphabetic knowledge by grouping their classmates' names by first letter (Easu and Emanuel) by last letter (Daisy, Kendy, Benny) and by the number of letters in the name (Travis, Dillan, JoAnna, Marcus). Ms. Doran explains that meaningful words (ones that hold meaning in our language) are formed by letters in a particular order. Ms. Doran then scrambles letters of students' names, and together they talk about why "nkedy" does not mean the same thing as "Kendy."

As students work with classmates' names they are developing familiarity with words that matter to them. Very few words carry as much significance as one's name, and so this activity plays an important role in providing authentic experiences in code breaking work.

Another literacy event that promotes alphabetic knowledge is for beginning readers to make their own alphabet books. Students are introduced to a large number of alphabet books at the writing center. The books range from silly and fanciful, such as *Chicka Chicka Boom Boom* (Martin & Archambault, 1989), *Old Black Fly* (Jim Aylesworth, 1992), and *Alphabet Under Construction* (Fleming, 2002), to those that depict common artifacts in the community such as *The Graphic Alphabet* (Pelliter, 1996) and *Eating the Alphabet: Fruits and Vegetables from A to Z* (Ehlert, 1989). Students use these books as models for their own alphabet books.

Invitation for the classroom

What do we notice about our names?

Read and discuss the story *Chrysanthemum* (Henkes, 1991). Chrysanthemum is a young mouse who loves her name until she goes to school and her classmates tease her about her name. Chrysanthemum's teacher steps in and shares with the children her own name, which is also the name of a flower. The children learn that all names are unique and special.

In small groups, have children write their names on name cards (cut sentence strips work quite well). Encourage all children to write their names even if they do not write it conventionally. For those children, talk about the differences between how the teacher writes the name and how the child writes the name.

Ask those in the small group to talk about what they notice about their names—similarities and differences (e.g., number of letters, similarity of letters).

As an extension, have children enter their names in the computer. Each name can be printed on a separate sheet of paper. Students can write or draw about themselves. The pages can be bound for a class book.

(Adapted from Kathy Egawa)

Text Set of Alphabet Books

- Sneed, B. (2002). *Picture A Letter*, New York: Dial Publisher.
- Ehlert, L. (1996). *Eating the Alphabet, Fruits and Vegetables from A to Z,* San Diego, CA: Red Wagon Books.
- Pelletier, D. (1996). *The Graphic Alphabet (Caldecott Honor Book)*, New York: Scholastic.
- Agee, J. (2003). *Z Goes Home*, New York: Hyperion Books for Children.
- Slate, J. (2003). *Miss Bindergarten Has a Wild Day in Kindergarten (Miss Bindergarten Books),* New York: Puffin.
- Lester, M. (2002). *A is for Salad*. New York: Putnam.

Environmental print, words that are on bulletin boards, hallways, signs, food labels, billboards, and other places provides additional opportunities for beginning readers to notice how letters are arranged in words. As they read cereal box labels, potato chip bags, and juice cartons, for example, children can discuss the letters in the words, copy them into their writing notebooks, and think about other places where they have seen those letters. Calkins (2001) talks about how this work would be complicated and difficult for young children if the focus were on spelling the words, but at this point it is not on spelling. Rather, their attention is on how letters appear in various places and within many words they see in the classroom, at home, in school hallways, and in stores. This alphabetic knowledge supports beginning readers and writers as they develop strategies for reading and writing texts.

making words

A strategy developed by Cunningham & Cunningham (1992) whereby students manipulate letters to form a series of words.

word lists

A strategy of creating words with similar letter patterns.

Making words (Cunningham & Cunningham, 1992) and **word lists** are two common invitations that enable young readers and writers to practice word patterns and letter–sound correspondence. In **making words**, students manipulate letters to form a series of words. The words often progress from simple two-letter words to more complex words using all of the letters. Following a reading of Kevin Henkes' *Lilly's Purple Plastic Purse* (1996), a group of first graders are given the following letter cards: a, i, s, c, p, t, l.

Invitation for the classroom

Sorting Letters and Words

Children can manipulate letters into groups or words. Magnetic letters on pizza pans or cookie sheets are quite common in early primary classrooms. Foam and wood letters in tubs are also good resources to have. Children can group letters based on a criteria (e.g., vowels, consonants). They can also manipulate the letters into a number of words. This open exploration of letters encourages creativity.

The consonants and vowels are typically different colors. The teacher calls out a series of words (for example, "pat, it, cat"), and the children are instructed to make the word with their letter cards. The following words are dictated: at, it, pat, sat, cat, lip, sip, pit, tip, slip, spat, slit, scat, splat, split. The final word is one that uses all of the letters. Students are challenged to determine what the word is based on the story that they have just heard (plastic). The *making words* strategy is different than the common activity of constructing as many words as you can from another word, in that the letters are not initially provided in the context of one word—the letters are simply listed for the children.

Word lists can be created for almost any purpose. In this particular strategy example, Ms. Williams, a first grade teacher, wanted her young readers to focus on letter patterns found in words. She selected three words from the story, *There Was an Old Lady Who Swallowed a Fly,* which was a familiar story to the students. She wrote "an" "old" and "lady" on three pieces of chart paper and underlined the spelling pattern for each word.

Ms. Williams grouped the students into three groups and gave each group one of the pieces of paper (and colored marker). Each group created a list of words with the same spelling pattern as the underlined part of the word. After a few minutes, students moved to another chart and began adding words to the list. To identify which words have been added, Ms. Williams reminded the groups to write only in the color that was provided. Here are the words that the students came up with.

Students constructed a large number of words that often are considered to be more sophisticated and complex. Because the boundaries in this activity are less defined and the focus is on letter patterns, not sound patterns, students draw upon their vast repertoire of word knowledge to create many words. *Word lists* are useful references for students to use in their reading and writing.

high-frequency words

Sight words that readers frequently encounter.

HIGH-FREQUENCY WORDS. *High-frequency words*, also known as sight words, are essential for children to learn. When children recognize and understand these common words, they read more fluently. Additionally, when beginning readers read high-frequency words with ease, they gain confidence in themselves as readers, and this confidence allows them to take risks with more challenging texts.

Fry's "Instant Words" (Fry, Kress & Fountaukidis, 1993) contains a list of the 100 most frequently used words in reading materials. Pinnell and Fountas (1998) identified the following 24 words (which are a part of the 100-word list) that kindergarten children should learn.

TABLE 7.3
Fry's 24 Most Frequently Used Words for Kindergartners

a	he	no	an	I	see	and	in
she	am	is	so	at	it	the	can
like	to	do	me	up	go	my	we

These words, like other high-frequency words, cannot be decoded easily, nor do they carry much meaning. They primarily serve to hold sentences together.

Young readers need an arsenal of words they recognize; therefore, teachers should include frequent opportunities for students to gain experience with these commonly used words. Teachers should use everyday pieces of literature and predictable books such as *Are You My Mother?* (Eastman, 1986), *The Grouchy Ladybug* (Carle, 1977), and *I Went Walking* (Williams, 1996) to highlight high-frequency words in context.

MINI-LESSONS FOR CODE BREAKING. Dahl et al. (2001) discuss a number of strategies for developing code breaking skills. These strategies are not a comprehensive list, but provide a way for children to connect their knowledge of letters and sounds to their independent reading and writing.

- **Use onset and meaning to figure out a word.** Children can simultaneously use the beginning letters of a word with their sense of meaning for the sentence to decode an unfamiliar word.
- **Sound out a word by elongating its sounds.** This is a familiar strategy, known as "sounding out." This strategy encourages readers to stretch out the sounds from left to right, noticing all the sounds in the word.

analogy

Noticing patterns in words to decode unfamiliar words.

- **Using pattern knowledge to figure out words.** This strategy involves using word patterns and analogies to decode unfamiliar words. *Analogy* (Goswami, 1991, 1988) is the process of noticing patterns and differences in words. Using what we know about familiar words helps us to decode unfamiliar words. When Deanna, a first grader, comes to the unfamiliar word "sting" in the sentence "The bee *sting* hurt my arm," she uses her knowledge that the /-ing/ in *sting* is similar to a word she knows, *sing*. Deanna makes the analogy that *sing* is like *sting* and is therefore able to decode the word.

- **Understanding variation in complex letter–sound relations.** Children need to be aware that letter–sound relationships are variable. This strategy is about which choice to make when working with words that have dipthongs, digraphs, and the variable sounds for the letters *c* and *g*. Teachers help children see that some words are exceptions and do not follow expected patterns.
- **Voice print matching to focus attention word by word.** This strategy involves looking at the exact word at the same time it is being said. This one-to-one matching reinforces the concept of the word, particularly when multisyllabic words are read. Teachers often use big books to support this strategy.

Strategies for code breaking are taught to provide children with paths of action so that they may successfully decode unfamiliar words.

All of the invitations presented for code breaking have occurred in the context of literature and everyday writing. When teachers approach code breaking practice as an integral aspect of a literacy program and not as an isolated activity, their curricular decisions will reflect a more integrated and holistic model of literacy. Teachers make decisions based on the needs of their students. Some students require more focused and explicit discussions of simple sound–symbol relationships; other students have internalized this knowledge and are ready to examine more sophisticated and complex language patterns and structure. In either case, learning how to break the code when unfamiliar words appear in text is a critical practice in the four-resource model.

Becoming a text participant

Children are active meaning makers as they listen to stories being read aloud, as well as when they read and write their own texts. ***Text participant practices*** involve particular cognitive strategies that include activating prior knowledge, predicting, organizing, questioning, summarizing, and visualizing. These strategies should be a part of early reading instruction. In many classrooms, however, text participant practices are limited to asking questions of the text and perhaps working on sequencing or cause and effect. While these are important, there should be more teaching of text meaning practices so that readers become strategic in how they process the information presented in the text.

text participant practices

Focus on the cognitive strategies of activating prior knowledge predicting, organizing, questioning, summarizing, and visualizing.

MAKING CONNECTIONS. A common strategy for the text participant practice for teachers to introduce to beginning readers is making connections to the text. When a group of young readers listened to their teacher read *Owen* (Henkes, 1993), a story of a young mouse that needs to give up his security blanket, they began to share their own stories of favorite, loved treasures that are hard to give up. The stories and insights that children generated in this discussion supported their own meaning making process.

Code breaking	Text participant
Text user	Critical practices

Beginning readers also make connections among different pieces of literature. Teachers will often encourage children to think about other texts or stories that they know that are similar to the one being read. For example, a teacher may read a collection of stories by the same author and talk with students about commonalities among the stories (e.g., characters, setting, language patterns). Inviting children to explicitly make connections is an important aspect of developing strategic comprehension skills.

schema

A mental set or representation.

Making connections to personal experiences and to other pieces of literature is possible because of how knowledge is stored in the mind. We have what are known as **schemas** (Anderson & Pearson, 1984), which are like file folders in our mind. This abstract representation helps us understand how the mind organizes and remembers all the concepts learned over a period of time. When we gain new information or knowledge, we "file" it in the folder that has other similarly linked ideas. We organize the material to make it easier to retrieve at a later date. When a key word or concept is encountered, readers access this information system, pulling forth the ideas that will help them make connections with the text so they can create meaning. The schemas that we have in our mind are based on our prior experiences and cultural backgrounds. This is why a group of children may construct different interpretations of a text. Much of our understandings depend on whether or not we have that particular schema to attach the new idea to. When teachers read a story, such as *Stellaluna* (Cannon, 1993), children may construct a number of ideas around Stellaluna's new life of acting like a bird and not a bat.

Schema can be organized by associations, categories, examples, and meaning. To illustrate, when Jasmine looks through the book *Beware of Storybook Wolves* (Childs, 2001), she recognizes a character, the wolf, from another story, *Little Red Riding Hood* (Wegman, 1993). Jasmine is building a schema for what storybook wolves are like and the kinds of trouble they cause. She also looks through Seymor Simon's (1993) nonfiction text, *Wolves*, to get a picture of what wolves really look like as compared to the fictional stories. She uses this connection to support her meaning making of the story she is currently reading.

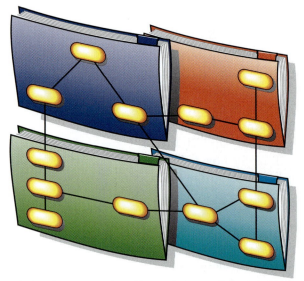

A visual representation of how schema are interconnected.

Invitation for the classroom

Sequencing Questions

Encourage children to ask questions that are on their minds. In doing so, children come to see that reading is about learning, and that their questions matter in the larger context of the reading event. When there are many questions, the teacher may want to keep track of them. The more factual based questions can be answered quickly. Questions more interpretive in nature may be used to start discussions or lead to inquiry projects.

MAKING PREDICTIONS AND INFERENCES. Making predictions and inferences are important as beginning readers come to make sense of words on a page. Teachers regularly engage students in "picture walks" where they peruse the cover of the story, thinking about what the story may be about (based on the pictures and illustra-

tions). Children are then asked to look through the book, focusing on the illustrations. This helps children gain a sense of what the story might be about before attending to the words in the story. An alternative to a picture walk is literature webbing. *Literature webbing* is an opportunity for children to make predictions about the events in a story. The teacher writes or draws story events on cards. The cards are mixed up, and children predict the order of events by placing the cards in clockwise order. The teacher reads the story; following the reading, the children confirm or correct their predictions by returning to the cards.

literature web

A strategy that encourages students to predict the sequence of events in a story.

Inferences are made as readers 'read between the lines.' "It is the strategic process of generating assumptions, making predictions, and coming to conclusions based upon giving information in the text and in illustrations" (Richards & Anderson, 2003, p. 290). As children combine information presented in the text with their own background experiences, they create connections that go beyond the author's exact words and images. Teachers can introduce inferencing and predicting to young readers by modeling and asking questions. Teachers can model how to reason, make assumptions, and come to conclusions (Richards and Anderson, 2003). Richards and Anderson created the "How do you know" questioning strategy to develop children's inferencing and predicting skills. This strategy helps children make connections between given and implied information.

VISUALIZING. Children create mental pictures and images while listening to stories being read by the teacher or another adult. They may also visualize characters and settings in stories that they are beginning to read on their own. Beginning readers use their background knowledge to create these mental images and associations.

Invitation for the classroom

How do you know?

- Read a picture book aloud, and stop where students should make an inference.
- Ask a question that prompts students to infer important information about the story.
- When students respond, confirm their answer and ask, "Did the author say that?"
- Follow-up this question with, "How do you know?"
- Encourage students to continue making inferences and predictions about the story. Have students explain how they figured out the various connections.

(Richards and Anderson, 2003)

Invitation for the classroom

It Doesn't Have to Be this Way

- Select a story that students are familiar with but that will appeal to them.
- Show students the cover and read the title. Ask students to predict what they think the story is about.
- Record their predictions.
- Read the story, stopping at the appropriate places to confirm earlier predictions.
- Prior to the end of the story, stop and summarize the story thus far.
- Have students draw what they see as the ending to the story.
- Share the different endings.
- Compare each student's ending with the one in the text.
- Have students point out ways that their own endings connect with the portions read aloud.

(Adapted from LaDonna Helm)

Teachers often ask children to close their eyes to visualize the scene, or they may ask children to draw pictures of the scenes and characters. The mental energy children use to create these mental pictures helps them to recall information as well as increase inferencing and prediction skills (Gambrell & Bales, 1986).

Visualizing can also be used in writing. When children are drafting stories, they can close their eyes or use drawings to help them imagine what they want their writing to say. Children can use description and sensory details to make their writing more engaging and vivid.

These text meaning practices, among others, are critical as young children learn how to examine and articulate their own assumptions and conclusions about the materials they are coming across in various settings.

Understanding how texts are used

text use practices

Focus on the varied purposes that texts serve.

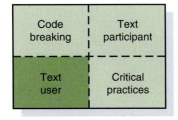

Another integral part of the beginning reading process is discovering the purposes that texts serve. In ***text use practices*** students come to know that people read for different purposes. Readers focus on different aspects of a text depending on if the text is fiction, nonfiction, magazine, brochure, maps, or road signs. For beginning readers, focusing on text use practices happens in the context of everyday experiences in the classroom. For example, Ms. Garcia's second graders read about the habits and habitats of hamsters in a book about caring for hamsters because they recently acquired a hamster for the classroom. This factual information provided a pathway to learning the best ways of caring for their new class pet. Down the hall in Ms. Williams's first grade classroom, her students are reading and talking about how poems create an emotional response and how authors use words to create pictures in a reader's head. In sorting out the ways of reading a text, these beginning experiences with text structures and purposes help children learn that people read for various purposes.

One way to promote text use is to ask questions of the text in relation to other books and texts the students know.

- How does this story start?
- What are some other books that start this way?

Invitation for the classroom

Creating a Story Map

Story maps are useful for helping children examine the structure of stories they are reading.

- Read a story that highlights the structure you are working with (narrative, expository).
- Create a story map skeleton on the board or as a skill sheet for children to complete.
- Have children work together to complete the diagram.

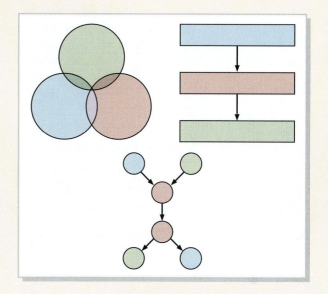

- What are some other ways the author could have started the text?
- What are some of the different sections in the book?

Another important strategy to work on with students in text use practices is the idea that texts (narrative, expository, poetry) carry with them particular structures. Discovering how narrative texts are written and organized helps children predict what is coming next, store information in the appropriate schema, and recall information with increased accuracy and completeness. Inviting students to consider how texts are used for different purposes and how they are constructed with different elements contributes to their growing sense that texts serve particular purposes and that these purposes are meaningful to becoming lifelong readers.

Thinking critically about texts

How can a teacher encourage young readers to use texts as a tool for learning? One way is to analyze texts to see how different groups of people are represented (Wilson, 2002). **Critical practices** involve a reader challenging the dominant perspective by asking questions of the text—how the story or event might be told from a different point of view, which voices and/or perspectives are not presented in the text; in a nutshell, critical practice involves asking why things are the way they are. Critical practices in primary classrooms are apparent through inquiry questions, literature discussions, and what's-on-my-mind conversations in the classroom.

Working from a critical practices perspective, Mr. Gentry, a multi-age primary teacher, introduces *Freedom Summer* (Wiles, 2001), a story of two young boys, one white and one black, living in the small southern town in the United States during the racially turbulent 1960s. At one point in the story laws are changed and all businesses and public places including the town swimming pool are open for all residents. The townspeople decide, however, decide to close the pool and fill it in with tar, so that no one can use the pool, especially the black citizens. The vivid illustrations invoke feelings of sadness for the two boys, as well as hope at the end of the story when they both walk

critical practices

Focus on challenging the status quo, taking multiple perspectives, investigating sociopolitical issues, and taking action.

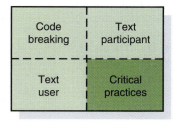

Invitation for the classroom

KWL charts

KWL charts are very common in classrooms where students are engaged in pursuing inquiry questions. Students create a KWL chart, which highlights what they already **know** about a topic, what they **want** to know or learn, and what they **learned** as a result of the reading and talking. This chart then can be the springboard for more refined and extended inquiry work.

why did the blak peopol
Coldinst Siwim in the pool?
why did the children clen to porch?
why did the peopol came to work at the pool?
why did joe and John Henry was Stering at the ster?

Why did the black people couldn't swim in the pool?
Why did the children clean the porch?
Why did the people come to work at the pool?
Why did Joe and John Henry was staring at the stairs?

Why did the wekers close the Pool?
Why did they ran to the Pool?
Whx dldinst were close
Why werethastetin at the steres

Students' questions for *Freedom Summer*

Why did the workers close the pool?
Why did they ran (run) to the pool?
Why didn't wear clothes?
Why were they staring at the stairs?

into the general store together. Mr. Gentry invites discussion throughout the reading of this story. He then asks students to compose questions about the story.

The students' questions and responses to the text were more complex and sophisticated than anticipated by their teacher. When opportunities are made available for young readers to question concepts and ideas presented in stories and other text materials, their reading practices are further extended and they begin to use reading as a tool for learning about the world, rather than just learning to read.

The four reading practices—code breaking, text meaning, text use, and critical practices—are the cornerstone of an effective beginning reading program. Children in kindergarten, first, and second grade should have opportunities to decode text, make connections with text, consider the use and purpose of the text, and respond critically to texts perhaps by challenging dominant perspectives and the status quo. How much focus each of these four practices receives in the classroom depends on the needs and interests of the students. Some students require more attention on code breaking, while others need to better understand text use practices. To address the varied abilities, needs, and desires of children in a classroom, a multifaceted approach to literacy development, such as the reader/writer workshop, is needed.

Creating Connections 7.1

Select one of the four practices. Considering the goals of the practice, select a children's literature title that will best highlight the identified goal. Develop an invitation or strategy lesson that can be taught to a beginning reader.

Reader/writer workshops for beginning readers

In Ms. Bridge's kindergarten classroom a reader/writer workshop is in full gear. Some children are gathered around her as she reads from a big book format of Eric Carle's (1968) *The Very Hungry Caterpillar*, while other children in a small group peruse a text set of materials on caterpillars and butterflies (e.g., *Home at Last: A Song of Migration* by Sayre, 1998; *From Caterpillar to Butterfly*, by Deborah Heiligman, 1996; and a life cycle chart). In a far corner of the room, two students write in their notebooks about their observations of caterpillars in the science center; and still others focus their attention on constructing a list of words with the same initial sound as the highlighted words on the chart (<u>c</u>aterpillar and <u>b</u>utterfly).

Each reading and writing event in this classroom engages children in meaning making by accessing their knowledge of language processes, experiences with texts, and their understandings of how the world works.

Creating a routine for primary grade reading and writing workshops

Routines are necessary for teachers and students to effectively manage the literacy development process and the scope of literacy knowledge and experiences that children bring into the classroom. The glimpse into Ms. Simon's classroom literacy practices in the opening vignette demonstrates the implicit role that routines play in designing meaningful and effective literacy instruction. For example, Ms. Simon set a time to introduce and reread familiar stories to students during shared reading. This routine offers students a concentrated time to work on words and word structures. Ms. Simon has regularly scheduled writing and sharing routines so that her students can share their writing with their classmates and comment on the book they are reading as a group. As a result of these consistent routines, the children begin to recognize the behaviors and actions that are expected in these events. When Ms. Simon rereads predictable texts, students know they can also read along, saying the words. Through her modeling of reading practices during shared reading events, her students begin to learn how to interact with text. Jose and Carlos come to know that during "microphone time" they will share their writing with others in the class, and that the response to their writing will matter. The established routines create learning environments that allow students to demonstrate their knowledge, experiences, and connections with texts in multiple ways.

Although reader/writer workshops should have a variety of reading and writing events and routines, this approach does not have a prescribed format or particular texts and engagements that must be included. Teachers can choose materials, grouping patterns, and strategy instruction based on the needs of the students.

TECHNOLOGY LINK

http://www.learner.org/ channel/libraries/ readingk2/sinnett/index. html

Visit John Sinnet's kindergarten classroom to see how he incorporates a writer's journal into his reading curriculum.

The following structures work well in primary grade classrooms:

- Read aloud favorite stories as well as new ones
- Conduct a mini-lesson to introduce or remind students of a specific strategy
- Conduct shared and guided reading events
- Provide opportunities for writing notebooks
- Offer literature discussions
- Implement independent reading and/or partner reading
- Have reading conferences
- Take time to reflect on the day's work

These literacy events enable teachers to work closely with beginning readers and writers—to support their growth and development in literacy processes. In the next section, these workshop routines and corresponding strategy work are further detailed.

Mini-lessons

The mini-lesson is an opportunity to bring together the whole group or a small group of children to learn about a new strategy for reading. In primary grade reading and writing workshops, mini-lessons can be drawn from a variety of assessments, including running records, miscue analysis, kidwatching notes and observations, responses on surveys and questionnaires, and reflections from retellings (see Chapter 9 on assessment for descriptions of these assessments and others). The content of a mini-lesson should be based on student needs.

Mini-lessons in primary grades may center on any part of the reading process, including but not limited to:

- extending children's reading time
- handling tricky words
- noticing first letters
- reading across the word (not just looking at the beginning letters/sounds)
- rereading to see what makes sense
- talking about books
- using what you already know to learn new words (word families)
- inviting others into a book
- understanding how to get big ideas from texts

Reading and responding

In reader/writer workshops for beginning readers and writers, there are a number of opportunities for children to engage with and respond to texts. Through read alouds, shared reading, literature discussions, and independent reading and writing, children are able to construct their own understandings, as well as learn how others responded to the story.

READ ALOUD IN WORKSHOP SETTINGS.   There cannot be enough said about the importance of reading aloud to children. In 1985, the National Commission on Reading concluded, "the single most important activity for building the knowledge required for eventual success in reading is reading aloud to children" (p. 23). In his classic book, *The Read-Aloud Handbook*, Jim Trelease (1989) argues for reading aloud to children of all ages. Trelease and other educators (Anderson, Hiebert, Scott, & Wilkinson, 1985; Cullinan & Galda, 1998) suggest that teachers, parents, care-givers, and older siblings read aloud to young children to entertain, explain, arouse curiosity, and inspire. They also state that by reading aloud:

- A child's brain is conditioned to associate reading with pleasure (because the environment is often pleasing).
- A child's background knowledge and experiences are enhanced.
- A child's storehouse of experiences are increased by hearing about people, places, and events that are not a part of their actual lives.
- Vocabulary development is strengthened.
- Connections between and among other texts are made possible.
- Fluent reading is modeled by a more capable reader.
- Ideas for their own writing and storytelling are provided.
- Book handling knowledge and concepts of print are developed.
- New forms of language, styles, and sentence structures are introduced.

With reading aloud taking such an important role in the development of young readers, it is important to consider the best picture books for reading aloud, how to evaluate those texts, and the best approaches to reading aloud to children.

QUALITY PICTURE BOOKS FOR READING ALOUD.   Picture books are popular in primary grade classrooms. There are a number of outstanding picture books ap-propriate for young children that range in genre, style, and content. Fiction, fantasy, nonfiction, historical fiction, biography, folklore, science fiction, and poetry can all be found in picture book format. It is important to select picture books that cap-ture students' interests, stretch them as readers, and reflect the diverse backgrounds

Did you know. . .

There are a number of professional organizations and websites that offer resources for identifying high-quality picture books to read aloud. A few include:

Booklinks. A publication by the American Library Association (www.ala.org/BookLinks).

Choice Lists by the International Reading Association. *The Reading Teacher* publishes the list of choices (teacher and student) each October (http://www.reading.org/re-sources/tools/choices.htm).

Carol Hurst's website on children's literature. http://www.carolhurst.com/profsub-jects/reading/readingaloud.html.

Jim Trelease's *Handbook of Reading Aloud*. An excerpt of his favorites is found at http://www.trelease-on-reading.com/rah_treasury.html.

Notable Books for a Global Society. A special interest group of the International Read-ing Association (www.tcnj.edu/~childlit/index.htm).

of the children in the classroom and in the world (Cullinan & Galda, 1998). Children need to see themselves and others reflected in the stories they hear.

When evaluating texts for reading aloud, consider:

- the text's literary elements,
- how language works,
- the accuracy of knowledge,
- presentation of content, and
- how language and illustrations extend emotions.

TECHNOLOGY LINK
http://www.duluth.lib.mn.
us/YouthServices/Book-
lists/Multicultural.html
This website lists authors
and titles that reflect the diversity of children and their
families in the United States
and around the world.

Stories that are too simple in language or in content may not sustain a meaningful conversation. For example, *Hop on Pop* (Dr. Seuss, 1963), while great for working on phonemic awareness and rhyming, does not elicit a meaningful conversation because there is a limited theme or storyline to engage students.

When selecting books that accurately portray diverse cultures, consider books that help young readers connect their own experiences to those presented in the story, identify contributions of all peoples, and foster respect and mutual understanding for those of other backgrounds and cultures. Culturally diverse perspectives need to be examined in ways that seek to present diversity in all its complexity and depth.

APPROACHES TO READING ALOUD. Reading aloud is often conducted with the whole class. Teachers will bring the class together to enjoy a new story or an old favorite. Repeated readings of a high-quality story contribute to children's meaning making processes. Children often ask to hear stories over and over again. In doing so, young readers are able to tease out the subtleties of language and themes that appear in high-quality texts. They are able to delve deeper into the storyline and construct more sophisticated and complex responses.

Teachers encourage students to *interact* with the text as it is being read, stopping at particular points in the reading for discussion and conversation. Barrentine (1996) suggests teachers prepare for effective read alouds by:

- previewing and reading the story prior to the read aloud,
- thinking about reading goals and strategies to highlight,
- identifying places in the text to seek students' predictions about the story,
- anticipating where to build upon children's background knowledge to make sense of the text,
- thinking about questions and ways of responding to students,
- being prepared to alter plans based on how students respond to the story, and
- planning ways for students to explore and extend the story in personal and exciting ways.

Ms. Hammel, a multi-age kindergarten to second grade teacher often reads aloud to her students. She uses texts that have rich language, multiple layers of meaning, and interesting characters. Taking an interactive approach, Ms. Hammel invites her students to respond throughout the reading of the story. On this particular day, she reads the story *Hope* (Monk, 1998), about a young biracial girl who learns the history behind her name and learns to be proud of her biracial heritage. While visiting her Aunt Poogie, Hope, the young girl, encounters a family friend who asks if she is "mixed." This comment disturbs Hope until her Aunt Poogie explains how she is from generations of faith "mixed" with lots of love. At this point in the story, Hope and her Aunt Poogie are at an open-air market and run into a family friend. Read through the following interaction between Ms. Hammel and her students. Then, notice how she engages her students in the text and calls on them to develop their own meaning based on personal experiences.

MS. HAMMEL: [reading] *They chatted on about who had died, and who married and who divorced, who had new babies and then Aunt Poogie put her arm around my shoulder and said, 'Violet, I bet you can't guess whose baby this is?' Miss Violet looked over her glasses and down her nose at me. She gestured for me to turn around and [inaudible]. Prudence, this child doesn't favor a soul in your family.' 'She's Eve's little girl. You remember Eve don't you? My brother Jack's daughter?' 'Oh my, yes!,' Miss Violet said, 'well she enough has her mamma's big brown eyes.'*

CARLY: Like mixed up.

ELLIOT: Because she's lighter skin and they both got dark skin.

MS. HAMMEL: Okay, darker skin and she's talking about a mix. What do you think she means by that Jasmine? How can that be a mix?

JASMINE: I'm mixed (said very quietly)

MS. HAMMEL: Okay. In your family you have. . . [mother, father, brother, sister?]. Your mother is. . .[white, or brown, or black]?

JASMINE: White.

MS. HAMMEL: And your dad is?

JASMINE: Brown.

MS. HAMMEL: Brown. And so together it is like a mix. And that's what she's noticing about this girl.

> What is the purpose of this question?

Ms. Hammel continues reading.

MS. HAMMEL: *Well Aunt Poogie put up her hand like a traffic cop. Rolled her eyes and set her mouth in a very sharp voice. Violet, what on earth do you think? And after that they said their good byes. And we finished our shopping and went home.*

MS. HAMMEL: Well what kind of reaction did Aunt Poogie have when Violet said that Hope was mixed? She was kind of angry about this, right?

SIENNA: That somebody's mixed.

MS. HAMMEL: Yeah, do you think that makes any difference when someone is mixed, or biracial?

STUDENTS: No.

MS. HAMMEL: Well why not Sienna?

SIENNA: Because. . .just because it's different skin, it's not like what we do. And like what you're like and what you think you'll be like. Yeah skin doesn't have anything to do with how they feel.

MS. HAMMEL: Okay, so really she's just looking at the outside appearance of this little girl, isn't she?

SIENNA: It doesn't matter what your skin is like. It doesn't matter.

> How does Ms. Hammel enable Sienna to "think aloud?"

Jasmine and other students begin to compare their skin tones on their hands. Ms. Hammel notices this and asks,

MS. HAMMEL: If we all put our hands out and put them next to each other, will all of our hands be the same color?

STUDENTS: No (in unison).

MS. HAMMEL: You put your hands beside each other and you looked at your hand color. And they were a little different weren't they?

STUDENTS: Yeah.

> When students compare their skin tones, how does this help students to extend their meaning of the text?

DARREN [Student]:	I've got a little red around mine.
MS. HAMMEL:	Would you say that makes one person better than another? Somebody has lighter skin.
SIENNA [Student]:	No! It's the same skin.
MS. HAMMEL:	Okay, so we're all different. Is different something that we should be upset about?
STUDENTS:	No (in unison).
MS. HAMMEL:	It's something we could be happy about.
JASMINE:	We're all a different color.
JOESEPH:	I'm not white.
BRADY:	I discovered that all kids in this class probably have different skin color.
MS. HAMMEL:	Okay, and what does that mean if we all have different skin color?
BRADY:	It doesn't matter, but if people make fun of their skin color then they can tell an older person. Like their parents.
MS. HAMMEL:	Okay. So we have people we can talk to about this. In this situation Aunt Poogie and Violet ended up leaving. They left the situation because I wonder if the Aunt felt like the little girl might be sad? Do you think there would be any sadness here?
STUDENTS:	Yes.
SIENNA:	When that girl, it was like what I just said. When she just made fun of her skin color, because when the girl has a different skin color and she was mixed and she wasn't. She said, that she has a different skin color than the one.
MS. HAMMEL:	You guys are having a great session here. Let's go on and find out what happens in the story.
[reading]
The ride home was quiet. Most quiet ride I can remember. Finally I asked, what did Miss Violet mean? Is the child mixed? Aunt Poogie stroked my head with one hand and said, "baby don't you pay Miss Violet never mind." All the way home I thought about what Miss Violet had said. All through my afternoon snack. All through helping Aunt Poogie snap the fresh green beans. All through dinner. All through brushing my teeth. Even when I said my prayers. I could not stop hearing Miss Violet say, my goodness. Is that child mixed?
MS. HAMMEL:	What do you think she was thinking from that day?

> What are some of the ways Ms. Hammel invites students into the conversation?

In this exchange, Ms. Hammel provides students with opportunities to connect their personal experiences with the fictional world of the story. She pushes her students to challenge the perspective offered in the story. Students saw the racism and prejudice in the simple statement "she's mixed" and challenged the idea that being different is a problem. Ms. Hammel was also receptive to the children's talk about their own skin color as they took time to compare their hands with each other. These insights and others are made visible through read alouds that encourage students to engage with the text.

> ### Creating Connections 7.2
>
> Read to a small group of kindergarten or first grade students. If possible, tape-record the conversation. What questions/comments arose during the read aloud? How did you respond to the student(s)?
>
> Share your experiences with classmates.

SHARED READING EVENTS. Teachers often work with students on reading strategies through shared reading (Holdaway, 1980) and guided reading (Fountas & Pinnell, 1996). In a **shared reading** event, a teacher generally reads from a big book version of a book that is relatively easy to memorize. Using texts of these types helps children learn how print works, story structures, word recognition, and how books can be a source of enjoyment as well as information. There are six types of books that provide these learning opportunities (McCraken & McCraken, 1995)

- **Rhythmic books.** The rhythm and predictable language enables children to anticipate upcoming words.

- **Repetitive books.** These books contain repetitive lines that children can learn and chime in.

- **Cumulative books.** This type of text continually builds each page by repeating text from previous pages and adding a new line of text with each new page.

- **Basic Sentence Pattern Books.** In this type of book, a basic sentence pattern is used to provide support for the reader.

- **Two-part books.** This type of text reads like a conversation in which a question is asked and a response is given with a subsequent two lines.

- **Information books.** These books do not follow a storyline; they are instead full of information about content-related topics. Use of information books is a good way to support students as they learn vocabulary, facts, and concepts.

During a shared reading event, a teacher may focus on code breaking and text meaning practices. The teacher begins by having children look closely at the cover of the book and asking them to make predictions about the story. The teacher may ask students to think about what the title of the story means. The teacher records these observations on chart paper that can be referred to later. The teacher reads the story for students to enjoy. Then, in a second reading, the teacher may encourage stops at predetermined points to discuss specific words and their spelling/sound patterns. Words with similar letter–sound patterns can be searched for in the text, highlighted and recorded on the chart paper.

The following excerpt is from a shared reading event in Ms. Doran's kindergarten class. Ms. Doran worked with children on distinguishing sounds at the beginning of words. Wyatt and a few of his classmates experienced difficulty with letter–sound relationships. Within the group are Cassidy and Esperanza who are English Language Learners. Ms. Doran decided to bring these students together to work on single consonant letters at the beginning of words. She selected a big book version of *Brown Bear Brown Bear What Do You See?* (Martin, 1992) because of the simple, predictable language pattern throughout the text. The brown bear in the story is asked a number of times what he sees, and in each case it is a colorful animal.

MS. DORAN:	This morning we are going to listen and talk about a story we read last week, *Brown Bear, Brown Bear, What Do You See?* As we look at the cover, what is the first thing that we notice?
WYATT:	A brown bear.
MS. DORAN:	That's right. There is a brown bear on the cover. Let's remember what the brown bear sees.

Ms. Doran began reading the story. After a few refrains, many of the children in this group start to chant the refrain, "Brown bear, brown bear, what do you see? I see a [supply-

---

shared reading

An interactive reading experience where teachers read aloud and focus students' attention on how print works, story structures, and word recognition.

> ### Creating Connections 7.3
> As you read through the excerpt, note the ways in which Ms. Doran responds to the students' comments.

ing the appropriate animal] looking at me." Esparanza, however, did not say anything. She watched intently as Ms. Doran turned each page. As Ms. Doran continued to read, most of the students chanted the refrain throughout the rest of the
story.

Ms. Doran:	Wow, you all really seem to be able to read this story. Let's go back to some of the words and think about what letters they start and end with. Let's start with brown bear. What letter do you see at the beginning of these two words?
Cassidy:	B.
Ms. Doran:	Yes, that's the letter "b."

At this point, Ms. Doran put a frame around the letter "b" in "brown" and "bear" by
using an index card that has a center cut out. She wrote "bear" and "brown" on a
piece of chart paper. Ms. Doran also sketched a picture of a bear and used a brown
marker to sketch a swatch of brown color.

Ms. Doran:	I wonder if we have other animals in here that also start with the letter b. Let's look through the pages and if you see an animal that has the same beginning letter as *brown* and *bear*, tell me to stop and we can write it down on our list.

Ms. Doran turned the pages slowly and at the same time reread the story. Students
also read along. Esparanza began to mimic other students as they said "brown bear"
when it was read in the refrain.

Deidra:	Stop, I see red bird.
Ms. Doran:	Good catch. *Bird* does start the same way as *brown* and *bear*. Let's add it to our list. What are the letters in the word bird? We know it has a "b."
Wyatt:	A
Patrick:	No, not an "a."
Ms. Doran:	You are right Patrick. This time it isn't an "a," but an "i" and then we have a "r." What is our last letter?
Cassidy:	B.
Ms. Doran:	bird. Bird has a "b" at the beginning and a "d" at the end.

At this point, Ms. Doran drew a quick sketch of a bird next to the word. She felt this
would help Esparanza make the connection to the word *bird*.

Esparanza, recognizing the picture of the bird, said, "pajaro" (the Spanish name
for bird).

Ms. Doran:	Yes, that is pajaro. In English we call it bird. Back to our story, are there other animals that start with a b?

Students looked intently at the text. They do not come up with any other animals
that start with a "b."

Ms. Doran:	well, we don't have many words on our B list from this book, but I bet we can add a few words that we already know. I'll put a box around these words to help us remember we saw them in this book. What are some other words we know that start with the same letter and sound as bird and bear?
Deidra:	ball.

The group continued to name words for the list, and Ms. Doran wrote them down.
These words were transferred to the word wall, and they became a resource for all
of the children to have access to when working in writing notebooks or reading independently.

Shared reading events enable the teacher to model and support the use of cues and self-monitoring reading strategies. Other possible formats for shared reading include echo reading and choral reading. *Echo reading* is when the teacher reads a line and the students repeat the same line, echoing the teacher. *Choral reading* is when students read along with the teacher.

> ### Shared Reading
> Teacher leads, students participate
> *Materials*: Enlarged texts visible to students (big books)
> *Choice*: Usually teacher's choice
> *Grouping*: Whole group or small group
> *Purpose*:
> To teach concepts about print and print conventions
> To analyze textual features; word study
> To teach comprehension and interpretation
> To enlist varied forms of response
> Readers benefit from highly visible demonstrations of the reading process. Concepts and conventions of print are made very accessible for them. Examination of textual features (letters, word parts) helps develop an understanding of alphabetic principle and the nature of written language.

LITERATURE DISCUSSIONS. Literature discussions offer further opportunities for students to interact with a text and draw meaning from it. Unlike a read aloud event where the teacher is reading to the whole class, literature discussions are usually comprised of small groups of students (4–6) who are interested in the same topic or have similar inquiry questions. With beginning readers, the teacher often reads the text to the small group of students, and while reading, encourages questions and comments along the way. In doing so, the teacher creates an environment that supports the notion that literacy development involves being a problem poser; that literacy is a socially constructed enterprise; and that taking an inquiry stance contributes to richer, more complex understandings. Through these literature discussions, children begin to make sense of the text and their place in the world.

When selecting texts for literature discussions, it is important to choose titles that reflect literary merit, are interesting to students, and represent events and characters of diverse ethnicity, cultural heritage, class, and gender (Wells, 1997). The most common genre to use for a literature discussion is fiction, but nonfiction texts work quite well. For example, many young readers are fascinated by books about animals (particularly sea animals), insects and birds, space, and places in the world. Literature discussions should provide opportunities to learn about issues that are significant to students' lives, such as love, hate, greed, justice, generosity, friendship, revenge, growing up, dying, and facing challenges (Raphael & Boyd, 1997, p. 74).

Literature discussions in beginning reading classrooms are important to developing a comprehensive reading program. Young readers are able to build a repertoire of comprehension strategies, while at the same time taking a more critical stance toward the issues presented. Within literature discussions, readers discover information, learn about themselves and others, and consider how they are positioned in the larger world.

INDEPENDENT AND PARTNER READING. Independent reading is often the heart of a reading workshop. First, children select texts to read for extended periods. This reading time gives beginning readers an opportunity to "lose themselves in the text." For beginning readers, the challenge is to help them select texts that are appropriate to their interests, needs, and strengths. Texts can range from easy concept books and wordless books, to predictable books, picture books, easy chapter books, kids' magazines, nonfiction texts, maps, environmental print, and poetry. Independent reading time should be used to push a reader to the edge of his or her comfort level. However, it is important that the young reader return to old favorites so that they can take a break from challenging work while continuing to work on their reading.

During independent reading time, children interact with texts in a variety of ways. Beginning readers may approximate reading behaviors, often constructing their own story to match the illustrations. They draw upon their knowledge of how stories are structured, anticipate upcoming events, how language is used in stories, and their memories of what happened from an earlier reading of the text. Beginning readers may also begin to identify familiar words and begin the process of reading conventionally. During other times, readers may retell the story, share favorite parts with the teacher or other students, write about texts in a journal, draw pictures, or act out parts of the story.

Independent reading time may include a mixture of independent and partner reading. By asking children to read a text together, or to share their favorite text with a partner, they learn that reading is a social activity and that sharing and talking about texts with others is important. In Ms. Fisher's first grade classroom, her students have opportunities to partner read in the reading loft—an area of the classroom where children can climb a ladder and be surrounded by texts as they sit on comfortable cushions. One afternoon, Ramon, Kevin, Everilda, and Victor were in the reading loft. Ms. Fisher overheard Ramon explain to Everilda, "I am just reading this book [*Tacky the Penguin*] to Kevin in Spanish 'cause that is what he knows." A few minutes later, Victor wanted to hear the story so Ramon read it in English. Ramon told the story, including the story's rap style song, "How many toes does a fish have?" As the story was revisited, the four readers constructed new understandings, building on the experiences and knowledge of their reading partners.

Writing

For beginning readers and writers, independent writing time offers children opportunities to try out unfamiliar words and structures, and to begin to learn the purposes of writing. In reader/writer workshop classrooms, children have access to their writing journals or sourcebooks, as well as to a variety of writing tools and materials. Chapter 6 offered a list of possible tools and materials to support independent writing.

When starting off with a writer's workshop, children will focus on personal narratives. They will draw and write about their families and other life experiences. As children become more accustomed to the routines and structures of writer's workshop time, they gradually begin to add details to their work (both the pictures and the words). Children are invited to share these pieces with others in the author's chair. In these experiences, the focus for children is not on the spelling or correctness of their work, but on the celebration of taking risks in writing—trying out new ideas and forms. In Ms. Bomer's classroom, two of her young writers decided to draft a "First Days of School" story. They worked on this story for a couple of days, each taking turns writing and sharing ideas. At the same time, another young writer, Makayla, decided to write her own story, "The Footprint," fashioned after *Are you my mother?* (Eastman, 1960). In another classroom, Ms. Cobb asks her first graders to write applications for the various classroom jobs that are available. She believes it is important for children to have authentic purposes for writing. Many of the children choose their independent writing time to compose their reasons for wanting a particular classroom job. In all of these classrooms, the children are engaged in writing for authentic and purposeful reasons.

Reading and writing conferences and record keeping

Reading and writing conferences allow teachers to assess their students' literacy strengths and to determine areas where a student may need additional instruction (Gill,

2000; Rhodes & Dudley-Marling, 1996). On any given day, a teacher can schedule two to three reading and/or writing conferences with individual students. These conferences are brief (5-10 minutes per child) and usually take place during independent reading and writing time.

During a reading conference, a teacher may ask a child to talk about what he or she is reading, to read aloud to the teacher, to retell the book, or to set personal reading goals. Sometimes the teacher shares particular strategies for making sense of the text. Reading conference forms allow teachers to keep track of their students' progress. The infor-

The foot print

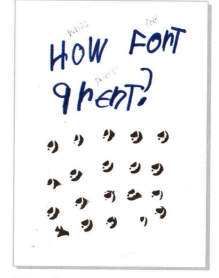

Whose foot print?

Are they his? No they are not

Are they hers? Yes they are hers

First day of school

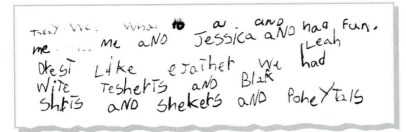

First day of school (cont.)

then we got ar bidd oti ... ... be. ei
sind ae binerandwe put it in ae bae fae
and the bell whet ring ring ring and we walked
out of are class and got on the bus and rodde
it hone riy mom was standing there I said
good by to Jessic and got of the bus
and ran tomy mom and kissd her and
gave her a hug, it absa icksting day
but was I was glad to be hom !

First day of school (cont.)

tybaH
calindr
I wood n ot rit num brs
mese. I will rit nubrs
net. I thek i wood like

Calendar
I would not write numbers messy. I will write numbers
neat. I think I would like

the gobl

the job
Job applications

mation gained in the reading conference should be used to plan instruction and to form the "as-needed" strategy groups for shared and guided reading events. Chapter 5 offered an invitation on conducting a reading conference. For beginning readers, it is important to act as a coach (Calkins, 2001). In a coaching conference you intervene as gently as you can, with the goal of trying to develop unconscious reading habits. Because beginning readers are new to the process, it is important to only work toward one major goal rather than pulling the beginning reader in different directions.

Similarly, in writing conferences with beginning writers, the teacher should focus the attention on one aspect of the young writer's work, even when there are multiple areas that need attention. In writing conferences, teachers can note what children know about directionality in writing, spacing, letter–sound correspondence, and spelling patterns. Teachers can also note if the young writer understands that writing is to convey ideas and thoughts.

Offered here are three slightly different forms for reading conferences that may be helpful in designing your own form (Figures 7.2, 7.3, and 7.4). In the first form, Ms. Doran lists the students she will see that day. For each student, Ms. Doran records the text selected, what was observed, the strategy work offered, and whether or not this work should be considered in a mini-lesson for others.

Page
hall monitor will i
be that ridr down
for the bad choss
and the good choss.

Hall monitor will I be that writer down for the bad class and
the good class.

Date	Text Shared/talked about	Noted observation	Strategy offered	Mini-lesson
Tiffany	The Napping House	T has read this text a number of times in independent reading. Reads at a very quick pace without much attention to the text	Showed T how to use her finger to track the words as she says them	
Darious	Pokemon cards	D shared his cards with me reading the names of the characters. I don't think he can read the characters without the pictures	Talked with D about how he uses pictures to support his reading	Picture cues to help when words are unfamiliar
Joseph	Little Bear	J miscues. Thought for taught Aboard for obey. commented that he used first letter cues for unfamiliar words	Showed J how to ask himself if the word made sense in the context of the sentence	Questions to ask ourselves while reading...does that make sense?

FIGURE 7.2 Daily conference sheet.

In the second form, Ms. Simon has a separate sheet for each child and records across time the work accomplished during reading conferences. These forms are kept in a student's personal folder so that Ms. Simon can refer to these forms when talking with parents.

Conference form

Name *Alicia*

Date	Text shared	Noted observation	Strategy offered
9.16			

FIGURE 7.3 Conference form for each student.

A third type of conference form identifies all of the children on one sheet. The notes are brief for each student, but Ms. Keller can quickly identify which students have not had a conference during the week

In a recent publication on conferencing, *One to One: The Art of Conferencing with Young Writers*, (2005) Calkins, Hartman, and White remind us that record keeping can help teachers take on new priorities, to notice strengths of their readers and writers, and to establish new goals and directions for the reader/writer

Week of __October_ 15-19_____				
Charles	Rohi	Jayvon	Thuy	Marcus
DeAndre	Sasha	Roberto	Trung	Jessica
Leslie	Everilda	Leah	Katlyn	Samantha
Monica	Astrid	Omer	Abel	Arlet
Dylan	Gilberto	Laureno	Imani	Edith

FIGURE 7.4 Conference form listing all students for the week.

workshop. What we need to remember is that whatever the form, it should be used to guide instruction and not merely to serve as a requirement for reader/writer workshop structures.

The teaching structures that make up the reader/writer workshop offer explicit and focused attention on code breaking practices, text meaning practices, text use practices, and critical practices. Students engage with texts from multiple vantage points and come to see that reading is more than deconstructing the sounds in a word, locating rhyming words, or retelling their own stories. Reading is all of these aspects of word analysis, comprehension, and more. The reader/writer workshop model for younger readers provides readers with literacy experiences that cut across many purposes and genres.

Connections to standards and benchmarks

A reading program for beginning readers that emphasizes code breaking, text meaning, text use, and critical practices will meet and exceed state and district standards and benchmarks. By using the routines and structures highlighted in a reading workshop, beginning readers will have many experiences with texts in authentic and meaningful ways. Typically, standards for kindergarten and first grade reading programs emphasize code breaking practices, with some attention to text meaning practices. Occasionally, there will be a standard that focuses on text use and critical practices. For most states, academic standards are meant to serve as a guideline for instruction. In other words, if you teach kindergarten or first grade, there is an expectation that your students will be able to accomplish the standards outlined for that particular grade level. In a recent review of three state departments of education websites (California, Georgia, and Indiana), the standards for kindergarten and first grade were similar. The following chart illustrates a sample of standards identified for first grade in English/Language Arts for these three selected states. Notice there is quite a bit of overlap with the guiding principles from IRA/NA-EYC outlined earlier in the chapter. Also notice that the level of specificity varies from state to state.

> ## Creating Connections 7.4
>
> Go to your state department of education website and review the standards for kindergarten, first-, or second grade in English/ Language Arts. How do the standards align with the four-resource model?

Reading Standards for First Grade in Three States

	Code Breaking	Text Participant	Text Use	Critical Practices
California (listed is the general overview of the standard. California has further delineated the standard into substandards or skills)	Students understand the basic features of reading. They select letter patterns and know how to translate them into spoken language by using phonics, syllabication, and word parts. They apply this knowledge to achieve fluent oral and silent reading.	Students read and understand grade-level-appropriate material. They draw upon a variety of comprehension strategies as needed (e.g., generating and responding to essential questions, making predictions, comparing information from several sources).	Students read and respond to a wide variety of significant works of children's literature. They distinguish between the structural features of the text and the literary terms or elements (e.g., theme, plot, setting, characters).	
Indiana	Word recognition involves the understanding of the basic features of words: word parts, patterns, relationships, and origins. Students use phonics, context clues, and a growing knowledge of English and other languages to determine the meaning of words and become fluent readers.	Comprehension involves understanding grade-level-appropriate material. Students develop strategies such as asking questions and making predictions. Response to grade-level-appropriate literature includes identifying story elements such as character, theme, plot, and setting, and making connections and comparisons across texts.	Students develop strategies for identifying and analyzing text structure, organization, perspective, and purpose.	Literary response enhances students' understanding of history, culture, and the social sciences.
Georgia (Georgia does not have an overview of the standards. The listed standards are categorized by concepts of print, phonemic awareness, phonics, fluency, and comprehension. Georgia further delineates the standards into smaller substandards or skills.	The student demonstrates knowledge of concepts of print. The student demonstrates the ability to identify and orally manipulate words and individual sounds within those spoken words. The student demonstrates the relationship between letters and letter combinations of written words and the sounds of spoken words. The student demonstrates the ability to read orally with speed, accuracy, and expression.	The student uses a variety of strategies to understand and gain meaning from grade-level text.		

Creating Connections 7.5

As you review the chart, what engagements and teaching structures would best support each standard?

Use your blog to share your thinking with classmates.

In Closing

This chapter on beginning reading instruction identified a number of key concepts that lead to effective and meaningful reading instruction in primary grade classrooms. The guiding principles and continuum of development suggest that beginning readers learn quite a bit about language and word structure and the notion that graphic symbols carry meaning. Luke and Freebody's four reading practices set the stage for considering the types of engagements that should be a part of every beginning reading classroom. Instruction in primary grades often emphasizes code breaking and text meaning practices. Text use and critical practices are also necessary for a balanced reading program. Throughout the chapter a number of resources, lists, and strategies were presented to address these practices in meaningful and authentic ways.

The reader/writer workshop model creates a literacy program that best meets the needs of individual readers in the classroom. Beginning readers engage with texts on many levels, while participating in whole class read alouds, small group shared and guided reading events, purposeful literature discussions, and independent reading and writing. Teachers address the individual needs of the students through mini-lessons, shared reading, and reading and writing conferences. The reader/writer workshop approach for beginning readers creates a literacy program that meets and often exceeds state and local standards, while at the same time creating a literacy environment that encourages children to actively participate and to construct meaning from the texts they are reading and composing.

Terms to Remember

Analogy *(192)*

Code breaking practice *(184)*

Critical practices *(197)*

High-frequency words *(192)*

Integrated approach *(185)*

Literature web *(195)*

Making words *(190)*

Phonemic blending *(186)*

Phonemic segmentation *(186)*

Prescriptive approach *(184)*

Schema *(194)*

Shared reading *(205)*

Text participant practices *(193)*

Text use practices *(196)*

Word families *(187)*

Word lists *(190)*

Resources for More Information

Barrentine, S. J. (1996). Engaging with reading through interactive read-alouds. *The Reading Teacher*, *50*, 36–43.

Calkins, L., Hartman, A., & White, Z. (2005). *One to one: The art of conferencing with young writers*. Portsmouth, NH: Heinemann.

Dahl, K. L., Scharer, O.L., Lawson, L. L., & Grogan, P.R. (2001) *Rethinking phonics: Making the best teaching decisions*. Portsmouth, NH: Heinemann.

Gill, S. (2000). Reading with Amy: Teaching and learning through reading conferences. *The Reading Teacher*, 53(6), 500–509.

Teale, W. & Yokota, J. (2000). Beginning reading and writing: Perspectives on instruction. In D. Strickland & L. Morrow (Eds.), *Beginning reading and writing* (pp. 3–21). Newark, DE: International Reading Association.

Questions for Further Reflection

- Why do you suppose code breaking practices have dominated beginning reading instruction?

- Reread the vignette that opened this chapter. Which practices are most evident in Ms. Simon's teaching of *There Was an Old Lady Who Swallowed a Fly?* Which are least evident?

- Why is it important to have a range of text materials in your classroom library?

- How do the examples and illustrations of classroom practices in this chapter compare to classrooms you have observed?

CHAPTER 8

Intermediate and Accomplished Readers and Writers

Ms Bell Discovers Her Fifth Grade Readers

A turning point in my career occurred when I realized the importance of linking literacy and student involvement. I began my second year of teaching with a reading workshop in my classroom. While students read independently, I conducted individual conferences. As the first couple of months progressed I became increasingly concerned that some of the boys in my class were not embracing the workshop with enthusiasm. A pattern began to develop in the normal daily reading routine: a group of boys would wait for me to become involved with other students, then proceed to engage in their own interests. One morning I noticed a group of three boys had gravitated to the far corner of the room. Experience has taught me that when a group of boys huddle together during independent reading sessions they are usually attempting to cover-up some off-task activity. As I approached the boys I heard faint whispers of "Shhhh!" and "Here she comes!" emanating from the huddle. This was immediately followed by a mad rustling of papers and "innocent" looks as each one in the group pretended to be totally engaged in a book. Even though I allowed students to choose their own materials for independent reading, I was suspicious when I saw one boy reading an informational text about puppies while his buddy next to him was totally engrossed in a recent issue of an *American Girl* magazine. Whatever they were disguising as "reading" was now hidden behind one of the boys.

"How's the reading going, guys?" I asked while taking a second glance at their materials. They looked at me and nodded politely. There were a few incoherent mumbles as they continued to stare at the books in front of them. I stooped down on the floor for a closer look. I looked at the first boy who was holding the *American Girl* magazine and inquired, "Tell me about what you are reading." I watched his eyes quickly scan the open page in front of him as he struggled in vain to find a reasonable answer to my question. He then looked up at me with a sheepish grin, knowing he had been caught.

After a few moments, I thought it best to rescue him from his embarrassing situation. I said to him and the other boys, "I know you all were not reading about puppies and 'American girls,' so tell me what you were *really* interested in over here."

Reluctantly, one boy removed a piece of paper and two smaller magazines from behind his back. The magazines were from a popular role-playing cartoon on TV. The boys were casting sideways glances at each other as I thumbed through the magazine and scanned the piece of paper. They had been writing a list of characters from the magazine and the attributes they possessed. The group shifted around nervously as they were half expecting me to confiscate their valuable items. "Tell me more about this," I inquired, pointing at the piece of paper.

Thus began an informative explanation about how every creature worked. They described the physical characteristics of each along with the special moves that they made

for fighting and defense. The boys took turns reading different statistics while interjecting other tidbits of information. The excitement in their faces and enthusiasm in their voices showed me this was something they were really interested in. Not only were they reading, but they were using higher level thinking skills to create and expand their knowledge. We became engaged in an active dialogue that I had been unable to experience with them in the past.

As I sat there listening, I realized how well they were applying literacy skills. After the boys finished explaining everything they knew about the subject, one of them asked if I was going to keep their valuable materials. Instead, I told them I was going to investigate other sources to help them learn more information. We discussed meeting the next day to review our findings. The excitement in the group was high, and one boy exclaimed that he was going to create a list at home that night.

Over time, I met with that group of boys a couple of times a week to discuss the latest developments in their readings and information gathering. We discovered there were chapter books and other magazines about the topic and characters. The boys started meeting more frequently, especially before school and during recess to compare new facts and discuss their latest readings. They even began a notebook that had important information and short stories they had created.

The thing that amazed me most was that they were engaged in reading. Previously, reading was not a priority for this group of boys as demonstrated by their daily routine of avoidance tactics. Now it was completely the opposite! Not only were they reading, but I was having a difficult time convincing them to stop once the period was over. As the year progressed, other students became interested and asked to

I wonder

- What important instructional decisions did Ms. Bell make to encourage her students to read?

- In what ways did Ms. Bell demonstrate the important role of reading and writing to her struggling fifth grade boys?

join the group. They also branched out into other topics and genres that suited their interests. I observed how each student became an active contributor and participant within their group once they were enthusiastic about their text. Allowing them to explore something they were interested in led to better comprehension and knowledge that transferred into other subjects, especially in their writing.

I was able to build lifelong learning skills in reading by working with my students' interests. They were more willing to listen to what I had to say and the strategies I was teaching them. Maybe they did not have a passion for reading that I, as a reading teacher, would like to see, but I was glad to see a firm foundation being built. This is an important skill that I think many intermediate teachers need to examine more closely.

Chapter Overview

Recent research and policy have focused on beginning readers and writers. There has been concerted effort from policy makers and curriculum developers to address the first few years of a child's reading and writing life. While this is extremely important, there is also a need to continue supporting children in their reading and writing as they move into middle and upper grade classrooms. The needs of intermediate and accomplished readers and writers vary significantly. They begin to navigate the cueing systems (graphophonemic, syntactic, and semantic) with relative ease. They are able to preview texts, decode unfamiliar words, read with fluency and intonation, make inferences, and comprehend and analyze storylines. In this chapter, the guiding questions include:

- What are the guiding principles and characteristics of intermediate and accomplished readers and writers?
- How do teachers implement the four reading practices (code breaking, text meaning, text use, and critical practices) in grades 3 through 6?
- How do teachers establish and maintain reading and writing workshops in intermediate classrooms?
- What are the mechanisms for linking instructional decision making to academic standards?

Guiding principles for intermediate and accomplished readers and writers

Children expand their repertoires of reading and writing strategies as they participate in various literacy events. Earlier chapters introduced the notion that there are diverse models and ways of thinking when it comes to teaching children to read and write. Some teachers and researchers are invested in an approach that isolates the reading and writing process and has children learning each aspect individually (part to whole), while other teachers and researchers believe that language and the cueing systems should not be divided out and learned separately (whole to whole). Of course, there are nuances to each of these positions. What is necessary in creating a productive and effective literacy curriculum is to consider that students need to be engaged in curriculum that is meaningful in their lives. To offer students a curriculum that is meaningful, teachers should address the specific characteristics and needs of intermediate and accomplished readers and writers. As illustrated by Ms.

Bell in the opening vignette, she was able to introduce new genres and reading strategies to her students by bringing in texts and materials that they were interested in learning more about.

In addition to recognizing the importance of incorporating multiple and everyday texts into the curriculum (*Guiding Principle #6* from Chapter 1), the teacher may also want to:

- invite students into a curriculum that operates from a perspective that literacy is socially and culturally situated; (*Guiding Principle #1*)
- provide opportunities for children to be problem-posers and inquiry oriented; and (*Guiding Principle #4*)
- encourage students to use their background knowledge and cultural understandings to make sense of the text. (*Guiding Principle #5*)

The next section offers a view of what it means to be an intermediate and accomplished reader and writer in classroom settings.

Characteristics of intermediate and accomplished readers

Children enter third through sixth grade with a range of skills and strategies related to literacy development. Most will be reading chapter books and will continue their development of phonics, comprehension, vocabulary and fluency. As children move from primary to middle grade classrooms, they encounter increasingly difficult and varied texts presented through a wide array of media (i.e., chapter books, textbooks, and websites). Not only are they required to comprehend and use such texts, but they are also expected to create similar texts on their own and in collaboration with others.

Continuing with the IRA/NAEYC document first introduced in Chapter 6 about emergent readers and writers, the final phase (Phase 5: Independent and Productive Reading and Writing) addresses the characteristics of reader and writers in third grade. To extend into fourth through sixth grades, a number of sources (e.g., Report of the New Jersey Task Force on Middle Grade Literacy Education and the International Reading Association) were consulted. Tables 8.1 and 8.2 highlight the reading skills of children in these grades, as well as offer suggestions for various literacy activities to address those skills.

With these guiding characteristics of intermediate and accomplished readers in place, the next section details how the four-resource model can be implemented to help teachers meet these objectives.

The four-resource model for intermediate and accomplished readers and writers

Similar to a primary grade curriculum, a curriculum organized around the four-resource model invites more experienced readers and writers to consider that reading and writing are for *something;* that one does not learn to read and write just to "do school." Recall that this is an integrated model with students accessing and using each practice, depending on what is being accomplished with the text (Fig. 8.1).

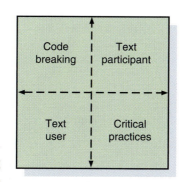

FIGURE 8.1 Four-resource model.

Phase 5a: Independent and Productive Reading and Writing (Grade 3)

In **third grade,** children continue to extend and refine their reading and writing to suit varying purposes and audiences.

Third Graders:	To Promote Literacy, Teachers Can:	Literacy Engagements for the Classroom
• Read fluently and enjoy reading.	• Provide opportunities daily for children to read, examine, and critically evaluate narrative and expository texts.	• Independent reading • Partner reading • Literature discussions
• Use a range of strategies when drawing meaning from the text.	• Encourage children to use writing as a tool for thinking and learning.	• Response logs • Writing notebooks • Writing conferences
• Use word identification strategies appropriately and automatically when encountering unknown words.	• Teach children to examine ideas in texts.	• Independent reading • Mini-lessons • Reading conferences
• Recognize and discuss elements of different text structures.	• Provide opportunities daily for children to read, examine, and critically evaluate narrative and expository texts.	• Independent reading • Literature discussions
• Make critical connections between texts.	• Create a climate that engages all children as a community of literacy learners.	• Literature discussions • Partner reading • Writing notebooks
• Write expressively in many different forms (stories, poems, reports).	• Teach children to examine ideas in texts. • Encourage children to use writing as a tool for thinking and learning. • Continue to create a climate that fosters critical reading and personal response.	• Author's chair • Independent writing • Mini-lessons • Author's celebration
• Use a rich variety of vocabulary and sentences appropriate to text forms.	• Extend children's knowledge of the correct use of writing conventions.	• Independent writing • Mini-lessons • Writing conferences • Author's chair
• Revise and edit their own writing during and after composing.	• Extend children's knowledge of the correct use of writing conventions.	• Independent writing • Mini-lessons • Writing conferences • Author's chair
• Spell words correctly in final writing drafts.	• Emphasize the importance of correct spelling in finished written products. • Extend children's knowledge of the correct use of writing conventions.	• Independent writing • Mini-lessons • Writing conferences • Author's chair

Phase 5b: Independent and Productive Reading and Writing (Grades 4–6)

In **fourth through sixth grades,** children continue to extend and refine their reading and writing to suit varying purposes and audiences.

Fourth through Sixth Graders	To Promote Literacy, Teachers Can:	Literacy Engagements for the Classroom:
• Use a number of different strategies to make sense of and remember what they read: use prior knowledge, question, visualize, make connections, determine importance, draw inferences, use fix-up strategies, and synthesize.	• Provide opportunities daily for children to read, examine, and critically evaluate narrative and expository texts. • Teach children to examine ideas in texts. • Encourage children to use writing as a tool for thinking and learning.	• Independent reading • Partner reading • Literature discussions • Reading response logs • Reading conferences • Independent writing • Author's circles • Writing conferences
• Anticipate the structures that they will find in text and use these text structures to aid comprehension.	• Provide opportunities daily for children to read, examine, and critically evaluate narrative and expository texts.	• Independent reading • Literature discussions • Reading conferences • Mini-lessons
• Apply word analysis skills to decode new vocabulary and polysyllabic words.	• Model strategies and provide practice for identifying unknown words.	• Independent reading • Reading conferences • Literature discussions • Mini-lessons
• Develop meaningful and authentic purposes for reading and writing.	• Continue to create a climate that fosters critical reading and personal response. • Encourage children to use writing as a tool for thinking and learning. • Create a climate that engages all children as a community of literacy learners.	• Independent reading • Literature discussions • Reading response logs • Mini-lessons • Inquiry projects and presentations • Independent writing
• Can pinpoint when meaning breaks down.	• Encourage children to use writing as a tool for thinking and learning. • Model strategies and provide practice for identifying unknown words	• Independent reading • Reading conferences • Mini-lessons • Writing conferences • Independent writing
• Connect reading and writing with their life and their learning inside and outside of school.	• Create a climate that engages all children as a community of literacy learners. • Provide opportunities daily for children to read, examine, and critically evaluate narrative and expository texts. • Continue to create a climate that fosters critical reading and personal response.	• Independent reading • Reading conferences • Mini-lessons • Writing conferences • Independent writing • Author's circles • Author's chair
• Develop critical perspectives toward what they read, view, and hear.	• Create a climate that engages all children as a community of literacy learners. • Provide opportunities daily for children to read, examine, and critically evaluate narrative and expository texts. • Continue to create a climate that fosters critical reading and personal response.	• Literature discussions • Reading conferences • Mini-lessons • Reading response logs • Presentations and sharing • Inquiry projects

Code breaking	Text participant
Text user	Critical practices

Code breaking for intermediate and accomplished readers

Readers in grades 3 through 6 are typically quite comfortable with the graphophonemic cueing system. They know the sounds that represent all of the letters and letter combinations. Knowing the 41 onsets and 38 rimes enables readers to decode thousands of words. These readers are also able to decode word chunks on a consistent basis (e.g., recognizing the word "mat" in matter, or "cap" in captain).

word study

Examining the shades of sound, structure, and meaning of words.

WORD STUDY STRATEGIES. The focus for code-breaking practices in these grades is to consider **word study** strategies. Word study involves examining "shades of sound, structure, and meaning" (Bear & Templeton, 1998, p. 223). It is about teaching children how to examine and think about words as they read and write. "Teachers who address word-knowledge components as integrated features rather than isolated subskills encourage students to make connections across sources" (Bloodgood & Pacifici, 2004, p. 251).

While spelling is an integral aspect of word study, the direction in this section is to understand how readers make sense of words and texts that are unfamiliar. Word study involves teaching processes and strategies for examining and thinking about the words readers read and write. Bear and Templeton note that when thinking about word study, there are three types of information that can be drawn upon: alphabetic, pattern, and meaning.

- **Alphabetic**. Alphabetic strategies refer to letter/sound correspondence. Emergent and beginning readers use alphabetic strategies to match letters and sounds in an obvious left to right fashion (e.g., m-a-t). Revisit the strategy work in Chapter 7 that focuses on the alphabetic principle for more information.

- **Pattern**. Pattern knowledge is more complex because it requires readers to consider words from a right to left perspective—to know, for example, if the word contains an "e" at the end, as in *make* or *rake*, that it will impact how the vowel is pronounced. Pattern knowledge also requires readers to note whether vowels are short, long, or if a consonant is doubled in multisyllabic words with vowel-consonant-consonant-vowel (VCCV) patterns or vowel-consonant-vowel patterns (VCV) (e.g., talent, pilot, mitten.)

- **Meaning**. Just as word families have similar spellings, meaning families have to do with what the words mean. Readers can begin to explore and appreciate the relationships in meaning families. Some words have consistent spelling and meaning despite differences in pronunciation. Meaning families often include affixes (prefixes and suffixes) as well as base words and their derivations. As readers begin to make these connections among words that belong in the same meaning family (e.g., ocean/oceanography/oceanic) their vocabularies increase and it becomes easier to understand why certain words are spelled/pronounced the way they are.

prefix

An affix that attaches to the beginning of a word.

suffix

An affix that attaches to the end of a word.

One type of meaning family is affixes. Affixes are word parts—**prefixes** and **suffixes**—that attach themselves to words and in doing so, change the meaning of the word. For example, when *im* is placed in front of *possible*, making the word *impossible*, meaning is changed from something that can happen to something that cannot happen. Sometimes the affix is a single letter, such as "s" for making words plural (e.g., cat**s**) or the affix may be a word in and of itself, like "super" in the word *superstore*. When students learn a selected number of prefixes and suffixes, their ability to decode a large number of words dramatically increases. Over thirty years ago researchers noted that

TABLE 8.1
Inflectional Suffixes

Verb tense	*-ed in opened*
	-ing in opening
Plurality	*-es in beaches*
	-s in monkeys
Comparison	*-er in faster*
	-est in cutest

66 percent of the words that contained prefixes were comprised of the following prefixes: *un, re, in, im, il, ir, dis, en, em,* and *non* (Carroll, Davis, and Richman, 1971). Eighty-two percent of words that contain suffixes involved one of the following: *-s/-es, -ed, -ing, -ly, -er/-or, -ion/-tion/-ation/-ition,* and *–able/–ible.*

There are two categories for suffixes. One category is **inflectional** (Table 8.1), meaning that it changes the tense of the verb, indicates plurality, or demonstrates comparison. These suffixes impact the syntax of the sentence.

The other category is **derivational**. These suffixes show a meaning relationship of the word to the root word. Derivational suffixes include: *ly, ness, y, er/or/ar, tion.* For example, the words *inventor* and *invention*. Both inventor and invention have a relationship with the word *invent*.

Root words are words or word parts that come from other languages, such as Greek and Latin. Knowing about these word parts will support readers as they encounter text, particularly text with unfamiliar words. For example, knowing the root word *jour* (day or daily) supports understanding of words such as journey, journal, and journalist.

inflectional suffix

The suffix changes the tense of the verb, indicates plurality, or demonstrates comparison.

derivational suffix

Show a meaning relationship between the word and the root word.

root word

Word or word part that comes from another language.

Invitation for the classroom

Roots and Branches

In this activity, students place a root word in the center of a web or tree trunk created on chart paper. In groups of three to five, students record derived words around the root or on branches in a different color. As an extension, students can also record the word meanings in a separate color.

Roots and Branches is something that can be a part of the daily routine around code-breaking practices.

Adapted from Bloodgood & Pacifici, 2004.

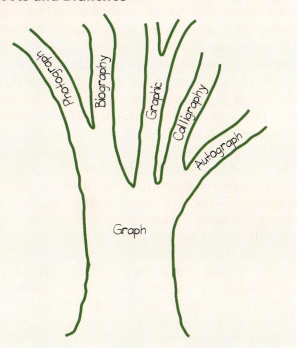

Another opportunity to work with words in an authentic and meaningful context is to engage in word sorts. Introduced to word sorts in Chapter 7 for beginning readers, a variation of word sorts in upper grades involves students paying close attention to spelling patterns. In word sorts, students are asked to explicitly think about how words are similar and/or different. This work helps students attend to unfamiliar words as they construct generalizations about words and related word patterns. In the following word pattern sort (adapted from Bear and Templeton, 1998), words with long ā sounds are placed on a grid. Students are then asked to sort the words according to the letter patterns and sounds heard.

walk	cave	nail	said
may	lay	tall	faint
gain	sail	hail	lane
paste	tray	paid	can
rain	land	mate	chase
range	flat	frame	chain

Walk (cvc)	**Cave (cvce)**	**Nail (cvvc)**	**Lay (cvv)**
tall	mate	sail	say
can	frame	hail	may
land	chase	paid	tray
flat	lane	chain	
	*paste	faint	
	*range	gain	
		rain	

*These two words extend the CVCE pattern to CVCCE pattern

Word hunts are a way to extend the knowledge gained in word sorts. After students study a pattern in word sorts, they can return to stories and texts they are reading to find words that go with a specific pattern. For example, students may be asked to hunt for words that contain a particular consonant and vowel patterns.

Word study work also includes understanding the distinctions between homographs and homophones/homonyms. *Homographs* are words that are spelled the same, but have different pronunciations and meanings; while *homophones/homonyms* are words that sound the same but have different spellings and meanings. Other invitations for focusing attention on code breaking include homophone dictionary and connections between writing and spelling.

Word study strategies are important in developing proficient and effective readers. As readers gain experience in working with derivational word patterns and affixes, their vocabulary increases, as does their ability to decode unfamiliar and more complex words.

DEVELOPMENTAL WORD STUDY AND SPELLING. Code-breaking practices in the intermediate and upper grades also involve opportunities to focus on issues related to spelling. Just as word analysis strategies are best attended to in the context of authentic reading and writing, so are strategies around spelling. Teachers will often use students' writing journals and compositions to highlight confusing and problematic words. For most students, there is very little randomness as to how they spell words. Students form and test hypotheses about what words look and sound like. For example, when Ashanti spelled "jeraf" (giraffe), she consciously attended to the spelling pattern of cvc (raf) to make a /ă/ sound.

In a study conducted by a group of teacher researchers (Dahl, Barto, Bonfils, Carasello, Christopher, Davis, Erkkila, Glander, Jacobs, Kendra, Koski, Majeski, Mc-

TECHNOLOGY LINK
http://pbskids.org/lions/songs/

Brian McKnight and Cleo the Lion sing this song about homophones.

homographs

Words with same spelling but different pronunciation and meaning.

homophone/homonym

Words that are pronunced the same but have different spelling and meaning.

Invitation for the classroom

Class Homophone Dictionary

There are a number of homophones (words that sound the same and are spelled differently) that intermediate and accomplished readers and writers may confuse.

Using a blank book with stenciled letters at the top, have students record homophones on the appropriate page. Students can cross reference homophones that begin with different letters (I and eye). Students can write definitions, synonyms, and sentences as part of the entry. This supports spelling–meaning connections.

B	
bee	be
brake	break
blew	blue

C	
cent	sent
cereal	serial
cheap	cheep
cell	sell

Homophone Reference List

bare	bear	
be	bee	
blew	blue	
break	brake	
cent	sent	
ceiling	sealing	
cereal	serial	
dear	deer	
die	dye	
due	dew	do
eight	ate	
feet	feat	
flew	flu	
flower	flour	
hall	haul	
herd	heard	
hire	higher	
hour	our	
know	no	
lesson	lessen	
made	maid	
mail	male	

meet	meat	
minor	miner	
nose	knows	
pair	pear	
pale	pail	
pause	paws	
piece	peace	
road	rode	
sale	sail	
seen	scene	
sees	seas	
side	sighed	
some	sum	
steel	steal	
tale	tail	
there	they're	their
threw	through	
to	too	two
wait	weight	
waste	waist	
weather	whether	
whole	hole	

Connell, Petrie Siegel, Slaby, Waldbauer, & Williams, 2004), students' strategies shifted across the developmental stages of word study. Recall in Chapter 6, stages of spelling were identified as random marks, prephonemic, early phonemic, letter naming, and transitional (Temple, et al., 1993). These stages are appropriate for primary grade readers and writers. For those in grades 3 through 6, there are additional categories to determine a student's development in spelling (Invernizzi, Aboudzeid & Gill, 1994; Templeton, 1991). These categories include:

Invitation for the classroom

How do you say . . .

Homographs are words that are spelled the same but are pronounced differently [*wind* (/wind/, /wīnd/), *wound* (/woond/, /wound/), or *live* (/liv/, /līv/)].

Using a list of homographs, have students construct sentences that clearly indicate the word's meaning. Discuss with students how there is a relationship between stress and grammatical function (nouns and adjectives typically are stressed on the first syllable, while verbs usually carry a second syllable stress).

The drama club will *present* their show next Tuesday. I looked all over the house for her birthday *present*.

Within Word In this stage, children recognize that the system includes more than letters and sounds. They begin to note that there are patterns that relate to sounds in indirect ways (long vowels receive extra silent letters, such as *bake*, *train*, or *height*).

Syllable Juncture Children in this stage acquire the meaning units contained in the spelling of polysyllabic words, words that have more than one syllable (e.g. competition). At the point were the syllables join, students learn there may be one letter, double letters, three letters or letters may be dropped (brag to bragging; make to making). This stage also focuses on stress, syllables, and vowel alterations. Where the accent is for a word will determine whether letters are added (equip to equipped; offer to offered).

Derivational-consistency Children explore words based on spelling/meaning relationships. Their word knowledge is becoming more abstract as they work within and between syllables in polysyllabic words. In this stage, children learn that words that are related in meaning are often related in spelling, regardless of pronunciation (e.g., impose/imposition; labor/laboratory).

Teachers can point out to students what they know and then compare this to what students are trying to spell. Students should have the opportunity to examine, manipulate, and make decisions about words according to categories of similarities and differences (Invernizzi, Aboudzeid & Gill, 1994). One particular instructional approach that encourages students to make visible their thinking is the Directed Spelling Thinking Activity developed by Jerry Zutell (1996).

In addition to the Directed Spelling Thinking Activity, spelling conferences also reveal students' strategies for spelling. Dahl et al. (2004) noted that students used a range of strategies for determining correct spellings. Figure 8.2 identifies the most common strategies.

1. Visualizing: drawing upon one's visual memory for words
   - Remembering words from books
   - Picturing words
   - Trying alternatives
2. Making connections: use known information to generate new spelling
   - Using word families and analogies
   - Starting with known patterns
   - Building words
3. Focusing on sounds: working with letter–sound relationships
   - Sounding out
   - Chunking
4. Reflecting: looking back on spellings, revisiting words, and checking for accuracy
   - Verifying spelling
   - Correcting errors
   - Checking resources
5. Combining information
   - Using multiple strategies
   - Using a strategy routine

FIGURE 8.2 Strategies students use for spelling.
Adapted from Dahl et al., 2004.

Much of the learning students do around spelling is the result of incidental word learning. Students pull words from authentic texts, work with them outside of the context, and put them back into meaningful contexts. In doing so, students integrate vocabulary, grammar, and spelling instruction. Having access to wide reading materials encourages readers to broaden their vocabularies and to expand their conceptual understanding of words and word patterns.

READING WITH FLUENCY. Fluency, one of the core areas in the No Child Left Behind (NCLB) legislation, is gaining increased attention in current reading curriculum and programs. According to the National Reading Panel report (2000), fluency relates to speed, accuracy, and proper expression. Early concepts of fluency related to the notion of reading smoothly and with expression. Now there is a focus on automatic and rapid word identification. In the early 1990s, researchers with a skills orientation (e.g., Marilyn Adams and Keith Stanovich) noted that fluency was an important skill and that in order to determine fluent readers, timed reading tests were administered (Weaver, 2002). Students who read fast on these tests were touted as better readers than those that read more slowly or those who struggled to complete the test in the allotted time. Yet it is often the case that a reader who reads rapidly and in some cases with expression, may not be attending to meaning making. We have all experienced this when asked to read something aloud. We focus on how we are saying our words, rather than what the words are saying. There is a pervasive perception that speed equates with competence. This is why many children respond to questions about what makes a good reader with comments about reading "fast."

TECHNOLOGY LINK

http://www.learner.org/channel/workshops/teachreading35/session2/index.html

This Annenberg website provides teachers with videos and supplemental professional development resources on fluency and word study in the intermediate grades.

Creating Connections 8.1

Consider children you know who are not fluent readers. How can you model and demonstrate fluent reading through out the day? What literacy engagements and activities will develop fluency?

Share your thinking with classmates through your blog.

Invitation for the classroom

DSTA (Directed Spelling Thinking Activity)

Determine the spelling pattern to emphasize, such as long vowel with silent e, or doubling of consonants when adding endings to single syllable words.

Select a group of words that demonstrates the pattern, a group that provides a contrast, and a few words that are exceptions. For example, the long i sound with silent e pattern might use these words:

> demonstrates pattern: ice, write, bike, bite, strike, ripe, line, hive

> contrast: tip, pin, did, fit, mist, big, wind, sick

> exceptions: sign, light, why

Begin with a brief spelling test. While a general introduction to the task is fine, do not provide any information regarding the spelling pattern.

If the words are well selected, there should be a mix of correct and incorrect spellings. Have students discuss what they were thinking as they spelled the words. After a few words are discussed, students begin to make their own connections across words and use these connections to revise or confirm their guesses.

Following a discussion, a word sort activity enables students to consider categories for their words, further verbalizing their thinking about why particular words belong in particular categories.

Students can then add their own words to the lists.

Adapted from J. Zutell (1996).

Fluency is not fixed or static. It changes, depending on what readers are reading, their familiarity with words, and the amount of practice in reading aloud. Context greatly influences how quickly readers read. What is the text about? Is it familiar to the reader? Allen Flurkey's work in the late 1990s indicated that reading rates vary across texts, that pauses often correlate to the types of miscues and strategies a reader is employing. He suggests that teachers and researchers focus on "flow," which is "a reader's dynamic response to a text, of speeding up and slowing down, acceleration and deceleration across a text" (1997, p. 155). There is an ebb and flow to reading that corresponds to the type of text, the reader's familiarity with the topic, and the context in which the text is presented. When readers are more familiar with a text, there is a greater likelihood that they read aloud with relative ease, while also making meaning of the text.

Many teachers in intermediate and upper grades struggle with ways to work on fluency (or flow) so that readers are confident in their abilities to orally read a text and at the same time construct meanings of the text. For most readers, fluency develops over time and through extended opportunities to practice reading texts, both orally and silently. Calkins (2001) talks about how books that are most appropriate for working on fluency in intermediate grades are those that are relatively easy, have long sentences, use authentic and natural language (language that is similar to how we talk), and contain many high-frequency words. Readers can cruise through these without much difficulty. Texts that have fragmented or unnatural language (similar to basal materials or decodable texts) do not provide adequate support for working on fluency.

> What Does Good Reading Sound like?
>
> Read like your talking, not choppy.
>
> Use a good reading voice, Don't exaggreate.
>
> Try to look ahead for ~~person~~ punctuation so that you ~~would~~ aren't caught off guard.
>
> Don't skip sentences.
>
> Schyler F.

Invitation for the classroom

Cutting

The teacher selects an excerpt from a piece of young adult literature that can be read dramatically and appreciated apart from the longer selection. Portions of the text not useful for the dramatic reading can be eliminated (cut). The teacher describes for students the book, including details about the author and his or her other works.

The excerpt is divided into sections, and each student is responsible for rehearsing his or her section. Students are encouraged to read their selections both silently and orally, highlighting unfamiliar or troublesome words.

Students are then paired together to rehearse their sections.

Students then perform their oral interpretations to other classmates, teachers, and administrators.

Adapted from Goodson & Goodson, 2005.

How can teachers support students as they become fluent and proficient readers? One way is through an instructional approach known as ***repeated readings***, whereby a student reads aloud a passage a number of times, and receives guidance and feedback on the quality of pace, intonation, and phrasing. Teachers can have students tape-record themselves as they read the passage. Then students listen to and critique the tape during reading conferences. Using a familiar text to work on fluency is key because the reader attends to reading with clarity, smoothness, and appropriate phrasing and intonation.

repeated readings

An instructional approach whereby a student reads aloud a passage a number of times with guidance and feedback on pausing, intonation, and phrasing.

Repeated readings are different than traditional "round robin" reading structures. In round robin structures, children read orally, but it is often the first time they have seen the text, and they are asked to only read a small amount of text. While teachers use this structure to attend to fluency, it is rarely achieved with this one shot at reading. For most of us, it takes practice to read a text with expression and accuracy. In contrast, repeated readings enable the reader to practice with a text a number of times, developing appropriate intonation and phrasing.

Other structures that support fluency work include:

- *Choral reading*: Students read aloud simultaneously in a group. This enables less fluent readers to be a part of the oral reading without having to read aloud alone.

- *Partner reading*: Two readers are paired to read a text aloud. The less fluent reader hears a model of fluent reading, while the more fluent reader helps with word recognition and provide feedback. Following these partner-reading engagements, students can share in larger discussions what they observed about their partner's reading.

- *Reader's theater*: Readers rehearse and perform a text that is rich in dialogue. Readers do not memorize the text, but over the course of rehearsing become quite familiar with it.

- *Independent reading time*. Readers have the opportunity to read texts they are interested in and for extended periods of time. There is no clear evidence that independent silent reading facilitates fluency, but the more reading students do, the greater the likelihood of becoming more efficient and fluent readers.

- *Read alouds*. Read alouds offer students opportunities to hear fluent reading. The teacher models for students how to sound like one is talking and how to scan ahead for punctuation marks to indicate intonation.

Students perform a Reader's theater script.

For intermediate and accomplished readers and writers, code-breaking practices focus on word analysis strategies (expanding their repertoire of new words to read and spell) as well as developing fluency in reading. Code breaking enables readers and writers to grow in their understanding of how words and language work.

TECHNOLOGY LINK
http://www.aaronshep.com/rt/

This site provides resources and tips for conducting Reader's Theater with children

Code breaking	Text participant
Text user	Critical practices

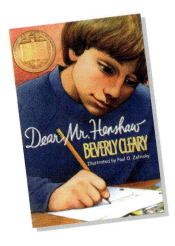

Text participant practices with intermediate and accomplished readers

Readers in third, fourth, fifth, and sixth grades participate in many kinds of literacy engagements throughout the instructional day. Reading and writing are seen as social practice in that students often work together as partners, in small groups, and as part of a whole class experience. These varied and multiple structures encourage readers to share their thinking and understandings of the text. They read and write different genres—narrative, expository, comic, websites, etc. Each of these genres contributes to intermediate and accomplished readers' repertoire of reading experiences. How readers define themselves as readers is very much a part of the text participant role. Readers bring to the reading event their knowledge and experiences of being a reader both in and out of the classroom. They draw upon their life histories, experiences, and cultures to form connections to the text. In this process, they make meaning from the text.

To illustrate the connections children make as they engage with text, a fourth grade teacher is reading *Dear Mr. Henshaw* (Cleary, 1984) as an after-lunch read aloud time. *Dear Mr. Henshaw* is the story of Leigh Botts who begins writing to his favorite author Mr. Henshaw. Through the letters, readers come to understand how Leigh feels about his parents' divorce, missing his dad, being the new kid in school, and adjusting to all of the changes taking place in his life. The students are asked to

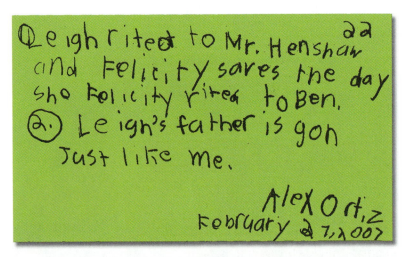

1. Leigh [writed] to Mr. Henshaw and Felicity saves the day she Felicity writes to Ben.

2. Leigh's father is gone just like me.

Alex and Brisli's post it notes for Mr. Henshaw.

write their thinking while they are listening to the story. On one particular afternoon, Brisli, an ELL student, focused on unfamiliar words that she wanted to know, while Alex commented that like Leigh, his own father is no longer living with him.

The text participant practice is quite common in reading instruction for intermediate and accomplished readers. Teachers and students are no longer singularly focused on code breaking and consequently spend a good portion of the instructional time drawing upon their prior knowledge and experiences to make sense of their current text. During read aloud events, literature discussions, and other reading opportunities, teachers often ask questions that encourage readers to consider what they know from their own experiences and how this information connects to what they are listening to and reading about in the text.

Creating Connections 8.2

Recall your own reading instruction in these grades. How much of the time was focused on text participant practices?

Share your responses with classmates in your blog.

Emphasizing the meaning of a text includes:

- accessing literal meanings from the text;
- drawing inferences;
- making links and connections to prior knowledge and experiences;
- interpreting texts; and
- constructing figurative meanings in texts.

To support readers in attending to these aspects, teachers and students may engage in the following activities and invitations: reading easy books with understanding, comprehension strategies, and building vocabulary.

READING EASY BOOKS WITH UNDERSTANDING. To build readers' confidence as they transition into the intermediate and upper grades, students should occasionally read books that are below their instructional level. Readers do not always have to encounter more difficult text. This is especially true for young readers who are just gaining their confidence around reading. When they read books that are easy, their sense of what it means to be a reader is developed. They begin to see how reading is more than merely decoding words on a page; they learn that accomplished and proficient readers construct meanings, read with clear, strong voices, and read with fluency.

In the beginning of the school year, the teacher may want to observe and monitor the activities that occur during sustained silent reading time (or independent reading time). Recall how Ms. Bell observed what some of her boys were doing during their independent reading time. She noted that they were not engaged in the materials and tried to look busy when she approached them. In similar classrooms, there are students who flip through book after book, without a clear sense of what the story is about. There are students who find reasons to be out of the classroom during this time (bathroom, office, etc.). Or there are students who watch everything else that is going on in the classroom. For these students, it may be worthwhile to more closely observe and document what they are doing during this time. For example, a teacher can join the reader and ask, "Can you tell me about this book? I don't know it." Or, "Can you read your favorite part for me?" Or, "What's happening on this page?" If it becomes apparent that the text is too difficult for the reader, the teacher can invite the reader to consider the idea that the book is too challenging. When this happens, the teacher might suggest that good readers determine when a book is too challenging or difficult.

Mini-lessons can introduce the notion that reading easy books is just as critical and important as reading texts that challenge them as readers. The focus of the mini-lesson is to provide children with tools to access when they are selecting among a range of text. One tool is for the reader to ask a series of questions about the text (Calkins, 2001).

Questions for readers to ask:

- Do I understand what this book is about?
- Do I feel like a strong reader?
- Can I read this book without stumbling over words?

Have students preview several texts using these questions. As they do so, students can quickly determine which books are at an "easy" level and which books are at a more "difficult" level.

VOCABULARY DEVELOPMENT INSIDE TEXT PARTICIPANT PRACTICES. Vocabulary has been identified as another key component of reading achievement in the National Reading Panel report (2000). Children with well-developed vocabularies are often the same children who engage in reading and writing on a regular basis. We learn words by being with words. On average, students add 2000–3000 words each year to their reading vocabularies (Anderson & Nagy, 1992; Beck & McKeowen, 1991). This means that students learn from six to eight new words each day, which is a sizable achievement. In any classroom there can be great differences in the range and number of words that children are exposed to. The differences can greatly impact what children are able to understand and make sense of in literacy events. Children with richer vocabularies are able to understand new ideas much easier than children with limited vocabularies.

There is quite a distinction between spoken and written language. Spoken language is not as rich or complex as written language because speakers are able to use gestures and tone to convey the idea, whereas with spoken language the writer must rely on interesting words to convey the thought. Children will likely encounter words in their literature selections and textbooks (e.g., restore, delve) that are not a part of their everyday speaking vocabulary. For ELL students, this is particularly true and the challenge to develop a rich vocabulary is even greater. There is a tendency to assume that because an ELL student is conversationally proficient, she is also proficient in understanding written vocabulary. When the ELL student struggles in reading, it may be that the vocabulary and not a reading disability is the issue.

Vocabulary knowledge is more than just knowing the definition of a word. Definitions of words provide only a surface understanding of the word. Traditionally, students are asked to look up definitions of words and use them in sentences as part of their vocabulary work. The problem is that students do not recognize the subtle nuances in the English language and will often use the word in the wrong way. To know a word, students need to encounter it in many different contexts, see how the word's meaning changes as a result of different contexts, and to see how its meaning relates to words around it (Texas Reading Initiative, 2002).

It is important for students to internalize the meanings of words—to learn beyond the low-level definition phase. The Texas Reading Initiative (2002) identified a number of effective strategies to support vocabulary development, including:

Encouraging wide reading
Wide reading involves introducing students to genres and texts that they are not necessarily familiar with. Students who read more and read more chal-

lenging texts will develop their vocabulary knowledge at a faster rate than students who typically read only those texts that they are familiar with.

Exposing students to high-quality oral language

Oral language is central to developing a rich and complex vocabulary. Introducing students to more sophisticated language through read alouds and storytelling are two possibilities for increasing vocabulary knowledge. High-quality children's literature regularly uses language that "talks over students' heads," but remains engaging and interesting for children to listen to and read.

Promote word consciousness

Word consciousness is playing with language. Students who are word conscious enjoy learning new words and engaging in word play. Word conscious activities include limericks, puns, jokes, anagrams, and crossword puzzles. Students can also pay close attention to the differences in how people speak in different situations. Chapter 2 offers invitations that encourage children to become language detectives and notice how words are used.

Provide explicit instruction of specific words and modeling of independent word-learning strategies

Explicit instruction and modeling are important aspects of vocabulary development. Effectively teaching vocabulary involves using definitional and contextual information and active learning. **Definitional vocabulary work** involves having students identify a number of aspects of the word. For example, Ricky, a fifth grader completed the following chart on the word "nimble."

    Contextual vocabulary work information asks students to learn words in context. To do this, students can write sentences, create scenarios, and dramatize new vocabulary words.

definitional vocabulary work

Invites student to identify a number of aspects of a word, such as definition, synonym, antonym and category.

contextual vocabulary work

Invites students to learn words in context through sentences, scenarios, and drama.

Word to know	Nimble
Dictionary definition	Quick, light, and agile in movement
Synonyms	Deftly, dexterously
Antonyms	Awkward, clumsy
Category	Way of moving
Real life example	I nimbly climbed to the top of the tree in my backyard
Picture	

Invitation for the classroom

Four Square

Four Square, similar to concept maps, enable students to learn word meanings conceptually.

Ask students to fold a piece of paper into fours.

In the upper left section of the paper, write the target word.

In the upper right section of the paper, provide a definition of the word, using the dictionary for support.

In the lower left section of the paper, provide some examples and nonexamples of the target word (these can also be drawings).

In the lower right section of the paper, write a sentence with the target word.

While definitional and contextual approaches to vocabulary development are available, teaching word meanings as concepts is a more effective approach. Students establish connections among context, their prior knowledge, and the concepts or words being taught (Stahl, 1999). *Concept of Definition Maps* are graphic displays that show common elements of a dictionary definition. These elements include (1) the category to which the word being defined belongs (What is this?), (2) some characteristics of the word (What is it like?), and (3) some specific examples and some nonexamples of the word. Students refer to context, their prior knowledge, and dictionaries to find the elements needed to complete the map.

Vocabulary development plays a key role in becoming an effective reader and writer. Helping students achieve a robust vocabulary will support their own growth and development as a proficient and effective literacy user.

Invitation for the classroom

Vocabulary Squares

In this invitation, students draw upon their linguistic and visual knowledge to develop word meaning knowledge. To begin, students self-select words that are interesting and/or confusing from texts they are currently reading (narrative or expository)

1. Students are given two 5-in. squares of paper. One is for the rough draft, the other for the final, clean copy.
2. The square contains the following information:
   a. word at the top
   b. short definition at the bottom
   c. a picture or symbol in center that illustrates the word
3. Have students use a black pen in their final copy.

Collect the squares and reduce them on the copy machine until the square is about $2\frac{1}{2}$ in. Approximately 12 squares can fit on a single $8\frac{1}{2} \times 11$ sheet of paper. Duplicate the sets of squares for each student and distribute as a vocabulary packet.

Students can use these vocabulary packets when encountering unfamiliar words in their reading.

CONNECTING TO THE MEANING OF A TEXT. Comprehension is a primary goal in the text participant practice. Comprehension is a general term that includes five processes. Following are five types of processes that support comprehension (Irwin, 1991):

Microprocess—chunking ideas into phrases for more fluent reading.

Integrative process—inferring connections among ideas in the text by noticing pronoun substitutions, cause and effect, and words, such as however, unless, and also.

Macroprocess—taking in the whole of the text or story and summarizing ideas.

Elaborative process—using background knowledge and experiences to make connections to the readers' own lives, other literature, and the world.

Metacognitive process—where readers monitor their own understandings

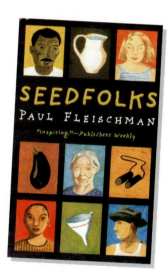

For many readers and teachers, these processes seem to be elusive—some readers comprehend with ease, others struggle even when they are reading all of the words. Teachers can support readers as they make sense of texts by focusing on these processes. Adapted from Tompkins (2004), Table 8.2 identifies classroom activities that aid the comprehension process.

Even though microprocesses are listed in this section, the activities that support it are more appropriate to the code-breaking practices [see previous section for a more complete discussion of choral reading and fluency]. To highlight the integrative process, teachers may ask students clarifying questions that bring to the readers' attention relationships at the syntactic level (e.g., pronoun substitution, connective words such as also, however, because). The macroprocess may also involve asking questions to understand the whole of the story. For example, when fourth grade students read *Seedfolks* (Fleischman, 1997), the story of a blighted neighborhood transformed when a young girl plants a few lima beans in an abandoned lot, the teacher may ask the following questions:

- Where do the characters live? What are the clues that tell you where they live?
- What kind of building do Kim, Ana, and Wendell live in? What season is it where they live? How do you know?
- What did Ana discover when she dug in the vacant lot? How did she feel about what she'd done?
- What could Gonzalo do that his father and great-uncle could not do?
- What did Leona want to change about the vacant lot? How did she change the situation? Was it difficult or easy work?
- What did Sam notice about the people in the garden on a busy Saturday?

TABLE 8.2
The Comprehension Process and Related Activities

Comprehension Process	Activities in the Classroom
Microprocesses	Practice choral reading to encourage readers to chunk texts in appropriate sections for fluent reading.
Integrative processes	Focus student attention on syntactic level connections in the text to infer relationships.
Macroprocesses	Use graphic organizers to determine which ideas are more or less significant to the storyline.
Elaborative processes	Hold literature discussions that focus on text to text, text to world, and text to self connections.
Metacognitive processes	Demonstrate think aloud strategies.

graphic organizer

A visual that makes explicit relationships and/or connections.

think aloud

A strategy that encourages readers to stop and reflect on their own metacognitive processes.

Children make sense of texts by learning to differentiate between more and less important ideas in the story. **Graphic organizers** offer students opportunities to generate ideas on paper and to consider relationships and connections. Graphic organizers come in many forms depending on the work that it is being used for. Common graphic organizers include webbing charts, Venn diagrams, flow charts, data charts, clusters, and T-charts (see Figure 8.3).

Elaborative processes focus on ways to extend the author's meaning and intention. Within this process, readers access their background experiences and knowledge to make sense of text. Three common connection strategies include:

- Text to text
- Text to self
- Text to world

Text-to-text connections are connections readers and writers make between and among texts. When Ms. Elrod's fifth graders read *Each Little Bird that Sings* (2005), they noted that the author, Deborah Wiles, also wrote *Love Ruby Lavender* (2001) and *Freedom Summer* (2001). This is one type of connection that highlights a commonality in one author across texts. Another type of text to text is when students comment that the character in one story reminds them of a character in another story. Students are moving between and among texts to make these connections and are seeing meaning making as extending beyond an individual text.

Text-to-self connections are when a number of personal connections are fostered. Students in Ms. Jordan's third grade classroom read *The Story of Ruby Bridges* (Coles, 1995). This story recounts Ruby Bridge's experience of being the only African American child to attend a New Orleans elementary school after a court order of desegretation in 1960. After reading the story, Arman records a personal connection to the character, Ruby.

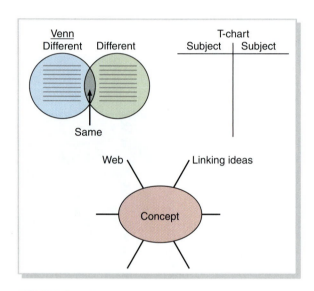

FIGURE 8.3 Graphic organizers.

Arman's text to self connection.

Ruby is black. I am black, we are not the same in every way but we do have some things in common. We both stick out in a crowd, we have nice teachers. We both go to school. We both have been to church, we both went to a court.

Text-to-world connections move beyond the personal experience to link to world knowledge. Very often, text-to-world comments that students make enable them to question and problematize issues presented in the text. The text-to-world connections may reside in the critical practices. In Ms. Paynter's fifth grade class, a group of students reads *Fly Away Home* (Bunting, 1993) with a group of first and second graders in Mr. Love's and Ms. Creek's classroom. As a result of reading this story about a homeless father and son who live in an airport, the group decided to host a food drive at the school. They wrote a letter to the principals to announce the food drive during school announcements.

Metacognitive processes are probably the most difficult for readers. In this process, the reader becomes aware of how they are thinking about a story; they become aware of their thought process. **Think aloud** is a strategy that encourages readers to stop and reflect on their own process as

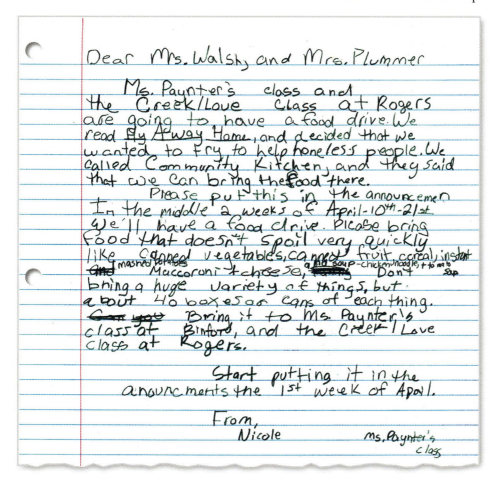

Dear Mrs. Walsh, and Mrs. Plummer

Ms. Paynter's class and the Creek/Love class at Rogers are going to have a food drive. We read Fly Away Home, and decided that we wanted to try to help homeless people. We called Community Kitchen, and they said that we can bring the food there.

Please put this in the announcemen In the middle 2 weeks of April-10th-21st We'll have a food drive. Please bring food that doesn't spoil very quickly like Canned vegetables, canned fruit, cereal, instant ~~and~~ mashed potatoes Maccoroni + cheese, ~~and~~ soup-chicken noodle, + tomato. Don't Soup bring a huge variety of things, but about 40 boxes or cans of each thing. ~~Can you~~ Bring it to Ms. Paynter's class at Binford, and the Creek/Love class at Rogers.

Start putting it in the anouncments the 1st week of April.

From,
Nicole   Ms. Paynter's
                                class

Nicole's letter to principals.

Invitation for the classroom

Creating Reading Bookmarks

Students can create bookmarks that remind them of different metacognitive strategies to use while reading. Suggestions for the bookmarks include:

Before Reading

- What is my **goal?**
- Can I **predict** what the text is about?

During Reading

- Do I **understand** what I am reading?
- Does the text **connect** with something I already know?
- Could I **explain** what I am reading to someone else?

After Reading

- Could I tell someone the **main idea** of this text?
- Do I need to **reread** any of the text?

they read a particular text. When demonstrating a think aloud, the teacher will stop reading at a particular point and make explicit the thinking that the teacher is doing at that specified point in the text. The demonstration helps less-experienced readers identify their own thinking patterns as they engage with text.

Table 8.3 identifies major comprehension strategies and corresponding reading behaviors as noted by the National Reading Panel's report (2000) and Low (2001).

Invitations to develop text participant practices involve reading journals, literature discussions, asking questions, creating character grids, and retelling stories. Encouraging students to ask questions of the text they are reading positions them as active readers, rather than passive readers. Questions can range from literal level questions that check for understanding to questions that are more interpretive in nature. When students ask their own questions, they are seeking to uncover uncertainties in the text. To facilitate this process, the teacher can record students' questions on a large chart after the text has been read, and students can work together in small groups to answer the questions. The work students engage in as they discuss their responses is more complex than if the teacher poses questions and a couple of students answer. (See critical questions in the "Critical Practices" section to push the questions to a new level of interpretation.)

TABLE 8.3
Key Comprehension Strategies and Reading Behaviors

Major Comprehension Strategies	Reading Behaviors Related to the Strategy
Control of the reading process	Tracks reading rate, speed Marks text Engages in self-study
Monitoring comprehension	Clarifies by asking questions Uses interrelated strategies Creates images Uses metacognitive strategies Engages in think alouds and reflections
Utilizes background knowledge	Relates one text to another Activates prior experiences and knowledge about the world and language Recognizes connections between parts of texts through past experiences Has knowledge of format and structure of various texts through past experiences
Interactions with text	Rereads Retells Skims Scans Reads orally Takes the text and does something
Developing word relations	Derives word meaning Recognizes words Uses context to derive meaning Uses close procedures Explores word functions
Utilization of text itself	Recognizes that stories are made up of a series of events or episodes that are systematically organized Infers relationships between events Examines the text, structure, content, and vocabulary Talks about how language works

Invitation for the classroom

Character Grids

Character grids enable students to focus on the behaviors and actions of characters throughout the story. Have students compare similarities and differences across characters in different versions of a particular story. Cinderella stories work well in this invitation.

Climo, S. (1989). *The Egyptian Cinderella*. HarperCollins.

Jackson, E. (1994). *Cinder Edna*. Lothrop.

Karlin, B. (1989). *Cinderella*. Little Brown, 1989.

Louie, A. L. (1982). *Yeh-Shen, A Cinderella Tale from China*. Philomel Books.

Martin, R. (1992). *The Rough-Face Girl*. Putnam.

Minters, F. (1994). *Cinder-Elly*. Viking.

San Souci (1989). *The Talking Eggs: a Folktale from the American South*. Dial Books for Young Readers.

San Souci (1994). *Sootface: An Ojibwa Cinderella Story*. Doubleday Books for Young Readers.

Steptoe, J. (1987). *Mufaro's Beautiful Daughters: An African Tale*. Lothrop, Lee & Shepard.

As students read the different versions, they record the main character's character traits. Students identify similarities and differences among the characters.

RETELLING AS AN AVENUE FOR UNDERSTANDING. One reason we want students to participate and engage in texts is to experience the delight of responding to texts in ways that matter—that hold significance for the reader. Retelling is a process whereby readers share and talk about the salient features of what they had just read (or in the case of read alouds, what they had just listened to). In a retelling, it is important to encourage readers to go beyond the generic aspects of the story. When Ms. Olsen read *The Yellow Star: The Legend of King Christian X of Denmark* (Deedy, 2001) to her class, many of her students responded with comments that did not push towards new understandings. Derrick's comment of "he was brave" served only to remind his peers that he had a general sense of the story. But more could be said about what the King of Denmark had done to save his countrymen from Nazi concentration camps. Ms. Olsen sees these comments as emerging understandings, and so she encourages her students to say more about what they are thinking. After Derrick notes that the king was brave, Ms. Olsen asks him why he thought this. This simple move enabled Derrick to say more of his thinking about how the king's decision to sew a star on his clothes when he isn't Jewish showed that he had compassion for his countrymen.

A few days later, when Ms. Olsen returned to this story and reread the text, she then asked her students to partner with each other and retell as much of the story as they could from beginning to end. Encouraging readers to work sequentially with a story supports their abilities to sequence and helps them to rethink what they have listened to or read. Retellings focus readers on constructing meanings of texts that are not just about *anything* but are connected to the text in some way (Calkins, 2001).

Text participant practices are essential to creating an effective and meaningful experience with text. For many intermediate and accomplished readers, text participant practices are at the heart of the work they do in reading and writing. The next two practices, text use and critical practices, are beginning to receive more attention in research and in classrooms.

Text use with intermediate and accomplished readers and writers

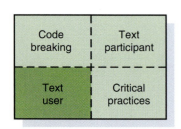

Intermediate and accomplished readers and writers interact with a variety of genres, including picture books, early chapter books, short stories, poetry, newspapers, informational texts, magazines, and everyday texts (e.g., gaming and sporting cards, cereal boxes, book club order forms). Critical to their development as readers is understanding that texts are designed for particular purposes. Readers may wonder how the composition of the text influences what one does with the text, as well as what some other options and alternatives are for the text.

As readers and writers investigate the texts available to them in the classroom and beyond the classroom, they begin to notice distinctive features that shape a text in a particular way. Text user practices invite readers to consider not just the content of the text (as in text participant practices) but also how the text is used. A central question to ask is "What is this text for, here and now?" Teachers may want to highlight the various design features and structures of different genres by asking students to consider the following questions (adapted from *Learning, Teaching and Assessment Guide, www.ltag.education.tas.gov.au*):

Questions for Text Use Practices

- What do you notice about the way this text looks?
- Which special features does this text have?
- What is the purpose of this text?
- Which text type is this? How do you know?
- In what ways is this text like others you have read?
- In what ways is this text different from the last one you read?
- How can you find information in this text?
- If you wrote a text like this, which words would you make sure you used?
- If you wrote a text like this, what title would you give it?
- If you were going to put this text on the web, what changes would you make?

- How would this text change if you were to use these ideas in a poem or a brochure or a poster?
- What title would you give this image?
- Who might have taken this picture? From where might it have originated?

Following these questions, readers may ask more specific questions related to the text they are working with, for example, a newspaper, a medicine bottle, or a recipe.

- How do newspaper headlines work? Why are they so large?
- How is the text on the medicine label designed to alert someone taking the medicine what to do if there are complications?
- Is the recipe written in a way that is easy to follow?

These questions are among the many that can be asked of any text. While this practice is one that does not seem to have much significance in more traditionally organized curriculums (it is typically not on a scope and sequence chart), it is a practice that moves readers to consider how reading and writing are socially situated. Texts are composed to achieve particular goals. Writers want to sell something if working on an advertisement, want to convey knowledge if working on a factual report, and want to share personal experiences if drafting a personal narrative. These decisions impact the structure and design of the text, which ultimately impact the ways in which readers read the text.

Text user practices are not as prevalent in elementary literacy programs, and yet this practice supports readers as they make decisions about how to read a particular text. This practice involves understanding the purposes of texts and using texts for different social and cultural functions. The design features and organization of the different texts signal to readers that not all texts are read in the same way.

> ### *Creating Connections 8.3*
>
> Make a list of five potential topics or themes to teach in an intermediate or upper grade classroom. For each topic consider the range of texts that can be used, as well as authentic reading and writing activities for students. Share your thinking with classmates.

Invitation for the classroom

What do you know about [type of genre]?

Invite students to brainstorm a list of descriptors for a particular genre. From the list of descriptors, create a definition of that genre. Now begin a conversation on what other aspects of the genre they may have not included. Talk about the design features of the genre that support the purposes it has for the reader.

Extension

As an extension of what do you know about [genre], have students compare the features of two genres (e.g., advertisement and report). This highlights the way in which genres use linguistic and organization features to establish text purpose and audience.

Adapted from Lorraine Wilson.

Invitation for the classroom

Exploring Comics as a Genre

In this invitation, students examine the characteristics of comics. There are different types, including historical, political, illustrated classics, funnies, superheroes, and contemporary (graphic novels).

Engage students in a discussion of the different types of comics. Bring in samples from newspapers, magazines, and comic books. Have students look through the different examples. In small groups, students should discuss what is similar and different among the types of comics.

- Is there dialogue? How is it presented?
- What are the characters doing? How is that shown?
- What is the shape of the comic frames? What does that represent?
- How is action shown?
- What happens from one frame to the next?

Encourage students to draft their own comics, keeping in mind the following points:

- Layout is important when combining images and text.
- Page layout and design can represent different organizational models, especially for storytelling. For example, a page with many frames can represent an ongoing scene with a lot of action. Larger frames with a great deal of detail may be an artist's attempt to set a forthcoming scene. Even page divisions add a certain element of story organization.
- Comics manipulate space on a page to guide the reader and affect the interpretation of the story.

Adapted from Lisa Storm Fink.

Critical practices with intermediate and accomplished readers

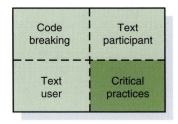

Critical practices invite readers and writers to reflect on and interrogate the texts in ways that challenge commonly held beliefs and understandings. Through critical practices, students come to understand that texts are not neutral; that they are connected to particular world views; and that there may be different viewpoints presented on the same topic. As readers in third through sixth grade gain experience with a wide range of texts, it is possible to broaden their understandings of reading to be more than decoding or comprehension, but that reading critically is about the social, historical, political, and economic context in which it was produced. While this may seem far-reaching for elementary students, there are a number of accounts (Comber, 2000; Heffernan, 2004; Vasquez, 2003) that demonstrate how elementary age readers and writers participate in critical literacy events.

Recently, Ms. Janasiewicz's fourth grade students began studying Presidents of the United States as part of their social studies curriculum. Most of the students in her classroom are English Language Learners from all parts of the world. Ms. Janasiewicz asked each student to select a president and read more about the president from a collection of biographies in the classroom. As students read, they were asked to record some of their questions, interesting points, connections, and surprises (QuICS). Their questions and comments suggest that these students are able to take on a more critical response to the material (Figure 8.4).

Along with QuICS, other invitations to support readers' critical practices while reading and writing include creating postcards, one long idea, and critical questions.

FIGURE 8.4 Students' QuICS about U.S. presidents (Andrew Jackson and George W. Bush).

Invitation for the classroom

Creating Postcards

Students can make visible the types of texts they have read over a period of time by making postcards for the texts they have read. Students can draw a picture on one side that is reflective of the theme and write comments about the text on the back of the postcard. Students should use this opportunity to reflect on significant issues that the story brought to the surface. Make these postcards available for students to look through—maybe by placing them in a decorative basket near the classroom library. Ask students to discuss the comments made on the postcard.

Adapted from Randy and Katherine Bomer.

Invitation for the classroom

One Big Idea

To encourage more complex thinking, engage students in a discussion that lasts for several class periods. Choose a topic that continues to show up in students' conversations and written responses. Don't focus on the main idea or theme of a text. Instead, choose a topic that is nagging in the heads of readers (e.g., fairness, gender). Post the topic on a piece of chart paper and over the course of several days, students have discussions, look for evidence in their reading, make connections to outside events, and write in their journals.

Invitation for the classroom

Critical Questions

Critical questions are not a part of a checklist of questions to work through, to "understand" the story. Rather, critical questions problematize the text and encourage readers to consider alternative positions and interpretations. Listed here are some general questions that provide a starting place for critical discussions.

- Whose voice is heard/not heard in this story?
- Who has the "power" in this story?
- Who does not have power in this story?
- How does this text make you feel about social issues and justice?
- What are other points of view for this story?
- Who else could tell this story?

Reader/writer workshop structure for intermediate and accomplished readers and writers

Chapter 7 established the parameters and structure for reader/writer workshops in primary grade settings. In many ways the routines are similar with mini-lessons, read alouds, literature discussions, independent reading and writing, and conferences. Teachers in grades 3 through 6 are able to further refine these structures, thereby enabling students to establish and negotiate their own learning. Each of the routines are expanded upon by addressing the types of texts most common in third through sixth grades, mini-lesson topics to move students forward, and strategies for shifting literature discussions from primarily teacher facilitated to peer facilitated.

Text Set on Civil Rights and School Integration

- *Ellington Was Not a Street* by Ntozake Shange. New York: Simon & Schuster Books for Young Readers, 2004.
- *The Story of Ruby Bridges* by Robert Coles. New York: Scholastic, c1995.
- *Through My Eyes* by Ruby Bridges. New York: Scholastic Press, 1999.
- *The School is Not White!: A True Story of the Civil Rights Movement* by Doreen Rappaport. New York: Jump at the Sun / Hyperion Books for Children, c2005.
- *Remember: The Journey to School Integration* by Toni Morrison. Boston : Houghton Mifflin Co., 2004.
- *Remember the Bridge: Poems of a People* by Carole Boston Weatherford. New York: Philomel Books, c2002.

Text sets for intermediate and accomplished readers

As noted earlier in the chapter, readers in third through sixth grades exhibit even more diverse strengths and weaknesses than in the primary grades. In these grades, there will be readers who have difficulty with various phonic concepts, as well as readers who are quite eager to read more complex and sophisticated texts. The materials that these readers interact with change dramatically. In addition to engaging picture books, intermediate readers begin to read chapter books and are introduced to content area texts in science and social studies.

Text sets work particularly well when there is a diverse range of readers because text sets offer a variety of genres (fiction, nonfiction, poetry, everyday), reading abilities (from easier picture books to complex chapter books), and complexity of ideas presented on the issue. Text sets are often designed around a unifying theme or author. For example, an author text set might include texts by Paul Fleischman or Kevin Henkes. A focus study text set might center on the topic of civil rights or new world explorers.

Text sets can be used in a variety of ways. In some classrooms, the whole class works with one text set, so it is necessary to have multiple copies of texts. In other classrooms, it may be that a smaller group of students works with a text set depending on their interests. For example, Mr. Lee's fifth grade students are working in focus study groups studying new world explorers. Mr. Lee used the school and public library to create four

different text sets on different explorers (i.e., Columbus, Ponce de Leon, Magellan, and de Soto). He spent time putting these sets together, but is aware that the materials may change as new information and questions are pursued by the readers in that group. Students regularly bring new materials to add to the text set, giving the text set a sense of flexibility and a feeling of being current.

The variation of texts in these text sets enables all of the students to access and use the materials and information. No matter what text is selected within the set, a student contributes knowledge and information to the group in literature discussions, when creating graphic organizers and maps, and in partner reading.

Two students working on a focus study.

Mini-lessons in reader/writer workshops for intermediate and upper grades

Knowing that readers in these grades exhibit a wide range of strengths and weaknesses, it will be important to maximize what readers are bringing to the reading event. Mini-lessons, as noted in Chapters 5 and 7, provide teachers with opportunities to teach with the learner in mind, rather than teaching because that is the next lesson in the basal series. Mini-lessons are often based on critical teaching moments, and the teacher is able to capitalize on this moment in a way that is meaningful and significant to the learners in the classroom. Mini-lessons offer strategies that students can use to become proficient and effective readers. In intermediate and upper grades, mini-lessons on reading may focus on the following (Calkins, 2001):

- Goals for reading. What kind of reader do you want to be?
- How can you talk about books with your friends?
- What makes a good reading partner?
- How can you make your literature discussion group productive?
- How can you respond to nonfiction texts?
- How can all voices be heard in a literature discussion?
- How do you select books to read?
- How can you move from details of the story to the big idea?
- How can your use of sticky notes improve reading comprehension and response?

- How can you learn how to skim materials?
- What features and structures do nonfiction texts have?
- What are some reading rituals?

In writing, the focus may include:

- How can you extend your writing time?
- How can you provide comments that encourage the author to continue?
- How can you work with a writing partner?
- How do you develop our own list of writing territories to help you find topics on which to write?
- What can you do when you are stuck?
- How can you develop interesting leads to your stories?
- How can you identify structures in nonfiction texts that you might want to also try out?
- How can you learn how to help peers by giving good feedback?
- How can you begin to write about issues of social justice?

The lists for both reading and writing are endless. Mini-lesson topics are generated from students' needs.

Literature discussions with intermediate and accomplished readers and writers

Students in grades 3 through 6 are often experienced literature discussion participants. They have contributed in read aloud settings, shared reading settings, and in their literature circles with peers. Because there is some familiarity with literature discussion formats, these readers extend beyond the literal meanings of the text and consider how their connections (personal and world) play a role in the ways in which meanings are constructed and negotiated.

A significant goal that many teachers have with their literature discussions in these grades is to move them beyond the "I like/don't like this book" or "My favorite part is . . ." stance. These comments do not push the readers to consider alternative possibilities for their understandings or to see how others interpreted the text. Literature discussions should be opportunities for readers to have not only "grand conversations" (Eeds & Wells, 1989) but to also have critical conversations. Bomer and Bomer (2001) describe that it is not enough to ask critical questions in literature groups or during class meetings, but that

> . . . children need to know how to have good conversations that build on and follow a line of thinking . . . they need to learn how to listen and respond to one another in a way that creates connections and builds a conversation history over time.

Teachers in grades 3 through 6 often have students select a book for literature discussions. Usually there are four to six choices in each round of literature discussions. To help children decide which book they may be most interested in, teachers conduct book walks/talks with a group of books. In these book talks, the teacher offers a summary of the story, why it is compelling, and who might be interested in reading such a book. Depending on how the room and time are organized, the students can then sign up to be a part of a particular literature discussion group.

After students select a book, the teacher then negotiates and works with the groups to determine the reading schedule (e.g., how many pages/chapter per week, plan for finishing the book, how often the teacher will join the conversation, type of presentation). Students meet in their groups depending on the schedule and use their time sharing new discoveries, interpretations, wonderings, and possibilities. The conversation often revolves around issues the readers want to address, as well as places they were confused or want more discussion about. One strategy that helps students stay focused on the text is to have reading journals that students bring with them to the group. In these journals, students note confusing words, places they didn't understand, interesting ideas, and other things they may be thinking about. The teacher checks in with each group as they read and discuss their book.

Creating Connections 8.4

Observe a group of third, fourth, fifth, or sixth grade readers in a literature discussion group. What kinds of support do the students have or need in order to be successful participants? Share your observations in your blog.

Reading and writing conferences

Reading and writing conferences are brief 5–10-minute meetings between a student and the teacher. In these meetings, the focus may be on reading, whereby the student may talk about what he or she is reading, retell the story, or read aloud to the teacher. The teacher may offer suggestions and strategies to extend the reader. Sharon Gill (2000) identified three roles she assumed while working with her students in reading conferences.

TEACHER ROLES DURING READING CONFERENCES.

- *Collaborator:* Share in the reading event by telling the reader an unknown word or reading a particularly difficult section of the text. The collaborator maintains an informal and positive environment.

- *Demonstrator:* Make your own (the teacher's) reading strategies explicit to the reader. Demonstrate how and when to use particular reading strategies in the context of reading connected text. This provides the reader with authentic examples of reading strategies in use.

- *Kidwatcher (Observer):* Take notes of the reader's miscues, actions, and behaviors during a reading conference. Through these observations and assessments, the teacher provides the reader with strategy lessons that attend to the needs of the reader. The following questions may be considered during a reading conference:

  - Is the student excited to read and share what she or he is reading?
  - Did the student spend too long on one page indicating she or he was struggling to decode the words?
  - Was the student able to retell the story in detail or was there only a general gloss of the story?
  - When asked, does the student think this book is too confusing, just about right, or too easy?
  - Is the student reading outside his or her interest, meaning is she or he taking risks with new books?

The time teachers take to kidwatch and consider what the student already knows about a text is critical to moving him or her forward in ways that are meaningful to the reader. Reading and writing conferences put the student at the center, not the curriculum or literacy program. Through conferences, teachers send messages to students that the work they do as readers and writers is important. They begin to build relationships with students in ways that cannot be accomplished in other settings. For students, reading and writing conferences are an opportunity to have individual and focused attention from the teacher. It is a time when students can have their literacy needs met and their questions answered.

 ## Connections to standards and benchmarks

The four reading practices (code breaking, text meaning, text use, and critical practices) are clearly evident when held up to state level standards and benchmarks throughout the country. In Chapter 7 we looked at three states—California, Georgia, and Indiana—to determine how closely aligned a reading program designed with the four practices in mind, as well as a reader/writer workshop structure, were to achieving the predetermined standards and benchmarks for early readers. What happens to those readers in grades 3 through 6?

	Code Breaking	Text Participant	Text Use	Critical Practices
California (listed is the general overview of the standard. California has further delineated the standard into substandards or skills)	Students understand the basic features of reading. They select letter patterns and know how to translate them into spoken language by using phonics, syllabication, and word parts. They apply this knowledge to achieve fluent oral and silent reading.	Students read and understand grade-level-appropriate material. They draw upon a variety of comprehension strategies as needed (e.g., generating and responding to essential questions, making predictions, comparing information from several sources). In addition to their regular school reading, students read one-half million words annually, including a good representation of grade-level-appropriate narrative and expository text (e.g., classic and contemporary literature, magazines, newspapers, online information).	Students read and respond to a wide variety of significant works of children's literature. They distinguish between the structural features of the text and the literary terms or elements (e.g., theme, plot, setting, characters).	

	Code Breaking	Text Participant	Text Use	Critical Practices
Indiana	Students understand the basic features of words. They see letter patterns and know how to translate them into spoken language by using phonics (an understanding of the different letters that make different sounds), syllables, word parts (un-, re-, -est, -ful), and context (the meaning of the text around a word). They apply this knowledge to achieve fluent (smooth and clear) oral and silent reading.	Students read and respond to a wide variety of significant works of children's literature, such as classic and contemporary literature, historical fiction, fantasy, science fiction, folklore, mythology, poetry, songs, plays, and other genres. In addition to regular classroom reading, students read a variety of nonfiction, such as biographies, books in many different subject areas, magazines and periodicals, reference and technical materials, and online information.	Students use appropriate strategies when reading for different purposes. Describe the differences of various imaginative forms of literature, including fantasies, fables, myths, legends, and other tales.	Students evaluate new information and hypotheses (statements of theories or assumptions) by testing them against known information and ideas. Compare and contrast information on the same topic after reading several passages or articles.
Georgia	The student understands and acquires new vocabulary and uses it correctly in reading and writing. The student uses letter–sound knowledge to decode written English and uses a range of cueing systems (e.g., phonics and context clues) to determine pronunciation and meaning.	The student consistently reads traditional and contemporary literature (both fiction and nonfiction) as well as magazines, newspapers, textbooks, and electronic material. The student demonstrates comprehension and shows evidence of a warranted and responsible explanation of a variety of literary and informational texts.	The student identifies and uses knowledge of common textual features (e.g., paragraphs, topic sentences, concluding sentences, glossary). The student identifies and uses knowledge of common graphic features (e.g., charts, maps, diagrams, illustrations). The student identifies and uses knowledge of common organizational structures (e.g., chronological order, cause and effect).	

In Closing

This chapter on intermediate and accomplished reading instruction provides an overview of the guiding principles and continuum of development that students in grades 3 through 6 attend to. In many cases, the skills and strategies are refinements of those skills and strategies learned in previous grades. The four resource model continues to be the framework by which the chapter is organized. Code-breaking practices in grades 3 through 6 involve understanding word patterns and the role of affixes. Text participant practices are most concerned with comprehension strategies and developing ways for students to transact with the text. Vocabulary development is important as intermediate and accomplished readers begin reading more sophisticated and complex texts. Vocabulary work can either be definitional or meaning based. The meaning-based work has more staying power, with readers learning the nuances of language. Text use and critical practices encourage students to take a closer look at the text, to identify the purpose it serves, and to take on a questioning stance. Resources, strategies, and technology links were provided to support the four-resource model in intermediate and upper grade classrooms.

The reader/writer workshop also remains as the structure by which to organize an effective literacy curriculum. The routines (read aloud, mini-lesson, independent reading and writing, literature discussions, and conferences) are further refined as readers and writers negotiate their own learning. Literature discussions begin to play a more central role in the curriculum, as students learn how to facilitate these discussions. The reader/writer workshop approach for intermediate and accomplished readers and writers creates a literacy program that meets and often exceeds state and local standards, while at the same time creating a literacy environment that encourages students to actively participate and to construct meaning from the texts they are reading and composing.

Terms to Remember

Contextual vocabulary work *(233)*
Definitional vocabulary work *(233)*
Derivational suffix *(223)*
Graphic organizer *(236)*
Inflectional suffix *(223)*
Homographs *(224)*
Homophone/homonym *(224)*

Prefix *(222)*
Repeated readings *(229)*
Root word *(223)*
Suffix *(222)*
Think aloud *(236)*
Word study *(222)*

Resources for More Information

Bear, D. R., & Templeton, S. (1998). Explorations in developmental spelling: Foundations of learning and teaching phonics, spelling, and vocabulary. *The Reading Teacher, 52*(3), 222–242.

Calkins, L. (2001). *The art of teaching reading.* Portsmouth, NH: Heinemann.

Eeds, M., & Wells, D. (1989). Grand conversations: An exploration of meaning construction in literature study groups. *Research in the Teaching of English, 23,* 4–29.

Heffernan, L. (2004). *Critical literacy and writer's workshop: Bringing purpose and passion to student writing.* Newark, DE: International Reading Association.

Invernizzi, M., Abouzeid, M., & Gill, J. T. (1994). Using students' invented spellings as a guide for spelling instruction that emphasizes word study. *Elementary School Journal, 95*(2), 155–167.

Questions for Further Reflection

- What aspects of the four-resource model for literacy instruction in grades 3 through 6 do you find yourself identifying with most easily?

- What literacy events in grades 3 through 6 have you observed that align with the four-resource model?

- How can teachers organize and structure literature discussions in ways that have all children engaged and participating?

- Why do you think students in these grades commonly experience the fourth grade slump, where reading and writing becoming increasingly more difficult?

Effective Assessment Practices for Reading and Writing

Ms. Taylor Invites Alternative Response

I am an Early Intervention Program teacher and everyday I meet with nine third grade students to work on their reading and writing skills. These nine students are in my class because they are considered to be "at risk" for failing the reading and math portion of the CRCT (Criterion-Referenced-Competency Test), a high-stakes standardized test given in my state. The school is a high achieving school, and if these students do not pass the test in the third grade, they do not move to the fourth grade. While the school's population was predominately Caucasian, nearly half of my students were students of color. Emmanuel's parents emigrated from Africa and Melvin's family recently moved to the United States from El Salvador. Neither of these students received any ELL support. Other students, like Caleb, had processing difficulties with language and commented daily that they hated reading.

What may seem surprising is that these students are fairly strong readers. I know this because I regularly assess them in ways that are more reflective of the work they do in the classroom. For example, early in the school year they read *Sister Anne's Hands* by Maribeth Lorbiecki (1998), a story about an African American Catholic Nun teaching in an all white school in the 1960s. This story sparked a lot of conversation so we delved into a unit on civil rights. We also read *White Socks Only* (Coleman, 1996) and *The Story of Ruby Bridges* (Coles, 1995) as well as information books about the civil rights movement and about Dr. Martin Luther King, Jr. We viewed photographs of the era and had discussions about my life as a child in the 1960s.

As part of their work, I had students use reading journals to record their thinking as we read and learned about the civil rights movement. Just after reading *Sister Anne's Hands*, some of the responses were as follows:

10/12 (Emanuel)

"Why didn't the kids like her because she was black and a kid though an paper airplane at the black bord then she read it she felt sad. Then she got posters the white people and the black people the kids felt shocked to see the photos. I felt like if I had a heart that would open the door for my life and maybe faithful instead of being mad like a soulid rock in the ground."

10/13

"I felt like if I were in the 60s when the try to break our hearts in half like has are hope and fait was gone but I am one of them and it would feel like I had to go to the to the park it would say colored people only I din't want this to happen but it did.

10/12 (Melvin)

I wonder why did a kid throw a piece of airplane paper at the thecher becase ther parints didn't tea them any maners. Becase there parents said it was O.K. because when his or her diad mom wher little ther perints said to be mean to black or brown people because that's how the perents rased them.

10/12 (Caleb)

I wonder why did one of the kids throw a paper airplane to the teacher

Didn't the kids like her

10/13 (Caleb)

When I am sad

I feel lonely

I feel glad

Sum time and

Sumtimes I feel stooped I

Know haou sister Anna felt

These journal writings provided me with important information about my students' ability to comprehend and respond to text. I could see that Emmanuel is a heartfelt writer, and that he would benefit from work on text to self and text to text connections. Caleb's journal revealed that he doesn't have the language abilities that Emmanuel has, but he makes meaningful text to self connections in ways that Emmanuel cannot. So, although at first glance it might seem that Emmanuel's writing is more advanced than Caleb's, a more thorough analysis reveals more about Caleb's comprehension strategies. Melvin's journal entry also indicates great insight into the story and a strong ability to make text to self connections. As a second language learner, he would benefit from additional support in vocabulary and spelling development. Melvin also needed to work on singular and plural pronouns and didn't have much of a grasp on the purpose of conventions.

I used the notes from these journal entries to guide my daily discussions with the groups as we reread the story and read new stories about the civil rights movement. A month later as the unit was ending, the following entries were in their journals:

I wonder. . .

● In what ways does Ms. Taylor's assessment practices align with the guiding principles of literacy development as described in chapter one?

● What are some ways that Ms. Taylor can inform parents of their child's growth and development in reading and writing?

● What other aspects of the reading and writing process might you be able to glean from the writing samples?

11/15 (Emanuel)

I rember when berenan and joby were teasing me because it made me feel like her in the story. Is it real? My Connections is when I felt like I was ruby walking down the sidewalk going inside a white school and crowd is shuoting out you I just go inside

11/16 (Caleb)

I remember when my brother pick on me. how did the wite men torn into a chikin? Pawourless

11/16 (Melvin)

What happened to the chicin man? I made a canichon when she got pickt on. What did she rost an egg Why did she get wopt.how did the chicen man get powers.

Using students' responses to text provided me with a glimpse into the sophisticated understandings that these students constructed throughout the unit on the civil rights. I was able to learn much more about them as readers and writers than I would have if I had administered a traditional end of unit test.

Chapter Overview

Effective literacy teachers depend on knowing students' interests, abilities, and experiences with texts in varied contexts. How one reads when curled up with a favorite book, when researching information for an inquiry project, or perusing the latest fashion magazine while waiting for the dentist is important information for the teacher to be aware of when planning and implementing curriculum. Teachers closely monitor and assess children's reading and writing behaviors as they work with them over time in a variety of situations.

We can see from Ms. Taylor's discussion of her students' abilities and successes in her classroom that there are many different ways in which students can demonstrate their understandings of text. The criterion referenced test that Ms. Taylor referred to revealed but one glimpse into a child's thinking process. Assessing the students' reading journals provided Ms. Taylor with a richer, more complex view of her students' comprehension processes. This chapter focuses on how to assess students' strengths in reading and writing. Many of these assessments are accomplished while students participate in meaningful and authentic literacy events.

This chapter is designed to enhance a teacher's ability to make informed decisions about instructional and assessment practices. Building on the discussion in chapter 3 about initial assessments, such as reading interviews, interest inventories and questionnaires, and kidwatching notes, the assessment practices in this chapter offer teachers an understanding of the complexity of the reading and writing processes that students attend to when engaged in meaningful literacy practices.

The following questions guide the discussion:

- What are the differences between formative and summative assessments?
- Why has there been a recent proliferation of tests and assessments, particularly at the elementary level?
- What is the teach-assess-reflect cycle? And what are the effects of this cycle?
- What are the differences between traditional and alternative assessment practices?
- How do teachers gather information to be used for assessment purposes?
- What various assessment practices are linked to code breaking, text participant, text use, and critical practices?

Formative and summative assessments

The purpose of assessment is to support and enhance students' learning. Assessments should be accurate, thoughtful, and supportive because they are crucial in enhancing students' growth and development. Assessments are used to make decisions about a student's progress on a continuous basis. There are two different approaches to assessments—formative and summative. Teachers use **formative assessments** to measure progress *during* the activity. Formative assessments give teachers information about students' strengths and weaknesses as they participate in a literacy event. Teachers can use this information within the context of instruction to make informed choices about how to adapt teaching and learning to meet students' needs. Formative assessments generally document learner growth over time; emphasize students' abilities, rather than their deficits; and are conducted on an ongoing basis. Examples of formative assessments include: class discussions, reading and writing conferences, journal writing, observations, and any other activity/aspect of classroom learning.

On the other hand, **summative assessment** is used to sum up what a student has learned in a given point of time. Summative assessments usually describe student learning, teacher ability, and school accountability at predetermined points in students' careers and in the academic year (Afflerbach, 2002). They also are connected to predetermined benchmarks and standards. Summative assessments provide information on how to group and compare students. These assessments usually come in the form of standardized, high-stakes tests. Other examples of summative assessments include end of chapter tests, final exams, and report cards.

formative assessments
Ongoing assessments that measure progress in the context of the activity.

summative assessments
Assessments that sum up what a student has learned at a predetermined point in time.

 # The proliferation of assessments

In the past 10 years, there has been a substantial increase in the number of summative assessments teachers are mandated to administer during the instructional year. One reason for this proliferation is NCLB legislation, which focuses on accountability and achievement (see Chapter 1 for a more complete discussion). NCLB mandates that all children in grades 3 through 8 take an annual state reading/language arts test (along with math and science). The belief is that by assessing students annually on these disciplines, teachers and students will ultimately be held accountable for the learning that is occurring in the classroom. Many states and districts mandate additional tests. For example, in a Texas school district, fourth grade students take an average of 13 district and state mandated tests in a nine-month period (Dooley, 2005). In other states, testing is just as plentiful. Georgia Department of Education requires that students in the elementary grades (K-5) take the Georgia Kindergarten Assessment Program (GKAP), writing assessments at grades 3 and 5, norm referenced (ITBS) at grades 1, 3, and 5, as well as criterion referenced (Georgia CRCT) in language arts, reading, mathematics, social studies, and science in grades 1–5. These lists only represent those tests that are considered large-scale and standardized. There are also a number of alternative and locally created assessments that teachers incorporate into their instructional day. Not only has the number of assessments required in schools increased, but there is a tremendous increase in the number of commercially produced, large-scale assessment tests available to early literacy teachers (K-3) (Paris & Hoffman, 2004). In 1990 there were approximately 20 commercial reading tests that a school district or state might choose from,

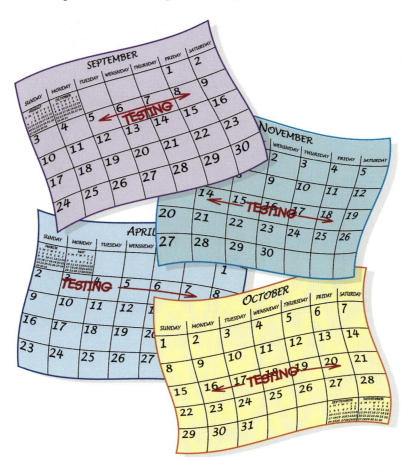

and just 10 years later, there were more than 148 tests (Stallman & Pearson, 1990; Pearson, Sensale, Vyas, & Kim, 1998). The tests not only increased in number but also in the skills to be assessed. Many of the tests focus on word knowledge, sound and symbol concepts, literacy and language concepts, and comprehension.

In addition to commercial assessments, there are locally produced assessments available. Meisels and Piker (2001) identified over 80 types of locally produced, non-commercial assessments that teachers could use in their kindergarten to grade three classrooms. These assessment practices included observation, checklists, constructed responses, running records, anecdotal notes, oral response, and others. The proliferation of assessment and accountability has many teachers wondering if they are doing nothing more than "teaching to the test." Teachers face a daunting task in trying to select which assessment tools, and how many assessments, will best serve their purposes and those of their students.

Purposes for assessments

There are a number of purposes teachers and other stakeholders have for assessing students in literacy development. One reason there is an increase in summative assessments (standardized tests) is to make comparisons across schools and districts. Under NCLB, a decision has to be made every year about whether or not a school is meeting state-established achievement goals. Some assessment practices, such as state-specific standardized tests, are developed to measure students' achievement in reading. Each state has determined a score that students must achieve on the state test in order to be considered proficient in language arts and reading. These test scores provide state departments of education and district level administrators with information as to whether or not schools are meeting adequate yearly progress (AYP). To make this determination, states compare the percentage of students in each school who meet proficiency standards to the statewide goals. State and district administrators review test results from individual schools to make decisions about funding and curriculum.

A more localized purpose for assessing students in literacy development is to better understand individual achievements. Large-scale assessments do not attend to this level of specificity; yet, it is this knowledge of the individual child that is more helpful to teachers, parents, and students. There are many formative assessment practices that are better suited for understanding the daily, ongoing practices in the classroom. Often referred to as alternative (because they are alternatives to the large-scale and standardized assessment tests), these assessments rely on teacher judgment and are not streamlined in the ways large-scale assessments are. They are context sensitive, meaning the assessment is directly tied to the activities in the classroom. The purpose for these alternative assessment practices is to enable teachers to make informed decisions about their teaching, curriculum, and what will best serve the student's interests and needs. Alternative assessments will be discussed in detail later in the chapter.

So far, two purposes for assessment have been shared: providing schools with information to judge the effectiveness of the school and collecting information on individual students to facilitate the learning process. Rhodes and Shanklin (1993) identified four additional purposes for assessment:

- to discover how an instructor's teaching has affected the learning process;
- to sharpen the quality of the teacher's observation and recording skills;
- to have information about a student's progress and achievement to share with others, and;
- to assess curricular strengths and weaknesses that will guide staff development.

The audiences and purposes for assessment are as varied as the different assessment practices. As teachers and other stakeholders consider the purposes behind different assessment practices, it is important to note that tests (in particular, large-scale, standardized tests) only capture a very small piece of the picture. Most of us attend to only a very small amount of all the possible things in the world (Weaver 1992). Tests take this idea even further. Only a slice of what a student knows or is able to do is assessed, with results somehow representing the whole of what a student knows.

> ### *Creating Connections* 9.1
>
> Reflect back to your own elementary school experience. What assessments were you given as a student? What are some of your memories around these assessments? Did the assessment fit the instruction and curriculum?
>
> Share your memories with classmates.

Assessing children on a variety of tasks and concepts provides a more complete picture of the student as a learner. Each student engages with the learning process in a slightly different and unique way. They bring to the literacy event prior knowledge experiences, and linguistic and cultural ways of being.

Literacy assessments reveal ideologies about learning and literacy

Literacy assessment practices, in concert with instructional practices, reveal the beliefs and values one has about literacy development. Recall the different ideological perspectives and models of schooling around teaching, learning, and literacy presented in Chapter 1—industrial, inquiry, and critical. These perspectives and models also influence teachers' assessment practices. Assessment practices aligned with an industrial model reflect standardization and uniformity. This can be seen in the large-scale, standardized testing measures currently sweeping the country. All students in a particular grade are given the same test at the same time, with the same amount of time to complete the test. There is little, if any, acknowledgment that students come to the test with different experiences and knowledge.

Teachers who view literacy from an industrial, or as noted in Chapter 4, a bottom-up perspective, will most likely use assessment practices that address individual skills that make up the reading process. The assessments often focus on discrete skills that can be easily measured, such as identifying parts of speech, correct usage of punctuation, determining the main idea of a reading passage, and selecting correctly spelled words. These assessments are more often decontextualized, which means they are not connected to the everyday activities in the classroom.

To illustrate, recall Ms. Day's first grade classroom from chapter one. Initially, her instructional decisions ascribed to an industrial model of accountability and standardization. Throughout the school year, Ms. Day has focused students' attention on learning discrete skills. As she and her grade level colleagues moved through the prescribed curriculum, there were benchmark tests and end-of-unit tests to accomplish. Ms. Day's students' progress in literacy development was determined by how well they did on the various tests. This narrow focus contributes to a stifled and static curriculum. In Ms. Day's classroom there will be children who do not perform very well on these tests and there may be high-stakes decisions made about their abilities and competencies.

Assessment practices that embody an inquiry or critical ideological perspective recognize that there are many possible ways to view a student's learning trajectory. Within this perspective, teachers regularly understand that literacy is a process con-

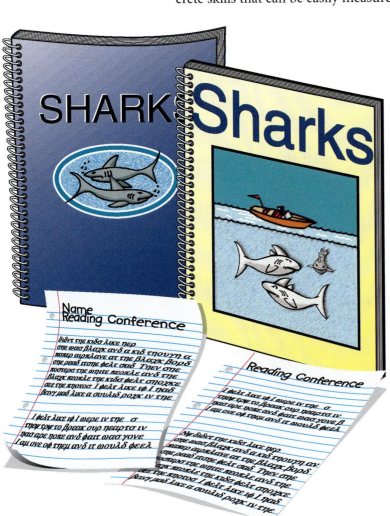

Inquiry journals and reading conference forms.

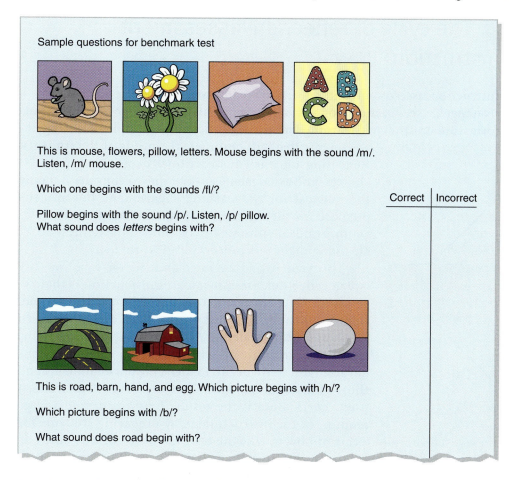

Sample page of benchmark test on phonemic segmentation.

structed over time and through a variety of artifacts, or student work. Literacy is seen as multifaceted, diverse, and complex. Literacy develops as a result of meaningful interactions and experiences with others and texts. Consequently, the assessments also mimic the ongoing everyday experiences with others and texts.

If Ms. Day were to take an inquiry or critical perspective toward teaching and learning, her assessments would capture students' learning across their interests and work. For example, Ms. Day decides to use a portfolio system to document her students' progress as they inquire about sharks and shark attacks in Florida. She negotiates with her students as to the types of artifacts to collect over time. Students mention their inquiry journals which houses their questions, research notes, and drawings of sharks. In addition, Ms. Day also collects reading and writing conference sheets that students have had around the texts they are reading on sharks. As Ms. Day reviews the individual portfolio for each student she has a much better understanding of the different strengths and weaknesses her students bring to the classroom.

Creating Connections 9.2

Ask a classroom teacher to share with you some of her or his assessments that are used in the classroom. As you review these assessments, consider these questions:

- What view or perspective of literacy is revealed in the assessment?
- What aspects of literacy are assessed?

📖 The cycle of reflection–assessment–instruction

Instruction, assessment, and reflection are intimately connected. In fact, it is a recursive cycle. Teachers conduct classroom-based assessments to gather information on students' learning and use this information to plan learning engagements that will best meet the needs of the students. Reflecting on one's instructional decisions, curricular choices, and assessments enables one to consider not only the purpose for the learning engagement, but also the purpose for the different assessments used in the classroom. Frank Serafini (2002) developed the Reflective Cycle to highlight this process (see Figure 9.1).

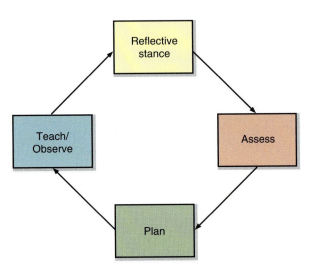

FIGURE 9.1 Reflective cycle for assessment and instruction.

The result of an integrated and recursive pathway between reflection, assessment, and instruction is that assessment practices and instruction are closely connected. In recent history, only a portion of this cycle has driven much of curricular decisions. Many teachers and administrators worried about performance on state-level standardized tests have begun to focus the curriculum around those skills and standards that are on the test. A "test prep" curriculum is the result. Teachers devote a large amount of the instructional day preparing students for these tests—both in terms of how to take the test (knowing there is only one correct answer) and what skills and concepts are on the test (e.g., locating main idea, summarizing, sequencing, grammar). Because of the energy and time devoted to preparing students for such tests, there are high expectations for students to perform well on the tests. The cycle, however, is incomplete because teachers rarely reflect on the resulting information to make informed decisions about curriculum. By the time the results are published, students have progressed onto the next grade and the teacher has a new group of students to work with. In these instances, assessment is driving instruction, but only for the reason to perform well on the assessment, not to necessarily improve instruction and/or learning.

The reflective component of this cycle is critical for teachers to understand the purposes behind the assessments they are implementing. Teachers can easily learn how to administer an assessment, but the larger issue is determining for what purposes those assessments serve. Only when one adopts a reflective stance and is willing to critically examine his or her teaching practices, does a more effective assessment and instruction plan emerge. Teachers with this reflective stance are able to better meet the needs of the individual students in the classroom. The reflective cycle complements the assumptions that Sharon Murphy (2001) identifies as guiding premises for authentic assessment practices.

- The child constantly makes predictions about the world.
- Assessment practices can highlight particular strengths and abilities, as well as conceal particular strengths and abilities.
- Assessment practices that are situated in everyday activities and events are more likely to yield richer information and data.

- There is a relationship between teaching and learning that is not always causal; children learn much that they were not taught.

Through the reflective cycle, teachers are able to value and assess literacy practices and events that occur in and out of school. Rather than capturing one moment in a child's life at school, assessment should be geared toward recording the shifting patterns in growth and development (Anthony, Johnson, Mickelson, & Preece, 1991) so that reflection, curriculum, and assessment become unified.

stakeholders

A group of people interested in the results of summative assessments.

high stakes tests

Assessments that have consequential outcomes.

Who is interested in assessment? High stakes for parents, teachers, and schools

The results generated by various assessment practices impact more than just the student and the teacher. There are many *stakeholders*—state department and district administrators, policy makers, researchers, politicians, and the public—who are interested in how well students are performing in school. There is a real desire to compare schools with schools, districts with districts, and states with states. Large-scale, standardized tests are usually used to make these comparisons. These tests become known as *high stakes* because there are consequential outcomes for students, teachers, and schools. "These outcomes may include student promotion or retention, student placement in reading groups, school funding decisions, labeling of schools as successful or failing, and the degree of community support for a school" (Afflerbach, 2004 p 2).

The popularity of standardized tests in the educational system is because the public generally finds these tests to be familiar. Rarely are there adults who have not had the experience of taking high-stakes tests. And with increased efforts in accountability, there are more and more standardized tests being administered, particularly in grades 3 through 8. The public also believes tests of this kind are fair and reliable. There is a perception that because students are tested under similar conditions that the tests are unbiased and that all children have equal opportunities to demonstrate knowledge.

So, who is interested in student achievement? Table 9.1 offers a glimpse into how assessment practices serve particular stakeholders, the type of information collected, and how frequently students are assessed (Farr, 1992).

School board and community members often contribute to discussions about assessment and accountability.

TABLE 9.1
How Assessment Practices Serve Stakeholders

Audiences	The Information Is Needed to	The Information Is Related to	Type of Information Collected	When Information Is Collected
Students	Identify strengths and areas of improvement	Individual	Specific to the assessment	Daily
Teachers	Plan instruction	Individual students and small groups	Specific to the assessment	Daily
Parents	Monitor progress of child	Individual student	Specific to the assessment	Periodically
School, district, and state administrators	Judge effectiveness of curriculum, materials, and teachers	Groups of students	Related to broad standards established by district and state; norm and criterion referenced	Annually and/or by term
General public and policy makers	Judge school quality and accountability	Groups of students	Norm reference; criterion referenced; broad goals	Annually

 # Traditional assessment

Traditional reading assessments are common throughout the United States. These summative assessments are most often designed to provide district-wide and national comparisons of children's reading achievements using commercially produced reading tests. Formal achievement tests, such as norm-referenced and criterion-referenced tests, and informal reading inventories are popular examples. These assessments are commercially produced. They provide a partial picture of a reader's strengths and areas for improvement.

Standardized and multiple choice tests

Standardized and multiple-choice tests have dominated much of the educational discourse around literacy development. Used primarily for evaluating schools and systems, these tests are considered to be uniform and reliable. They can effectively compare children across schools, districts, and states. Comparisons of this sort can be useful to make general statements about the current state of affairs of the educational system. For example, the National Assessment of Educational Progress (NAEP) is a standardized test that is given periodically in the fourth, eighth, and twelfth grade. The test is designed to measure reading comprehension in the areas of reading for literary experience, reading for information, and reading to perform a task. NAEP results are then reported to consider comparisons across states and other jurisdictions and to track changes in student achievement over time in grades 4, 8, and 12. NAEP does not report on individual students or schools. The results of NAEP are not used to make decisions at the school level.

> ### *Creating Connections 9.4*
>
> Link to the NAEP website (http://nces.ed.gov/nationsreportcard/about)
>
> Compare the trends in reading since 1990. What do you notice about reading achievement in grades 4 and 8?
>
> How do these trends compare to the public's perception of reading achievement in the United States?

There are two categories of standardized tests—***norm-referenced*** and ***criterion-referenced***. Norm-referenced tests compare student performance to a cross section of students at that same grade level in other parts of the country. The Scholastic Aptitude Test (SAT) and Iowa Test of Basic Skills (ITBS), among others, are norm-referenced tests. Norm-referenced tests are not aligned with curriculum, but are developed as a way to differentiate and sort students into particular categories. Norm-referenced test scores are distributed on a bell curve, with half the students scoring above the 50th percentile, and half of the students scoring below the 50th percentile.

The other category is criterion-referenced, and these tests are designed to assess students' knowledge based on predetermined criteria. Many states have moved to criterion-referenced tests to measure accountability in learning. In theory, everyone can pass a criterion-referenced test. Criterion-referenced tests are linked to curriculum. In many states and school systems, criterion-referenced tests have become the singular measure by which students are evaluated on their skills and knowledge. These tests are known as high stakes because of the consequences of failing these particular tests. If students do not achieve a predetermined level of competence, they are often mandated to attend summer school and are required to retake the test. If they continue not to pass, these students are then retained in the previous grade.

The standardized tests that children take in elementary school usually have two categories for literacy development: language and reading. In the language category, students are asked to consider analogies, usage, sentence construction, and vocabulary. A sample test question in language for second grade is:

Which word means only one?

a. we

b. me

c. them

A third grade question may look like this:

When Bob threw the ball above his head, the ball hit the <u>seeling</u>. Which word should replace the underlined word to make the sentence correct?

a. *sealing*

b. *ceiling*

c. *cieling*

d. *seeing*

These sorts of questions are discrete and do not reflect the richness or complexity of language development. Additionally, the test questions measure what is known as textbook English, or Standard English, and not necessarily the competence that students have as they navigate and codeswitch in a variety of contexts.

A second area that is commonly tested is literature. This section of the test usually involves reading short passages and then answering a series of questions related to the main theme, title, or other aspect of the passage. The challenge here is that readers bring a set of experiences to the passage that may make the meaning different than what is

norm-referenced

Tests that compare student performance to a cross section of students at the same grade in other parts of the country.

criterion-referenced

Students are assessed on predetermined criteria.

Did you know. . .

America's public schools administer more than 100 million standardized exams each year, including IQ, achievement, screening, and readiness tests.

Source: The testing explosion: www.fairtest.org.

available as an option on the test. This variation, while celebrated in literature discussions, book talks, and reading journals, is not valued on the standardized tests. To illustrate this point, the book *First Grade Takes a Test* (Cohen, 1995) highlights how a young child deliberates over a couple of possible responses on a test question, because his experiences suggest a viable, but incorrect response (according to the test maker). For many students this scenario is quite common. The reading passages and corresponding questions do not encourage different kinds of responses.

Standardized tests are inevitable. There are millions of dollars tied up in the production and scoring of standardized tests for school systems throughout the country. What is important in the context of learning how to effectively teach reading and writing is that for many students and teachers these test questions do not reflect what it means to be a reader and writer in the twenty-first century. The questions demonstrate only a fraction of all that is needed to be a proficient reader and writer. With that in mind, then, teachers need to consider other forms of assessment as viable mechanisms for determining a reader's strengths and areas for improvement. According to Paris and Hoffman (2004), there is not one best assessment or even best assessment type. Teachers should draw upon multiple measures to make informed decisions about the students in their classrooms and the direction of their reading and writing curriculum.

Informal reading inventory and qualitative reading inventory

Informal reading inventory (IRI)

Reading assessment that is individually administered to determine a student's reading level.

Unlike most standardized assessments that are administered in group settings, ***informal reading inventories (IRI)*** are individually administered. IRIs include graded word lists, reading passages, and comprehension questions. These assessments are designed to help a teacher determine a student's reading level and reading strengths and needs. IRIs assess word recognition, word meaning, reading strategies, and comprehension. One advantage that IRI has over standardized tests is that an IRI more closely resembles an authentic reading event. Students read a whole story or passage. The follow-up comprehension questions range from literal to interpretive and inferential. The results of an IRI are used to make approximate decisions at the classroom level about the appropriate reading level (easy, instructional, or frustration). These reading levels are often used when teachers place students in needs-based groups for guided reading.

Qualitative reading inventories (QRI) are similar to IRIs in that they use graded word lists and passages to assess oral and silent reading (Leslie & Caldwell, 2001). However, there are a few differences. In QRIs, the selected reading passages are both narrative and expository. This enables the teacher to determine a student's strengths and weaknesses in both genres. QRIs also address a student's prior knowledge by asking questions designed to ascertain whether a student is familiar with the topic. In addition, QRIs provide three ways of assessing comprehension: student unaided recall, questions without look-backs, and questions with look-backs. Look-backs enable the teacher to differentiate between comprehension and memory (Leslie & Caldwell, 2001). A student may comprehend while reading but then forget when asked a specific question. If a student can find the correct response during a look-back, the teacher can assume that comprehension is occurring during the reading.

To administer an IRI or QRI, students are first given a list of words to read. This list is a starting point for determining what level to begin testing. Students read the words while the teacher records those read automatically, those read with some delay, and those read incorrectly. For the QRI, students are then asked to provide a prediction and/or are asked questions that elicit prior knowledge. Reading the passage is the next step. This can be done either orally (with miscues recorded) or silently (noting how long it takes

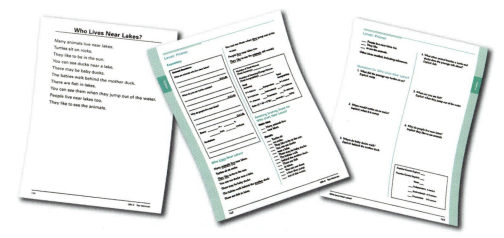

Sample pages from a Qualitative Reading inventory.

Source: From Leslie, Lauren & Joanne Caldwell *Qualitative Reading Inventory*, 3/e. Published by Ally and Bacon, Boston, MA. Copyright © 2001 by Pearson Education. Reprinted by permission of the publisher.

the reader). It is recommended that children in grades K–2 read orally, while in grades 3–6, a combination of oral and silent reading is used. Students are then asked to retell the story to the best of their ability. Comprehension questions follow the reading. Based on all of the information gathered, a student's reading level is determined.

Traditional assessments, while common in many classroom settings, do not provide complete information about a student's progress in reading and writing. Assessments that focus a bit closer on the reader's and writer's behaviors and thought processes are important to consider. Additionally, assessments should be embedded or integrated into the daily work that students accomplish. The next section identifies a number of alternative assessments that are viable options for teachers in classroom settings.

Alternative assessment practices

The past 30 years have seen considerable growth in the area of alternative literacy assessments. Recent research in literacy development (Gee, 2004; Barton & Hamilton, 2000; Street, 1995) indicates that literacy practices and the corresponding literacy assessment practices are much broader and more complex. No longer is literacy just about reading and writing static material, but children are learning to read and write in high-tech, multimodal worlds. It is essential that assessment practices align with these more sophisticated ways of interacting with text.

Characteristics of alternative assessments

Alternative assessment practices are designed to gain a more complete picture of reading and writing processes and to determine how individual children respond to particular literacy events. For the most part, alternative assessments are formative in nature. Characteristics of alternative assessments include that they:

- occur on a daily basis as part of the ongoing reading and writing opportunities;
- involve a variety of reading and writing events;
- focus on students' processes and products;
- honor multiple perspectives; and
- bring together data from several sources.

alternative assessments

Assessments that are designed to better capture a student's learning process.

triangulation

Using multiple sources of information to determine a pattern.

Alternative assessments are located inside everyday reading and writing events. Through authentic reading and writing events, the teacher is able to more accurately assess a student's use of the cueing systems (graphophonemic, syntactic, semantic, pragmatic). For example, Ms. Taylor in the opening vignette used her students' reading responses as documentation of the ways in which her students comprehended *Sister Anne's Hands*. When needed for parent conferences, report cards, and cumulative comments, Ms. Taylor will be able to draw upon those notes and student work to make informed decisions about the next instructional steps in the curriculum.

Alternative assessment practices pay attention to students' processes and products. Products, such as responses on comprehension questions and writing samples, provide some information. But it is also important to understand how students arrive at particular responses or what they were aiming to do with their written composition. Students' in-process thinking provides new insights into how they use reading and writing strategies. Self-assessments, such as reflections focused on one's achievements and progress, encourage students to clarify and articulate their thinking and reasoning.

Honoring multiple perspectives is a critical aspect of alternative assessments. When teachers consider a student's range of assessments (e.g., answers on a reading interview, a miscue report, self-reflection, and scores on a standardized test), the teacher is able to triangulate the information. *Triangulation* is bringing together multiple data sources to search for patterns in the responses. The teacher considers how all of the information fits together to develop a more complete picture of the student's literacy knowledge and skills.

Additionally, teachers value alternative assessments that are less public and less visible to parents and other stakeholders (Paris & Hoffman, 2004) because alternative assessments more closely identify the individual student's strengths and weaknesses. Gaining this type of information helps teachers to more effectively plan for and teach students at their appropriate instructional level.

Types of alternative assessment practices

There are a number of different types of assessment practices that teachers have access to. Recall that Meisels and Piker (2001) noted more than 89 noncommercial assessment practices that are classroom based. This section focuses on those alternative assessments that are most commonly used by teachers in elementary classrooms. There are two general categories: document/observation and responsive listening. Some of the assessments, such as miscue analysis and running record, can cross over into both categories. The boundaries between these categories are flexible and dynamic.

Documentary/observation

Documentary/observation comprises the majority of assessment practices that are readily available in classrooms. Teachers are interested in recording the interactions and behaviors students have with texts. Teachers spend time observing and documenting such interactions in the form of miscue analysis, running records, anecdotal records, checklists, and portfolio collections of work samples. These assessments enable teachers to interpret students' behaviors, actions and the artifacts produced (work samples). Implicit within these assessment practices are two assumptions: (1) "the knowledge children have about literacy will be demonstrated in observable ways; and (2) the environment is conducive to allowing for such demonstrations" (Murphy, 2001, p. 373).

MISCUE ANALYSIS. *Miscue analysis* is one of the most informative assessment tools for understanding the reading process and how readers attend to the cueing systems. Charting the miscues, analyzing them, and assessing the retelling make a nearly invisible process, the reading process, a more visible process. Miscue analysis is an attempt to capture what real readers do with real text.

What are miscues? A *miscue* is an unexpected response to printed text. It may come in the form of an omission, substitution, or insertion of another word. According to K. Goodman (1969), these miscues are not random errors, but are based on predictions and hypotheses the reader has about the different cues. The purpose of documenting miscues is to help the reader develop more effective strategies (both language cues and cognitive cues) when dealing with texts.

As you may remember from Chapters 2 and 4, the language cueing systems include:

- *graphophonemic:* attending to sounds, spellings, and phonic relationships.
- *syntactic:* attending to the grammar or structure of the language.
- *semantic:* attending to the meaning of the words.
- *pragmatic:* attending to the context.

In addition to the language cueing systems that readers draw upon to make sense of the text, they also draw upon their cognitive cues. These cues relate to what the reader intends to do with the text in the moment of reading. The cognitive cueing systems include:

- *infer:* guessing information needed based on partial information.
- *sample:* selecting the most productive and useful cues.
- *predict:* anticipating information is coming.
- *confirm:* self-monitoring for meaning making.
- *correct:* reconstructing text and recovering meaning.

Readers orchestrate these cues and their background experiences and knowledge to bring meaning to the text. The orchestration of all of this sometimes produces unexpected response to the text. Figure 9.2 highlights the most common markings for miscue analysis.

Analyzing readers' miscues while reading authentic and real text provides a clear view, or a "window" into how the reading process works (Martens, 1997, p. 600). Without such a process, we are left with a simplistic view that some students just can't read, or that they have poor reading proficiency. Miscue analysis highlights the various aspects of the reading process, thereby allowing the teacher to see what hypothesis the reader is drawing upon as the reading event occurs. Miscue analysis helps teachers see that readers are knowledgeable language users; that readers usually make reading and writing errors for a reason; and that readers have a variety of strengths that teachers can access and build upon.

RETROSPECTIVE MISCUE ANALYSIS. In recent years, Y. Goodman (1996), P. Martens (1998), and others (Y. Goodman & Flurky, 1996; Moore & Gilles, 2005) have involved the student's reflective thinking in the miscue analysis process. This is known as *retrospective miscue analysis* or *RMA*. Asking readers to consider their own miscues provides them with opportunities to develop an understanding of themselves as readers. Students reflect on their reading behaviors, strengths, and areas that need work.

The RMA can also be accomplished when readers select their own miscues to discuss. This involves them in the whole process, and the preceding questions can

---

miscue analysis

The process of documenting and analyzing a reader's miscues while reading a passage of text.

miscue

An unexpected response to printed text—omission, substitution, or insertion of another word.

retrospective miscue analysis (RMA)

Includes the reader's reflective comments during a miscue analysis.

Substitutions

Substitutions are shown by writing the miscue directly above the word or phrase.

comfortable

He was sitting comfortably in the carriage.

Omissions

Omissions are marked by circling the omitted language structures.

"I can do all that," replied the husband.

Insertions

Insertions are shown by marking a proofreader's caret at the point of insertion and writing the inserted word or phrase where it occurs in the text.

some

"Now I've got more work to do," said the man.

Regressing and Abandoning a Correct Form

Abandonments are marked by drawing a line from right to left to the point at which the reader went back to repeat but abandoned the expected text. An inscribed AC is used to indicate this type of regression. In this example, the reader first reads *head against the wall*, then rejects this possibility and produces the more sensible *hand against the wall.*

(AC) *hand*

"How many times did I hit my head against the

wall?" she asked.

Regressions or Repetitions

Linguistic structures that are reread are underlined to explicitly show how much the reader chose to reread. Regressions are marked by drawing a line from right to left to the point at which the reader went back to repeat. A circle inscribed with an R designates simple repetitions. Multiple repetitions, words or phrases that are repeated more than once, are underlined each time they occur.

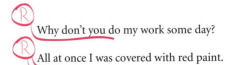

(R) Why don't you do my work some day?

(R) All at once I was covered with red paint.

Regressing and Correcting the Miscue (Self-corrections)

Self-corrections are marked by drawing a line from right to left to the point at which the reader went back to repeat in order to correct the miscue. A circle inscribed with a C indicates a correction.

The markings in this example show that Gary predicted *horses* (which he repeated twice), followed by a correction to *houses*, followed by the substitution *of* for *and*, followed by the correction to *houses and roads*. His multiple attempts are written and numbered in the order of occurrence above the sentence.

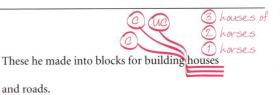

These he made into blocks for building houses

and roads.

Substitutions Often Called Reversals

An editor's transposition symbol shows which words have been reversed.

I sat looking down at Andrew.

Was something wrong with Papa?

FIGURE 9.2 Markings for miscue analysis.

Source: Adapted from Goodman, Y. (1995) Miscue Analysis for Classroom teachers: Some procedures and some history, *Primary Voices, v. 3(4), 5–9.*

Invitation for the classroom

Conducting a Miscue Analysis

The following process adapted from Y. Goodman, D. Watson, & C. Burke (1987) is how to best approach miscue analysis.

Materials:

- tape recorder
- a piece of text that is unfamiliar and slightly challenging to the reader
- a typed version of the story for the teacher to mark
- pencil

Procedure:

1. Sit next to the reader if possible and explain that you want to know what s/he does when reading.
2. Let the reader know that she or he is being taped so that you can listen to the reading again.
3. Remind the reader that there may be words that are unfamiliar and that she or he should do what she or he does when reading alone—skipping, guessing—but that she or he should continue reading and constructing meaning.
4. After the reading, ask the reader to retell the story and what was happening.

   If the reader needs support during the retelling, you may consider asking these questions:

   Tell me more about. . .
   After . . . what happened?
   Why do you think (event) happened?
   Why do you think (character) did that?
   Was there anything in the story that you thought was (funny/sad/strange, etc.)?
   When appropriate follow up the reader's response with "Why do you think so?"
   Or "What in the story made you think so?"

Try not to provide information to the reader, but allow her/him to expand on what she or he has said.

Analysis and Scoring:

There are three ways to analyze and mark the oral reading portion of the assessment.

Option 1: This is the simplest form. As the reader reads, follow along and mark any miscues with a + or −. This method will help the teacher develop a "miscue ear." The + and − indicate whether or not the miscue was a good miscue (contributes to meaning making) or a bad miscue (disrupts meaning making). The teacher can discuss these with the reader.

Option 2: Use basic miscue marking to note the reader's miscues.

Option 3: Complete Option 2 and then ask the following questions for each miscue. Read the sentence as the reader completes it.

   Question 1 examines the syntax (grammar) of the sentence:
Does the sentence sound like an acceptable language structure within the reader's dialect and within the context of the story?   Yes   No

   Question 2 examines the semantics/pragmatics (meaning) of the sentence:
Does the sentence make sense within the reader's dialect and within the context of the story?   Yes   No

Note: A sentence can have meaning (Y) only if it has an acceptable English structure. Questions 1 & 2 can only be coded either YY, YN, or NN. A coding of NY is not possible.

Question 3 considers the possibility of a change in the meaning of the sentence: *Does the final sentence the reader produced change the meaning of the printed text?*

      No

  Partially   (There is a minor inconsistency, loss, or change of an idea, incident, character, sequence, or concept in the story.)

     Yes   (There is a major inconsistency, loss, or change of an idea, incident, character, sequence, or concept in the story.)

Note: Meaning change can be considered ONLY when there is meaning present. So, Question 3 can *only* be coded if Questions 1 and 2 are coded YY. For sentences without meaning, a dash indicates they cannot be coded for Question 3 (i.e., YN- and NN-).

Question 4 examines the attention the reader paid to graphic features of the text. *How much does the reader's substitution, even if it was corrected, graphically resemble the text item?*

    H — High. Two out of three parts in the word, or 50% or more of the letters in each word, are similar.

    S — Some. One out of three parts in the word, or at least one letter in each word, is similar.

    N — None. The two words have no parts or letters that are similar.

To answer Question 4, consider only one-word-for-one-word substitutions that are "complete" words (not partial words), even if they were corrected. If multiple responses were given, look at the first complete one to examine the cues the reader paid attention to first. (Since insertions and omissions have no text word for comparison, Question 4 is not asked for them.)

Note: Repeated miscues are coded for Question 4 only the first time they occur, so the data is not inflated. Function words, such as articles and pronouns, are NOT considered repeated miscues, however, because of their role in marking relationships in the text. So, function words are coded for Question 4 every time they occur as a one-word-for-one-word substitution.

also be asked. The RMA allows readers to have more control over their reading process and to become empowered readers. They become more articulate about the reading process and their abilities as readers.

Did you know. . .

Here is a listing of resources to learn more about miscue analysis and retrospective miscue analysis. Use these resources to view examples and scoring guides.

Davenport, M.R. (2002) *Miscues, Not Mistakes*. Portsmouth, NH: Heinemann.

Goodman, Y. M., & Marek, A. M. (1996). *Retrospective Miscue Analysis: Revaluing Readers and Reading*. Katonah, NY: Richard C. Owen.

Goodman, Y.M., Watson, D.J., & Burke, C. (2005). *Reading Miscue Inventory: From Evaluation to Instruction*. Katonah, NY: Richard C. Owen.

Wilde, S. (2000) *Miscue Analysis Made Easy: Building on Students' Strengths*. Portsmouth, NH: Heinemann.

Both miscue analysis and retrospective miscue analysis are intensive assessments that require quite a bit of time to administer. Most teachers are not able to conduct these assessments on each student. Through observations and other informal assessments, teachers generally select students that exhibit puzzling behaviors to conduct a miscue analysis or retrospective miscue analysis.

RUNNING RECORDS. Running records, another formative assessment, are designed to assess the reader's fluency when reading aloud. Similar to miscue analysis (but not as time intensive), running records track the number of miscues a reader makes while reading a text. A student's fluency is then used to determine if a particular reading passage is too difficult, at the appropriate instructional level, or too easy for the student.

Running records are conducted in the moment so there is less preparation needed than with miscue analysis. The following steps are guidelines for conducting running records.

Conducting a Running Record

- Select a book that approximates the child's reading level. Explain to the child that he or she will read out loud as you observe and record his or her reading behavior.

- Sit next to the child so that you can see the text and the child's finger and eye movements as he or she reads the text.

- As the child reads, place a check mark above each word that is read correctly.

- If the child reads incorrectly, record above the word what the child reads. Record other marks as needed (substitutes, omits, repeats, pronounces incorrectly, or doesn't know the word).

- If the child is reading too fast for you to record the running record, ask him or her to pause until you catch up.

> **TECHNOLOGY LINK**
> http://www.readinga-z.com/
> newfiles/levels/runrecord/
> runrec.html
>
> This site provides information and forms to use when conducting running records.

Invitation for the classroom

Conducting a Retrospective Miscue Analysis

Retrospective miscue analysis is conducted after students have participated in a standard miscue analysis procedure.

- Select a number of high-quality miscues to discuss with the student. The preselected miscues should highlight the reader's strengths to help her or him realize that they are using strategies to support meaning making.

- Ask the reader to listen to the audiotape and follow along with the original text. After listening to the tape, engage the reader in a discussion about the selected miscues. Help the reader to explore possible reasons for the miscues. The following questions begin to uncover how the reader's knowledge of language helps to resolve problems faced in the text (Y. Goodman 1996):
  - Does the miscue make sense? Does it sound like language?
  - Did you correct your reading of the word? Should it have been corrected, or did you read it correctly the first time?
  - Why did you make the miscue?
  - Does the word in the text look like the word that you used? Does it sound like it?

- Be sure to pay attention to the reader's behavior as he or she reads. Is the child using meaning (M), structural (S), and visual (V) cues to read words and gather meaning?
- Intervene as little as possible while the child is reading.
- If the child is stuck and unable to continue, wait 5–10 seconds and tell him or her the word. If the child seems confused, indicate the point of confusion and say, "Try again."

Following the reading, the teacher calculates the number of words read correctly. This percentage can be used to determine if a particular text is at the reader's instructional level. The criteria for determining a student's instructional level is:

- *Independent level:* 95 percent–100 percent words read correctly.
- *Instructional level:* 90 percent–94 percent words read correctly.
- *Frustration level:* fewer than 89 percent words read correctly.

Keep in mind that these are not strict criteria. The different levels are to serve as guidelines. Readers work and make sense of text when they are interested in the ideas. So a text with seemingly difficult words that appears beyond a reader's instructional level may very well be text that captures the reader's attention and motivation. The converse is also true: A text that does not capture the reader's attention may be perceived by the reader as difficult and hard to make sense of, even though the number of words pronounced correctly exceeds 89 percent.

The recorded miscues can be further analyzed to determine how to support the reader's growth in the reading process. The teacher can categorize the miscues into visual, syntactic, and meaning. The teacher uses this information to learn whether the reader is overly dependent on one particular strategy (i.e., sounding words out; substituting words that have similar initial letters, such as *self* for *scarf*). The teacher may also ask the reader to retell the story to determine the reader's understanding of the text. All of this information is used to guide instruction.

Running records are a common assessment practice that many teachers do during guided reading or as they circulate and work with individual children. Because children are constantly learning (even when you don't think they are paying attention), it is important that running records do not overtake your reading time. In one early primary classroom, Ewa, a first grader, conducted her own running record on her friend Brooke as she read *The Crazy Quilt* (Avery, 1994).

CHECKLISTS. Checklists are an opportunity to gather general information about a

First grade student's example of a running record.

reader in a relatively quick way. They do not provide the in-depth view of the reading process that miscue analysis or running records do, but teachers can gain an overview of how the reader responds to texts, the reading environment, and motivation for reading. Checklists can serve as reminders for the types of information to assess. They also inform other stakeholders about what is valued in the classroom, district, or other levels. Table 9.2 is a checklist adapted from Weaver, Gillmeister-Krause, and Vento-Zogby (1996).

TABLE 9.2
Reading Process Checklist

	Usually	Often	Sometimes	Not Yet
Motivation				
To what extent does the reader show an interest in texts?				
To what extent does the reader choose reading over other possible activities?				
To what extent does the reader set goals for reading?				
Reading Strategies				
To what extent does the reader use effective strategies, such as predicting, monitoring comprehension, and other "fix-it" strategies when meaning has gone awry?				
To what extent does the reader read for meaning?				
To what extent does the reader make connections among books, experiences, and background knowledge?				
To what extent does the reader talk about what she or he is reading?				
To what extent does the reader employ word level skills to unfamiliar words?				
Reading Environment				
To what extent does the reader read across genres?				

Source: Weaver, C, Gillmeister-Krause, L. & Vento-Zogby, G. (1996) creating support for effective literary education: workshop materials and handarts. Portsmouth, NH: Heinemann.

Checklists come in different forms, for different purposes. The previous checklist is designed to address the reading behaviors and strategies of one reader. Another form may be developed to better understand how a reader is doing in a particular literacy event, such as a literature discussion (Figure 9.3).

Or, a third option is to develop a checklist that is focused on the nuances of one particular aspect of reading. In this example, the checklist is centered on story retelling (Figure 9.4).

Checklists are most effective when the teacher and students determine what is important about the reading and writing process and then develop checklist statements that identify those areas that are critical to becoming a successful reader in that class. These checklists add meaning and value to the assessment practices by closely attending to what is perceived as most important in the reading process.

Checklists are sometimes published with prescriptive reading programs. One issue with these prepackaged checklists is they may not be as valuable as personally developed checklists. Someone else's understandings of what is important can be limiting to what the teacher and students value in a particular classroom. Many teachers develop checklist items with the children. These add a greater degree of meaning and value in the classroom.

CLASSROOM OBSERVATIONS AND ANECDOTAL RECORDS. Classroom observations are both commonplace and daunting. Teachers constantly observe what is

Name _____

Date	Makes connections to other texts, experiences	Contributes to discussion	Initiates the discussion	Acknowledges others' comments	Speaks confidently	Asks questions

FIGURE 9.3 Literature discussion checklist.

	Usually	Often	Sometimes	Not Yet
Retold entire story: Beginning, middle, and end				
Understood major ideas				
Used background knowledge during retelling				
Used correct usage during retelling				
Retold story fluently				
Used age-appropriate vocabulary				
Told the story in sentences that made sense				

FIGURE 9.4 Storytelling checklist.

going on in the classroom. And yet, it is difficult to know what to focus on, how to record the observations, and then what to do with the information. In addition, teachers have a large number of other responsibilities to attend to while in the classroom. An efficient record-keeping system is critical so that anecdotal notes can be used effectively to make informed decisions about curriculum and student growth.

Most teachers develop their own system for collecting anecdotal records. Some teachers use a notebook with a student's name on each page. Over the course of the week, the teacher notes observations for each child. When it comes time to complete report cards and conduct parent conferences, the anecdotal records from the notebook can be used to make informed decisions. An advantage of the notebook is that it keeps the notes in one central location. However, it is difficult to remember to write in the notebook, to comment on each student in a regular manner, and to know what to focus on. Unfortunately, notebooks are too often used to record social behavior and not growth or progress in literacy development (Anthony, et al., 1991).

As an alternative to using a notebook, some teachers use one sheet that focuses on a specific area or skill. This one-sheet observation method (Figure 9.5) attends to the need to regularly comment on each student and have a focus. The focus of the sheet might be retelling, predictions, connections, confidence, or interests. The teacher writes each student's name in a small box on the sheet. During the week, the teacher can record phrases and information in each student's box. Having all of the students listed on one page enables the teacher to quickly see who needs to be observed. The focusing area provides a frame of reference that is connected to the curricular goals. This reduces the teacher's observations to key aspects and helps the teacher move beyond the more obvious social behavior comments.

Responsive listening assessments

Responsive listening attends to how children generate a set of hypotheses about the ways in which literacy practices operate. There is much knowledge waiting to be revealed. Responsive listening assessments include retellings, literature discussion, and reading and writing conferences.

Week: 7		Charlie	Dana	Brennen	Lukas	Maddy	Autumn
Focus: Predictions		Eliza	Jacob	Michael	Sean	Kassey	Kileigh
Dharma	Karen	Scharlene	Tomas	Olivia	Jose	Blanca	Victor
George	Michelle	Ricardo	Veronica	Mary	Paul	Ernesto	Hannah
Caleb	Kevin	Meghan	Alex	Paige	Rose	Patrick	Caroline

FIGURE 9.5 Sample one-sheet observation.

RETELLINGS. Retellings are a powerful way to understand the richness of student's ability to synthesize, interpret, and recast the text (Anthony, Johnson, Mickelsson, & Preece, 1991). Teachers often conduct retellings as part of a miscue assessment. In a miscue assessment, the retelling occurs after the student has read the text aloud. The teacher asks the student to retell the story in as much detail as possible.

Retellings may also occur outside of the more standard miscue analysis. In these instances, retellings can be oral or written. The goal of retelling is to provide students with opportunities to highlight and emphasize those aspects of the text that are most salient and interesting to the reader. Different than interpretations constructed during literature discussions, retellings are geared to assess how closely the reader's interpretations/predictions are to the original source. The listed criteria may be useful when using retellings as a form of assessment:

- Does the reader attend to the following literary elements of the story: characters, setting, plot, climax/solution?
- Does the reader include all of the relevant story episodes and events?
- Does the reader express emotion as she or he is retelling the story?
- Does the reader conclude the retelling accurately?

GROUP DISCUSSIONS. Group discussions offer teachers opportunities to assess the meaning making process while students are reading and discussing a particular text. Discussions encourage authentic and meaningful talk among students. Students share their understandings, seek to clarify places of confusion, and create more expansive understandings. A difference between retellings and discussions is that students often extend their thinking in a discussion, as they work to clarify and interpret text. In these discussions, teachers can assess comprehension, as well as give value to divergent thinking, other points of view, and how children negotiate their understandings with others (Figure 9.6). The conversation provides a way for the teacher to come away with better understandings of what the students may need instructionally.

To effectively assess a discussion as a component of responsive listening, teachers may want to focus on questions such as:

- Do students bring insights or divergent perspectives into the discussion? How are these responded to?
- Do students invite others to share differing points of view?
- What connections are made between the text and the self, the world?
- Do students recognize there may be more than one interpretation or point of view?

By listening carefully to the ways in which students respond to texts, teachers can begin to better understand how students are making sense of texts.

Group Members _Nancy, Maddie, Imani, Monica_

Date _Feb. 26_ Book title _Each Little Bird That Sings_

Amount of participation (list names under each category)

A great deal	Medium	None
Maddie	_Nancy_	_Imani_
	Monica	

What discussion skills do students need to work on?
Listening to each other
building on what was said

FIGURE 9.6 Responsive listening assessment: Group discussion.

READING AND WRITING CONFERENCES. Reading and writing conferences are opportunities to assess the meaning making processes that students engage in as part of the literacy process. The conference structure is not necessarily an assessment practice, but the information gathered as a result of conferencing with a student provides the teacher with a glimpse into how the student interprets texts as well as composes texts. During a conference the teacher may ask the student to share reflections on a particular text. Reading conferences enable the teacher to gain a more detailed picture of the reader's abilities to construct meaning from texts that have been self-selected, while writing conferences reveal the student's composing strategies. Conferences also provide the teacher with information about the student's comfort level with a particular text, the types of connections made to other texts and experiences, and why the reader or writer has selected this particular text to work with. This information can be considered as teachers develop their classroom libraries and plan mini-lessons during reader/writer workshop.

> ### Creating Connections 9.5
> Interview a teacher who uses various forms of alternative assessments. What does this teacher see as the benefits and challenges of the assessments she or he uses?

Gathering information to use in assessing readers' and writers' growth in literacy development

Collecting and analyzing the information that teachers need to make informed decisions regarding instruction and curriculum can be overwhelming. There are at least 20 children in the classroom, loads of possible data sources, and virtually no time to organize and analyze what all the data means. Is every student product important to use as a source of information? Do all literature discussions need to be audiotaped in order to determine a student's involvement in the group? No. Rather what you will want to do is to consider which data sources will provide the information that you seek. Anthony, et al. (1991) suggest that teachers keep the following guidelines in mind to manage the process of gathering information.

Guidelines for Choosing Data to Use in Assessing Students

Does the task (and the student product/process associated with the task):

- use authentic text in naturally occurring school literacy events (reading conferences, reading aloud, literature discussions)?
- use familiar language (not framed as a test question)?
- involve the (re)construction of meaning (constructing one's own interpretation)?
- require integrated behavior (drawing upon reading, writing, listening, and speaking)?
- involve a context (meaningful and authentic to the learning environment)?
- generate implications for instruction (what mini-lesson is best suited for this learner)?

Not every assessment will meet all of these criteria, but the more criteria met the more useful and meaningful the assessment will be to the teacher and the students.

Portfolio Systems

Portfolio systems are more than collections of students' work in folders to be reflected upon only during special events, such as Open House and parent conferences. As an assessment practice, the purpose of the portfolio is not to store individual pieces of work, but to document the growth and development of a student's learning process within an instructional program. With a portfolio as evidence of a student's learning process, it is possible to construct a portrait, "one that a teacher and student can learn from long after the isolated moment of assessment" (Wolf, 1989, p. 39).

Portfolios are described in many different ways depending on the purpose and audience. Sometimes portfolios are created by students to be used in classroom settings as a way to represent themselves to others. At the other end of the spectrum, government agencies use information collected in the portfolio to make policy decisions and determine how to distribute resources. There are many ambiguities about how to define portfolios, but a widely accepted definition comes from the Northwest Evaluation Association and is further refined by Arter and Spandel (1992):

> a purposeful collection of student work that tells the story of the students' efforts, progress, or achievement in [a] given area(s). This collection must include student participation in selection of portfolio content; the guidelines for selection; the criteria for judging merit; and evidence of student reflection. (p. 36)

Recently, Cohen and Wiener (2003) identified common and essential features of literacy portfolios:

- Entries are collected in semipermanent folders.
- The artifacts selected for a portfolio are the result of collaboration between student and teacher. Criteria for a portfolio collection should be jointly established.
- The artifacts in a portfolio represent a purposeful review of a student's abilities, growth in accomplishments, or demonstration of a student's best work.
- Students' reflections are critical in a portfolio and ultimately lead to a sense of ownership.
- Artifacts selected for a portfolio represent chronological development. Therefore, all artifacts should be dated.
- Artifacts reflect authentic classroom activities and are not constructed for the sake of the portfolio. There is variety in the types of artifacts collected.
- Portfolios often contain additional material, such as teacher observations, checklists, or other informal assessments.

These general criteria or features for portfolios are helpful as teachers and students begin to construct literacy portfolios that provide a picture of an individual student's interests, abilities, goals, learning strategies, and outcomes.

WRITING PORTFOLIOS. Writing portfolios contain evidence of both process and product (Cohen & Wiener, 2003). Writing portfolios have a long history, evolving from the writing folders. In most elementary classrooms, students have writing folders that house their writing drafts over a period of days or weeks. They may also have lists, notes, comments from peers, and multiple revisions. As students move through the writing process and create many different pieces, they need a place to store the finished pieces. The writing portfolio becomes a repository for this work. The biggest distinction between the writing folder and portfolio is that the pieces in the portfolio are purposefully selected based on criteria and goals.

READING PORTFOLIOS. Similar to writing portfolios, reading portfolios also include artifacts that reflect process and product. The portfolio becomes a way for students to engage in thoughtful reflection about what and how they read. Reading portfolios should include measures that reflect and analyze:

- decoding and vocabulary skills,
- comprehension skills,
- responses to reading across content and for different purposes, and
- reading interests and attitudes

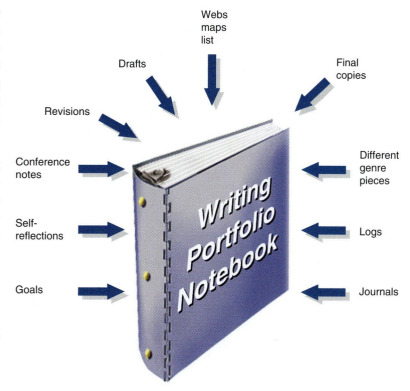

Assessment practices align with code breaking, text meaning, text use, and critical practices

So far the discussion on assessment has focused on the general characteristics, structure, and organization of traditional and alternative assessment practices. For the remainder of the chapter, more specific assessments are highlighted and linked to the four reading practices (code breaking, text participant, text use, and critical) profiled in earlier chapters. As students participate in each of the four reading practices, there are opportunities to gather data to determine which practices need more attention in terms of student development and understandings and in curricular invitations. Table 9.3 lists the assessments that are most useful for each of the reading practices.

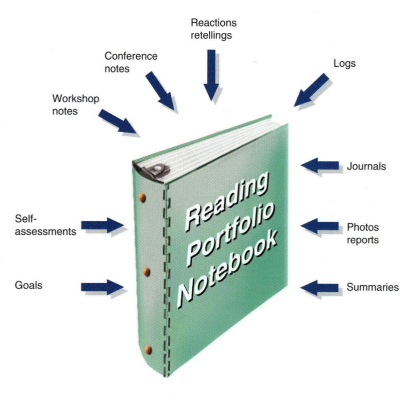

TABLE 9.3
Reading Practices and Types of Assessments

Reading Practice	Literacy Events and Activities That Attend to:	Assessments (formal and informal)
Code breaking		
• Alphabetic awareness • Phonemic awareness • Concepts of print • Spelling	• Observations of book handling and tracking • Observations of songs, rhymes, repetitions • Word games • Observation of ability to generate/identify sounds • Writing journals	• Checklists of letter–sound knowledge • Running records • Anecdotal notes • Yopp-Singer Phonemic Awareness test • Miscue analysis • Clay's concepts about print (see Chapter 6) • Informal and qualitative reading inventories
Text Participant		
• Drawing on own experiences • Comparing own experiences with text • Understanding how a text works • Gain meaning from texts and illustrations	• Literature discussions • Retellings • Reading conferences • Response logs and other work samples • Personal reading lists • Interest inventories	• Retellings (both as a part of miscue analysis and not a part of miscue analysis) • Group Discussion Charts • Informal and qualitative reading inventories
Text Use		
• Understanding that different texts serve different purposes • Using a variety of texts appropriately • Recognizing there are options and alternatives with text • Knowing that a text's use determines the composition and genre of the text	• Literature discussions • Reading conferences • Work samples	• Personal reading lists • Response logs • Literature discussion charts • Self-reflections
Critical Practices		
• Recognizing that texts are not neutral, that they represent particular views • Understanding that texts influence the reader • Noting that texts position readers • Recognizing that the author has a purpose for creating a text	• Reading conferences • Literature discussions • Reflections • Work samples	• Self-reflections • Response logs • Literature discussion charts

Code breaking assessment

Recall that code breaking practices focus on decoding, spelling, and a general understanding of patterns and conventions in the text. Readers engaged in code breaking practices pay attention to alphabetic awareness, phonemic awareness, word building, and spelling. Literacy events that best support code breaking practices include:

- reading and writing environmental print
- shared reading
- guided reading
- independent reading
- independent writing

For emergent and beginning readers, teachers can use the Concepts about Print and Concepts of Screen assessments detailed in Chapter 6 to gain a picture of how children interact with environmental print, texts, and computers in the classroom and play centers. To consider interactions with environmental print, a teacher may ask children to read the label from a common snack food (such as goldfish crackers). Then the teacher asks the following questions:

- Can you point to where it says "goldfish crackers"?
- Can you find another place it says "goldfish crackers"?
- How do you know it says goldfish crackers?
- Tell me more about what else is on this box?

Additionally, the teacher may observe how children read environmental print in a variety of contexts. Building on the work of Harste, Woodward, and Burke (1984), and later from the Test of Early Reading Ability by Reid, Hresko, and Hammil (1989), the teacher can ask the child to read from the actual label, then move to a photocopy of the label, and then to a handwritten version of the label. This process documents children's knowledge of writing, as compared with drawing, and to see what they already know about the relationship between letters and sounds.

Early literacy teachers may want to use a more standardized approach to documenting children's understandings of phonemic awareness and phonics. Recall the emphasis in recent years on phonemic awareness as a predictor of successful reading. Phonemic awareness is the ability to distinguish sounds in the speech stream. A common assessment is the Yopp–Singer Phonemic Awareness (see Figure 9.7). This assessment measures a child's ability to distinguish and say separate phonemes in different words. The teacher asks the child to listen to the word (*ride, go, dog,* etc.) and then say each sound in the word (notice that it isn't a test that asks children to identify particular letters, but sounds). Not all children need to spend considerable amounts of instructional time on phonemic awareness. This assessment enables teachers in the early grades (kindergarten and first) to identify children who may need more support with phonemic awareness.

To score the test, a child receives credit for those words that are correctly segmented into the appropriate phonemes. No partial credit is given. Children who score high on the test are said to be phonemically aware. Children who correctly segment some of the words are emerging into their understandings of phonemic awareness, and children who segment only a few words are in need of more literacy events that highlight sounds and language play.

Children's understandings of phonics can be assessed through their writing. Children demonstrate their knowledge of letter–sound relationships through the choices they make in spelling. Teachers can assess their growth in this area by examining and classifying the misspelled words in the writing journals and drafts. For example, Ms. Donavan has her first grade students write a daily entry in their journals. She responds to the students' writing, thereby providing an authentic audience and context. As students share their thoughts and ideas, Ms. Donavan notes the types of words students struggle with as they write. She has created a spelling analysis chart that helps her identify children's current understandings (see Figure 9.8). This information becomes useful as Ms. Donavan plans her own spelling program.

The Reflective Cycle for assessment leads to a more cohesive and meaningful literacy program for children. In the case of the Yopp–Singer assessment, the teacher can note which children would benefit from literacy events that emphasize rhyme, alliteration, and language pattern play. Texts selected for read aloud and shared reading events can target particular sounds and language patterns.

Miscue analysis and running records also offer teachers a window into how readers access the graphophonemic cueing system to decode the text. Through these assessments, the teacher can document which children overuse this cueing system. In reading conferences and mini-lessons, teachers can provide alternative strategies for students to consider.

Yopp–Singer Test of Phoneme Segmentation.

Score (# correct) _____

Name _____

Date ☐ fall _____
☐ winter _____
☐ spring _____

Directions: Today we're going to play a word game. I'm going to say a word and I want you to break the word apart. You are going to tell me each sound of the word in order. For example, if I say **old**, you should say /o/ /l/ /d/. Let's try a few together.

Practice items: (assist in segmenting, if necessary)   ride (3)   go (2)   man (3)

Test items: (Circle those items that the student correctly segments; incorrect responses are recorded on the blank line following the item.)

1. dog _____	12. lay _____
2. keep _____	13. race _____
3. fine _____	14. zoo _____
4. no _____	15. three _____
5. she _____	16. job _____
6. wave _____	17. in _____
7. grew _____	18. ice _____
8. that _____	19. at _____
9. red _____	20. top _____
10. me _____	21. by _____
11. sat _____	22. do _____

(Hallie Kay Yopp grants permission for this test to be reproduced. The author acknowledges the contribution of the late Harry Singer to the development of this test.)

FIGURE 9.7 Yopp—Singer Test of Phoneme Segmentation.

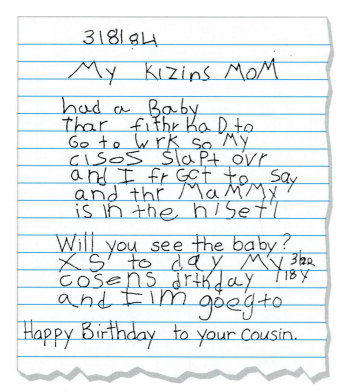

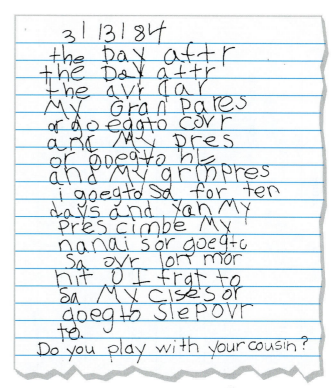

My cousin's mom had a baby. Their father had to go to work so my cousins slept over and I forgot to say and their mommy is in the hospital. Will you see the baby? Yes, today. My cousins birthday and I'm going to. Happy Birthday to your cousin.

The day after. The day after the [ ] my grandparents are going to cover and my dress [ ] and my grandparents going to stay for 10 days and [ ] my nana is going to stay over longer more [ ] I forgot to say my cousins are going to sleep over too.

Text participant assessments

A text participant assessment is based on how the reader participates, or interacts with a story. For example, after reading *Shiloh* (Naylor, 1991), a story about finding and adopting a puppy, a student relates her experience of finding a lost puppy and taking it home. In text participant assessments, the focus is on how readers make meaning from what has been read. As readers make sense of words on pages, they draw upon prior knowledge and experiences, compare their experiences with those in the text, construct literal and inferential meanings, and understand that texts are constructed to make meaning. Reader's prior knowledge is constructed from their lived experiences at home and in the community, personal and cultural values and beliefs, and memories. A reader's ability to understand a text is largely determined by the prior knowledge and experiences brought to the text.

Unfortunately, many assessments that attend to text participant practices assume that there is only one correct answer to a question (Anthony, et. al, 1991). The reader's response must match the interpretation that has been determined by the teacher (or whoever wrote the assessment). A more productive way to think about comprehension and students' understandings of text is to consider the plausibility of a reader's interpretation. Does the reader draw upon information in the text, as well as his or her own personal connections, experiences, and knowledge to con-

> ### Creating Connections 9.6
>
> Choose some writing samples from a child. Identify the misspelled words. Create an analysis chart and categorize the errors. Based on the number of errors in each category, what instructional decisions can you make for this young speller?
>
> Share your reflections with a classmate.

Word	Child's Spelling	Phonic Alternatives		Faulty auditory perception	Analysis of Structure						Unclassifiable
		Reasonable Alternatives (including homophones)	Alternatives Not Conforming to Spelling Precedent		Letters Omitted	Letters Added	Letters Transposed	Letters Substituted	Doubling Errors	Similar Visual Configuration	

FIGURE 9.8 Spelling analysis chart.

struct a response? This way of thinking about comprehension and meaning making may illuminate the notion that texts carry multiple interpretations and meanings.

To assess text meaning participant practices, teachers collect needed information through authentic literacy events including read alouds, literature discussions, retellings, reading conferences, book shares, and work samples.

Read alouds offer opportunities for students to construct meaning from the texts they hear. Children actively listen and respond to the story as the teacher reads the text and engages them in conversations. Before Ms. Taylor began reading *Sister Anne's Hands* (Lorbiecki, 2000) to her group of third grade students, she asked them to think about a previously read story, *Baseball Saved Us* (Mochizuki, 1995). Students were encouraged to recall events in the story and to make connections to an earlier story, *Trail of Tears* (Bruchac, 1999). As the students talked, Ms. Taylor noted on her observation sheet (Figure 9.9) which students contributed to the discussion. She also documented various comments students shared.

These notes help Ms. Taylor see how children respond to various texts. She is interested in the level of connections children make across texts, experiences, and their own personal background knowledge. When teachers record students' comments during a conversation it is difficult to capture all of the statements. On some occasions, Ms. Taylor may want to tape record the conversation to replay at a later date. Reviewing the tapes provides opportunities to hear aspects of a conversation that may be previously missed. Ms. Taylor may also invite students to listen to their tape-recorded conversations as they reflect on how well they work together as a group.

Book shares offer a venue for assessing comprehension as well as the students' reading interests and attitudes. After reading a book during their independent reading time, students can share their reactions and connections to a story, as well as a summary of the story. Teachers can gauge a student's text participant roles in these informal book shares.

Readers bring to the event their own histories and backgrounds. During literature discussions and reading conferences, the teacher may be inclined to ask the following questions to better understand the thought processes of the students as they navigate texts.

- What connections does the reader make to other texts, experiences, events?
- How does the reader make these connections visible to others?

There are many ways a student can make visible their thinking about a particular story. Work samples and artifacts are often collected as part of a portfolio and might include response logs, sketch to stretch drawings, story maps, and literary

Date _10/15_

Patrick	Emmanuel	Caleb	Matthew
They both got caught (connection between Trail and Baseball) had to be guarded	Her hands are black	She's a nun She's black and no one in the class is black	Both attacking Pearl Harbor Tells her about God
Abby			
She's Catholic; she's a part of the church; I'm Catholic			

FIGURE 9.9 Observation sheet for text participant practices.

Book shares offer teachers a glimpse into what students value in a story.

interviews. These documents and projects are assessed by the teacher based on predetermined criteria (see Figure 9.10). Teachers may also ask students to reflect on the work samples and to share these reflections (written or oral) with peers, administrators, or other teachers.

Text use assessments

Text use practices encourage readers to consider how the purposes behind the text help to shape its form, whether it is a narrative, expository, advertisement, etc. In other words, what is the text's purpose? Is it an advertisement, an argument, or an entertaining story? Literature discussions, retellings, book shares, and other literacy events are opportunities for students to reveal their understandings of how genres are crafted for various purposes. Within events such as personal reading lists, interviews, literature discussions, and reading conferences, a teacher may assess a student's engagement and understanding of the text use practices.

Personal reading lists and response logs reveal the types of texts students are typically reading at any given time. Within these documents, teachers may see the quality and level of response from the students. As part of the reading list and response log, teachers can ask additional questions to uncover the purposes behind reading and reading particular texts.

- What goals does the reader have for the text?
- How does the reader view this text (as difficult, easy, relevant, irrelevant, interesting, dull)

Critical practices assessments

Critical practices refer to how readers challenge the status quo as well as begin to understand the ways in which texts position them as readers and literacy users. With critical practices, readers demonstrate their awareness that texts are constructed by others with particular values, viewpoints, and ways of thinking. Reading does not happen in a vacuum, or only inside the reader's head. Rather, readers bring to the reading event their social and cultural lives.

How does a teacher gather information about students' critical abilities? The most common events for gaining insight into students' critical thinking are literature discussions, response logs, and reflections. In any of these events the teacher may ask the following questions:

- What sort of reader is she or he in the situation (gender, race, class, top group, middle group, bottom group)?
- What identity is taken up in the text?
- What identity does the reader take up?

Aligning assessment practices to the four reading practices demonstrates the importance of linking assessment and instruction. Assessment practices (both alternative and traditional) should measure a wide range of skills through a variety of formats and responses. The diversity of the assessment practices incorporated into the four reading practices signals that there are many ways to attend to progress that children make as they become proficient and effective readers and writers.

Reading Responses	5	4	3	2	1
Understanding of Reading	• An Insightful understanding of key issues in the reading • Draws significant conclusion about issues	• A strong understanding of issues in the reading • Draws solid conclusions about issues	• An adequate understanding of issues in the reading • Draws satisfactory conclusion about issues	• A partial understanding of the issues in the reading • Lacks conclusions about issues or forms inaccurate ones	• A minimal understanding of issues in the reading • Lacks conclusions about issues or forms inaccurate ones
Use of Support Information	• Accurate and appropriate use of a variety of examples and references to the text. Support for ideas and opinions is precise and thoughtfully selected	• Accurate and appropriate use of examples and reference to the text to support ideas and opinions	• Satisfactory use of examples and references to the text to support ideas and opinions	• Uses few details or examples from the text to support ideas and opinions	• Lacks details or examples from the text to support ideas and opinions
Organization	• Logical and effective organization of ideas	• Logical organization of ideas	• Adequate organization of ideas	• Weakness in organization of ideas	• Lacks organization of ideas
Quality of Expression	• Rich, effective language • Skillful use of sentence variety • Consistent use of accurate conventions	• Specific descriptive language • Sentence variety • Minimal errors in conventions that do not interface with communication	• Appropriate language • Some sentence variety • Satisfactory use of accurate conventions	• Occasionally uses inappropriate or incorrect language • Sentence makes sense but has little variety • Errors in conventions may interfere with communication	• Inappropriate or incorrect language • Lacks accurate sentence structure • Errors in conventions that interfere with communication • Errors do not interfere with communication

Name _____

Title of Book _____

Date _____ Rating _____ Comment _____

Suggestions _____

FIGURE 9.10 Reading response rubric used by a fifth-grade teacher.

From: Cohen, J. (2003). Literacy portfolios improving assessment teaching and learning. Upper Saddle River, NJ: Pearson Education.

In Closing

The multitude of reading and writing assessments available to teachers and students provides teachers with many opportunities to effectively evaluate students' strengths and areas that need improvement in reading and writing. How teachers view the role of assessment often depends on the ideological perspectives that one holds about learning and teaching. Traditional assessments, those that adopt more simplistic procedures, such as multiple choice and standardized tests, are aligned with an industrial model of learning. These type of assessments are not linked directly to ongoing curricular decisions, but are used to compare school and district performance. Alternative assessments, on the other hand, provide teachers with a more complete picture of the learner's growth and progress in literacy development. There are many different types of assessments from documentary and observational to responsive listening. Such assessments include miscue analysis, running records, retellings, checklists, and anecdotal notes.

With all the different assessment practices available for students and teachers, it is critical to keep in mind that the focus for any assessment is to provide information that can lead to more effective curricular decisions. Assessment practices should provide teachers, parents, district level personnel, and other stakeholders with information that can be used to shape curriculum as well as describe student and school achievement in relation to district and state reading and writing standards.

Terms to Remember

Alternative assessments *(265)*

Criterion-referenced *(263)*

Formative assessment *(255)*

High stakes tests *(261)*

Informal reading interview (IRI) *(264)*

Miscue analysis *(267)*

Miscue *(267)*

Norm-referenced *(263)*

Portfolio systems *(278)*

Retrospective miscue analysis *(267)*

Stakeholders *(261)*

Summative assessment *(255)*

Triangulation *(266)*

Resources for More Information

Afflerbach, P. (2002). The road to folly and redemption: Perspectives on the legitimacy of high-stakes testing. *Reading Research Quarterly*, 37, 348–360

Anthony, R., Johnson, T., Mickelson, N., & Preece, A. (1991). *Evaluating literacy: A perspective for change.* Portsmouth, NH: Heinemann.

Goodman, Y. (1995) Miscue Analysis for Classroom teachers: Some procedures and some history, *Primary Voices*, v. 3(4), 5–9.

Martens, P. (1997). What Miscue Analysis Reveals about Word Recognition and Repeated Reading: A View through the "Miscue Window." *Language Arts*, 74(8), 600–609

Rhodes, L. K., & Shanklin, N. L. (1993). *Windows into literacy: Assessing learners*, K-8. Portsmouth, NH: Heinemann.

Serafini, F (2002), Reflective practice and learning, *Primary Voices* K–6, 10(4), 2–7.

Questions for Further Reflection

- Traditional assessment practices continue to be a driving force in curricular decisions, student placements, and funding for districts. What conversations can you have with parents and other teachers to begin advocating for more diverse measures of assessment?

- What role should miscue analysis play in a reading curriculum and to what extent?

- As a teacher, what do you see as the potential value of assessment?

- What difficulties or challenges do you anticipate as you administer alternative assessments in classroom settings?

CHAPTER 10

Facilitating Meaningful Literature Discussions

Ms. Wilson's Fourth Grade Students Talk About The Mouse and the Motorcycle

A group of seven fourth graders participating in a classroom book club contemplate the plight of Ralph, a mouse, as he is about to take a motorcycle out for a nighttime spin in Beverly Cleary's classic story, *The Mouse and the Motorcycle* (1990 c.1965). At this point in the story, Keith, a young boy who befriends Ralph, lets him take the motorcycle out for a night of adventure. Ralph, who had never ventured far away from home, was thrilled at the possibilities that awaited him. After a close call in being seen by the hotel manager, Ralph returns home and climbs up into Keith's pajama pocket for safety.

The students in this book club meet without me on a regularly basis. I have four groups going at the same time, and each day I sit in on one group's conversation. Students are learning how to participate in a book conversation on their own. There are no pre-determined questions for them to answer or summaries to write. Early in the school year, I tape record the conversations so that I can listen to them later in the day and determine possible next steps. *The Mouse and the Motorcycle* group began talking about their favorite parts of the story and their different interpretations of the events. The group members included Clark, Robert, Elizabeth, Elaine, Kelly, Marcy, and Michelle. Clark, a self-assured reader in this group is the first to offer comment. Elaine, who is a less confident reader, follows with her own favorite part of the story. Elizabeth, also a confident reader, steps in and challenges Elaine's understanding of the story:

CLARK: I like the part where he rides the motorcycle.
ELAINE: I liked the part when he was riding the motorcycle down the hall and the dog heard him and then he [said] okay okay I'll take you for a walk. And then Ralph talked to the old man.
ELIZABETH: Matt? [referring to the bellman of the hotel]
ELAINE: yeah
ELIZABETH: He's not an old man. He's. . .
CLARK: How do you know?
ELAINE: They said, Matt the old man.
ELIZABETH: Does it say that?
ELAINE: It did
CLARK: Don't read it. Don't read it. Blah Blah Blah
ELAINE: Be quiet.

In this excerpt, Clark, the self-assured reader was able to challenge his peers; he did not need to justify his interpretation or listen to what his peers were offering as possibilities. Elaine tries to assert her own position by confirming that her interpretation is accurate and giving Clark a directive, "be quiet." As the conversation moved on, Marcy waited patiently to interject her ideas,

ELIZABETH:	How can the motorcycle go when there is no motor on it?
KELLY:	Cause the boy already told him.
CLARK:	Cause it is a magical moment. [students talking over one another—cannot understand what is said]
ELAINE:	It's make believe. It's not a true story.
ELIZABETH:	But if it were true, how could it go?
KELLY:	It's fiction. [more talking on top of each other]
CLARK:	Oh, come on. It's just fiction. You can't believe fiction.
MARCY:	Well maybe . . . what he can't, what the mouse probably was doing was having one foot on the pedal and one foot to move.
CLARK:	Fiction can't be (unintelligible).

I wonder . . .

- For these fourth grade readers, where does meaning reside? In the text? In their experience? In the negotiation of ideas? In all three?

- What roles do these readers take on when discussing the text?

- If you, as a teacher, were to enter into this conversation, what observations could you make?

- What questions would support these readers in their interpretations of this story?

A few days later, the students in the book club meet again. At this meeting, each member brings a list of their own questions to ask each other.

CLARK:	Why does Ralph like the motorcycle?
KELLY:	Because he is getting tired of walking all over the hotel?
CLARK:	bbzzzzzz. How can he walk all the way around the hotel?
KELLY:	Well, not around it. He's getting tired of walking. [students again are talking on top of each other]
KELLY:	I think he likes the motorcycle because he is tired of walking.
ROBERT:	I think he just . . . I think he likes it because he sees something new and you've never seen it before and you like it
KELLY:	like a Porsche
ROBERT:	I don't know, I think he likes it. He probably just likes it.
CLARK:	Robert's turn.
KELLY:	No my turn.

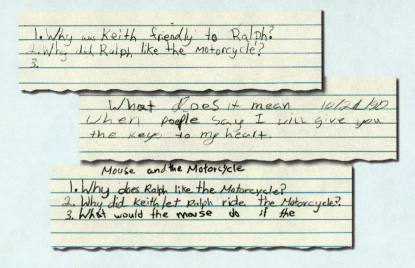

1. Why was Keith friendly to Ralph?
2. Why did Ralph like the motorcycle?
3.

What does it mean   10/21/10
when people say I will give you
the keys to my heart.

Mouse and the Motorcycle

1. Why does Ralph like the Motorcycle?
2. Why did Keith let Ralph ride the Motorcycle?
3. What would the mouse do if the

At this point, I interrupt the students to talk about how literature discussions are opportunities for everyone to engage and participate. We begin to talk about how people can have different interpretations or understandings of the story, and what is important is to make sure that everyone has a chance to share their thinking. I introduced the idea that maybe there needed to be some guidelines for the students as they worked together. This group thought that was a good idea. I left them to brainstorm a list of what it might look like and sound like to be a good literature discussion participant.

Chapter Overview

Literature discussions, mentioned throughout the previous chapters, are an important component of effective literacy instruction. They can be implemented in every grade and conducted in a variety of ways—from teacher-facilitated and structured discussions to student-led, informal discussions. Literature discussions may involve an entire classroom of students, a group of children, or even just a few children interested in a particular story. The discussion may appear to be very structured a question and answer format or loosely structured, similar to an informal conversation.

Many of the ideas presented in this chapter are the "behind the scenes" or hidden influences in literature discussions, meaning that this work is often not visible to an observer in the classroom. An observer might not notice that students have a different purpose for reading the text than the teacher, or that students construct interpretations based on the text and their own understandings. What is visible, however, is the effect of these "hidden influences" on literature discussions.

In this chapter, you will learn how to implement and facilitate effective literature discussions in the classroom. You will also learn strategies that support the complex nature of sharing one's thinking about a book or other text. After reading this chapter, you will be able to answer the following questions:

- How can teachers promote meaningful literature discussions?
- What roles do teachers and students assume in teacher-led discussions and student-led discussions?
- What is meant by interpretive authority and social positioning?
- Why is flexibility of stance and interpretive authority important in literature discussions?

An inside look: Two very different literature discussion groups

The discussion of *The Mouse and the Motorcycle* in the opening vignette involved only students who selected this text. Other students in that class were busy reading their selections, such as *Number the Stars* (Lowry, 1989), *Holes* (Sachar, 1998), and *Because of Winn Dixie* (DiCamillo, 2000). In each group, students decided on how much they would read before meeting and how long it would take them to read the entire selection. These decisions were then shared with Ms. Wilson who recorded

their expectations and goals on a chart. The *Mouse and the Motorcycle* group decided to read four chapters a week and to meet every other day. As they met for their discussions, it became apparent that a couple of students were taking over the conversation and not listening to everyone's responses.

In contrast, Ms. Taylor's third grade students (from chapter 9) all read *Sister Anne's Hands* (Lorbiecki, 1998) as part of their language arts block (see vignette in chapter nine). Recall that this is a story about an African-American nun teaching in a Catholic school in the early 1960s. One day a cruel message about Sister Anne is written on a paper airplane. Sister Anne turns the painful incident into a powerful learning experience for Anna and her classmates. At the end of the school year, Sister Anne is transferred to a school in Chicago. The students in Ms. Taylor's class wonder why Sister Anne left the school at the end of the year. They questioned whether it was her own decision to move or if she was forced to leave. Students listened intently to each other's interpretations of the story as they considered who would force Sister Anne to relocate and why. They also wondered why the parents don't want Sister Anne to be their children's teacher.

CALEB:	She was black.
EMMANUEL:	No one in the class was.
MARVIN:	Maybe they are racist.
RYAN:	What's that?
MARVIN:	hate people from Africa and Mexico

The discussion about the story does not end with a final comment from the students or their teacher. Instead, students continue to think and wonder about the story as they spend time writing in their response journals. The discussion about racial difference and prejudice, and the follow-up work in response journals appears to happen effortlessly. The multiple ways that Ms. Taylor's students responded to *Sister Anne's Hands*—reading, talking, and writing about the story—contribute to the ways in which they understand and interpret the themes of the story for themselves.

Ms. Taylor's discussion group has a different tone than the discussion group from Ms. Wilson's class. Ms. Taylor offered opportunities for students to examine their own interpretations in light of what others may have said. They were genuinely interested in what their classmates had to say. In *The Mouse and the Motorcycle* group, however, students were beginning to position members of the group as experts who know correct answers, and others as nonexperts. They did not work to build upon each other's comments, but rather talked over each other. While these two groups were organized differently (one was student led and the other teacher facilitated), it is the "behind the scenes" work that often results in effective literature discussions for entire classrooms or in small groups. Effective literature discussions do not just happen. Literature discussions develop as a result of key decisions about:

- texts
- group participants, and
- ways of responding.

Teachers must take into account the goals, purposes, texts, and assessments of the discussion in order to bring about meaningful conversations among their students.

Goals for literature discussions

Literature discussions, book clubs, and literature-based instruction have become a way of curriculum life for teachers in all grades. There are a number of goals teachers have for implementing literature discussions. For example, an initial goal may be to have students identify particular details of the text in a public forum. More substantive goals may be for students to:

- share their understandings and interpretations of the text with each other,
- listen to others' interpretations, and
- construct negotiated responses that build from the comments of group members (as in the earlier comments about *Sister Anne's Hands*).

Initial goals are achieved when readers focus on comprehending the story. Asking students to identify details and literary elements are a part of this initial goal. As students move beyond this initial level, they share their own interpretations of the story. They begin to discover worlds outside their own individual, lived experiences. These interpretations reveal students' social, cultural, and political backgrounds. Literature discussions provide a space for students to hear how others interpreted the story, thereby broadening their own individual understandings. Literature discussions also offer students space in the curriculum to engage in critical practices—to problematize, challenge, or question longstanding beliefs. In doing so, students' interpretations are more complex and substantive.

Imagine a group of second graders having a culminating discussion about the classic story, *Charlotte's Web* (White, 1952). As part of the discussion, the teacher encourages students to consider what makes a main character. One student, Marc, believes that Charlotte is the main character, because of the story's title, "Why is it called *Charlotte's Web*?" His classmate, Oliver, disagrees and states, "Wilbur was in the beginning and the end of the story so he was the main character. Charlotte was just in the middle and a little in the end." For Oliver, the main character is defined by presence in the story. As the two classmates disagree about who is the main character in the story, they learn that there may be a range of understandings and a variety of ways that authors develop main characters. Later, the teacher shifts the conversation to a discussion of the theme. Jillian offers her understandings of the main events, "Charlotte saving Wilbur" to which Phillip adds "Friends help friends." Phillip's ideas of friendship may reveal his own beliefs about what friends are. In this literature discussion, students construct interpretations that are tied to their own understandings of text and the world around them.

The goals for a literature discussion become apparent as teachers make a number of important decisions regarding the texts, the purposes, and the group itself. How teachers and students participate in literature discussions is often determined by the particular goals they want to achieve. This decision is in many cases implicit in the types of responses and interpretations accepted within the discussion.

How readers make meaning from a text: Reader response theory

Reader response theory plays an important role in effective literature discussions. Recall that in chapter 4, readers and writers transact with the text, meaning that they construct interpretations of the text based on their own experiences and histories. As a result of a negotiation between the reader and the text, new interpretations are developed that may contribute to the overall understanding of the text. In this section, key insights into **reader response theory** are examined in light of conducting effective literature discussions in elementary classrooms.

reader response theory

Focuses on the reader or audience rather than the author or text.

Readers bring their sociocultural backgrounds to the text

Reader response theory suggests that readers are not passive participants in the reading event (Fish, 1980; Langer, 1995; Rosenblatt, 1938, 1978). Instead, readers play an integral role in the meaning making process by bringing their own social, cultural, and historical ways of participating in the discussion group. Children learn from previous experiences (mostly in school settings) the ways in which people talk about stories, what information is valued and privileged, and how to interact with others within the context of a literature discussion.

> ### Creating Connections 10.1
>
> What experiences and knowledge do you bring to a literature discussion? What contributing factors influence how you respond in such settings?
>
> Share your thinking with classmates.

Earlier in the chapter when Ms. Wilson's fourth grade students discussed *The Mouse and the Motorcycle*, each child brought to the group their own way of participating in the group, based on their individual backgrounds and experiences. The comments Clark made to Elizabeth and Elaine about his interpretation of the story did little to support a collective building of information about the story. Instead, his comments positioned him as an authority within the discussion. Elaine's history as a struggling reader was reflected in her peers' comments, as they discounted what she had to say. Clark, Elaine, and Elizabeth are typical of how many students interact in literature discussions. The spheres of influence (see Figure 10.1), such as how to interact with others, the texts used, and the value of the literature discussion in the larger literacy picture all contribute to what is meant by a literature discussion in a particular classroom.

FIGURE 10.1 Spheres of influence that contribute to a reader's interpretation of text.

Readers transact with the text

transaction

A relationship between the reader and the text, whereby what is interpreted is mediated by the reader's experiences and background.

Readers not only read with the text, but they also *transact* with the text (Rosenblatt, 1938, 1978). A **transaction** is a two-way process, whereby the reader brings to the reading event his or her prior experiences about the world and at the same time entertains a multitude of possible interpretations offered by the text. Gaining an understanding of the text along with its characters and themes is a dynamic, reflective, and introspective process. The newly constructed interpretations that come as a result of the transaction do not reside solely "in" the text or "in" the learner, but happen as a result of a negotiation between the two. As such, multiple interpretations can be considered. And while there is an extended range of interpretations, reader response theory (Figure 10.2) suggests that acceptable responses take into account both the text and each reader's cultural background and individual uniqueness (Chase & Hynd, 1987). Moreover, readers make meaning that is personal but situated within the text.

Following is a discussion between a group of first and second graders in Ms. Hammel's class. They are talking about *Tomás and the Library Lady* (Mora, 1997). *Tomás and the Library Lady* is the story of a young boy whose family works the farm fields in Texas and Iowa. Constantly moving between the two places is difficult, and Tomás finds refuge in the stories his grandfather tells. Papa Grande tells Tomás there are more stories in the library. Tomás meets the library lady who introduces him to the world of books.

MS HAMMEL'S FIRST AND SECOND GRADE STUDENTS DISCUSS *TOMÁS AND THE LIBRARY LADY*. Ms. Hammel begins her literature discussion time by reminding students about another story they read that addressed migration. This story was about the monarch butterfly and how these butterflies migrate to Mexico. Ms. Hammel then introduces the idea that people also migrate to different places. She reads the first few pages of *Tomás and the Library Lady* and comments:

Ms. Hammel: Tomás said he was tired and that his car was tired. Do you think this is a move across town? Sounds like it's a long distance from Texas to Iowa.

Ms. Hammel then poses a question she wants students to consider, "Why do people move?"

Hannah: to go to a different place
Keith: to find a new house

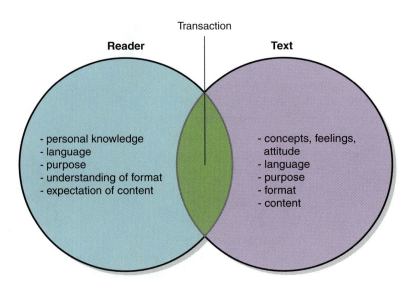

FIGURE 10.2 Reader response theory: Transaction between reader and text.

BRANDIE:	to visit family
MS. HAMMEL:	It might be that they want to live near their family. Some of you live close to grandparents.
HERNAN:	I live with my grandparents.
ENRIQUE:	They may go for sabbatical.

Ms. Hammel, knowing that Enrique's father, a professor at the local university, had recently taken a sabbatical to Mexico, asks Enrique to explain what sabbatical is. Following the explanation, Ms. Hammel invites two more students into the discussion:

MS. HAMMEL:	Scott and Chania were discussing this yesterday; why were you going to have to move?
SCOTT:	A new landlord.
MS. HAMMEL:	This new landlord is refusing their section eight, and the section eight is to provide housing at a lower cost. Avery, you said you are getting ready to move, why?
AVERY:	We have a new house because my mommy is going to have a baby and we needed to have more rooms.
JAIME:	We moved because of the cockroaches.
MS. HAMMEL:	That's another reason. Jaime you were just talking about the conditions of your place causing you to want to move. It sounds like there are a lot of reasons why people move and as we continue the story, let's think about why Tomás and his family are moving. Is Tomás's family moving because of one of the reasons you listed, or is there another reason?

At this point, Ms. Hammel continues to read the story.

This interchange between Ms. Hammel and her students reflects how readers transact with the story. They draw upon their own experiences with moving to make initial connections with the text. As Ms. Hammel reads about Tomás and his family's migration between Texas and Iowa, students consider other reasons why people move. Through this process, students construct an interpretation that extends beyond their own experience and that of the text. These negotiated responses illustrate that there was no single correct way of responding to the literature (and to Ms. Hammel's question). Students were encouraged to construct their own meanings as they listened to the story and considered what they knew about why people move. Meaning was not lying in wait to be "discovered" by the reader; nor was it solely in the experiences the students brought to the text. The negotiation of ideas between students' experiences and those presented in the text led to a more complete understanding about the complexities of why people relocate to other places.

Judith Langer (1995) contributes to reader response theory by suggesting that responding to text is a process of **_envisionment_**. Building on the notion of a transaction, envisionment is defined as

envisionment

Dynamic sets of ideas, images, questions, anticipations, and hunches that a reader has while reading, speaking, or writing.

> text worlds in the mind and they differ from individual to individual. They are a function of one's personal and cultural experiences, one's relationship to the current experience, what one knows, how one feels, and what one is after. Envisionments are dynamic sets of related ideas, images, questions, disagreements, anticipations, arguments, and hunches that fill the mind during every reading, writing, speaking, or other experience when one gains, expresses, and shares thoughts and understandings. (p. 9)

Did you know. . .

Since 1987, the Center on English Learning & Achievement (CELA) has been conducting research dedicated to gaining knowledge to improve students' English and literacy achievement. CELA has maintained its reputation as being objective in a field that is often contentious, while expanding its contributions to include, for example, knowledge about successful preparation and ongoing support for effective teachers. Teachers, coordinators at the school, district, and state levels, and other policymakers in particular use the Center's website and print materials to inform their decisions and work to improve student literacy achievement.

http://cela.albany.edu/

TECHNOLOGY LINK

http://www.learner.org/channel/libraries/engagingliterature/responding/

Rich Thompson facilitates a literature discussion with his fourth grade students. He assumes the role of engaged reader and uses the discussion not only to support student contributions, but to model additional ways they might approach the literature.

In classroom literature discussions where readers are encouraged to transact with the text and construct sets of related ideas or envisionments, students have opportunities to consider and reconsider texts from multiple perspectives. As the first and second grade readers in Ms. Hammel's class illustrate, their understandings of why people move and subsequently, why Tomás's family is moving, reside in the negotiation of individual perspectives and in those presented in the text. How children convey their interpretations to the group and which interpretations carry more validity within the group depend on the stance, interpretive authority, and the social position of those in the literature discussion group. These influences, often hidden to the casual observer, can help teachers establish meaningful and effective literature conversations in the classroom. In the following sections, each hidden influence is examined with strategies offered to make these influences more visible in classroom interactions and literature discussions.

Stance: A reader's attitude and purpose

stance

The attitude or purpose one has for reading.

When you pick up a novel for the beach or a manual on how to fix your DVD player, do you enter into the text with the same purpose or attitude? Most likely you do not. *Stance* refers to the attitude and purpose a reader has for reading a selected text. Stance can also refer to how one engages in a literature discussion. There are many dimensions to stance, including *literary/strategic, contextual, and ideological* (Flint, Lysaker, Riordan-Karlsson, & Molinelli, 1999; Flint & Riordan-Karlsson, 2001). Figure 10.3 demonstrates how these dimensions are interconnected and as students construct meaning from a text, traces of these dimensions are apparent in their comments.

literary/strategic dimension

Reader's attention is focused on textual cues.

THE STRATEGIC/LITERARY DIMENSION: IS THE TEXT FOR INFORMATION OR ENJOYMENT? One of the first things we all do when looking at a text is look for cues such as pictures, diagrams, or special sections. These cues tell us whether the text is fiction or nonfiction. And what we know about fiction and nonfiction will help us determine the purpose we have for reading the text. This is what is meant by *literary/strategic dimension*. The reader's attention is focused on textual cues and purposes for reading. Textual cues, such as pictures, diagrams, text organization, special sections, headings, etc., help readers decide which literary stance to take. When paging through a book, a reader may notice that there are no special pull-out boxes of texts, diagrams, words in bold font, or glossaries. Without these textual cues, the reader may assume that the text is fiction with characters, settings, and plots. On the other hand,

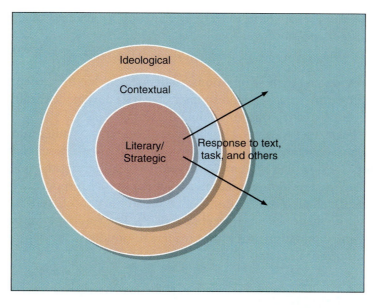

FIGURE 10.3 Dimensions of stance.

if such cues are noticed, including two-column formats and defining words in the context of the paragraph, the reader may assume that the text is nonfiction. Readers use these cues to determine how they may approach the text—as something to gain information from or to enjoy as a story.

Thinking about the author's purpose is another part of literary/strategic stance. As a reader considers the author's purpose for writing, and their own purpose for reading, the reader gains a sense of what the text might be about. Authors generally write to entertain, inform, explain, promote thinking, or persuade. Teachers can ask students these questions to highlight what the author's purpose may be:

- Why did the author write this?
- What does the author want me to learn from this?

These questions help readers to better understand the text and to develop interpretations of it. This interaction with the text ultimately contributes to an effective literature discussion or other literacy events.

Readers also need to consider their own purposes for reading. As they begin to read, have students respond to these questions:

- What is my plan? Why am I reading this text?

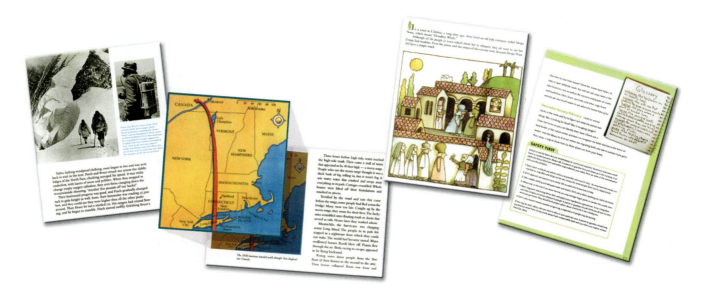

- Am I reading this to learn information, or am I reading this to enjoy the experience and/or story?
- What is important to me in reading this text?

By responding to these questions, readers learn what they will gain as a result of the reading experience. These responses may shift during the reading event, depending on the internal reasons for reading the text.

There are two general purposes for reading—to gather information or to have an emotional response, "a lived through experience" (Rosenblatt, 1978). These two purposes are called ***efferent literary stance*** (reading to gather information) and ***aesthetic literary stance*** (reading for an emotional response). These purposes (or stances) fall on a continuum, from a predominately efferent stance to a predominately aesthetic stance (Rosenblatt, 1978). The reading experience is not an all or nothing orientation, but rather readers respond to a text with more emphasis towards one or the other stance.

efferent literary stance

Attention is towards gathering information from a text.

aesthetic literary stance

Attention is towards having an emotional response to the text.

> ### *Creating Connections* 10.2
>
> Put together a collection of texts on a particular topic. Identify the predominate stance that the texts may be read from.

Figure 10.4 provides an overview of how a literary/strategic stance is constructed.

Adopting an efferent literary stance means to seek out and process information. An efferent literary stance is generally more predominant when students read expository or nonfiction texts, including content area textbooks (e.g., social studies or science textbook) and picture books, such as Seymor Simon's *Hurricanes* (2003). An efferent stance is most commonly adopted when the reader is trying to gain information about a particular process, event, or concept. Readers adopt an efferent stance when researching texts for information. For example, reading a science passage about the layers of the earth may evoke an efferent stance from the reader. The Internet is often read from an efferent stance. Experienced web page readers scan the text quickly searching for key-

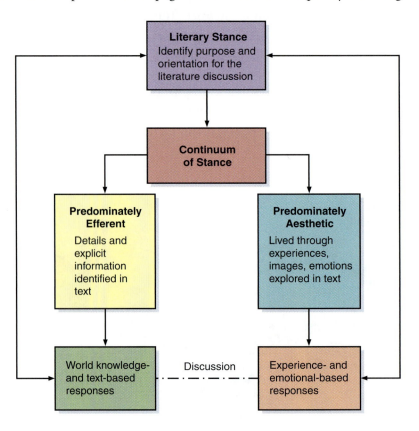

FIGURE 10.4 Reader's orientation to text.

words or bits of information. An efferent stance may also be adopted for narrative texts when teachers and students selectively attend to the literal details of the text, such as characters' names, progression of events, or where the story takes place.

An aesthetic literary stance, on the other hand, is what most readers adopt when they talk about the theme and their emotional responses to the fictional or narrative text. An aesthetic stance focuses the reader's attention on the more private aspects of the text—the feelings, images, and emotions that are evoked as a result of reading. When someone "escapes" into a text, they are taking an aesthetic stance toward the material. Many of us have this experience when reading a novel on a rainy Saturday or enjoying a poetry reading at a local bookstore. When children read *Charlotte's Web* (White, 1952) for the first time, for example, an aesthetic stance is sure to emerge. Young readers may experience happiness when Fern, the farm girl who cares for Wilbur, is able to keep Wilbur from imminent death, and children may experience sadness when it becomes apparent that Charlotte, the spider, is dying. In literature discussions, an aesthetic stance is often evoked when readers discuss themes of the book.

> ### *Creating Connections 10.3*
> Think about the literature discussions you have been involved in. What was your predominate stance while engaged in the discussion?

The aesthetic stance involves not only a personal response but may also include a social, cultural, and/or political response to a text (Lewis, 2000). When readers encounter texts whose characters and storylines are about cultures and life experiences that are very different from their own, their abilities to identify and make personal connections may be challenged. In such instances, a reader's orientation or purpose for reading may involve more social and political aspects, thereby broadening the notion of aesthetic stance. For example, when reading *Sold* (McCormick, 2006), an adolescent reader may not be familiar with the slave trade of young women in India. As the story is read, she responds to the events by considering how young women in her own country are treated and begins to take a more political stance towards issues of human rights.

In addition to taking a particular stance toward a text, readers also come to the text with different intentions. Intention lies between the purposes and attitudes one has toward reading and the actual act of reading (Ruddell & Unrau, 1997). During literature discussions a reader's intention becomes explicit through the types of responses that are constructed. Interpretations may be based on experience, emotions, world knowledge, or the text. Experience- and emotion-based interpretations are formed from prior experiences and personal reactions or connections to concepts and ideas presented in the text. These responses are in keeping with an aesthetic stance. Text-based and world knowledge responses align themselves with an efferent stance. Figure 10.5. Adopting a Literary Stance with *Charlotte's Web* explores the possibilities.

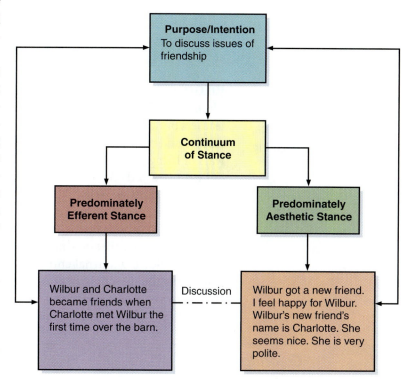

FIGURE 10.5 Adopting a literary stance with *Charlotte's Web*.

As the figure demonstrates, friendship was identified as an important concept to discuss. If the reader responds with a predominately efferent stance, the interpretation is more text based in nature. If a student responds aesthetically, the interpretation will have traces of personal experience and emotions. Adopting particular stances along the continuum is fluid and dynamic, meaning that the stance can change over the course of a discussion or literature selection. The adopted literary stance is "not fixed, but instead is situated within the context of a particular moment, place, and set of readers and texts" (Lewis, 2000, p. 257). Readers may begin with one stance and through questions and interpretations revisit the ways in which they are reading the text.

CONTEXTUAL DIMENSION: WHERE DOES THE DISCUSSION OCCUR? The *contextual dimension* of a literature discussion refers to the environment where the discussion occurs, including the structure of the event and how it will be enacted. Will the discussion be a small group or large group? Will the discussion be teacher directed or student led? Will there be a series of questions posed to the group or will the group participate in an open conversation about the text?

Hanssen (1990) poses a number of contextual questions for teachers to keep in mind when conducting a literature discussion group:

- Should the discussion group be a large group or a small group?
- Which story or book will be read and who chooses it?
- Should the teacher participate in the discussion?
- When should a group meet and who decides when the group will meet?
- Will the text be read silently or out loud?
- Will students read the text while the group is together or before the group meets?

Responses to these questions speak to the deliberate decision making that occurs for effective discussions to take place. Meaningful and productive literature discussions do not just happen; they are a result of careful planning and consideration.

IDEOLOGICAL DIMENSION: WHAT BELIEFS DOES THE READER HAVE? The *ideological dimension* involves the beliefs, values, and understandings that readers and teachers bring to a text. Drawing upon one's sociocultural background and experiences, readers and teachers adopt various ideological stances about learning, teaching, and ways of being in the world as they enter into literature discussions. Ideologies are socially constructed (Bloome & Bailey, 1992). "The community in which we live, the social relationships we form, the groups we belong to, the meanings ascribed to certain cultural artifacts and beliefs, and our political values situate and constitute our ideological stance towards literacy events" (Flint, et al., 1999). Texts are read and discussed from a perspective that depends on one's ideological stance.

The following journal entries appeared in a primary multi-age classroom (ages 6–8) where the students had questions and concerns about the United States' response to the terrorist events of September 11, 2001. As they listened to their teacher read *Sami and the Times of the Trouble* (Heidi, 1992), a story of a young boy and his family living in Beirut during wartime, they began to ask questions about their own lives and surroundings, and compose meaningful comments in their own journals. Students shared these drawing and comments with each other in a group conversation.

---

contextual dimension

The environment in which the discussion takes place.

---

ideological dimension

Involves the reader's beliefs, values, and understandings.

> *Creating Connections* **10.4**
>
> Take a look at the last five texts (books, magazines, newspapers, websites) you read. What literary/strategic stance did you adopt to read them? Share your findings on your blog.

These students' comments and responses to the tragedy of September 11 indicate that students as young as 6 are able to construct their own beliefs and perspectives about the ways in which the world operates. Issues surrounding friendship, loyalty, defense, and power are a part of these comments.

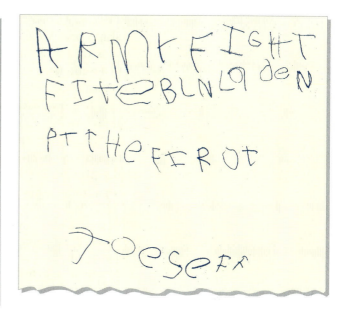

Dear Sami I'm so sorry this is going to happen. There are so many bombs but I don't like it I know this [is] not fun. I know you are sad and scared. I know this is scary. And I know this is bad.

Army fight. Fight Bin Laden put the fire out.

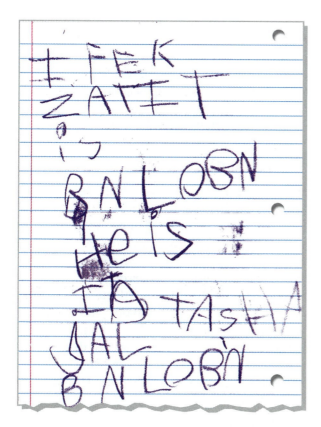

I think that is Bin Laden. He is in jail Bin Laden

(drawing of Osama Bin Laden in jail)

Teachers also bring their ideological stance to the classroom and these stances impact instructional decisions. Decisions about how to teach, what to teach, and what to assess are guided by beliefs about the teaching and learning cycle (Cunningham & Fitzgerald, 1996). These beliefs are shaped by past experiences, memberships in various groups, academic and professional preparation, and relationships with others (Bloome & Bailey, 1992; Kamberelis & Scott, 1992). Instructional stances influence the pedagogical approach for a particular literacy event. For example, when a teacher values and expands on the multiple interpretations offered by her students during a literature conversation, the teacher's perspective of literacy is one that is based in social, cultural, and historical contexts. She recognizes that students learn from each other, that they bring their own backgrounds and knowledge to the reading event, and that this knowledge is based on the children's own histories.

Additionally, the teacher recognizes that students bring to the classroom a range of processes in which to understand the text. To further illustrate this point, consider fifth grade teacher Ms. Reiner's explanation of why she wants her students to read authentic pieces of literature:

I want students to know that they are not the only ones going through a particular problem or issue, like fighting with your parents or friends, or worried about being 'cool,' or knowing that peer pressure is something we all go through. I also want them to see that events that happened in history have stories behind them, that real people were affected, and that we can make decisions that are more informed if we know some of the stories.

Ms. Reiner's comments make clear her own belief that through reading children come to know their world and themselves better. Her ideological stance suggests that reading is a broader endeavor than simply identifying the main idea or vocabulary words. Reading for this teacher is more robust and enables her to select texts that her students may be interested in reading. Her students benefit from talking about texts and addressing issues and problems that matter to their sense of self.

All three dimensions of stance—literary/strategic, contextual, and ideological—intersect and are a part of the readers' interpretations and responses. Readers talk with each other about a text, pose questions, challenge perspectives held by each other and those in the text, and make visible their beliefs. The interplay of these dimensions influences the way in which children understand and find meaning in texts.

Making stance visible in literature discussions

Although stance is an integral part of a literature discussion, the highlighted excerpts throughout this chapter illustrate that, in general, stance is not a visible aspect of the literacy event. It is a hidden influence that greatly impacts the direction of the discussion group, as well as the outcomes of it. While a student's personal stance and a teacher's instructional stance should be in agreement, often there is a misalignment of these stances. When this happens, teachers become frustrated because they do not believe the students are trying their best or adequately comprehending the text. Students worry that they don't know what to do. These common sentiments by both teachers and students lead to ineffective literacy engagements.

An example of a misalignment of stances is when Ms. Sherridan a student teacher in Ms. Wilson's class asked the students to visualize an early scene from *Island of the Blue Dolphin* (O'Dell, 1990). In this early chapter, the author establishes the idea that there are many sea otters floating off the coast of the island.

MS. SHERRIDAN: Picture in your mind, what are you seeing?
        ELAINE: You see water and you see brown things in the water

MS. SHERRIDAN:	So what are the sea otters doing?
ELAINE:	Playing
MS. SHERRIDAN:	Lying on their backs, cruising around, laying there looking at the sky. He's having fun; he's just playing there
ELIZABETH:	When I went to WaterWorld
MS. SHERRIDAN:	Elizabeth, we don't need stories. We need to get this read.
ELIZABETH:	I saw a sea otter
MS. SHERRIDAN:	At WaterWorld?
ELIZABETH:	No, umm . . .
MS. SHERRIDAN:	At Marine World?
ELIZABETH:	Marine World

Ms. Sherridan's purpose and intentions were more along the lines of a predominately efferent literary stance. She wanted the students to visualize a scene from the story. When Elizabeth attempted to construct a response more reflective of an aesthetic and personal experience, it was in opposition to what Ms. Sherridan had in mind. Consequently, a misalignment occurred, thereby limiting the potential and overall effectiveness of the literature discussion.

To promote effective literature discussions, the teacher's stance and the students' stance need to be in sync with each other. Teachers and students can talk about their goals in the literature discussion. Why do people read? How does sharing ideas increase comprehension? How do new ideas develop in the course of the literature discussion? The following invitations are designed to make explicit why stance is important to consider and how students may benefit from such discussion.

> ### Creating Connections 10.5
>
> Discuss with a teacher his or her reasons for having students read a particular literature selection. Considering the multiple dimensions of stance, what might you say about this teacher's perspective about literacy development?

In Ms. Rodriquez's second grade classroom, students use the *Looking Backwards and Beyond* strategy. Ms. Rodriquez asked students to review the story *Strega Nona* (de Paola, 1988). Strega Nona is a Grandma Witch with magic powers. She helps everyone in the town with their troubles, including curing headaches, finding husbands, and curing warts. Because Strega Nona is old, she hires Big Anthony to help her with chores around the house. Strega Nona has a pasta pot that turns into a magic pasta pot when she sings to it. One day, when Strega Nona is gone, Big Anthony uses the magic pot and feeds everyone in town. Unfortunately, he cannot make the pasta stop and soon there is pasta all over town. Strega Nona returns

Invitation for the classroom

Looking Backwards and Beyond

This strategy encourages readers to reflect on their interpretations of the text in light of having read the whole text. Adaptations have been made to highlight the influence of stance.

- How did the textual cues and elements of the text (i.e., chapter headings, pictures, headings, italicized words, etc.) contribute to how you "read" the text?

- Think about why the author ended the story the way she/he did. What type of ending would change how you read the book?

- Lay some of the books you know well next to this one. Did you read them with the same purpose and intention in mind? How are they similar? How are they different?

Adapted from L. Calkins.

and fortunately saves the day. The students were quite familiar with the story. To begin the conversation, Ms. Rodriguez posed the following question,

MS. RODRIGUEZ:	When you read *Strega Nona,* what clues did you use to know this story would be fiction?
MARCIA:	There were funny pictures.
MS. RODRIGUEZ:	Okay, the pictures helped to tell us that this story might be fiction. What other clues did you use?
TERRENCE:	Their names.
MS. RODRIGUEZ:	Can you say more, Terrence, about what you mean?
TERRENCE:	Big Anthony and Strega Nona. These names are not real. Nobody has the name Strega Nona.
MS. RODRIGUEZ:	Oh, I see. Terrence is thinking that the author used names that don't seem real. Remember that Strega Nona is not her real name, but the name that everyone in the town called her. It means Grandma Witch. So, Strega Nona is a nickname. Terrence, I like how you are thinking about how the author created characters to tell the story, rather than writing a story about real people and real events.
PHILLIP:	I think that the magic pot was a clue.
MS. RODRIGUEZ:	Absolutely, Phillip. Have you ever heard of a magic pasta pot before?
STUDENTS:	Noooo.
MS. RODRIGUEZ:	Right, the magic pasta pot is a big clue that this story is fiction. When you were reading this story, did you think about being in the town with all the pasta?
DARIAN:	Ewwww, I would eat up the whole plate. And more and more and more.
ALIS:	Yuck, I couldn't eat that much. I would be sick.
MS. RODRIGUEZ:	Yeah, I don't think I would want that much pasta either. So, we know that this story is one that is made up, or fiction. When we read fiction stories, we often will be happy or sad or have some kind of feeling about the characters and what is happening to them. We are going to move now to our response journals, and as you write today you might want to think about how you feel about one of the characters, Strega Nona or Big Anthony, and if what he or she did was right.

The brief discussion between Ms. Rodriguez and her students illustrates how she was able to address genre and stance in a way that made sense to the students. Although she did not use the terms genre and stance, she did make it explicit that fictional stories are ones that we often have emotional reactions to.

Teachers can also begin to work with students on the purposes one has for reading a text. It is important to begin making visible what teachers and authors have in mind for a text, so that students can also consider their own purposes for engaging in the material. Some possible questions may include:

Creating Connections 10.6

Interview two or three children (ages 6–12) about why they read and what they hope to gain from the experience. Share with classmates your findings about the different dimensions of stance these students seem to be putting into place.

- Think about the teacher's purpose for assigning this text.
- Think about why the author wrote this text.
- Think about why you are reading this text. What might be interesting in this text?

Invitation for the classroom

What Does Stance Do?

Invite students to consider the following questions about purpose and intention. These questions should promote conversations about how texts are structured differently; how readers enter into reading events with different purposes and foci; and how readers have choices about the stance they adopt toward a text.

- Why do people read (nonfiction, newspapers, magazines, fiction stories, advertisements, etc.)?
- How is reading during Drop Everything and Read (DEAR) or Sustain Silent Reading (SSR) time different than reading your social studies or science textbook?
- Why do authors write in different ways for the different books?

Invitation for the classroom

Questions Reveal Stance

Invite students to make a chart of the types of questions they ask when engaged in a literature discussion. One student may be selected to record the questions for a group's conversation. After the discussion, have students chart the questions on a continuum from efferent (seeking factual information) to aesthetic (seeking personal, social, political interpretations). As students talk about the nature of the question and where it fits on the comparison chart, they may come to see how various questions lead the discussion a particular way and signify a particular stance toward the text. A comparison chart for *Tomás and the Library Lady* conversation with the first and second graders serves as an example.

> **Tomas and the Library Lady**
>
> **Factual Questions**
> (book centered)
>
> What did Tomas learn at the library?
>
> Why did Tomas want to go to the library?
>
> How far is it between Texas and Iowa?
>
> Where is Tomas from?
>
> Who told Tomas to go to the library?
>
> **Feeling Questions**
> (personal, social)
>
> What kind of books do you like to read?
>
> Why do people move? What are some reasons you have moved?
>
> Do you have to pay to go to the community kitchen?
>
> Why did they drive a rusty car?

Invitation for the classroom

Questions That Push for One Stance or Another

When discussing a piece of text, teachers can ask these general questions to support students taking a particular stance toward a text.

Aesthetic Stance:

- What do you think about the story?
- Tell anything you want about the story.
- What was your favorite part? Tell about it.
- Has anything like this ever happened to you? Tell about it.
- Does the story remind you of anything? Tell about it.
- What did you wonder about? Tell about it.
- What would you change in the story?
- What else do you think might happen in the story?
- What would you say or do if you were a character in the story?
- How do you think the characters felt?

Efferent Stance:

- What was the main idea of the story?
- What did the author mean by . . .?
- Tell the order of the story events.
- Describe the main characters.
- Explain the characters' actions.
- What other stories are like this one? Compare the stories.
- What was the problem in the story? How did the author solve the problem?
- How did the author make the story believable?
- Is it fact or fiction?

Adapted from C. Cox (1999)

Interpretive authority: How students react to each other's comments

Students listen to each other during literature discussions.

Literacy events are shaped not only by the content to be learned or discussed, but also by the level of participation and engagement of those participating. Language use plays an important and vital role as students respond to texts, tasks, and each other. Students use language to share their understandings and knowledge, as individuals and as members of communities. Halliday (1975), Vygotsky (1978), and Britton (1993) suggested that language use transforms thinking. It is through language that we come to express and make sense of our experiences and our place in the world. Our interactions with others shape and define meanings of words and how they are used in various contexts.

When students engage in literature discussions, they are able to appropriate and build upon each other's ideas and those of the authors. In doing so, students' various interpretations of the literary work emerge. These newly constructed interpretations often have traces of others' comments. As students continue to build on each other's comments, they take the interpretations to new levels.

Participation structures include how students enter the discussion, take turns in conversations, share relevant ideas and information, and understand different ways of engaging in the discussion. These interaction patterns play a significant role in how texts are understood and negotiated in the socially-situated context of the classroom.

Through opportunities to talk with others, new understandings emerge. However, all talk is not the same and it is through interpretive authority that students and teachers determine which responses are viable and contribute to the discussion, and which responses are not as valid in the eyes of the participants.

Interpretive authority involves who is talking, what the speaker is saying (content), and how other group members react to the comment (Flint & Riordan-Karlsson, 2001). Interpretive authority also:

> takes into account how teachers and students judge the viability and validity of responses shared within literacy events. This authority is dependent on a number of factors, including but not limited to, social awareness, reading ability, and social positioning. (p. 91)

When students and the teacher gather for a literature discussion, the multiple dimensions of stance become central to determining interpretive authority. How a text is read, the structure of the discussion, and the beliefs that participants hold will elicit responses that some deem more valuable than others. While there are multiple and shifting roles for teachers and students, there are distinctive patterns of interpretive authority within various literature discussion structures. Table 10.1 provides an overview of what the roles are that teachers and students assume; where meaning is located; and who has or does not have interpretive authority.

interpretive authority

When teachers and/or students judge the viability and validity of a response.

TABLE 10.1
Literature Discussion Formats

	Teachers' Role in the Discussion	Students' Role in the Discussion	Where Meaning Resides	Level of Interpretive Authority
Teacher-led	Teacher directs and evaluates.	Students respond when asked questions.	Meaning is usually based in the text or with the teacher.	Teacher usually assumes high levels of authority, particularly when invoking an evaluator role.
Student-led	The teacher is generally not present.	Varies depending on the participants (initiator, informer, evaluator, negotiator, speculator, and many more).	Varies in the text, in the participant, and in a negotiation among participants.	Individual students will carry more authority, depending on perceived reading ability, social position, and stance.
Teacher-led, but student-centered.	Teacher facilitates, models, and scaffolds effective discussion strategies.	Varies depending on the participants (initiator, informer, evaluator, negotiator, speculator, and many more).	Usually in the negotiation among the participants	The teacher and students will share authority in constructing meaning of the text.

Teacher-led discussions

Teacher-led formats often follow a conversational pattern known as Initiate, Respond, and Evaluate (I-R-E) (Cazden, 1988; Mehan, 1979). The teacher will *initiate* a question, students will be asked to *respond* to the question, and the teacher will *evaluate* the students' responses before moving to the next discussion point. The following excerpt from a discussion group led by Mrs. White, a fourth grade teacher, illustrates the IRE format. Mrs. White and her students discuss *Otherwise Known as Sheila, the Great* (Blume, 1972), the classic tale of 10-year-old Sheila Tubman. Sheila wonders if she is the outgoing, witty, and capable Sheila the Great, or the secret Sheila, who's afraid of the dark, spiders, swimming, and dogs. She faces these fears one summer while visiting Tarrytown, New York. In this excerpt, Mrs. White initiates a discussion about chapter thirteen, where the girls in the neighborhood have created slam books (books with derogatory statements) about each other.

MRS. WHITE:	Jimmy, what do you think happened in chapter thirteen?
JIMMY:	They were scared on the hay wagon
MRS. WHITE:	That's not a part of chapter thirteen. I don't think there are any hay wagons in chapter thirteen. Chapter thirteen, something really serious happened.
DEANNA:	The girls decided to write mean things about each other in those little books and they all got mad at each other.
MRS. WHITE:	Yes, and what made the girls start throwing airplanes around?
TAMARA:	They did these little books that said mean things.

In this excerpt, the teacher controls and maintains the conversation. She had a particular interpretation of the text in mind. For her, the location of meaning resided *in the text*. Mrs. White expected students to recall information directly from the text. When this occurs, the text is viewed as the authority, and the teacher assumes the interpretive authority to determine if students have accurately recalled the information. She takes on the role of being the evaluator.

Student-led discussions

TECHNOLOGY LINK
http://www.kidsreads.com/
clubs/index.asp

Kidsreads helps kids find information about their favorite books, series, and authors. Reviews of the newest titles, interviews with the authors, and special features on great books are included.

Student-led discussion groups often do not have the teacher present. Students are responsible for reading and discussing the text on their own. In these instances, the discussion is often harder to follow because the students typically talk over each other. In teasing out what does get said, however, there generally are multiple ideas being built upon. The nature of interpretive authority, then, is more fluid because students will use a variety of ways to determine whether the interpretation or response is acceptable in moving the conversation forward. Students use their knowledge of the reader's social position within the class and reading abilities to decide how to receive the response. For example, when the fourth graders from Ms. Wilson's class (remember from the beginning of this chapter they read *The Mouse and the Motorcycle*) met months later to talk about Sharon Bell Mathis's (1975) book *Hundred Penny Box*, they used their knowledge of how each one was positioned in the class as a reader (for example, strong vs. not a strong reader), as well as who they perceived had knowledge of the world to establish interpretive authority in the group.

Hundred Penny Box highlights a young boy's relationship with his great-great aunt who is 100 years old. Aunt Dew has a box of 100 pennies, one for each year of her life. As she pulls the pennies out one by one, she reflects on her life and shares these memories with Michael, the young boy. The following conversation highlights what students know about Aunt Dew, the elderly, and dying.

MARCY: I think that Michael's mom shouldn't make Aunt Dew [take a nap] because she might not fall asleep at the dinner table.

ROBERT: She might die in her sleep.

MARCY: I think . . .

ROBERT: How would she [Aunt Dew] know if it's [special mahogany box] missing?

ELAINE: Can't she say her prayers, "Now I lay me down to sleep," that one? And, "If I should die before I wake, I pray the Lord my soul to take."

ROBERT: Yeah, but . . .

ELAINE: I don't know the long one.

KELLY: I don't know the ones in English, cause I say them in Spanish, cause I went to CCD in Spanish.

This discussion is quite different than the teacher-led discussion. The meaning explored in this discussion group was not just in the text, but *in the negotiation* among learners' experiences and what they were reading in the text. For example, Elaine and Kelly brought their personal knowledge of why you say prayers before you sleep. Robert and Marcy stayed close to the text and tried to extend their understandings based on what the text was offering. The roles these readers assumed were those of catalysts and initiators instead of evaluators. As such, interpretive authority was shared among the participants.

> ### Creating Connections 10.7
> It is important to form literature discussion groups that bring together students of varying abilities in reading. How will you ensure that all of the readers in the group are able to have their interpretations heard and valued in the group?

THE EVALUATOR ROLE IN STUDENT-LED DISCUSSIONS. Readers with little experience in student-led literature discussions where multiple and varied interpretations are accepted, may think that someone has to evaluate the response based on previous experiences and expectations with texts, including how to behave, how and when to talk, and how to interact with texts (Allen, Moller, & Stroup, Moller, 2003). Students that view themselves as "good readers" will frequently take on the evaluator role, while students with less confidence in reading will generally acquiesce to those classmates who are perceived to be better readers and have a greater understanding of the text. An example of this dynamic is a conversation between two readers talking about an event in the story *Island of the Blue Dolphin* (O'Dell, 1990). As the following dialogue illustrates, Michelle is the more confident reader in this exchange. She locates meaning in the text and ultimately holds more interpretive authority.

KARA: But it didn't say what the women wanted

MICHELLE: [reads from the text] *I could hear cries of delight from the women in the bush.* Cries of delight. Happy.

KARA: So the women were happy. Michelle, can I write 'the women were yelling because they were so happy?'

Remember Ms. Wilson's class discussion of *The Mouse and the Motorcycle?* The students maintained a close read of the text. Clark, a confident reader, assumes a more authoritative role in the group. Recall that the students are talking about their favorite part of the story. Here is how the group's discussion continues:

ELIZABETH:	I like the part when Matt, when Matt, when mouse asked
CLARK:	Sshh, let her talk
ELIZABETH:	When Ralph asked Matt for a favor and then, where was it, open the door a crack and Ralph zoomed into the room and the mom, "Augh a mouse" and said that she was going to report it to the management because she didn't think there should be a mouse.
MARCY:	I liked the part when the mouse was on the motorcycle
KELLY:	I liked the part when Ralph went up the boy's sleeve
CLARK:	I liked all of it
ELIZABETH:	Yeah, but you've read the whole thing
CLARK:	I know
ELAINE:	I liked the part when Ralph went up the sleeve too. That's the funniest part
CLARK:	That must tickle

In the opening vignette, you may recall that Elaine relied on the text to support her answer, "*They said* Matt the old man", while Elizabeth, unsure of her interpretation, asked "Does *it say* that?" These two learners viewed the text as the source of meaning. Clark, however, did not follow Elaine and Elizabeth's reliance on the text to support an interpretation; rather, he stated the information as a known fact.

Early on, Clark's ability to challenge Elizabeth's interpretation revealed his social status within the peer group. He did not have to justify his interpretation for it to be accepted by the group. When Clark mentioned that he liked all of it and Elizabeth replied with, "Yeah, but you've read the whole thing," Clark merely asserted, "I know." Clark's challenge to Elizabeth caused Elaine to assume a defender role to protect her interpretation. Consequently, Elizabeth did not carry much status with Clark, Elaine, or in the group in general. She was challenged and then she questioned her own interpretation, as though she could be incorrect. To gain some status in the group, Elizabeth decided to recall her favorite section of the text. This gave her some confidence in knowing that she could recall text with ease (a skill generally praised by her teachers). As students engage in student-led discussions, how they go about responding to each other's comments and interpretations should be discussed as they consider what it means to participate in literature discussions.

Literature discussions can be difficult to assess, particularly when the teacher is not a part of the conversation. Tape recording the sessions and listening to them at a later date is one way to check in with students. In doing so, the teacher can begin to tease out the different roles and stances the students take on when working with classmates. Another possibility is to have children complete reflections on their process, as well as their understandings of the text. These forms are easily created based on students' experiences and needs.

Teacher-led, student-centered discussions

In teacher-led, student-centered discussions, the teacher models, scaffolds, provides explicit instructions, and encourages students taking on more responsibility within the conversation (Raphael & Au, 1998; Short, Kaufman, Keiser, Kahn, & Crawford, 1999; Wells, 1997). When teachers are participants and active listeners in the conversation and not merely directors, patterns of interpretive authority emerge that locate meaning in the negotiation of ideas and texts. Earlier in the chapter, we saw how

Name Aimee   # 6

The book I read was Voices in the Park

Group members were: Clayton, Riley, Ian, Jordon

Rate your enjoyment of working in your group (3 = outstanding, 2 = good, 1 = okay)

I enjoyed working in my group   1 ② 3

because: Sometimes it was so-so and sometimes it was fun.

Our discussion about the book made me think about : Stereo types

Our presentation: We made a mural of Stereo types and Prejuduce.

Next time we get together with our 1st/2nd grade buddies I would like to: Have different gloups + Stories

Reflection forms from Aimee and Susannah.

A Friday Morning Reflection

Name Susannah

The book I read was fly away home

I enjoyed working in my group   1   ②   3
because I wokte hrea I got avry thing Done

Our discussion about the book made me think about homo iss Pepol

Our presentation i thot it was Grat Becuase we roooe wiot of Books

Next time we get together with our 5th grade buddies I would like to Stwy

a gif rt Book

Ms. Hammel's first and second graders discussed *Tomás and the Library Lady*. Now let's examine how Ms. Reiner's fifth grade students respond to the book.

MS. REINER'S FIFTH GRADE STUDENTS DISCUSS *TOMÁS AND THE LIBRARY LADY.*

Ms. Reiner:	Okay, how would we like to begin this conversation?
Amber:	I don't know (*giggling*).
Ms. Reiner:	I think Nathan and Alicia might begin our discussion. *(Whispers of Elisa are made by various students)*
Ms. Reiner:	Elisa. Okay and Anne. [Anne has her hand raised] Anne, I'll remember you. Which question do we want to address?
Elisa:	Can we give a topic?
Ms. Reiner:	Sure.
Elisa:	Why did they go to Texas?
Nathan:	Because they had to work.
Than:	Work
Elisa:	Don't they grow potatoes in Iowa?
Nathan:	They have corn.
Alicia:	They do grow a lot of corn.
Nathan:	It wasn't a vacation or anything.
Ms. Reiner:	I'm not sure that that's as closed of a question as you think it is. Right from the beginning, what made them go to Iowa?
Suzanne:	Maybe they pay more to their workers.
Elisa:	Maybe they can't get a job in any other state.
Alicia:	Huh?
Suzanne:	Yeah, but maybe they get paid more.
Than:	to work, more work
Anne:	Maybe they like know somebody in Iowa and they've been there before.
Nathan:	Well, obviously they've been there before. *(Students begin speaking over each other.)*
Nathan:	Maybe they grow better corn there, so they get paid more.
Suzanne:	Maybe they just like that corn, because maybe they have a better place for them to live.
Anne:	Oh, oh, oh. *[Ann raises her hand, waving it energetically, excited to speak.]* Maybe in other places they have more people living in one house than they do in Iowa.
Ms. Reiner:	That's a good question. Where would they stay?

This discussion highlights the notion that the teacher, Ms. Reiner, took on a facilitator role, a role that encouraged students to expand their thinking. She provided opportunities for the students to start the line of questioning. As participants, the students and the teacher shared the role of interpretive authority. They constructed multiple possibilities about why Tomás and his family migrated between Iowa and Texas. Students began to explore the nature of migrant farm life, as well as economic realities of working in the fields. By sharing the interpretive authority among students and the teacher, expanded understandings and interpretations were constructed about the text.

Encouraging readers to share interpretive authority during literature discussions

Classrooms will always have students that are more proficient in the reading process than others. Some students will have a greater sense of social positioning in the classroom; and some students will construct interpretations based on their own experience, and show more ease in the negotiation of text. Because of this, promoting interpretive authority has to be more than offering students "task" oriented roles such as *timekeeper*, *recorder*, and *reporter*. These roles do not push students to consider alternative interpretations, to challenge the text or each other, or to negotiate for more complex and rich understandings. Teachers need to encourage a sense of shared authority. This can be accomplished by focusing students' attention on how they respond to each other, the types of questions pursued in a discussion, and how alternative meaning-making processes might elicit broader notions of what it means to be a reader.

> ### Creating Connections 10.8
>
> Observe a small group of students engaged in a literature discussion. What are the various roles these students adopt? Who seems to have more interpretive authority in the group? Share your insights with the teacher and your classmates.

Invitation for the classroom

QAR (Question-Answer Relationship) Strategy

This strategy, encourages students to generate and classify questions based on their own experiences and background knowledge. There are four categories of questions that highlight the relationship between the text, the reader, and the transaction that occurs in meaning making. To implement QAR, the teacher or student constructs questions that fit into four categories:

Right there: These questions ask for information that is explicitly located in the text.

Think and search: These questions are text-centered but the response is inferred from a variety of sources within the text.

Author and you: The questions ask for information that combines what is learned in the text and students' personal experiences.

On my own: The questions ask for information that is primarily from the students' background and experiences.

The range of questions enables participants to speculate, challenge, defend, and inquire, thereby promoting higher levels of comprehension and reflection. The questions provide participants with ways of connecting to the text through their background experiences, world knowledge, text information, and imagination. As participants read the text and discuss the questions, they begin to consider how each other constructed various responses and how alternative meanings may contribute to pushing the conversation forward.

Adapted from T. Raphael (1982, 1986) and Raphael & Pearson (1985)

Invitation for the classroom

Save the Last Word for Me

How can a teacher encourage multiple perspectives during a literature discussion? This strategy, has readers construct interpretations based on their own experiences, histories, cultural values and beliefs, and group memberships. This strategy demystifies the notion that there is one "right" interpretation.

- While students are reading a text, have them jot down on index cards any words, ideas, or phrases that capture their attention.
- On the other side of the card, the reader writes what these words mean to them.
- Students come together to share their work. One student begins by reading the phrase or quotation on his or her card. The other students respond to the quotation. The student who read the quotation "has the last word" about why that particular phrase was important based on what was written on the backside of the card and the discussions that just occurred.

Adapted from C. Burke (1996)

Invitation for the classroom

Fishbowl Strategy

The fishbowl strategy enables teachers and students to reflect "in the moment" about the types of responses and reactions occurring in a conversation. To set up the strategy, the teacher asks a group of four to six students to sit in a close circle, while the remaining students sit around the group. The students in the middle are in essence, in the fishbowl.

Who talked?	What was said?
Elizabeth started	She asked, why did they go to Texas?
Nathan	for work
Elizabeth	Don't they grow potatoes in Iowa?
Nathan	They have corn
Alicia	A lot of corn
Nathan	It wasn't a vacation or anything

The teacher initiates a discussion with the students in the smaller group. Those in the outer circle observe and record interaction patterns and what information was discussed. In other words, who talked and what was said.

Following the discussion, the teacher opens the conversation for the observers to share their impressions and comments. This strategy is designed to make more visible the implicit patterns of talk in the discussion.

Adapted from P. Scherer (1997)

Supporting the reader in having a flexible view of the text

Stance and interpretive authority have a collective impact on how the text is understood. Flexibility in adopting various stances and who has the authority to make public and visible a particular response is central to navigating between the two hidden influences. What does it mean to be flexible in assuming a range of stances toward texts? How does flexibility in recognizing sources of meaning contribute to students' understandings of the text, tasks, context, and of each other?

Flexibility, much like Rosenblatt's efferent/aesthetic literary stance continuum, may also be positioned on a continuum (Flint and Riordan-Karlsson, 2001). Figure 10.6 illustrates the continuum of flexibility for stance and interpretive authority. At one end of the continuum, teachers and students embody a flexible perspective toward texts, tasks, and others when they consider multiple sources of meaning amidst a variety of possibilities. Literature discussions and other literacy events, such as inquiry projects that use technology, often enhance this notion of flexibility because of the nonlinear nature of websites and of inquiry questions. Students' purposes for reading often shift between efferent and aesthetic, as do the ways in which they demonstrate their knowledge and understandings.

At the other end of the continuum, teachers and students adopt a less-flexible perspective toward texts, tasks, and each other when they are not able to entertain alternatives in the literature discussion. The lack of flexibility may lead to narrowly defined ways of engaging in a literature discussion. When this occurs, there is little room to accept an interpretation that is different from the larger group.

It is important for teachers and students to consider the impact of flexibility of stance and interpretive authority, as well as on the meaning making process. The interpretations and ideas negotiated among teachers and students as a result of flexibility and openness to alternative stances and sources of meaning lead to richer and more complex insights.

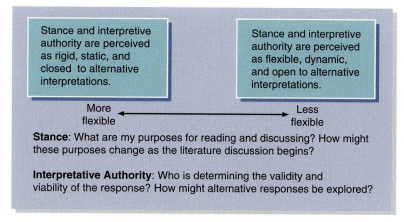

FIGURE 10.6 Continuum of flexibility within stance and interpretive authority.

In Closing

Literature discussions are immensely popular literacy events in classrooms, from kindergarten to college. Teachers and students read and discuss literature with varying purposes and goals; these variances can result in different ways in which texts are interpreted, as well as who has the interpretive authority within the group. As readers construct multiple interpretations for a particular text, these interpretations often reflect the students' background experiences. In some cases, discussions are opportunities for teachers and students to author their own words, their own actions, their own lives.

Broadening our conceptions of what a particular stance or purpose may be, the ways in which children enter into and participate in literature discussions, and the types of responses and interpretations they construct is crucial. Literature discussions offer a venue for examining the influential role of stance and interpretive authority. In classrooms where the teacher offers teacher-led, student-centered discussion formats, more thoughtful and enriching conversations emerge. Teachers can scaffold and support students' tentative comments and questions as students struggle to construct interpretations that move the conversation forward and make a difference. Ultimately, stance influences one's authority to negotiate interpretations of texts. When readers are aware of stance and interpretive authority, they become more reflective and critical readers.

Terms to remember

Aesthetic literacy stance *(300)*

Contextual dimension *(302)*

Efferent literacy stance *(300)*

Envisionment *(297)*

Ideological dimension *(302)*

Interpretive authority *(309)*

Reader response theory *(295)*

Literary/strategic dimension *(298)*

Transaction *(296)*

Stance *(298)*

Resources for More Information

Allen, J., Moller, K. J., & Stroup, D. (2003). "Is this some kind of soap opera?": A tale of two readers across four literature discussion contexts. *Reading & Writing Quarterly*, 19(3), 225–251.

Flint, A. S., & Riordan-Karlsson, M. (2001). *Buried treasures in the classroom: Using hidden influences to enhance literacy teaching and learning.* Newark, DE: International Reading Association.

Langer, J. A. (1995). *Envisioning literature: Literary understanding and literature instruction.* New York: Teachers College Press.

Lewis, C. (2000). Limits of identification: The personal, pleasurable, and critical in reader response. *Journal of Literacy Research*, 32, 253–266.

Short, K., Kauffman, G., Kaser, S., Kahn, L., & Crawford, K., (1999). "Teacher-watching": Examining teacher talk in literature circles. *Language Arts*, 76(6), 377–385.

Questions for Further Reflection

- Why is it important to consider where meaning resides for readers?

- What roles do you typically assume during literature discussions with peers and/or with children?

- How can kidwatching skills increase our knowledge of students' positions in literature discussions? What does this knowledge do for you as you plan effective and meaningful literature discussions?

chapter 11

Reading to Learn: Using Nonfiction and Electronic Media to Support Literacy Development

Mr Gallagher and Ms Reiner Invite Their Students to Inquire

It's our "Back to School Open House" and Sarah approaches us. "Can you give me some idea of what kinds of research we'll be doing this year?" she asked. We had studied a nearby working class neighborhood last year during our *Indiana History* year of study. We explained that our focus would be *U.S. History* this year, paying close attention to early exploration and culture. Sarah went on,

> I met my mom's friend this summer. She asked me about my school. I told her that I was in this multi-age class and I had studied Women's Rights a couple of years ago. She's 85 years old and has been working on Women's Rights almost her entire life. She sent me this packet since it's Women's Equity Day, the 85th Anniversary of the constitutional amendment for women's right to vote this Friday. Here, look, there's a purple sash, articles, and placemats. I was wondering if our class could do something. Can I study Women's Rights again this year?

This abbreviated conversation epitomizes what keeps us passionate about literacy. We team teach a class of approximately 50 kindergarten through sixth grade students. Many of the students, can and do, like Sarah, talk about school with outsiders in meaningful ways. Sarah's choice to study the history of women's rights again means that subject is still important to her. She knows there is more to learn and is suggesting this significant anniversary will be important to us all. She approached us to talk about curriculum.

This was not something we planned for all summer. This student embarked on an unknown journey two years ago. Her focused study did not end with her presentation. She shared her passion with others through conversation and writing and happened to cross paths with someone else who had the same passion. Now these two people were having a positive rippling effect on our class. It reminds us of something we've heard Jerry Harste say, "It's [trying on critical perspectives] not a topic we're done with but a perspective to stay with us the rest of our lives."

On the third day of school, which was Women's Equity Day, our class watched several clips of the PBS video *Not for Ourselves Alone, The Story of Susan B. Anthony and Elizabeth Cady Stanton*. Students' focus study logs were open and they were furiously taking notes. Students regularly asked that the tape be rewound so they could hear different segments again. During another work session that same day, some students looked at the website www.nwhp.org while others looked at our current and previous U.S. history textbooks, Joy Hakim's *A History of US Reconstructing America* 1865–1890 and other books from the women's text set including *Created Equal: Women Campaign for the Right to Vote (1840–1920)* (Rossi, 2005). *You Want Women to Vote, Lizzie Stanton?* (Fritz, 1995), and T.

Boweis (2005), *How the Amazon Queen fought the Prince of Egypt*. We constructed text sets as a way to gather resources from different perspectives and provide a rich collection of varied information.

When students leave for the day, instead of closing our door during these challenging times, we talk and write about what we do and why we do it. Sometimes we're tempted to take a break from this kind of work but realize we cannot afford to do that. There are always new families in our room and new administrators in our school and our school district. We know we have to be proactive in order to create the world where we want to live as teachers and citizens.

Our overall sense of hope comes from our students. Like holistic teachers everywhere, we believe in celebrating individual student strengths and nurturing growth. In our multi-age classroom there are no artificial grade boundaries to constrain learning potentials. Students' willingness to ask questions and ponder complexities with fresh insight is refreshing and invigorating. Their ability to read and think critically gives us the energy to continue what we do and share our passion about literacy.

I wonder. . .

- In what ways do Mr. Gallagher and Ms. Reiner demonstrate responsiveness to students in their classroom?

- What do you think about reading a nonfiction text during read aloud time?

- How do you envision a curriculum that values the interests that students bring into the classroom? Be specific.

Chapter Overview

An inquiry-based curriculum that primarily uses nonfiction texts is usually reserved for intermediate grades and above. Throughout most of the twentieth century, it was believed that young children would not be able to comprehend such texts and that the focus needed to be on learning to read. This stance assumed that reading was an object to be studied, and not a tool to enhance or further learning.

Recent accounts in early literacy classrooms, however, challenge this perception (Vasquez, 2003; Comber, 2000). Children pursue questions that matter, research important topics, and share significant learning with classmates and others. In doing so, they use texts in meaningful and purposeful ways—to locate information, to broaden understandings, and to offer a place to challenge and critique. Writing also becomes more relevant as they use their writing to reflect, respond, and present new thinking.

Although inquiry studies may seem peripheral to the work that many policy makers and administrators believe *needs* to happen in classrooms, inquiry-based learning and the use of nonfiction texts greatly enhance and inform the work that is going on in classrooms. While Mr. Gallagher and Ms. Reiner had not anticipated a continued inquiry into women's rights, they were able to provide opportunities and materials for their students to take on such important issues because they valued students' interests and experiences. A literacy curriculum focused on inquiry affords teachers and students with opportunities to embrace the guiding principles established in Chapter 1. One of the principles, *"Literacy practices are learned through inquiry"* is at the center of this chapter, but the remaining principles are also evident. Through inquiry, students come to see how literacy is socially and culturally constructed, how multimodal texts contribute to learning, and how students bring to the forefront their own lived experiences and knowledge to build a foundation for new learning. Inquiry also acknowledges that literacy practices are purposeful and linked to broader social goals.

This chapter focuses on how readers and writers of all ages can engage in inquiry projects and focus studies to transform their learning. As a way to understand the role of inquiry in literacy development, this chapter addresses the following questions:

- What does an inquiry-based curriculum entail?
- How do teachers effectively use nonfiction texts for inquiry learning?
- What reading and writing strategies do teachers focus on when using nonfiction texts?
- How can teachers create learning experiences that highlight a variety of multiliteracies and technologies?

Using inquiry-based learning across the curriculum

"Without one's own serious and sincere questions one cannot creatively understand anything other or foreign."

(Bakhtin, 1986, p.11)

Children are naturally inquisitive. They ask numerous questions about their environment, their communities, why things happen, and how things work. Many of us have experiences with young children as they learn how to participate in the communities in which they are raised. They often use "why" and "how come" questions while exploring the world around them. Their questions and interests expand as they enter school.

Elementary teachers often teach content areas (science, social studies, mathematics) in a static, isolated fashion that begins and ends with facts. In math, for example,

Did you know . . .

In 1993 the Center for Inquiry (CFI) in Indianapolis opened five classrooms in a wing of IPS School #92, taking in 100 students in grades K–5. Now CFI is its own school with over 280 students in grades K–8.

In 2006 the second CFI opened its doors to 200 students in grades K–6 at School #84. Grade 7 will be added in the fall of 2007 followed by grade 8.

That makes almost 500 students in Center for Inquiry schools in Indianapolis.

http://www.302.ips.k12.in.us/

Three digit subtraction worksheet 1   Name_____

Three Digit Subtraction Worksheet 1

Find the answer.

A
$$\begin{array}{r} 700 \\ -\ 600 \\ \hline \end{array}\qquad \begin{array}{r} 332 \\ -\ 121 \\ \hline \end{array}\qquad \begin{array}{r} 222 \\ -\ 102 \\ \hline \end{array}\qquad \begin{array}{r} 545 \\ -\ 345 \\ \hline \end{array}\qquad \begin{array}{r} 237 \\ -\ 124 \\ \hline \end{array}$$

B
$$\begin{array}{r} 399 \\ -\ 125 \\ \hline \end{array}\qquad \begin{array}{r} 478 \\ -\ 110 \\ \hline \end{array}\qquad \begin{array}{r} 664 \\ -\ 423 \\ \hline \end{array}\qquad \begin{array}{r} 761 \\ -\ 430 \\ \hline \end{array}\qquad \begin{array}{r} 844 \\ -\ 442 \\ \hline \end{array}$$

C
$$\begin{array}{r} 429 \\ -\ 318 \\ \hline \end{array}\qquad \begin{array}{r} 902 \\ -\ 701 \\ \hline \end{array}\qquad \begin{array}{r} 737 \\ -\ 426 \\ \hline \end{array}\qquad \begin{array}{r} 874 \\ -\ 273 \\ \hline \end{array}\qquad \begin{array}{r} 295 \\ -\ 110 \\ \hline \end{array}$$

D
$$\begin{array}{r} 503 \\ -\ 101 \\ \hline \end{array}\qquad \begin{array}{r} 661 \\ -\ 111 \\ \hline \end{array}\qquad \begin{array}{r} 840 \\ -\ 630 \\ \hline \end{array}\qquad \begin{array}{r} 403 \\ -\ 201 \\ \hline \end{array}\qquad \begin{array}{r} 299 \\ -\ 137 \\ \hline \end{array}$$

E
$$\begin{array}{r} 694 \\ -\ 120 \\ \hline \end{array}\qquad \begin{array}{r} 578 \\ -\ 321 \\ \hline \end{array}\qquad \begin{array}{r} 526 \\ -\ 201 \\ \hline \end{array}\qquad \begin{array}{r} 464 \\ -\ 103 \\ \hline \end{array}\qquad \begin{array}{r} 603 \\ -\ 101 \\ \hline \end{array}$$

F
$$\begin{array}{r} 789 \\ -\ 388 \\ \hline \end{array}\qquad \begin{array}{r} 457 \\ -\ 341 \\ \hline \end{array}\qquad \begin{array}{r} 288 \\ -\ 117 \\ \hline \end{array}\qquad \begin{array}{r} 446 \\ -\ 223 \\ \hline \end{array}\qquad \begin{array}{r} 859 \\ -\ 159 \\ \hline \end{array}$$

Schedule
Reading   *8:00 – 9:30*
Skills   *9:30 – 10:00*
Math   *10:00 –10:45*
Recess   *10:45 –11:00*
Social Studies   *11:00 –12:00*
Lunch/Recess   *12:00 – 1:10*
DEAR   *1:10 – 1:30*
Science   *1:30 – 2:15*
Specials   *2:15 – 2:45*

children complete worksheets of math problems, while in social studies they read the information from the textbook and answer a series of follow-up questions. Current curricula in science, social studies, and mathematics is designed to cover as much content as possible, without regard for how the content fits with broader curricular aims. Students read from the textbooks with the perspective that all of the information is equal in importance to the reader. And the content is often divided into artificial categories that bear little resemblance to how individuals learn and retain knowledge (Fenimore & Tinzmann, 1990). For example fourth grade social studies content focuses on state history—categories may be how the state was settled, the growth and development of the state, and current issues facing the state. Too often the recitation of literal level information is at a premium; with too little time spent on how the concepts integrate and work together.

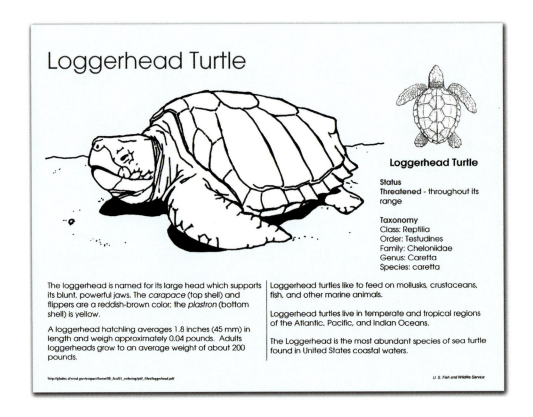

Loggerhead Turtle

Loggerhead Turtle

Status
Threatened - throughout its range

Taxonomy
Class: Reptilia
Order: Testudines
Family: Cheloniidae
Genus: Caretta
Species: caretta

The loggerhead is named for its large head which supports its blunt, powerful jaws. The *carapace* (top shell) and flippers are a reddish-brown color; the *plastron* (bottom shell) is yellow.

A loggerhead hatchling averages 1.8 inches (45 mm) in length and weigh approximately 0.04 pounds. Adults loggerheads grow to an average weight of about 200 pounds.

Loggerhead turtles like to feed on mollusks, crustaceans, fish, and other marine animals.

Loggerhead turtles live in temperate and tropical regions of the Atlantic, Pacific, and Indian Oceans.

The Loggerhead is the most abundant species of sea turtle found in United States coastal waters.

http://glades.sfwmd.gov/empact/home/08_fcs/01_coloring/pdf_files/loggerhead.pdf

U. S. Fish and Wildlife Service

Inquiry, like reading, is an "all at once" process (Berghoff, Egawa, Harste, & Hoonan, 2000). When children are engaged in inquiry, they predict and confirm, question and experiment, collect and synthesize. Children's questions are not usually bounded by a particular content or discipline. Rather, their questions and the research around their questions cross different disciplines (e.g., Are clouds heavy? Why are clouds white?). Children are more deeply engaged in their work when the work isn't broken up into small time blocks for different subjects. Implementing an inquiry-based curriculum involves not just a text, but the whole world around the text.

Key principles of an inquiry-based curriculum

There are a number of key principles that an **inquiry-based curriculum** is based upon (Berghoff, Egawa, Harste, & Hoonan, 2000; Duvall, 2001; Harste, 2001).

- *Inquiry-based curriculum is a philosophical stance that embraces a sense of inquisitiveness.* It requires that the teacher and students be comfortable in asking "why" and "how."

- *Inquiry-based curriculum requires that students have personal ownership in the curriculum.* By having students pursue their own questions, they develop a stronger sense of investment and higher motivation for engaging in the curriculum. This was evident in the work going on in Mr. Gallagher and Ms. Reiner's classroom. Sara was greatly invested in learning more about women's rights and consequently, she was an active learner in the classroom.

- *Inquiry-based curriculum encourages students to become thoughtful risk takers.* They learn that it is part of the process to make mistakes; to value revision and reflection.

- *Inquiry-based curriculum embraces the collaborative, social nature of learning.* Students work together as they ask questions, pursue information, and share findings.

- *Inquiry-based curriculum involves building background knowledge and making relevant connections.* In order for students to ask insightful questions, have thoughtful conversations, and make deep connections they have to expand their background knowledge on the topic. Inquiry-based curriculum invites students to make connections not just from fact to fact, but fact to concept. These deeper connections encourage students to authentically investigate their questions.

- *Inquiry-based curriculum uses diverse sources of knowledge to construct meanings.* When children engage in an inquiry-based curriculum, they use not only their personal knowledge but also their knowledge of how disciplines are organized to make sense of their questions. For example, if students were to study migration patterns of birds, they would ask questions and seek answers from the perspective of scientists, historians, artists, and mathematicians. In doing so, they begin to see how their understandings can be represented in a number of different ways.

- *Inquiry-based teaching requires that teachers and students are active participants.* As students pursue various interests and questions, teachers must observe and confer with them in order to be aware of what students know and what will stretch their thinking. Teachers match their teaching to the needs, questions, and insights of their students.

inquiry-based curriculum
A curriculum that starts with questions and through research and experimentation students gain new insights and understandings.

TECHNOLOGY LINK
http://www.inquiry.uiuc.edu/index.php

The Inquiry Page is more than a website. It's a dynamic virtual community where inquiry-based education can be discussed, resources and experiences shared, and innovative approaches explored in a collaborative environment.

- *Inquiry-based curriculum involves reading, writing, listening, and speaking.* Students effectively engage in inquiry studies by integrating language practices—reading, writing, speaking, and listening. They draw upon what they are reading across multiple sources as information for their own writing. They share ideas with others, listening for new directions and possibilities. Working on inquiry studies takes place throughout the instructional day in literature circles, community circles, reading and writing conferences, shared and guided reading events, among many other venues.

- *Inquiry-based teaching uses a broad range of materials, including non-fiction texts and websites.* Materials collected for inquiry studies invite students to think about their questions rather than provide answers. Students read across a number of different texts to find relevant and useful information and perspectives on the topic. They explore a variety of genres and read texts of varying difficulty and purposes to gain new understandings of their topic of interest.

These principles are important as teachers and students embark on an inquiry-based curriculum. Four of these principles—problem posing, topic selection, integration of language processes, and sources of knowledge—are examined in greater detail. Later, the roles of nonfiction in literacy development, as well as technology are explored.

Problem posing

The questions that matter are those that are personal and constructed by the students ("I have a bull mastiff, named Isabelle, I think mastiffs are the biggest dog there is. But Colin says his great dane is bigger and faster than my dog. Is that true?"). These questions sit at the center of the curriculum. An inquiry curriculum isn't just about a series of questions with complementary answers. There is not a one-to-one correspondence between the question and the answer. Inquiry-based learning pushes beyond the who, what, where, and when questions. Students are asked to consider "what does this mean?" and "How can I use this information?" (Owens, Hester, & Teale, 2002). For example, children may use the information gathered about the distinctions between great danes and bull mastiffs when thinking about how dogs help people with disabilities. Inquiry-based learning "is more about unpacking the complexity of issues, than it is about coming up with simple solutions to complex problems" (Harste, 2001, p. 10).

Inquiry is a process that involves both problem posing and problem solving (Freire, 1985; Short, Harste, & Burke, 1996). Inquiry involves immersing oneself in a topic and having time to explore the topic by asking meaningful questions and systematically investigating those questions. The most difficult part of any inquiry is problem posing—finding questions that matter. When students first begin asking questions, they frequently ask what Tower (2000) referred to as "small questions" (for example, "What is the largest breed of dog?"). These questions are factual and often only one source is needed to locate the answer. Rather, inquiries should consider "big questions," ones that do not have a simple, single answer and where multiple sources are needed. As big questions ("How did dogs evolve from wolves?") are considered and researched, smaller questions get answered ("How many breeds of dogs are there? Which ones are most like wolves? What is the smallest dog breed?"). The role that questions play in the inquiry is to "provide a kind of structure for critical information gathering-—to look through texts and other materials in such a way that it is possible to sort relevant from irrelevant, important from unimportant. . ." (Sheingold, 1987, p. 81).

Students must have time to "muck around" with their topic before pursuing any questions (Short, Harste, & Burke, 1996). The more complex and bigger questions surface as a result of having time to read and peruse various texts and materials. As students engage in these early investigations of their topic they begin to ask more interesting questions (Why do people use dogs for protection? What things can dogs do for blind people? Why do dogs come in all shapes and sizes?)

> ### Creating Connections 11.1
>
> If you had the opportunity to investigate an area of interest (not necessarily related to learning how to teach reading and writing), what sorts of questions/topics would you pursue?
>
> Jot down a few of your questions.
>
> What steps would you take to follow up on your questions?
>
> Share with your classmates through your blog.

Topic choice

Inquiry-based learning depends on students pursuing their own interests and questions. Often, in the early stages when students seem to be interested in a hundred different topics, they struggle in identifying topics that are not too broad, too narrow, too difficult, or too easy. There are a couple of ways to approach this dilemma. Teachers may guide student choice for inquiry projects by asking students to select topics that align with broader themes such as migration, change, family histories, world events, and so forth. Teachers may also ask that students identify a predetermined number of things/facts/ideas known about the topic. Having a little bit of information about a particular topic seems to result in more focused inquiries, rather than starting from scratch, where the potential for a "too big" inquiry is quite high.

On the other hand, teachers can foster inquiries by sparking interest in a topic that students may not consider on their own (Owens, Hester, & Teale, 2002). Some students may not select a topic because they do not have any prior knowledge—of bird migration, for example—and through a teacher's introduction on the topic, new inquiries emerge ("Why do birds migrate? Which varieties? Do any of them migrate to our town?").

Integrating reading and writing strategies

Inquiry-based learning is open-ended and unfinished. It is not the objective of inquiry to teach specific reading or writing skills. Rather, the primary goal is learning about the inquiry topic; and students use language processes—reading, writing, listening, and speaking—as tools to investigate these topics. Students naturally engage in reading and writing as they examine and explore their topic. Inquiry-based learning uses reading and writing as tools for learning, not objects of learning. It may not be necessary to have a predetermined time for reading and writing instruction because students are actively engaged in reading and writing as they pursue their questions and wonderings. Students read across a number of different texts to find relevant and useful information and perspectives on the topic. They explore a variety of genres and read texts of varying difficulty and purposes to gain new understandings of their topic of interest. Writing includes posing questions, recording information, and reflecting on learning. This means that the writing happens throughout the inquiry process. Moreover, reading and writing are intertwined as the topic is explored.

To illustrate, consider how Ms. Verma, a second grade teacher, incorporates reading and writing into her inquiry curriculum. Ms. Verma's second grade students embarked on an inquiry about insects. She put together a set of books that highlights varieties of insects, as well as scientific concepts, such as observation and comparing and contrasting information. Included in the text set are *Bug Faces* (Murawski, 2000), *Magic School Bus Spins a Web* (Cole, 1997), *Children's Butterfly Site* (http://bsi.montana.edu/web/kids-butterfly/), *100 Things You Should Know About Insects & Spiders* (Parker & Flegg, 2004)

TECHNOLOGY LINK
http://www.units.muohio.edu/dragonfly/

Project Dragonfly provides children with opportunities for inquiry-based learning.

Diary of a Worm (Cronin, 2003) *Creepy, Crawly, Baby Bugs* (Markle, 1996) and *Fireflies* (Brinkloe, 1986). The children listened to these texts during read aloud time, read them in independent and partner reading events, and engaged in whole and small group discussions. Insects, such as beetles, fireflies, and ants were available to observe. Children recorded their understandings in journals and on charts. Ms. Verma focused some of her strategy work on observation (What did you notice about this bug?) and comparing and contrasting (How are these alike and how are they different?). As students worked on this inquiry, Ms. Verma introduced them to text structure, mainly compare and contrast. She asked students to create a graphic organizer that compares and contrasts different bugs (see Figure 11.1). The students then came together to share their thinking and make further observations about insects. These initial opportunities to read or write during inquiry are necessary as students build theories, enlist others for support, communicate understandings, and plan further investigations (Flint & Bomer, 2002).

Sources of knowledge and the teacher's role

Harste (1994) identifies three sources of knowledge that inquiry cuts across: *personal and social knowing; disciplines;* and *sign systems.* Personal and social knowing relates to the personal experiences that a student brings to the question. Children

FIGURE 11.1 Graphic organizer for compare/contrast.

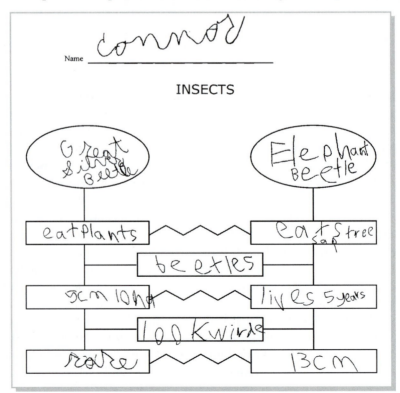

living on the coast of California will have a different relationship and knowledge of the ocean than children living in the Midwest. One's personal experiences of living near an ocean influence the questions asked. The second knowledge source is the disciplines (biology, government, history, earth science, etc.). These knowledge sources are often taught as discrete subjects in school and are usually reduced to a series of facts (Short & Burke, 1996). What is important in an inquiry are not the bits and pieces of information, but rather the multiple perspectives that emerge from the disciplines. To illustrate, the general topic of the ocean may be further explored through the lens of history (How has the ocean influenced people's movement around the world?), science (Why do whales migrate? Why is the water salty?) and/or geography (How much of the world is covered by water? How many people rely on the ocean for food?). These questions invite different perspectives on the general topic and encourage students to develop more complex understandings.

The third knowledge source is using sign systems to create and communicate understandings. The *sign systems* (language, art, music, drama, etc.) are not to be added on as frills and extra activities, but should be used to better understand the inquiry topic. Students may view paintings of ocean scenes to examine the human connection to the ocean, create graphs and charts to detail animal and plant life, and listen to waves to determine cycles. The multiple sign systems are tools for expanding understandings and gaining new perspectives.

sign systems
Ways of constructing and communicating knowledge.

While the three knowledge sources comprise a way of thinking about inquiry curriculum, the roles that teachers take on also signify a change from more traditional forms of curriculum. Pataray-Ching and Roberson (2002) note that in inquiry-oriented classrooms, teachers:

- assume an inquiry stance—they are also inquirers and learners.
- encourage students to view the world as problem posers—what questions do they have?
- organize their instructional time to provide in-depth explorations of topics.
- observe students from a "kidwatching" perspective; as inquirers trying to learn all one can about the student as a learner.
- encourage multiple ways of knowing and through multiple sign systems.
- organize classroom experiences so that students are accountable for their learning through reflections, sharing, and documenting their progress.

In classrooms where teachers establish an inquiry curriculum, students come to see learning as a lifelong endeavor. They begin to ask personally meaningful and relevant questions that are situated in their own experiences, and they begin to view the world as a place where there are many questions to investigate (Pataray-Ching & Roberson, 2002). One important aspect of an inquiry-based curriculum is using nonfiction texts to support children's questions and wonderings.

TECHNOLOGY LINK
http://www.thirteen.org/edonline/concept2class/inquiry/demonstration.html#classrooms

In these video clips teachers are using inquiry-based learning in real classrooms.

The role of nonfiction in developing readers and writers

Recent studies indicate that the current state of affairs for the use of nonfiction texts in elementary classrooms is quite poor. Across 20 first grade classrooms that Duke (2000) observed, she discovered that the children had an average of 3.6 minutes a day of exposure to nonfiction texts. In this same study, she also noted that less than

14% of classroom material
is nonfiction

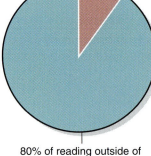

80% of reading outside of
school is nonfiction

ten percent of the classroom libraries were comprised of informational texts. Yopp and Yopp (2000) found that of the 126 early elementary teachers they surveyed, only 14% of their materials for read aloud were informational. An earlier study conducted by Hoffman and Roser (1993) discovered that of the 500+ teachers surveyed, not one nonfiction title was provided as a top title used for read aloud. Teachers often do not introduce nonfiction to students until in the upper grades (fourth grade and up) because of the perception that nonfiction texts are mostly used for reading to learn, not learning to read.

These and other statistics suggest that young children have few opportunities or exposure to nonfiction texts. And while there is minimal exposure to this genre, children actually spend a great deal of time engaged with nonfiction texts outside of classroom settings. Approximately 80% of what students read outside of school is informational in nature. They read magazines and trading cards related to hobbies and sports, flyers, brochures, environmental texts, and Internet sites. In fact, 96% of text that appears on Internet websites is expository (Kamil & Lane, 1998). By the time students reach middle school, 75% percent of their reading demands involve nonnarrative materials (Moss, 2004). In fact, most of what is read as an adult is expository (newspaper, magazine articles, Internet sites, work-related documents, instructions, etc.).

Why nonfiction matters

Familiarity with nonfiction texts in elementary classrooms is important to developing proficient and effective readers. 50% to 80% of the material on standardized tests is expository (Moss, 2004). With such a large percentage of the reading passages expository, it is critical for teachers to encourage nonfiction reading in the classroom. A lack of opportunities with this type of text may be one reason that many students experience the "fourth grade slump," where they do not do as well as in previous years on achievement tests, content area reading, and other assessment measures.

Children enjoy reading nonfiction material.

Many states include nonfiction reading in their state standards and benchmarks. Most states require that by the end of third grade children will be proficient readers of nonfiction texts, including expository tradebooks, discipline-oriented textbooks (science and social studies), websites, and other texts (see Table 11.1). There are increased expectations for children to read, write, and learn from informational texts because there is greater access to information. Additionally, children will be expected to make more sophisticated moves with nonfiction texts, including locating, understanding, evaluating, and synthesizing information. Inviting children to read nonfiction texts provides diverse contexts to problem solve and critically think.

Why are nonfiction texts important in the classroom? One very important reason is because children are intrinsically interested in reading nonfiction. Given the opportunity, many students become deeply engaged in reading nonfiction texts, and very often prefer such texts (Caswell & Duke, 1998; Guillaume, 1998; Palmer & Stewart,

TABLE 11.1

Standards for Nonfiction Reading

A sampling of states with standards related to reading nonfiction text. These standards represent grades 2 and 3.	
Georgia	Interprets information from illustrations, diagrams, charts, graphs, and graphic organizers
Indiana	Use knowledge of the author's purpose(s) to comprehend informational text
Pennsylvania	Read and understand essential content of informational texts and documents in all academic areas
Utah	Locate facts from a variety of informational texts (e.g. newspapers, magazines, books, other resources)

2003). Palmer and Stewart (2003) discovered that first, second, and third grade students selected nonfiction titles 63% of the time when asked to select books they thought they would like to read. Children's motivation to read is often determined by the types of texts and genres available to them. Having access to nonfiction titles is critical in fostering engaged reading for many students.

Inviting children to use nonfiction for inquiry-based and content-area learning

Most teachers want their students to be literate, civic-minded, and problem posers. In order to achieve these goals, teachers need to offer students opportunities to engage with texts that support children's inquisitive and curious nature. Nonfiction texts serve as a vehicle for supporting children's questions, interests, and experiences. Jeff Wilhelm (1998) comments, "Nonfiction provides a context for our learning and situates it. It allows us to be ethnographers by observing and entering into other worlds and experiencing these places, people and times that are often at a distance from us" (pp. 217–218).

Nonfiction texts are plentiful, yet teachers rarely use nonfiction in their reading instruction. What has been known for many years, however, is that children, especially boys, gravitate to nonfiction in ways that are not supported in classroom settings (Smith and Wilhelm, 2002). Figure 11.2 lists questions for teachers to ask themselves to help them integrate nonfiction texts across the curriculum.

Nonfiction texts can be used as a springboard into new curriculum and inquiries. Through nonfiction use, children begin to develop knowledge about the world around them. They ask questions and imagine possibilities. For example, Ashley, one of Ms. Suttle's fourth grade students, put into the "What's on my Mind" basket a comment regarding the amount of chores she has at home. This sparked a

TECHNOLOGY LINK

http://www.ncte.org/elem /awards/orbispic-tus/106877.htm

List of Orbis Pictus award winners for outstanding nonfiction from NCTE. This site provides an overview and criteria for the Orbis Pictus Award. Scroll down to the bottom of the page to locate the past winners links by year.

- What do I want children to learn in school?
- How does nonfiction fit into the purposes and goals established for the classroom?
- What role do I, the teacher, play in mediating children's use of the broad array of texts available (nonfiction tradebooks, Internet sites, newsmagazines, etc.)?
- How can the purposes for reading and writing informational texts be shaped to mirror out-of-school literacy purposes?

FIGURE 11.2 How do I integrate nonfiction texts across the curriculum?

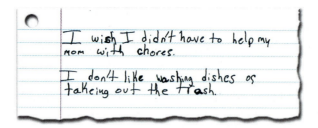

Ashley's comments on chores.

conversation among her classmates about their chores and how chores might be different in other parts of the world. In response to the students' interest in this topic, Ms. Suttle put together a text set to introduce the notion of child labor to her students. They read a number of expository texts that discuss child labor and the rights of children. In their quest, they came upon the texts *Kids at Work: Lewis Hine and the Crusade against Child Labor* (Freeman, 1998) and *Stolen Dreams: Portraits of Working Children* (Parker, Engfer, Conrow, & Engfer, 1997).

Nonfiction texts build comprehension skills and encourage students to engage in critical thinking. Ms. Suttle's students continued to develop their comprehension skills as they predicted, synthesized, and inferred information from the texts they were reading. They created comparison charts of their lives and those of children in other parts of the world, such as India, Nepal, and Mexico. The students gained more complex and sophisticated language and vocabulary as they read the stories in these texts. As the students read these texts, they challenged their own understandings of what it means to work, why it is so different in other places, why things are the way they are, and what they might imagine as possibilities for the future. The reading of these texts, along with others, promoted an inquiry stance as these students began to conduct inquiry projects related to child labor.

In the next section, ways to evaluate and locate high quality nonfiction texts are presented.

Evaluating nonfiction texts

There has been an explosion of nonfiction titles for young readers in libraries, bookstores, and inside basal anthologies. In past years, many titles were poorly written, lacking clear structure and sufficient text processing signals, such as overviews, topic or main idea statements, or summaries. However, in recent years, there have been

Invitation for the classroom

Linking to Nonfiction

Ask students to look through your classroom library of nonfiction texts. (You may also want to include more texts from the school or local library.) Offer a broad selection so that there is at least one book that will interest each child. As students look through the books, ask them to think about personal connections to the texts. Have each student select one or two books they have a personal connection to. Once students select their books, have them take a few minutes to write their connection to the topic/book. Share these notes with other classmates as an introduction into nonfiction, and as a way to become familiar with the range of interests reflected in the classroom.

Adapted from Jerry Harste.

attempts to improve the quality of nonfiction texts available for elementary aged readers and writers (Hiebert, 1999; Moss, 1997). Nonfiction titles are becoming more diverse and responding to timely issues (Iraq war, natural disasters such as the tsunami in southeast Asia, and presidential elections). They are packed with information in forewords, author's notes, annotated glossaries, and indices.

Given the proliferation of nonfiction titles available to students and teachers, it is important to select high-quality, nonfiction literature that encourages thinking and provides new information for students; appeals to students visually; has credible authors and accurate factual information; and offers clear organizational structures such as headings, table of contents, indices, and common formats such as question-and-answer or comparing and contrasting.

Recognizing that expository text structures vary from fiction, it is important to provide students, in all grades, with multiple opportunities to access and use nonfiction texts in a variety of ways. Nonfiction texts encourage students to gain a depth of knowledge in content areas, such as social studies and science.

CATEGORIES OF NONFICTION TEXTS. Children need to have a variety of texts at their disposal, as well as rich experiences with these texts. There are different types of nonfiction texts that should be available for students in classroom and school libraries. Included in the categories of nonfiction texts are: concept books, identification, procedural, biography, and informational storybooks.

CONCEPT. Concept books are designed to explore characteristics of an abstract idea (e.g., colors, numbers, size, seasons). Much of the information is carried in the illustrations of these texts that are particularly for younger readers. Concept books ask the reader to generalize and see patterns. Examples of concept books are *Shapes, Shapes, Shapes* (Toban, 1996), *Breathtaking Noses* (Machotka, 1992), and *Pie in the Sky* (Ehlert, 2004).

IDENTIFICATION. Identification texts are those that use mostly labels and diagrams to present the information. Examples include *DK Eyewitness Series* (e.g., *Oceans*, 2004; *Volcanos and Earthquakes*, 2004; *Reptiles*, 2000; and *Sharks*, 2004).

PROCEDURAL. These are "how to" books and are found in a wide range of domains— science, cooking, crafts. Most of these books have a material section and a series of steps to accomplish the task. Temporal words (first, next, last) are regularly used. Examples include *Pretend Soup* (Katzen & Henderson, 1994), *Earning a Ride: How to Be a NASCAR Driver* (Woods, 2003), and *Take A Look Around: Photography Activities for Young People* (Varriale, 1999).

Criteria for choosing nonfiction texts

Choose texts with:

- **New information to encourage young children's thinking.** High-quality, nonfiction conveys at least some information that the reader may not already know, but would very much like to.

- **Appealing design, format, and writing style.** Nonfiction texts that speak directly to the young reader are appealing. The language used in the text is lively and engaging. These texts often use well-designed graphics and illustrations. Photographs, diagrams, maps, drawings, charts, and figures are the types of illustrations used.

- **Accurate facts.** A critical component of high-quality nonfiction is to provide accurate and up to date information for the reader. People of different abilities, race, and culture should be represented fairly and without stereotype. Readers should also note the credentials of the author(s). This helps in determining if the author is able to speak with any conviction and authority. Along with the author's experiences and credentials, it is also important to distinguish between what is known and what is believed to be true (e.g., scientists think, perhaps).

- **Good organization.** High-quality children's nonfiction texts have clear organizational structures. Compare-contrast, question-answer, cause-effect, description, and sequence are common expository structures. Headings and subheadings are also frequent. Many nonfiction texts do not need to be read from cover to cover, and the organizational structure helps students determine which areas of the text to read.

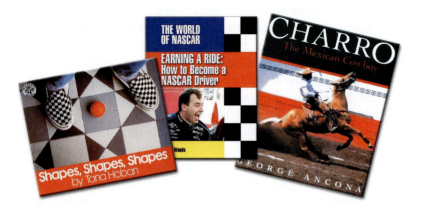

BIOGRAPHY. Biographies convey information about a person's life and experiences. Common features of biographies include chronological organization, explanation of the importance of the person's life, and narratives that describe life events. There are a number of biographies for famous people (sports figures, Presidents), as well as not-so-famous people, but whose accomplishments are important (scientists, civil rights workers). Examples include *The Boy on Fairfield Street* (Krull, 2004), *Sammy Sosa: Amazing Athletes series* (Savage, 2004), and *Dare to Dream: 25 Extraordinary Lives* (Humphrey, 2005).

INFORMATIONAL STORYBOOKS. Some texts blur the genre boundaries between fiction and nonfiction. These texts, such as *Magic School Bus* series (Cole & Degan) and *Diary of a Worm* (Cronin, 2003) provide excellent introductions into expository because they carry a narrative structure which is familiar, but also provide facts and information. These informational storybooks often encourage multiple readings because it is difficult to manage all of the information in one sitting.

It is important for students to have access to and to use nonfiction texts that cut across the different categories. In doing so, they come to see how information is presented in a variety of formats. The next section highlights opportunities for incorporating nonfiction reading into an effective literacy curriculum.

Incorporating nonfiction into a reading and writing curriculum

Josh, an avid reader in third grade, is struggling to read his fifth grade social studies textbook. He opens up to the designated page and within minutes has lost interest in what he is reading. It seems like he is reading the words but there isn't any meaning attached to the words. Josh is able to decode the words, yet he doesn't recognize the way the information is laid out. He finds it difficult to make sense of the information presented in the textbook. Josh's reading background suggests that he has limited experiences in reading expository text. He usually reads science fiction and adventure stories.

Josh's experiences as a reader are not uncommon. Many students read fiction quite comfortably and struggle to read nonfiction. They often approach the nonfiction text with the same mindset as reading a narrative, thinking about plot, theme, and characters, not facts, figures, and headings. Yet, expository text structure is quite different. The differences create dissonance in the reading event, and in a short amount of time engaged and avid readers become disengaged readers.

Students quickly lose interest in reading. Teachers can support students by explicitly pointing out the differences in how one reads nonfiction and fiction texts. Frequent and repeated use of nonfiction texts, along with strategy work contributes to students' abilities to navigate among many different types of texts. Structures for incorporating nonfiction reading and writing into the curriculum include reading aloud informational books, providing reading time for nonfiction, and reading nonfiction along with fiction.

Read informational texts aloud

One way to increase the amount of exposure students have to nonfiction texts is to read aloud from nonfiction selections, including books, magazines, newspapers, and websites. Teachers often link the nonfiction text to a current inquiry or focus study occurring in the classroom or in a particular discipline, such as social studies, science, mathematics, and art. Integrating nonfiction reading into the areas of study that are currently in place in the classroom helps students make important connections across texts and topics. In Mr. Rupp's fifth grade classroom in Georgia, the students initiated an inquiry into the Trail of Tears. The inquiry came about because one student in the class wondered about people being displaced from their homelands, and if it ever happened in the United States. Mr. Rupp invited students to examine issues related to displacement and offered to put together materials for an inquiry on Trail of Tears. He gathered materials from the National Historic Trail (http://www.rosecity.net/tears/trail/retrace.html) to share with students. One piece Mr. Rupp read aloud was entitled "National Historic Trail," which provided students with some background information on the Trail of Tears. Following this read aloud, the students worked in small groups to discuss what they had heard, and to consider additional issues they wanted to read about. Because Mr. Rupp believes it is important to read around an issue before asking questions, he does not ask students to create a list of questions at this point in the inquiry. As the inquiry continued, Mr. Rupp read aloud nonfiction material (journal entries, interviews, historical accounts, etc.) to provide students with information, and to allow them to experience a variety of categories and forms of nonfiction texts.

Children as young as 5 and 6 are already sensitive to the differences between nonfiction and storybooks (Duke and Kays, 1998). By reading aloud nonfiction texts, children are able to:

- hear how language is used,
- learn new linguistic features that are different from stories,
- learn how the text is structured,
- hear text that may be too difficult to read on one's own, and
- observe how more competent readers may not read a text in a linear fashion.

Many nonfiction texts do not have storylines to follow and are designed to be read in nonlinear formats. A reader may begin on any page depending on the information a reader is seeking. When reading aloud texts that are not necessarily read from beginning to end, the teacher may highlight how readers use the index and table of contents to determine where to go in the text. These mini-lessons on structure serve as important scaffolds.

Provide time to read in content areas

Students need to know that reading in the content areas is not just reading the required textbook section. There should be time set aside to read other materials, including literature, that support the topic of study. Independent reading time inside of social studies or science or any other content area supports children's continued

Sample twin texts

Fiction	Nonfiction
For younger readers	
Stellaluna by Janell Cannon	*Bats* by Celia Bland
Cloudy With a Chance of Meatballs by Judi Barrett	*Comets, Meteors, and Asteroids* by Seymour Simon
Red Leaf, Yellow Leaf by Lois Ehlert	*Why Do Leaves Change Color?* by Betsy Maestro
The Tree That Would Not Die by Ellen Levine	*A Tree Is Growing* by Arthur Dorros
The Apply Pie Tree by Zoe Hall	*Apples of Your Eye* by Allan Fowler
Old Bear by Jane Hissey	*How Teddy Bears Are Made* by Ann Morris
Amazing Grace by Mary Hoffman	*The Story of Ruby Bridges* by Robert Coles
Aunt Harriet's Underground Railroad in the Sky by Faith Ringgold	*"Wanted Dead or Alive:" The True Story of Harriet Tubman* by Ann McGovern
The Maestro Plays by Bill Martin Jr	*What Instrument Is This?* by Rosmarie Hausherr
Listen Buddy by Helen Lester	*Communication* by Aliki
Postcards From Pluto: A Tour of the Solar System by Loreen Leedy	*Do Stars Have Points?* by Melvin & Gilda Berger
Flatfoot Fox by Eth Clifford	*Foxes* by Emilie U. Lepthien
I'm Going to Be a Firefighter by Edith Kunhardt	*Fire!* by Joy Masoff
The Whales by Cynthia Rylant	*Whales* by John Bonnett Wexo
The Foot Book by Dr. Seuss	*What Neat Feet* by Hana Machotka
The Butter Battle Book by Dr. Seuss	*Always to Remember: The Story of the Vietnam Veterans Memorial* by Brent & Jennifer Ashabranner
A Happy Tale by Dorothy Butler	*Sky Pioneer: A Photobiography of Amelia Earhart* by Corinne Szabo
For older readers	
Thunder on the Tennessee by G. Clifton Wisler	*A Nation Torn Apart* by Delia Ray
Hiroshima by Laurence Yep	*Sadako and the Thousand Paper Cranes* by Eleanor Coerr
A Picture of Freedom: The Diary of Clotee, a Slave Girl by Patricia McKissack	*Rosa Parks: My Story* by Rosa Parks with Jim Haskins
West to Opportunity: The Diary of Teresa Angelino Viscardi by Jim Murphy	*Children of the Wild West* by Russell Freedman
Voyage on the Great Titanic: The Diary of Margaret Ann Brady by Ellen E. White	*Ghost Liners* by Robert D. Ballard
The Egypt Game by Zilpha K. Snyder	*Pyramids* by Anne Millard

From Camp, D. (2000). It takes two: Teaching with *Twin Texts* of fact and fiction, Reading Teacher, Vol. 53, Issue 5, pp. 400–409.

TECHNOLOGY LINK

List of nonfiction books to support science and social studies

Science:
http://www.nsta.org/ostbc

Social Studies:
http://www.socialstudies.org/resources/notable/

access and opportunities to read for meaning. Students are able to further develop their abilities to become proficient readers in a variety of settings. Continuing with Mr. Rupp's classroom, he facilitates nonfiction reading during the students' social studies time. Students read sections of the social studies textbook alongside other texts, including *Trail of Tears* (Bruchac, 1999), another with the same title *Trail of Tears* (Stein, 1993), and a website on the Cherokee tribe and the Trail of Tears (http://kathyschrock.net/webquests/LAMB/Cherokee.htm). Mr Rupp encourages his students to record important details throughout their reading of these various sources. These notes will support students in their discussions of issues around the Trail of Tears and relocation of Native Americans.

Pairing nonfiction with fiction

Earlier chapters talked about creating text sets that included both fiction and non-fiction texts. One place to start in creating text sets is to create what Camp (2000) called "Twin Texts." Twin texts are two texts (one fiction and one nonfiction) paired together on the same topic. Pairing nonfiction with fiction encourages reading across different types of texts. The fiction selection often provides the contextual setting for a topic, while the nonfiction text capitalizes on children's enthusiasm for facts. Twin texts help students to see how one book may "facilitate understandings of other books and issues" (Short, 1991, p. 2).

Reading strategies for nonfiction and content area reading material

The reading strategy work throughout the various chapters is certainly applicable to nonfiction texts. This section, however, highlights various strategies that may be more useful when working with nonfiction texts.

Code breaking strategies for nonfiction text

One of the biggest challenges a reader encounters when working with nonfiction texts is unfamiliar vocabulary. Students often comment that nonfiction texts have "too many hard words" and they often "don't know what the words mean" (even if they can pronounce them). When students come across too many unfamiliar "high concept" words, they are less likely to make connections to their existing background knowledge, to comprehend the text easily, and make inferences (Rupley, Logan, & Nichols, 1999). While vocabulary work is not particular to nonfiction text (as noted in Chapters 7 and 8), new and unfamiliar words are often a stopping point for many readers when reading nonfiction.

- Content area vocabulary words are tied directly to the concepts being learned. While reading from a social studies textbook, a fourth grader may come across the words "specialize" and "interdependent" while learning these concepts for the first time during a lesson in economics.
- Knowing new vocabulary is essential for understanding the concepts attached to content area reading. In the preceding example, the reader will not understand the concepts associated with specialization and interdependence if unable to accurately define these terms.

Invitation for the classroom

Linking Something Old with Something New

This strategy builds on the importance of background knowledge and experiences. Students will come across unfamiliar words as they read nonfiction texts. Select a few stopping points as places to discuss these unfamiliar words. As students talk about what they are reading, find ways to link their understandings to words and phrases that may be unfamiliar. Students can then draw upon their background knowledge and experiences to begin building connections to the new information.

- New vocabulary words in a content area are often related to each other (i.e, economic terms, science terms, history terms).

We all have memories of learning lists of vocabulary words. For many of us these memories include writing definitions, with little, if any, retention of what the words meant when we actually read the words in the textbook. The words were often selected by the teacher (most likely pulled from the teacher's edition of the textbook). The isolated activity of defining words was often an unproductive act. Readers rarely learn words by copying definitions from the dictionary.

Gaining word knowledge and using code breaking practices require a complex process of integrating unfamiliar words with experiences and knowledge the reader brings to the text—his or her schema (Greenwood, 2002). Therefore, a more constructive way to encourage vocabulary learning is to draw upon words that readers will most likely come across in their reading. Selecting words from contextual reading situations integrates vocabulary instruction into wider reading opportunities and emphasizes word meanings that relate to comprehension (Blachowicz & Lee, 1991). In addition to teaching vocabulary words in context, the following strategy work may better support code breaking practices inside nonfiction texts.

For example, when Allison, grade 2, read about the fur coat of big cats (lions, tigers, cheetahs) and viewed the picture of a tiger hiding in the grass, she talked about how the tiger was hard to see. Her teacher asked Allison if she could think of words that might be related to the idea of "hard to see." Allison came up with "hiding," "not be seen" and "can't find." As she talked, her teacher also mentioned the word "camouflage." Allison seemed to understand the term and when she came across it in the text—"Black leopards and jaguars spend most of their time in shady forests, where their dark fur gives them good camouflage"—she was able to immediately make the connection that the black leopards and jaguars were trying to hide. This strategy supports active code breaking processing by having students consider what possible words may appear in the content of their content reading.

Word mapping, a strategy that was developed by Schwartz and Raphael (1985), is a graphic representation of a word and focuses on three questions: What is it? What is it like? What are some examples? Rossenbaum (2001) extends this work to encourage deep processing of words.

Code breaking practices focus on supporting readers as they learn to manipulate words, to see similarities and differences, and to consider multiple definitions and shades of meaning.

Invitation for the classroom

Word Mapping

Students are asked to select difficult words to map. These words should be drawn from their reading and inquiry projects. They consider the context in which the word was used to locate appropriate definitions, antonyms, synonyms, and alternative forms of the word. Students are also asked to create an original sentence that uses the word appropriately.

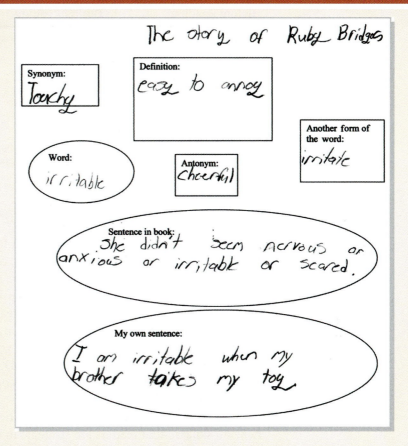

Invitation for the classroom

Connect the Words

Select an important theme, word, or phrase that students have been studying. Write this in the center box.

Ask students to select two or three important words associated with the theme and to write them in the ovals at the outer corners of the graphic.

In pairs, ask students to think aloud and generate the connections between the important words and the theme. Record the connections in the square boxes.

Pairs should ask each other, "How does this word related to that word?"

Have pairs share their connections.

Adapted from Zwiers (2004).

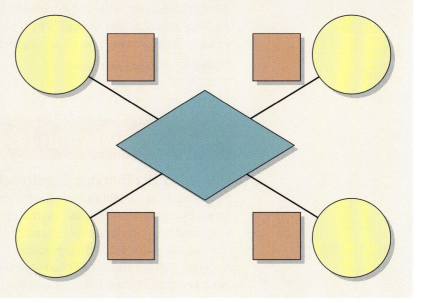

TABLE 11.2
Comprehension Strategies for Nonfiction

Before Reading	During Reading	After Reading
Predicting	Making connections	Summarizing
Accessing prior knowledge	Questioning	Creating graphic representations
	Visualizing	
	Inferencing	
	Using text structure to identify main ideas	
	Paraphrasing Clarifying	

Text participant strategies for nonfiction texts

Nonfiction texts prove to be more difficult for some readers because of the varied text structures (e.g., cause/effect, sequence, compare/contrast). There is less familiarity with these structures than with more common storybook structures where characters, setting, plot, and conflict/resolution are apparent. There are a number of strategies that teachers can model for readers as they interact with nonfiction texts to better support their meaning making processes. Some of the strategies are timeless, and in fact, you may use them as you read textbooks and other informational materials. Kletzien and Dreher (2004) noted that nonfiction texts are particularly useful for developing these common comprehension skills before, during, and after reading (Table 11.2).

The following strategy work and invitations support developing these comprehension skills so that readers are strategic in their meaning making processes.

Invitation for the classroom

Contrast Charts

During reading, students create a chart that lists what they know or are familiar about the topic and areas that they do not know, and what students do not know. After reading, students use the chart as a place to begin conversations and inquiries. Readers focus attention on what they already know in relation to the text.

Adapted from Yopp and Yopp, 1996b.

Invitation for the classroom

SQR3 (Survey, Question, Read, Recite, and Review)

Before reading, students *survey* the text by perusing through the pages, noticing pictures, photographs, captions, charts, etc. They will often also notice the cover and talk about their previous experiences and/or knowledge of the topic. The teacher will ask *questions* that focus on predicting. The text is then *read*, either orally or silently depending on the students. Following the reading, students are asked questions that were generated before the book was read. This facilitates their abilities to recall and recite information, drawing on their understandings of the text. Finally, students have opportunities to *review* the information and concepts learned. More questions are often asked, such as:

- What did you learn in reading this text?
- Would you like to read another book on this topic?
- Did the book have the information you were hoping to learn?

Invitation for the classroom

Get One-Give One

This invitation supports the social nature of learning and helps students to tap into and build their background knowledge for a text.

- Using the topic that is being studied, have students write down ideas related to the topic (1–4).
- Have students circulate around the room and exchange their ideas for at least three different ideas from other students (5–8).
- After several minutes, have students regroup and share with the class ideas they heard from others.

Adapted from Kagan, 1997.

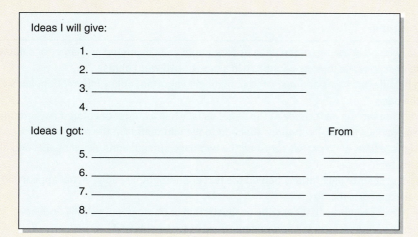

Ideas I will give:

1. _____
2. _____
3. _____
4. _____

Ideas I got: From

5. _____   _____
6. _____   _____
7. _____   _____
8. _____   _____

Text use strategies for nonfiction texts

Text use practices for nonfiction texts involve students being able to effectively determine and understand the purpose for the text and the organizational features of nonfiction texts. While nonfiction texts are written to provide readers with information, it is important that students are able to distinguish the nuanced purposes of nonfiction texts—to inform and/or persuade.

Invitation for the classroom

Learning about Organizational Features of Nonfiction Texts

In this invitation students explore the organizational features of nonfiction texts, such as labels, captions, headings, fonts, and so forth.

Bring together a collection of nonfiction texts around a particular topic or issue (migration, civil rights, environment). Have enough copies for students to browse through the books. The books should also showcase a variety of organizational features.

Have students browse through the books looking for the organizational features that make the books interesting and engaging. Explain to students that nonfiction texts have several different features that set them apart from fiction books and that some of these features can be used in their own writing.

Engage students in a discussion about their findings. The following prompts to engage students in the discussion:

- Would anyone like to share a page that they found interesting or well organized?
- What makes the page interesting or well organized?
- Did anyone else find a similar feature in the books they were looking at?
- When browsing through the books, what features immediately caught your attention?

Have students discuss the different organizational features found in their texts. A chart can be created to identify the purpose of the organizational features.

Allow students, either independently or with a partner, to browse through the nonfiction texts again to find examples of the different organizational features. Model how students can use Post-it notes to mark the features and write notes to remind themselves of what they want to share.

Organizational Features of Nonfiction Texts

Organizational Feature	Description
Headings	Usually found at the top of the page or paragraph; usually printed in a larger or colored font; describes the topic or paragraph in a one- or two-word phrase
Font	Can be different styles or sizes; used to highlight important or key information; adds variety to the page
Sidebars	Boxed information on the side of the page; usually has a border or colored background; often provides text or illustrations that add to the information in the main text
Borders	Designs or lines of color that surround the two-page spread; adds visual appeal and often fits the topic
Backgrounds	Blocks of color or illustrations behind the text or photographs; adds visual appeal and usually supports the text
Captions	One to two sentences that describe an illustration or photograph; usually appears underneath the picture, but sometimes above or to the side of it
Labels	Often added to photographs or illustrations to provide more information to the reader
Diagrams, charts, graphs, tables	Used to show written or additional information in a different and simple way; provides visual appeal to a two-page spread
Did You Know facts	One to two sentences that provide a hook to the two-page spread; usually provides interesting or fascinating facts that will grab the reader's attention
Photographs and illustrations	Adds visual appeal to the page; provides support for the written text

Adapted from Emily Manning.

Invitation for the classroom

Text Transformation

In this invitation, students transform a text into a different genre. They can turn a textbook chapter into a newspaper article, poster, biography, interview, or news program.

Discuss with students how different genres serve different purposes.

Model the types of thinking skills that students should make evident in their text transformations, including cause and effect, sequence, and persuasion.

Ask students to identify the most important information in the original text. What did the author of the original text want readers to remember? A graphic organizer may be helpful to capture the main idea and supporting elements for the new version.

Have students write their transformed text.

Adapted from Zwiers, 2004.

Critical practices strategies for nonfiction texts

One of the most important aspects when working with nonfiction texts is to support readers' growing awareness that they need to be critically literate. Nonfiction texts provide opportunities for readers to confirm and/or challenge the information presented. Teachers can support students in learning which information is central to their inquiry and which information is secondary or nonessential to their inquiry. As readers read across texts (multiple texts on the same issue) they can learn to take on a more critical stance.

The invitations presented for working with nonfiction texts inside of the four resource practices are just a few examples. There are many more that can be created and implemented in classrooms, kindergarten to sixth grade. Content area vocabulary, background knowledge, comprehension strategies, and organizing large amounts of information are critical aspects to meeting the needs of students as they face increasingly complex expository materials in and out of classroom settings.

The next section of this chapter moves to discussing reading and writing nonfiction texts in multimodal environments.

Invitation for the classroom

Circle of Questions

This strategy allows readers to critique a text and to learn that not every question can be answered in one particular text.

- Arrange students in small groups. Ask each group to brainstorm a list of questions they have in relation to a topic the class is studying. Then, bring the groups together and record each groups' top two questions on a piece of chart paper.
- Through discussion, categorize the questions and have each group select a category to work with.
- Have students reread the text and record their answers. As a whole class, discuss whether the text adequately addressed the question(s). If not, ask readers where they think additional information could be found.

Adapted from Sampson, Sampson, & Linek, 1994/95.

Invitation for the classroom

R.I.T.E.

The R.I.T.E strategy—*Read, Interrogate, Tell and Explore* encourages students to make thoughtful predictions prior to reading a text and to search for information as they read. Readers must use their analytical skills to determine if the information is relevant to their needs. In this adaptation, readers first consider what they know about the topic, then they speculate on various details of the topic, and finally, they set a purpose for reading. The goal of this strategy is for readers to compare the data in the text with their own speculations and to see if they are correct. As readers begin reading, they interrogate the text. Questions readers may ask include:

- Is this fact true?
- What evidence in the article would lead me to believe the fact is either true or false?
- Is there any way, within the limits of the article, to test the truthfulness of the fact?
- What do I know about the fact itself that would lead me to think it is true or false?

In the tell section, students work in small groups to share their thinking and to further problematize the text. The explore aspect is an opportunity for readers to read other texts to compare and contrast facts and information.

Adapted from Polette, 2002.

Nonfiction texts in multimodal environments

Technology influences almost every aspect of our daily lives. Most people have computers and Internet access, either at work, home or at the library; have cell phones, pagers, and PDAs; and have videogames, televisions, DVD players, and digital video recorders. Children in today's classrooms and those that you will teach in the near future are growing up in environments where much of this is readily accessible. They are learning the codes and ways of interacting with these various technologies. Many children are experiencing technology in rapidly different ways than most of their teachers.

Not only is the definition of literacy changing, but so too are the ways in which children decode texts, make meaning, and critique available information. The rapidly changing technologies require teachers to be more informed about how to use technology in the classroom in ways that make sense for learning and teaching, as well as broaden our own understandings of how children make use of these multimodal technologies.

There seems to be a growing divide between the literacy experiences occurring in classrooms and the kinds of experiences available in out-of-school contexts (home, community centers, playground, etc). In classrooms, children most often read various books (i.e., picture, textbooks, young adult novel) and sometimes, news magazines. Out-of-school contexts provide children with access to texts that are multimodal and multidimensional, such as websites, graphic novels, search engines, instant messaging, and video games. Students are busy constructing their own sense of self and identity in these texts and at the same time discounting the relevancy of what schools have to offer. Gee, Hull, and Lankshear (1996) note that "if learning is

Did you know . . .

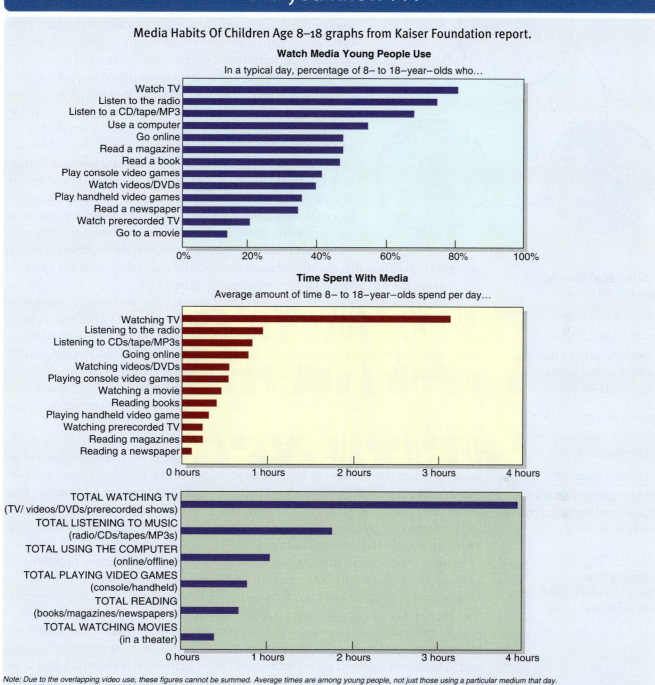

Media Habits Of Children Age 8–18 graphs from Kaiser Foundation report.

Watch Media Young People Use

In a typical day, percentage of 8– to 18–year–olds who...

- Watch TV
- Listen to the radio
- Listen to a CD/tape/MP3
- Use a computer
- Go online
- Read a magazine
- Read a book
- Play console video games
- Watch videos/DVDs
- Play handheld video games
- Read a newspaper
- Watch prerecorded TV
- Go to a movie

(0% – 100%)

Time Spent With Media

Average amount of time 8– to 18–year–olds spend per day...

- Watching TV
- Listening to the radio
- Listening to CDs/tape/MP3s
- Going online
- Watching videos/DVDs
- Playing console video games
- Watching a movie
- Reading books
- Playing handheld video game
- Watching prerecorded TV
- Reading magazines
- Reading a newspaper

(0 hours – 4 hours)

- TOTAL WATCHING TV (TV/ videos/DVDs/prerecorded shows)
- TOTAL LISTENING TO MUSIC (radio/CDs/tapes/MP3s)
- TOTAL USING THE COMPUTER (online/offline)
- TOTAL PLAYING VIDEO GAMES (console/handheld)
- TOTAL READING (books/magazines/newspapers)
- TOTAL WATCHING MOVIES (in a theater)

(0 hours – 4 hours)

Note: Due to the overlapping video use, these figures cannot be summed. Average times are among young people, not just those using a particular medium that day.

to be efficacious, then what a child or an adult does now as a learner must be connected in meaningful and motivating ways with 'mature' (insider) versions of related social practices" (p. 4). Moreover, it is critical that teachers make school experiences and the literacy practices associated with such experiences more relevant to students' lives. In the next section, we look at ways for teachers to bring these new modes for literacy into the classroom.

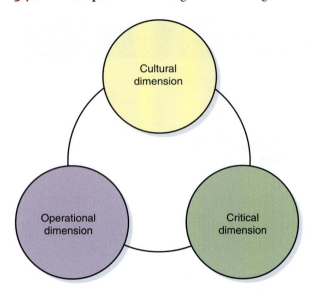

FIGURE 11.2 Dimensions of multimodal literacy.

multimodal literacy

Literacy practices that are carried across multiple sites/texts/or media.

operational dimension

Knowing how to operate the technology.

cultural dimension

Knowing that technology use is in relation to creating specific meaning.

critical dimension

Knowing how to problematize and evaluate software and other resources.

Dimensions of multimodal literacy

Multimodal literacy is not something to tack onto the bottom of the curriculum; to save for significant research projects, or to entice an unmotivated and struggling reader. Similar to inquiry-based curriculum, we need to think about multimodal literacy as being integrated into the instructional day, so that the technology (whether it is pencil and paper, powerpoint slides, video, email notes, etc.) is the means by which understandings are constructed and shared. Durrant and Green (2000) identified three dimensions of learning that focus on how technology use and *multimodal literacy* may be conceptualized in classroom practice. These dimensions complement the notion that literacy is socially situated, by considering the contextual aspects of literacy and technology. With these dimensions, one does not start with "skills" and "how to" in a vacuum, but this learning is always in context. Additionally, the dimensions are not hierarchical, but rather work together seamlessly to address literacy practices (Figure 11.2).

How can technology and other modes of literacy be used in the classroom? First, readers need to know how to work computers or operate any of the technology. This first dimension is the *operational dimension.* Much like code breaking practices, the operational dimension is interested in the "how to" and technical competence. Understanding how the technology operates (turning the machine on, plugging devices into the computer), the mechanics of keyboarding, and how to function within the operating system (creating and locating files, opening databases, etc.) are within this dimension.

The second dimension, *cultural dimension,* refers to the notion that technology use is always in relation to creating specific meanings. We use technology to get things done in the world—to inform, to stay connected, to achieve our own purposes (and others). This dimension is closely related to how readers engage with texts as text participants. The focus is on meaning making, whether it is by reading texts on paper or by using powerpoint to structure a presentation. We bring our own experiences and understandings to the text and technologies.

Thirdly, the *critical dimension* draws upon students' abilities to problematize and evaluate software and other resources (websites and programs). In much the same way as the critical practices in reading and writing challenge and problematize texts, so to can issues of access, power, and equity be challenged in relation to technology resources. How am I to read/write a particular text? How does availability to various technologies support and/or hinder students' trajectories in learning? What about issues of power and access? Who determines how much and when a student uses technology? Who selects various software programs for students to use? These questions manifest themselves within the critical dimension.

Durrant and Green (2000) are careful to note that there is not an exact mapping between the dimensions they identified and the four-resource model. However, both frameworks consider how literacy and texts (and technologies) are socially constructed.

Integrating electronic media into literacy instruction

Students' increasing awareness of technology requires teachers to take a more proactive role in integrating technology into the curriculum. The edges are blurring between visual and verbal modes, so that meaning making is becoming more multimodal (Kress, 1997). Readers and writers use a variety of sign systems (music, art), as well as still and moving images and icons to construct texts that are very different from the texts that most teachers work with. Students also are much more facile in communicating with global media technologies (instant messaging, email) in ways that differ significantly than more traditional modes of communication.

What makes technology work successfully in some places and not in others? How do some teachers infuse technology seamlessly into the curriculum, so that it is not an added burden or something extra to worry about? To build the bridges between technology and literacy instruction, Labbo and Reinking (1999, p. 481) identified five goals:

New digital technologies should be

- available for literacy instruction and
- used to enhance the goals of conventional literacy instruction.

New digital technologies should be used to

- positively transform literacy instruction,
- prepare students for the literacy of the future, and
- empower students.

These goals, while not groundbreaking, are important to keep in mind as we consider the possibilities of integrating technology with literacy instruction. The first goal, availability, is critical in moving technology from the periphery (and in computer labs) into classrooms, where students have regular access during instructional time. The rapid development of new technologies continues to challenge schools and districts to keep current, as do equity issues in terms of which schools benefit from technology and which schools do not have readily available access.

The second and third goals—enhancing and transforming literacy instruction—are important goals, as teachers and students consider ways in which technology can further support literacy learning. There are a number of innovative and exciting opportunities for children to access and use technologies in meaningful ways to enhance and support literacy development. The earlier "drill and skill" programs, while still available in many classrooms, do not enhance or transform learning in any significant way. Ineffective practices do not magically improve through the use of technology. Rather, opportunities to use the Internet broaden students' reading beyond the textbook and encourage more critical stances. They are learning to read new forms and new genres.

The fourth and fifth goals are related to looking into our future. If we are to prepare students to be literate in this new century, it requires that teachers and schools encourage technology use that is meaningful to students' lives. Reading and authoring texts that embody multimodal characteristics (e.g., nonlinear reading, experimenting with format, fonts, graphics) enables students to construct unique and often more complex texts than what they can do with traditional, more static technologies and tools.

TECHNOLOGY LINK
http://www.learner.org/channel/workshops/teachreading35/session5/index.html

Dr. Donald Leu addresses new reading and writing strategies in using the Internet to promote literacy development.

Types of communication technologies available to students.

Creating Connections 11.2

Interview a teacher about his/her use of technology in their literacy curriculum.

What are some of the concerns or issues that the teacher encounters when trying to integrate technology in meaningful and productive ways?

Effective teachers are aware of these new technologies and how they are changing the ways in which readers and writers work. Rather than relying on conventional school-based literacy activities and tasks (writing research reports; reading young adult novels), teachers are coordinating multiple texts, formats, and genres and asking students to create multimodal projects that include print-based texts, graphics, video streaming, audio, and pictures (Grisham, 2001). Teachers who work to more effectively integrate technology into their literacy instruction offer a transformative literacy curriculum that will contribute to meeting the needs of a literate population.

Linking electronic media with informational literacy

Technology is often used with inquiry-based learning and focused studies. In today's learning environments, children have more access in locating relevant information to better understand their topic. Technology use also supports children's abilities to organize and present their new information in engaging ways (e.g., powerpoint slides that include video clips, music clips). The following chart highlights the processes children encounter in inquiry projects and how technology contributes to the learning. This list is not exhaustive, but demonstrates that many of the skills students are asked to do can be accomplished using technology in meaningful ways.

All of the information processing skills in Table 11.3 can be attended to with basic computer programs and Internet access. More sophisticated programs with many "bells and whistles" are not necessarily critical for the goals of integrating technology into a literacy program. Students need to know how to select, evaluate, and synthesize the vast amount of information into something that makes sense. Technologies are avenues to enhance and support the learning that is already taking place in many classrooms.

TABLE 11.3
Literacy Skills that Use Information Technology

Information Process	Information Technology Possibilities
Defining and planning	• Brainstorm a list using a word processor • Creates concept webs with software programs • Create inquiry proposal with appropriate headings and room for note-taking
Locating	• Use library computer keyword search • Browse various related websites • Google search • Refine searches to reduce irrelevant hits
Selecting and Noting	• Use skimming and abstracts to select relevant material • Use word processor or other feature for note-taking • Use cut and paste features of word processing program
Organizing	• Use slides to organize ideas • Create headings/subheadings
Presenting	• Create a multimodal presentation with music, video, moving images • Use draw/paint software tools • Engage in formatting work (font, spacing) • Create posters

Scaffolding reading and writing strategies with electronic media

Reading and writing are no longer just "linear" and "static" enterprises. With the advent of hypertext, much of our reading and writing in digital formats is multilinear and dynamic. Reading websites, CDs, and DVDs requires that we scan and search for the information we seek, whether it is in the form of icons, images, links, texts, or video clips. Readers have choices as they interact with multimodal texts—choices that are not typically available in more static and traditional forms (book pages). Writers also experience a different kind of composing process when using digital technologies. They can compose in multilinear formats (create links and buttons), import icons and images, add other technologies (video and music), and experiment with fonts and formats. There are no predetermined or standard ways to read and write such texts. The reader or writer is able to choose where to start, where to go next, and which buttons or links to pursue.

Invitation for the classroom

Students conduct WebQuests by exploring WebQuests topics on the Internet. WebQuests are designed to use students' time well, to focus on using information rather than looking for it, and to support students as they problem solve, process information, and collaborate.

WebQuests can be designed around any topic. For example, there are WebQuests on:

Chocolate: http://www.btcs.org/tutorials/WebQuests/chocolate/
Winter Celebrations: http://jets.utep.edu/helen_ball/awauson/winter/adriawauson/index.htm
Solar System: http://www.teachtheteachers.org/projects/SPierce/index.htm
Figurative Language: http://bugges.wcpss.net/Do%20You%20Know%20What%20It%20Means.htm

To learn more about WebQuests and to learn how to create your own, visit:
http://webquest.sdsu.edu/
http://webquest.sdsu.edu/designsteps/index.html

Adapted from Dodge (1995).

In Closing

The reading diet for students in the primary or early grades has historically been dominated by narrative and fiction texts. Much of this is changing, however, particularly with the recognition that children are quite interested in learning about the social and natural world. An inquiry-based curriculum invites students and teachers to examine and explore the world around them. Students pursue their own interests, ask insightful questions, read and write a variety of texts, and consider a range of possibilities in presenting their new understandings.

Nonfiction texts are a central component of inquiry-based curriculum. It is noted that reading nonfiction materials is perhaps the most common type of reading, from how-to manuals and newspapers to websites about a particular topic. In recent years, there has been a proliferation of high-quality nonfiction texts that are accessible for young children. Through nonfiction reading and writing, children are able to answer real questions and solve real problems. There are different categories of nonfiction texts—concept books, identification, procedural, biography, and informational storybooks. Teachers support nonfiction reading by engaging students in a variety of strategy lessons that highlight text structure, making connections, and comprehending.

Multimodal environments further enhance an inquiry-based curriculum. Students use a variety of sign systems and technologies to construct meaning of texts. They engage with different forms of texts, from print based to digital. The edges between these various forms of text are blurring, bringing together both visual and verbal modes. As students and teachers begin to incorporate digital technologies into the reading and writing curriculum, it should be noted that these new technologies should support and enhance the literacy curriculum.

Terms to Remember

Critical dimension *(346)*
Cultural dimension *(346)*
Inquiry-based curriculum *(325)*
Multimodal literacy *(346)*
Operational dimension *(346)*
Sign systems *(329)*

Resources for More Information

Berghoff, B., Egawa, K., Harste, J., & Hoonan, B. (2001). *Beyond reading and writing: Inquiry, curriculum, and multiple ways of knowing.* Urbana, IL: National Council Teachers of English.

Duke, N. K., & Kays, J. (1998). "Can I say 'once upon a time'"? Kindergarten children developing knowledge of information book language. *Early Childhood Research Quarterly,* 13, 295–318.

Harste, J. C. (2001). What Education as Inquiry Is and Isn't. In S. Boran & B. Comber (Eds.), Critiquing Whole Language and Classroom Inquiry (pp. 1–17), Urbana, IL: National Council of Teachers of English.

Labbo, L. D., & Reinking, D. (1999). Negotiating the multiple realities of technology in literacy research and instruction. *Reading Research Quarterly,* 34, 478–492.

Moss, B. (1997). Using children's notification tradeboocks as read-alouds. *Language Arts,* 72(2), 122–126.

Pataray-Ching, J., & Robertson, M. (2002). Misconceptions about a *Curriculum-as-Inquiry* Framework. *Language Arts,* 79(6), 498–506.

Questions for Further Consideration

- Why is it important to have a well stocked nonfiction library in the classroom?

- What experiences have you had in using digital technologies to enhance literacy instruction?

- Ask a group of children to provide you with possible questions to study. What would be your next step in planning an inquiry curriculum to support their questions?

Working with Struggling Readers and Writers

Rakwaun can be described in one word, *eager*. Eager to be involved, eager to please, eager to learn. It is easy to be overlooked in a classroom of 34 students, especially when 98% of the students are classified as below the poverty line and your classroom is located in an urban, public school labeled "failing." Rakwaun is anything but overlooked, partially because of his enthusiasm for being involved and partially because the "failing" label assigned to this school does little to describe the authentic learning taking place within its walls.

Being a "failing" school does have its advantages. In Chicago, schools with this label are given a literacy coach to work with students and teachers. This role is loosely defined and takes a different shape throughout the district. Literacy coaches are required to offer professional development for teachers and assist in classrooms to ensure that students are receiving appropriate literacy instruction.

As a literacy coach, I work in many classrooms with a variety of students and teachers at different places in their literacy development. Some days I model a lesson for a teacher, and other days I work with a small group of students who need additional support and help in literacy. No matter what my purpose when entering the classroom, "eager" is my favorite kind of teacher and student to work with. This makes our fourth grade classroom one of my favorite places to be. There you will find Rakwaun with his hand up, whether he is seated in the front row, back corner, or working with a small group on the floor. You will also see his teacher learning right along with her students.

I can walk into this classroom any time during the instructional day and see literacy development interwoven into activities and curriculum—whether it's science, math, or language arts. Charts filled with Post-it notes display student thinking and cover the walls. Students have independent reading boxes on their desks, which contain books they have chosen to read, and their reader's and writer's notebooks to record thoughts they may have while reading these books. Books in clearly labeled baskets can be found to meet readers' needs. Strategies are listed on how to choose the right book for one's reading. Students are invited to explore nonfiction books, favorite fourth grade classics, as well as books in languages other than English. These teaching tools are used and used often. The books in the reading boxes have Post-it notes overflowing from between the pages and the charts are layered five or six deep in places where a new topic is added right over the previous as the wall space has been exhausted.

I support the fourth grade teacher by conferencing with individual students. These conferences take place during the reader/writer workshop time. While they are a time investment, there are great benefits as teachers begin to know their students in more complex ways. Rakwaun is one student that benefits greatly from such conference time. Rakwaun was given the Qualitative Reading Inventory at his grade level and he performed quite poorly. Although his oral reading is confident and with much expression, and he self-corrects for sentence fluency, Rakwaun's comprehension scores give him a lower than grade level status. He shows weakness in all areas including story retelling and implicit and explicit question answering. Through conferring with Rakwaun, his strong desire to please becomes apparent.

One of the drawbacks of his motivation to please is that he places all of his focus on reading perfectly and none of his efforts on understanding what he is reading. Rakwaun's need to please goes further—he will not admit that he does not know an answer to a question. Rakwaun invents stories based upon what he remembers, which is often just a title, and then answers all questions as if this is the story he has just read. A teacher who has been communicating with Rakwaun will quickly see a disconnect when someone like myself offers the scores on the latest assessment they have administered. Reading and writing conferences offer a whole look into the student as an individual and help to guide development.

Literacy coaches also are available to help plan for instruction. After administering formal assessments to Rakwaun and some of his classmates and conferring with them about their reading and writing, I can now plan with Mrs. Buttle, the fourth grade teacher, to help meet the needs of these unique learners in her classroom. The formal assessments tell me that Rakwaun needs to work on self-monitoring skills. I accomplish this by modeling how I monitor my own reading. I place a short passage on the overhead projector. After reading a section of it, I stop and write a reflection of what I had just read on a sticky note. If I can't do this, I reread what I just read. After Rakwaun has time to practice this, I role play with him to show him how to do this while reading orally with a partner. A section is read orally then the reader or listener does the retelling. These mini-lessons do not need to take long and can be done for a small group of students or even for the entire class. The goal is for these students to have a specific strategy to practice during their own reading.

Ms. Buttle and I want to encourage Rakwaun's interest in reading and writing about nonfiction. Rakwaun may need to focus on expanding his writing of nonfiction texts. His writer's notebook offers many short entries. Some on the same topic; many on nonfiction. Rakwaun knows a lot about spiders, so this is a good topic for him to write about. Students cannot write about what they do not know. Rakwaun's piece about "Extremely Weird Spiders" can be used as an example to show how he can look inside his writing to find places to go into further detail. In a conference with Rakwaun, we read through

I wonder. . .

- What role does Mrs. Laughlin play in supporting the literacy development in this fourth grade classroom?

- What are the structures that Rakwaun's teacher has in place to support his growth and development in literacy?

- How does Rakwaun's teacher demonstrate that she values what he brings to the literacy event and to learning?

March 30, 2006

Dear Mrs. Buttle,

The book I'm reading now is Extremely Weird Spiders By: Sarah Lovett. The book is nice because it tells me where spiders live and what they do.

Also, did you ever know that books can teach you diffrent facts? Yep, it sholl can like for enstence, a wolf spider has 8 eyes! I thought all spiders had 2. Another example, a black widow spider has a family called the Theridindae. I thoght spiders lived on there own.

Thats why I say books can teach us to, no afence but they can. Maby thats why you have us read every night. Write back soon!

Sincerely,
Your Student
Rakwaun H.

Rakwaun's writing notebook entry.

Dear Rakwaun,

What genre is Extremely Weird Spiders? You seem to have learned a lot about spiders from this book. Do you think you know a lot more about spiders because of this book? I read a lot of books on Spain. I have history books on Spain, geography books on Spain, and so much more. It is my favorite country. Since I have read so much about Spain, I am almost an expert. Do you think you could read more books about spiders so you could be an expert? I also write about Spain a lot because I know so much. Maybe you can use what you have learned and write about that in your writer's notebook.

Rakwaun's teacher's response in the notebook.

this piece and look for topics to read more about. Rakwaun could read and write about orb weavers, types of webs, other weird spiders, and so forth. Once he sees that he already has the seeds of writing in his notebook, he can create a complete piece of writing on spiders; Rakwaun can go back into his notebook to begin this new piece.

Chapter Overview

Children in preschool through grade six are learning to read and write a variety of texts and materials in different contexts. Throughout the chapters in this book there have been multiple discussions on ways to organize and structure a literacy curriculum that effectively meets the needs of all readers and writers in the classroom. The four resource model attends to all aspects of the reading process and the reader/writer workshop structure provides the flexibility (both in terms of materials and in lessons) needed to develop a literacy curriculum that is authentic and meaningful. For students like Rakwaun, a reader/writer workshop forum provides opportunities to explore and draft texts that have captured students' interests. While Rakwaun appears as a struggling reader on some assessment measures and may be targeted for additional support, the reading conferences provide his teacher and the literacy coach with other views of him that demonstrate how much he is capable of doing.

This chapter extends the conversation about literacy practices and development to consider what it might mean to be a struggling reader and/or writer. Guiding questions include:

- What are the different ways in which students may struggle with reading and writing?
- What role does motivation and engagement play in supporting struggling readers and writers?
- What strategies are most effective for increasing students' motivation and engagement?
- What intervention programs are successful for struggling readers and writers?
- What does it mean to teach literacy to all children?

Factors that contribute to struggling reading and writing

In every classroom there are children for whom literacy practices are a struggle. Termed "at risk," "struggling," "slow readers," "poor readers," or "remedial readers," these ***struggling readers*** are often one or more years below their respective grade level as determined by a battery of assessments, both formal (criterion-referenced tests) and informal (teacher observation, anecdotal notes). When students reach the intermediate and upper grades, reading is a precursor for completing many of the tasks in the classroom. If students are unable to read and write proficiently, their academic performance begins to spiral downwards. They are likely to experience frustration as they move into middle school and beyond. What are some factors that may impinge upon a student's abilities to be successful in reading and writing? Cognitive processing, motivation, and teacher beliefs and attitudes are three possible factors.

struggling reader

Usually one or more years behind their grade level.

Cognitive processing

Cognitive processing difficulties influence the extent to which a student understands a given text. Some students struggle with code breaking practices. They may not recognize many words or have much knowledge of letter–sound relationships. Other students may find that text participant practices are difficult—they are able to say the words but meaning is not attached to those words. They do not know that reading should make sense, or that they should use their prior background and context to determine what is coming next in the text. And still other readers may not know how to set goals, recognize that text is structured differently for different purposes, or how to apply fix-it strategies when comprehension breaks down (Worthy and Invernizzi, 1995; Hall, 2007). Cognitive processing difficulties may be evident when students are not able to initiate purpose, recognize meaning, sample details, connect facts, select important sentences, predict, infer, make connections, engage in self-correcting behaviors, and retain what is read or written (Ruddell & Ruddell, 1994). Table 12.1 highlights the difference between struggling and effective literacy users in key aspects of the reading process.

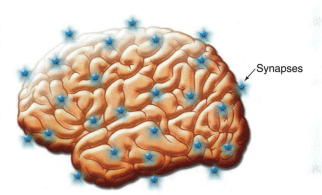

Synapses

Connections (synapses) between the brain's cells (neurons) create neural networks (a collection of associated neurons through synapses). It is these neural networks that provide the foundation to perception and the ability to learn.

Motivation and engagement

In addition to cognitive processing difficulties, motivation and engagement also play a significant role in how struggling readers respond to literacy events and practices. A number of researchers (Guthrie & Wigfield, 2000; O'Flahavan, Gambrell, Guthrie,

TABLE 12.1

Differences between Struggling and Proficient Literacy Users.

Reading and Writing Skills	Struggling Reader and Writer		Proficient Reader and Writer
Word Identification	Limited	→	Automatic
Vocabulary	Underdeveloped	→	Proficient
Fluency	Disjointed	→	Effortless
Comprehension	Narrow	→	Expansive

Stahl & Alvermann, 1992; Veenman, 1984) have concluded that lack of motivation is a primary concern for many classroom teachers. Oldfather (1993) suggests that motivation can make the difference between learning that is temporary and superficial and learning that is permanent and internalized.

Struggling readers are seemingly unmotivated and lack self-confidence in their abilities to read and write. They very often have a negative history towards reading and writing. This history plays a role in how students see themselves as readers and writers, and how they respond to new literacy events in the classroom. Sometimes students will use avoidance and/or disruptive behaviors to draw attention away from the fact that they are not reading (Guthrie & Davis, 2003; Hall, 2007). They may procrastinate and deliberately avoid putting forth any effort.

Students with low motivation and engagement are also faced with low self-confidence and low self-esteem around literacy. They are aware that their curricular choices and texts are not the same as their peers and begin to doubt their own abilities to succeed in literacy related activities and tasks. As they continue to struggle, they begin to develop expectations that reading and writing are too hard and that they are unable to participate. This lack of self-efficacy impacts the decisions that students make around literacy. They may say to themselves that there is no reason to continue reading because they are not going to succeed.

Lack of involvement in literacy practices is initially seen as why they are struggling. But as students get older they begin to attribute their struggles to luck, task or text difficulty, or the availability of help (McElroy, Goetze, & Beach, 1997; Shell, Colvin, & Bruning, 1995). A cycle develops, whereby at-risk readers and writers struggle. Because they are not engaged in the reading and writing materials, they are not working on various skills and strategies to improve their abilities. The challenge then is how to effectively break the cycle and teach students that exhibit some cognitive processing difficulties and/or motivation difficulties to become effective and proficient readers and writers.

The National Reading Research Center (1997) identified a number of key ideas related to motivation and reading:

- Engaged readers are knowledgeable, strategic, motivated, and socially interactive.
- Instruction should be systematic and integrated with quality literature.
- Motivation to read and reading ability are a synergistic, mutually reinforcing phenomenon.
- Thinking and talking about books promote children's critical understandings of what they read.
- The use of multiple texts, as opposed to a single textbook, fosters students' interests.
- Using analogies between unfamiliar and familiar concepts aids students' learning.

TECHNOLOGY LINK
http://www.ala.org/ala/ya
lsa/booklistsawards/quick
picks/07qp.htm

This site identifies books that teenagers will pick up on their own and read for pleasure. The list is geared to the teenager who, for whatever reason, does not like to read.

intrinsically motivated
Seek reading and writing because of personal interest and desire.

extrinsically motivated
Seek rewards and praise when engaged in reading and writing.

Ultimately, providing students with the skill to read and learn is not enough. Students must also develop the intrinsic motivation to read and learn. *Intrinsically motivated* readers and writers are those that seek reading and writing because of personal interest and desires to learn, relax, escape or empathize (Block, 2003). *Extrinsically motivated* readers and writers work for rewards and praise from others, such as Pizza Hut's BookIt program and Accelerated Reader points. What teachers strive for is developing readers and writers that have a love of learning and begin to develop their own reasons for reading and writing.

Did you know . . .

More than 20 percent of adults read at or below a fifth grade level—far below the level needed to earn a living wage (National Institute for Literacy, Fast Facts on Literacy, 2001).

Good readers in fifth grade may read 10 times as many words as poor readers over a school year (Nagy and Anderson, 1984).

According to the 2003 National Assessment of Educational Progress (NAEP), 37 percent of fourth graders and 26 percent of eighth graders cannot read at the basic level; and on the 2002 NAEP 26 percent of twelfth graders cannot read at the basic level. That is, when reading grade appropriate text these students cannot extract the general meaning or make obvious connections between the text and their own experiences or make simple inferences from the text. In other words, they cannot understand what they have read. (National Assessment of Educational Progress).

Out-of-school reading habits of students has shown that even 15 minutes a day of independent reading can expose students to more than a million words of text in a year (Anderson, Wilson, & Fielding, 1988).

Forty-four percent of American fourth grade students cannot read fluently, even when they read grade-level stories aloud under supportive testing conditions (NAEP, Pinnell et. al, 1995).

Teacher beliefs and attitudes

In addition to the difficulties students may have in cognitive processing and motivation, teacher beliefs and attitudes play a role in how students see themselves as readers and writers. Teachers' practices are firmly rooted in their beliefs about teaching and learning. Recall in Chapter 4 how ideologies about teaching and learning set the stage for the types of theories and curriculum that are made available for students. The type of curriculum then shapes how students view literacy practices. For struggling readers, the teacher's beliefs and attitudes may be even more prominent.

Teachers need to have opportunities to articulate their beliefs when working with struggling readers and writers. Maxson (1996) found that when the teachers in her study were provided opportunities to articulate their strongly held beliefs about learning in general, and struggling readers in particular, they very often were implanting practices that aligned with their beliefs. Many of the teachers held onto an "all children can learn" belief and as a result sought out additional resources, strategies, and methods to best meet the needs of the children. Teachers that work to meet the children where they are at (linguistically, cognitively, socially) will offer a diverse range of methods, pedagogy, and environments, with a singular goal of meeting students' needs.

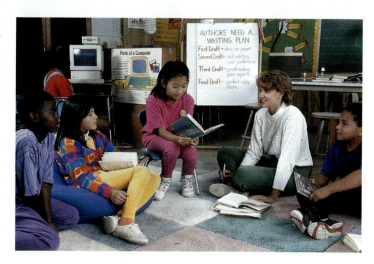

In the next section, reader characteristics and behaviors are identified as well as the evidence a teacher may use to determine students' needs. Following that, a discussion of how to implement a reader/writer workshop structure to support struggling readers and writers, as a possibility of accelerating the learning for these students is offered.

📖 Identifying struggling readers and writers during literacy events

Teachers draw upon a number of sources of information to determine if students are struggling with texts and/or literacy events. This information comes from state reading tests, miscue analysis, qualitative reading inventories, running records, reading and writing interviews, reading and writing conferences, retellings, and kidwatching notes. For example, Ms. Galfi uses some of her time during reader/writer workshop to take notes and confer with her students to determine if there are any issues or concerns she needs to be aware of. On one particular day early in the school year, Ms. Galfi noticed that DeAnna was just sitting there, staring off into space as the other kids bent anxiously over their books and reading logs. A few minutes into the workshop time, DeAnna insisted that she needed to use the bathroom. Ms. Galfi has noticed that DeAnna frequently asks to go to the bathroom during workshop time, so she decided to conference with her the following day. During the conference, she asked DeAnna to make a list of the kinds of things she liked to read and write. DeAnna said that she liked flowers and horses. Ms. Galfi asked DeAnna to write down the words *flowers* and *horses*. DeAnna stared blankly at her. "What sound do you hear at the beginning of *flowers*?" Ms. Galfi asked. "Ffff," DeAnna replied making the /f/ sound. She then said,

"What letter makes that sound?" "F," said DeAnna. "Right, *flower* starts with an F, so start by writing that down." Again, her comment was met with a blank stare. She began to wonder if DeAnna knew how to write an "F," so she told her to look at the alphabet above the chalkboard to find the letter F and copy it down. DeAnna was not able to pick it out from the other letters until Ms. Galfi pointed out the picture of the fish right above it. Ms. Galfi recorded this information on her observation sheet. She will use the knowledge from this conference to develop strategies for providing additional support and help for DeAnna. She decided that DeAnna would benefit from opportunities to participate in shared reading experiences, where she could focus on letter–sound patterns, including onsets and rimes.

What other characteristics and behaviors might struggling readers and writers exhibit? Literacy researchers (Valencia, Riddle, & Buly, 2004; Weaver, 2002) have identified and labeled these behaviors and the possible evidence for such actions. In most cases, readers are not weak in all areas of the reading process (e.g., word identification, comprehension, fluency), but are generally challenged in one area. Table 12.2 lists the characteristics and the types of evidence that teachers may use in determining possible teaching strategies to further support struggling literacy users.

TABLE 12.2
Struggling Reader Characteristics and Possible Evidence

	Reader Characteristics	Possible Evidence that a Reader May be Struggling
Automatic Word Caller	Reader doesn't seem to know that reading should make sense. Reader is able to decode words quickly and for the most part accurately.	• Word identification is strong, usually at or above grade level. • Reader cannot tell much about the selection even if the selection is appropriate for the reader's prior knowledge.
Struggling Word Caller	Reader struggles with both word identification and meaning. Reader has uneven expression and phrasing. Reader doesn't seem to know that reading should make sense.	• Reader sounds out a lot of words and settles for words that don't fit the context. • Reader cannot tell much about the selection even if the selection is appropriate for the reader's prior knowledge. • Reader says she or he can't read.
Word Stumbler	Reader doesn't recognize many words or have much knowledge of letter–sound patterns. Reader overrelies on context to determine words. Reader's initial attempts at reading are choppy and slow.	• Reader tells the story more from the pictures than the words on the page. • Reader skips or misreads a huge portion of the words. • Reader substitutes many words to preserve meaning. • Reader says s/he can't read.
Slow Comprehender	Reader doesn't seem to monitor comprehension. Reader has good word knowledge and understands that reading should make sense.	• Miscues often do not fit the grammar or meaning. • Reader does not automatically decode multisyllabic words. • Reader cannot tell what the selection is about, even texts that are appropriate to his or her interests. • Reader says that she or he doesn't like to read.
Slow Word Caller	Reader doesn't read fluently or efficiently. Reader lacks confidence and often thinks that reading means saying all the words correctly.	• Reader reads in a monotone, reads through punctuation marks and otherwise reads aloud without appropriate intonation for an audience. • Reader struggles again and again to get each word not recognized on sight.

Instructional practices for struggling readers and writers

There is a perception that struggling readers and writers are deficit in some way (e.g., linguistically, cognitively, socioeconomically) and that they need to be remediated prior to receiving regular class instruction. Struggling readers and writers are often supplied with a remedial curriculum. They are regularly provided a curriculum that is watered down, slowed down, presented in a more isolated fashion and focuses on specific skills and drills (Johnston & Allington, 1991). Struggling readers also experience a curriculum that emphasizes code breaking and phonics at the expense of text participant and critical practices. There are very few opportunities for students that struggle with reading to work on meaning making strategies. Additionally, Roller (1996) notes that struggling readers are provided less wait time for self correction to take place as compared to proficient readers. Teachers and others

TECHNOLOGY LINK
http://www.learner.org/
channel/workshops/
teachreading35/session7/
index.html.

In this session, literacy expert Dorothy Strickland discusses key elements of
effective instruction that
build on student diversity
and promote effective learning. You will learn strategies
for differentiating instruction to maximize learning
for all of your students.

will immediately jump in and provide the appropriate word for the struggling reader rather than allowing the student to try out various reading strategies to decode and make sense of the word. More of the same but at a slower pace does very little to enhance a struggling reader's self-confidence. Students are quite aware of the differences in each other's curriculum and expectations. For the struggling reader, she or he may feel even less motivated and engaged in literacy practices. The slower pace continues to push these students farther and farther behind, thereby creating even more of an academic gap between those that struggle and those that are proficient.

A reader/writer workshop structure is an appropriate structure to support struggling readers and writers in the classroom. Because there is flexibility within the structure and all students are not completing the same tasks and activities at the same time, it is more difficult for classmates to signal out those that are struggling. With a focus on personalizing instruction to meet the needs of each individual, teachers can implement a range of literacy strategies to attend to the varied strengths and needs that each student displays. For struggling readers, teachers can take a closer look at the role of interest and background and scaffolding in motivating struggling readers. They can also modify read alouds, independent reading time, and comprehension monitoring strategies.

Interest and background

Interest and background knowledge play an important role in readers' abilities to make sense of text. Interest fosters a desire to know more, while background knowledge on the topic enables readers to draw upon what they already know to support comprehension. When students are interested and engaged in the topic or material, they often can read texts that are above their normal reading level. Children who indicate they are interested in the text are also more likely to "try harder" and say they "want to learn more." (Mizelle, 1997, p. 16). This is why struggling readers need to explore a range of texts and not be relegated to a particular reading level as determined by a prescriptive program. It is important for teachers to be knowledgeable about students' interests. Recall in Chapter 3 how Ms. White provided Jacob with books and websites on soccer because she was aware of his interests through questionnaires and interest inventories. Jacob responded by actively reading and engaging with the materials.

All children like to be considered experts at something and so this is a great avenue to explore with struggling readers and writers. They are not often seen as experts due to their inabilities to effectively read (and this skill clouds the judgment of many, peers and teachers included). When struggling readers and writers are seen as experts, they gain much needed confidence. Ms. Carrier, a third grade teacher, invites students to share their interests and passions with the class community. She has numerous occasions throughout the instructional day where students share and talk with each other. This sharing enables students to make visible their own interests. Ms. Carrier records these interests, and as opportunities become available she asks students to become resident experts. Recently, Ms Carrier noted that one of her struggling readers paid particularly close attention during morning meeting when the topic of caring for the class pets (fish and hamsters) came up. The students were reading an article in the Weekly Reader about how to care for exotic pets and Tobias talked a lot about caring for his own pets at home (turtle and a dog). Ms. Carrier asked Tobias if he could create a checklist that shows how much work he does to care for his animals. Tobias agreed and in the process of creating the checklist, he

FIGURE 12.1 Tobias' materials on caring for pets.

went to the school media specialist for suggestions on books and websites that provide information on caring for pets. Tobias brought these materials into the classroom and shared with his classmates some information he learned (Fig. 12.1). As a result of noticing Tobias' interest, Ms. Carrier provided Tobias with a way into literacy and encouraged him to continue learning more about animal care.

Read alouds to extend comprehension

Struggling readers, particularly in the intermediate and upper grades, can usually comprehend and appreciate texts that are far more demanding than what they can read on their own. Read alouds can be used to engage students in comprehension strategies because they encourage active participation through open-ended questions. Students can be exposed to texts that are interesting and will help prepare them for materials that they will likely experience as their word identification improves (Ganske, Monroe, & Strickland, 2003). During read-aloud events, teachers can model comprehension strategies through think alouds and explicit demonstrations of what good readers do when reading. Think alouds require a reader to stop periodically, reflect on what is happening in the text, and relate orally what reading strategies are being used. "By thinking aloud during a read aloud, teachers can demonstrate the kind of self-questioning, reacting, and visualizing in which they engage (e.g., *I'm wondering* why the little boy keeps asking this question; or *I'm confused* by that idea, so *I'll read it over again*; or *I'm picturing* the dark clouds in the sky.)(Ganske, Monroe, & Strickland, 2003, pp.123–24).

Teachers can also read aloud authors that write across levels of difficulty (e.g., Cynthia Rylant, Lois Lowry, Tomi DePaola). The teacher can read the more difficult text during a read aloud and invite students that need more support to read other stories by the author for independent reading time.

Independent reading time

For struggling readers and writers, independent reading and writing time is usually not their favorite time of the day. It can be seen as an extension of time spent on the very skill they struggle with. To support struggling readers and writers during

Invitation for the classroom

Think Aloud

The "Think-Aloud" strategy helps students make predictions about the text; compare and contrast events, ideas, and characters; visualize the information that is described in the text; and make connections to prior knowledge. It is important for teachers to model how to engage in a think aloud.

Provide students with a passage from a text they are currently reading. As you read it aloud, stop periodically and comment. There are a variety of responses that you can make, including imagery/visual responses, making connections to personal experiences, making connections to other texts, predictions, stating confusion, and stating understanding.

Ask students to reflect on the types of comments and responses you made while reading. Students can create bookmarks to remind them of the different responses they can make.

Have students work in small groups and practice thinking aloud as they read various passages from a text.

independent reading and writing time, teachers can modify the time to better meet students' needs. One possibility is to create buddy reading partnerships. When grouping students into pairs, it is ideal if the pairs are comprised of an intermediate or upper grade struggling reader with a primary grade reader. This arrangement allows the older reader to be a reading model for the younger student. Most often the materials selected for this reading event are easy books (ones that younger readers enjoy). The struggling older reader now has a purpose for reading easy books. Before reading the book to the younger reader, the struggling reader should practice (as all professional readers do before reading to an audience). This enables the struggling reader to work on fluency in an authentic manner. The buddy reading partnership provides the necessary purpose for engaging struggling readers in reading and for building self-esteem around literacy practices.

Teachers can combine shared and independent reading time, so that while some students are actively reading on their own, struggling readers may be receiving additional instruction with the teacher. Teachers can use shared reading as a time to provide explicit instruction on phonics, comprehension, and/or fluency work. See Figure 12.1 for additional suggestions for promoting independent reading with struggling readers.

Scheduling easy reading time to gain confidence

All readers in the classroom need time during the instructional day to read texts and materials that are below their instructional level. Teachers can coordinate this time to bring together students that are struggling with more proficient readers so that there are good reading models available for struggling students to observe.

> **A Selection of Books to Use with Buddy Reading Partnerships**
>
> Adams, A. (1971). *A Woggle of Witches*. New York: Scribner.
> Barrett, J. (1970). *Animals Should Definitely Not Wear Clothing*. New York: Antheneum.
> Brown, M. (1995). *Arthur's Christmas Cookies*. Boston: Little, Brown.
> Carle, E. (1995). *The Fireflies*. New York: Harcourt.
> DeRegniers, B.S. (1964). *May I Bring a Friend?* New York: Antheneum.
> Emberley, B.A. (1995). *Drummer Hoff*. New York: Simon & Schuster.
> Hogrogian, N. (1971). *One Fine Day*. New York: McMillian.
> Hogrogian, N. (1995). *Good Night, Owl*. New York: Simon & Schuster.
> Keats, E. (1962). *The Snowy Day*. New York: Viking.
> Keats, E. (1965). *Peter's Chair*. New York: Harper & Row.
> Kellogg, S. (1973). *Leo, The Late Bloomer*. New York: Dutton.
> Lobel, A. (1968). *The Comic Adventures of Old Mother Hubbard and Her Dog*. New York: Bradbury.
> Sendak, M. (1963). *Where the Wild Things Are*. New York: Harper & Row.
> Sendak, M. (1973). *Noisy Nora*. New York: Dial.

In Ms. Elrod's fourth grade classroom, she has students meet with her after recess for 15 minutes to share in some easy fun reading. The group changes each day, but Ms. Elrod ensures that her most struggling students are a part of the group on a more frequent basis. Because she includes her stronger, more proficient readers in the group, the students do not suspect that this work was for the "low group." As the children come in from recess they check the white board to see if their name is listed. If it is, they meet in the library corner. If their name is not listed, they continue reading their independent selection. The materials that Ms. Elrod has in the basket are easy picture books that students are familiar with. While the children are reading the books, Ms. Elrod does not work with students on comprehension. She may talk with them about figuring out unfamiliar words but the intention is for student to gain confidence in their reading.

TECHNOLOGY LINK

http://childrensbooks.about.com/od/toppicks/tp/hi_lo_books.htm

Booklists for reluctant readers. The books are at the reader's interest level (**"hi"** stands for "high interest") but written at a lower reading level (**"lo"** stands for "low readability") to encourage reading. Kids and teens reading below grade level are more apt to want to read a book if it is not only at their reading level but also at their interest level.

hi/lo books

Books that are high interest but written at a lower reading ability.

FIGURE 12.1
Promoting Independent Reading with Struggling Readers

- Create a classroom library that contains books for all reading abilities, from two years below to at least two years above grade level.
- Increase the number of nonfiction texts in the classroom library. Nonfiction books are often high interest and contain text features (headings, graphics, pictures) that support reading.
- Conduct book talks on easier books. Students like to read books that teachers enjoy and recommend.
- Encourage reading books in a series. Series books enable students to use their knowledge of characters to make sense of new plots and situations.
- Allow time for students to present their own books in book talks.

A Selection of Books for Reluctant Readers in Grades 4 through 6

Avi (1993) *Nothing But the Truth*. Avon Flare Books
  A student's suspension for singing "The Star-Spangled Banner" in homeroom becomes a national issue.
Brooks, Bruce (1993) *Boys Will Be*. H.Holt
  Celebrates being a boy and discusses a variety of "boy stuff", including caps, sports, mothers, and friends.
Bunting, Eve (1991) *The Hideout*. Hucourt Brace Jovanovich
  Andy hides out in a luxurious San Francisco hotel and stages his own kidnapping.
Byars, Betsy. (1988) *The Pinballs*. ABC-Clio
  Three lonely foster children are tired of being bumped from home to home like pinballs.
Clements, Andrew (1996) *Frindle*. Simon & Schuster Books
  Nick invents a new word to combat a teacher's love of the dictionary and things quickly get out of hand.
Coville, Bruce (1993) *Aliens Ate My Homework*. Pocket Books
  A tiny spaceship lands in Rod's science project and aliens ask his help in catching an interstellar criminal.
Fleischman, Paul (2004) *Seedfolks*. Harper Trophy
  A trash-filled inner city lot turned into a productive garden beautifies a city block and changes city souls.
Howe, Deborah (2006) *Bunnicula*. Aladdin Paperbooks
  Chester the cat tries to warn his human family that their new bunny is a vampire.
Levine, Gail Carson (1997) *Ella Enchanted*. HarperCollins
  Ella struggles against the childhood curse that forces her to obey any order given to her.
MacLachlan, Patricia (1991) *Journey*. Delacorte Press
  Abandoned by his mother, Journey feels his past has been erased until his grandfather restores it to him.
Paulsen, Gary (1999) *Hatchet*. Aladdin Paperbooks
  After a plane crash, Brian learns how to survive in the wilderness with only the aid of a hatchet.
Scieszka, Jon (1995) *The Time Warp Trio* series.Viking
  Three boys find themselves taking hilarious trips through time due to the gift of a mysterious book.
Spinelli, Jerry (2004) *Maniac Magee*. Little, Brown, & Co
  After his parents die, Jeffrey Lionel Magee's life becomes legendary for athletic and other feats.
Yolen, Jane (1990) *The Devil's Arithmetic*. Puffin Books
  Time travel places Hannah in the middle of a small Jewish village in Nazi-occupied Poland.

Scaffolding

scaffolding

Individual support to help bridge the gap between what a learner knows and can do with what a learner needs to know in order to succeed.

Scaffolding is often used to describe actions that teachers take to provide support and guidance to struggling readers. Because less-accomplished readers and writers tend to engage in literacy events that they are already familiar with, scaffolding provides opportunities for these students to engage in new tasks. In many instances, ***scaffolding*** refers to the activity before, during, and after a reading event that is intended to help a struggling or novice reader. Similar to the scaffolding that is on a building, a teacher's scaffolding should be gradually withdrawn as a student develops independent reading skills and strategies. Graves and Graves (1994) suggest that scaffolding should be treated as "a flexible framework that provides a set of options from which you select those that are best suited for a particular group of students reading a particular text for a particular purpose" (p. 5). Figure 12.2 offers a framework for considering the level of scaffolding needed in a particular literacy event.

When teachers provide appropriate scaffolding to struggling readers and writers, they create a learning environment that presents challenges in a supportive context; provides security through successful risk taking on a daily basis; and includes opportunities for students to begin assuming responsibility for their learning (Block, 2003).

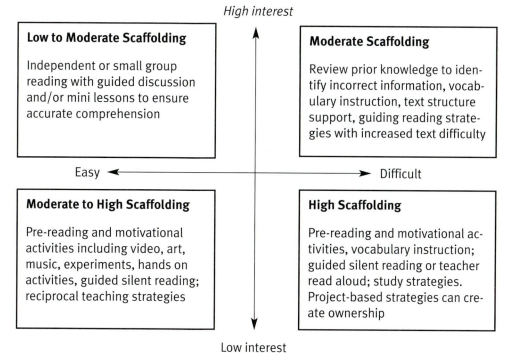

High interest

Low to Moderate Scaffolding

Independent or small group reading with guided discussion and/or mini lessons to ensure accurate comprehension

Moderate Scaffolding

Review prior knowledge to identify incorrect information, vocabulary instruction, text structure support, guiding reading strategies with increased text difficulty

Easy ← ——————————————→ Difficult

Moderate to High Scaffolding

Pre-reading and motivational activities including video, art, music, experiments, hands on activities, guided silent reading; reciprocal teaching strategies

High Scaffolding

Pre-reading and motivational activities, vocabulary instruction; guided silent reading or teacher read aloud; study strategies. Project-based strategies can create ownership

Low interest

FIGURE 12.2 Levels of Scaffolding
Figure by Dorie Combs (2004)

Comprehension monitoring strategies

A significant issue with struggling readers is their inability to effectively comprehend text. Harris and Hodges (1995) note that comprehension is the "intentional thinking during which meaning is constructed through interactions with text and reader" (pg. 207). As identified in the listing of characteristics of struggling readers, students may be able to effectively decode words and read with some fluency, but are unable to retell what was read or comprehend with any degree of success. There are a number of strategies that students can engage in to monitor their own comprehension and notice when it is breaking down. Figure 12.3 is a flow chart developed by Jeff Wilhelm that students can use to monitor their comprehension. This flow chart can be adapted for any level of reader and is useful to have hanging as a reminder for students, or as a book mark for students to refer to when they sense their comprehension is breaking down.

All students can use the identified strategies that support struggling readers. They are designed to be implemented in reader/writer workshop structures, whereby the teacher is working in small groups and individually with students. Because the reader/writer workshop structure enables students to grow and develop as individual readers and writers, teachers can more directly attend to the individual needs of each student. Some students require more time to process the information, while others struggle when reading particular formats or genres of text. The

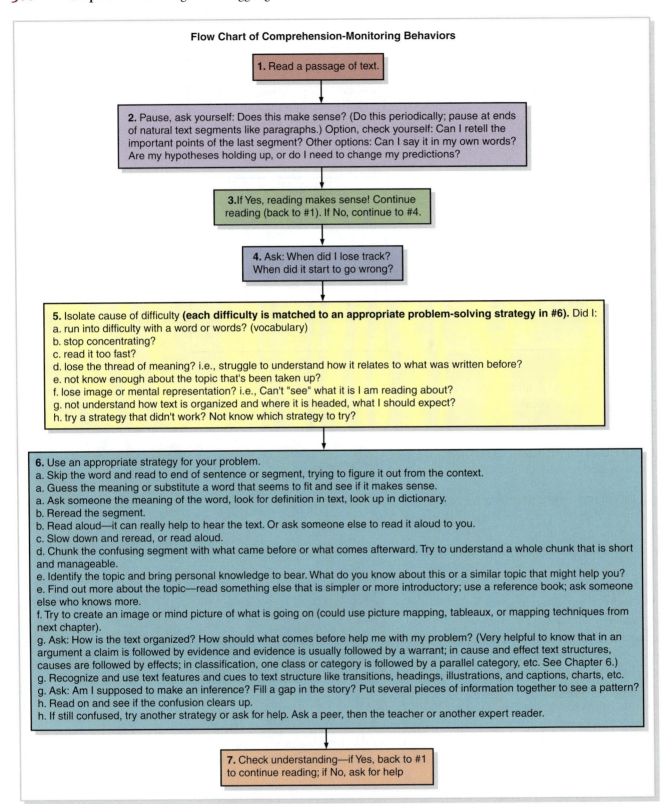

FIGURE 12.3 Flow Chart to Help Students Monitor Their Comprehension.

Flow chart by Jeff Wilhelm
http://content.scholastic.com/content/collateral_resources/pdf/r/reading_bestpractices_comprehension_flowchartofbehavior.pdf .

Invitation for the classroom

Main Idea Questioning

This strategy lesson, helps children manage the complex series of information-processing tasks involved in proficient reading. Readers are asked to think about the meaning of a text as it is read.

While students are reading a paragraph of their text, ask them to:

THINK: Think as you read each sentence: What is the author saying?
BUILD: Put the ideas together and build meaning.
SUMMARIZE: What is the main idea of the text?
QUESTION: Choose a question word (who, what, when, where, why, how) and build a question about the main idea of the text.
ASK: Ask your main-idea question and consider the answer.

Adapted from Lubliner (2004).

Invitation for the classroom

Reflecting Questions Back to the Student

Reflecting questions back to students asks them to (a) elaborate, (b) think metacognitively, (c) solve problems, and (d) support their answers.

Elaboration

Does this make you think of anything else you read?
Did you like this more or less than the last thing you read? Why?
What parts of this text did you particularly like?
If you had a chance to talk to the author, what would you say?
Why is this an important story to share?

Metacognition

How would you feel if _____ happened?
Why did you choose this selection to read?
Can you describe your thinking?
What do you know that you did not know before reading this?
Did your thoughts and feelings change?

Problem Solving

What do you need to do next?
How did you solve this problem?
What do you do when you get stuck?
What do you do when you don't understand the content?
Can you think of another way we could do this?

Supporting Answers

Why is this one better than that one?
What are your reasons for saying that?
How did you know that?
Do you have good evidence for believing that?
What did you (or author) mean by _____?

Adapted from C.C. Block (2003).

reader/writer workshop supports this variation as flexible grouping routines are implemented, text sets are provided, and students have ample time to participate in uninterrupted reading and writing.

In the best case scenario, there will continue to be students who struggle with school-based literacy events and tasks. In some districts, there is more pressure to perform to established state standards. When schools do not achieve these benchmarks, districts may implement whole school reform efforts to combat the perceived failing status of a school. The next section describes reform efforts that are centered on literacy development and achievement.

> ### Creating Connections 12.1
>
> Think about a student who may be struggling with reading and writing. As you consider the actions and behaviors of the student, what initial actions can you take to support this reader or writer in classroom literacy events?
>
> Share your thinking with classmates on your blog.

Literacy reform efforts for struggling schools

adequate yearly progress (AYP)

The minimum level of improvement that states, school districts, and schools must achieve each year.

School systems and districts are under enormous pressure to achieve ***adequate yearly progress (AYP)*** as determined by various measures including standardized tests in reading and mathematics. Many schools, particularly those in high-needs urban settings, do not achieve AYP and are required to develop a school improvement plan to address the areas of concern. The school improvement plan often includes a literacy reform effort that focuses on early literacy and ways to increase academic achievement.

Five of the most widely disseminated "off the shelf" reform models include *Reading Recovery, Literacy Collaborative, Four Blocks, Success for All (SFA),* and *America's Choice.* Two of the five reform models (SFA and America's Choice) are school-wide initiatives that include literacy materials, professional development for teachers, and trained coaches to monitor implementation. Other similarities across the models include:

- a substantial amount of time for the literacy block (90 minutes to 2 hours),
- a mixture of whole class and small group instruction, regular phonics practice, and
- the use of leveled or simplified texts for beginning reading.

In the next section, each major literacy reform model is described.

Reading Recovery

Reading Recovery, developed by Marie Clay (www.readingrecovery.org), is an early intervention program designed to help the lowest achieving first graders. Students receive intensive one-on-one daily tutoring for a period of up to 20 weeks. The daily sessions last thirty minutes. A Reading Recovery teacher

---

Characteristics of Literacy Reform Efforts Designed to Increase Success for Struggling Readers and Writers

- **Early intervention.** The primary grades (K–2) are often the target for many intervention programs. Identifying students early in the process will help to close the academic gap between those that struggle and those that do not. Screening assessments are conducted to identify children who are behind the prerequisite literacy and language-related skills.

- **Systematic reading program.** Reform efforts have in place a systematic reading program that contains essential components of the reading process. The content is carefully sequenced within a grade level and across grade levels.

- **Explicit lesson delivery.** Instruction is highly explicit. Student performance is carefully monitored and corrections are immediately provided to prevent children from developing serious error patterns or misconceptions.

- **Data-driven instruction.** Assessments are used to initially identify students. Progress assessments are used to ensure that students are making adequate progress.

- **Prioritization of available time and resources.** The primary concern is to provide children with the time and resources to achieve grade-level expectations and standards.

will usually work with four to five students a day. According to Gay Sue Pinnell, Reading Recovery is a "balanced approach within which powerful components work together to enable young, initially struggling readers to strategically process written texts" (Pinnell, 2000, p. 10).

There are three components to Reading Recovery: (1) a diagnostic survey, (2) tutoring session, and (3) teacher training. The diagnostic survey (Clay's Observational Survey of Early Literacy Achievement) is conducted on each student, and the results are used to make instructional decisions when working with the student. Each tutoring session consists of:

- reading familiar stories,
- repeating a reading of a story heard the day before,
- working with letters and or words using magnetic letters,
- writing a story,
- assembling a cut up story
- introducing and reading a new story.

Throughout the session, the teacher demonstrates problem-solving strategies and provides support for the reader to develop effective reading strategies. The teacher training component is extensive, with teachers learning the theories and practices of effective reading instruction in a year long intensive course.

Reading Recovery focuses on 10 components of the reading process. These components are closely aligned with the work of the National Reading Panel and their report on effective literacy instruction (see Table 12.3).

TABLE 12.3
Aspects of Reading Recovery Model

1. Phonological Awareness	Teach students to hear the sounds in words
2. Visual Perception of Letters	Teach students to perceive and identify letters of the alphabet
3. Word Recognition	Teach students to recognize words
4. Phonics/Decoding Skills	Teach students to use simple and complex letter–sound relationships to solve words in reading and writing
5. Phonics/Structural Analysis	Teach students to use structural analysis of words and learn spelling patterns
6. Fluency/Automaticity	Develop speed and fluency in reading and writing
7. Comprehension	Teach students to construct meaning from print
8. Balanced, Structured Approach	Provide a balanced approach so that literacy develops along a broad front and students can apply skills in reading and writing
9. Early Intervention	Intervene early to undercut reading failure
10. Individual Tutoring	Provide one-to-one assistance for the students who are having the most difficulty

Literacy Collaborative

Literacy Collaborative, developed by Irene Fountas and Gay Su Pinnell (www.lcosu.org), is designed to extend the principles of *Reading Recovery* to whole class instruction. The Literacy Collaborative is a five-year commitment, with the first year designated to training the literacy coordinator and the school leadership team. Grades two through four are implementation years, where teachers participate in 40 hours of professional development on how to implement the framework. By the fifth year, all teachers should be implementing the literacy framework in their classrooms. The Literacy Collaborative uses a "train the trainer" model of professional development, whereby a literacy coordinator receives training in Literacy Collaborative theory and pedagogy and reproduces the training for colleagues at the school site. The literacy coordinator also conducts on-site lesson demonstrations and coaching.

The Literacy Collaborative framework for literacy development includes word and language study, reader workshop, and writer workshop. There is flexibility with each of these areas in terms of content, student groupings, time frames, and level of teacher-directed instruction (Fountas & Pinnell, 2006). Literacy events within the blocks involve teacher read alouds, followed by group discussion of text meaning, word study lessons with high frequency words, small group reading instruction focused on reading strategies, independent or partner reading, and independent writing.

Leveled texts are a key feature of the Literacy Collaborative. Remember from Chapter 5 that leveled books are used primarily in guided reading groups, and that the text has been controlled in some fashion (readability, features, or letter–sound patterns). During small group reading, students work on previewing and predicting skills. After silent or quiet oral reading, the teacher asks comprehension questions. Unlike Success for All, the Literacy Collaborative takes a much more embedded approach to phonics instruction. Phonics generalizations are taught more informally as children encounter words in their reading.

Four Blocks

Four Blocks developed by Pat Cunningham and Dorothy Hall (www.wfu.edu/fourblocks) is a comprehensive language arts program initially designed for the primary grades. The program includes four aspects of literacy development: (1) guided reading, (2) working with words, (3) writing, and (4) independent reading. Each block has 30 minutes of instruction. The Four Blocks reform effort does not offer a scripted approach to reading and writing. Rather, teachers make decisions about what and how they are going to teach. The only structure Four Blocks has is that the children should be exposed to each of the blocks on a daily basis.

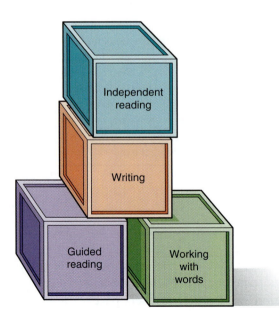

Beginning with the Guided Reading block, teachers plan direct, explicit instruction that focuses on skills and strategies in comprehension. Most of the time this work is with the whole class rather than in small groups. Four Blocks creators believe that all children need the same skills (prediction, establishing prior knowledge, vocabulary development). It is assumed that for children who see the work as "too easy," there are opportunities in the other blocks to meet their instructional needs. And, this is also true for students who find the work is "too difficult." The Guided Reading block exposes children to a wide range of literature. Children are encouraged to respond to literature during this block of time.

The Working with Words block of time is devoted to phonics and word study. Children learn to read and spell high-frequency words. Time is spent on reviewing and adding words to the word wall. Children practice new and old words by using visual, auditory, and kinesthetic experiences—looking at the words, saying the words, clapping or snapping the letters, writing the words on paper, and self-correcting the words with a teacher.

The Self-Selected Reading block is when teachers conduct read alouds and when children read books that are "on their level." The teacher selects the texts for read aloud depending on students' interests or connections to other aspects of the curriculum (science or social studies themes). The teacher also organizes collections of books to be placed in bins or buckets for students to access as they engage in self-selected reading. The teacher will often conduct reading conferences during this time and generally at the end of this block of time, a few children will share what they have been reading in a "reader's chair."

The Writing Block includes a mini-lesson on writing (mechanics, grammar, or content), opportunities for children to draft, revise, and edit their own pieces, writing conferences with the teacher, and author's chair.

The Four Blocks reform effort for primary grades has been extended to the upper grades—*Big Blocks*. Similar in implementation, Big Blocks includes the four necessary components of the language arts program. There are differences in the content in each block. For example, in the Working with Words, the focus moves from recognizing and spelling high-frequency words to working with content area vocabulary. Another difference is that teachers often extend the time in each block to at least 45 minutes because of the nature of the work they are doing with students.

Success for All

Success for All (SFA) developed by Nancy Madden and Robert Slavin (www.successforall.net) is a comprehensive reform effort that targets high-poverty, disadvantaged schools and student populations. This effort focuses on prevention and early intervention, so that all children will finish third grade reading on grade level. At the center of the program is 90 minutes of uninterrupted reading instruction. The 90 minutes are usually broken into 20 minutes of story sharing and retelling (listening comprehension in grades 2 and above), 50 minutes of instructional time, and 20 minutes of oral language development (silent reading in grades 2 and above). In kindergarten and first grade, the 50 minutes of instructional time are designed for children to read with the teacher. Students in first grade progress through carefully sequenced and phonetically controlled readers developed by SFA. Each story is taught over a three-day period. The teacher follows a script that explicitly presents phonics generalizations and patterns, sight words, and word patterns. Reading instruction focuses on phonemic awareness, auditory discrimination, and sound meaning. Students chorally read or read in pairs the story a number of times. The teacher is provided detailed scripted lessons for read-aloud discussions.

In grades 2 through 5, students read from school-selected or district-selected reading materials, basals, and/or trade books. Students work in four-member teams on activities built around their reading materials. The team structure motivates children to stay on task and help each other learn. In these grades, instruction focuses on comprehension skills, such as finding the main idea, retelling, asking questions, sequencing, making predictions, using graphic organizers, understanding the difference between fact and opinion, understanding cause and effect, and using words in context. Fluency is strengthened through paired and repeated readings. Students also work on identifying literary elements, vocabulary, and writing skills.

America's Choice

Similar to *Success for All, America's Choice* is a comprehensive school reform effort (www.ncee.org/acsd) designed to improve literacy and mathematics in grades K–12. *America's Choice* focuses on internationally benchmarked performance standards, as well as standards at the state and local level. The literacy component of this reform effort is consistent with the National Reading Panel's report for reading instruction: phonemic awareness, phonics, fluency, vocabulary, and comprehension. This alignment ensures that America's Choice can be considered in school systems with Reading First funding. At the elementary level, there is a $2\frac{1}{2}$ hour daily block of literacy instruction: 30 minutes of skill instruction (phonics, grammar, spelling, and diction), one hour of reading instruction, and 1 hour of writing instruction. Teachers organize their instruction in a myriad of ways from whole class to small group instruction. Because it is a comprehensive program, the teachers are provided with daily lesson plans, classroom activities, homework assignments, books for classroom libraries, and more.

As part of the reform effort, America's Choice incorporates professional development into the model. Teachers participate in teacher study groups and professional learning communities.

The school-wide reform efforts in literacy are attractive to many school systems and districts struggling to meet adequate yearly progress. While there are significant differences in how literacy is approached in each of the aforementioned models, research shows that there is improvement in word reading, word attack, and phonemic awareness with all of the reform models (Tivnan & Hemphill, 2005). This should not be surprising because this is a significant component in all of the models. However, there appears to be minimal gain in students' abilities to meet grade level expectations in reading comprehension and vocabulary development.

It is also interesting to note that some of the reform efforts have appropriated labels such as "reader workshop" and "writer workshop." The ways in which these components are implemented within the reform efforts are generally more prescriptive and structured than what is typically meant by "reader workshop" and "writer workshop."

The literacy reform efforts listed here and others are designed to increase the academic achievement of struggling readers and writers. While these efforts have varying degrees of success with teachers and students, becoming an effective literacy teacher means teaching into the needs of all students in your classroom—regardless of the program you might use to enhance literacy.

> ### *Classroom Connections* 12.2
>
> Interview teachers in your local school system to determine if any comprehensive school reform models for literacy achievement are implemented in the schools. What reactions do the teachers have to such efforts?

Teaching all children to lead literate lives in the twenty-first century

Children are redefining what it means to be literate in the twenty-first century. They seamlessly navigate between and among texts in a variety of forms and formats, from traditional print-based materials to interactive web-based materials. As they effectively demonstrate their abilities to work with such materials, it is necessary for teachers to teach *into* the individual needs and strengths of each student. Students come into our classrooms with a range of strengths, experiences, background, knowledge, and needs. The guiding principles outlined in Chapter 1 are not just for students that are on track for successful literacy experiences, but should also be considered for students that find reading and writing events challenging and difficult. Restated here in Figure 12.4, these guiding principles are a reminder that literacy practices are far more complex than merely calling out words and answering literal level questions.

These principles are the foundation for developing and implementing a meaningful and effective literacy curriculum for all children. As teachers embrace these principles and make them central to their literacy curriculum, students experience a curriculum that is generative, student centered, and has application beyond the classroom walls.

Figure 12.4
Guiding Principles for Effective Literacy Instruction.

- **Principle #1: Literacy practices are socially and culturally constructed.** Reading and writing practices are not isolated events, but rather involve social and cultural understandings. Struggling readers benefit from participating in collaborative reading and writing events.

- **Principle #2: Literacy practices are purposeful.** Literacy should be purposeful and take social goals into consideration. It is important for struggling readers and writers to see the value and purpose for the literacy event.

- **Principle #3: Literacy practices contain ideologies and values.** Literacy practices are not neutral; they carry with them ideas, beliefs, and values on how the world should be organized. The types of materials and curricular decisions made available for struggling readers and writers reflect the beliefs and assumptions of what struggling readers are capable of doing.

- **Principle #4: Literacy practices are learned through inquiry.** There are many ways to approach the teaching of reading and writing, and by taking on a problem-posing stance, new insights may be uncovered. Struggling readers and writers should have opportunities to participate in inquiry-based curriculum.

- **Principle #5: Literacy practices invite readers and writers to use their background knowledge and cultural understandings to make sense of texts.** Essential to making sense of texts is drawing upon students' background experiences and knowledge. Struggling readers and writers come into the classrooms with a range of experiences that need to be acknowledged as they navigate texts.

- **Principle #6: Literacy practices expand to include everyday texts and multi-modal texts.** Everyday materials (flyers, brochures, song lyrics, advertisements, etc.) and multimodal texts can be used to teach reading and writing. Struggling readers and writers will benefit from a diverse set of reading and writing materials.

Working toward such a curriculum requires that teachers begin to ask a different set of questions. Based on the work of Tomlinson (2003) and the ideas in Chapter 1 regarding a teacher's vision, the following questions may seem straightforward, yet the answers are much more complex and require that teachers embrace a perspective that all children have potential for learning regardless of their life circumstances, ethnic and cultural backgrounds, and language abilities. The most fundamental question is:

Do I intend to teach each individual child to be a proficient and engaged reader and writer?

Answering this question in the affirmative means that a teacher must consider how to reach children who struggle with the reading and writing processes. Where can a teacher begin? First, remember that children enter into the literacy curriculum from various points of entry and bring with them diverse perspectives on learning. Earlier in the chapter, you read Tobias' list of pet care responsibilities. This is just one example of how teachers teach *into* students' needs. Tobias's teacher noticed how engaged Tobias was during the morning meeting conversation and constructed a pathway for him to be recognized for his knowledge and interest. Throughout all of the chapters, the teachers have engaged in kidwatching and reflection to determine the next best step in a child's literacy development. Other questions that encourage teachers to teach *into* the students' needs and experiences are:

- What are my students' particular interests and needs?
- What are my students' strengths?
- What can I do to ensure that each student works at the highest level of thought and production possible?
- What would it take to tap the motivation already within this learner?
- How might I adapt the agenda to work for the student?
- What circumstances will be the most effective catalyst for this student's development?
- How do I support each student's movement toward being an expert reader and writer?

These questions focus on developing excellence and equity in the classroom. Individuals are at the center of each question. The responsibility lies with the teacher to adapt the activities and curriculum, rather than positioning the student in a deficit model of learning. Because the focus is on the students' interests and not on the labels they may have been encumbered with, students can work across groups and opportunities. They are not confined to a particular experience because of their abilities or lack of abilities in literacy development.

Creating Connections 12.3

Return to your discussion of what reading is in the first chapter. How might you revise your initial discussion?

In Closing

Teaching all students in a classroom means that a teacher is committed to providing instruction that highlights the differences that individual children exhibit and not aim for a "one size fits all" model and hope for the best. In every classroom there will be children for whom reading and writing are not easy. This may be because of cognitive processing concerns, language difficulties, lack of motivation or engagement, or teachers' beliefs and attitudes. Struggling readers and writers often receive a curriculum that is slowed down and singularly focused (most often on code breaking strategies). This pushes struggling readers further and further behind with less and less motivation to continue.

To effectively meet the needs of struggling readers and writers, and in fact all readers and writers in a classroom, the teacher can organize a literacy curriculum that includes: planning literacy as a socio-critical practice, differentiating instruction with the reader/writer workshops, using the four-resource model for authentic literacy instruction, and maintaining a long-term view of literacy.

Plan Literacy as a Socio-critical Practice

Literacy is first and foremost a social practice. Teachers must go beyond the classroom to think about the lives and experiences of children. Teachers should plan for the big picture (Wilson, 2002). They do this by drawing upon their own beliefs about teaching and learning, about language, and literacy. They think about the kind of curriculum they want to implement in the classroom. As Harste reminds us, curriculum is a "metaphor for the lives we want to lead." Teaching literacy from a socio-critical perspective recognizes that reading is more than breaking the code. Literacy practices involve readers taking on multiple perspectives, engaging in social action, disrupting the commonplace, and focusing on sociopolitical issues (Lewison, Flint, & Van Sluys, 2002).

Differentiate Instruction with Reader/Writer Workshops

The reader/writer workshop approach as described throughout this text is one approach to literacy instruction that supports the varying interests and needs of students. Reader/writer workshop structure differentiates and personalizes instruction for students through mini lessons, literature discussions, independent reading and writing time, and conferences. Students are celebrated for their own accomplishments as they reflect on their progress and set new goals for themselves.

Use the Four-Resource Model for Authentic Literacy Instruction

The four-resource model for literacy development enables teachers to infuse the curriculum with literacy events and practices that are authentic and meaningful to emergent, novice, and accomplished readers and writers. Children not only learn to be code breakers and text participants, but also text users and text analysts. These resources are not hierarchical or discrete. "The proposition here is that all of these repertoires are variously mixed and orchestrated in proficient reading and writing. The key concept in the model is necessity and not sufficiency—each is necessary in new conditions, but in and of themselves, none of the four families of practices [resources] is sufficient for literate citizens/subjects" (Luke & Freebody, 1999, pp. 7–8). The four-resource model helps teachers and students move toward a more socially just society by inviting readers and writers to examine why things are the way they are. By infusing the four-resource model into the literacy curriculum, teachers offer students challenges and possibilities that prepare them to participate in a multimodal, multicultural global context.

Maintain a Long-Term View of Literacy

Today, teachers are often bogged down with mandates and prescriptions for literacy development. *No Child Left Behind* legislation has left many teachers believing that their major responsibility is to improve test scores, which essentially means that they are teaching for short-term results. And yet when teachers have a long-term view of what literacy is all about, "students' intellectual development and reading achievement are better served by practices that foster the desire to read" (Worthy, Turner, & Moorman, 1998, p. 302). This text is designed to offer teachers with possibilities in their teaching to teach for long-term results. Literacy development is not a discipline to be taught, but a means to understand and make a difference in the world.

Terms to Remember

Adequate yearly progress (AYP) *(368)*

Struggling reader *(355)*

Intrinsically motivated *(356)*

Extrinsically motivated *(356)*

Hi/Lo texts *(363)*

Scaffolding *(364)*

Resources for More Information

Hall, L. (2007). Understanding the Silence: Struggling Readers Discuss Decisions About Reading Expository Text, *Journal of Educational Research,* 100(3), 132–141.

Johnston, P., & Allington, R. (1991). Remediation. In R. Barr, M. L. Kamil, P. Mosenthal, & P. D. Pearson (Eds.), *Handbook of reading research: Vol. 2,* (pp. 984–1012). White Plains, NY: Longman Publishing Groups.

Roller, C. M. (1996). *Variability, not disability: Struggling readers in a workshop classroom.* Newark, DE: International Reading Association.

Tivnan, T. & Hempkill, L. (2005). Comparing four literacy reform models in high-poverty schools: Patterns of first-grade achievement. *Elementary School Journal,* 105 (5), 419–442.

Tomlinson, C. A. (2003). *Deciding to Teach Them All,* Educational Leadership, 61(2), 5–11.

Valencia, S.W., & Riddle Buly, M. (2004) Behind test scores: What struggling readers really need. *The Reading Teacher,* 57(6), 520–531.

Questions for Further Consideration

- What mechanisms and resources can you advocate for to support struggling readers and writers in classroom settings?

- Reflecting on the previous chapters in the book, identify particular chapters and/or sections where the guiding principles were clearly evident. How might you use this information to begin conversations with teachers and administrators in the field?

- How do you envision literacy in the twenty-first century? What does it mean to live a literate life?

- What resources (human and material) will you need to teach a reader/writer workshop? How might you begin to acquire those resources?

APPENDIX A

Newberry Award Winners (1922–present)

The Newbery Medal is awarded annually by the American Library Association for the most distinguished American children's book published the previous year. The Newbery Award became the first children's book award in the world. Its terms, as well as its long history, continue to make it the best known and most discussed children's book award in this country.

Date	Title/Author/Publisher

2000s

2007 **The Higher Power of Lucky** by Susan Patron, illustrated by Matt Phelan (Simon & Schuster/Richard Jackson).

2006 **Criss Cross** by Lynne Rae Perkins (Greenwillow Books/HarperCollins).

2005 **Kira-Kira** by Cynthia Kadohata (Atheneum Books for Young Readers/Simon & Schuster).

2004 **The Tale of Despereaux: Being the Story of a Mouse, a Princess, Some Soup, and a Spool of Thread** by Kate DiCamillo, illustrated by Timothy Basil Ering (Candlewick Press).

2003 **Crispin: The Cross of Lead** by Avi (Hyperion Books for Children).

2002 **A Single Shard** by Linda Sue Park (Clarion Books/Houghton Mifflin).

2001 **A Year Down Yonder** by Richard Peck (Dial).

2000 **Bud, Not Buddy** by Christopher Paul Curtis (Delacorte).

1990s

1999 **Holes** by Louis Sachar (Frances Foster).

1998 **Out of the Dust** by Karen Hesse (Scholastic).

1997 **The View from Saturday** by E. L. Konigsburg (Jean Karl/Atheneum).

1996 **The Midwife's Apprentice** by Karen Cushman (Clarion).

1995 **Walk Two Moons** by Sharon Creech (HarperCollins).

1994 **The Giver** by Lois Lowry (Houghton).

1993 **Missing May** by Cynthia Rylant (Jackson/Orchard).

1992 **Shiloh** by Phyllis Reynolds Naylor (Atheneum).

1991 **Maniac Magee** by Jerry Spinelli (Little, Brown).

1990 **Number the Stars** by Lois Lowry (Houghton).

1980s

1989 **Joyful Noise: Poems for Two Voices** by Paul Fleischman (Harper).

1988 **Lincoln: A Photobiography** by Russell Freedman (Clarion).

1987 **The Whipping Boy** by Sid Fleischman (Greenwillow).

1986 **Sarah, Plain and Tall** by Patricia MacLachlan (Harper).

1985 **The Hero and the Crown** by Robin McKinley (Greenwillow).

1984 **Dear Mr. Henshaw** by Beverly Cleary (Morrow).

1983 **Dicey's Song** by Cynthia Voigt (Atheneum).

1982 **A Visit to William Blake's Inn: Poems for Innocent and Experienced Travelers** by Nancy Willard (Harcourt).

1981 **Jacob Have I Loved** by Katherine Paterson (Crowell).

1980 **A Gathering of Days: A New England Girl's Journal, 1830–1832** by Joan W. Blos (Scribner).

1970s

1979 **The Westing Game** by Ellen Raskin (Dutton).
1978 **Bridge to Terabithia** by Katherine Paterson (Crowell).
1977 **Roll of Thunder, Hear My Cry** by Mildred D. Taylor (Dial).
1976 **The Grey King** by Susan Cooper (McElderry/Atheneum).
1975 **M. C. Higgins, the Great** by Virginia Hamilton (Macmillan).
1974 **The Slave Dancer** by Paula Fox (Bradbury).
1973 **Julie of the Wolves** by Jean Craighead George (Harper).
1972 **Mrs. Frisby and the Rats of NIMH** by Robert C. O'Brien (Atheneum).
1971 **Summer of the Swans** by Betsy Byars (Viking).
1970 **Sounder** by William H. Armstrong (Harper).

1960s

1969 **The High King** by Lloyd Alexander (Holt).
1968 **From the Mixed-Up Files of Mrs. Basil E. Frankweiler** by E. L. Konigsburg (Atheneum).
1967 **Up a Road Slowly** by Irene Hunt (Follett).
1966 **I, Juan de Pareja** by Elizabeth Borton de Trevino (Farrar).
1965 **Shadow of a Bull** by Maia Wojciechowska (Atheneum).
1964 **It's Like This, Cat** by Emily Neville (Harper).
1963 **A Wrinkle in Time** by Madeleine L'Engle (Farrar).
1962 **The Bronze Bow** by Elizabeth George Speare (Houghton).
1961 **Island of the Blue Dolphins** by Scott O'Dell (Houghton).
1960 **Onion John** by Joseph Krumgold (Crowell).

1950s

1959 **The Witch of Blackbird Pond** by Elizabeth George Speare (Houghton).
1958 **Rifles for Watie** by Harold Keith (Crowell).
1957 **Miracles on Maple Hill** by Virginia Sorensen (Harcourt).
1956 **Carry On, Mr. Bowditch** by Jean Lee Latham (Houghton).
1955 **The Wheel on the School** by Meindert DeJong (Harper).
1954 **...And Now Miguel** by Joseph Krumgold (Crowell).
1953 **Secret of the Andes** by Ann Nolan Clark (Viking).
1952 **Ginger Pye** by Eleanor Estes (Harcourt).
1951 **Amos Fortune, Free Man** by Elizabeth Yates (Dutton).
1950 **Door in the Wall** by Marguerite de Angeli (Doubleday).

1940s

1949 **King of the Wind** by Marguerite Henry (Rand McNally).
1948 **The Twenty-One Balloons** by William Pène du Bois (Viking).
1947 **Miss Hickory** by Carolyn Sherwin Bailey (Viking).
1946 **Strawberry Girl** by Lois Lenski (Lippincott).
1945 **Rabbit Hill** by Robert Lawson (Viking).
1944 **Johnny Tremain** by Esther Forbes (Houghton).
1943 **Adam of the Road** by Elizabeth Janet Gray (Viking).
1942 **The Matchlock Gun** by Walter Edmonds (Dodd).
1941 **Call It Courage** by Armstrong Sperry (Macmillan).
1940 **Daniel Boone** by James Daugherty (Viking).

1930s

1939 **Thimble Summer** by Elizabeth Enright (Rinehart).
1938 **The White Stag** by Kate Seredy (Viking).

1937   **Roller Skates** by Ruth Sawyer (Viking).

1936   **Caddie Woodlawn** by Carol Ryrie Brink (Macmillan).

1935   **Dobry** by Monica Shannon (Viking).

1934   **Invincible Louisa: The Story of the Author of Little Women** by Cornelia Meigs (Little, Brown).

1933   **Young Fu of the Upper Yangtze** by Elizabeth Lewis (Winston).

1932   **Waterless Mountain** by Laura Adams Armer (Longmans).

1931   **The Cat Who Went to Heaven** by Elizabeth Coatsworth (Macmillan).

1930   **Hitty, Her First Hundred Years** by Rachel Field (Macmillan).

1920s

1929   **The Trumpeter of Krakow** by Eric P. Kelly (Macmillan).

1928   **Gay Neck, the Story of a Pigeon** by Dhan Gopal Mukerji (Dutton).

1927   **Smoky, the Cowhorse** by Will James (Scribner).

1926   **Shen of the Sea** by Arthur Bowie Chrisman (Dutton).

1925   **Tales from Silver Lands** by Charles Finger (Doubleday).

1924   **The Dark Frigate** by Charles Hawes (Little, Brown).

1923   **The Voyages of Doctor Dolittle** by Hugh Lofting (Stokes).

1922   **The Story of Mankind** by Hendrik Willem van Loon (Liveright).

APPENDIX B

Caldecott Award Winners (1938–present)

Established in 1937, The Caldecott Medal is awarded to the artist of the most distinguished American Picture Book for Children published in the United States during the preceding year. This medal is to be given to the artist who has created the most distinguished picture book of the year and named in honor of the nineteenth-century English illustrator Randolph J. Caldecott.

Date	Title/Author/Publisher

2000s

2007	**Flotsam** by David Wiesner (Clarion).
2006	**The Hello, Goodbye Window** illustrated by Chris Raschka; text by Norton Juster (Michael di Capua/Hyperion).
2005	**Kitten's First Full Moon** by Kevin Henkes (Greenwillow Books/HarperCollins Publishers).
2004	**The Man Who Walked Between the Towers** by Mordicai Gerstein (Roaring Brook Press/Millbrook Press).
2003	**My Friend Rabbit** by Eric Rohmann (Roaring Brook Press/Millbrook Press).
2002	**The Three Pigs** by David Wiesner (Clarion/Houghton Mifflin).
2001	**So You Want to Be President?** illustrated by David Small; text by Judith St. George (Philomel Books).
2000	**Joseph Had a Little Overcoat** by Simms Taback (Viking).

1990s

1999	**Snowflake Bentley,** illustrated by Mary Azarian; text by Jacqueline Briggs Martin (Houghton).
1998	**Rapunzel** by Paul O. Zelinsky (Dutton).
1997	**Golem** by David Wisniewski (Clarion).
1996	**Officer Buckle and Gloria** by Peggy Rathmann (Putnam).
1995	**Smoky Night** illustrated by David Diaz; text by Eve Bunting (Harcourt).
1994	**Grandfather's Journey** by Allen Say; text edited by Walter Lorraine (Houghton).
1993	**Mirette on the High Wire** by Emily Arnold McCully (Putnam).
1992	**Tuesday** by David Wiesner (Clarion Books).
1991	**Black and White** by David Macaulay (Houghton).
1990	**Lon Po Po: A Red-Riding Hood Story from China** by Ed Young (Philomel).

1980s

1989	**Song and Dance Man** illustrated by Stephen Gammell; text by Karen Ackerman (Knopf).
1988	**Owl Moon** illustrated by John Schoenherr; text by Jane Yolen (Philomel).
1987	**Hey, Al** illustrated by Richard Egielski; text by Arthur Yorinks (Farrar).
1986	**The Polar Express** by Chris Van Allsburg (Houghton).
1985	**Saint George and the Dragon** illustrated by Trina Schart Hyman; text retold by Margaret Hodges (Little, Brown).
1984	**The Glorious Flight: Across the Channel with Louis Bleriot** by Alice & Martin Provensen (Viking).
1983	**Shadow** translated and illustrated by Marcia Brown; original text in French: Blaise Cendrars (Scribner).
1982	**Jumanji** by Chris Van Allsburg (Houghton).
1981	**Fables** by Arnold Lobel (Harper).
1980	**Ox-Cart Man** illustrated by Barbara Cooney; text by Donald Hall (Viking).

1970s

1979	**The Girl Who Loved Wild Horses** by Paul Goble (Bradbury).
1978	**Noah's Ark** by Peter Spier (Doubleday).
1977	**Ashanti to Zulu: African Traditions** illustrated by Leo & Diane Dillon; text by Margaret Musgrove (Dial).
1976	**Why Mosquitoes Buzz in People's Ears** illustrated by Leo & Diane Dillon; text retold by Verna Aardema (Dial).
1975	**Arrow to the Sun** by Gerald McDermott (Viking).
1974	**Duffy and the Devil** illustrated by Margot Zemach; text retold by Harve Zemach (Farrar).
1973	**The Funny Little Woman** illustrated by Blair Lent; text retold by Arlene Mosel (Dutton).
1972	**One Fine Day** retold and illustrated by Nonny Hogrogian (Macmillan).
1971	**A Story** retold and illustrated by Gail E. Haley (Atheneum).
1970	**Sylvester and the Magic Pebble** by William Steig (Windmill Books).

1960s

1969	**The Fool of the World and the Flying Ship** illustrated by Uri Shulevitz; text retold by Arthur Ransome (Farrar).
1968	**Drummer Hoff** illustrated by Ed Emberley; text adapted by Barbara Emberley (Prentice-Hall).
1967	**Sam, Bangs & Moonshine** by Evaline Ness (Holt).
1966	**Always Room for One More** illustrated by Nonny Hogrogian; text by Sorche Nic Leodhas, pseud. [Leclair Alger] (Holt).
1965	**May I Bring a Friend?** illustrated by Beni Montresor; text by Beatrice Schenk de Regniers (Atheneum).
1964	**Where the Wild Things Are** by Maurice Sendak (Harper).
1963	**The Snowy Day** by Ezra Jack Keats (Viking).
1962	**Once a Mouse** retold and illustrated by Marcia Brown (Scribner).
1961	**Baboushka and the Three Kings** illustrated by Nicolas Sidjakov; text by Ruth Robbins (Parnassus).
1960	**Nine Days to Christmas** illustrated by Marie Hall Ets; text by Marie Hall Ets and Aurora Labastida (Viking).

1950s

1959	**Chanticleer and the Fox** illustrated by Barbara Cooney; text adapted from Chaucer's Canterbury Tales by Barbara Cooney (Crowell).
1958	**Time of Wonder** by Robert McCloskey (Viking).
1957	**A Tree Is Nice** illustrated by Marc Simont; text: Janice Udry (Harper).
1956	**Frog Went A-Courtin'** illustrated by Feodor Rojankovsky; text retold by John Langstaff) (Harcourt).
1955	**Cinderella, or the Little Glass Slipper** illustrated by Marcia Brown; text translated from Charles Perrault by Marcia Brown (Scribner).
1954	**Madeline's Rescue** by Ludwig Bemelmans (Viking).
1953	**The Biggest Bear** by Lynd Ward (Houghton).
1952	**Finders Keepers** illustrated by Nicolas, pseud. (Nicholas Mordvinoff); text by Will, pseud. [William Lipkind] (Harcourt).
1951	**The Egg Tree** by Katherine Milhous (Scribner).
1950	**Song of the Swallows** by Leo Politi (Scribner).

1940s

1949	**The Big Snow** by Berta & Elmer Hader (Macmillan).
1948	**White Snow, Bright Snow** illustrated by Roger Duvoisin; text by Alvin Tresselt (Lothrop).
1947	**The Little Island** illustrated by Leonard Weisgard; text by Golden MacDonald, pseud. [Margaret Wise Brown] (Doubleday).
1946	**The Rooster Crows** by Maud & Miska Petersham (Macmillan).
1945	**Prayer for a Child** illustrated by Elizabeth Orton Jones; text by Rachel Field (Macmillan).

1944   **Many Moons** illustrated by Louis Slobodkin; text by James Thurber (Harcourt).
1943   **The Little House** by Virginia Lee Burton (Houghton).
1942   **Make Way for Ducklings** by Robert McCloskey (Viking).
1941   **They Were Strong and Good** by Robert Lawson (Viking).
1940   **Abraham Lincoln** by Ingri & Edgar Parin d'Aulaire (Doubleday).

1930s
1939   **Mei Li** by Thomas Handforth (Doubleday).
1938   **Animals of the Bible, A Picture Book** illustrated by Dorothy P. Lathrop; text selected by Helen Dean Fish (Lippincott).

Orbis Pictus Award Winners (1990–present)

The Orbis Pictus Award is an annual award to promote and recognize excellence in the writing of nonfiction for children. The name *Orbis Pictus* commemorates the work of Johannes Amos Comenius, *Orbis Pictus—The World in Pictures* (1657), considered the first book planned for children.

Date	Title/Author/Publisher

2000s

2007 **Quest for the Tree Kangaroo: An Expedition to the Cloud Forest of New Guinea** by Sy Montgomery. Photos by Nic Bishop (Houghton Mifflin).

2006 **Children of the Great Depression** by Russell Freedman (Clarion Books).

2005 **York's Adventures with Lewis and Clark: An African-American's Part in the Great Expedition** by Rhoda Blumberg (HarperCollins).

2004 **An American Plague: The True and Terrifying Story of the Yellow Fever Epidemic of 1793** by Jim Murphy (Clarion Books).

2003 **When Marian Sang: The True Recital of Marian Anderson: The Voice of a Century** by Pam Munoz Ryan, illustrated by Brian Selznick (Scholastic).

2002 **Black Potatoes: The Story of the Great Irish Famine, 1845–1850** by Susan Campbell Bartoletti (Houghton Mifflin).

2001 **Hurry Freedom: African Americans in Gold Rush California** by Jerry Stanley (Crown).

2000 **Through My Eyes** by Ruby Bridges, Margo Lundell (Scholastic Press).

1990s

1999 **Shipwreck at the Bottom of the World: The Extraordinary True Story of Shackleton and the *Endurance*** by Jennifer Armstrong (Crown).

1998 **An Extraordinary Life: The Story of a Monarch Butterfly** by Laurence Pringle (Orchard Books).

1997 **Leonardo da Vinci** by Diane Stanley (Morrow Junior Books).

1996 **The Great Fire** by Jim Murphy (Scholastic).

1995 **Safari Beneath the Sea: The Wonder World of the North Pacific Coast** by Diane Swanson (Sierra Club Books).

1994 **Across America on an Emigrant Train** by Jim Murphy (Clarion Books).

1993 **Children in the Dust Bowl: The True Story of the School at Weedpatch Camp** by Jerry Stanley (Crown Publishers, Inc.).

1992 **Flight: The Journey of Charles Lindbergh** by Robert Burleigh illustrated by Mike Wimmer (Philomel Books).

1991 **Franklin Delano Roosevelt** by Russell Freedman (Clarion Books).

1990 **The Great Little Madison** by Jean Fritz (Putnam).

APPENDIX D
Assessment Forms

TEACHER–STUDENT READING CONFERENCE FORM

Name   Date

Text title

Type of text (picture book, chapter book, magazine, etc.)

Points discussed?

Strategies used?

Recommendations?

Next steps?

Additional comments

Date of next Conference

READING CONFERENCE AND GOALS

Name: Date

Begin time   End time

Bring to your conference a book you are currently reading or working with

Title

Is this book too easy, just right, or challenging? How do you know?

Tell me what this book is about so far.

What are your reading plans with this book? How much time will you need to complete the book? What will you do after you finish this book?

What are your goals for reading? Possible areas to consider include:
- Rereading when meaning is unclear, when something doesn't make sense
- Think about what you are reading and what is happening
- Make sure you can decode and understand almost all of the words in a book
- Think about why characters act and behave as they do
- Make connections to your own life
- Try reading in another genre
- Extend the amount of time you read daily
- Learn different parts of stories (e.g., main idea, setting, plot, conclusion)
- Learn new strategies for decoding unfamiliar words

My goals:

Name:
Book Title:
Date:

BOOK CELEBRATION PLAN

For my book celebration project I will create a(n) _____

_____

I think this project is a good one because _____

_____

I will be working with _____

_____

Why is this an important part of the story? _____

_____

_____

_____

_____

Book pages I will use	Quotes from that page

On the back of this sheet, draw a sketch of your project

CONCEPTS ABOUT PRINT (CAP) ASSESSMENT TOOL (MARIE CLAY)

Print Concept	Teacher Asks Student to	Student Response
1. Front cover	Show me the front of this book.	
2. Back cover	Show me the back of this book.	
3. Title	Show me where the name of the story is.	
4. Print carries messages	Show me where the words of the story are.	
5. Beginning of the story	Show me with your finger where I start reading.	
6. Left to right; top to bottom	Show me with your finger which way I go as I read the page.	
7. Return sweep	Where do I go then?	
8. One to one matching bottom	You point to the words as I read the story.	
9. First word	Show me the first word on this page.	
10. Last word	Show me the last word on this page.	
11. Word	Point to one word on the page; now two words.	
12. First letter in a word	Point to the first letter in this word.	
13. Last letter in a word	Point to the last letter in this word.	
14. One letter/two letters	Point to one letter in this word; point to two letters in the word.	
15. Letter names	Show me three letters on this page, and tell me the names.	
16. Capital letter	With your finger, show me a capital letter on this page.	
17. Small letter	With your finger, show me a small letter on this page.	
18. Period	What is this called? Or what is this for?	
19. Question mark	What is this called? Or what is this for?	
20. Exclamation mark	What is this called? Or what is this for?	
21. Quotation mark	What is this called? Or what is this for?	
22. Comma	What is this called? Or what is this for?	

The last few concepts (18–22) may not be attended to until well into kindergarten or even first grade.

CONCEPTS OF SCREEN CHECKLIST (TURBILL, 2001)

Child's name: _____   Date:

Skills		Not yet	Can do with help	Beginning to do on own	Can do on own
Mouse	Move mouse with one hand				
	Use index finger on left side of mouse				
	Match mouse and cursor				
	Use mouse to click in right place				
	Use double click to open icons				
	Use click and drag				
Programs	Turn on computer				
	Locate appropriate program on desktop				
	Open program				
	Close program				
Navigation	Recognize basic icons and their functions — Cross to close				
	Next page				
	Next activity				
Directionality	Scroll				
	Knows how to move to an activity				

Computer at Home	Yes	No
Programs child uses at home		

Confidence	Seems frightened of computer	Prepared to observe others and try	Quite confident	Very confident

Any other points of interest that you've noticed (e.g., helping others, very interested in activity)

DAILY CONFERENCE SHEET

Date	Text Shared/ Talked About	Noted Observation	Strategy Offered	Mini-Lesson

INDIVIDUAL LITERATURE DISCUSSION FORM

Name _____

Date	Text Shared	Noted Observation	Strategy Offered

READING PROCESS CHECKLIST

Name _____   Date _____

	Usually	Often	Sometimes	Not Yet
Motivation To what extent does the reader show an interest in texts?				
To what extent does the reader choose reading over other possible activities?				
To what extent does the reader set goals for reading?				
Reading Strategies To what extent does the reader use effective strategies such as predicting, monitoring comprehension, and other "fix it" strategies when meaning has gone awry?				
To what extent does the reader read for meaning?				
To what extent does the reader make connections among books, experiences, and background knowledge?				
To what extent does the reader talk about what s/he is reading?				
To what extent does the reader employ word level skills to unfamiliar words?				
Reading Environment To what extent does the reader read across genres?				

LITERATURE DISCUSSION CHECKLIST

Name _____

Date	Makes Connections to Other Texts, Experiences	Contributes to Discussion	Initiates the Discussion	Acknowledges Others' Comments	Speaks Confidently	Asks Questions

Yopp–Singer Test of Phonemic Segmentation

Student's name _____ Date_____

Score (number correct) _____

Directions: Today we're going to play a word game. I'm going to say a word, and I want you to break the word apart. You are going to tell me each sound in the word in order. For example, if I say "old," you should say "/o/-/l/-/d/." (Administrator: Be sure to say the sounds, not the letters, in the word.) Let's try a few together.

Practice items: (Assist the child in segmenting these items as necessary.)

      ride   **go**   **man**

Test items: (Circle those items that the student correctly segments; incorrect responses may be recorded on the blank line following the item.)

1.	dog	_____	12. lay	_____
2.	keep	_____	13. race	_____
3.	fine	_____	14. zoo	_____
4.	no	_____	15. three	_____
5.	she	_____	16. job	_____
6.	wave	_____	17. in	_____
7.	grew	_____	18. ice	_____
8.	that	_____	19. at	_____
9.	red	_____	20. top	_____
10.	me	_____	21. by	_____
11.	sat	_____	22. do	_____

The author, Hallie Kay Yopp, California State University, Fullerton, grants permission for this test to be reproduced. The author acknowledges the contribution of the late Harry Singer to the development of this test.

STORYTELLING CHECKLIST

Name _____

Date _____

	Usually	Often	Sometimes	Not Yet
Retold entire story: Beginning, middle, and end				
Understood major ideas				
Used background knowledge during retelling				
Used correct usage during retelling				
Retold story fluently				
Used age-appropriate vocabulary				
Told the story in sentences that made sense				

Next steps:

RESPONSIVE LISTENING ASSESSMENT: GROUP DISCUSSION

Group members _____

Date _____

Book title _____

Amount of participation (list names under each category)

A great deal   Medium   None

What discussion skills do students need to work on?

Mini-Lessons

Listed is a collection of mini-lesson topics that can be introduced to children, K–6th grade.

Reading

- How can you extend your time in reading and writing?
- How do you handle tricky words?
- How can you learn to notice first letters in words?
- How can you read across the word (not just looking at the beginning letters/sounds)?
- How can you learn to reread to see what makes sense?
- How can you talk about books?
- How can you use what you know to learn new words (word families)?
- How can you invite others into a book?
- How do you get big ideas from texts?
- Goals for reading. What kind of reader do you want to be?
- How can you talk about books with your friends?
- What makes a good reading partner?
- How can you make your literature discussion group productive?
- How can you respond to nonfiction texts?
- How can all voices be heard in a literature discussion?
- How do you select books to read?
- How can you move from details of the story to the big idea?
- How can using sticky notes improve reading comprehension and response?
- How can you learn how to skim materials?
- What features and structures do nonfiction texts have?
- What are some reading rituals?

Writing

- How can you extend your writing time?
- How can you provide comments that encourage the author to continue?
- How can you work with a writing partner?
- How do you develop your own list of writing territories to help you find topics on which to write?
- What can you do when you are stuck?
- How can you develop interesting leads to your stories?
- How can you identify structures in nonfiction texts that you might want to also try out?
- How can you learn how to help peers by giving good feedback?
- How can you begin to write about issues of social justice?

Glossary

adequate yearly progress (AYP)   The minimum level of improvement that states, school districts, and schools must achieve each year.

aesthetic literary stance   Attention is toward having an emotional response to the text.

affixes   Linguistic elements that are added to words to change the meaning.

alternative assessments   Assessments that are designed to better capture a student's learning process.

analogy   Noticing patterns in words to decode unfamiliar words.

author circles   Strategy designed to facilitate children sharing works in progress.

authoring cycle   A model for writing development that highlights the transactional nature between reading and writing.

autonomous model   Sets of literacy skills and competencies are separate from the situations in which they are used.

basal reading series   A comprehensive set of materials designed for the purpose of teaching reading.

code breaking practice   The focus is on the letter–sound relationship and the structure of words.

codeswitch   A linguistic term meaning to alternate between one or more languages, dialects, or registers in a single stretch of talk.

cognitive psychologist or bottom-up theory   Learning to read is based on a series of small discrete steps from the simplest to the most complex.

concepts about print   An assessment tool to identify young children's awareness of literacy concepts.

concepts of screen   An assessment to determine children's understandings of digital media.

concepts of words   An assessment tool to identify young children's awareness of literacy concepts.

contextual dimension   The environment in which the discussion takes place.

contextual vocabulary work   Invites students to learn words in context through sentences, scenarios, and drama.

contrastive perspective   A perspective that accepts nonstandard language use.

correctionist perspective   A perspective that attemps to correct any nonstandard language use.

criterion referenced   Students are assessed on predetermined criteria.

critical dimension   Knowing how to problematize and evaluate software and other resources.

critical model   Raises questions about power, gender, social structures, and identity, offering a more global context for learning.

critical practices   Focus on challenging the status quo, taking multiple perspectives, investigating sociopolitical issues, and taking action.

critical theory   Invites teachers and students to problematize and question current beliefs on practices.

cueing systems   Sets of cues or clues built into the structure and patterns of the language.

cultural dimension   Knowing that technology use is in relation to creating specific meaning.

cultural mismatch   To view students from a deficit perspective based on cultural and/or linguistic differences.

culturally relevant pedagogy   Teaching into the academic and social needs of culturally and linguistically diverse students.

decodable text   A part of phonics-oriented basal programs that starts with the smallest units of language and progresses upwards to more meaningful units.

definitional vocabulary work   Invites a student to identify a number of aspects of a word, such as definition, synonym, antonym, and category.

derivational suffix   Show a meaning relationship between the word and the root word.

dialect   A variety of language used by people in a particular geographic region.

digital language experience approach   Children use digital media to compose language experience stories.

DR-TA format   Directed reading–thinking activity to promote comprehension.

ebonics   Systematic and rule-governed language variety spoken by many African American students.

efferent literary stance   Attention is toward gathering information from a text.

emergent literacy   A perspective that focuses on the informal learning of literacy in home, preschool, or kindergarten settings.

environmental print   Text found in the environment (signs, posters, billboards, boxes).

envisionment   Dynamic sets of ideas, images, questions, anticipations, and hunches that a reader has while reading, speaking, or writing.

etymology   The study of word origins.

experience view   Children need to experience prerequisite skills to accelerate readiness.

extrinsically motivated   Seek rewards and praise when engaged in reading and writing.

flexible grouping   Children are placed in groups based on common interests, strengths, or needs.

formative assessment   On-going assessments that measure progress in the context of the activity.

four-resource model   A comprehensive view of reading that includes code breaking of text participant, text user, and critical practices.

funds of knowledge   Historically accumulated resources, knowledge, and competencies that families and community members have.

graphic organizer   A visual that makes explicit relationships and/or connections.

guided reading group   Flexible reading groups based on students' needs. Leveled texts are commonly used.

halliday + model   Extends the Halliday model (learning language, learning about language, and learning through language) to include learning to use language to critique.

hi/lo books   Books that are of high interest but written at a lower reading ability.

high frequency words   Sight words that readers frequently encounter.

high stakes   Assessments that have consequential outcomes.

ideological dimension   Involves the reader's beliefs, values, and understandings.

ideological model   Literacy is not a generalized culture-free process, but a set of specific practices in particular social contexts.

ideologies   Systems of beliefs that people carry with them as they navigate their daily living.

independent reading/ sustained silent reading   A time during the reader/writer workshop where students read selections of their own choosing.

industrial model   A model of education which focuses on standardization.

inflectional suffix   The suffix changes the tense of the verb, indicates plurality, or demonstrates comparison.

Informal reading inventory   Reading assessment that is individually administered to determine a student's reading level.

initiate-respond-evaluate (IRE)   An interaction pattern whereby the teacher initiates a question, students respond, and the teacher evaluates the response.

inquiry model   Suggests that learning is best achieved when students make decisions about their own learning process.

inquiry-based curriculum   A curriculum that starts with questions, and through research and experimentation students gain new insights and understandings.

integrated approach   Code breaking is taught by using authentic pieces of literature.

interactive journals   Teachers and students write to each other in a journal. They ask questions, share experiences, and record ideas.

interpretive authority   When teachers and/or students judge the viability and validity of a response.

intertextuality   The process of constructing links between text and one's experiences to other texts, or to outside knowledge.

intrinsically motivated   Seek reading and writing because of personal interest and desire.

kidwatching   The process of closely observing children's learning processes as they occur in various settings.

language experience approach   A strategy whereby the teacher writes the story as a child tells it. The story is then read by the teacher and child.

literary/strategic dimension   Reader's attention is focused on textual cues.

literature web   A strategy that encourages students to predict the sequence of event in a story.

literature-based basal   Incorporates contemporary and classic literature in student anthologies. Vocabulary, comprehension, and phonics skills are introduced in the beginning.

making words   A strategy developed by Cunningham & Cunningham (1992) whereby students manipulate letters to form a series of words.

maturation view   Mental age is a determing factor in whether formal reading instruction should begin.

mini-lesson   Short, focused instructional session where strategies are introduced and discussed.

miscue   An unexpected response to printed text—omission, substitution, or insertion of another word.

miscue analysis   The process of documenting and analyzing a reader's miscues while reading a passage of text.

morpheme   Smallest linguistic unit that carries meaning.

multicultural texts   Picture books and young adult novels that portray and honor diverse languages and cultures.

multimodal literacy   Literacy practices that are carried across multiple sites/texts/or media.

No Child Left Behind (NCLB)   Federal legislation to improve the state of education.

norm-referenced   Tests that compare student performance to a cross section of students at the same grade in other parts of the country.

onsets   Part of the single-syllable word that precedes the vowel.

operational dimension   Knowing how to operate the technology.

orthography   The study of how language is organized in written text.

phoneme   Is the smallest unit of sound in the language.

phonemic awareness   To consciously attend to sounds in the language.

phonemic blending   Ability to articulate the sounds of the word together.

phonemic segmentation   Ability to segment a word into the individual sounds or phonemes.

phonetics   Studying how we articulate and segment various phonemes.

phonics   Association between letter and sounds.

phonics-first approach   Instructional materials and pedagogy that focuses on letters and sounds as the primary component of learning to read.

phonics-oriented basal   Provides explicit and systematic instruction in phonics. Stories are designed to teach letter–sound correspondence.

portfolio systems   A collection of student work that documents growth and progress over time.

prefix   An affix that attaches to the beginning of a word.

prescriptive approach   An approach to literacy instruction that teaches code breaking and other skills through an explicit and systematic manner with controlled texts.

psycholinguistics or top-down theory   Meaning is central to the reading process. The emphasis moves from meaning to letters/sounds.

reader response model   Readers transact with the text, creating new understandings based on prior experiences.

reader response theory   Focuses on the reader or audience rather than the author or text.

reader/writer workshop approach   Structure for teaching reading and writing that individualizes instruction.

Reading first initiative   A federal initiative to apply scientifically based reading research and instruction in grades K–3.

reading readiness   A perspective that believes that children need to be taught a series of prerequisite skills prior to reading and writing.

register   Language used for a particular purpose or in a particular setting.

retrospective miscue analysis   Includes the reader's reflective comments during a miscue analysis.

rimes   Part of the single syllable word that includes the vowel and all succeeding consonants.

root word   Word or word part that comes from another language.

scaffolding   Individual support to help bridge the gap between what a learner knows and can do with what a learner needs to know in order to succeed.

schema   A mental set or representation.

scientifically based reading research (SBRR)   Involves the application of rigorous, systematic, and objective procedures to obtain reliable and valid knowledge.

shared reading event   An interactive reading experience where teachers read aloud and focus students attention on how print works, story structures, and word recognition.

sign systems   Ways of constructing and communicating knowledge.

skills-based approach   Instructional materials and pedagogy that focus on discrete skills in learning to read.

stakeholder   A group of people interested in the results of summative assessments.

stance   The attitude or purpose one has for reading or writing.

status of the class   An organizational technique to keep track of student progress.

storybook reading   A literacy event that usually involves an adult or older child reading to a younger child.

struggling reader   Usually one or more years behind their grade level.

suffix   An affix that attaches to the end of a word.

summative assessments   Assessments that sum up what a student has learned at a predetermined point in time.

syntax   The study of the rules or "patterned relations" that govern the way words combine.

talking books   Multimedia products that incorporate text, sound, and images to tell the story.

text participant practice   Focus on the cognitive strategies of activating prior knowledge predicting organizing, questioning, summarizing, and visualizing.

text sets   Collections of books and other materials that are organized around a particular theme or concept.

text to self   Connection is based on personal experience.

text to text   Connection is to another piece of text.

text to world   Connection is to a larger world on social events or issues.

text use practices   Focus on the varied purposes that texts serve.

think aloud   A strategy that encourages readers to stop and reflect on their own metacognitive processes.

trade books   Books that are not designed to specifically teach reading. Generally trade books are found in libraries and bookstores.

transaction   A relationship between the reader and the text, whereby what is interpreted is mediated by the reader's experiences and background.

transactional theory   Reading is seen as a transaction—a negotiation between the reader and the text.

triangulation   Using multiple sources of information to determine a pattern.

virtual school bags   A concept whereby a teacher considers the knowledges, skills, and ways of being that children carry with them in a virtual back pack.

whole language model   Reading is seen as an all-encompassing act involving the 4 cueing systems (graphophonemic, syntactic, semantic, and pragmatic).

word family   Words that share the same rime pattern.

word lists   A strategy of creating words with similar letter patterns.

word study   Examining the shades of sound, structure, and meaning of words.

References

Adams, M. J. (1990). *Beginning to read: Thinking and learning about print.* Cambridge, MA: Massachusetts Institute of Technology.

Afflerbach, P. (2002). The road to folly and redemption: Perspectives on the legitimacy of high-stakes testing. *Reading Research Quarterly,* 37, 348–360.

Afflerbach, P. (2004). *High stakes testing and reading assessment.* National Reading Conference Policy Brief. Presentation at the University of Maryland, September 2004.

Allen, J., Moller, K. J., & Stroup, D. (2003). "Is this some kind of soap opera?": A tale of two readers across four literature discussion contexts. *Reading & Writing Quarterly,* 19(3), 225–251.

Allington, R. (1993). *Reducing the risk: Integrated language arts in restructured elementary schools.* Report 1.8. National Research Center on Literature Teaching and Learning.

Anderson, J. (1995). How parents perceive literacy acquisition: A cross-cultural study. In W. Linek & E. Sturdevant (Eds.), *Generations of literacy: The seventeenth yearbook of the College Reading Association* (pp. 262–277). Harrisburg, VA: College Reading Association.

Anderson, R., Hiebert, E., Scott, J., & Wilkinson, I. (1985). *Becoming a nation of readers.* Washington, DC: US Department of Education, The National Institute of Education.

Anderson, R. C., & Pearson, P.D. (1984). A schema-theoretic view of basic reading processes. In P.D. Pearson (Ed.), *Handbook of reading research.* New York: Longman.

Anderson, R. C., & Nagy, W. E. (1992). The vocabulary conundrum. *American Educator,* 16(4), 14–18, 44–46.

Anthony, R., Johnson, T., Mickelson, N., & Preece, A. (1991). *Evaluating literacy: A perspective for change.* Portsmouth, NH: Heinemann.

Arter, J. A., & Spandel, V. (1992). Using portfolios of student work in instruction and assessment. *Educational Measurement: Issues and Practice,* 11, 36–44.

Atwell, N. (1987). *In the middle: Writing, reading, and learning with adolescents.* Portsmouth, NH: Heinemann.

Au, K. H. (1980). Participation structures in a reading lesson with Hawaiian children: Analysis of a culturally appropriate instructional event. *Anthropology and Education Quarterly,* 11 (2), 91–115.

Au, K.H., & Mason, J. M. (1983). Cultural congruence in classroom participation structures: Achieving a balance of rights. *Discourse Processes,* 6 (2), 145–167.

Auerbach, E. (1989). Toward a socio-contextual approach to family literacy. *Harvard Educational Review,* 59(2), 165–181.

Ayers, W. (2004). *Teaching toward freedom: Moral commitment and ethical action in the classroom.* Boston, MA: Beacon Press.

Bahktin, M. (1935/1981). "Discourse in the Novel." In *The dialogic imagination: Four essays by M. M. Bakhtin,* ed. M. Holquist; trans. C. Emerson and M. Holquist, pp. 259–422. Austin: University of Texas Press.

Bahktin, M. (1986). Speech genres and other late essays. Austin: University of Texas Press.

Banks, J. (2004). Multicultural education: Characteristics and goals. In J. Banks & C. A. Banks (Eds.), *Multicultural education: Issues and perspectives* (5th edition). Boston, MA: Allyn and Bacon (pp. 1–26).

Barnitz, J. G. (1997). Emerging awareness of linguistic diversity for literacy instruction. *The Reading Teacher,* 51(3), 264–266.

Baron, D. (2005). *Do you speak American?* Retrieved June 23, 2007 from Official American Website: http://www.pbs.org/speak/.

Barrentine, S. J. (1996). Engaging with reading through interactive read-alouds. *The Reading Teacher,* 50, 36–43.

Barton, D., & Hamilton, M. (2000). Literacy practices. In D. Barton and M. Hamilton (Eds.), *Situated literacies: reading and writing in context.* Florence, KY: Routledge, Taylor, Francis.

Barton, D., and Hamilton, M. (1998). *Local literacies: A study of reading and writing in one community.* London: Routledge.

Beck, I. L., & McKeown, M. G. (1991). Conditions of vocabulary acquisition. In P. D. Pearson (Ed.), *The handbook of reading research* (Vol. 2, pp. 789–814). New York: Longman.

Bear, D. R., & Templeton, S. (1998). Explorations in developmental spelling: Foundations of learning and teaching phonics, spelling, and vocabulary. *The Reading Teacher, 52*(3), 222–242.

Berghoff, B., Egawa, K., Harste, J., & Hoonan, B. (2000). *Beyond reading and writing: Inquiry, curriculum, and multiple ways of knowing.* Urbana, IL: National Council Teachers of English.

Bissex, G. L. (1980). *Gnys at wrk: A child learns to write and read.* Cambridge, MA: Harvard University Press.

Blachowicz, C., & Lee, J. (1991). Vocabulary development in the literacy classroom. *The Reading Teacher,* 45, 188–195.

Block, C.C. (2003). *Literacy difficulties: Diagnosis and instruction for reading specialists and classroom teachers* (2nd ed.) Boston, MA: Allyn & Bacon.

Bloodgood, J. W., & Pacifici, L. C. (2004). Bringing word study to intermediate classrooms. *The Reading Teacher, 58*(3), 250–263.

Bloome, D. & Bailey, F. (1992). Studying language and literacy through events, particularity, and intertextuality. In R. Beach, J. Green, M. Kamil, & T. Shanahan (Eds.) *Multiple disciplinary approaches to researching language and literacy* (pp. 181–210). Urbana, IL: NCTE & NCRE.

Bloome, D., & Katz, L. (1997). Literacy as social practice and classroom chronotopes. *Reading and Writing Quarterly: Overcoming Learning Difficulties,* 13(3), 205–25.

Bomer, K. (2005). *Writing a life: Teaching memoir to sharpen insight, shape meaning, and triumph over tests.* Portsmouth, NH: Heinemann.

Bomer, R., & Bomer, K. (2001). *For a better world: Reading and writing for social action.* Portsmouth, NH: Heinemann.

Bond, G. L., & Dykstra, R. (1967). Coordinating center for first-grade reading instruction programs. Minneapolis: University of Minnesota.

Bourdieu, P. (1986). The forms of capital. In: Richardson, J. G. (Ed.) *Handbook of theory and research for the sociology of education* (pp. 241–258). New York: Greenwood Press.

Brabham, E., & Villaume, S. (2002). Leveled texts: The good news and the bad news. *The Reading Teacher,* 55(5), 483–441.

Brisk, M. (1998). *Bilingual education: From compensatory to quality schooling.* Mahwah, N.J.: L. Erlbaum Associates.

Britton, J. (1993). *Language and learning.* New Hampshire: Boynton/Cook Publishers.

Bruner, J. (1986). *Actual minds, possible worlds.* Cambridge, MA: Harvard University Press.

Bruner, J. (1990). *Acts of meaning.* Cambridge, MA: Harvard University Press.

Bullivant, B. M. (1989). Culture: It's nature and meaning for educators. In J. A. Banks and C. A. Banks (Eds.), *Multicultural education: Issues and perspectives* (pp. 27–45). Boston: Allyn & Bacon.

Burnett, C., & Myers, J. (2002). "Beyond the frame": Exploring children's literacy practices. *Reading,* 36(2), 56–62.

Burns, M. S., Griffin, P., & Snow, C. E. (1999). *Starting out right: A guide to promoting children's reading success.* Washington, DC: Commission on Behavioral and Social Sciences and Education.

Cadiero-Kaplan, K. (2002). Literacy ideologies: Critically engaging the Language Arts curriculum. *Language Arts,* 79 (5), 372–392.

Calkins, L. M. (1983). *Lessons from a child: On the teaching and learning of writing.* Exeter, NH: Heinemann Educational Books.

Calkins, L. M. (1986). The art of teaching writing. Portsmouth, NH: Heinemann.

Calkins, L. (2001). *The art of teaching reading.* Portsmouth, NH: Heinemann.

Calkins, L., Hartman, A., & White, Z. (2005). *One to one: The art of conferencing with young writers.* Portsmouth, NH: Heinemann.

Callins, T. (2004). Culturally responsive literacy instruction. National Center for Culturally Responsive Education Systems (NCCREST). U.S. Department of Education, Office of Special Programs.

Cambourne, B. (1995). Toward an educationally relevant theory of literacy learning: Twenty years of inquiry. *The Reading Teacher*, 49(3), 182–190.

Carroll, J. B., Davis, P., & Richman, B. (1971) *The American Heritage word frequency book*. Boston: Houghton Mifflin.

Caswell, L. J., & Duke, N. K. (1998). Non-narrative as a catalyst for literacy development. *Language Arts*, 75 (2), 108–117.

Cazden, C. B. (1988). *Classroom discourse: The language of teaching and learning*. Portsmouth, NH: Heinemann.

Chaffel, J., Flint, A. S., Pomeroy, K., & Hammel, J. (2007). Young children, social issues, and critical literacy: Stories of teachers and researchers. *Young Children*, 62(1), 73–81.

Chall, J. (1967). *Learning to read: The great debate: An inquiry into the science, art, and ideology of old and new methods of teaching children to read, 1910–1965*. New York: McGraw-Hill.

Chamot, A., & O'Malley, W. (1994). Instructional approaches and teaching procedures. In K. Spangenberg-Urbschat & R. Pritchard (Eds.), *Kids come in all languages: Reading instruction for ESL learners* (pp. 82–102). Newark, NJ: International Reading Association.

Chapman, M. (1994). The emergence of genres. Written communication, 11, 3, 348–380.

Chase, N., & Hynd, C. (1987). Reader response: An alternative way to teach students to think about text. *Journal of Reading*, 30, 530–540.

Chera, P., & Wood, C. (2003). Animated multimedia 'talking books' can promote phonological awareness in children beginning to read. *Learning and Instruction*, 13(1), 33–53.

Clay, M. M. (1967). The reading behavior of five year old children: A research report. *New Zealand Journal of Educational Studies 2*, (1) 11–31.

Clay. M. M. (1975). *What did I write?* Portsmouth, NH: Heinemann.

Clay, M. M. (1998). *By different paths to common outcomes*. York, ME: Stenhouse Publishers.

Clay, M. M. (2000). *Concepts about print: What have children learned about the way we print language?* Portsmouth, NJ: Heinemann.

Cohen, J., & Wiener, R. B. (2003). *Literacy portfolios: Improving assessment, teaching, and learning*. Upper Saddle River, NJ: Merrill.

Coltrane, B. (2003). *Working with young English language learners: Some considerations*. Washington, DC: ERIC Clearinghouse on Languages and Linguistics. Available at http://www.cal.org/resources/digest/0301coltrane.html.

Comber, B. (2000). What really counts in early literacy lessons, *Language Arts*, 78(1), 39–49.

Comber, B. (2001). Critical literacies and local action: Teacher knowledge and a new research agenda. In B. Comber & A. Simpson (Eds.), *Negotiating critical literacies in classrooms*. Mahwah, NJ: L. Erlbaum Associates (pp. 271–282).

Combs, D. (2004). A framework for scaffolding content area reading strategies. *Middle School Journal*, 32(2), 13–20.

Cook, M. (2005). 'A place of their own': Creating a classroom 'third space' to support a continuum of text construction between home and school. *Literacy*, 39(2), 85–90.

Cooper, P. (2005). Literacy learning and pedagogical in Vivian Paley's 'storytelling curriculum'. *Journal of Early Childhood Literacy*, 5(3), pp. 229–252.

Cullinan, B. E., & Galda, L. (1998). *Literature and the child*. Fort Worth: Harcourt Brace College Publishers.

Cunningham, J. W., & Fitzgerald, J. (1996). Epistemology and reading. *Reading Research Quarterly, 31* (1), 36–60.

Cunningham P., & Cunningham J. (1992). Making words: Enhancing the invented spelling-decoding connection. *The Reading Teacher*, 46 (2), 106–116.

Dahl, K. L., Scharer, O.L., Lawson, L. L., & Grogan, P.R. (2001). *Rethinking phonics: Making the best teaching decisions*. Portsmouth, NH: Heinemann.

Dahl, K. L., Barto, A., Bonfils, A., Carasello, M., Christopher, J., Davis, R., Erkkila, N., Glander, S., Jacobs, B., Kendra, V., Koski, L., Majeski, D., McConnell, E., Petrie, P., Siegel, D., Slaby, B., Waldbauer, J., & Williams, J. (2004). Connecting developmental word study with classroom writing: Children's descriptions of spelling strategies. *The Reading Teacher*, 57(4), 310–319.

Dantas, M. (1999). Ways of seeing literacy learning: A review of major perspectives. Educational Report #32, The Ohio State University.

Department of Tasmania Education (2007). *Learning, teaching, and assessment guide*. Retrieved on June 29, 2007 from http://www.ltag.education.tas.gov.au/.

Dewey, J. (1990). *The school and society; and, the child and the curriculum*. Chicago: University of Chicago Press.

Dickinson, D., McCabe, A., & Sprague, K. (2003). Teacher rating of oral language and literacy (TROLL): Individualizing early literacy instruction with a standards-based rating tool. *The Reading Teacher, 56*(6), 554–565.

Dixon, C. Green, J. Yeager, B., Baker, D., & Franquiz, M (2000). "I used to know that": What happens when reform gets through the classroom door, *Bilingual Research Journal, 24*(1/2), 1–14.

Dodge, B. (1995). Webquests: A structure for active learning on the World Wide Web.

Dooley, C. (2005). One teacher's resistance to the pressures of test mentality. *Language Arts, 82*(3), 214–221.

Duffy, G. G. (1998). Teaching and the balancing of round stones. *Phi Delta Kappan, 79*, 777–780.

Duke, N. K. (2000). 3.6 minutes per day: The scarcity of informational texts in first grade. *Reading Research Quarterly, 35*, 202–224.

Duke, N. K., & Kays, J. (1998). "Can I say 'once upon a time'"? Kindergarten children developing knowledge of information book language. *Early Childhood Research Quarterly, 13*, 295–318.

Durrant, C., & Green, B. (2000). Literacy and the new technologies in school education: Meeting the li(IT)eracy challenge. *Australian Journal of Language and Literacy Education, 23*(2), 89–108.

Durkin, D. (1966). *Children who read early: Two longitudinal studies*. New York: Teachers College Press.

Duvall, R. (2001). Inquiry in science: From curiosity to understanding, *Primary Voices K-6*, 3–9.

Edelsky, C., Altwerger, B., & Flores, B. (1991). *Whole language: What's the difference?* Portsmouth, NH: Heinemann.

Eeds, M., & Wells, D. (1989). Grand conversations: An exploration of meaning construction in literature study groups. *Research in the Teaching of English, 23*, 4–29.

Egawa, K. (2002–07). Name talk: Exploring letter–sound knowledge in the primary classrom. Retrieved on August 10, 2007 from www.readwritethink.org.

Egawa, K., & Harste, J. C. (2001). What do we mean when we say we want our children to be literate? Balancing the literary curriculum: A new vision. *School Talk, 7*(1), pp. 1–8.

Eisner, E. (1990). Implications of artistic intelligences for education. In W. J. Moody (Ed.), *Artistic intelligences: Implications for education* (pp. 317–342). New York: Teachers College Press.

Ericson, L., & Juliebo, M. F. (1998). *The phonological awareness handbook for kindergarten and primary teachers*. Newark, DE: International Reading Association.

Farr, R. (1992). Putting it all together: Solving the reading assessment puzzle. *The Reading Teacher, 46*(1), 26–37.

Flesch, R. (1955). *Why Johnny can't read—and what you can do about it*. New York: Harper.

Fennimore, T. F., & Tinzmann, M. B. (1990). What is a thinking curriculum? Retrieved on June 29, 2007 from www.ncrel.org/sdrs/areas/rpl_esys/thinking.htm.

Fink, L. S. (2002–2007). Comics in the classroom as an introduction to genre study. Retrieved on June 29, 2007 from www.readwritethink.org.

Fish (1980). *Is there a text in this class? The authority of interpretive communities*. Boston, MA: Harvard University Press.

Flint, A. S., Lysaker, J., Riordan-Karlsson, M. E., & Molinelli, P. (1999). Converging and intersecting views: An investigation of stance in four independent classroom studies. *48th Yearbook of the National Reading Conference* (pp. 340–353). Chicago, IL: National Reading Conference.

Flint, A. S., & Riordan-Karlsson, M. (2001). *Buried treasures in the classroom: Using hidden influences to enhance literacy teaching and learning*. Newark, DE: International Reading Association.

Flint, A. S., & Bomer, R. (2002). Inquiry-based instruction. In B. J. Guzzetti (Ed.), *Literacy in America: An encyclopedia of history, theory, and practice*. Santa Barbara, CA: ABC-CLIO.

Flurkey, A. (1997). *Reading as flow: A linguistic alternative to fluency*. Unpublished doctoral dissertation. Tucson, AZ: University of Arizona.

Fountas, I. C., & Pinnell, G. S. (1996). *Guided reading: Good first teaching for all children*. Portsmouth, NH: Heinemann.

Fountas, I. C., & G. S. Pinnell. 2006. *Teaching for Comprehending and Fluency, Grades K-8: Thinking, Talking, and Writing about Reading*. Portsmouth, NH: Heinemann.

Franquiz, M. E., & de la Luz Reyes, M. (1998). Creating inclusive learning communities through English language arts: From chanclas to canicas. *Language Arts*, 75(3), 211–220.

Freire, P. (1970). *Cultural action for freedom.* Cambridge: Harvard Educational Review.

Freire, P. (1973). *Education for critical consciousness.* New York: Seabury Press.

Freire, P. (1985). *The politics of education: Culture, power, and liberation.* South Hadley, MA: Bergin & Garvey.

Freeman, D., & Freeman, Y. (2000). Meeting the needs of English language learners. *Talking Points*, 12 (1) 2–7.

Fry, E. B., Kress, J. E., & Fountoukidis, D. L. (1993). *The reading teacher's book of lists.* Englewood Cliffs, NJ: Prentice Hall.

Galda, L., Cullinan, B. E., & Strickland, D. S. (1993). *Language, literacy and the child.* Fort Worth, TX: Harcourt Brace Jovanovich College Publishers.

Gallas, K. (1997). Story time as a magical act open only to the initiated: What some children don't know about power and may not find out. *Language Arts*, 74(4), 248–255.

Ganske, K., Monroe, J. K., & Strickland, D. S. (2003). Questions teachers ask about struggling readers and writers. *The Reading Teacher,* 57(2), 118–128.

Gambrell, L. B., & Bales, R. J. (1986). Mental imagery and the comprehension-monitoring performance of fourth- and fifth-grade poor readers. *Reading Research Quarterly, 21,* 454–464.

Gay, G. (2000). *Culturally responsive teaching: Theory, research, & practice.* New York: Teachers College Press.

Gee, J. P. (2004). *Situated learning and literacy: A critique of traditional schooling.* New York: Routledge.

Gee, J. P., Hull, G., & Lankshear, C. (1996). *The new work order: Behind the language of the new capitalism.* Boulder, CO: Westview Press.

Gentry, J. R. (1982). An analysis of developmental spelling in GNYS at WRK. *The Reading Teacher*, 36, 192–200.

Gill, S. (2000). Reading with Amy: Teaching and learning through reading conferences. *The Reading Teacher*, 53(6), 500–509.

Gollnick, D. M. (2002). Incorporating linguistic knowledge in standards for teacher performance. In C. Adger, C. Snow, & D. Christian (Eds.), *What teachers need to know about language* (pp. 103–112). Washington, DC: Center for Applied Linguistics.

Goodman, K. S. (1965). A linguistic study of cues and miscues in reading. *Elementary English, 42,* 639–645. Reprinted in K. S. Goodman, *Language and literacy: The selected writings of Kenneth S. Goodman* (Frederick V. Gollsch, Ed.; Vol. 1, pp. 115–120). Boston: Routledge and Kegan Paul.

Goodman, K. S. (1968). *The psycholinguistic nature of the reading process.* Detroit, MI: Wayne State University Press.

Goodman, K. S. (1969). Analysis of oral reading miscues: Applied psycholinguistics. *Reading Research Quarterly,* 5(1), 9–30.

Goodman, K. S. (1986). *What's whole in whole language?* Portsmouth, NH: Heinemann.

Goodman, K. S. (1989). Whole language research: Foundations and development. *The Elementary School Journal,* 90, 208–221.

Goodman, Y. M. (1978). Kid watching: An alternative to testing. *National Elementary Principal,* 57(4), 41–45.

Goodman, Y. M. (1990). *How children construct literacy: Piagetian perspectives.* Newark, DE: International Reading Association.

Goodman, Y. M. (1995). Miscue analysis for classroom teachers: Some procedures and some history, *Primary Voices,* 3(4), 5–9.

Goodman, Y. M. (1996). At the critical moment: RMA in classrooms. In Y. Goodman & A. Marek (Eds.), *Retrospective miscue analysis* (pp. 189–201). Katonah, NY: Richard C. Owen Publishers.

Goodman, Y. M. (2003). *Valuing language study: Inquiry into language for elementary and middle schools.* Urbana, IL: National Council of Teachers of English.

Goodman, Y. M., & Altwerger, B. (1981). Print awareness in pre-school children: A working paper. a study of the development of literacy in preschool children. Occasional Paper No. 4, University of Arizona.

Goodman, Y. M., Watson, D., & Burke, C. (1987). *Reading miscue inventory: Alternative procedures.* New York: R. C. Owen Publishers.

Goodman, Y. M., & Goodman, K.S. (1994). To err is human: Learning about language processes by analyzing miscues. In R. B. Ruddell & N. J. Unrau (Eds.), *Theoretical models and processes of reading* (pp. 620–639). Newark, DE: International reading association.

Goodman, Y. M., & Flurkey, A. (1996). Revaluing and Revelations, In Y. Goodman & A. Marek (Eds.), *Retrospective miscue analysis* (pp. 107–118). Katonah, NY: Richard C. Owen Publishers, Inc.

Goodson, F. T., & Goodson L. A. (2005). You oughta use the periods and stuff to slow down: Reading fluency through oral interpretation of YA lit. Voices from the *Middle* 13(2) 24–29.

Gonzalez, N., Moll, L., Tenery, M. F., Rivera, A., Rendon, P., & Gonzales, R. (1995). Funds of knowledge for teaching Latino households. *Urban Education*, 29(4), 444–471.

Goswami, U. (1988). A special link between rhyming skill and the use of orthographic analogies by beginning readers. *Journal of Child Psychology & Psychiatry & Allied Disciplines*, 31 (2), 301–311.

Goswami, U. (1991). Learning about spelling sequences: The role on onsets and rimes in analogies in reading. *Child Development*, 62(5), 110–123.

Graves, D. (1982). *Writing: Teachers and children at work*. Portsmouth, NH: Heinemann.

Graves, M. F., & Graves, B. B. (1994). *Scaffolding reading experiences: Designs for student success.* Norwood, MA: Christopher-Gordon.

Greenwood, S. (2002). Making words matter: Vocabulary study in the content areas. *Clearing House* 75, 258–263.

Griffith, P., & Leavell, J. (1995). There isn't much to say about spelling . . . . or is there? *Childhood Education*, 72, 84–90.

Grimes, J. E., & Grimes, B. F. (1996). *Ethnologue: Language family index to the thirteenth edition of the Ethnologue.* Dallas, TX: Summer Institute of Linguistics.

Grisham, D. L. (2001, February). Making technology meaningful for literacy teaching: A webquest. Retrieved August 10, 2007 from http://www.readingonline.org/editorial/edit_index.asp?HREF=/editorial/february2001/index.html.

Guillaume, A. M. (1998). Learning with text in the primary grades. *The Reading Teacher,* 51, 476–486.

Gutiérrez, K., Asato, J., Santos, M., and Gotanda, N. (2002). Backlash pedagogy: Language and culture and the politics of reform. *The Review of Education, Pedagogy, and Cultural Studies,* 24(4), 335–351.

Guthrie, J. T., & Davis, M. (2003). Motivating struggling readers in middle school through an engagement model of classroom practice. *Reading and Writing Quarterly,* 19, 59–85.

Guthrie, J. T., & Wigfield, A. (2000). Engagement and motivation in reading. In M. L. Kamil, P. B. Mosenthal, P. D. Pearson, & R. Barr (Eds.), *Handbook of reading research* (Vol. 3) (pp. 403–422). Mahwah, NJ: Erlbaum.

Hall, N. (1998). Real literacy in a school setting: Five-year-olds take on the world. *The Reading Teacher*, 52(1), 8–17.

Hall, L. (2007). Understanding the silence: Struggling readers discuss decisions about reading expository text, *Journal of Educational Research,* 100 (3), 132–141.

Halliday, M. (1975). *Learning how to mean: Explorations in the development of language.* London: Edward Arnold.

Hamilton, M. & Barton, D. (2001). Editorial: Broadening the study of reading. *Journal of Research in Reading*, 24(3), 217–221.

Hammerness, K. (2003). Learning to hope of hoping to learn: The role of vision in early professional lives of teachers. *Journal of Educational Change,* 2, 143–163.

Hanssen, E. (1990). Planning for literature circles variations in focus and structure. In K. G. Short & K. M. Pierce (Eds), *Talking about books: Creating Literate communities* (pp. 199–209) Portsmouth, NH: Heinemann.

Harris, K. R., & Graham, S. (1996). *Making the writing process work: Strategies for composition and self regulation.* Cambridge, MA: Brookline Books.

Harris, T. L., & Hodges, R. E. (1995). *The Literacy Dictionary: The vocabulary of reading and writing.* Newark, DE: International Reading Association.

Harste, J. C. (1990). Inquiry-based instruction. *Primary Voices, K–6,* 1(1), 3–8.

Harste, J. C. (1994). Literacy as curricular conversations about knowledge, inquiry, and morality. In M. Ruddell & R. Ruddell (Eds.), *Theoretical models and processes of reading* (4th ed., pp. 1220–1242). Newark, DE: International Reading Association.

Harste, J. C. (2001). What education as inquiry is and isn't. In S. Boran & B. Comber (Eds.), *Critiquing whole language and classroom inquiry* (pp. 1–17), Urbana, IL: National Council of Teachers of English.

Harste, J. C., & Carey, R. F. (1979). Comprehension as setting. In J. C. Harste and R. F. Carey (Eds.), *New perspectives in comprehension*. Bloomington, IN: Indiana School of Education, 1979.

Harste, J. C., Burke, C. L., & Woodward, V. A. (1982). Children's language and world: Initial encounters with print. In J. Langer &. M. Smith-Burke (Eds.), *Bridging the gap: Reader meets author* (pp. 105–131). Newark, DE: International Reading Association.

Harste, J. C., Woodward, V. A., & Burke, C. L. (1984). *Language stories & literacy lessons.* Portsmouth, NH: Heinemann Educational Books.

Hartman, D. K. (1992). Intertextuality and reading: Reconceptualizing the reader, the text, the author, and the context. *Linguistics and Education, 4*(3 & 4), 295–311.

Hartman, D. K. (1995). Eight readers reading: The intertextual links of proficient readers using multiple passages. *Reading Research Quarterly, 30*(3), 520–561.

Harvey, S., & Goudivas, A. (2000). *Strategies that work: Teaching comprehension to enhance understanding.* York, ME: Stenhouse Publishers.

Heath, S. B. (1983). *Ways with words: Language, life and work in communities.* Oxford: Cambridge University Press.

Heffernan, L. (2004). *Critical literacy and writer's workshop: Bringing purpose and passion to student writing.* Newark, DE: International Reading Association.

Heffernan, L., & Lewison, M. (2005). What's lunch got to do with it? Critical literacy and the discourse of the lunchroom. *Language Arts, 83*(2), 107–117.

Hefflin, B. R. (2002). Learning to develop culturally relevant pedagogy: A lesson about cornrowed lives. *Urban Review, 34*(3), 231–250.

Helm, L. (2002–07). It doesn't have to end that way: Using prediction strategies with literature. Retrieved on August 10, 2007 from www.readwritethink.org.

Hiebert, E. H. (1999). Text matters in learning to read. *The Reading Teacher, 52*(6), 552–566.

Hoffman, J. V., Roser, N., Salas, R., Patterson, B., & Pennington, J. (2000). Text leveling and little books in first grade reading. Report # 1–010. Center for the Improvement of Early Reading Achievement, Ann Arbor, MI.

Hoffman, J. V., & Roser, N. L. (1993). Reading aloud in classrooms: From the modal toward a 'model.' *The Reading Teacher, 46*(6), 496–503.

Holdaway, D. (1980). *Independence in reading: A handbook on individualized procedures.* Gosford, Australia: Ashton Scholastic.

Howard, G. R. (2001). *We can't teach what we don't know. White teachers in multiracial schools.* Teachers College Press, New York.

Hudelson, S. (1984). Kan yu ret an rayt en ingles: Children become literate in English as a second language. *TESOL Quarterly 18*(2), 221–237.

Hymes, D. (1972/1986). Models of the interaction of language and social life. In John Gumperz & Dell Hymes (Eds.), *Directions in sociolinguistics: The ethnography of communication* (pp. 35–71). London: Basil Blackwell.

Iaquinta, A. (2006). Guided reading: a research-based response to the challenges of early reading instruction. *Early Childhood Education Journal, 33*(6), 413–418.

Invernizzi, M., Abouzeid, M., & Gill, J. T. (1994). Using students' invented spellings as a guide for spelling instruction that emphasizes word study. *Elementary School Journal, 95*(2), 155–167.

Irvine, J. J., & Armento, B. J. (2001). *Culturally responsive teaching: Lesson planning for elementary and middle grades.* Boston: McGraw-Hill.

Irwin, J. W. (1991). *Teaching reading comprehension process* (2nd ed.), Boston: Allyn & Bacon.

Jimenez, R. T. (2004). More equitable literacy assessments for Latino students. *The Reading Teacher, 57*(6), 576–578.

Johnston, P., & Allington, R. (1991). Remediation. In R. Barr, M. L. Kamil, P. Mosenthal, & P. D. Pearson (Eds.), *Handbook of reading research: Vol. 2* (pp. 984–1012). White Plains, NY: Longman Publishing Groups.

Jordan, N. (2005). Basal readers and reading as socialization: What are children learning? *Language Arts, 82*(3), 204–213.

Kagan, S. (1997). *Cooperative learning,* San Clemente, CA: Kagan Cooperative.

Kamberelis, G., & Scott, K. (1992). Other people's voices: The coarticulation of texts and subjectivities. *Linguistics and Education,* 4, 359–403.

Kamil, M., & Lane, D. (1998). Researching the relation between technology and literacy: An agenda for the 21st century. In D. Reinking, M. C. McKenna, L. D. Labbo, & R. D. Kieffer (Eds.), *Handbook of literacy and technology: Transformations in a post-typographic world* (pp. 323–341). Mahwah, NJ: Erlbaum.

Kantrowitz, B., & Hammill, R. (1990). The reading wars, *Newsweek,* 116, (10), 8–12.

Katz, L. G., & Chard, S. C. (1989). *Engaging children's minds: The project approach.* Norwood, NJ: Ablex Pub. Corp.

Kletzien, S. B., & Dreher, M. J. (2004). *Informational text in K–3 classrooms: Helping children read and write.* Newark, DE: International Reading Association.

Kress, G. (1997). *Before writing: Rethinking the paths to literacy.* London: Routledge.

Kress, G., & Jewitt, C. (2003). Introduction. In C. Jewitt and G. Kress (Eds.), *Multimodal literacy* (New York: Peter Lang), 1–18.

Kuby, P., Goodstadt-Killoran, I., Aldridge, J., & Kirkland, L. (1999). A review of research on environmental print. *Journal of Instructional Psychology,* 26, 173–183.

LaBerge, D., & Samuels, S. (1974). Toward a theory of automatic information processing in reading. *Cognitive Psychology,* 6, 293–323.

Labbo, L. D. (2000). 12 things young children can do with a talking book in a classroom computer center. *The Reading Teacher,* 53(7), 542–546.

Labbo, L. D., & Reinking, D. (1999). Negotiating the multiple realities of technology in literacy research and instruction. *Reading Research Quarterly,* 34, 478–492.

Labbo, L. D., & Kuhn, M. (2000). Weaving chains of affect and cognition: A young child's understanding of CD-ROM talking books. *Journal of Literacy Research,* 32(2), 187–210.

Labbo, L. D., Eakle, A. J., & Montero, M. K. (2002). Digital language experience approach: Using digital photographs and software as a language experience approach innovation. Retrieved August 10, 2007 from http://www.readingonline.org/electronic/elec_index.asp?HREF=labbo2/index.html.

Ladson-Billings, G. (1995). Toward a theory of culturally relevant pedagogy. *American Education Research Journal,* 35, 465–491.

Ladson-Billings, G. (2001). *Crossing over to Canaan: The journey of new teachers in diverse classrooms.* San Francisco: Jossey Bass.

Langer, J. A. (1995). *Envisioning literature: Literary understanding and literature instruction.* New York: Teachers College Press.

Lankshear, C., & Lawler, M. (1993). Schooling and revolution. In C. Lankshear and P. L. McLaren (Eds.), *Critical literacy: Politics, praxis, and postmodern.* Albany, NY: State University of New York.

Leland, C. H., & Kasten, W. C. (2002). Literacy education for the 21st century: It's time to close the factory. *Reading & Writing Quarterly,* 18(1), 5–15.

Leland, C., Harste, J. C., Ociepka, A., Lewison, M., & Vasquez, V. (1999). Talking about books: Exploring critical literacy: You can hear a pin drop. *Language Arts,* 77(1), 70–73.

Leslie, L., & Caldwell, J. (2001). *Qualitative reading inventory, Edition 3.* New York: Longman.

Lewis, C. (2000). Limits of identification: The personal, pleasurable, and critical in reader response. *Journal of Literacy Research,* 32, 253–266.

Lewison, M., Flint, A. S., & Van Sluys, K. (2002). Taking on critical literacy: The journey of newcomers and novices. *Language Arts,* 79(5), 382–392.

Lindfors, J. W. (1999). *Children's inquiry: Using language to make sense of the world.* New York: Teachers College, Columbia University.

Lotherington, H. (2004). Emergent metaliteracies: What the Xbox has to offer the EQAO. *Linguistics & Education,* 14 (3/4), 305–319.

Low, M. (2001). *Making episodes, making connections: A reading comprehension assessment tool. The REL's Pacific CHILD Project, Year One Product.* Honolulu, HI: Pacific Resources for Education and Learning.

Lubliner, S. (2004). Help for struggling upper grade elementary readers. *The Reading Teacher,* 57(5), 430–438.

Luke, A., & Freebody, P. (1997). Shaping the social practices of reading. In S. Muspratt, A. Luke, and P. Freebody (Eds.), *Constructing critical literacies* (pp.185–223). Catskill, NJ: Hampton Press.

Luke, A., & Freebody, P. (1999, August). Further notes on the four resources model. Retrieved June 23, 2007 from www.readingonline.org/past/past_index.asp? HREF=/research/luke-freebody.html.

Manning, E. (2004). Using science texts to teach the organizational features of nonfiction. Retrieved on August 10, 2007 from www.readwritethink.org.

Martens, P. (1997). What miscue analysis reveals about word recognition and repeated reading: A view through the "Miscue Window." *Language Arts*, 74(8), 600–609.

Martens, P. (1998). Using Retrospective Miscue Analysis to Inquire: Learning from Michael. *The Reading Teacher*, 52(2), 176–80.

Mason, J. M., & Allen, J. B. (1986). A review of emergent literacy with implications for research and practice in reading. In E.Z. Rothkopf (Ed.), *Review of research in education*, v13, (pp. 3–47). Washington, DC: American Educational Research Association.

Mason, J. M., & Sinha, S. (1992). Emerging literacy in the early childhood years: Applying a Vygotskian model of learning and development (Technical Report No. 561). Urbana Champaign, IL: University of Illinois.

Maxson, S. (1996). The Influence of Teachers' Beliefs on Literacy Development for At-Risk First Grade Students. Paper presented at the Annual Meeting of the American Association of Colleges for Teacher Education (48th, Chicago, IL, February 21–24, 1996).

McCarthey, S., & Hoffman, J. (1995). The new basals: How are they different? *The Reading Teacher*, 49 (1), 72–76.

McCracken, M. J., & McCracken, R. A. (1995). *Reading, writing, and language* (2nd ed.). Winnipeg Manitoba, Canada: Peguis.

McElroy, L., Goetze, S., & Beach, S. (1997). At risk learners part 1: Learning the cycle, *Reading Psychology*, 18(2), 173–182.

McGee, L., & Richgels. D. (1996). *Literacy's beginnings. Supporting young readers and writers.* (2nd ed.): Boston: Allyn & Bacon.

McGee, L., & Purcell-Gates, V. (1997). Conversations: So what's going on in emergent literacy? *Reading Research Quarterly*, 32, 310–318.

McKenna, M. C., & Kear, D. J. (1990). Measuring attitude toward reading: A new tool for teachers. *Reading Teacher*, 43(9), 626–639.

Mehan, H. (1979). *Learning lessons: Social organization in the classroom.* Cambridge, MA: Harvard University Press.

Meisels, S. J., & Piker, R. (2001). *An analysis of early literacy assessments used for instruction* (Tech. Report.). Ann Arbor, MI: Center for the Improvement of Early Reading Achievement (CIERA).

Meyer, D., Madden, D., & McGrath, D. (2004). English language learner students in the U.S. Public Schools; 1994 and 2000. *Education Statistics Quarterly*, 6(3), 1–2.

Miller, L., (1998). Literacy interactions through environmental print. In R. Campbell (Ed) *Facilitating preschool literacy* (pp. 100–118). Nemark, DE International Reading Association.

Mills, H., O'Keefe, T., & Jennings, L. B. (2004). *Looking closely and listening carefully: Learning literacy through inquiry.* Urbana, IL: National Council of Teachers.

Mills, H., & Clyde, J. A. (1990). *Portraits of whole language classrooms.* Portsmouth, NH: Heinemann.

Mizelle, N. B. (1997). Enhancing young adolescents' motivation for literacy learning. *Middle School Journal*, 28(3), 16–25.

Moll, L. C., Amanti, C., Neff, D., & Gonzalez, N. (1992). Funds of knowledge for teaching: Using a qualitative approach to connect homes and classrooms. *Theory Into Practice*, 31(2), 132–141.

Moore, R., & Gilles, C. (2005). *Reading Conversations: Retrospective miscue analysis with struggling readers, grades 4–12.* Portsmouth, NH: Heinemann.

Morphett, M. V., & Washburne, C. (1931). When should children begin to read? *Elementary School Journal* 31, 496–501.

Moss, B. (1997). Using children's nonfiction tradebooks as read-alouds. *Language Arts,* 72(2), 122–126.

Moss, B. (2004). Teaching expository text structures through information trade book retellings. *The Reading Teacher*, 57(8), 710–718.

Moss. G. (2001). Seeing with the Camera: Analysing children's photographs of literacy in the home. *Journal of Research in Reading*, 24(3), 279–292.

Nagy, W. E. (1988). *Teaching vocabulary to improve reading comprehension.* Urbana, IL: ERIC Clearinghouse on Reading and Communication Skills.

Nagy, W., & Scott, J. (2001). Vocabulary processes. In M.L. Kamil, P. B. Mosenthal, P.D. Pearson & R. Barr (Eds.), *Handbook of reading research: Volume III* (pp. 269–283). New York: Longman.

National Academy of Sciences (2000). *Eager to learn.* U.S. Department of Education.

National Association of Early Childhood Education (1998). Learning to read and write: Developmentally appropriate practices for young children. *Young Children*, 53(4), 30–46.

National Center for Educational Statistics (2002). 1999–2000 schools and staffing survey: Overview of the data for public, private, charter, and Bureau of Indian Affairs Elementary and Secondary Schools. Washington DC. US Dept. of Education, Office of Educational Research and Improvement.

National Clearinghouse for English Language Acquisition (2006). The Growing Numbers of Limited English Proficient Students (1994/5–2004/5). Retrieved on June 23, 2007 from National and Regional Data and Demographics. Website: http://www.ncela.gwu.edu/policy/states/reports/statedata/2004LEP/GrowingLEP_0405_Nov06.pdf.

National Education Association (2003). Status of the American Public School Teacher, 2000–2001. Washington, D.C.

National Institute of Child Health and Human Development (2000). *Report of the National Reading Panel. Teaching children to read: An evidence-based assessment of the scientific research literature on reading and its implications for reading instruction* (NIH Publication No. 00–4769). Washington, DC: U.S. Government Printing Office.

Necochea, J., & Cline, Z. (2000). Effective educational practices for English Language Learners within mainstream settings. *Race, Ethnicity and Education*, 3(3), 317–332.

Neuman, S., (2001). *Access for all: Closing the book gap for children in early education.* Newark, DE: International Reading Association.

Neuman, S., & Roskos, K. (1990). Play, print, and purpose: Enriching play environments for literacy development. *The Reading Teacher*, 44, 214–221.

Neuman, S., & Roskos, K. (1991). The influence of literacy-enriched play centers on preschoolers' conceptions of the functions of print. In J. Christie (Ed.), *Play and early literacy development* (pp. 167–187). Albany: State University of New York Press.

Newkirk, T. (1989). *More than stories: The range of children's writing.* Portsmouth, NH: Heinemann.

O'Flahavan, J., Gambrell, L. B., Guthrie, J., Stahl, S., & Alvermann, D. (1992, August/September). Poll results guide activities of research center. *Reading Today*, p. 12.

Oldfather, P. (1993). What students say about motivating experiences in a whole language classroom. *The Reading Teacher*, 46, 672–681.

Owens, R., Hester, J., & Teale, W. (2002). Where do you want to go today? Inquiry-based learning and technology integration. *The Reading Teacher*, 55, 616–626.

Palmer, R. G., & Stewart, R. A. (2003). Nonfiction trade book use in primary grades. *The Reading Teacher*, 57 (1), 38–48.

Paley, V. G. (1981). *Walley's stories: Conversations in the kindergarten.* Cambridge, MA: Harvard University Press.

Paley, V. G. (1992). *You can't say you can't play.* Cambridge, MA: Harvard University Press.

Paley, V. G. (1997). *The girl with the brown crayon.* Cambridge, MA: Harvard University Press.

Paris, S., & Hoffman, J. (2004). Reading assessment in kindergarten through third grade: Findings from the Center for the Improvement of Early Reading Achievement. *The Elementary School Journal*, 5, 199–217.

Papert, S. (1993). *The children's machine: Rethinking school in the age of the computer.* New York: Basic Books.

Pataray-Ching, J., & Roberson, M. (2002). Misconceptions about a Curriculum-as-Inquiry framework. *Language Arts*, 79(6), 498–506.

Pearson P. D., Sensale, L., Vyas, S., & Kim, Y. (1998, December). *Early literacy assessment: A marketplace analysis.* Paper presented at the annual meeting of the National Reading Conference, Austin, TX.

Piaget, J. (1959). *The language and thought of the child*, 3rd ed. London: Routledge & Kegan Paul.

Pinnell, G. S. (2000). *Reading recovery: An analysis of a research based reading intervention.* Columbus, OH: Reading Recovery Council of North America.

Pinnell, G. S., & Fountas, I. (1998). *Words matter: Teaching phonics and spelling in the reading/writing classroom*. Portsmouth, NH: Heinemann.

Polette, K. (2002). R.I.T.E. Reading: Constructing meaning by finding out what is "wrong" in an informational text. *Gifted Child Today magazine*, v25(2) 36–41.

Pransky, K., & Bailey, F. (2002). To meet your students where they are, first you have to find them: Working with culturally and linguistically diverse at-risk students. *The Reading Teacher*, 56, 370–383.

Pratt, A. C., & Brady, S. (1988). Relation of phonological awareness to reading disability in children and adults. *Journal of Educational Psychology*, 80, 319–323.

Purcell-Gates, V. (1995). *Other people's words: The cycle of low literacy*. Cambridge, MA: Harvard University Press.

Quigley, B. A. (1997). *Rethinking literacy education: The critical need for practice-based change*. San Francisco: Jossey-Bass Publishers.

Raphael, T. (1982). Question-answering strategies for children. *The Reading Teacher*, 36, 186–190.

Raphael, T. (1986). Teaching question answer relationships, revisited. *The Reading Teacher*, 39, 516–522.

Raphael, T. E., & Pearson, P. D. (1985). Increasing students' awareness of sources of information for answering questions. *American Educational Research Journal*, 22, 217–236.

Raphael, T. E., & Boyd, F. (1997). Writing for reflection and understanding: A Book ClubProgram component. In S. I. McMahon & T. E. Raphael (Eds.), *The "Book Club" connection: Literacy learning and classroom talk* (pp. 69–88). New York: Teachers College Press, Columbia University.

Raphael, T.E., & Au, K. (Eds) (1998). *Literature based instruction. Reshaping the curriculum*. Norwood, MA: Christopher Gordon Publishers.

Redd, T. M., & Webb, K. S. (2005). *A teacher's introduction to African American English: What a writing teacher should know*. Urbana, IL: National Council of Teachers of English.

Read, C. (1971). Preschool children's knowledge of English phonology. *Harvard Educational Review*, 41, 1–34.

Reid, D. K., Hresko, W.P., & Hammil, D. D. (2001). *Test of early reading ability*. Austin, TX: Pro-Ed.

Rhodes, L. K., & Dudley-Marling, C. (1996). *Readers and writers with a difference: A holistic approach to teaching struggling readers and writers*. Portsmouth, NH: Heinemann.

Rhodes, L. K. & Shanklin, N. L. (1993). *Windows into literacy: Assessing learners, K–8*. Portsmouth, NH: Heinemann.

Richards, J. & Anderson, N. (2003). How do you know? A strategy to help emergent readers make inferences. *The Reading Teacher*, 57 (3), 290–293.

Richgels, D. J. (2004). Paying attention to language. *Reading Research Quarterly*, 39 (4), 470–477.

Robb, L. (2002). Multiple texts: Multiple opportunities for teaching and learning. *Voices from the Middle* (9)4, 28–32.

Roller, C. M. (1996). *Variability, not disability: Struggling readers in a workshop classroom*. Newark, DE: International Reading Association.

Rosenbaum, C. (2001). A word map for middle school: A tool for effective vocabulary instruction. *Journal of Adolescent & Adult Literacy*, 45, 44–49.

Rosenblatt, L. (1938). *Literature as exploration*. New York: D. Appleton-Century Company.

Rosenblatt, L. (1978). *The reader, the text, the poem: The transactional theory of the literary work*. Carbondale, IL: Southern Illinois University Press.

Roskos, K., & Christie, J. (Eds.) (2000) *Literacy-enriched play settings: a broad-spectrum instructional strategy*. Mahwah, NJ: Lawrence Erlbaum.

Ruddell, R. B., & Unrau, N. J. (1997). The role of responsive teaching in focusing reader intention and developing reader motivation. In J. T. Guthrie & A. Wigfield (Eds.), *Reading engagement: Motivating readers through integrated instruction* (pp. 102–125). Newark, DE: International Reading Association.

Ruddell, R., & Ruddell, M. R. (1994). "Language acquisition and literacy processes." In R. Ruddell & M. R. Ruddell (Eds.), *Theoretical models and processes of reading (4th ed.)* (pp. 448–468). Newark, DE: International Reading Association.

Rupley, W., Logan, J., & Nichols, W. (1998). Vocabulary instruction in a balanced reading program. *The Reading Teacher*, 52(4), 336–346.

Rybczynski, M., & Troy, A. (1995). Literacy-enriched play centers: Trying them out in the 'real world.' *Childhood Education, 72*(1), 7–13.

Sampson, M. B., Sampson, M. R., & Linek, W. (1995). Circle of questions. *The Reading Teacher, 48*(4), 364–365.

Scarborough, H. S. (1990). Very early language deficits in dyslexic children. *Child Development, 61*(6), 1728–1744.

Scherer, P. (1997). Book club through a fishbowl: Extensions to early elementary classrooms. In S. I. MacMahon and T.E. Raphael (Eds.), *The book club connection: Literacy learning and classroom talk.* New York: Teachers College Press.

Schweiker, K., & Schweiker, W. (1993). Research Findings on Awareness, Acceptance, and Practice of Emergent Literacy Theory. Paper presented at the Annual Meeting of the Eastern Educational Research Association (Clearwater Beach, FL, February 17–22, 1993).

Serafini, F. (2002). Reflective practice and learning. *Primary Voices K–6, 10*(4), 2–7.

Shannon, P. (1990). *The struggle to continue: Progressive reading instruction in the United States.* Portsmouth, NH: Heinemann.

Schwartz, R. M., & Raphael, T. E. (1985). Concept of definition: A key to improving students' vocabulary. *The Reading Teacher, 39*(2), 198–205.

Sheingold, K. (1987). Keeping children's knowledge alive through inquiry. *School Library Media Quarterly, 25*, 80–85.

Shell, D. F., Colvin, C., & Bruning, R. H. (1995). Self-efficacy, attributions, and outcome expectancy mechanisms in reading and writing achievement: Grade-level and achievement-level differences. *Journal of Educational Psychology, 87*, 386–398.

Short, K. G. (1991). Intertextuality: Making connections across literature and life (Report No. CS213180). Tucson, AZ: University of Arizona (ERIC Document Reproduction Service No. ED 342 001).

Short, K. (1999). The search for 'balance' in a literature-rich curriculum. *Theory into Practice, 38*(3), 130–137.

Short, K. G., & Burke, C. (1991). *Creating curriculum: Teachers and students as a community of learners.* Portsmouth, NH: Heinemann.

Short, K. G. & Burke, C. (1996). Examining our practices and beliefs through inquiry. *Language Arts, 73*, 97–104.

Short, K. G., Harste, J. C., w/ Burke, C. (1996). *Creating classrooms for authors and inquirers.* Portsmouth, NH: Heinemann.

Short, K., Kauffman, G., Kaser, S., Kahn, L., & Crawford, K. (1999). "Teacher-watching": Examining teacher talk in literature circles. *Language Arts, 76*(6), 377–385.

Smith, F. (1988). *Understanding reading: A psycholinguistic analysis of reading and learning to read.* Hillsdale, NJ: L. Erlbaum Associates.

Smith, F. (1992). Learning to read: The never-ending debate. *Phi Delta Kappan, 73*(6), 432–440.

Smith, M., & Wilhelm, J. (2002). *"Reading don't fix no Chevys:" The role of literacy in the lives of young men.* Portsmouth, NH: Heinemann.

Smitherman, G. (1977). *Talkin and testifyin: The language of black America.* Boston: Houghton Mifflin.

Snow, C. E., Burns, M. S., & Griffen, P. (1998). *Preventing reading difficulties in young children.* Washington, DC: National Research Council, National Academy Press.

Stahl, S. (1999). *Vocabulary development.* Cambridge, MA: Brookline Books.

Stauffer, R. (1969). *Directed reading maturity as a cognitive process.* New York: Harper & Row.

Stauffer, R. (1980). *The language-experience approach to the teaching of reading.* New York: Harper & Row.

Stallman, A. C., & Pearson, P. D. (1990). Formal measures of early literacy. In L. M. Morrow and J. K. Smith (Eds.), *Assessment for instruction in early literacy* (pp. 7–44). Englewood Cliffs, NJ: Prentice Hall.

Stanovich, K. E., Cunningham, A. E., and Cramer, B. B. (1984). Assessing phonological awareness in kindergarten children: Issues of task comparability. *Journal of Experimental Child Psychology, 38*(2), 175–190.

Street, B. V. (1984). *Literacy in theory and practice.* New York: Cambridge University Press.

Street, B. V. (1995). *Social literacies: Critical approaches to literacy in development, ethnography, and education.* New York: Longman.

Strickland, D. (2001). The role of parents and grandparents in children's cognitive development: Focus on language and literacy. White House Summit on Early Childhood (July 27, 2001).

Strickland, D. S., & Shanahan, T. (2004). Laying the groundwork for literacy. *Educational Leadership, 6* (6), 74–77.

Sulzby, E., & Teale, W. (1991). Emergent literacy. In R. Barr, M. Kamil, P. Mosenthal, & P. D. Pearson (Eds.), *Handbook of reading research, Vol. II* (pp. 727–757). New York: Longman.

Teale, W. H., & Sulzby, E. (1986). *Emergent literacy: Writing and reading.* Norwood, NJ: Ablex.

Teale, W., & Yokota, J. (2000). Beginning reading and writing: Perspectives on instruction. In D. Strickland & L. Morrow (Eds.), *Beginning reading and writing* (pp. 3–21). Newark, DE: International Reading Association.

Temple, C., Nathan, R., Burris, N., & Temple, F. (1993). *The beginnings of writing,* 3rd ed. Boston: Allyn and Bacon.

Templeton, S. (1991). Teaching and learning the English spelling system: Reconcepulizing method and purpose. *Elementary School Journal,* 92, 185–201.

Terry, M. (2006). The importance of interpersonal relations in adult literacy programs. *Educational Research Quarterly,* 30 (2), 30–43.

Texas Reading Initiative (2002). Promoting Vocabulary Development Components of Effective Vocabulary Instruction. Austin: Texas Education Agency.

The American Heritage Dictionary of the English Language (4th ed.) (2000). Boston: Houghton Mifflin Company.

Thomson, P. (2002). *Schooling the rustbelt kids: Making the difference in changing times.* Crows Nest, NSW: Allen & Unwin.

Tivnan, T., & Hemphill, L. (2005). Comparing four literacy reform models in high-poverty schools: Patterns of first-grade achievement. *Elementary School Journal,* 105(5), 419–442.

Tomlinson, C. A. (2003). Deciding to teach them all. *Educational Leadership,* 61(2), 5–11.

Tompkins, G. E. (2004). *Literacy for the 21st century: Teaching reading and writing in grades 4 through 8.* Upper Saddle River, NJ: Pearson/Merrill/Prentice Hall.

Tower, C. (2000). Questions that matter: Preparing elementary students for the inquiry process. *The Reading Teacher,* 53, 550–557.

Trelease, J. (1989). *The new read-aloud handbook.* New York: Penguin Books.

Turbill, J. (2001). A researcher goes to school: The integration of technology into the early literacy curriculum. *Journal of Early Literacy,* 1(3), 255–279.

U.S. Department of Commerce (1996). *Current population reports: Population projections of the United States by age, sex, race, and Hispanic origin, 1995–2050.* Washington, DC.

Valencia, S. W., & Riddle Buly, M. (2004). Behind test scores: What struggling readers really need. *The Reading Teacher,* 57(6), 520–531.

Van Allen, R. (1976). *Language experience activities*: Boston, MA: Houghton Mifflin.

Vasquez, V. (2003). What engagement with Pokémon can teach us about learning and literacy. *Language Arts,* 81(2), 118–125.

Vasquez, V. (2003). *Getting beyond "I like the book": Creating space for critical literacy in K-6 classrooms.* Newark, DE: International Reading Association.

Vasquez, V. (2004). *Negotiating critical literacies with young children.* Mahwah, NJ: Lawrence Erlbaum Associates.

Veenman, S. (1984). Perceived problems of beginning teachers. *Review of Educational Research,* 54(2), 143–178.

Villegas, A. M., & Lucas, T. (2002). *Educating culturally responsive teachers: A coherent approach.* Albany, NY: SUNY Press.

Vygotsky, L. S. (1978). *Mind in society: The development of higher psychological processes.* Cambridge: Harvard University Press.

Watson, D. (1989). Defining and describing whole language. *Elementary School Journal,* 90, 130–141.

Weaver, C. (1990). *Understanding whole language: From principles to practice.* Portsmouth, NH: Heinemann.

Weaver, C. (2002). *Reading process and practice.* Portsmouth, NH: Heinemann.

Weaver, C., Gillmeister-Krause, L., & Vento-Zogby, G. (1996). *Creating support for effective literacy education: Workshop materials and handouts.* Portsmouth, NH: Heinemann.

Wells, Gordon. (1997). Learning to be literate: Reconciling convention and invention. In S.I. MacMahon, and T. E. Raphael (Eds.), *The book club connection: Literacy learning and classroom talk* (pp. 106–116). New York: Teachers College Press.

Whitehurst, G. J., & Lonigan, C. J. (1998). Child development and emergent literacy. *Child Development,* 68, 848–872.

Whitmore, K., Martens, P., Goodman, Y., & Owocki, G. (2004). Remembering critical lessons in early literacy research: A transactional perspective. *Language Arts,* 82(4), 296–307.

Wilhelm, J. (1998). Big stuff at the middle level: The real world, real reading, and right action. In R. Bamford & J. Kristo (Eds.), *Making facts come alive: Choosing quality nonfiction literature K–8.* Norwood, MA: Christopher Gordon.

Wilhelm, J. (2001). *Improving comprehension with think aloud strategy.* New York: Scholastic.

Wilson, L. (2002). *Reading to live: How to teach reading for today's world.* Portsmouth, NH: Heinemann.

Wilson-Keenan, J., Solsken, J., & Willett, J. (2001). Troubling stories: Valuing productive tensions in collaborating with families. *Language Arts,* 78(6), 520–528.

Wolf, D. (1989). Portfolio assessment: Sampling student work, *Educational Leadership,* 46(7), 35–39.

Wolfram, W., Adger, C. T., & Christian, D. (1999). *Dialects in schools and communities.* Mahwah, NJ: L. Erlbaum Associates.

Wolfram, W., & Schilling-Estes, N. (1998). *American English: Dialects and variation.* Oxford: Basil Blackwell.

Worthy, J. & Invernizzi, M. (1995). Linking reading with meaning: A case study of a hyperlexic reader. *Journal of Reading Behavior,* 27(4), 585–603.

Worthy, J., Turner, & Moorman, M. (1998). The precarious place of self-selected reading. *Language Arts,* 75(4), 296–304.

Yopp, H. (1988). The validity and reliability of phonemic awareness tests. *Reading Research Quarterly,* 23, 159–177.

Yopp, H. (1995). A test for assessing phonemic awareness in young children. *The Reading Teacher,* 49(1), 20–29.

Yopp, R. H., & Yopp, H. K. (2000). Sharing informational text with young children. *The Reading Teacher,* 53, 410–423.

Zecker, L. B. (1999). Different texts, different emergent writing forms. *Language Arts,* 76(6), 483–492.

Zutell, J. (1996). The directed spelling thinking activity (DSTA): Providing an effective balance in word study instruction. *The Reading Teacher,* 50(2), 98–108.

Zwiers, J. (2004). *Building reading comprehension habits in grades 6–12: A tool kit.* Newark, DE: International Reading Association.

Children's Literature References

Ada, A. F. (2001). *Gathering the Sun.* New York: Harper Collins.

Anacona, G. (1999). *Charro: Mexican Cowboy.* San Diego, CA: Harcourt.

Ashman, L. (2003). *Rub-a-dub sub.* San Diego, CA: Harcourt.

Avery, K. (1994). *The Crazy Quilt.* Tuscan, AZ: Good Year Books.

Aylesworth, J. (1992). *Old Black Fly.* New York: Holt.

Bear, J. B. (1994). *The Frog and the Princess and the Prince and the Mole and the Frog and the Mole and the Princess and the Prince.* Berkeley, CA: Tricycle Press.

Blume, J. (1972). *Tales of a Fourth Grade Nothing.* Santa Barbara, CA: Cornerstone Books.

Blume, J. (1972). *Otherwise Known as Sheila, the Great.* New York: E. P. Dutton.

Brinkloe (1986). *Fireflies: Story and Pictures.* New York: Aladdin Books.

Brothers Grimm (1981). *Little Red Riding Hood.* Mahwah, NJ: Troll Associates.

Bruchac, J. (1999). *Trail of Tears.* New York: Random House.

Bower, T. (2005). *How the Amazon Queen Fought the Prince of Egypt.* New York: Atheneum Books for Young Readers.

Bunting, E. (1993). *Fly Away Home.* New York: Clarion.

Bunting, E. (1996). *Going Home.* New York: HarperCollins Publishers.

Cannon, J. (1993). *Stellaluna.* San Diego, CA: Harcourt Brace Jovanovich.

Carle, E. (1979). *The Very Hungry Caterpillar.* New York: Philomel Books.

Carle, E. (1988). *Have You Seen My Cat?* New York: Philomel Books.

Carle, E. (1996). *The Grouchy Ladybug.* New York: HarperCollins.

Child, L. (2001). *Beware of the Storybook Wolves.* New York: Arthur A. Levine Books.

Cleary, B. (1965). *The Mouse and the Motorcycle.* New York: W. Morrow.

Cleary, B. (1981). *Ramona Quimby, Age 8.* New York: Morrow.

Cleary, B. (1984). *Dear Mr. Henshaw.* New York: Harper Trophy.

Cohen, M. (1980). *First Grade Takes a Test.* New York: Greenwillow Books.

Coleman, E. (1996). *White Socks Only.* Morton Grove, IL: A. Whitman.

Cole, J. (1986). *The Magic School Bus at the Waterworks.* New York: Scholastic Inc.

Coles, R. (1995). *The Story of Ruby Bridges.* New York: Scholastic.

Cronin, D. (2003). *Diary of a Worm.* New York: Joanna Cotler Books.

Deady. K. W. (2001). *Great White Sharks.* Mankato, MN: Capstone High-Interest Books.

Deedy, C. A. (2000). *The Yellow Star: The Legend of King Christian X of Denmark.* Atlanta, GA: Peachtree.

Christopher, C. (2000). *Soccer Duel.* New York: Little, Brown & Young.

Davis, L. (1998). *Susan B. Anthony: A Photo-illustrated Biography.* Mankato, MN: Bridgestone Books.

dePaola, T. (1979). *Oliver Button is a Sissy.* New York: Harcourt Brace Jovanovich.

dePaola, T. (1988). *Strega Nona.* New York: Simon & Schuster.

DiCamillo, K. (2000). *Because of Winn Dixie.* Cambridge, MA: Candlewick Press.

Dorling Kindersay Publishing Staff (2000). *Soccer (Eyewitness Book Series).* New York: DK Publishing.

Dorling Kindersay Publishing Staff (2004). *Oceans* (Eyewitness series). New York: DK Publishing.

Dorling Kindersay Publishing Staff (2004). *Volcanoes and earthquakes.* (Eyewitness series). New York: DK Publishing.

Dorling Kindersay Publishing Staff (2004). *Reptile.* (Eyewitness series). New York: DK Publishing.

Dorling Kindersay Publishing Staff (2004). *Sharks.* (Eyewitness series). New York: DK Publishing.

Duncan, P. E. (2003). *The Worrywarts.* New York: Harper Collins.

Dr. Seuss (1957/1985). *The Cat in the Hat.* New York: Random House.

Dr. Seuss (1963). *Hop on Pop.* New York: Beginner Books.

Eastman, P. D. (1998). *Are You My Mother?* New York: Random House.

Ehlert, L. (1989). *Eating the Alphabet: Fruits and Vegetables from A to Z.* San Diego, CA: Harcourt Brace Jovanovich.

Ehlert, L. (2004). *Pie in the Sky.* Orlando, FL:Harcourt.

Ernst, L. C. (2002). *Three Spinning Fairies: A Tale from the Brothers Grimm.* New York: Dutton Children's Books.

Farris, C. K. (2003). *My Brother Martin: A Sister Remembers Growing Up with the Rev. Dr. Martin Luther King, Jr.* New York: Simon & Schuster Books for Young Readers.

Fleishman, P. (1997). *Seedfolks.* New York: Harper Collins.

Fleming, D. (1991). *In the Tall, Tall, Grass.* New York: H. Holt.

Fleming, D. (2002). *Alphabet Under Construction.* New York: Henry Holt.

Forward, T. (2005). *The Wolf's Story: What Really Happened to Little Red Riding Hood.* Cambridge, MA: Candlewick.

Freeman, D. (1968). *Corduroy.* New York: Viking.

Freeman, R. (1994). *Kids at Work: Lewis Hine and the Crusade Against Child Labor.* New York: Clarion Books.

Fritz, J. (1995). *You Want Women to Vote, Lizzie Stanton?.* New York: Putnam.

Greenaway (1999). The *Big Book of Bugs!* New York: Welcome.

Hamilton, V. (2003). *Bruh Rabbit and the Tar Baby Girl.* New York: The Blue Sky Press.

Harvey, M. (1996). *Women's Voting Rights.* New York: Children's Press.

Heidi, F. (1992). *Sami and the Times of the Trouble.* New York: Clarion Books.

Heiligman, D. (1996). *From Caterpillar to Butterfly.* New York: HarperCollins.

Henkes, K.(1991). *Chrysanthemum.* New York: Greenwillow Books.

Henkes, K. (1990). *Julius, Baby of the World.* New York: Greenwillow Books.

Henkes, K. (1993). *Owen.* New York: Greenwillow Books.

Henkes, K. (1996). *Lilly's Purple Plastic Purse.* New York: Greenwillow Books.

Henkes (2003). *Olive's Ocean.* New York: Greenwillow Books.

Hoban, T. (1986). *Shapes, Shapes, Shapes.* New York: Greenwillow Books.

Hooks, B. (2002). *Be Boy Buzz.* New York: Hyperion Books for Children.

Humphrey, S. M. (2005). *Dare to Dream!: 25 Extraordinary Lives.* Amherst, NY: Prometheus Books.

Katz, B. (2001). *A Rumpus of Rhymes: A Book of Noisy Poems.* New York: Dutton Children's Books.

Katzen, M., & Henderson, A. (1994). *Pretend Soup and Other Real Recipes: A Cookbook for Preschoolers & Up.* Berkeley, CA: Tricycle Press.

Krull, K. (1997). *Lives of the Athletes: Thrills, Spills (and What the Neighbors Thought).* San Diego, CA: Harcourt.

Krull, K. (2004). *The Boy on Fairfield Street: How Ted Geisel Grew Up to Become Dr. Seuss.* New York: Random House.

Lauber, P. (1996). *Hurricanes: Earth's Mightiest Storms.* New York: Scholastic.

Lewellyn , C. (1998). *The Best Book of Bugs.* New York: Kingfisher.

Lewellyn, C. (1999). *The Best Book of Sharks.* New York : Kingfisher.

Lichtenheld, T. (2000). *Everything I Know About Pirates: A Collection of Made-up Facts, Educated Guesses, and Silly Pictures About Bad Guys of the High Seas.* New York: Simon & Schuster Books for Young Readers.

Long, M. (2003). *How I became a Pirate.* San Diego, CA: Harcourt.

Lorbiecki, M. (1998). *Sister Anne's Hands.* New York: Dial Books for Young Readers.

Lowry, L. (1989). *Number the Stars.* Boston: Houghton Mifflin Co.

Machotka, H. (1992). *Breathtaking Noses.* New York: Morrow Junior Books.

MacLachlan, P. (1985). *Sarah, Plain and Tall.* New York: Harper & Row.

Martin, B. (1970). *Brown Bear, Brown Bear, What Do You See?* New York: Holt, Rinehart and Winston.

Martin, B. & Archambault, J. (1989). *Chicka Chicka Boom Boom.* New York: Simon & Schuster Books for Young Readers.

Mathis, S. B. (1975). *The Hundred Penny Box.* New York: Viking Press.

McCormick, P. (2006). *Sold.* New York: Hyperion.

McKissack, P. (1986). *Flossie and the Fox.* New York: Dial Books for Young Readers.

Mochizuki, K. (1993). *Baseball Saved Us.* New York: Lee & Low.

Monk, I. (1999). *Hope.* Minneapolis, MN: Carolrhoda Books.

Mora, P. (1997). *Tomas and the Library Lady.* New York: Knopf.

Munsch, R. N. (1993). *The Paperbag Princess.* Buffalo, NY: Discis Knowledge Research.

Myers, W. D. (2004). *I've Seen the Promised Land: The life of Dr. Martin Luther King, Jr.* New York: HarperCollins Publishers.

Naylor, P. R. (1991). *Shiloh.* New York: Atheneum.

O'Dell, S. (1990). *Island of the Blue Dolphins.* Boston, MA: Houghton Mifflin Company.

Parker, D. L., Engfer, L., & Conrow, R. (1997). *Stolen Dreams: Portraits of Working Children.* Minneapolis: Lerner Publications Co.

Parker, S. & Flegg, J. (2004). *100 Things You Should Know About Insects & Spiders.* Broomall, PA: Mason Crest.

Paterson, K. (1987). *Bridge to Terabithia.* New York: Harper Trophy.

Paulson, G. (1999). *Hatchet.* New York : Aladdin Paperbacks.

Pelliter, D. (1996). *The Graphic Alphabet.* New York: Scholastic.

Pienkowski, J. (1981). *Dinnertime.* London: Orchard Books.

Rappaport, D. (2001). *Martin's Big Words: The Life of Dr. Martin Luther King, Jr.* New York: Hyperion Books for Children.

Rossi, A. (2005). *Created Equal: Women Campaign for the Right to Vote, 1840-1920.* Washington, DC: National Geographic.

Rowling, J. K. (1998). *Harry Potter and the Sorcerer's Stone.* New York: Arthur A. Levine Books.

Rylant, C. (1982). *When I Was Young in the Mountains.* New York: Dutton.

Sachar, L. (1998). *Holes.* New York: Farrar, Straus and Giroux.

Salkeld, A. (2000). *Mystery on Mt. Everest.* New York: Scholastic.

Savage, J. (2005). *Sammy Sosa.* Minneapolis: LernerSports.

Sayre, A. P. (1998). *Home at Last: A Song of Migration.* New York: Holt.

Simon, S. (1993). *Wolves.* New York: HarperCollins.

Simon, S. (2003). *Hurricanes.* New York: HarperCollins.

Slepian, J. & Seidler, A. (1967). *The Hungry Thing.* Chicago: Follett.

Smith, D. J. (2002). *If the World Were a Village: A Book About the World's People.* Toronto: Kids Can Press.

Sobol, D. J. (1963). *Encyclopedia Brown, Boy Detective.* New York: T. Nelson.

Starbright Foundation (2001). *Once Upon a Fairy Tale: Four Favorite Stories.* New York: Viking.

Stein, R. C. (1993). *Trail of Tears.* Chicago: Children's Press.

Taback, S. (1997). *There Was an Old Lady Who Swallowed a Fly.* New York: Viking.

Trosclair (1973). *Cajun Night Before Christmas.* Gretna, LA: Pelican Pub. Co.

Varriale, J. (1999). *Take a Look Around: Photography Activities for Young People.* Brookfield, CT: Milbrook Press.

Wells, R. (1992). *Bunnycakes.* New York: Puffin.

Wells, L. (2003). *Bunny Party.* New York: Puffin.

Wheeler, L. (2004). *Bubble Gum, Bubble Gum.* New York: Little, Brown and Co.

White, E. B. (1952). *Charlotte's Web.* New York: Harper.

Wiles, D. (2005). *Each Little Bird That Sings.* Orlando, FL: Gulliver Books/Harcourt.

Wiles, D. (2001). *Love, Ruby Lavender.* San Diego, CA: Harcourt.

Wiles, D. (2001). *Freedom Summer.* New York: Atheneum Books for Young Readers.

Willimas, S. (1990). *I Went Walking.* San Diego, CA : Harcourt Brace Jovanovich.

Wood, A. (1984). *The Napping House.* San Diego: Harcourt Brace Jovanovich.

Woods, B. (2004). *Earning a Ride: How to Be a Nascar Driver.* Maple Plain, MN: Tradition Books.

Woodson, J. (2001). *The Other Side.* New York: Putnam's.

Wyeth (1998). *Something Beautiful.* New York: Bantam Doubleday Dell.

Text and Illustration Credits

Chapter 10, p. 293: Book cover of *Holes*, by Sachar, L. (1998). New York: Farrar, Strause, and Giroux.

Chapter 10, p. 299: Reprinted with permission of Simon & Schuster Books for Young Readers, and imprint of Simon & Schuster Children's Publishing Division from *Strega Nona* by Tomie dePaola. Copyright © 1975 Tomie dePaola.

Chapter 10, p. 299: From *Mystery on Everest* by Salkeld, A. (2000). National Geographic Society.

Chapter 11, p. 321: Reprinted with permission of Atheneum Books for Young Readers, an imprint of Simon & Schuster Children's Publishing Division from *How the Amazon Queen Fought the Prince of Egypt* by Tamara Bower. Jacket illustrations copyright © 2005 Tamara Bower.

Chapter 11, p. 321: From *You Want Women to Vote, Lizzie Stanton*, by Jean Fritz © 1995. Illustrations copyright © 1995 by DyAnne DiSalvo–Ryan. G. P. Putnam's Sons, a division of Penguin Group (USA) Inc. All rights reserved.

Chapter 11, p. 321: From *Created Equal, Women Campaign for the Right to Vote*, By Ann Rossi, Copyright © 2005 National Geographic Society. Reprinted with permission of the National Geographic Society.

Chapter 11, p. 321: From *Women's Voting Rights* by Miles Harvey. Published by Children's Book Press.

Chapter 11, p. 328: Book cover from Creepy, *Crawly Baby Bugs*, by Sandra Markle. © 1996. Published by: Walker and Company.

Chapter 11, p. 328: Book cover from THE MAGIC SCHOOL BUS SPINS A WEB by Joanna Cole, Illustrated by Bruce Degen. Illustrations copyright © 1997 by Bruce Degen. Reprinted by permission of Scholastic Inc.

Chapter 11, p. 328: © Children's Butterfly Site. The Children's Butterfly Site is a science resource made available by the USGS National Biological Information Infrastructure (NBII) Program. The site is jointly managed by the NBII Mountain Prairie Information Node and the Big Sky Institute at Montana State University. http://bis.montana.edu/web/kidsbutterfly.

Chapter 11, p. 334: Book cover from *Shapes, Shapes, Shapes* (1986) by Tana Hoban. HarperCollins Children's Books.

Chapter 11, p. 334: Book cover from *The World of Nascar Driver* by Bob Woods. Copyright © 2004 by Tradition Publishng Company, LLC. HarperCollins Children's Books.

Chapter 11, p. 334: Book cover from CHARRO, Copyright © 1999 by George Ancona, reprinted by permission of Harcourt, Inc. This material may not be reproduced in any form or by any means without the prior written permission of the publisher.

Chapter 11, p. 336: Camp, D. (2000, February). It takes two: Teaching with twin texts of fact and fiction. The Reading Teacher, 53(5), 400–408. Reprinted with permission of the International Reading Association.

Chapter 12, Fig. 12.2: Reprinted with permission from National Middle School Association. Combs, D. (2004). A Framework for Scaffolding Content Area Reading Strategies. Middle School Journal, 36, (2), p. 14, November 2004. National Middle School Association.

Chapter 12, p. 361: From *Welcome to Petpourri.* http://www.avma.org/careforanimals/kidscorner/default.asp.

Chapter 12, p. 361: Book cover from *All About Pets: Turtles* by Martha E. H. Rustad. Copyright © 2002 Capstone Press. All rights reserved.

Chapter 12, p. 361: Book cover from *Kitten Care* by Kime Dennis. Copyright © 2004 Dorling Kindersley Limited.

Appendix A: The John Newbery Medal. Association for Library Service to Children, American Library Association.

Appendix B: The Randolph Caldecott Medal. Association for Library Service to Children, American Library Association.

Appendix C: The Orbis Pictus Award. National Council for Teachers of English.

Photo Credits

Chapter 1

P. 3: (swoosh, right) Ellen Ford/John Wiley & Sons, Inc. **P. 5:** blend/Punchstock. **P. 6:** (left) SUPERSTOCK. **P. 6:** (right) PhotoDisc, Inc./Getty Images, Inc. **P. 9:** (top) Book cover from "Scholastic Q & A: What Do Sharks Eat For Dinner" by Melvin and Gilda Berger, illustrations by John Rice. Illustrations © 2001 by John Rice. Reprinted by permission/Scholastic, Inc. **P. 9:** (bottom) From "the Truth About Great White Sharks © 2000 by Mary M. Cerullo (text); Jeffrey L. Rotman (photographs). Used with permission of Chronicle Books LLC, San Francisco/Chronicle Books. **P. 9:** Cover of "The Best Book of Sharks" by Claire Llewellyn. © Kingfisher Publications Plc 1999. Reprinted by permission of Kingfisher Publications Plc, an imprint of Houghton Mifflin Company. All rights reserved. **P. 12:** Elizabeth Crews/The Image Works. **P. 15:** Purestock/SUPERSTOCK. **P. 16:** Digital Vision/Media Bakery. **P. 21:** Stock Connection/Punchstock.

Chapter 2

P. 25: (swoosh, right) BananaStock/Media Bakery. **P. 28:** Blend Images/Media Bakery. **P. 49:** Tom Rosenthal/SUPERSTOCK.

Chapter 3

P. 58: Used by permission of HarperCollins Publishers. **P. 59:** (swoosh, right) Bob Daemmrich/The Image Works. **P. 61:** Purestock/Punchstock. **P. 64:** blend/Punchstock. **P. 73:** "Corduroy" by Don Freeman © 1968 Viking Children's Books/Penguin Group USA Inc. **P. 74:** Jacket Cover from "Something Beautiful" by Sharon Dennis Wyeth. Used by permission of Random House Children's Books, a division of Random House, Inc.

Chapter 4

P. 84: (top) /Sovfoto/eastfoto. **P. 84:** (bottom) Bill Anderson/Photo Researchers, Inc. **P. 85:** (swoosh, right) Corbis Digital Stock. **P. 85:** Hulton Archive/Getty Images/NewsCom. **P. 95:** Used by permission of HarperCollins Publishers. **P. 95:** Book cover from "the Magic School Bus Inside A Hurricane" by Joanna Cole and Bruce Degen. Illustrations © 1995 by Bruce Degen. Reprinted by permission/Scholastic, Inc. **P. 98:** stockbyte/Punchstock. **P. 103:** Ellen Ford/John Wiley & Sons.

Chapter 5

P. 113: (swoosh, right) Martin Heitner/SUPERSTOCK. **P. 125:** Ellen Ford/John Wiley & Sons. **P. 130:** Bananastock/Punchstock.

Chapter 6

P. 145: (swoosh, right) Digital Vision/Media Bakery. **P. 149:** The Sacramento Bee/Anne Chadwick Williams/Zuma Press. **P. 152:** Dennis MacDonald/Age Fotostock America, Inc. **P. 153:** Brand X Pictures/Media Bakery. **P. 167:** Photodisc/Media Bakery. **P. 170:** Liquid Library/Media Bakery. **P. 171:** Corbis Digital Stock.

Chapter 7

P. 179: (swoosh, right) Banana Stock/Media Bakery. **P. 185:** Mark DuFrene/Contra Costa Times/Zuma Press. **P. 186:** Digital Vision/Punchstock. **P. 193:** Francisco Cruz/SUPERSTOCK. **P. 195:** Jacket photography © 1992 Joe Mcdonald; jacket © 1993 HarperCollins Publishers/HarperCollins Publishers. **P. 195:** "Red Riding Hood" by James Marshall © 1993 Picture Puffins/Penguin Group USA Inc. **P. 195:** Reproduced by permission of Hodder and Stoughton Limited. **P. 199:** Elizabeth Crews/The Image Works. **P. 200:** Ellen B. Senisi/The Image Works.

Index